I Belong To:

Please return me

to my owner.

Thank You!

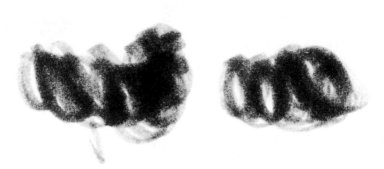

CATHERINE BOOTH

tee-totaler
82
86-
138

Catherine Booth in 1869

CATHERINE BOOTH

The Story of her Loves

by

CATHERINE BRAMWELL-BOOTH

HODDER AND STOUGHTON

Printed in Great Britain
for Hodder and Stoughton Limited
St. Paul's House, Warwick Lane, London, E.C.4
by Willmer Brothers Limited, Birkenhead

Dedicated to

THE WOMEN OF THE SALVATION ARMY

FOREWORD

by Frederick Coutts, C.B.E., General of The Salvation Army

(International leader 1963-1969)

A fresh and comprehensive appreciation of the life and influence of the Army Mother is long overdue, and we are indebted to her eldest grand-daughter, Commissioner Catherine Bramwell-Booth, for undertaking this.

William Booth has had his fair share of biographers, but no serious study of Catherine has appeared in this country since that written by W. T. Stead in 1900. Yet she was a woman who combined in a unique way a happy private life with a commanding public life.

There was never any need for her to seek on the platform any form of compensation for what she was denied in the home. "Ever your loving Catherine," she wrote to William when their friendship was young, and this she remained to the end. To husband and home her heart was given.

But equally was her heart possessed by the conviction that she— and all Christian women with her—should not be denied the liberty of prophesying. So from Whit Sunday, 1860, in the Bethesda Chapel, Gateshead, to Thursday, June 21, 1888, in the City Temple, London, her public ministry went from strength to strength by reason of what her eldest son described as her simplicity of manner allied to her gift of lucid statement.

Being dead, Catherine Booth still speaks—and will speak to many through these pages.

London
1969

AUTHOR'S PREFACE

This book is my attempt to write a study of Catherine Booth, the first woman Salvationist, known as the Mother of The Salvation Army; and to trace her influence on the Army's development. As I pondered the possibility of doing this, a hope suddenly made itself at home in my mind, that the book might be, as it were, a telescope bringing her into focus for people today. During the years of preliminary study I have lived in her thoughts, searched out her motives, become familiar with her idiosyncrasies; felt my pulse quicken as I have been drawn along by her zeals; experienced a longing to be young again, that I might better emulate her example. And from that useless longing came another hope, a hope, growing as I wrote, that my version of Catherine's story might be an inspiration and a challenge to some young men and women to venture all, as she did, in faith's certainty that "God is enough for us".

Today it is difficult to grasp how rapidly The Salvation Army grew in its first twenty-five years. But whether one considers the number of its converts, the strict discipline enjoined upon its soldiers, the place accorded to women in its ranks, the spread of its activities to other lands, or the variety of its practical works of mercy, The Salvation Army is a phenomenon unmatched in religious history. It is invidious and fruitless to try to discern how much in all this was William Booth's share and how much was Catherine's. As I see it they were so completely one, their loves and aims were fused in such fashion, that their individual contribution cannot be disentangled.

Had Catherine Booth an exaggerated concept of woman's capacity to influence the world? Today doors to education, to the professions, to politics (all closed in my grandmother's time) are open to her equally with men. Would Catherine be disappointed that woman's freedom to enter these spheres has not resulted in raising standards of integrity and in the protection and cherishing of the young? She believed that women were pre-eminently fitted for leadership in the moral sphere. But then her hopes of what women might do in the world always premised Christian women. She had no faith in the basic betterment of mankind apart from God. Her eager heart would grieve, I think, that woman's right to preach Christ is not, even now, universally recognized. "Whether the Church will allow women to speak in her assemblies can only be a matter of time..." she wrote in 1860. Would she feel that to have waited a hundred years was too long?

If I have given prominence to William Stead's opinions in Catherine's story, it is because he is the only one of her contemporaries, apart from her family, who made more than a brief record of their impressions of her. He was acquainted with all the Booths, and came close to Catherine in friendship and understanding. He did not become a Salvationist and so remained independent of loyalties to the Army, but he was sincerely religious and in touch with the religious and political thought of the day. An intelligent, sensitive spirit, with a sturdy individualistic outlook, Stead made an impact on his time. Lord Fisher in his *Memories* described him as "one of the best friends I ever had, and in my opinion the greatest of all journalists of his day ... He was absolute integrity and he feared no man". It has been reassuring to me to find Stead's views on Catherine Booth often coinciding with my own, and convenient that at times he should express them rather than I.

ACKNOWLEDGEMENTS

A happy part of writing this book has been the kindness of those who have aided me:

At the very beginning my adorable and ever beloved Mother who helped with the reading—in part deciphering—of some of my grandmother's letters.

My sisters Mary, Dora and in particular Olive, who has enmeshed herself in the toils of checking and ordering references and in the drudgery of typing and re-typing alterations and additions.

My dearly loved friend and former fellow officer in the Salvation Army, Catherine S. Lamb, whose earthly journey has now ended, who gave me so lavishly of her time to discuss and criticize the book and who at her own request and to my relief undertook the final typing of the script.

These dear ones share in any good the book may do, for without the encouragement they gave me I doubt whether I should have persevered with it to the end.

I am grateful to my comrade George Hurren to whom I turned for comment and advice from a Salvationist's outlook; as also to the late Captain A. Richmond Henderson, R.N., who read the pages and gave me a churchman's views. His advice and our discussions were not only helpful with the book but ranging far afield remain for me a delightful memory.

Thankfully I acknowledge the ready permission given by Mr. St. John Ervine and the publishers, William Heinemann Ltd., to include certain quotations from *God's Soldier*.

Catherine Bramwell-Booth.

March 1969.

CONTENTS

page

ILLUSTRATIONS

BOOK ONE

Awakening of Love for God

"To love Thee with all my heart is all my desire."*

"Lord Thou knowest that I love Thee, but I want to love Thee more."*

"I want more faith. I want to walk more by faith and not by feelings."*

"I regarded conformity to the will of God as true religion even from childhood."

—In a love-letter to William Booth.

"I don't believe in any religion apart from doing the will of God."
—In a letter to her mother.

"I know the religion of Jesus is a *reality* just as I know I live and breathe and think."

—In a love-letter to William Booth.

"If the Gospel were less mysterious, it would lack one of the characters of the Divine signature."

—In a love-letter to William Booth.

"I feel the power to leave myself and my all in the hands of God."*

"I know not what He is about to do with me, but I have given myself entirely into His hands."*

"Sinners do not understand and cannot appreciate the joys of the spiritual Kingdom ... one of the chief of these enjoyments is knowing and loving God."

—From a public address.

*From Catherine Mumford's Journal written in her teens.

1

The keen north country air strikes chill in the room where, through the drawn blinds, a mild unshadowing light illumines the waxlike stillness of a little child's form. He is beautiful in death; but estranged by that motionless sleep; changed into something mysterious, awesome. The picture of him, as he lies there, will not fade from the memory of his small sister Catherine staring, as only a very young child can stare, unknowing, unconcerned, upon the face of death. The scene will still be vivid when nearly sixty years later she said, "I was scarcely more than two years old but I can remember to this day, the feeling of awe and solemnity with which the sight of death impressed my baby-mind . . . the effect has lasted to this very hour."[1]

That day, she sat erect in her mother's arms, dark curls clustering close about her small head, its poise on the slender neck giving, even so early, an impression of dignity to the fragile-looking child. But had you seen her then, it would have been the eyes you would have noticed. A sweet little face, "all eyes", dark eyes, not blue like those of the woman in whose arms she sits, for little Catherine Mumford favours her father rather than her mother. This sight of death was her first memory of life. It marked her mind, and made death a familiar fact; an unforgettable reality in her world. She once said, "I am sure that many parents enormously underestimate the capacity of children to *retain* impressions made upon them in early days."[2] Was that first glimpse of death one of the things which, as she grew older, impelled her to peer beyond it? Thoughts of God had already awakened in her and thoughts of death would now stay with her also.

Two inestimable advantages enriched the child born on January 17, 1829, at Ashbourne in Derbyshire. The first, that she was given to a Christian home, where God was honoured and spoken of, and the wonders of His works discussed naturally and unaffectedly. There was no conspiracy of silence about religion there. The life of the mind and spirit was cultivated, perhaps to the detriment of the body at times, but if so not for lack of love, but only for lack of knowledge of more health-giving methods. Her other happy fortune was that she was welcomed: no tinge in that Ashbourne home of the poisonous lie so destructive of family life that children are "encumbrances" to be avoided. The Mumfords lost three sons in infancy and while another son John was born in 1833, Catherine was always treasured as a special gift by her mother. There is hardly a trace of John's existence in the family correspondence. I gather that he went to boarding-school from a reference in a letter to a box used by him at

17

school. He went to America when he was sixteen where he prospered and established a family.

As Catherine's mind unfolded she unconsciously imbibed a sense that the family is the object of God's love; the home the garden where this life's most exquisite joys flower—in fact, she experienced the civilizing effects of the principles of religion as revealed in the Bible. From her little daughter's earliest years Catherine's mother talked to her about God and led her to feel that to please Him was the chief purpose of life. The child had a strict upbringing, but seems never to have regretted it. Of her mother she wrote, "The longer I live the more I appreciate my mother's character. She was one of the Puritan type. A woman of sternest principles and yet the embodiment of tenderness. To her, right was right no matter what it might entail. She had an intense realization of spiritual things. Heaven seemed quite near, instead of being a far-off unreality."[3] Mrs. Mumford had strong views about the undesirability of leaving children too much to the care of servants and little Catherine did not spend her infancy relegated to a nursery, but was largely in her mother's company. A lively, noticing child, she picked up her "letters" almost without teaching and could read at three. By the time she was five she had begun her education in earnest. From what Catherine tells I picture the scene, Mrs. Mumford sitting upright in a high-backed, high-seated chair, leaning slightly sideways and supporting a large open volume on the arm of the chair. At her side, perched on a stool, so that her eyes should be above the book, stands little Catherine, reading aloud in a clear, childish treble.

The book from which she reads is the Bible. The child is already familiar with many of its stories; and now, reading from the Book for herself, she begins gradually to love the Bible; it becomes one of the essentials of life. Her young mind is nourished by it, absorbing its ideals, its warnings and precepts. Her active imagination feeds upon its awesome delineations; on its thunders, visions, voices: on its mountains, rivers, trees, gardens and deserts, sea and stars. Its passages are the magic carpet by which the "long, long thoughts of youth" range and soar; not among the mere figments of human creation but with the Divine; with the eternal verities; with angels and devils, with the powers of darkness and of light. The rhythm of its cadences makes a measure in her mind and, most thrilling of all, it clothes her conception of God, so that she comes to feel that she knows Him, at least knows her own version of Him. Soon the stool is no longer needed to bring the page within reach; the baby-treble gradually becomes a full bell-like tone, readily expressive of the emotions of the reader. When she is famous as a public speaker, her voice will be described by journalists as a "beautiful voice, with a clear, ringing note in it",[4] "a sweet rich voice". Constant reading aloud helped to develop it; also, and this was very important for her future, Catherine grew accustomed to the sound of her own voice. She learned to control and use it to fit her feelings as she read. Mrs. Mumford was training better than she knew. By the time the child was twelve years old she had read the Bible aloud straight through *eight* times! There were other text books but the Bible continued to hold chief place. As she grew older, her own spirit began striving to find its way, to reconcile the contradictory aspects of truth, of God Himself. The child was sometimes preoccupied, absorbed by some inner vision or conflict, but of this her mother knew nothing. She marked the kindling light in her daughter's eyes, the flush upon her cheeks, or the unwelcome paleness there and, observing her, came by degrees to feel that there was something incalculable, self-contained, in the child.

It was to her mother more than to any other human influence that Catherine owed the early awakening of the strong moral sense inherent in her nature. She tells that from three years of age and onward there were sometimes tears at good-night time, and the "confession" of something the child thought "wrong". She could not go to sleep until her tender spirit felt forgiven and comforted with a sense of God's love. Her mother never excused the fault, nor attempted to explain away the child's distress. Conscience was a reality before babyhood was well passed, and, promptly obedient or not, Catherine never challenged its authority. It was her own experience as a child that established in her mind the opinions she expressed with surprising authority to her betrothed, William Booth, on the religious instruction of the young. She wrote ". . . it seems to me that in this respect error of a very serious nature is almost universally prevalent in Methodist teaching. It seems to be the *first* and most important and eternal duty to drill into the mind an idea of *estrangement* from God, a conviction of moral degeneracy and actual alienation. Now *I* conceive that in direct opposition to this mode, the *first idea,* the very foundation of a religious training, should be to impress the young heart with a sense of God's *fatherhood,* His tenderness and love toward mankind generally. The young soul should be *drawn towards God,* not repulsed from Him. Work this conviction into the mind of a child and *then* show it the obligation it is under to regard God's will in all things and to keep His commandments (not failing to explain their import and spirit, according to the child's understanding) and the conscience of even a little child will testify to their reasonableness and righteousness. Let these two ideas, first God's fatherhood and love; second, the obligation arising out of this relationship to keep His commands, take possession of the mind of a child and they will *produce* a sense of moral degeneracy far *deeper* and more influential than could be produced by any other means. If the parent or teacher were continually re-iterating the fact of his being a sinner from morning to night, in the child's ears, it would produce no *consciousness* of it in his heart,

19

but let him be *thus* instructed, and he will *feel* bitterly that there is antagonism between his soul and God's holy law. He will understand better the nature and consequences of sin than all the abstract teaching in the world could explain, and thus will the foundation of true conversion be laid deep in his own experience; for when the plan of redemption comes to be unfolded to his mind and heart, he will at once receive it as in harmony with his settled ideas of God's character. He will look upon it as an expression of a Father's love, rather than a scheme to appease an angry judge."[5]

Catherine had an unusually intense nature; this was manifest even in infancy. To her play was serious. She cared for her dolls with a conscientious fervour very amusing to her parents. Every little detail must be attended to or their small owner was unhappy. Her sense of responsibility for them increased as she grew older and her "care" for them did not become "hitty-missy". She soon began making their clothes. Mrs. Mumford was a very good needlewoman especially in embroidery of various kinds; she helped her little daughter, and the skill acquired in making garments for her dolls stood Catherine in good stead when it came to living on little. She enjoyed playing the more since her imagination was not blunted by artificial stimulation, nor deformed by what was ugly or vicious as it is for so many children today. Hers was furnished with things clean and beautiful, and was so vivid, that to her the imagined often became more real than reality! Whatever form playing took, it engrossed her and was at the moment a serious affair; that was her attitude to life. Discussing her on one occasion with her eldest daughter I mentioned this trait. "Why, yes," was the reply, "she *was* serious, living was to her a *very* serious thing, she *felt* things so deeply."

2

In early childhood there were moments when the vehemence of Catherine's emotions induced in her a flaming unselfconsciousness that overwhelmed all natural objecting instincts. By nature she was reserved, shy, but when roused she would act in a manner that seemed to be quite at variance with her nature; with a boldness that had nothing to do with *feeling* bold. At such times an unreflecting confidence possessed her, a self-obliterating intensity of emotion. Many, especially women, are capable of this self-forgetfulness in moments of danger or acute stress. The thing to be remarked in Catherine is the kind of circumstance that awakened it; and the swiftness of the change in her from lamb to lion. For example, see her at nine or so bowling her hoop and running lightly beside it

20

down the road, when she becomes aware of a noisy crowd advancing; sees, in a flash, a manifestly drunken lout being dragged along by a policeman, and at their heels a mob of boys and youths, jeering and laughing. In an instant the child is at the man's side, she takes his hand in hers, hoop and stick tucked under her other arm. Thus they progress to the police station. Imagine the company approaching! The child's figure in incongruous contrast to the dishevelled sot; her head held high, her eyes flashing, her cheeks scarlet with mingled pity and scorn. At that moment there is, and all her life will be, "a hot spring of indignation" in her, ready to leap up in the presence of cruelty and injustice. But it was not the mere motion of impulse that took her to the drunkard's side, it was something much deeper. Stead* wrote of her, "It is well to note with what passionate sympathy she regarded those who were suffering, whether they were drunkards or animals, so long as they were sentient beings. Up to the very last this was one of the dominant notes of Mrs. Booth's life."[6] This was not an acquired gift, Catherine never needed to *pray* for compassion, it welled up unbidden and would have flowed forth, whatever the manner of her life, though without religion it might well have narrowed to the exclusive channel of personal feelings. As it was, it gave her a bias in favour of the weak, of the oppressed and suffering, of minorities in almost any field. The "drunk" in the policeman's grip was no doubt a sight to shrink from, but there was no one on *his* side, so she must be.

She had to pay in exhaustion, physical and nervous, for her lavish compassions. Once, when quite a small girl, having seen sheep goaded in the street, she rushed home to fling herself on a couch in a "speechless paroxysm of grief", nor could such tears be quickly quenched. Again and again when still a child, she would fly out of the house to remonstrate with some person she had caught sight of ill-treating an animal. Early in their acquaintance her lover was to learn how she felt about dumb creatures. In the first year of their engagement, when he had a circuit in Lincolnshire, she wrote to him, "Frisking lambs, pretty creatures! I sometimes see them in the Brixton Road, being driven by rude, inhuman boys and men with great thick sticks, and often so lame that they can scarce walk... You will think I am unaltered in my peculiar feelings toward the brute creation, and so I am (except that I feel more deeply). I would rather stay at home than endure what I often do in going a walk."[7] Cruelty to animals remained one of the major problems of the universe for her. Toward the end of her life she said, "I have suffered so much over what appeared to be the needless and inexplicable sorrows and pains of the animal creation—as well as over those of the rest of the world,

* W. T. Stead, (1849-1912). Journalist, editor of *Pall Mall Gazette*, founder and editor of the *Review of Reviews*. Social reformer.

that if I had not come to know God by a personal revelation of Him to my own soul, and to trust Him because I knew Him, I can hardly say into what scepticism I might have fallen."[8]

We may well note here that *Orders for Soldiers* (that is members of The Salvation Army) contains the following instructions: "The Salvation Soldier will have a kind heart and will deal lovingly with all those with whom he is associated. Especially will he manifest love and gentleness in his connection with . . . the animal world. Cruelty will be impossible to him . . . Not only will he avoid inflicting unnecessary hardship on animals, but he will, as far as he has opportunity, be ever willing to lend a hand to save or relieve any suffering creature that he comes across."[9] This book, *Orders and Regulations for Soldiers of The Salvation Army,* was written by William Booth in 1878, revised by Bramwell Booth, the Army's succeeding General, in 1927, and it is still in force in The Salvation Army in all parts of the world. Little Catherine Mumford, stamping her feet and shedding her bitter tears in anguish that she could not do more to protect ill-treated animals, never could have imagined what was to be her share in the creation of a vast religious body which would require of its adherents "love and gentleness" to animals, and issue "orders" against cruelty! Surely this is not an unimportant result of her influence on The Salvation Army? No other religious association to this day has, so far as I know, given kindness for the *creature's* sake, for sweet pity's sake, a definite place in its ordinances, teaching and practice.

If firm convictions in the moral sphere were inculcated and fostered in Catherine by her mother, it was through her father that she early developed that wide outlook on men and affairs which was hardly less important in fitting her for her future. In Mrs. Mumford's realm there was no latitude for independence of thought, but in her father's domain it was invited and encouraged. He had an active, even original mind in a practical way. For example, he was among the first to take a share in bringing in trams and himself experimented in the making of perambulators; his daughter was to possess one of his first for her own children. It was made to take to pieces and fold flat for transportation. John Mumford was an attractive personality, a jolly, good-looking, intelligent fellow, full of quick enthusiasms. When Catherine was nearly five, in 1833, continuing his business as a coachbuilder, he removed to his native town of Boston in Lincolnshire. There he threw himself into the newly developing temperance movement with zeal; he gave lectures, and his home became a centre of temperance interests. Leading advocates of the cause visited him; there were lively discussions, John Mumford's small daughter listening. She was like her father in some ways, and soon shared his new interest. The two talked and counter-talked. The child's mind was so quick to grasp a point, her repartee so apt, herself so engaging (especially when lost to all but the excitement of the moment) that to her father, and often

22

to his friends, her presence was a welcome pleasure. At first playfully on their part, and later quite as one of themselves, she shared in the talk. Her mind was seething with ideas. There was so much to explore, to enquire into, so much waiting for expression, that talking, for her, was an exciting adventure. Who could tell where it might lead? She and her father often found themselves in opposite camps, which only stimulated resourcefulness.

This freedom for fearless expression in talk was an important ingredient in Catherine's education. Mrs. Mumford was so afraid of harmful influences that she seldom allowed the child to go outside the home. Catherine had few acquaintances, and no friends of her own age. Reserved by nature, this isolated life, and especially the absence of youthful company, might well have centred the child's thoughts too much on herself. As it was, her father proved a healthy and stimulating intellectual companion. For him it must have been more than normally a delight to lead his clever little daughter into the world of his own interests; to debate with her all kinds of things, and in the jolly heat of argument to forget that he was not always the example to her in religion that he ought to be.

On temperance father and daughter were in complete agreement and only vied with each other in finding more telling points for their attack on the evils of strong drink; on her part, at least, a genuine conviction was established which was never to be shaken. In her brief reminiscences she declared, that at seven years of age, "I had washed my hands of strong drink."[10] Growing prematurely out of childhood in the Boston of the late eighteen-thirties, Catherine read avidly all to be found on the temperance question, became secretary of the junior branch of the local temperance society, and was busy in a practical way, helping to arrange meetings and raising subscriptions. What more could she do to further the cause, she asks herself? *Write!* We do not know how the thought kindled, perhaps when reading some article that she felt was a weak statement of the case. Heart beating faster at the thought, she decides that the venture is to be attempted. Good-nights are promptly said, her bedroom door locked, and by the light of a candle she sets about her writing. Never at a loss for words, and thoroughly convinced of the rightness of her opinions, pen flies over paper, leaving a small untidy script in its wake. How can one write carefully and at the same time quickly enough to catch one's thoughts? Even when copied she fears her childish handwriting may betray her age to the editor. A friend is allowed to share the secret. He copies and dispatches. This first attempt, and others, duly appear in various magazines to which her father subscribes. Catherine, keeping her secret, for the writings are anonymous, is happily excited. This is a fine way of having her say, of laying down the law, without drawing attention to herself!

There were other enthusiasms in her childhood. Her imagination

23

was seized upon by the state of the heathen, especially negroes, because they seemed to her to be the most oppressed and defenceless. She sat, an eager young listener, at all missionary meetings within her reach. What could she *do*? She collected money from her acquaintances, gave up sugar, and practised other denials to swell her fund; felt an intense desire to get more *done*. Oh, why were people satisfied with doing so little when the need was so terrific! She says of that time, "I can remember a sort of inward pity for what I thought then the small expectations of the church . . . I can remember how disappointed I felt at the comparatively small results which seemed to give satisfaction . . ."[11]

3

Catherine loved her father. In childhood she felt a freedom with him never experienced with her mother. A year or two later there slips into the end of a letter to her mother, "dear mother, I wish we knew each other better". Without thinking much or at all about it, the child felt her father understood her, they were companionable. If he had maintained his spiritual life, father and daughter would have drawn closer as her mind developed, and become lifelong friends. As it was she found him a delightful and affectionate companion. Writing to her betrothed once, she said that she felt uneasy at something "my father said. I am so sorry you should take any notice of it . . . the fact is he is a real tease."[12] He praised her sallies in conversation and encouraged her, sometimes on lines her mother would rather have suppressed. I found a phrase in one of the love-letters which might throw light on her girlhood. She said to her lover: ". . . I can do nothing under discouragement . . . it always unnerves me."[13] Perhaps Mrs. Mumford's high standards and rather narrow outlook had a disheartening effect on Catherine who had a tendency to depreciate anything to do with herself. From her letters it is evident that love of nature was early awakened in her. She wrote to her lover, "I shall never forget seeing the hills of Dovedale when I was seven years old . . . the impression, indefinite tho' it is, will never be effaced."[14] By the time she was in her teens she was enamoured of sea, sky and all the loveliness of the land. Until they left Boston her father kept a horse, a usual thing in those days, as a car is today. Driving in the countryside became one of her keenest joys. Probably her father took her with him on business trips and she learned to enjoy taking the reins into her own hands. She wrote once, "I am exceedingly fond of riding (not omnibuses) in open vehicles, until I came here I was used to it from a child. It always had a wonderful effect on my spirits. I used to drive very well." I like to picture the vivacious little girl chattering to her father as they drive along. She hears the larks singing and notices the loveliness of light and shade. She breathes the country air and learns to like what she once wrote of as "that free, sweet, wholesome kind of smell".

But something happened when she was twelve years old that changed the gay companionship between father and daughter. Then Catherine experienced her first deep grief. At this time she had a dog, a much loved retriever named Waterford. The two went everywhere together. One can easily imagine what this creaturely friendship meant in the child's life. The dog was devoted to his young mistress and she to him, the more because, as she tells, "I had no child companion." He used to lie outside her bedroom door and if he heard the sound of weeping would whine to be let in "that he might in some way manifest sympathy and comfort me". She lost this dog in a tragic manner. The circumstances were etched on her memory and clear as on the day it happened when, toward the end of her life, she recorded the story. "Wherever I went the dog would follow me about as my self-constituted protector, in fact we were inseparable companions. One day Waterford had accompanied me on a message to my father's house of business. I closed the door, leaving the dog outside, when I happened to strike my foot against something and cried out in sudden pain. Waterford heard me, and without a moment's hesitation came crashing through the large glass window to my rescue. My father was so vexed at the damage done that he caused the dog to be immediately shot. For months I suffered intolerably, especially in realizing it was in an effort to alleviate my sufferings that the beautiful creature had lost its life. Days passed before I could speak to my father, although he afterwards greatly regretted his hasty action, and strove to console me as best he could."[15] This happening deeply affected Catherine. She never afterwards felt the same toward her father. For a time he seemed to be almost a stranger. There was more than grief for the loved companion in the resentment that closed her lips for days and gave her months of inner suffering.

There had already begun to emerge in her an innate sense of justice, a strong critical judgment, the faculty to weigh and reason and then to decide. A tribunal arose in her own breast before which she did not flinch to arraign, not only herself and her own doings, but also the doings of the great ones of the earth. Napoleon was adjudged "the embodiment of selfish ambition". Caesar passed muster better, for "though by no means an attractive character . . . he appeared to me to desire the good of his country, and not merely his own aggrandizement".[16] These girlish verdicts were of no importance to anyone but herself. But to *her*, her *own* conclusions began to matter much and will matter more. What she believed, and what her thought, in the inner realm of her being began to loom large. There was an unsuspected strength behind the emotional façade of her nature. She searched the Bible in earnest now to find her own conclusions. The bedtime prayers were no longer shared with her mother. To her lover, William Booth, she once wrote ". . . the light and influence of His Holy Spirit has attended me from earliest infancy, and often excited in my childish heart struggles, hopes and fears of no ordinary nature; though such struggles were hid in the penetralia of my own spirit, and unknown to any mortal."[17] The episode of the dog's death and the turmoil of heart that ensued, may well have precipitated the spiritual conflict about which she did not open her lips until years afterwards.

We know that Mrs. Mumford noted a failure of health and spirits. She may have felt, with a mother's quick intuition, that the child was withdrawing too much into herself. Could it be that there was too much of praying and reading? Whether or not, Mrs. Mumford decided that it would be good for Catherine to go to school. A lady who attended the same chapel in Boston as the Mumfords had become friendly. She was a woman of unusual ability and, even more important to Catherine's mother, a sincere Christian. Principal of a girls' school, it was she who persuaded Mrs. Mumford to let Catherine become one of her pupils. School opened the door for Catherine to associate with girls of her own age; she was twelve, and she received a host of new impressions. The child did not find herself at a disadvantage educationally; and she now applied herself with happy ardour to her lessons. She was soon on good terms with pupils and teachers; was early made monitor and by common consent her version of any incident was accepted without question. All had soon learned that nothing could induce Catherine Mumford to tell a falsehood. History was her favourite subject; she showed special aptitude for composition, liked geography and longed to visit other lands. Arithmetic was her bugbear. She said afterwards that she thought this was because it was taught in a "senseless way". Later, mathematics attracted her. The time passed happily. One of her rare references to youthful delights is to these school days. She was joyous, and soon began to indulge her love of teaching by coaching those who were not so quick at their lessons.

But not all school memories were happy ones. That intense nature of hers gave trouble, made her outbursts of temper increasingly a misery to herself, especially in retrospect. She came in for a share of teasing because she was thought to be a favourite of the Principal. The outcome was a wholesome, if stormy, experience for Catherine. How *unjust* to blame her for Miss X's praise! And when her contradictions only provoked the teasers to more teasing, Catherine's fury would break forth. When the flare-up was over she was ready to exaggerate her share of the blame and freely expressed her regrets. She felt she was worse than others thought her; for when she was angry she was very, very angry—she alone knew how angry. It was the force of the *inner* storm that brought so deep a sense of condemnation. It was comparatively easy to tell her schoolfellows that she was sorry, but they did not know how wicked her feelings had been. She knew! And that knowledge taught her much about her own heart, brought, too, the humiliation and pain that followed failure to act as she knew she ought.

In her studies she revelled; got into the way of taking a book with her when walking in the lanes near home; applied herself too closely perhaps? In those days comparatively little attention was given to the physical needs of growing children; indeed, little was known of essentials for health. Children of middle-class homes were often worse off than their poorer country neighbours in the matter of fresh air and vitamin-rich foods. In 1843, when she was fourteen years of age, serious curvature of the spine showed itself. The brief school-days came to an abrupt end. For months Catherine must lie on her face in a kind of hammock. Here was a trial for her active nature, but from it came the freedom to study to her heart's content, and in the main to make her own choice of books. Mrs. Mumford made no attempt to resume control of her daughter's education. The school Principal had, doubtless, assured her that Catherine was as advanced as girls of the day needed to be and that therefore she need not trouble with further studies unless she liked. She *did* like. She used her enforced inactivity to immerse herself in religious history and theology. Who, if anyone, advised what books she should choose? We do not know. Perhaps her father. Perhaps the Principal of her school, who would surely still be interested in her pupil and continue to visit the house as an acquaintance. Catherine was already an omnivorous reader and had access to religious magazines of the day; references to books in these may have interested her. We do know that during this time she read and studied a number of books on doctrine and on Church history, including the translated works of Mosheim and Neander. From these and similar books she gained her knowledge, and an informed appreciation, of the first centuries of Christianity with a precocious understanding of the teachings and problems of the early Church.

Such reading provided her with a foundation of facts, a safeguard when conflicting doctrines came up for judgment. For instance, from Mosheim she learned that the Calvinistic teaching had no foundation in the doctrine of the early Church. Calvin's doctrine of predestination, as expounded in Catherine's own day, had become a stumbling block to many sincere souls; aspects of the teaching were over-emphasized until the whole was sometimes so distorted as to be as much an "error" as those Calvin sought to combat. Wesley's works held high place with her, as became a child of Methodism. Wesley's convert, Fletcher of Madeley, and especially his treatise, *Checks to Antinomianism,* greatly influenced her. From this she drank in the full force of

27

Fletcher's fervid exposition and refutation of the doctrine of pre-destination. It was well for The Salvation Army that Catherine Mumford thoroughly sifted this question and that she reached conclusions that enabled her to help many people in the years to come, and to define Salvation Army doctrine on the question. Finney's writings and biography, his lectures on theology in particular, and other theological books were first read through and then perused and annotated. Catherine made epitomes of the chief contentions of the authors whose works impressed her. The facsimile of a page of her notes on *Butler's Analogy** serves as an example. Butler's conception of life as a school gave her a reasoned confirmation of the truth already discerned in the Bible. Her mind yielded assent, and the effect may be traced in her letters and sermons. Dr. Laura Petri† says, "Catherine Booth never forgot her call and never forsook her role as teacher in this school."[18] Biographies attracted her and from them she imbibed an immense variety of knowledge of people. At fifteen or thereabouts she tried hard to cope with Newton's‡ elaborate work on prophecy. She made notes, looked up references, and then, for one of her years, arrived at a notable conclusion. Stead said of this, "with the swift decisiveness of her nature, she brushed away the whole art and mystery of prophecy-mongering. A sensible decision, and one due to her intense practicability, which next to her native gift of humour saved her from many a 'pitfall'."[19] Her view was that "since so many able and learned people differed regarding the matter, it would be unwise for me to spend time and effort in striving to come to any clearer conclusion."[20] Speculations relieved the solemnity of the themes engaging her. She was made thoroughly happy to find that Wesley and Butler envisaged the possibility of a future life for animals. Reading from her couch, her thoughts travelled in a world of ever-opening vistas. Questions new to her sprang up on all sides. Old truths were met clothed in new garments. She was thinking, thinking, praying too, but thinking. It was at this time that the foundations of her intellectual beliefs were well and truly laid.

In these two years, from fourteen to sixteen, Catherine was engrossed with problems of doctrine, philosophy and theology. It is well to realize that these studies were genuinely her choice, entered into to satisfy the demands of her own mind, and to meet the questions that kept on springing up there. During her fifteenth year she faced a mental and spiritual crisis. She felt her thoughts were sinking into confusion amidst contradictory theories; as if she were

* *Analogy of Religion* by Joseph Butler, theologian (1692-1752), Bishop of Britol, Dean of St. Paul's, etc. See facing page 30.

† Laura Petri, Doctor of Philosophy, author; wrote a Life of Catherine Booth, *Catherine Booth och Salvationismen*, 1925.

‡ Sir Isaac Newton, philosopher, scientist (1642-1727).

drifting into a mental mist. Then abruptly she came to a decision that was like taking a leap from the lines authority laid down. It set her on a path of independence that might have proved highly dangerous; might have led her into scepticism. She decided to *reject all theories* which contradicted her *own* ideas of right and wrong. The resulting fury, almost frenzy, of reading, arose partly from the necessity she felt for putting "all theories about God" to the test of this decision. Note that her attitude was not merely a revolt against authoritarian belief, common enough in adolescence, but that it included a recognition of her individual responsibility to *justify* to her own mind each rejection; with the corollary that theories *not* so rejected *must* be accepted as truth; to reject any of *these* would henceforth be to rebel against God. Reading her letters, lectures and sermons, it is surprising to find how comprehensively the doctrines and disciplines of The Salvation Army are to be found in them. She was indeed to be the teacher of the people, and her teaching was sound teaching. It was in these two years of immobility that Catherine wrestled with questions and fought through confusing theories to a clear conception of truth, and was enabled to accept dogmas from which she never departed.

Mrs. Mumford nursed Catherine devotedly, feared a little for her, seeing her so absorbed in study, but by now she was getting used to her daughter's excited distractions. Writing, after her marriage, to her mother, and waxing enthusiastic about some plan, Catherine says, "I know you will say, 'There goes Kate again!'" Mrs. Mumford gave up trying to curb her. Gradually the little daughter slipped away. She was in process of becoming what Begbie called "an able, masterful and brilliant young woman ... a terror to the loose thinkers and careless talkers of her little circle".[21] The spinal trouble yielded to treatment. After more than a year of lying prostrate, Catherine was allowed to be up a little daily. Probably the child was too energetic, for pain in the back continued in some measure all through her life. At twenty-three she had electric and other treatment for noticeable curvature, and fitfully feared being permanently "deformed". A doctor attending her when she was twenty-four examined her back. In a letter to William Booth at the time, Catherine wrote, "After examining the bones from top to bottom, he said 'Why, I see nothing the matter with it. That back is all right.' 'Yes,' mother said, 'but you should have seen it twelve months ago.'"[22]

At fifteen the chief of the pleasures, that permission to be about brought, was to go to chapel. Throughout her childhood Sunday was a day of happy experiences. It brought her in contact with people; the crowd, the singing, the stir of life and, at an early age, the sermon; all attracted her, fed her thoughts. Mrs. Mumford welcomed the resumption of chapel-going. She hoped it might break the spell of the books, and distract Catherine, who was still too much of an invalid

29

for her mother's peace of mind. Visitors, in the shape of cousins from Derby, put in an appearance. Possibly their stay in the home was the result of a little scheming on Mrs. Mumford's part. One of the cousins is a fine-looking young man of quick intelligence. Catherine has been acquainted with him in desultory fashion as long as she can remember. Always a favourite of his, she now seems suddenly grown-up and his equal. Her scintillating talk entrances him; he finds her girlish beauty very appealing, irresistible when her eyes smile into his, as she fervently expounds some theory or listens, alert, to his account of something or other. He is very soon in love with her. Catherine likes him. He is attentive, sympathetic, clever too. Her heart goes out to him in a pleasurable sort of way. His company is a happy interlude; it might easily become a necessity. What if it did? He is not religious as she understands religion; still, she could reason, she knew, with effect, surely it would not be hard to win him for God? He wants to please her, to agree with her? Clearly, then, she is the one who could lead him into truth?

So days, weeks pass; but as Catherine's feelings become more engaged, she thinks more deeply about him and hears conscience speak in the familiar words, "Be ye not unequally yoked together with unbelievers." However much she likes him she cannot evade the fact that the young man is as yet an "unbeliever". In spite of this, her heart inclines towards him; she feels the stirring of something new within, and her mind becomes all turmoil. In some strange way she finds herself compelled to argue on both sides. He goes with her to chapel, his eyes on her rather than on the preacher. He scratches clever little sketches on the pew in front to attract her attention to himself; a harmless ruse, he thinks, but it tends to mark his lack of piety, and troubles rather than amuses her. He goes away. They correspond. He returns, his ardour increases. For a time Catherine shrinks from repulsing him; but presently she knows she must. She dare not go against God's express command. So the farewell is said, tenderly, and Catherine must, I fancy, never have been more desirable to her young lover than when she was striving to solace him for his loss of her. "It cost me a considerable effort at the time," she afterwards wrote, but she learned from her own heart's experience to counsel others who might be drifting into disobedience to God in like circumstances. She asks, "What says your own conscience about accepting that unconverted lover? I entreat you, obey! Never mind what friends say, what inclination says, what apparent interest says; they all *lie* if they contradict God!"[23] Catherine was now on the verge of sixteen and shortly after the young man had his dismissal, the Mumfords went to London, making their home in Brixton.

Butler's Analogy

Chapter 1st. ...

4

The move to London was a great event in Catherine's life. Once installed in the new home she is all eagerness to see for herself something of the city's historical monuments. St. Paul's, the Palace of Westminster, the Abbey, all delight her and surpass her expectations. She goes to the National Gallery and elsewhere, as strength allows; thinking new thoughts of man's greatness from these works of his hands. This widening of experience was good for her. The wonders and beauties of the past are wholesome food for thought at sixteen, and Catherine's enthusiastic nature made her especially responsive. Then in London there were opportunities for listening to sermons of a different type from those within reach at Boston. Exeter Hall was in its hey-day and eminent speakers were to be heard there. The chapel Mrs. Mumford attended was a larger, more influential centre than any Catherine had known before. As her health improved, she longed for opportunity to pursue her studies. A few years later she wrote of her discontents at this period: "I have often ... wished I had been born with a mind *content* to feed on the empty husks in which I have seen others take so much delight, rather than be conscious of the possession of powers which must lie dormant and talents uncultivated and desires and hopes which could never be realized. I have been ready to demand of the Lord why He made me thus and deprived me of the means to that culture and improvement which He had so lavishly bestowed upon others who neither valued nor used them."[24] These stirrings of ambition came, in part at any rate, from her growing perception that she was possessed of mind and will different from, if not superior to, those of her acquaintances. Did she now perhaps for a time feel it a disability to be a girl?

The novelty of being in London recedes. Catherine is again left much to her own devices. Reading and studying go on; there are walks and drives in the nearby country. She goes with alacrity to the new chapel of which her mother has become a member, but within her lies a new unrest. Hungry for knowledge, for reason's certainties, as she has been, she now longs for an inner witness: the *rest* of certainty in the soul's secret place. Her thoughts begin to turn inwardly to herself. Hitherto her energies of mind and heart have been largely taken up with things outside herself. Catherine is not introspective by nature. Her preoccupation with religion was not induced by interest in her own state, nor, as such, in her own religious experience, which was a straightforward, sincere and childlike desire to please God. The active, practical vigour of her powers had been engaged outside herself. This will be true of her all her life.

She is not primarily interested in her own feelings, but in her relation to God and to others. In all her thirst to *know* about God, about mankind's history, the vital force of her thought is not concerned with herself, but with the deep mysteries of God and of her duty to Him; with thoughts akin to what she once called "an overwhelming, a prodigious thought, *that Christ shed His blood for every soul of man*". Now, on the threshold of her seventeenth year, questions arise, disturbing, insistent, related to her own heart. Has she the assurance of her *own* salvation? Knowing so much *about* God and man's conception of Him, does she know Him by *personal revelation of Him* to her own soul? This for her now becomes the supreme question; her whole future hangs upon the answer.

She looks back and cannot remember a time when she did not pray to God and want to please Him. She said, "I had the strivings of God's Spirit all my life, since I was about two years old." Is such consciousness of God in infancy more common than is generally supposed? Jacques Lusseyran, writing of his earliest recollections, says: "I knew very early, I am quite sure of it, that . . . another Being concerned Himself with me and even addressed Himself to me. This Other I did not even call God. My parents spoke to me about God, but only later. I had no name for Him. He was just there . . . My religion began like this."[25] Catherine's narrative continues, "My dear mother has often told me how she went upstairs to find me crying, and when she questioned me, I said I was crying because I had sinned against God . . . All through my childhood I was graciously sheltered by a watchful mother from outward sin and, in fact, brought up a Christian."[26] Memory confirms all this, yet the question persists. She asks herself, "Do I know God by a personal revelation of Him to my own soul?" There are no unforgiven outward sins to separate her from God. But there have been sins. Those outbursts of temper when at school come to her mind. The death of her dog when she was twelve and the mental suffering that lasted for three months afterwards, is five years away, but still vivid to her mind's eye, as it will be all her life. The nature of the temptation which then assailed her she never brought herself to tell. But as we search out her soul's experience from the records of her life and words, we are justified in surmising. I am convinced of its nature. Read what she said of it herself, take it literally; it is an account of something that really happened to her. Do not shy away from the old-fashioned wording. "When not more than twelve," she wrote to William, her betrothed, "I passed through such an ordeal of fiery temptation for about the space of three months as but to reflect on makes my soul recoil within me; at that age I frequently watered my couch with my tears, and the billows of the Almighty seemed to go over me. Many a time my whole frame has trembled under the foul attacks of the adversary, and his attacks were so subtle and of such a nature that I could not then on pain

Bramwell Booth's favourite portrait of his mother

William Booth in 1856, from a portrait to mark his evangelistic ministry in Sheffield

Catherine Mumford shortly before her marriage in 1855

of death have revealed them to anyone ... So I endured alone and unaided by any earthly friend these fearful conflicts of soul ... But the storm passed, and my mind regained in great measure its former vivacity."[27] In my opinion we are justified in connecting what Catherine thus recounts with the experience she passed through at the death of her dog, about which she said "for months I suffered intolerably". Her age fits, and surely there could not have been *two* such periods in the same year? Further, it is evident that there was something more than grief for the loss of a loved companion in the child's resentment against her father and the inner tumults which followed. She was young and unacquainted with evil. She saw her father in a new light and he would never be the same to her as before. Her anguish at the mere remembrance of this experience excludes the idea that it was in the nature of sorrow for sin such as she had felt before, or merely deep regret at the vehemence of her resentment against her father. She had often asked for and received forgiveness. But "these fearful conflicts of soul" that she felt she could not "on pain of death have revealed to anyone" must have been something darker; a temptation that shook her to the very depths of her being. What then? She confided in no one. She felt alone, alone in the universe. Her whole being trembled under the "attacks of the adversary"; and "his attacks were so subtle!" What if he insinuated the question: *Is there a God?* To one whose whole life has been passed in the company of thoughts about God, and who has grown up with the conception of the world and all beloved objects as in His keeping, the shock of recognizing that unbelief is possible can be devastating. Even to be aware of the temptation to doubt seems to be a pollution; as she herself described to William, it was a "foul" attack. Dr. Laura Petri reaches the same conclusion. She says "there is real ground for the assumption that this fierce conflict in childhood concerned nothing less than faith in God's existence."[28]

Catherine, child though she was, might at this time have become an atheist. The strength of temptation lies in the vulnerability of the character assailed. This child, the logical strength of whose mind was that she must *reconcile* all things; who could not tolerate injustice, or pretence, must herself be "satisfied", or reject all profession of faith. Judging from what we know of her character before and after this conflict, it seems to me inevitable that at some time in her life this battle in the mind for faith must have been fought; the fool's verdict "there is no God" faced and rejected.

This is the first serious crisis in Catherine's soul's life, perhaps the most important. She withstood the enemy's assault, his subtle approach was rejected. The free spirit, "unaided by any earthly friend", owned and worshipped God, turned from the unreasonable horror and darkness of a godless universe as from something unbelievable. "My mind," she said, "gained its former vivacity." Significant this, of

B

the nature of the conflict. It was in some manner a subjection of her thoughts, the assent of her *mind* to God. After this conflict Catherine was no longer only a child. She has discovered herself. Nothing so completely reveals to man his own importance as a person, as does his individual recognition of God, no matter at what age that avowal takes place. Once God is consciously admitted into man's universe that man ceases to be an ant in the ant heap, a grain of sand tossed by blind force; he becomes a creature related to his Creator. Catherine emerges from this encounter with the evil one, aware of herself in a new way. She sees herself a being able to stand erect and "enter into judgment with the Almighty"; she uses that expression of herself in the same letter as that in which she tells of the conflict. Henceforth God is not merely taken for granted as the perfect, all-powerful, all-loving Father in heaven of childhood's days. He becomes in a growing sense the all-pervading Presence who gives meaning to life and to death; the One who claims her love and confidence, and with whom all other loves are brought into harmony. The command "Thou shalt love the Lord thy God . . ." is no longer a counsel of perfection unattainable by ordinary mortals but a channel for the inexpressible longing of the human heart to adore and to know the Being whom faith reveals.

Always her logical mind forces Catherine back to sound beginnings. Theoretical knowledge must be substantiated by her own experience. It is this passion for winning an inner assent that led her when fourteen years old to reject, as she put it, "all theories *about* God and religion which contradicted my innate perception of right and wrong".[29] Harmony between her "innate perception" and her faith, between reason and belief was indispensable to her. We may call this the second crisis or phase in Catherine's spiritual development. It was not a fierce fight as was the first, but a rising tide of conviction. Here at fourteen it was established for her that the light of the Spirit in the soul must be at one with God's word in the Bible. This was to be a safeguard for her. Now was laid that foundation of "sound doctrine" which would protect and guide her and William Booth, The Salvation Army too. Speaking in after years she said of this experience, "I could not then put it into this language, but I remember distinctly the feelings of my soul. I said, 'All that is in me akin to goodness and truth God has put there, and I will never believe that what God has put in me contradicts what He has put into this Book [the Bible] . . . and thank God I came to the Scriptures for myself, which I recommend you to do. Don't imagine that the repugnant views of the character of God which have been forced upon you by professed theologians will form any excuse for your rejection of this Book or of the divine authority of it in the great day of account . . .' "[30]

At seventeen Catherine came to the third crisis in her religious experience. The matters that disturbed her were not concerned with faith in God; nor with conflicting dogmas. The question now is not, *is* there a God; nor, can I accept this or that conception of Him; but do I know Him by a personal revelation of Himself to my own soul? She felt that if the witness of the Holy Spirit to her own heart were not given, all her knowledge *about* God, *about* the practice of religion, would fail to satisfy.

In each phase of her soul's awakening the keynote of Catherine's cry is "*I* must know. *I* must find." And it is so now at seventeen when she comes to feel that she is uncertain whether she has experienced the change of heart about which she has read so much. She is now "determined to leave the question no longer in doubt". One of Satan's snares for her at this time, she tells, was this: "*You* must not expect such a change as you read of in books; *you* have been half a Christian all your life. You always feared God. You must content yourself with this..." and she goes on, "I was terribly afraid of being self-deceived. I said 'No, my heart *is* as bad as other people's, and if I have not sinned outwardly I have inwardly.' My foolish wicked heart had often been ready to enter into judgment with the Almighty. I said, 'I will never rest till I am thoroughly and truly changed, and know it as any thief or great outward sinner...' I refused to be saved by logic... faith is not logic, but logic may help faith... It seemed unreasonable to suppose that I could be saved and not know it." She could not recall any particular place or moment when she had definitely stepped out on the promises of God and received the witness of the Holy Spirit to her salvation. She now prays especially for this. Often she paces her room until early morning, reasoning, praying. Does this anguish of desire for assurance, she asks herself, mean that she is receiving new light? Or does it mean that she *is* already saved? The uncertainty saps her faith. The terrible fear of being self-deceived grows in her, spoils her praying and again and again her logical turn of thought forces her back to the conclusion which she has already accepted that "*it seemed unreasonable to suppose that I could be saved and not know it.*"[31] The determination to settle the question beyond doubt hardens; one way or the other she *must* know.

One night, wearied out, she places her Bible and hymn book as usual under her pillow, and in a last prayer asks, as she had done many times before, that she might awake to the assurance of her acceptance with God. Of this "struggle" and its issue she tells, "I cried for nothing on earth or in heaven, but that I might find Him Whom my soul panted after. And I did find Him...I knew Him, I can't tell how, but I knew Him. I knew He was well pleased with me."[32] It is in the morning hour, on waking, that she opens her hymn book, and reads:

35

> *My God, I am Thine,*
> *What a comfort divine,*
> *What a blessing to know that my Jesus is mine!*

She says "the words came to my inmost soul with a force and illumination they had never before possessed. It was as impossible for me to doubt, as it had been before for me to exercise faith. [Notice here that Catherine herself emphasizes *lack of faith* as the crux of the matter for her.] I no longer hoped that I was saved; I was *certain* of it. The assurance of my salvation seemed to fill my soul. I jumped out of bed and without waiting to dress ran into my mother's room and told her what had happened. Till then I had been very backward in speaking, even to her, upon spiritual matters. I could not open my heart to her. I was so happy I felt as if walking on air."[33]

It would be a mistake to conclude that the form of the third crisis in Catherine's spiritual development was entirely the outcome of Methodist teaching, as some have thought. Had the doctrine of conversion been unemphasized, even unknown, in her circle, her own need would still have driven her to seek the event under whatever name. Had she not found assurance of her individual acceptance with God, she must have renounced religion altogether. She could never have survived years of doubt and uncertainty. Her passionate love of truth barred the way to any profession tainted with unreality and on the other hand her sense of the logical begat convictions that allowed no rest until experience had been brought into harmony with them. Once convinced that if she were God's child it was *reasonable* she should know it, Catherine felt that there was only one road open to her, to seek until that knowledge were given; the alternative was to turn away from God altogether. The nature of the sins that burden the heart matters not at all; what each heart needs is to be reconciled to God, to possess by faith the assurance that Christ pardons and receives. Religious experiences are never identical. Souls pass through similar phases, there are recognizable features in the form experience takes but, when genuine, it is essentially individual, and is not capable of proof except to the consciousness of the partaker.

Catherine's experience was important not alone to herself but to The Salvation Army. Her preaching exercised a vital influence on its formative years. The majority of early converts in The Salvation Army were saved from flagrant sin; the assurance of forgiveness came swiftly, as an upleaping flame of joy, and but for Catherine Booth's own experience that assurance might all too readily have come to be associated with salvation from gross sinning alone. How clearly she taught that everyone, child or grown-up, stood in equal need of the inner witness of sonship, the secret token of acceptance with God; the knowledge that the free spirit has made its choice and submitted to God. "It does not signify," she once said, "how we are trained or what were the particular circumstances of our antecedent life; there comes a crisis, a moment when every human soul which enters the Kingdom of God has to make its choice of that Kingdom in preference of *everything* that it holds and owns as its world . . . and embrace and choose God."[34] On another occasion she declared, "Saving faith is not intellectual perception of the truth . . . if a mere intellectual perception of the truth were saving faith, the devil would have been saved long ago! There are tens of thousands of people in this country who have been taught that because they have received the facts *about* Jesus Christ into their minds, they are Christians. . . . Saving faith is not mere feeling on the subject of religion . . . it is the committal, the giving over of the soul and of the whole being to God. It means such a giving of himself up to God as constitutes him henceforth God's man . . . He wants you to say, 'Now, Lord, all the guilt of my past life is open to You, but You have promised to receive and save me . . . I come and put myself at the foot of the Cross *to be Yours wholly for ever.'* . . . I never knew a soul come to that in my life . . . who did not soon get flooded with light."[35]

It was early in the morning of June 15, 1846, when Catherine rushed in to share with her mother the joyful knowledge that she was "saved". The next few months were the happiest she had yet known. She felt a harmony in all her being. Her "enthusiastic, excitable nature" (this is her own description), released from the strain of the past striving, went free in an ecstasy of joy. She could not sing, had no ear for music, or now she would certainly have sung for joy. She became a member of the Brixton Methodist Church. In her honesty she had refused to do so before. To be a child of the Church before she had the assurance that she was a child of God would, she thought, have been to make a false profession. Catherine joined the weekly class meeting. Her class leader, a Mrs. Leay, wife of a retired minister of the circuit, helped her considerably: for one thing she insisted that Catherine should overcome her timidity, and take her turn in praying aloud and later to give her "testimony" as was the custom in Methodist Class Meetings. Sometimes Mrs. Leay kept the class waiting on their knees for five minutes for Catherine to begin! This learning to speak to God aloud in the presence of others was most valuable; it is unlikely that she could have brought herself to speak to a congregation had she not already been accustomed to pray aloud before people. The world owes something to Mrs. Leay for helping her new class member to win this freedom. She gained Catherine's confidence, who came to feel that here was one to whom she could speak of her heart's experience. "My mother in Christ," Catherine, at eighteen, called her.

It was a radiant daughter who sat beside Mrs. Mumford now, listening to the sermon. Able sermons were the rule in this more fashionable Brixton church, different in several ways from the homely chapel in Boston. Catherine, eager to *do something*, began to speak to acquaintances about Christ. For three months after her conversion she was possessed by joy. Hopes had changed into realities that brought a new security to all her precious things. Her joy gave her liberty to share with others her own experiences. The discovery that she was able to help some of them filled her heart with a new delight, a blend of wonder that God would deign to use her and of ecstasy when what she did was effective. For the time being this joy over-ruled her timidity and the dread of being in any sense singular which was natural to her.

After her conversion Catherine's desire to help others brought a new zest to her praying and increasingly prayer became a conscious communion with Christ. She sometimes rose from her knees feeling that she had received not merely temporary elevation of mind but new illumination of Truth that remained vivid all her life. She wrote to her lover of such an experience: "It was in secret communion with Him I realized the glorious vision ... Oh, the comfort and light which such a vision leaves! . . . I believe hell itself could not obliterate the view then given me..."[36] I think that it may have been during the period of exaltation which followed her conversion, that she found her faith invigorated when she actually voiced her prayers. She was more able to elude material environment and to enter, as it were, another dimension of thought. She said once, "When my mother had gone out I used to like to get alone and pray aloud". Some prayers, she felt, must be put into words that she could hear. Often she prayed pacing her room, her heart pent up with thanks-giving and desire. She was of a deeply emotional nature and in the early years of her spiritual life there were often tears for joy as well as grief when praying. She counted on prayer for the renewal of strength, for guidance and for light "to know the whole truth as it is in Jesus". She did not allow the mystery of prayer to prevent her praying; it was part of her soul's life, an expression of her love to God and of her love for others. When she became engaged to William Booth they often planned to be praying, each for the other, at the same hour. She hardly wrote a letter that did not include the plea "pray for me".

5

Since her conversion Catherine had grown much closer to her mother, who was an increasingly lonely woman. The shadow of a great grief began to blot out the sun of human happiness for her.

John Mumford had been an enthusiastic Methodist, a zealous and eloquent local preacher, when he won his wife out of a worldly, weathly home; then he thought himself called of God to become a minister, but resisted the conviction and gradually became engrossed in trying to make money. His ardour in God's service cooled, he ceased to preach, finally abandoning even the profession of religion, as also his "temperance" views. Under the stress of financial difficulties in business Mr. Mumford had begun to take an occasional glass of wine to brace himself. He was emotional and quickly grew depressed; a little more wine, and then still more was needed. Before long it took spirits to revive him, and Catherine and her mother had the unspeakable misery of watching him, whom they both loved, drift into the power of the hated "drink". This grief cut to the very quick of Catherine's soul. She had not discarded her childhood's convictions about temperance, and now all those theoretical arguments gained a bitter strength from this personal wound. It is likely that the depressing atmosphere in the home at this time, and her grief on her father's account, reacted on Catherine's intense nature with exaggerated force, predisposing her to the serious illness which showed itself in the September of 1846, when her life was endangered. A chill brought inflammation of the lungs and she was confined to her room all the winter. Physical weakness added to the effort of broaching spiritual matters in conversation. Timidity re-asserted itself. Gradually she lost her first freedom to speak of her Saviour, the ebullient glow of her joy cooled.

By May she was considered well enough to travel to Brighton. The air there was "so good", and there was an aunt with whom she could stay. Mrs. Mumford could not leave her husband. One suspects that it was loneliness and the fear that she might not recover that now caused Catherine to make the one attempt of her life to keep a diary. Normally she felt no need to analyse and record her feelings, nor was she interested enough in herself and her doings to take the time for writing about them for no particular purpose. What would be the use of it anyway? would have been Catherine's question. She was practical, almost utilitarian in her outlook on life; and this, linked to her energy and intenseness, led her to overstress the importance of "doing" things.

Her daughter's illness was a severe trial to Mrs. Mumford, who had not been able to accept it with resignation. Since the anxiety about Mr. Mumford, Catherine had become her mother's confidant. The journal shows how their roles are reversed. It is the daughter who plans to cheer and comfort, pleading with God for her parents. I think some may see, with me, a lovely foretaste of this spiritual concern for the multitude in the years to come, in the daughter's love and solicitude for those most dear to her. She learned how precious it is to plead with God for those we love. On the day after arrival in Brighton, and every day until her return home, she writes in her journal. All entries are in the same strain, and brief extracts or merely a phrase are enough to show the trend of her thoughts at this time, and to reveal something of what she was like.

May 12 [1847]. "I felt very ill in the train, but could lie down when I felt faint. My mind was kept calm, and while passing through some tunnels [we remind ourselves that trains were new in those days, and to pass through a tunnel meant pitch dark and fearful racket] I thought, should any accident happen amidst this darkness and hurry me into eternity, shall I find myself in Glory? and I felt I could say, even here, 'Lord, if it were Thy will to take me I could come, but how unworthy I am'."

May 13. "I feel very much cast down at the thoughts of being away from home ..."

May 14. "This morning while reading *Roe's Devout Exercises of the Heart,* I was much helped and enabled to give myself afresh into the hands of God, to do and suffer all His will. Oh, that I may be made useful to this family ... help me to display the Christian character ... I find much need of watchfulness and prayer, and I have this day taken up my cross in reproving sin ... Lord, follow with the conviction of Thy Spirit all I have said ... Oh, to be a Christian indeed and to *love Thee* with all my heart is all my desire. I do love Thee, but I want to love Thee more, I want to enjoy Thee more." These words express an attitude of mind. Catherine is beginning to enjoy God for what He *is,* independently of His works. She is on the way to say with Paul "I *know* in whom I have believed." In the secret place of her soul she has begun to rejoice in the beauty of God's *righteousness.* Her knowledge of what He *is* is beginning to be a sanctuary where she is safe from the despairs at man's wickedness and misery which, had she not possessed it, might have overwhelmed her spirit. She wrote once to William Booth, her betrothed, of her soul's experience before she had met him: "*God is so good.* If we could only see Him as He is ... Oh, let us pray and watch to get our eyes fully opened to behold His beauty."[37] She begins to prove for herself that in the contemplation of God "one delights in seeing the object loved, and the very delight in the object seen arouses a yet greater love".[38] To her lover, to her children and friends she often writes of "enjoying God". But back to her Journal in 1847.

May 15. "I was much blessed this morning at private prayer particularly in commending my dear parents into the hands of God. I sometimes get into an agony of feeling while praying for my dear father. O my Lord, answer prayers and bring him back to Thyself."

Sunday, May 16. "I went to chapel ... though I felt very poorly and my cough was very troublesome, which gave rise to wandering thoughts. At night I could not venture to chapel again but spent the time in reading to my dear aunt and the person in the house ...

40

I hope the Lord will make me useful here. I think the restitution of my health is *not* the only reason I am come. My dear aunt is in trouble about one of her children who is not a comfort to her..."

May 17. "This morning I felt very happy and held sweet communion with my Lord."

May 18. "I feel very poorly today... so exceedingly low and much inclined to fret... oh, for more patience and resignation... Lord, Thy will be done. Only let me *feel* that all I do is right."

May 19. "I went to class and felt blessed, but my mind is so excited at these times that it is a great exertion to speak. I am most blessed when alone in my room quietly... In the morning before I was up a lady came to see me through the instrumentality of Mrs. Leay. I found her to be a Christian, though not a Wesleyan, but this signified nothing." Note the sweeping finality of this judgment; the more significant that Catherine is herself a devoted Wesleyan. In later years she wrote to her lover, "I love all who love the Lord, I abhor sectarianism more and more."[39] Christian unity, she claimed, should be the unity of faith and love, not of form and method. Her view was incorporated in The Salvation Army discipline.

May 24. "I have been drawn out to pray for my dearest mother more than usual... and have this day received a letter which made me weep tears of joy. As soon as I had read it I kneeled down and gave full vent to the gratitude that overflowed my heart..."

May 25. "Felt poorly this morning; had rather a restless night. Wrote to my dear mother and felt blessed in so doing. May my letter prove a word in season to tend to establish her confidence in the Lord."

May 28. "A day of inward peace. I feel more resignation to the will of my Lord... I think I can say with truth and sincerity Thy will be done."

May 29. "I feel very poorly... I have written a letter today to my dear father. May God bless it to his soul."

The entry for *June 1* recalls her conversion. "I see the month's return that fixed my happy choice—twelve months this month I became a child of God... Oh, my gracious, loving Lord what records of Thy faithfulness and lovingkindness does the past present ... I feel ashamed before Thee of the numerous instances in which I have grieved the Holy Spirit and the many times my heart has been unbelieving and ready to doubt Thy faithfulness... Thy will be done only let me be Thine, whether suffering or in health, whether living or dying..." *Doing God's will,* being ready at every step on life's way to say, "Not my will, but Thine be done", is already for her the very essence of religion. "I regarded conformity to the will of God as true religion even from childhood," she told her betrothed. A few years later she wrote to her mother, "I don't believe in any religion apart from doing the will of God."

41

The journal continues, "I have posted a letter to my dear father filling two notes full. It is a really encouraging letter. Lord, accompany it with the influence of Thy Spirit . . . Mr. Wells asked me to pray in class but I did not and do not feel right about it. I was just going to begin when he began. I made the cross bigger than it really was but I have made up my mind tonight that I will never do so again. I will pray if I can at all . . ."

June 2. "This morning I was blessed in private prayer. I remained in bed until twelve. I felt very poorly with pain in my breast and shoulders. I have suffered a great deal with my back today . . . Oh, how I shall enjoy the kindness and attention of my dear mother when I again enjoy them. Lord, help her and undertake for us in our temporal difficulties . . ."

June 3. "This morning I was much blessed in prayer. I rose earlier and went out on the level and sat down on the seat to read Miss R.'s *Heart Exercises*. I felt a sweet calm overspread my mind. The beautiful scenery around, the tranquillity that reigned seemed well to suit me . . . I have had pain in my shoulder today and my back. Altogether the ways of God are mysterious and past finding out . . . I know not what He is about to do with me, but I have given myself entirely into His hands . . ."

June 4. "This morning I received a letter from my dear mother and one from my dear father, and afterwards was much blessed in praying for father, also in entreating the Lord's provision in temporal things. My dearest mother is a good deal tried just now, but I believe the Lord will provide. I felt faith this morning in praying for this. *O Lord help me more fully to trust in Thee, direct me in every step of my life . . . !*"

Sunday, 6. "I have been to chapel again tonight . . . and I have renewed my spiritual strength . . . Tonight, Lord, *Thou knowest that I love Thee, but I want to love Thee more.* The pain in the upper part of my back is so bad it seems worse at chapel than anywhere. I think it is with keeping it in one position so long . . . I feel today as if this earth will not long be my place. Well, Thy will be done, *only when Thou sendest let the messenger be love . . .*"

8. "This afternoon, for the first time in my life, I visited the sick and endeavoured to lead a poor young girl to Jesus. I think if spared this will be a duty I shall greatly delight in, but Thy will be done. Tonight at class meeting . . . I engaged in prayer . . . My heart beat violently but I felt some liberty."

June 10. "This day I have been framing new resolutions to be more devoted to God. I endeavoured to say a little to benefit my dear Aunt with respect to family prayer and was betrayed into *unprofitable reasoning* though I felt patience to try to do good. I think I shall be more careful in future . . . I have had severe pain in my left breast yesterday and today and through my chest . . . I called in with [name illegible] to have a tooth out, but the gentleman

42

said he feared I was too weak to undergo the operation. He said my pulse was feeble as an infant's and he thought the shock might bring mishap. He was very kind in giving me advice, and said he would try and make me something to relieve it. He thought I ought to have the care of a medical man here."

Tuesday, 15. "...it is twelve months today since I received the blessing of pardon...O my loving Lord, on looking back over the past year what cause I see to praise Thee...but keep me, whether I live or die, let it be to Thy glory."

One or two letters to her parents add a little to our knowledge of her at eighteen. She writes almost without a full-stop and runs on from subject to subject; in eight closely covered pages, in the letter from which I quote, there is no paragraph. "My very dear parents, thank you for your kind letters...I have been here a week today it has been a pleasant week and I hope by another week to feel much better, the weather has been lovely till today..." Then come details of expenses; it is evidently an anxiety to be a charge on her parents. "I don't wish you to be at any more expense for it costs me much more than we calculated upon but I can't help it...Maria [probably a cousin] seems very content, her disposition is so even it is not a little thing that will move her. I wish I had a little more of that evenness of temper but alas you know I am very irritable." Of Sunday: "If I am able I shall go to class in the afternoon and Maria is going with me to see what a class meeting is. Her church holds Calvinistic doctrine I went to her chapel once but could not *receive* all I heard, though I believe that the Minister was a true Christian, I am sorry she has received these opinions and endeavour by simple Scripture, which is the best weapon, to show her the true extent of the blessed atonement. She says I have thrown much light upon her mind."

Friday morning half past 11. "I have just returned from the beach it is a lovely morning but very rough and cold, the sea looks sublime, I never saw it so troubled, its waters...lash the shore with great violence, the sun shines with full splendour which makes the scene truly enchanting...There is a meeting in the Town Hall this evening at six o'clock of the Evangelical Alliance if I feel well I think of going...I wish I could see you, though I should not like to come home just yet the change is most agreeable to my feelings it is like a new world to me, I was heartily sick of looking at bricks and mortar. Oh, I love the sublime in nature it absorbs my whole soul I can't resist it, nor do I envy those who can, there is nothing on earth more pleasing and profitable to me than the meditations and emotions excited by such scenes as I witness here; I only want those I love best to participate my joys and then they would be complete...my kind love to you both and all enquiring friends. Excuse this scrawl and believe me to remain my dear parents Your affectionate daughter, Catherine."

43

As postscript a circle surrounded by dots and "kiss" written over it tells of the child in her, and the command not to let her letters lie about shows that she is beginning to look upon them as revealing something of her inner self not for the eye of a stranger. All her family letters are of this kind and she continually stresses her wish that the recipient should "burn this", "destroy this scrawl at once", "keep my letters locked up", and, as in these earliest ones, increasingly so to the last, she writes in a hurry. The "scrawl" she deplores but does not remedy, simply for lack of time or because her thoughts outrun her pen. Her letters from Brighton show her "concern" for others, ask for advice in helping Maria and freely blame herself for her own short-comings; that too will be characteristic of many of her letters: as see this: "My dearest Mother, I thank you very sincerely for your kind, nice long letter and especially as I know what an effort it is for you to write; don't fear for a moment that I should think you indifferent to my comfort how could I possibly think so, with so many proofs to the contrary, I thank you for your very kind and seasonable advice and I do pray and read the Scriptures with Maria, and she has prayed in my presence once, the *first time* she ever attempted it except alone. I hope the work is begun. I have had a deal of talk with her about election and Christian perfection the last of which she would not admit possible, I never felt clearer light on these points than now; oh the depth of the riches and the wisdom of God! Pray for me my very dear Mother I wish we knew each other better ... Believe me with all my faults and besetments, your affectionate and loving child Catherine." None of these letters is dated but the following extract is from the latest: "I should like to spend another week here it would be delightful, one only wants the needful and there seems to be plenty of it in Brighton but I don't happen on it! There are 'bills' all over the place offering rewards for lost articles but alas I have not been fortunate enough to find a mite yet though I often look out ... I should like to have got her [Maria] a brooch but I cannot ..."

Catherine's first Sunday back at home is a happy day, and she turns to her Journal to say, *June 20, 1847.* "Sunday was a day of peace and enjoyment. I went to chapel twice [an epitome of the sermons follows] I felt it good; my heart swelled at the thought of heavenly rest ... *I feel the power to leave myself and my all in the hands of God* ... He knows what is best; sometimes I think He will restore me to perfect health, though I never feel led to pray for this, but rather that I may glorify Him in death ... but whichever way, it will all be well ... I feel better in many respects for my visit. I suffer most from pain in my breast and shoulders and difficulty of breathing at times and general fever with a craving for food which I cannot satisfy."

Sunday, July 11. "Yesterday I felt so poorly that I could scarcely bear anything ... I can say Thy will be done. I have been reading from *Baxter's Saints' Rest* the importance of living a heavenly life on earth. I am determined to try."

Sunday, July 25. "I have not written in my journal this past week, it has been one of spiritual conflict and bodily weakness. I have felt as though I could not pray at times. Such rebellious thoughts and feelings have arisen in my mind as I cannot express, and irritability of temper ... This morning I went to Southwell with my dear mother and heard young Mr. Thomas* preach a beautiful sermon and I am going tonight. Lord bless me, Thou knowest I would not willingly grieve Thee ... and if I have given way now, forgive me through Jesus ... keep me to the end, save me whether by suffering or health, life or death, only let me be fully Thine."

Entries in the diary get further apart until so much as a month may separate them. In March 1848 it comes to an end.

October 4. "This time last year I was very ill. I had just commenced my six months' confinement by affliction but bless God I am able to attend to my Sunday School which increases fast. O that I may be able to sow some seed to the glory of God. I feel my responsibility is great."

October 21. "I have been reading a little of Mrs. Fletcher's life and have been blessed ... I believe it is possible to live by His grace without grieving the Spirit of God in anything, though I see this to be a very high state."

Saturday evening, December 25. "In contrasting my circumstances with last Christmas Day I see much cause for gratitude and praise ... Last Christmas Day I had kept my room for many weeks ... but this day I have enjoyed a measure of health and strength, so that I could go about and do as others ... on faithfully examining myself and looking back on the past year ... my heart has on various occasions been in some measure drawn from God, I mean experienced a deadness and dullness in spiritual things ... I have not been so constant over private prayer as I ought to have been ... I feel an earnest desire now I am entering another year to be more devoted to God ..."

Sunday, January 2, 1848. "... Tonight I desire to renew my covenant with the Lord, to be His more fully ... I have been writing a few daily rules ... but above all I am determined to search the Scriptures more attentively for in them I have eternal life. I have read my Bible through twice in sixteen months, but I must read it with more prayer for light and understanding ... *I feel I want more faith. I want to walk more by faith and not by feeling.*"

Monday, January 17, 1848. "Nineteen years this day I have lived in this world of sin and sorrow, but oh I have had many

* Dr. David Thomas (Congregational), Minister of Stockwell New Chapel, South London.

sweets mingled with the bitter, I have very much to praise my God for . . ."

January 21. "I have felt better this week in my mind, but am but very poorly in body . . . the weather is cold and that affects me. *My mind is often tossed with reasonings.* About my health I sometimes think I really am better, and then I feel so many bad symptoms that I think the disease must be inwardly ravening, this often harasses me, it seems such a state of suspense, but I know it is for want of more resignation. Oh, to lie passive in Thy hands . . . My dearest mother is very poorly. Oh my Lord support her and strengthen soul and body if it please Thee."

Sunday, February 6. "This morning I went to chapel . . . I believe if I get to the means oftener my soul would prosper better, still I know I might be blessed more at home if I lived in the spirit of prayer . . . I live too much by feelings instead of by faith for *it is faith that conquers all spiritual enemies.* I want constantly to look to Jesus . . . I can say it is my longing desire to glorify Him, to be more devoted to His service. I will in the strength of grace deny myself more . . . I have renewed my practice of abstaining from dinner on a Friday and butter in a morning, as I had discontinued it for some time . . . My dear mother is very poorly and much harassed . . . My dear father is a great trial to us."

The last entry, quoted in full: 24 (*Monday*). "Blessed be God I have felt better in my soul this last few days than I have done for some time; I have been more blessed in prayer and enjoyed a stronger confidence in God. Lord help me to be more faithful. I am very poorly. My side and breast are worse; Mr. Stevens my fresh doctor came to see me on Tuesday last. He is a very nice man and a preacher in our Society. He sounded my chest and thinks the left lung is affected, but he says there is no cavity in it and he thinks he can do me good."

The closely scribbled pages are proof that the journal was intended for the writer's eyes alone, even so, she seems never to have referred to it. Studying her letters and sayings, I am taken aback to find how consistent were her aspirations and dedications. Many of the phrases revealing her heart longings at eighteen fit almost to the letter with what she is saying forty years later and through all the time between. From her conversion to her death her soul's over-riding craving was to *love God more.* Can true love ever be satisfied? Is it not inherent in the mystery of man's nature that the lover *must* look forward to loving? Words must fail and fade into mere repetitions but the power of love leaps into renewed life, having in itself a principle of life, of self-propagation; something which the lover feels will never be quenched. Such words as "eternal", "unchanging", "everlasting", "for ever and ever", are in every true lover's vocabulary, and with them go vows that belong to the future as far ahead as the future can be imagined. All her life Catherine goes on saying to God, "I do love Thee but I want to love Thee more", and all the qualities of her nature were sanctified and strengthened by that love. All earth's loves were subordinated to her love for God, and sublimated by God's love for her and for the whole world. There is no streak of self-importance in her praying. All she receives from Him is of God's mercy; she claims nothing from God by her own merit, nothing more than God offers to all men. The journal also shows that Catherine knew that her lack of faith was the gravest obstacle to her soul's triumph in Christ. Between the paper covers of this penny exercise book may be found the confirmation of her son Bramwell's verdict that she was "by nature an unbeliever"; may be found too, that the emphasis in her battle for faith centred in the strength of the soul to submit to the will of God. This for her was of the very essence of Christianity. Throughout her life her love to God grew and with it the determination to please the Beloved which love engendered. Such living is only possible by faith. Faith then, continued to the end of her life, as it was in the beginning, the essential victory.

6

At nineteen, the Catherine we have seen reflected in her journal vanished; there are no more self-revealing records until her love-letters begin. Her health improves. She is able to be out and about more. She walks in the near countryside, goes to Exeter Hall to hear noted speakers, listening with increasingly critical ear to sermons. Her disappointment with herself, the sense of her own slow growth in Christlikeness, does not diminish her tendency to decide what is right for others. She discusses with her father and mother the causes of the decline in conversions in the Methodist Church as a whole, tends to blame the preachers, who, although often eloquent, yet fail to bring hearers to a decision. Ought not people to be helped to take a definite step? She went on reading, of course, and in particular reads the Bible, relating its teaching to her own spiritual experience now, and seeking from its pages satisfying answers to the myriad questions in her mind. She lets the Bible speak to her about her *own* needs, appropriates the promises of God in a more personal sense than before. Her prayers to be "prepared" for all are being answered; in learning to know her own heart she is unconsciously learning how to help others.

Before Catherine fell ill in the autumn of 1846, a dispute had arisen in the Wesleyan Church which led to a rupture in that body. Catherine was already a stout partisan when she wrote to her mother from Brighton, "I am indignant at the Conference for their base treatment of Mr. Burnett. But I quite expected it, when he gave a conscientious affidavit in Mr. Hardy's case. Well, it will all come down on their own pates!"[40] Nourished on the teaching of John Wesley and the hymns of his brother Charles, and by the biographies and sermons of early Methodists, Catherine wanted to see a return to the old-time fervour. She welcomed what was called the "Reform Movement" as a step to this end. The arbitrary action of Conference in banishing the American evangelist Caughey* had greatly disturbed many Wesleyans and strengthened the case of the "reformers" within their ranks. When they and those who followed them finally separated from the parent body they numbered well over a hundred thousand. Catherine read everything to be had bearing on the controversy, much of it aloud to her mother; together they entered into its every phase. Catherine went to meetings to hear protagonists and when Conference finally expelled certain ministers she attended a meeting at Exeter Hall where resolutions approving their attitude were adopted.

There was a good deal of excitement in Methodist circles. Catherine, with her characteristic enthusiasm, had made her sympathies known to her friends and when Conference required members of the church to abstain from attending any gathering of the Reformers, she was advised by her dear Mrs. Leay to withdraw her support, or, at least, not to speak about her views. But Catherine considered the decisions of Conference were neither just nor right. To be silent would be to pretend an agreement she did not feel, and would, in her view, be almost as bad as to abandon the injured party. When remonstrated with, she only the more eagerly expressed her opinions and her reasons for sticking to them. It had not occurred to her that the end of this might be her own expulsion! When the possibility, with consequent separation from friends in the chapel circle, was pointed out to her, she was hurt. Here was a new kind of wound, and at the hand of friends. Tears welled up in her eyes, but that did not prevent their kindling! There was nothing to argue about now she felt; what she might lose personally weighed nothing, nothing at all. As to a suggestion that it might be to her *advantage* to remain a member of the more influential section of the church, if it carried any weight it was in an opposite direction to that intended. She continued to express her opinions and when the time came for renewing the quarterly membership ticket, hers was withheld.

Catherine Mumford was expelled from the Wesleyan Church not for any breach of church doctrine or discipline, but for showing that her sympathies were with the already expelled ministers. She was young and ardent. "Nursed and cradled in Methodism," she says of

* Rev. James Caughey (Methodist), American evangelist. Exercised a profound influence on William and Catherine Booth.

herself, referring to this time. "I loved it with a love which has altogether gone out of fashion among Protestants for their church. Separation from it was one of the first great troubles of my life."[41] After her death *The Methodist Times* recorded: "Mrs. Booth, the greatest Methodist of our generation is gone ... We call her a Methodist for she was born a Methodist and brought up a Methodist, and a Methodist she would have remained to this hour, if mankind's hardness and intolerance had not driven her out ... of the Methodist fold."[42] The expelled Reformers opened a chapel at Binfield near the Mumford home and Catherine and her mother began to attend there, for it followed that Mrs. Mumford would not remain in fellowship with the body that had expelled her daughter. Catherine was asked to take the senior girls' Bible Class, with a membership of fifteen, varying in age from sixteen to nineteen years. Many hours were spent in preparation of the lessons; and prayer meetings were held with those of the girls who cared to stay after the ordinary class was over. These were encouraged to pray aloud and it was a joy that the membership increased, and that a number were converted. As to the Reformers, Catherine said, "I was greatly disappointed. I had hoped in my simplicity they would bring back the fervour and aggressiveness of bygone days. Instead of this everything was conducted very much in the ordinary style and I soon became heartily sick of the spirit of controversy."[43]

The recent financial stress at home eased. Had it not been for Mrs. Mumford's own money, the position would have been serious. It was at about this time that she began to supplement their income by taking a paying guest. He sometimes accompanied Catherine and her mother to lectures and evidently brought new interest into the house. The Reform chapel was at rather a distance, and walking there was often beyond Catherine's strength, especially in bad weather. This led to attendance at a nearby Congregational Church where there was an exceptionally good preacher, Dr. David Thomas. She delighted in his sermons and was helped by them. One Sunday, however, he said something which she considered was derogatory to woman as a moral being. Catherine at once wrote to Thomas setting forth her own views. The treatise, for it amounts to that, may be found in Booth-Tucker.*[44] Begbie said, "Something of this brilliant young person's character, and her original genius, may be seen in this letter which she sent to a minister who had preached a sermon with which she disagreed. The modesty of the approach does not minimize the force and vigour of the attack; and certainly such views in the 'fifties were unusual, and in a girl of her age remarkable enough to draw attention."[45] First, she tells of her "profound

* Frederick de Lautour Booth-Tucker. Indian Civil Service. Became Salvation Army officer; wrote *Life of Catherine Booth.*

respect" and high esteem for the doctor's powers of intellect and heart. "But because I believe you love *truth*, of whatever kind, and would not willingly propagate erroneous views on any subject, I venture to address you. Excuse me, my dear sir, I feel myself but a babe in comparison with you. But ... in your discourse on Sunday morning ... your remarks appeared to imply the doctrine of woman's intellectual and even moral inferiority to man ... Permit me, my dear sir, to ask whether you have ever made the subject of woman's equality as a *being*, the matter of calm investigation and thought? If not, I would, with all deference, suggest it as a subject well worth the exercise of your brain ... So far as Scriptural evidence is concerned, did I but possess the ability to do justice to the subject, I dare take my stand on *it* against the world in defending her perfect equality. And it is because I am persuaded that no honest, unprejudiced investigation of the sacred volume can give perpetuity to the mere assumptions and false notions which have gained currency in society on this subject, that I so earnestly commend it to your attention. I have such confidence in the nobility of your nature, that I feel certain neither prejudice nor custom can blind you to the truth, if you will once turn attention to the matter."

"Scriptural evidence ... I dare take my stand on *it* against the world." She is pouring out her thoughts now, thoughts awakened and marshalled in those precious Bible reading days of early youth. The Bible is the foundation of her ideals, it is in all her thinking until she is "fully convinced" in her own mind. And then she is ready to "stand on *it* against the world." She now marshalls her argument. There are no hesitancies; it is indeed difficult to keep in mind the author in the shape of the unschooled Miss! One can imagine how intensely she feels about the subject as she writes ... "The day is only just dawning with reference to female education,* and therefore any verdict on woman as an intellectual being must be premature and unsatisfactory. Thank God, however, we are not without numerous and noble examples of what she may become, when prejudice and error shall give way to light and truth, and her powers be duly appreciated and developed ... I am quite sure your remarks implied more than you intended. For I cannot believe that you consider woman *morally* more remote from God than man, or less capable of loving Him ardently and serving Him faithfully? If such were the case, would not the Great and Just One have made some difference in His mode of dealing with her? But has He not placed her on precisely the same footing, and under the same moral government with her companion? Does she not sustain the same relation to Himself and to the moral law? And is she not exposed to the same penalties and an heir of the same immortality?

* Written in 1850. Women were not admitted to degrees until: London 1878; Oxford 1920; Cambridge 1948.

This being the case, I argue that she possesses equal moral capacity.

"Experience also on this point, I think, affords conclusive evidence. Who, since the personal manifestation and crucifixion of our Lord, have ever been His most numerous and faithful followers? On whom has the horrible persecution of past ages fallen with most virulence, if not on the sensitive heart of woman? And yet how rarely has she betrayed moral weakness by denying her Lord, or moral remoteness from Him by listening to the tempter! Has she not, on the contrary, stood a noble witness for Christ in scenes and circumstances the most agonizing to her nature, and with Paul literally counted all things (even husband and children) but loss for His sake? . . . Oh, the thing which next to the revelation of the plan of salvation endears Christianity to my heart is, what it has done, and is destined to do for my sex . . . All man-made religions indeed neglect or debase woman, but the religion of Christ recognizes her individuality and raises her to the dignity of an independent moral agent. Under the Old Testament dispensation we have several instances of Jehovah choosing woman as a vehicle of His thoughts and the direct and authorized exponent of His will." Here follow various biblical references. The text continues, "In the New Testament she is fully restored to her original position, it being expressly stated that in Christ Jesus there is neither male nor female, and the promise of the outpouring of the Spirit is no less to the handmaidens than to the servants of the Lord."

Catherine then refers to confusion between subjection and inferiority. Woman is to be subject, "not as a being", but only to her own husband, "this was imposed upon her expressly as a punishment for sin, and not on the ground of inferiority, intellectual or moral. Indeed, had this subjection existed prior to the fall, as the natural consequences of inferiority, there would have been no force in the words 'He shall be over thee'."

And now see this young woman's conception of husband and wife under Christ! ". . . the glorious provisions of Christianity come to those who are united in Christ . . . the wife may realize as blissful and perfect a oneness with her husband as though it [the curse] had never been pronounced. For while the semblance of it remains, Jesus has beautifully extracted the sting by making love the law of marriage, and by restoring the institution itself to its original sanctity. What wife would not be careful to reverence a husband, who loves her as Christ loves His Church? Surely the honour put upon woman by the Lord, both in His example and precepts, should make His religion doubly precious to her and render His sanctuary her safe refuge from everything derogatory or insulting to her nature! Oh, that Christians at heart would throw off the trammels of prejudice, and try to arrive at the truth on this subject! Oh, that men of noble soul and able intellect would investigate it, and then ask themselves and their compeers, *why* the influence of woman should be so under-

51

estimated ... If it be only *partially* true that those who rock the cradle rule the world, how much greater is the influence wielded over the mind of future ages by the *mothers* of the next generation than by all the young men living! Vain, in my opinion, will be all the efforts to impregnate minds generally with noble sentiments and lofty aspirations, while the mothers of humanity are comparatively neglected, and their minds indoctrinated from the schoolroom, the press, the platform, and even the pulpit, with self-degrading feelings and servile notions of their own inferiority! Never till woman is estimated and educated as man's equal—the literal 'she-man' of the Hebrew—will the foundation of human influence become pure or the bias of mind noble and lofty ... ! Oh, that the church generally would enquire whether narrow prejudice and lordly usurpation has not something to do with the circumscribed sphere of woman's religious labours, and whether much of the non-success of the Gospel is not attributable to the restrictions imposed upon the operations of the Holy Spirit in this as well as other particulars! Would to God that the truth on this subject, so important to the interests of future generations, were better understood and practically recognized.

"Forgive me, my dear sir, if I have spoken too boldly . . . I love my sex ... I desire above all earthly things their moral and intellectual elevation. I believe it would be the greatest boon to our race. And though I deeply feel my *own* inability to help it forward, I could not satisfy my *conscience* without making this humble attempt to enlist one whose noble sentiments on other subjects have so long been precious to my soul."

In closing, significantly, she declares her views are "independent and distinct from any society or association of whatever name ... I realize how imperfectly I have expressed myself. I hope, however, if there be anything worth your attention you will not despise it on account of its illogical expression ... Neither, I trust, will you judge me harshly for withholding my name. I began this letter hesitating whether I should do so or not. But there being nothing in it of a personal character or which can at all be influenced by the recognition of the critic, and it being the furthest from my thought to obtrude myself upon your notice, I shall feel at liberty to subscribe myself an attentive hearer."

Catherine feared that to reveal her youth—her early twenties—might result in a disregard of what she has to say, and there was no manner of doubt in *her* mind that *that* was deserving of attention. Her thoughts were not of herself as she wrote but of her sex and of the Church as a whole. On this question of woman's equality with man as a being, she believed that she had learned from God and that she had heard the attuning answer of her own judgment. She was conscious of the mysterious, but none the less real, link between *revelation* and the endorsement of finite reason which creates religious

52

conviction in the mind of man. She was not expressing *her* ideas; her part in them she felt was negligible; she merely clothed in her own words conclusions reached from study of the Scriptures. The truth worked in her mind like leaven; her thoughts, permeated by it, were no longer only her own. Conviction pent up within her impelled expression, she laid down the law with authority, for she believed it was not her law but Another's.

At twenty-three, save for pain in her spine, Catherine was in better health than for years. Her mother was more cheerful, chapel activities, while disappointing, were still the chief centre of interest, and she and her mother made new acquaintances among the Reform party. Some of these were of a more rough and ready type than Catherine had met hitherto. There was Mr. Rabbits, for instance. He was an old-fashioned Methodist who liked to hear "Amens" in chapel; a local preacher and a "light" in the Reform party. He began business, it was said, on a borrowed half-crown and by the time the Mumfords came to know him he owned several flourishing boot shops and was reputed to be a millionaire. A shrewd masterful person, he was full of energetic interest in his boot-making and in religion. He soon became a great admirer of clever little Miss Mumford, who was not afraid to stand up to him. He liked her all the better for that. He reckoned that she was the best judge of a sermon he knew. Besides, she was full of practical good sense, and Rabbits valued that. Catherine enjoyed talking to him. She had gained poise during these last years; had her feelings more in hand; was not so prone to speak and then to regret it afterwards. As she listened to Mr. Rabbits expounding his views on questions of the moment she was looking out on life with the hint of a smile about her lips. She had begun to think that she could put a good many things right had she her way! As she grew older she felt increasingly the intellectual limitations of her immediate circle and quite guilelessly remarked on finding herself "different". In later life she used to speak of "the dear Lord's idiot children", but she early knew that she was not one of them! It is clear from her love-letters that she herself felt that her "circumstances" had been frustrating, and she resented her lack of opportunity for education. Yet the onlooker cannot, I think, avoid the conclusion that the very circumstances which she would have changed were used to hedge her in, so that her spirit might appropriate its heritage in the Bible, and live on it, until her own convictions and principles were rooted and developed. Catherine herself came to value this. She once said, "Being so much alone in my youth, and so thrown on my own thoughts and those of the mighty dead as expressed in books, has been helpful to me."[46] What she wrote to her betrothed is the more worthy of note that it gives her own version of her upbringing while the time was still near and fresh to her memory, "I cannot tell you the gratitude I sometimes feel to God for having shielded me in childhood and early youth

53

from the giddy, flirty pleasures of the world. I have to mourn many *disadvantages* and grievous ones, but oh, I do feel the value of those I possessed. I do see the effects they have had on my heart and character. I see the importance of young minds being engaged with pure and weighty subjects, and the young heart shut up from the fascinations and allurements of unreal and pretended admiration. Oh if ever I have a daughter how I shall guard the sacred gem of a pure and unsophisticated mind, it is indeed a precious boon to its possessor . . ."[47]

The intensity of her nature, as well as her isolation, tended to magnify the conflicts of her own spirit. The sharp edge of her childhood's griefs stung and startled her into facing problems generally undiscerned until later in life. Catherine came up to them with a childlike directness. Sophistries had no power on her mind. Its "tossings" were the greater for that. Facts, often terrifying, could not be evaded; truth, as she saw it, was never within reach of tampering, could not be whittled away. To Catherine life was reality; not a shadow; not in any degree a stage from which to attract attention to herself; but stark, gorgeous, unaccountable reality; eternity impinged upon it. In her mind, from the nursery to the grave, there was room for height and depth, for extremes of joy and grief; room for God. She dwelt in growing awareness of God; and gave Him naturally, logically His place in her life. She saw God related to the individual soul of everyman—to herself—in everything. She learned to love Him, and what was perhaps more significant she *wanted* to love Him more.

If we are to understand her it is important that we should realize that her familiarity with God, her sense of His immanence, His every-day-ness, was not something forced upon her, not extraneous. It was like a spring of life in her that made it natural to her that she and the Almighty should be on speaking terms. Like Job, she exercised her right to contend with God; to plead, to disagree; to submit, and trust, and love, like Abraham and David, Peter and John, whom she felt she knew and understood. Her "God-awareness", the over-ruling force of her love for God, gave her, as nothing else could have done, a sense of safety, of assuredness in life, which fitted her to an amazing degree for her future. It balanced her sense of her own unworthiness which, without it, might often have kept her lips closed. It made her free from the limitations set by convention. She was not tamed by self-consciousness; she was hardly self-conscious at all. But God-conscious, yes, God-conscious always. She lived in the company of the "mighty dead", continuously sensible of the presence of the Holy Spirit, and by Him was made ready to do a new thing in the world. Catherine Mumford is an example of the beautiful effect that loving God has on personality. Pure love to God reacts on the qualities of human nature, invigorates them, so that when they are exercised they are more alive, warmer, more steadfast, more delicate, nearer in sympathy and understanding to God *and* to man. "Prepare me for all," she had prayed. And truly she was prepared: through her serious-minded, rather unusual childhood; through her sombre adolescence, God was leading her; she was being prepared to be:

A transcendent lover;

An exquisitely affectionate wife;

A mother of adoring sons and daughters;

A preacher of "irresistible eloquence";

One of the great figures of religious history;

A lawgiver to a new company of the redeemed on earth;

Mother of The Salvation Army.

And to be led, when at the height of her powers and influence, slowly, painfully, down into the valley of the shadow to meet death; to be strong and very courageous in that last conflict, as she had prayed forty years before she might be. To the end of her life the words she had used at eighteen would still be true for her. "I give myself afresh into the hands of God, to do, and to suffer, all His will."[48]

BOOK TWO

Catherine's Love for William Booth

"The more you lead me up to Christ in all things, the more highly shall I esteem you, and if it be possible to love you more than I do now, the more shall I love you."*

"The nearest our assimilation to Jesus, the more perfect and heavenly our union."*

"I read over the marriage service the other day and wept over it. Because others go and swear in the presence of God to do certain things and fulfil certain duties, without even reflecting on their nature and extent, that is no reason why I should do so."*

"Do you ever think how kind it was of God to make such a relationship a *holy* one, so that His own children may realize more bliss in it than any other?"*

"Any idea of lordship or ownership is lost in love . . . there will be mutual yielding wherever there is proper love, because it is a joy to yield our own will to those for whom we have real affection."*

"Our home . . . if we live in love, *as Christ hath loved us*—what a little heaven below . . ."*

"It is the highest ambition of my soul that you should be a man of God and live only to save souls."*

"Others may trim and oscillate between the broad and narrow path, but for us there is but one straight, narrow, shining path of perfect devotedness, and if we walk not in it we are undone."*

"That you love me so well, now you love the Lord better, makes me rejoice, and I feel now that I may love you as much as I like."*

"The thought of walking through life *perfectly united*, together enjoying its sunshine and battling its storms . . . is to me exquisite happiness, the highest earthly bliss I desire."*

*In love-letters to William Booth.

58

1

At eighteen Catherine Mumford had prayed, "Lord prepare me for all ..." Her thoughts then were of her immediate future, and in particular of that still recurring fear of early death. Would she recover? A few days before she had written in her Journal, "I feel today as if this earth will not long be my place. Well, Thy will be done, only when Thou sendest let the messenger be love ..." God's messenger to her was love; but to call her to life. Life more joyous, more fruitful in service, than anything she could have imagined. But before the heart had heard the voice of love, her judgment, what Stead afterwards called that "intense practicability" in her, laid down some essential prerequisites in the man she would take as husband. She wrote, "As quite a young girl I made up my mind. He must be a sincere Christian; not a nominal one, or a mere church member, but truly converted to God. I resolved that he should be a man of sense. I knew that I could never respect a fool, or one much weaker mentally than myself ... Another resolution I made was that I would never marry a man who was not a total abstainer, and this from conviction and not merely to gratify me." Unessential, but desirable, Catherine thought, giving imagination a little innocent freedom, was that "he" should be a minister. "I could be most useful to God as a minister's wife," she told herself; and, still looking into the future, she added to the desiderata that "he" should be "dark, tall and for preference called William!"[1]

William Booth was born in Nottingham in 1829, the same year as Catherine Mumford, and was brought up in the Church of England. His father, Samuel Booth, a speculating builder, had made and lost a fortune by the time William was twelve years old. This financial failure drastically changed the boy's prospects. He was taken from school and apprenticed to pawn-broking; because, in his father's opinion, "there was money in it". Soon afterwards Samuel Booth died leaving his wife and family in comparative poverty. At the age of fifteen William was converted in Wesley Chapel, Nottingham; and immediately he and one or two other lads began to hold street meetings in the slums of that city. Begbie says "... the lad went on with his street-preaching, his cottage prayer meetings, and his face-to-face encounters with notorious profligates; using means which startled orthodoxy and inventing methods wholly unsanctioned by traditional authority."[2] At twenty years of age William went to seek a better opening in London, but found it must still be in the now hated pawn-broking business. He lived in his employer's home, as was customary at the time, and had only Sunday to spend as he chose.

59

He chose to employ it by continuing his preaching, having brought with him recommendations from the Nottingham Wesleyan Circuit. The rule at the business was that he must be in by 10 p.m. or the door would be locked against him. William tells, "This law was rigidly enforced in my case, although he [the owner] knew that I travelled long distances preaching the Gospel . . . To get home in time, many a Sunday night I have had to run till out of breath, after walking long distances and preaching twice in the day."[3]

Curiously enough William was driven out of the Wesleyan Church after much the same arbitrary fashion as was Catherine. He took no interest in the Reform agitation, as she did, but from his zeal to preach in the streets was *suspected* of secret sympathy with the party and on this suspicion his membership ticket was withheld! No effort was made to keep in touch with young Booth; nor was there any word of enquiry about his views on the matter. When the local body of the Reformers heard of his expulsion, they passed a resolution inviting him to join them. This he did in June 1851, continuing as local preacher.

Mr. Rabbits was already acquainted with William Booth, had been present when he preached for the first time in Walworth chapel, and was delighted with his earnest manner, and the "Amens" with which the congregation responded. On that Sunday Rabbits took the young man home to dinner and, from then until his death, remained William Booth's staunch friend. Now Mr. Rabbits was rather proud of his young protégé, and when, after joining the Reform party, William Booth was appointed to preach at the chapel where Mrs Mumford and Catherine were members, Mr. Rabbits made a point of asking Miss Mumford what she thought of the sermon. "One of the best I have heard in this chapel,"[4] she answered.

Catherine next saw William at Mr. Rabbits' house, where he had invited some of the leading Reform members to "tea and conversation". Young Booth, who arrived late, was almost immediately pounced upon by his host to recite an American temperance piece. He tried to get out of it on the ground that few present were abstainers. However, Mr. Rabbits was inexorable and would accept no excuse. The fact that he was not an abstainer himself would, he was sure, prevent anyone present from feeling uncomfortable.

Picture the scene: the large, crowded, rather floridly furnished Victorian drawing room; the ladies' voluminous dresses filling and overflowing their chairs. Catherine, in lilac silk and velvet perhaps— she was fond of that colouring—spread her skirts about her in demure manner and settled to listen. An old lady gave me a vivid description of Catherine as she appeared in the pulpit in the quite early days of her public ministry. This would be about seven years after the tea party at Mr. Rabbits'. My old friend, who was sixteen at the time, said of Catherine ". . . she was dressed in lavender silk with a velvet jacket of darker shade, her bonnet had lavender in it too; her hair was jet black and curly and her cheeks rosy. As she talked her eyes sparkled and I thought she was the most lovely person I had ever seen." We may imagine her sitting in old Rabbits' drawing room, right elbow cupped in left hand, hand to cheek, alert, listening. Now and again she lifted her eyes and let them rest upon the dramatic young man. The recital over, silence, and the light rustle of silks and sighs as the ladies relaxed: then, someone said something in defence of moderate drinking. Now, for the first time, William heard Catherine's voice. Their eyes met, and while she, opposing, entered the discussion "with logic unmatched in that room",[5] William's grey eyes dwelt on her as if she were a point of light in surrounding dusk. No wine was taken with the refreshments served before the guests departed, a tacit acknowledgment of the force of the arguments advanced. Catherine and her mother drove away chatting about the party. There was only the most casual reference to the young reciter.

At eighteen, whilst still in Nottingham, William Booth had been encouraged by the Superintendent of the circuit to offer for the Methodist ministry. The doctor to whom he was sent for a report said that he was in no condition for so strenuous a life and advised that he should wait at least a year. In London, where he was a recognized local preacher, he raised the question again but was told that preachers were not needed. The invitation to join the Reformers revived his hopes. Early in 1852 Mr. Rabbits had a conversation with him, of which, and its results, William Booth tells, "Mr. Rabbits said to me one day 'you must leave business and wholly devote yourself to preaching the Gospel.' Impossible, I answered. There is no way for me. Nobody wants me. 'Yes,' said he, 'the people with whom you have allied yourself want an evangelist.'

"They cannot support me, I replied, and I cannot live on air.

" 'That is true, no doubt,' was his answer. 'How much can you live on?' I reckoned up carefully. I knew I should have to provide my own quarters and pay for my cooking . . . I told him that I did not see how I could get along with less than twelve shillings a week.

" 'Nonsense,' he said, 'you cannot do with less than twenty shillings a week, I am sure.' All right, I said, have it your own way, if you will, but where is the twenty shillings to come from?

" 'I will supply it,' he said, 'for the first three months at least.' Very good, I answered. And the bargain was struck then and there. I at once gave notice to my master, who was very angry and said, 'If it is money you want that need not part us.' I told him that money had nothing to do with the question, and that all I wanted was the opportunity to spend my life and powers publishing the Saviour to a lost world. And so I packed my portmanteau and went out to begin a new life."

He found quarters in the Walworth district, two rooms in the house of a widow at five shillings a week with attendance. He bought chairs and a bed, and a few other necessaries. "I felt quite set up, and fully prepared to settle quietly down to my work . . ."[6]

The day that follows his shopping day, a Good Friday, is William's birthday, April 10, 1852, his twenty-third. His spirits are high. He feels the day auspicious. What day indeed could be more truly a "good" day on which to begin his new life than this Holy Anniversary? Fearlessly, eagerly, he dedicates himself to God afresh. O happy day that finds him free from all conflicting claims. Free! Free! Free! He might shout for joy, leap even, but to "settle quietly down to my work" on *this* day is quite beyond him. He *must* walk abroad. He decides on a visit to a cousin who lives on the other side of London, at whose house he plans to spend the night. He strides along, unconsciously a conspicuous figure; tall, over six feet, thin as a rake, the energetic step giving an impression of vigour that counteracts the delicacy suggested by his build and pallor. There is no hair on his face at this time, only a fringe of soft beard at the sides and under the chin. He treads the pavements as if he were already in sight of his goal. No more planning wild expedients, as when, at twenty-one, he wrote to a friend, "You ask me 'what is your plan?' . . . go out to Australia as chaplain on board a convict ship . . . to preach to the very worst of men Christ's salvation." To this same friend he had lately written ". . . my inmost spirit is panting for the delightful employment of telling, from morn till eve . . . the glad tidings that mercy is free."[7] He breathes the sweet spring air, sweet even in Walworth, and feels that the sun is shining on his future way. (Surely it must have been shining on that day?) His thoughts are singing praises to God as he goes.

But he has no faintest premonition that this day is to bring to him the crown of all human joys, the perfect love of a heart to match his own. No hint stirs in William of the world eminence to be his sixty years hence. Kings and potentates will send greetings for that *last* birthday, tens of thousands among peoples will name him in their prayers and encompass him with their affection; but *now,* walking through Walworth, his thoughts are all of the "delightful employment" of telling that "mercy is free". Oh, the mercy of God! William Booth was musical and delighted in singing, all through the march of the sixty years that await him he will sing. When his grandchildren gather about him on festive days at home, there will always be singing; and a hymn to the tune of *The Mistletoe Bough*, with the refrain, "Oh, the mercy of God", will never be omitted. There was always a kind of "blessedness" on his countenance while we sang it; a slight lifting of the head (covered to the last by a mop of hair), a richness, sometimes a tremor in his voice as he led us in the refrain, which was sung over and over again, "Oh, the mercy of God".

On this day, in Walworth, God's mercy meets William Booth in the shape of Mr. Rabbits. He is in one of his masterful moods. He enquires where his young friend is going? To make a visit? Nonsense! He shall come instead to services in Cowper Street schoolroom. "But I insist." And William, too happy to mind where he goes, agrees. He is free! The sun is shining. Oh, the mercy of God! To these services comes Catherine Mumford. Catherine does not feel well enough to stay to the close of the evening meeting and, as a final touch of felicity to this fantastically happy day, William is asked to escort her home. It is hard to resist the thought that the warm-hearted, managing Mr. Rabbits has not had a hand in this! Be that as it may, William finds himself driving with Catherine to her home, alone with her for the first time.

Side by side she and William sit. The carriage rattles over the unpaved road. First from one side, then from the other, dim light from without spreads brief shadowy glimmer through the dusk within as they drive past the small pools of light round the street lamps. Remarks are made, their voices, surprisingly, sound normal! But presently each in secret realizes that this is a moment apart, a moment to be remembered *for ever.* The little space they occupy is suddenly illumined, and these two see one another; see one another— *and know*! From inside the closed carriage, travelling through the darkening streets, each looks up, and, like Jacob after the sun had set on that other evening long ago, sees heaven brought within reach of earth. Oblivious of their situation, each knows "The Lord is in this place." Yes! Neither of them ever doubts that. William wrote it was God Himself ". . . Who in a most wonderful and providential manner has brought us together, and then flashed into our hearts the sweet and heavenly feeling of a something more than earthly unison."* Nothing that happened to them afterwards had power to mar the gift, nor to tarnish the memory of the timeless moment when love made a shining pathway, from the carriage in which they sat, to heaven's gate: a pathway they would walk *together.* Catherine wrote long afterwards: "That little journey will never be forgotten by either of us . . . as William expressed it, 'it seemed as if God flashed simultaneously into our hearts that affection which . . . none of the changing vicissitudes with which our lives have been so crowded has been able to efface . . . We struck in at once in such wonderful harmony of view and aim and feeling on various matters that passed rapidly before us, that it seemed as though we had intimately known and loved each other for years and suddenly, after some temporary absence, had been brought together again. Before we reached my home we both . . . felt as though we had been made for each other."[8]

Arrived, the talk continues. "No doubt we drew each other out,"

* When five years had passed it was again Good Friday and April 10, and Catherine wrote of it to her parents as "the anniversary of our engagement".

Catherine says. "The conversation was lively and interesting, and my mother listened and had her say."[9] Catherine was almost at the end of her life when she records this, but the scenes of that Good Friday evening were as clear as yesterday. In Mrs. Mumford's presence, and though no word of love had been spoken, love bound the two young hearts as one; transmuted all their possessions into gifts for each other. Soon it was later than could be believed. Where was Mr. Booth going? Catherine discovered "he had purposed to stop at his cousin's. Instead of that he had got into this meeting and from this meeting had come on with me."[10] It was now far too late to walk to his cousin's and Mrs. Mumford invited him to stay the night. Catherine and William parted with formal handshake, the light of love shining on the brow of each as they looked smiling, fearless, into the other's eyes.

Once in his room and the door shut, William came suddenly back to earth. A tumult arose in his breast. Impossible to doubt that he had met the woman of his ideals: impossible to doubt that he had found *love;* yet this was contrary to all his plans. Only yesterday he had escaped from that galling business yoke. Today (was it really only today?) his way had seemed so plain, he had felt "fully prepared to settle quietly down to my work". Now he remembered that Mr. Rabbits' arrangement with him was but for three months! After that what? What indeed! One dark certainty drew ever nearer, became ever clearer, thoughts of wife and home were *not* for him. In the chill grey of Saturday morning (surely it was a chill grey day?) without having spoken a word of love, he walked away from the Mumford home.

For Catherine there was no such tumult, but instead a joyous assurance that this knowledge of love's all-embracing presence was of God's will for her. She said, speaking of that drive home, "It was curious, too, that both of us had an idea of what we should require in the companion with whom we allied ourselves for life; if ever such alliance should take place... and here we were, thrown together in this unexpected fashion, matching those preconceived characters, even as though we had been made to order!"[11] She was telling of her own heart's certainties when she went on to say, "We felt... that henceforth the current of our lives must flow together." To William, in one of her love-letters, she wrote recalling that first evening, "Twelve months tomorrow night I first leaned on your arm and you first came under our roof, may we indeed have cause to praise God throughout eternity for that meeting. We were strangers then and yet there was a strange sympathy of feeling which only kindred spirits feel."[12]

On that Saturday morning William had walked disconsolately from the door of her home. "But," Catherine recounts, "it was not many hours before he found himself at that door again." The disclosure of their feelings to each other was soon made and then to

Catherine's parents, Mr. and Mrs. Mumford

William and Catherine with their family in 1862: Katie, Emma,
Willie (Bramwell), Herbert (the baby) and Ballington

Catherine about 1863

Catherine, William poured out all that was seething within him: the "terrible controversy", the clash of desires that confused the issue for him: the awful fear that "it cannot, it must not, it shall not be." All this he told Catherine and she recorded it. They now met almost daily. They talked. Talked and prayed. Always at parting they knelt and prayed together, he prayed and she prayed. Their first resolve was that "nothing should be done in haste". Love declared, the fair fact of it acknowledged by both, betrothal was naturally the next step. *But only on one condition,* Catherine decrees. And then William came up against a quality in her hitherto unperceived by him: something adamant. Before she would accept the precious pledge of his love, William must be *convinced in his own mind that it was God's will.* William hesitated, asked himself if he were convinced that he would be doing God's will. He had no "revelation" about it. Might not new vows to Catherine now conflict with vows he had already made to God? Could he be sure that it would be right while his prospects were so poor? After one of his visits William wrote: "I *know,* I always knew, I was not worthy...Do not imagine I... question a word you have spoken. I love you."[13] Engagement or no engagement it is a solace to him to put the words on paper. In an undated letter written before breakfast, because it had been too late to call upon her by the time he was free the evening before, a Sunday, he said, "I need not tell you how often I thought of you the past day ...but perhaps I might tell you how the tone of your voice and the influence which attended your prayer followed me, and even in the pulpit blessed my soul." Catherine tells that they agreed on a period "during which time we were to seek Divine guidance...and to pray that God would show him whether in the peculiar circumstances in which he was placed it was His will that the union should take place."[14] William began to realize how high were her ideals, and as she told him in triumphant language her thoughts about God, he became conscious of the brightness of her soul's shining: and, perhaps the more harshly clear from that light, saw his own experience and circumstances as contrary to his hopes and incompatible with the possession of this sweet and vital creature. Dared he draw her into the chill of his uncertain lonely way?

After the fascination of that first evening had worn off, Mrs. Mumford looked on William Booth with a more critical eye. She heard of his circumstances; felt, and not unnaturally, that he had been precipitate in expressing his feelings for her daughter. A letter of William's told the effect of this on him: "The high estimation your mother has for you, led her, I conceive, to take a prejudicial view of my conduct and to make remarks which were unmerited and unjust and calculated to wrong my soul. But it is over now...your kindness to me...I have indeed been grateful for it and felt how undeserved it was."[15] At twenty-three William's capacity for

65

enthusiasm was like a rising tide in him: his zeal held an explosive quality that sometimes startled even himself! As he sat in the drawing-room of Catherine's home, his eyes resting on his Love, he saw the delicate variation of expression on her features as she talked, noticed the way she held her head, the grace of an occasional gesture; and felt a rush of joy as he realized afresh how beautiful she was. More beautiful than he remembered; forgetting that he had felt just the same when he had seen her the day before! He felt a mounting power within his breast like a great force rising under the pressure of his restraint; power to be and to do for his beloved, *all* that he *wanted* to be and to do. He became oblivious of his poor prospects, of Mrs. Mumford's displeasure and his mother's warnings. *He* did not reason, he *knew!* "I love you." "I adore you." "I *will* make you happy."

As for all natures capable of rising to heights of enthusiasm, he was prone to droop into depths of despondency. He reached now and then a point where the very thought of committing himself to an engagement, the obligations of which he might not be able to fulfil, frightened him. He wrote: "I believe you think me sincere ... I have no present probability of making circumstances such that I can ask you to share my home ... Moreover when I ponder over ... the darkness that hangs around me, I feel an involuntary shudder creep over me at the thought of an engagement ... I need not say the high place your character and disposition have in my esteem. I need not say how I regret for your sake, that I ever set foot in your home."[16] Again William wrote: "My dear Friend, I know not that I have anything to write about in any way cheering to your feelings ... I fear I have blocked up for ever any possible way of my being made a blessing to you. ... Darkness gathers thicker than ever round the path I tread, and doubt, gloom, melancholy and despair would tread me down. My resolutions are unbroken to live and die only for the salvation of souls ... I say nothing decisive, because I know nothing. I have neither advanced nor retrograded from the position I occupied when last we met."[17]

Now see Catherine's mingled grief and hope in the following letter: "My dear Friend ... My heart feels for you far beyond what I can express. Oh, that I knew how to comfort you in an indirect way ... You do grieve me by saying you fear you 'have blocked up every way of being a blessing to me'. *I tell you it is not so* ... and if you could look into my heart you would see how far I am from such a feeling. *Don't pore over the past.* Let it all go. Your desire is to do the will of God and He will guide you ... The words 'gloom, melancholy and despair' lacerate my heart. Don't give way to such feelings for a moment. *God loves you.* He will sustain you.

"The thought that I should increase your perplexity and cause you suffering is almost unbearable. Oh, that we had never seen each other. Do try and forget me, as far as the remembrance would injure your usefulness or spoil your peace ... if I cause you to err I shall never be happy again. Don't, I beseech you, take any step without some evidence *satisfactory* to your own mind of the will of God; think nothing about me ... May God bless and guide you into the path which will be most for His glory and your soul's interest is my constant prayer. Perhaps my writing this is injudicious. I feel my position unutterably or I should have said much more, but I cannot bear that you should feel as if no one cared for, or sympathized with you ... Yours affectionately, Catherine."[18]

The stand Catherine took was for William's sake. She knew that the very strength of his love, if pinioned as it were, by doubt of its legitimacy, would cripple his spirit; whereas love, that was his, with God's approval would bear him on wings. She was determined that he should not be allowed to take a step that later he might feel he *ought* not to have taken. Was *he* certain that their betrothal would be right, that was the only question for Catherine. Even for the sake of her happiness and his own William was too honourable to affect an assurance he did not feel. To her this betokened his "innate uprightness", and he knew that she "valued his sincerity". She knew that love's joyous abandon could only blossom from an experience rooted beyond doubt's assailing in the assurance of God's approval. Now they agreed to put all thought of an engagement aside, and to look upon each other as friends only. The perceptive may learn a lot about William Booth at twenty-three from his reply to a missing letter of Catherine's, and smile at him perhaps, though not unkindly I hope. "My dear Catherine, I have read and re-read yours of yesterday evening and in answer to it what can I say? My heart dictates what for the sake of your peace I dare not write, I mean, what I feel ... I will love you as my sister, as I love my dearest friend. I cannot afford to lose your friendship. I *should* be lonely then. We can meet now and then and talk about books and Christ and Heaven, *nothing more, can we not?*

"You say I am to tell you if you have acted unkindly; I cannot, for no such feeling toward me ever dwelt for a moment in your heart. I honour you, I worship, I adore, I have loved you, oh, perhaps more than ... but I forbear; I would not write about myself. I want you to be happy and in the future—but again I am rambling on to forbidden ground ... I will work harder, study more closely ... and seek to gain equilibrium for my spirits and employment for my thoughts. Fear not for *me,* if I love you at all, if you wish to know *how much I love,* measure it by my calmness and my willingness in any way to do as you wish. I will. If you wish to see me, name the time and then nothing positively preventing I will come, though it be *every* night or only every year. I have nothing to say but I still write on. You will allow me to write to you now and then? I will not ask an answer ... it seems to afford me unspeakable pleasure to be penning down words which I know will meet your eye, but I suppose I should feel this in writing to any other friend? . . . You have oftimes told me in triumphant language that 'God lives', now reap all the comfort possible from it yourself. The matter with me is in perfect abeyance, where it ought to have been all along. Not a feeling is shaken, not a tithe of my affection is destroyed. I write at random, I know not when nor where to leave off. Never mind me, forget me altogether so far as what I feel is concerned, but do not forget to regard me as a friend, as one who only waits to prove his friendship for you . . . I am sure you are the care of Heaven. *I know,* I always knew, I was not worthy of one so pure, so holy, so chaste, so good.

"Whatever you do, whatever you think, do not imagine I question a word you have spoken. I declare before the throne of Eternal Truth that *I do not.* I love you, I love you as dearly as ever and that love is grounded on the highest esteem. But calmly, Catherine, let us do His will. I am perfectly the master of my feelings," here William paused, sincerity compelled him to add, "at least to a great extent . . . May God comfort you now that I lack the power, and believe me to remain, Yours affectionately, Yours for ever in Jesus' love, William."[19]

To this letter Catherine says, "Come and see me." William came, he tried to be calm as they talked together. As always in her presence his hopes rose. Might he, after all, keep his hopes? He proposed that they should agree upon an engagement and wait and see how things turned out, though he confessed that his doubts about his circumstances were not dispelled. He could not say, much as he wished it, that he had received any special guidance. The next day he wrote again: "My dear Friend, I promised you a line. I write. I know no more now than I knew yesterday. I offered as you know full well then and there to make an engagement. You declined on what without doubt are good grounds, but still I cannot do more . . . You know the inmost feelings of my heart, and I can say no more than that I have not, as I could have wished, seen anything to intimate the will of God. If my circumstances had not been so benighted I might not have desired this . . . Now understand me. As I said yesterday, I offer now *a step in the dark.* I will promise you anything you wish *for your own dear sake* . . . You can write me your mind. I do not wish to trouble you for a long letter. Put down in a line what you think. If you decline, as yesterday, I ask the favour of being allowed to keep as sacred as my Bible and as full to me of inspiration, and as sacred to my inmost feelings, the notes I already have in your writing. As you wish you can keep or burn mine. I could almost trust you with the keeping of the title deeds of my soul's salvation, so highly do I esteem your character. Perhaps I write wildly. Excuse me. I began calm. After this is ended, this awful controversy, I shall call on you again. If you *accept* what I have stated, I will come on

Saturday. *If not,* I shall call as a friend in the course of a few days and show you how I bear the matter."[20]

Swiftly Catherine sent her reply. If to William an engagement seemed to be a "step in the dark", she would have none of it! But the steadfast light of her love shines clearly in this letter as already embracing the whole of life. Love and faith now so possessed her that nothing shall make her afraid, not even the fear that she might lose her beloved. *"My dear Friend,* I have read and re-read your note and I fear you did not fully understand my difficulty. It was not the *circumstances;* I thought I had fully satisfied you on that point, I thought that you felt sure that a bright prospect could not allure me nor a dark one affright me, if only we are one in *heart.* My difficulty, my *only* reason for wishing to defer the engagement, was that *you* might feel satisfied in your own mind that the step is right. To cause you to err would cost me far more suffering than *anything* else ... You say, if your circumstances were not so benighted you would not desire so striking an indication of God's will. I answer, if you are satisfied of *His* will, irrespective of circumstances, let circumstances *go* and let us be one, come what will ... if you feel satisfied on these two points, first, that the step is *not* opposed to the will of God, and secondly that I am calculated to make you happy, come on Saturday evening and on our knees before God let us give ourselves afresh to Him and to each other for His sake, consecrate our whole selves to His service, *for Him to live and die.* When this is done what have we to do with the future? We and all our concerns are in His hands, under His all-wise and gracious Providence. I wish you could see into my heart for a moment, I cannot transfer to paper my *absorbing* desire that *the will of God may be done* in this matter ... If you come on Saturday I shall presume that you are satisfied on those two points and that henceforth we are one."[21]

Note, Catherine spoke no word of love in this or any letter written to William before her betrothal to him.

William came. Hand in hand he and Catherine kneeled before God, "henceforth ... one". Nearly twelve months later she wrote, "We are one in *all things;* it will be twelve months on the 13th May since, bowed together at this sofa, we solemnly gave ourselves to each other and to God. If you will, we will always keep *that* as our real wedding day. It was so in the sight of God and in all the highest and holiest senses, the next is a mere legal knot, *that* was a moral and spiritual union of souls."[22] Kneeling, side by side, hand in hand to pray together, became a life-long custom. In a love-letter of 1853 Catherine writes of praying at agreed times, though apart, "Oh, how sweet to think that we do as truly meet, as really mingle desires and sympathies as if we knelt together with our hands clasped in each others, as we used to do."[23]

In Begbie's opinion the love of Catherine Mumford and William

69

Booth is "one of the most remarkable and charming love stories in the world—the love story of a man and a woman in whose hearts an extraordinary sense of religion had the uppermost place, to whom everything secular and human had a divine relativity, for whom God and His worship were the sovran ends of their existence ... Passion was there, deep and abiding, but passion restrained by duty and consecrated by devotion. An immense reverence for the woman characterized the love of the man, and a deep, self-sacrificing faith in the man and his destiny characterized the love of the woman."[24]

After their troth is plighted, Catherine wrote her first love-letter: "*My dearest William,* I fancy I see a look of surprise suffuse your countenance at the reception of this after such a recent visit. You will think it unnecessary and so it is, but I don't feel inclined for either reading or working just now. The evening is beautifully serene and tranquil according sweetly with the feelings of my soul, the whirl-wind is past ... Your sweet letter and kind visit have hushed its last murmurs and stilled every vibration of my throbbing heart-strings. All is well. I feel it is right and my soul praises God for the satisfying conviction. Most gladly does my soul respond to your invitation to give myself afresh to Him and to strive to link myself closer to you, by rising more into the likeness of my Lord; the nearer our assimilation to Jesus, the more perfect and heavenly our union. Our hearts are now indeed *one*, so one that disunion would be more bitter than death. But I am satisfied our union may become, if not more complete, yet more divine and consequently capable of yielding a larger amount of pure unmingled bliss. The thought of our walking through life together *perfectly united*, together enjoying its sunshine and battling with its storms, by softest sympathy sharing every smile and every tear, and with thorough unanimity performing all its momentuous duties, is to me exquisite happiness, the highest earthly bliss I desire ... We *have* acknowledged God from the beginning, we *have* sought His will ... and we do now love Him more for the love we bear each other ... satisfied that in each of our souls there flows a *deep undercurrent of affection.* We will seek grace to bear with the bubbles which may arise on the surface, or wisdom so to treat them as to increase the depth and accelerate the onward flow of the pure stream of love ... Though it is so short a time since I pressed your hand and said good night, I am joyfully anticipating your next visit; to see you and to hear your voice is always *happiness,* to bow with you before the throne of Grace and hear you dedicate your *whole self* to the service of God, and entreat His blessing and smile on our future, is perfect bliss. The more you lead me up to Christ in all things the more highly shall I esteem you, and *if it be possible* to love you more than I do now, the more I shall love you. You will be tired of this scrawl; at least I am ashamed of it, so till we meet again I must say farewell, though it is only in words. You are always present in my thoughts. Believe me, dear William, as ever your *own* loving Kate."[25]

"As ever!" Thus, swiftly love overruns time's limits, past and future; Catherine is William's "own" in love's eternity; as ever—for ever. And as to loving, she *knows* she loves William so much as it is possible for her to love. She knows that if in some future day or circumstance she discovers that it were possible for her to love him more, then she will love him more. The thought of ever loving him less does not arise, to her it is inconceivable. In a vivid, almost mundane, manner her love to God is stimulated by her love for William: "We do now love Him more for the love we bear each other." This is not presumption, nor some romantic phantasy, it is simply stating the fact. The converse is equally true. The more she loves God, the richer, the more steadfast becomes her love for William. She saw, if but dimly now, what she will see clearly later, the beautiful and awful truth that it is only when love to God takes second place to love for a human object that that love may distil poison capable of destroying love itself; whilst those who go on loving God first find their earthly loves thriving.

2

"Life now to me assumed altogether another aspect," Catherine tells. "The idea of the possibility of becoming a wife and mother filled my life with new responsibilities, but the thought of becoming a minister's wife made the whole appear increasingly serious. I assumed in imagination all these responsibilities right away, even as though they had already come, and at once set myself with all my might to prepare to meet them. I added to the number of my studies, enlarged the scope of my reading, wrote notes and made comments on all the sermons and lectures that appeared at all worthy of the trouble, started to learn shorthand in order that I might more readily and fully correspond with William."[26] This shorthand learning did not come to more than an occasional word in a love-letter, but the readiness to attempt new methods is typical of Catherine. Imagination boggles at the thought of the length to which her letters might have run had she and William mastered the medium! As it is, although she finds that writing tires her back more than anything, and inveighs against pens that "scratch" or "cut into the paper", her letters to William often run to two thousand words and more.

A letter of William's, written shortly after his engagement to Catherine, gives a picture of him arriving late in his small room feeling he cannot go to bed until he has written the dear name, although he had but just left her side. It is the expression of an immature mind, but it contains phrases that may well be called prophetic. Catherine's lack of musical proficiency was a disappointment to William who was very musical. To please him she set herself to learn to play the piano and struggled valiantly against the odds of her age, and a weak spine. William's letter, undated, gives the Walworth address and is headed Wednesday night, eleven o'clock: *"My dear Catherine,* I have just read over your pencillings ... I cannot go and lay me [down] until I have scratched some of my feelings on to paper. I *fear* the feelings of my heart, they are so intense, they may not be of long continuance so excited, perhaps better not, but I trust they will be deeper as well as calmer ... I *feel toward you* as I *never* did to *another* ... my heart beats in perfect unison with your own and I praise Him who redeemed me for the perfect treasure which in you I possess ... I cannot see you to tell you this, so ... I tell it you at a distance with my pen. Good night.

"Thursday morning ... I dare not tell you the hour, it is not early enough [evidently William already stood a little in awe of his "perfect treasure"!] ... Your prayers follow me, and if I love you more in one position than another, it is when on your knees, and if your voice soundeth unto me more harmonious and more musical at one time than another it is when pleading with the Author and Founder and Redeemer of the new and better Covenant. You have company today. I wish you social happiness. It is on my mind, I forgot to allude to it yesterday; try in some way or other to make it a gathering of spiritual profit (do not waste time on mere temperance conversation) but oh, talk about Christ. Launch right out on the subject ... If Mr. Rabbits is not there, pray yourself with them—this, if it be a cross, take it up. I should wish you to perfectly overcome all shyness on this point. Oh, to me this is far better than if you could bring forth music from the pianoforte or guitar. It is what I have yearned for in all my day dreams about a companion that [and here come the prophetic words, the italics are mine] *she should be willing and able to plead in public and in private* ...

"I have not for a moment had a doubt as to the propriety of declining any offers of business. I do not imagine my path is that way. I am yearning for a nobler work. For your dear sake I might desire the former, but I do not see even that ... My breakfast waits, my books are conjuring me not to slight them again today, as I did yesterday and many days gone by. Bayswater pulpit is frowning at me in the distance for my thoughtlessness and disrespect in not preparing for it, and I know full well that the wishes of that one, who so far as earth is concerned sits supreme ruler of my soul, are that I should give all diligence to study. Therefore believe me, dearest Catherine, to remain, Yours affectionately in Jesus' love and the best of bonds, William."[27]

A letter of Catherine's, which might be an answer to this one of

William's, shows that she is beginning to be anxious about his health and imploring him to "desist from unnecessary exertion". She does not know her William yet, nor that anxiety about his health and overworking will last all her life! *"My dear William,* I ought to be happy after enjoying your company all the evening but now you are gone and I am alone, I feel a regret consonant with the height of my enjoyment . . . the pleasure connected with pure, holy, sanctified love forms no exception from the general rule. The very fact of loving invests the being beloved with a thousand causes of care and anxiety, which if unloved would never exist, at least I find it so. *You* have cost me more real anxiety than any other earthly object ever did . . . I think I see you looking puzzled to conjecture the cause of my anxiety after such a satisfactory interview, and so many kind words which as they fell from your lips sank into my heart and will never be forgot . . . The next cause of anxiety is for fear you should get cold going home too thinly clad, surely you will not; I hope if you come tomorrow evening you will bring your greatcoat, my candle is just going out so I must say good night. May Heaven's best blessing descend and abide with you sleeping and waking. Yours in the fullest sense you can desire, Catherine.

"*Saturday morning.* I have several things to attend to but as I know if you still don't come you would like a line, I am determined you shall have one . . . I hope you will come tonight. It seems a long time since last night already, but if you don't, do be careful on Sunday. You know I would not in any way lessen your usefulness, but I must beg of you to desist from all unnecessary exertion. For instance, don't pray more than once in the prayer meeting *if there is anyone else to pray,* don't sit up singing till twelve o'clock after a hard day's work. Such things are not required by either God or man and remember you are not your own. Do forgive this scrawl."[28]

These first months of her engagement, Catherine said, were among "the happiest periods of my life, but for the gloomy view William was apt to take of our circumstances".[29] His was not a gloomy disposition, but it was natural that he should look to the future with an impatience very intolerant of the obstacles in his way. What a mercy for him that Catherine was within reach. Letters make it clear that into her sympathetic ear he could pour out his longings, fears and hopes. She was the first to recognize that as a preacher, paid from a private source, he could have no real authority even in the small group to which he was attached. Further, the leader of the local movement denied him reasonable opportunity to preach. They both agreed that the arrangement with Mr. Rabbits should come to an end when the three months were completed in July. Catherine was not anxious about the future. Perhaps she was too happy to be? Happiness and faith go well together. In her own words, "I felt quite certain that God would interfere on our behalf."[30]

In a love-letter she wrote, "Mr. Thomas called last evening . . . I do like him; he is one of the nicest men I ever conversed with . . . I really love him and his preaching gets better and better . . ."[31] It was no doubt with Mr. Thomas in mind that Catherine persuaded William to offer himself, as a candidate for the ministry, to the Independents, as Congregationalists were then called. She tells, "I argued that once settled in a Congregational pulpit, he could impart into his services and meetings all that was good and hearty and soul-saving in Methodism."[32]

William went to see Dr. Campbell,* one of their leading men who recommended that he should enter the Congregational College for Ministers at Cotten End. After passing various examinations and preaching trial sermons, Booth was accepted. On the day before that on which he was to enter college he was interviewed by Dr. George Smith, representing the governing committee, and told that by the end of the first term it was expected he would be ready to conform to the Calvinistic doctrine which was then the basis of Congregational theology. William was nonplussed! He had been assured by leading ministers of this church that he would not be required to preach any doctrine he did not honestly believe. However, on his way home from the interview he bought *The Rule of Grace,* one of the books he had been instructed to study. When he had read the first thirty pages he threw it across his room convinced that he could never adopt its teaching. Although Catherine had set her heart on his going to the college, she was in agreement with him that on this question of doctrine he could not yield. She says, "We were both saturated, as it were, with the broadest, deepest, highest opinions as to the extent of the love of God, and the benefit flowing from the sacrifice of Jesus Christ. We were verily extremists on this question." And she goes on to explain "the matter [of going to college] had been undertaken . . . at my own instigation and I had laboured to pilot him [William] through the many difficulties that barred the way; and now, all at once, my schemes were frustrated".[33]

Ways and means demanded that William should be employed at something. The little store of money with which he had left business was exhausted. The last sixpence he had in the world he had given to a poor girl dying of consumption the day before he was to have entered college. Surely no man ever held his scanty means more lightly! This matter of the last sixpence would never have been heard of had not Catherine treasured the memory, and it stands in such acute contrast to the character his detractors later gave him, that it is worth remembering. William was now penniless and having sold his bits of furniture, what was to happen? "So far as we could see

* Rev. John Campbell, D.D. (1795-1867), well-known Congregational minister. Editor of official periodicals for Congregational Union.

no other deliverance was in sight,"[34] Catherine recalls, but her faith in William and in God's providing did not waver. Meantime he was offered a room in the Mumford home. Deliverance, though not in sight, was not far off. A friend in London, hearing of enquiries for a preacher to undertake the oversight of a group of Reform societies in and around Spalding, recommended young Booth. Before many days had passed he was installed there. "To us this seemed a wonderful intervention indeed," says Catherine, "... if it had not meant parting".[35] Yet it was the parting that called forth the love-letters! These are not looked upon by either of them as anything worth preserving, except for the joy of possession. They are written for a lover's eye alone. Catherine often instructs William to "burn this", or pleads "really I am ashamed to send this unconnected scrawl. Do *this once* burn this out of sight."[36] Of another one she suggests, "perhaps it will be company for you in some lonely walks." She tells William "all yours have reached me ... five in number ... how often they have been read I cannot tell. I still wear them in my frock."[37]

In her letters Catherine reveals the beauty and strength of her love and at the same time the beauty and strength of her character. The discerning may find not only what her love dictates to William but also an expression of that self-obliterating intensity of emotion earlier remarked in her. Have any woman's love-letters ever been so little taken up with herself, with her own doings, or pleasures, or needs? She tells of her health, to please William when she is well, and when she is sick because it would not be honourable to hide it from him. They had been engaged nearly eighteen months when she wrote: "Do be happy about *me* ... I have never discouraged you about the *future,* neither our prospects nor our domestic happiness. It has only been about my health, and *that* I could not hide without evading your enquiries and acting deceitfully, and that I would scorn to do. *If I do not get well* and you feel it would be wrong to marry me I shall fully release you ... but my Love, God will be gracious to us. I think He will give me my health."[38]

William in his letters allows himself the luxury, for such it is to a lonely man, of complaining, "I feel uncommonly tired and weary this morning. My head aches," or, "I should have written you yesterday but was so unwell ..." Catherine constantly enquires after *his* health and gives advice, remarkably good advice too. She had a flair for common-sense treatment as distinct from fashionable foibles. Thus her opinions expressed to William in 1852 on the value of cod liver oil, and that fresh air was essential for health, or that having a cold sponge in the morning was invigorating, may be considered sound today. She wrote, "Be assured I will do all I can for my body," and then enquiries: "Do you think you hold yourself upright? Have you tried any exercises for the purpose? Have you attended to your feet?. .Washing the feet frequently is so conducive to health."[39]

75

He learned from her that foot comfort was important to a preacher and formed the habit of changing his woollen socks at least once and often two or three times a day. One should have it in mind that in their time the connection between dirt, drains and disease was only beginning to be understood. Smallpox, cholera and consumption were a continual menace.

In selecting passages from her letters I have chosen those that seem to me to reveal her thoughts and character. This means leaving out most of the common stuff of letters, such as local and family news; simply because there is no room for it in this book. For the same reason William's letters are almost excluded. For the most part they describe his services, his sermons and how he felt about them; the visiting of the sick, and his riding, driving and walking over the flat fen lands of his district. Catherine in contrast had little to do but practise the piano, pray for and write to her Love. Her letters led William along the road of self-examination. While she spoke with the voice of her love for him, he heard also the voice of God's messenger to his soul. As one reads her letters it is difficult to remember that the writer was only in her early twenties and that her experience was restricted to the narrow and sluggish current of life in her suburban home. Indeed it is impossible unless the atmosphere in which her soul had developed be taken into account; her familiarity with the Bible and all that had burgeoned in her mind from the truths she found there. She said, "Before I was fifteen years of age God had ... taught me ... that every act of our lives, every relationship into which we enter ... should be centred and bounded by God and His glory." Phillips Brooks describes such a state "... when the priority of existence is seen to rest in a Person, and the background of life is God; then every new arrival instantly reports itself to Him and is described in terms of its relationship to Him ... The priority of God! It is the great illumination of all living."[40] This was true for Catherine before she met William, and what was to come of it her future shows. What had already come of it by the time she was twenty-three these love-letters tell. The standards set forth in them by her, for herself and for her beloved, for his work and for their walk together through life stem from her sense of "the priority of God". Begbie says of them: "Some of these letters seem to me as beautiful love-letters as any in the world, reaching at times heights of religious inspiration hardly to be matched ... and sounding so unmistakable a note of truth and purity of aim that they do not suffer in the least from an occasional use of the now outworn vocabulary of Methodist fervour ... One of her letters indeed deserves to live (and probably will live) as one of the beautiful documents in the literature of mysticism* ... The letters are so spontaneous, so unconscious of

* Begbie does not specify which of Catherine's letters he had in mind.

publication, so intimate and yet so public, that they may be given in their fulness and with scarcely the interposition of a single comment."[41] Her love-letters have been described as "Puritan". St. J. Ervine* agrees, but adds, "it does not imply, as might be imagined by those who are unacquainted with the beauty of Puritan life and have heard only of its narrowness and restrictions, that emotional warmth is absent from them ... both his and hers are full of their preoccupation with religion and the warfare in which they were engaged; but the depth and beauty of their devotion is plain. These two never wavered in their love for each other for a second from the day on which they announced it to the day she died."[42]

Catherine's mothering of William was an expression of her love for him, a kind of language of the heart. She would teach him because she sees that he is capable of being made perfect, or almost. She sets about the fashioning delicately, with an unerring instinct for foster-ing the headship in him. Catherine has no notion of usurping his place. She perceives that to wound his self-esteem might irreparably injure the poise of their love. Again and again she makes him feel how much she needs *his* help. In one of the earlier letters to Spalding she says, "Remember the father is, and must be the *head* of his household." In another, "But I forget to whom I write. *You* know all this better than I do ..." And it is in the unconscious wisdom of her perfect sincerity and love's perfect confidence that she writes accentuating *her* need of *him*. "My own dear Love, Oh how I should like to see you tonight and to hear you speak to me in tones of sweet affection and encouragement. I feel my weakness and deficiencies most bitterly, and have shed some tears because of it . . . I have confidence in *you* as to battling with the trials of life, or I think I should sink into despair ... but *you* will be my defence and shield, my prop and succour, will you not dearest?"[43] In another letter telling of her sense of God's mercy: "Oh, help me to praise Him, and *help me* to serve Him, will you my dearest Love?"[44]

In her perception of the promise his future held, Catherine drew William up to her view. Hers was not the dominating and possessive influence often associated with highly developed maternal instincts, for, as she herself put it, "any idea of lordship or ownership is lost in love ... there will be mutual yielding wherever there is proper love, because it is a joy to yield our own will to those for whom we have real affection whenever it can be done with an approving conscience. This is just as true with regard to man as to woman."[45] William learned from her of this sweet mutual joy in yielding to one another. We know that he has seen what she was praying he might see, when, after one of his visits to London he wrote, "I can see plainly, my

* St. John Ervine, LL.D. Playwright and author. Wrote Life of William Booth *God's Soldier*, 1934.

77

dearest, that our influence over each other will be immense. I tremble when I think how much apparently during my last visit I exercised over you. Oh, my heart must be thoroughly Christ's . . ."[46]

Catherine's letters are closely written in a small swift hand; one has the impression that she could not write fast enough to set her thoughts on paper, and she often runs on without paragraphs filling every corner and then, sometimes, crossing the already covered pages. For clarity I have adjusted paragraphs and punctuation and left out some quotations from the Scriptures and of hymns. The reader must remember always that none of these letters is a prepared expression of thought. Each one is at the moment of writing the spontaneous outpouring of love and of love's hopes and fears. Does the distance in time justify revealing these intimacies between lovers to the cold glance of strangers? If reading the letters were to prove helpful to anyone, I think Catherine would consent. She wanted above all to *help* people, and I believe these letters will. At least they will help the reader to know Catherine herself. None the less, turning the pages I have felt a shiver of hesitancy as I read Catherine's *"take care* of my letters. I should not like any other eye to see them but your own." Dr. Laura Petri says, "Catherine Mumford's letters to William Booth form an original and brilliant part of Mrs. Booth's writings. The letters are quite outstanding in literature. Various interesting love-letters between great men and women have been published, but not just this kind."[47] No! For in a curiously complete sense the letters of Catherine's youth set forth the ideals, the plan on paper, of her life, and of the teaching and aims of The Salvation Army. She lived out the principles expressed in her love-letters, and her story is one more proof added to the many that the Bible standards for human behaviour are attainable by the help of the Holy Spirit. Wife and mother, Catherine became a saint, not of the cloister, but of the hearth; a being who from youth to death loved the Lord her God with all her heart and with all her soul and with all her strength and with all her mind. In every vicissitude of her life she could say to God with complete sincerity, "Lord, Thou knowest all things; Thou knowest that I love Thee."

3

Soon after William's arrival in Spalding he wrote what for him was a long letter. He was in lodgings and alone. The letter begins: "My dearest earthly Treasure, bless you a thousand times for your very kind letter just received; it has done my heart good . . . I have thought about you much and very affectionately the last few days . . .

I do not doubt our future oneness with regard to revivalism and about all things. I have such faith in our powers of utterance that we shall be able to make plain to each other what we mean and our love to each other, that when we can be brought to see truth held by the other we shall rejoice to adopt it. [This state of mind continued between them both till death parted them.] And although now I do not doubt I could bear with extravagance in a preacher or a prayer meeting which you would condemn . . . I do not blame you, so wait until the time comes, and we shall yet, I do not doubt, see with the same eyes . . . I have not the tact and talent that thousands have, and yet under their ministry how little do we see *done;* . . . I go to Him and say, I am nothing, Thou art my all in all. Try this, will you darling? Don't begin at the outside and aim at patching up this rent and that rent in your life, but go to Jesus and take the blessings of a pure heart at His hand . . ."

Note now the quick change of mood. He had been in bed with stomach trouble. "Oh, how I wanted your hand on my aching head . . . was really ill, thought much of you. Got better and went and preached, and came home and made a hearty dinner of goose, etc. . . . In the morning I had again to take brandy twice, and then I preached with some pleasure." He describes his meetings, good congregations, good results. He tells about the farms where he stays: the farmer "took me in his gig, I found his home quite a nice house, a large family of very nice and apparently well-educated children, a resident governess . . . I made an excellent dinner, and away we went to preach; service held in a large kitchen, which was quite full, about seventy present. Here I met Mr. Jonathan Longhatton. He told me that as a man of experience, I must take port wine, that he could tell by my voice and appearance that it would do me good. My health is of first importance. What do you say, dearest? After shaking hands we went in the gig again, and after a cold bleak ride I reached Holbeach, took tea with Mr. Peet, and preached . . . So that by the time I reach Spalding on Friday, after being absent seven days, I shall have preached, all well, ten instead of six sermons . . . if your health and my circumstances would warrant it, our wedding, instead of January '54 should be January '53. I remain, my darling, Yours as ever and forever, William. *To my dearest Love.* My position here is likely to be just to my own mind."[48]

All Catherine's letters, unless otherwise specified, are written from the Mumford home at 7 Russell Street, Brixton. "*My dearest William,* Here I sit alone in our comfortable little parlour." Thus begins the first letter I can find of Catherine's to Spalding. Part follows ". . . and now feel a strong inclination to talk with you a bit . . . You will be pleased to hear that we have spent a very comfortable Sabbath. We had a cold dinner and *all* went to Chapel this morning . . . I went to school in the afternoon and was received with great apparent pleasure by my class. Hope some seed of truth sank into their minds which will germinate another day. Had a wet walk home, *and no beloved one to meet me.* Have been praying earnestly for my dearest, that his sermon may find its way to the hearts of the people, and that his own soul may be abundantly watered. Felt it very good to draw nigh unto God. Oh, to live in the spirit of prayer. I feel it is the secret of real religion ... How much I have thought about you, I cannot tell, nay, I should say, when have you been absent from my thoughts ... and now, good night, another look at your portrait, and then I am off to bed. I have slept in your room ever since you went and have gone to bed much earlier, have not dreamed about you once, to my great disappointment; was pleased to hear you had about me; it would be a comfort to see you even in fancy.

"*Monday.* In consequence of going to bed earlier, I am able to rise earlier and hope soon to reap mental and physical improvement from it. For several mornings I have sponged all over in cold water, and dressed by the light of the lamp. I rest as many hours, only I get it at the right end of the night. I hope, my love, you will *not sit up late.* I am sure it is most injurious. Try to get to bed every night by ten o'clock. Don't let the pleasures of social intercourse with the very kind friends with whom you stay induce you to sit up late. Remember how it unfits you for early rising and study in the morning ... The post boy is just going past, singing that tune you liked so, about 'My master sell me',* etc. He frequently does, and there is nothing seems to cast such a shade over my heart. I hope it will soon be forgotten. It makes me feel such a sense of loneliness now I hear you sing it no longer ... I am delighted to hear you had such a good day and gave such satisfaction. Let us give all the glory to God and be encouraged. I *think* you did quite *right* in saying what you did about salary ... If they like you they will not lose you for the sake of a few pounds. However, try them fair, but as you are so happy amongst them I would not advise you to leave because of salary. I value your happiness *far, far* beyond any pecuniary advantages whatever.

"I am very sorry to hear you will have so little time to study. My dear, *you must have* it somehow, or you *will wear out.* They must lessen the labour; no man can sustain incessant toil without any recruiting time, either mentally or physically, and you must tell them so, after a time ... Loving you as fervently as ever, and rejoicing in your prosperity. I am yours in as full a sense as you desire, Kate.

"*Wednesday night.* I received your kind letter this morning [in which William tells of his further success, and the warmth of the

* Negro song "Why did my master sell me upon my wedding day?" The American novelist Harriet Beecher Stowe had lately published *Uncle Tom's Cabin* (1851) exposing the evils of slavery.

people toward him] ... I rejoice in the kindness and attention you
receive, but I rejoice with trembling. I know *how dangerous* it would
be to a heart far less susceptible of its influence than yours ... I feel
how dangerous it would be to *me*, and it fills me with the tenderest
anxiety for your spiritual safety. You have especial need for watchfulness and private intercourse with God. My dearest Love, beware
how you indulge that dangerous element of character, ambition.
Misdirected it will be everlasting ruin to yourself and perhaps to me
also. Let not self-aggrandizement fire it. Fix it on the Throne of the
Eternal and let it find the realization of its loftiest aspirations in the
promotion of *His* glory ..." She goes on to warn him of the danger of
"a perverted ambition, the exaltation of self instead of God ... I could
write sheets on the subject, but my full soul shall pour out its desires
to that God who has promised to supply all your need. In my
estimation faithfulness is an indispensable ingredient of all true friendship. How much more of a love like mine? You say 'Reprove, advise,
etc. as you think necessary'. I have no reproofs, my dearest, but I
have cautions, and I know you will consider them ... I am going to
post this and may as well fill it up, notwithstanding its prodigious
length."[49]

Catherine is perhaps over anxious that William should study. Almost
every letter commands or coaxes him to that end. One feels that
disappointment at the failure of the plan for his going to Cotten End
College is still with her. She writes, "I have been revolving in my
mind all day which will be your wisest plan under present circumstances. It appears to me that as you are necessitated to preach nearly
every evening and at places so wide apart, that it will be better to do
as the friends intimate and stop all night where you preach, and
not attempt to walk long distances after preaching. With a little
management and a *good deal of determination* I think you might
accomplish even more that way, as to study, than the other [i.e. to
come 'home' to a rented room]. Could you not provide yourself with
a small leather bag or case, large enough to hold *Castle's Educator*,
your *Bible* and any other book you might require for general
purposes, pens, ink, paper, and a *candle*, and presuming that you
generally occupy a room to yourself, could you not rise, say by six
o'clock every morning and convert your bedroom into a *study* till
breakfast time? After breakfast and family devotions could you not
again retire to your room and determinedly apply yourself to it till
dinner, when doubtless the friends who are *able* would gladly entertain you, and when not able you could pay for your dinner, and then
start on your journey to your evening appointment; get there for a
comfortable tea and do the same again. I hope, my dearest love, you
will consider this plan ... your appointments are not till evening and
you must spend your day somewhere. Will you not make up your
mind to surmount *every* obstacle, and *study*, either by hook or by

crook, as the country folk say. If you cannot, I would say give it up at once and risk the getting of a smaller circuit ... Try to restrain your voice as much as possible. Don't preach a bit louder than you talk. You might be heard distinctly by seven or eight hundred people. *Don't sing*, nor pray in prayer meetings oftener than is *necessary*. I am glad you live well ... I hope you don't forget to wage war with the drinking custom. Be out-and-out on that subject. I am glad Mr. Shadford [with whom William lodged] is a teetotaller; hope he is also anti-tobacco and snuff. Father is still a teetotaller.

"Tuesday afternoon. My dearest love, I thank you sincerely for your kind letter this morning. I like it better than any I have received since you went, there is a depth of feeling manifest ..." Referring to her proposal that William should study in the morning, she goes on, "... if you can adopt such a plan there would be no necessity for a pony, but it is for you to determine whether a settled home and keeping a pony would be better. At all events, it is of no use having one without the other, as it is impossible to *walk home* after preaching. I would not advise you to leave the circuit because of salary on any account, if they will give you £60, and there is a *prospect of studying*. But if you really see no possibility of studying don't stay for any amount of money ... Do not be over-anxious about the future. *Spalding will not be your final destination* if you make the *best of your ability*. I feel your kindly consideration for my future comfort, but do not be over-anxious, even about that. God will open our way if we faithfully serve Him and seek not our own happiness, but His glory ... "[50]

A couple of days later she is writing, "... I have thought very carefully over the plan proposed in my last in juxtaposition with your proposal to keep a pony, and at present I am in favour of the former ... but of course you are the best judge. I fear you are over-looking the care and attention a pony would require as well as food. If in the summer you could put it out to graze for nothing there would be the trouble of cleaning and 'cotching' as Sam says, which would cost you a good bit if you had to hire it done, but you will consider the matter well, I doubt not, and whichever way appears to promise the *most time for study, adopt it* ... I perceive, my love, by your remarks on the services you have held, that you enjoy less liberty in preaching in the larger places before the best congregations, than in the smaller ones. I am sorry, my love, for this, and am persuaded it is the fear of man which shackles you. Do not, my dear, give place to this feeling. Remember you are *the Lord's servant* and if you are a faithful one, it will be a small matter with you to be judged of man's judgment. Let nothing be wanting *beforehand* to make your sermons acceptable. But when in the pulpit, try to lose sight of their worth or worthlessness as far as composition is concerned, and think only of their bearing on the destiny of those before you, and your own responsibility to Him who has sent you to declare His gospel . . . How do you get on, my dear, for money? I think you must be rather put about. I have often wondered how you got on in that respect. Send me word in your next, and how you get your clothes washed, and what you pay for them. I hope to receive a letter tomorrow or Saturday . . . Write longer letters when you can. Write a bit when you have a minute or two disengaged [not so easy without fountain-pens!] never mind scrawl. I love to read them. Many a time do I feel thankful for the post. What should we do without it? . . . What you say about your love for me *sinks* into my soul, because I am persuaded that you write *no more* than you feel, therefore I draw all the comfort such kind assurances are calculated to convey, and I need not tell you how truly such love is reciprocated. You *know it*. Bless you, my dearest. *If you love me* I know we shall be happy together in any state of life God sees best for us. Oh, let us love Him more . . . Yours in tenderest affection, Cathy . . . I am very sorry you do not like my likeness. I never did think it a good one . . . I should like you to have a better one. Yours I like better than ever but it should be varnished. Shall I write to the young man about it? I fear I shall injure it, if it is not done soon."[51]

The next day she has word from William that his salary is to be eighty pounds a year; and writes: "*My beloved William* . . . If anyone who did not know me had seen me walk about the parlour, absorbed in tears . . . they would have thought I had received some very distressing intelligence, but they were tears of gladness and gratitude for the goodness of God . . . I did not expect more than £65, and your position being defined so exactly according to your own views, and their not desiring so many sermons as you supposed, is over and above anything *I* had even hoped. Let us praise the Lord and be encouraged.

"Of the kindness of the people I cannot speak. I can only *feel* its value . . . Mind, my love, that you sustain it *as a man*. Gentlemanly manners and kindness will not fail to do it. As a *preacher* study will not only enable you to maintain your present status, but attain a higher. You promise me *to do what you can;* if you do that, I have no fear . . . What you say about ensuring your life I highly approve, and shall estimate such an act as another proof of your practical affection for myself . . . We have found a very nice box in the loft which holds all your books first-rate. Send word where it must be directed and what day it must come. I will forward the victorine [fur tippet] tomorrow . . . I am sorry I overlooked the cold mornings in my scheme. It was not through want of thought or feeling for you, but from over-anxiety for your mental improvement. I find sponging [in cold water] a great preventative to susceptibility of cold. I believe it is an excellent thing. I wish you would try it. I think my health is generally better, and I believe my back is improving. Good afternoon.

I shall be too late [for post]. Yours in tenderest and most enduring affection, Cathy."[52]

Joyful and confident in faith after her conversion, Catherine had felt free to help others. Then, after her illness, her natural timidity asserted itself, and she became "tossed with reasonings". Her letters from time to time reveal her longing for the former spiritual joys: as in this letter. "My dearest William ... this afternoon I went to school, and enjoyed a few moments *sensible access* to God (oh, how sweet, like a sudden outburst of sunshine in a tempestuous night) before I commenced the duties of the class. I felt as I sometimes used to feel in brighter happier days, as if self were sinking, expiring, and for the moment, the glory of God *only* seemed to engage and rivet the eye of my soul, as the sublime object at which I must aim. Need I tell you that I had special liberty and pleasure in speaking to the children ... It is a glorious work in any way to be instrumental in winning souls. Oh, for *wisdom* and *grace* to do it in the best way, and having done all, to *feel* in our inmost souls our insignificance, and adore the condescending love which deigns to use *such* instruments for the accomplishment of so great a purpose.

"This evening I have spent alone. I have been particularly blessed in praying for you yourself, more than for a blessing on the Word; not, I think, because I feel more indifferent to its success, but because I seem to see such an intimate connexion between your personal experience of its powers and its practical effect upon those to whom you minister. My heart yearns over you. I should like to say much which I cannot write. I feel an inexpressible tenderness of soul in thinking about you ... The love I bear you, my dearest, is no superficial thing, nor do I think it is selfish. I feel your happiness and usefulness are paramount to every other consideration with me. I want you to be a man of God in the strictest sense ... I have been thinking, my love, of our future. I feel its brightness or obscurity rests with ourselves. Providential trials we shall have, *we would not* be without them, whereof all God's children are partakers, but we may, and oh, shall we not? live in the perpetual sunshine of each other's ardent affection, and God's unchanging love. Tell me, my love, whether it shall be so. I *should* like to hear you breathe out your determination and desire that it may be, before the Throne tonight, but, as that cannot be, join me on Xmas Day (at any hour you will name) in asking for grace so to live. Good night, my love, yours in the tenderest of bonds, Cathy.

"*Thursday afternoon.* I received both your letters ... With respect to your lodgings, if you expected to be at home altogether, or *nearly so*, I should consider 9/- reasonable, very; but as you are out so much I think it will be the most expensive way you can adopt. Is there no widow lady, a member of the Society, who would take you on your own terms, i.e. to cook etc. for you? If I were in your place

84

I would enquire well, and not decide hastily, but I doubt not you will do for the best. I think your washing very cheap indeed. If the circuit will engage to keep a pony, I should think it would be best to have one. I am very sorry to hear you are preaching so much this week. I thought the Committee did not require more than six sermons per week, if so, I think it is not wise voluntarily to work so hard, though you are so well. I fear for your chest if you overdo it. Remember, my dear, your body is not your own. The Lord requires its preservation for *His* service, and *I* am anxious that you should live out all your days ... Mother thinks there is a great improvement in the shape of my back, indeed I am wearing the shield quite tight to it. I often want you to put on my boots and goloshes. Father puts them on for me on Sunday morning. My general health is better than it has been for a long time ...

"*Friday afternoon* ... I received yours this morning, and was very pleased to hear you have been so fortunate in the selection of a home. It is very cheap to include the use of a parlour and coals, and yet, as you say, will be an advantage to the parties themselves ... Your calculations about furnishing exactly meet my views. I like your notions about having things *good* and comfortable *at first*. There is nothing like it ... Mention in your next *what* clothes you want. I am glad you intend getting a new suit. I am sure you need them, have them *good*. I wish you had left an order for them in London, I think you would have done better. I hope you will have a good season on the Watch Night. I will meet you at the solemn hour, all well. Let us breathe each other's name with the last breath of the old year."[53]

And two days after Christmas, "*My dearest Love* ... I have felt very anxious about your health, since hearing you were so poorly. I could not sleep last night for thinking about you. I do hope you are better. I fear, my love, you are not sufficiently careful as to diet. Do exercise self-denial when such things are before you as you have any reason to fear will disagree with you." William's circuit was in rich farming land and members of his congregation naturally offered their best fare to the youthful preacher. At twenty-three roast goose was a welcome repast after walking five or six miles. Had the nervous agitation of preaching not to follow, it would no doubt have agreed with William. But he was a man of unrestrainable energy. He set about his work in headlong fashion, and suffered from indigestion all his life. A page or two further on in Catherine's letter comes this outburst, "I am all anxiety about you; it is monstrous to think of preaching ten sermons in one week ... If you do so again I shall be quite angry. It is wicked. It is out of all reason." The writer is in calmer mood when telling that William's box had been dispatched. "We managed to make it hold all you require, by close packing ... write by return after you receive it. Unpack it carefully as, in sundry

85

little holes amongst the books, you will find two or three mince pies, which we send, not because we fear you will lack abundance of Xmas cheer but because we wish you to taste ours . . . In the little place for razors in the dressing-case you will find a lock of hair, and in a little square hole, the key, etc. My dear mother has mended your trousers. She says they are not done very nicely, but they will last a while, and then you must get a tailor to do them."

These paragraphs are among the interspersions that crop up, a sort of green turf footing between the leaps of thought into higher regions. This letter begins with a playful dig at William, and runs into a love passage, thus: "As I did not feel in writing tune yesterday or on Xmas Day, I will this evening give you a sketch of our Christmas enjoyment. Father dined at home and tho' our number was so small, we enjoyed ourselves very well. Your representative on the wall seemed to look down on our sensual gratification with awful gravity, manifesting an indifference to the good things of this life not at all characteristic of the original. I thought about you very, very much through the day. I could not but contrast my feelings with those of last year. *Then* my anxieties and affections were centred in objects whose love and care I had experienced through many changing years. *Then* I knew no love but that of a child, a sister, a friend, and I thought that love deep, sincere, fervent; perhaps it was, nay *I know it was*. But since then a *stranger, unknown, unseen* till within the last short year, has strangely drawn around himself the finest tendrils of my heart and awakened a new, absorbing affection which seems, as it were, to eclipse what I before deemed the intensity of love. *Then,* my anxieties were almost confined to *home; now,* this same stranger, like a magnet, draws them after him in all his wanderings, so that they are seldom *at* home. What a change in one short year. Can you solve the mystery? Can you find the reason?"

Catherine goes on to tell of her father. He "seemed the kinder", is "still a teetotaller and is abstaining altogether from the pipe . . . *don't forget him,* my love, at the Throne of Grace, help me and my dear mother to pray for him . . . Oh, for a Christlike sympathy for souls such as I used to feel when I have sat up half the night to plead for them. My dearest love, *this* is the secret of success, the weapon before which the very strongholds of hell must give way. Oh, let us try to get it again, let us *make up our minds* to win *souls* whatever else we leave undone . . . You ask my opinion about taking port wine. I need not say how willing, nay, how anxious I am that you should have anything and everything which would tend to promote your *health* and happiness, but so thoroughly am I convinced that port wine would do neither, that I should hear of your taking it with unfeigned grief. You must not listen, my dear, to the advice of every-one claiming to be experienced. Persons really experienced and judicious in many things not infrequently entertain notions the *most fallacious* on this subject. I have had it recommended to me scores of times by such individuals, but such recommendations have always gone for nothing because I have felt that ... *on that subject* I was the best informed. I have even argued the point with Mr. Stevens [her doctor] and I am sure I set him completely fast for argument to defend alcohol, even as a medicine. I am fully and for ever settled on the physical side of the question. I believe you are on the moral and religious, but I have never thought you were on the physical. Now, my dearest, it is *absolutely necessary*, in order to save you from being influenced by other people's false notions, that you should have a *settled, intelligent* conviction on the subject, and in order that you may get this I have been at the trouble almost to unpack your box, which was beautifully packed, to get out *Bachus*, in which you will find several green marks and likewise some pencillings, in three or four *sections*, which I hope you will read ... It is a subject on which I am most anxious you should be *thorough*. I abominate that hackneyed but monstrously inconsistent tale, *a teetotaller in principle,* but obliged to take a little for my stomach's sake! Such teetotallers aid the progress of intemperance more than all the drunkards in the land, and there are abundance of them amongst Methodist preachers ... Oh, my love, take every care of yourself, get everything *needful,* but flee the detestable drink as you would a serpent. Be a teetotaller in principle and *practice*, and in this respect by example and precept train up your sons (if ever you have any), in the way in which they *should go*.

"I am glad you *feel* the importance of the training of children. There is no subject on which I have felt and still feel more acutely. I have often looked upon a little child and felt my whole frame affected by the consideration that it were possible for me, sometime, to become a mother. The awful weight of responsibility wrapped up in that beautiful word has often caused my spirit to sink within me. Oh, if I did not fully intend and ardently hope to train my own (if ever blessed with any) differently to the way in which most are trained, I would pray every day, most earnestly, that I might never have any ... My dear, I hope you do not consider the arduous but *glorious* work of training the intellectual and moral nature of the child, solely the duty of the mother. Remember the father is, and must be ... the *head* of his household. Think for a few moments what is implied in being their *head*, their *ruler*, their *shepherd,* their *tender parent* ... As soon as you can afford it buy Abbot's *Mother at Home*, price 1/-, and lend it to some of the mothers you come in contact with ... It will do good, it is as much your duty to reprove as to exhort. Good night ... "[54]

A few days after this letter, only part of which is quoted, comes the New Year and a letter from Catherine headed "January 1, 1853. Twenty minutes past twelve o'clock." Of this one I quote about half:

"A happy new year to you, my dearest William, and abundance of peace and joy. I am all alone, my dear mother having gone to bed very unwell. I have just risen from my knees and as my first act (with the exception of impressing a kiss of purest affection on the lineaments of your features) I take my pen to salute you at this early hour of this new year's morning. A cold, unsatisfactory mode of salutation, but one which I am sure (as time and circumstances will allow no other) will be pleasing to you. If I *could* convey my feelings to paper I *would,* but my heart is too full for utterance; the Lord only knows and can fully understand the indefinable emotions of my soul tonight. Oh, that I could see you and tell you all my heart, but if you were here I could not find *language,* I could only throw myself into your arms . . . I seem as it were at this solemn moment to be poised on the ridge of time's highest billow, from whence I can see all the past and the possible future at a glance; and the mingled emotions of sorrow, gratitude, hope and fear excited by the scene almost overwhelm me . . . Sorrow entwines itself even into the sunniest spots which the future presents; the purest and noblest earthly joys I ever hope to realize are linked with pain and grief. What a complicated thing is human life. And you, my own dear Love, will help me to bear the sorrows of life, will you not? . . . My soul rejoices to have one to repose in, one to love, and one who I trust will fully understand me—and enter into my views and feelings and sympathize in all my joys and sorrows, some of which hitherto have been peculiarly *my own.* I must now retire, though I feel no desire for sleep . . .

"*Sunday night* . . . It has been a good day with me. I trust I am beginning to live a new spiritual life. My soul seems to be enlarging, my sympathies expanding. I trust my understanding strengthening. I hope it has been a profitable day to my dearest Love. Oh, for a few hours' communion, *I feel so much* that I cannot write, and I feel deeply, exquisitely, on account of the past.

"William, I think you will find me altered in some things when we meet again. I hope I shall find you altered. My Love, let us govern all our actions, small and great, by the precepts of the Word and the articles of conscience. Let us begin, nay, I trust we have begun, to live from *principles* so that we and all who may ever appertain unto us may be examples to others. Life never appeared so important to me as now. I never so fully understood its value and estimated its consequences, and never did I so firmly determine, so *earnestly begin* to improve all its privileges. Will you join me, my dearest? Will you struggle against every obstacle, fight with every temptation, and embrace every opportunity? Will you, William? Oh, tell me in your next that you will. What I say about my determination to improve is not idle talk. I have *already begun* and I am firmly determined to improve to the utmost of my ability every faculty God has given me. I intend to make myself *fit* to become a *mother,* and being that in

88

every sense, I shall be fit for any destiny which God may impose upon me. I shall throw aside all false delicacy and write freely to you, my Love, on every subject which I conceive to be connected with the future happiness of ourselves and ours. Do the same with me, let our hearts be as thoroughly known to each other on all such subjects as it is possible for them to be . . .

"*Monday afternoon* . . . I have been praying earnestly for you, my dear, and now after reading your Monday's letter I will notice one or two things omitted before. You say, my Love, that you never felt more desirous than now that we may in all things be fully and truly one. I love to read it, because I believe it is the true idea, the original intention of God, and the privilege of all believers united in *Him* . . . I believe two united in Him may realize as complete and blissful a union, morally and spiritually, as though the curse had never been pronounced. Else He has left incomplete the work of restoration. Till this true idea of marriage is better understood there will be few happy unions, few well-regulated families. Till the position and mission of woman is properly estimated and cared for, in vain shall we look for perfect *oneness* in parents, and real worth in children. The general system of female education is calculated to render woman anything but a helpmate to man and a judicious self-dependent trainer of children. How can it be expected that a being trained in absolute subjection to the will of another, and taught to consider that subjection her glory, as well as an imbecile dependence on the judgment of others, should at once be able to throw off the trammels of prejudice and training, and assume that self-respect, self-reliance and sound judgment which are indispensable to the proper discharge of maternal duties? It is altogether unphilosophical to expect such a thing. It would be a phenomenon in the history of mind without a parallel. Has it never struck you, my dear, in your frequent visits to houses where ill-behaved children and foolish mothers destroy your peace to enquire why it is thus? Surely it is not want of affection in woman's heart? . . . nothing but improper culture, consequent on the false notions entertained of her nature and vocation.

"Never till she is valued and *educated* as man's equal will unions be perfect, and their consequences blissful. One of the happiest omens for English homes and England's future glory—moral glory— is the light and enquiry spreading on this subject . . . I intend to make myself acquainted with those natural laws on the observance of which God has made health and happiness *so much to depend*, more fully than I am at present and I shall not fail to communicate to you the result of my studies on the subject. Will you so far honour my judgment as to be guided in some things by my advice? I am glad your box came nicely to hand . . . I am glad you like your little watch-pocket and lock of hair. I don't know how you could wear it except on a ribbon round your neck. It makes me smile—nevertheless I am quite agreeable. I would have some of yours put in a locket if I could afford it."[55]

"*My beloved William*, as it is my intention to *treat* you to a short letter..." so begins a letter that deals, among other things, with flannel shirts, table napkins and ink to be sent to him at William's request. Also it shows the writer longing for a sight of her Love. "I am very pleased to hear you think there is a prospect of your coming to see us in harvest time, but I had been anticipating seeing you *before then*. I thought of a spring trip to Spalding just when the fields and hedges were springing into life and verdure. But perhaps it will be impossible. I shall leave it entirely to you to decide... delighted with your account of the Quarterly Meeting at which your position was most *flattering*. Had I been present I should have listened to Mr. Rowland's eulogium of your conduct with a *thrill* of *delight*, but even in that happy moment, I should involuntarily have turned an anxious look upon *you* and in my heart have prayed that the well meant, sincere and, I doubt not, well deserved encomium might not have proved a siren's voice in your soul. Perhaps it would only have been the solicitude of love, which often sees dangers where there are none... I know you will not estimate yourself by what others say and think of you, but by what you *know* in your own heart... I think, my Love, you are far too sanguine in your hopes about your circumstances as to marriage, unless indeed you think the circuit will make you a handsome present. Don't indulge hopes and expectations which cannot be realized. Calculate judiciously."[56]

These remarks vexed William. His heart was set on being able to offer Catherine a home quickly. He longed unutterably for that; and it piqued him that his Love should be so swift to warn him of the dangers of flattery, the more because he knew she was right! He wrote off in haste a letter that Catherine read "with some surprise and grief... I think you could scarcely have read my letter or else must have mistaken either its import or its spirit... I am sure I am as jealous for the honour and independence of your position as you can possibly be. My advice to be judicious in your calculations about the time of our union was dictated by nothing but a *loving* consideration for *yourself* and I really am at a loss to conceive how it could have called forth a response so harsh and unkind. I had no idea of coming to Spalding *directly*. If you look at my letter you will find that I *mentioned spring* as the time I had thought of, but I shall abandon all thoughts of such a thing if there is the least danger of its making an unfavourable impression ... I often wish writing was easier to me. I should write longer and oftener... You will see by my letter I was put about. My heart is too sensitive and your letter seemed unkind. But my heart is quite right with you now. Good night my Love."[57]

Five days later, on the eve of her birthday, Catherine writes one of these "longer" letters. Some of the pages are missing and the carefully sewn sheets have come apart. From its worn condition I judge that William must have read this letter many times. It gives a history of Catherine's spiritual experience, and knowing something of what her life with William is to be, it is moving to read of her aspirations for herself and for her lover. Anxious for the future, William asked in his birthday letter to her if she can leave it with the Lord? She answers, "Yes, my Love, I can." The simplicity of her reply, the courage implicit in it, strikes the keynote of her whole life. One may judge the rush to get her thoughts down on paper from the number of small words she left out of this letter.

"*Sunday night.* January 16th '53. My dearest William, I am now closing the last day of my 23rd year. I have been reflecting on the circumstances and experiences of my past life, on its sins, sorrows, joys and mercies, and my soul is deeply moved by the retrospect, for though my short course has been marked by no very extraordinary outward events, I cannot but think that the discipline of soul through which I have passed has been peculiar and calculated to fit me for usefulness in the cause of God. I feel truly ashamed, now that clearer light seems to shine on the path in which the Lord has led me, of my continual murmurings and discontent because of the circumstances in which He has permitted me to be cast. Truly I have laboured under many disadvantages and have often thought my lot on that account very hard, but I now see and acknowledge the goodness of God in having made up for them by the bestowment of that without which all the advantages in the world would have availed me nothing, and above all, by the impartation [of] the light and influence [of His] Holy Spirit [which] has attended me from earliest infancy, and often excited in my childish heart, thoughts, struggles, hopes and fears of no ordinary nature, though such struggles were hid in the penetralia of my own spirit and unknown [to] any mortal . . . when not more than twelve I passed through such an ordeal of fiery temptation for about the space of three months as but to reflect on makes my soul recoil within me. At that age I frequently watered my couch with my tears, and the billows of the Almighty seemed to go over me. Many a time my whole frame has trembled under the foul attacks of the adversary and his attacks were so subtle and of such a nature, that I could not then, on pain of death, have revealed them to anyone. So I endured alone and unaided by any earthly friend these fearful conflicts [of] soul the effect [of] which soon became manifest in pale cheeks, failure of health and spirits, though the true cause was unknown. But the storm passed and my mind gained in a measure its former vivacity, my soul found some repose in Christ, which, alas, soon became disturbed and was ultimately lost. The fitfulness of childish feeling, the changes and enjoyments [of] youth and the absence [of] those helps I so much needed, induced

91

seasons of indifference and I frequently grieved the Holy Spirit . . . till at length I was roused to deep and lasting concern to become in all things conformed to His will [for] I regarded conformity to the will of God as true religion even from childhood . . . After that happy change I have often told you how much I enjoyed of His presence and how I went on for some time from strength to strength. Oh, if I had followed on in the same glorious path how different would have been my feelings tonight, but alas I left my first love and wandered from the side of my Saviour . . . The desires of a whole life to be consecrated [to] the service of God seem revived in my soul. I feel sometimes as though I could do or suffer anything to glorify Him who has been so wonderfully merciful to me . . .

"I have enjoyed a precious season in prayer tonight, such liberty to ask, such a melting of soul I have not for a long time experienced. I did not forget you, my dearest. No, I pleaded hard and earnestly for your complete consecration to God. Nothing but this, my dear William, will do for either *you* or *me*. Others may trim and oscillate between the broad and narrow path, but for *us* there is but *one* straight, narrow, shining path of perfect devotedness and if we walk *not* in it we are undone. I hope, my Love, you are determined to be altogether a man of God, nothing less will secure your *safety* or usefulness. God is not glorified so much by preaching, or teaching, or anything else, *as by holy living*. You acknowledge the possibility of 'going round the circuit and satisfying the people, without winning souls to God, to peace and heaven'. Yes, my Love, it is awfully possible and especially in your case; but to live a *holy life* without winning souls is just as *impossible*. Oh, be determined to know nothing amongst men but Christ, seek nothing amongst them but *His* exaltation, His mediational renown. God has graciously given you the desire of your heart, in opening your way to the ministry of His Gospel, and that in a sphere exactly suited to your predilection and views of truth . . . He is proving you, not *now* in the furnace of affliction and adversity, but in the sunshine of prosperity, in a path paved with kindness and *dangerously slippery*. Oh, watch, watch, the motions of your heart, scrutinize your motives, analyse your desires and aims, and keep your eye single . . .

"*Tuesday evening.* My dear Love, after reading over the preceding, I hesitate whether to send it or to begin a fresh sheet, but as there are some thoughts I should [like] you to know, and as writing is so unfavourable to my back, I must even let it pass, though there are some things I would omit if I had to write it over again. But I hope you will understand me. I never communicated so freely to anyone before the experiences of my heart, but *we are one* and therefore I do it without reserve . . . It is very possible that the knowledge which I have of my own heart and its susceptibility of praise and eulogium makes me overestimate *your* danger. I am apt to measure yours by what I feel my own would be in such circumstances, and herein perhaps, I err. But you will forgive me, because it is the error of affection and not of a disposition to criticize or find fault. Tell me in your next that you pardon the thoughts expressed above and don't be grieved at them.

"I am *very, very* sorry to hear you have planned yourself as often as three times on a Sunday and four times in the week ... I am sure neither you nor any other man can preach at that rate and give the people anything worth having. [Note, sermons were expected to last at least an hour in those days.] Time for study you must have, and time free from the flurry and excitements of other engagements or all is lost. Let this quarter suffice, be wiser next time. To be absent from home three weeks out of four would indeed be poor work to be married with, but nevertheless if I thought there was a real necessity for it, in order for the prosperity of the work of God, I could bear even that, but I am sure there will be no need for it. You say if you had a wife and a pony you should be all right. My advice is, don't have one till you can have both, and have neither until you can provide for them.

"I will attend to your wishes about the music. I will *do my best*, but my Love, don't expect too much. You don't understand the difficulties. Miss Tabart says I get on well and if I had begun young I should have excelled at it . . . I am miserably dissatisfied with my progress, but I will persevere and likewise enquire about a master ... I like Mr. Rabbits' note. Does he intend to make you a present of the boots? If so, it is very kind but how will he know the size? It would be a pity to have them too little. Good night. I must leave a little bit to fill up after I have been to Mr. Franks. Oh, the tedium of writing; when shall we be able again to converse without it.

"*Thursday afternoon.* I thank you, my Love, for the extra letter which I received yesterday morning ... I went to Mr. Franks yesterday and never since you went have I felt the need of your arm to lean upon as much as I did walking from the gate home ... I am very encouraged about my back ... I am sorry you feel anxious about the future. You ask me if I can leave it with the Lord? Yes, my Love, I *can*, I am doing so. I see it is my business to make the most of the present and *trust Him* to direct and provide for the future. Let us faithfully serve henceforth and He will make our way plain before us."[58]

4

The lovers first agreed to exchange one letter a week; soon there must be at least two, and presently they wrote daily. "There was no letter for me, dearest, this morning. I have got so used to receive one every morning that I feel lost without it," wrote Catherine. Of the many available I have chosen passages that reveal something of herself and what she feels about William, as in this undated one: "I do indeed want to lay my head on your bosom and tell you all my heart. I have felt quite childishly today...Oh *how I long to see you tonight* and to communicate the thoughts and feelings which throb in my bosom. Oh, my Love, let us live to [some] purpose while we do live. Oh, to be indeed 'light and salt' in our influence on all around us, right through life. Oh, to rise above the common beaten track of *professed* Christian life..."[59] And again "...I want to find in you my *earthly all;* I expect to do so; I feel too deeply to be able to write on this subject; whenever I try my tears blind me; you think I underestimate your love; why, my dearest, do you think so? *Tell me why?* Perhaps I write too fully all my fears and thoughts and hopes about the future, but oh, I feel the importance of the relationship we are to sustain to each other, and I *do* want *us both* to be prepared to fill it with as much *happiness* to each other, and glory to God, and good to *others,* as it is possible. Be assured, my Love, I *have* confidence in you. I believe what you say, but you know, William, I shall give up my all to you, my happiness, my life, my pride, and perhaps to some extent my eternal destiny, and is it unnatural for me sometimes to express a little anxiety? Believe me, *my own dear Love,* I have confidence in your professions and I never for one *moment* doubted the honourableness of your intentions. As to the time of our union, I am surprised you think it will be practicable so soon...In this I am sure, as in other things, I am ready to consider your happiness, but you must have a house before then. Whenever I come, I doubt not I shall love the people and feel an interest in the circuit second only to yourself, and I hope to be very useful in it. I must get more religion, and then all will be well. I must get *self* destroyed, and then the Lord may trust me to do good without endangering my own soul. I am glad to hear you say you love me best when you love Jesus most; it is a good sign; such love cannot be displeasing to Him. I hope we shall be able to love Him in each other, and each other in Him, and that the nearer our assimilation to Him, the nearer will be our assimilation to each other. Glorious possibility, *it may be so:* let us both resolve that it *shall.*"[60]

William's letters are for the most part undated but this is of the period: "*My own dear Kate*, With feelings of very great pleasure I snatch up my pen to write you a line—bless you, I would that I could see you and that I could rest me for a season by your side and tell you all my heart . . . I want you, your company, your comforting and consoling converse. I want you to hear me, to criticize me, to urge me on. I feel a desperate sense of loneliness . . . I want you, too, to help you, to make you happy, to bring you flowers, to show you my friends, for you to enjoy the sunshine with me, and the landscape and the Sabbath and sweet days; bless you I was never made to enjoy things *alone*."[61]

This from Catherine might well be a reply: "I have loved you better today, my dearest, than *ever* I did before. Your anxiety for my happiness, your kind encouragement has not been expressed in vain . . . talk of burning *that* letter. I would rather burn any of them than it. Be assured a kinder fate awaits it. It will lie under my pillow many a night yet and when supplanted by another as *loving*, it shall be provided with a safe and comfortable resting place *easy* of access . . . I feel your kindness in saying you will have a horse and gig . . . I am exceedingly fond of riding (not in London omnibuses) but in an open vehicle through a nice open country. I was used to it from a child until I came here, and it always had a wonderful effect on my spirits. Then what will it do when *you* are my driver and protector? . . . We were talking about being separated and Mother said all the people will be strange. You will have none of your own friends there. I said 'Oh, *yes*, I shall have *one* friend!' . . . Indeed I felt and still do feel, that with you, my Love, if you are loving and faithful, and I believe you will be, I could be happy in a wilderness . . . You will always let me pour out my soul to *you* won't you? You don't know half the gushing tenderness of my soul, William, not *half* the enthusiasm of my nature . . . But I shall make this letter as long as the last . . . Good night. I had so much to say . . . but I must write another time. Oh what a happiness when we can *talk* together again."[62]

A week later a letter runs to over 3,000 words recounting homely details, "I have just been reading over your two kind letters and learning off the loving words contained therein . . . You had a hard day on Sunday, your poor head might well ache. I wish I could have nursed it on my bosom, perhaps that would have relieved the pain, or at least have rendered you less sensible to it. But what a mercy you did not spend your strength for naught. My soul does praise the Lord for the glorious work He has begun . . . You have to encounter many influences adverse to the continuance, oh, if you have faith and *wisdom* all minor considerations may be lost in an overwhelming desire for the salvation of souls . . .

"I am very pleased with your account of the Sunday School. Such a class as you mention would indeed be a blessed sphere of usefulness. If I were only fit for it—but oh, my Love, you very much over-

95

estimate my qualifications. Such an undertaking requires much ability and *more than all* deep piety, real heart union with Jesus, such as I once enjoyed, such as I hope to enjoy again. Pray much for me... I think I am writing strange jargon tonight. Somehow I don't feel in tune so I will give over, but I must first tell you that last night my dearest father brought me a nice little watch for a present. I am to consider it a birthday gift... Good night. Oh, I should love a kiss.

"*Thursday evening*. My dearest Love... I have been ill all day." Catherine then described how she rose before 7 a.m. lighted a fire and set to practising. However pain and fainting overcame her, though "I have not time to be ill"; she hoped to be well enough to keep her appointment with Mr. Franks next day and then drifted into a soliloquy about loving in such a fashion as that when death parts them there will be "no tears of remorse—those bitterest of all tears... Oh, my dearest, pray for me. My soul is melted tonight; death and eternity have occupied my thoughts more today than usually. I see the uncertainty of all things...

"All you have said about Mr. Shadford has given me a favourable impression... but though I advise you to make him your confidant and adviser, I would again caution you against making *unnecessary* communications to him or anyone else... you say perhaps you have been too sanguine as to the time of our union, etc. I think so and therefore it has not hurt me. Don't be afraid to tell me *every phase* of your position and prospects, bright as well as gloomy. You think it [their wedding] would be better in January than autumn—'if we could wait'. My Love, I think it *will* be *much better*—if *you* can wait but I will solemnly consider *your* advantage in this matter—not my own fancy... The music tires me... But I am determined to persevere and do what I can and you desire no more, do you dearest? *Will you promise me the same with reference* to your studies? of so much greater importance. *Do* and I shall feel so encouraged... You say, my dear, you are getting quite slovenly, etc. Now William I do hope you will watch against this. With a little care and prudence you may *always appear to the best advantage*... Send me word whether you got the tooth powder, I sent you a recipe, if you have lost it I will send you another. I hope you will use it regularly. I like it very much. I am glad you got *Newton's Dissertations* cheap. Write your name in it. How do you get on with *Bachus?* I want to hear that your views on that important question are matured and *settled* for ever." And she tells him what material to get for "fronts" and what he should pay and "it is time to retire. I have much to say but I must not sit up... Good night my Love. Yours alike in all circumstances in undying affection.

"*Friday afternoon*. I have just risen from my knees after meeting you at the Throne of Grace. The Lord has blessed me. I could almost imagine you were kneeling by my side. Oh, when shall we again mingle our voices and clasp each other's hand, as well as unite in spirit? . . . I was off to Mr. Franks this morning by a quarter past eight, went with father to the gate. It was the coldest walk I ever had in my life . . . I feel much encouraged about my back . . . Mr. Franks says it progresses quite satisfactorily. [William's sister is coming up to town.] It will be nice to have a sister, *if she can love me.* You have written one of your letters at two or three times. I like that method. Try if you can [to] keep a sheet on the go and write a few words whenever you have a spare moment or feel *particularly loving.* You can bid me good night sometimes on paper as well as in fancy . . . I think Love if you get to bed by ten, and you told me you did, that you might rise at six without hurting you, and think what precious portion of quiet time this would redeem each week." And one last scrap of news in this gallimaufry of a letter ". . . we have lost poor puss . . . I feel so grieved, she was a faithful loving old thing. She endeared herself to me so much more that dreary sorrowful morning you went away. I am sure if you had seen her you would have liked her for my sake . . ." From which word I gather William did not much favour cats.

Catherine was often teased at home about her enthusiastic temperament; the warmth of her feelings she knew were sometimes an embarrassment. See this to William ". . . Your letters do not meet the yearnings of my heart, perhaps they *ought* to do. I wish my heart were differently constituted, I might be happier; but it *will* be extravagant and enthusiastic in spite of all my schooling. If ever I get to heaven what *rapture* shall I know. What a mercy that this is but a vestibule for a future existence—that my soul *may* enjoy a glorious future and realize not only the perfection of all its power, but the satisfaction of its hitherto insatiable desires."[63] One senses in many letters that she expects William to decry her ardent flights or to be "offended" as he sometimes is! It is not until they have been betrothed a year and eight months that she writes, "I never *knew* that you loved me *because* of my capacity for deep feeling; on the contrary, I have often felt discouraged from writing all I felt by the idea that you would count it extravagant enthusiasm or wild sentimentalism."[64] And only a few months before marriage she wrote on the same lines, "Believe me, my precious, I *do* strive against it. I *do* battle very hard, thou dost not know *how* hard, to conquer this apprehensive, sensitive, impetuous spirit . . . I *will* strive to be calmer . . . but I have so often failed and almost despair."[65]

This capacity for intense feeling helped Catherine perhaps more than any other of her natural qualities to take the place for which God was preparing her. It added to the power of her eloquence and made her able to inspire others to take action. Even in homely plans for husband and children her eagerness carried them with her. Her enthusiasm could make trivial things delightfully exciting and

97

in serious matters took her quite out of herself. Certainly her influence over William was strengthened by her "zeals". He might join her mother and father in laughing at her, but as a rule he let her persuade him! As an example of "trivial" enthusiasms it is amusing to trace the cold water question through successive stages. Catherine to William, "I do wish I could persuade you to sponge with cold water now the weather is warm. If you would do it one week, you would need no persuasion to continue it. The positive comfort (to say nothing of the *good* resulting) would abundantly repay the trouble. *I should be so pleased* to hear you were doing it, if it were only every other morning. Do, there's a dear."[66] When William was preaching as a travelling evangelist he wrote in a letter beginning "My dearest and most precious Sweet . . . have commenced washing my chest well with cold water every morning and then rubbing well and I fancy I have benefited much."[67] A few weeks before their wedding William writes, "I continue cold water bathing every morning." And twenty years later he tells his Love in a letter from America ". . . I surprise all my hosts by my pertinacious cold water operations in the morning. They are all for hot water, and hot rooms, etc."[68]

One of Catherine's letters evidently did not entirely please her lover, and her response gives us an idea of William's attitude and her own. But they are learning to know each other and come nearer after the small rift . . . "I did not intend what I said about your letters in the shape of *fault-finding*. My Love, let *us* be able to speak to each other about anything which we think might be better, without accusing each other of finding fault. If ever I write anything which you disapprove, *tell me at once,* and don't let it throw a cold chill over all your letter, leaving me to conjecture, perhaps causes the furthest from the true one. If I leave anything unsaid, which you think I should have said, tell me, and let me do the same, without feeling hurt. Let us be *one*. Let us love each other as ourselves. You ask me to love you with a love which will bear with *some* of your failings till we meet again. My love is equal to *all* your failings, and is no less likely to be *enduring* because it sees *some, as well as excellencies.* Is your love equal to *my* failings? . . . My soul is often humbled and depressed under a sense of them.

"*Friday afternoon.* My dearest William, I received your Tuesday's letter and for the first time feel at a loss how to answer it. I have not been happy since I first read it. You keep me too much in the outer world of mere circumstances. I cannot, I will not, be satisfied unless you let your *heart* commune with me. The state of the weather, and the conditions of the roads are interesting to me, because you have to brave the one and traverse the other. The minutae of your perambulations are always interesting, but if you have not time to write this, and *also* to communicate *some* of your *soul's thoughts, feelings, desires, hopes* and *fears,* I would rather be left to conjecture (with the aid of the Plan) as to where you are, how far you walk, etc., than to be deprived of *heart* communion ... with *me* nothing but a thorough sympathy of feeling and a free and unrestrained interchange of thought will be satisfactory. Do not call this finding fault, my dear ...

"You remember what sorrow you used to express because our intercourse had been so marred and clouded by your unsettled state of mind and anxiety about the future, and what beautiful and *loving* letters you used to promise me when you got settled and comfortable, but now you say that you can write letters on any subject but talk better on *this*. If you mean that you prefer oral communication because of its superior pleasure and facility, *so do I*, but *on that account only*, not because I feel shy to commit to paper my heart's deepest feelings, or ever find it difficult to fill a sheet *to you*. Hitherto out of the abundance of my heart my pen has written, perhaps too freely ... Don't think I forget your circumstances, the fatigue and consequent depression you must feel after so much exertion ... I don't agree with you in thinking that you would never have made a student. I believe *you would*, under some circumstances, and whatever I have said has only been to induce you to brace up your mind to grapple with the difficulties of your position."[69] A few days later Catherine is writing, "Oh, it will indeed be sweet, as you say, 'when we can whisper every thought and feeling into each other's ears and hearts', but, my dear, while this is impossible let us make up for it as far as we can by this only available mode of communication—writing ... My idea of the relationship we are to sustain to each other (nay, which we *do now* in heart and soul and interest sustain) was always that of a *perfect union* ... Let us be as careful about grieving each other as we are about hurting ourselves. I see more than ever that 'love is the fulfilling of the law' ... but I am forgetting to whom I write. ... *Monday*. My dearest Love ... I will try to make more allowance for your circumstances, when I read your letters in future, but, my dear, never again subscribe yourself my 'friend' *merely*. That day has gone by for ever, you are more to me than any friend can ever be, and so am I to you ..."[70]

The next letter I have chosen is noteworthy because for the first time Catherine sends William notes for a sermon she had herself composed. Mark her diffidence and also note that it was William who persuaded her to make the effort. Later on he will count on her for help of this kind and write in peremptory fashion: "I want a sermon on the flood, one on Jonah, and one on the Judgment. Send me some bare thoughts, some clear startling outlines."[71] Here are Catherine's remarks about that first essay of hers "... spent the remainder of the evening in writing a few thoughts on a text on which I opened, but I don't know whether I shall ever send them. I fear they would be no use to you; however, as you so wish me to send you some of my own, I will try to mature them a bit and send them *if* you will promise me never to tell anyone they are mine, *if you should think them worth anything.* And if you should not, honestly, do tell me so, for I have prayed earnestly for the Lord to give me some thoughts on some passages of His word, and solemnly promised that if He would do so no being but yourself should know with whom they originated, so that the glory (if they should be instrumental in doing good) may be His and not mine. I tell you this *only* to prevent you telling anyone *in case* you should be pleased with anything I may ever send you, which is so doubtful that I might almost safely have withheld the request. Yet perhaps I am not the best judge ... Let me tell you that to commit them to your knowledge and keeping is the strongest proof I can give you of my confidence. You are the first to whom I ever did so. Good night, my dearest Love, oh, I wish I could see you. You *must* come in May, if there are special trains. It will then be five months since we parted. Quite *long enough* to be without seeing each other, and you *promised* to come in six months the night before you went, so it will only be one month sooner."[72]

Five months without sight or sound of one another! What a difference a telephone would have made and how much nearer to Brixton Spalding would have been had one of William's friends there had a car. As it was the lovers must put up with the dessicated form of communication provided by letters and what one put in letters was sometimes misinterpreted! It is small wonder, particularly if we have in mind what Catherine called William's "whirlabout life", that there should be an occasional misunderstanding, even a hurt, in the course of their exchange of thought on paper. Face to face it would have been different, or at least so Catherine thought. To the onlooker it is evident that this absence from each other was necessary in order to give free play for uttering thought and counter-thought between them. Catherine herself came to feel this as she told William, "This long correspondence should have developed our character to each other, for my part I am sure I have written the very workings of my soul and I am sure you know me far better than you could have done by personal intercourse of twice or thrice the length of time ..."[73] Even in their separation, love was always uppermost to soften, in Catherine's case to restrain, too vehement expression, but had William been within sight and touch when she began pouring out her thoughts, for example on revivals, she would have perceived that he was not able to bear it; and then William might never have known what she felt on this and other questions. For them both, and for their work in the world, it was of utmost importance that they should agree on certain subjects. Agreement between two minds when thoughts have been freely and fully expressed is very different to superficial agreement which is liable to disruption because the depths have never been sounded. This man and woman were to walk through life agreed on all major matters. That unity was an immense advantage when it came to founding The Salvation Army, and in training up their children and converts. This tedious business of writing helped to plant and establish opinions in each of them, that would go on growing in strength and harmony. Also, it served to cool the heated retorts that might very well have shut off further exchange of opinion between them. To William, inaccessible, Catherine could write "...faithful as well as loving I must ever be", but to William, present in the flesh, a sense of his displeasure at what she was saying would have aroused an overwhelming impulse to console and caress the beloved which would have effectively stifled further words in argument, at any rate for the moment. But letters being perforce the *only* way of bridging their separation the lovers unknowingly provide us with a permanent account of the development of convictions vital to their own spiritual experience and for the great movement they brought into being.

Take this letter of Catherine's, for instance; she was a few weeks past her twenty-fourth birthday when she wrote it: "*My own dear William,* It is nearly ten o'clock, but I feel reluctant to retire to rest without holding a little converse with you. Would that I could do it in living, breathing words, but as that is impossible I must be satisfied with this poor substitute...I do hope you are well and have had a happy, useful day. I pictured you to myself this morning, and thought how I should love to hear you preach...I have pressed some warm and loving kisses on the cold outline of your dear features tonight. Oh, I trust *our* love will be *enduring* as life, deep as its lowest vale of adversity, high as its most towering mountains of pleasure, and broad as all its duties and awful responsibilities. Pray about the future, hope much, *intend* much...Your very kind and cheering letter came duly to hand yesterday morning, and though both *it* and Saturday's gave me great pleasure, I cannot divest myself of anxiety on your behalf...and I feel as if it would relieve me to tell you all my heart. Oh, my Love, I have felt acutely about you, I mean *your soul.* I rejoice *exceedingly* to hear how the Lord is blessing your labours, but as I stand at a distance and contemplate the scene of action and all the circumstances attending it, I tremble with apprehension for the object most beloved and nearest...my heart. I know how possible it is to preach and pray and sing and even *shout* while the heart is not right with God. I know how popularity and prosperity have a tendency to elate and exalt self, if the heart is not humbled before God. Try to get into that happy frame of mind to be satisfied if Christ be exalted, even if it be only by compelling you to lie at the foot of the Cross and look upon Him. If your happiness of soul comes to *depend* on the excitement of active service, what if God should lay His hand upon you and give you the cup of suffering instead of labour? Nothing but a heart in unison with His, and a will perfectly submitted, can then give peace. Watch against *mere animal excitement*

101

in your revival services. I don't use the term in the sense in which anti-revivalists would use it, but only in the sense in which Finney himself would use it. Remember Caughey's silent, soft, heavenly carriage; *he* did not shout. There was no necessity. He had a more potent weapon at his command than noise. I never did like noise and confusion—*only so far* as I believed it to be the *natural* expression of deep anxiety wrought by the Holy Ghost, such as the cries of the jailer, etc. Of *such* noise, produced by such agency, the more the better . . . I should not have troubled you with my views on the subject (indeed I think you know them pretty fully. If not, you will find them exactly in *Finney's Lectures on Revivals*, which I consider the most beautiful and common-sense work on the subject I ever read) only that you have been wondering how I shall enter into it *with you.*

"My dear, I trust as far as I have ability and grace I shall be ready to strengthen your hands in the glorious work by taking under my care, to enlighten and guard and feed, the lambs brought in under your ministry. I believe in instantaneous conversion as firmly as you do, at the same time I believe that half of what is called conversion is nothing of the kind and there is no calculating the evil results of deception in a matter so momentous. Great caution is necessary in dealing with enquirers, especially the young . . . I know you will rightly estimate what I have written. Don't think that I consider *your* danger greater than *my own* would be if placed in your circumstances. Alas, I of all beings should be most in danger of being vain-glorious and self-sufficient; and perhaps it is because I feel this that I am so anxious about you. However, tell me, my Love, in your next all about your *soul's secret experience.* Tell me whether you attend faithfully to private prayer and how you feel when *alone with God.* This is the surest test by which to judge of your state . . . I am so pleased to hear that you think yourself improving as a preacher. Of course you cannot but be conscious of the fact, and there is no harm in your expressing it to *me.* I only wish I could hear you . . ."[74]

William's answer to this letter distressed Catherine. She wrote, "Your letter came to hand about an hour since and I can attend to nothing till I have written you a line in reply. I never was more *surprised* in my life than on reading it to find the aspect my last seemed to wear in your eyes. I am sure, dearest, the state of your own *mind* makes all the difference to your interpretation of my letters. You should not read mine as you would a stranger's, you should bear in mind what I am, and what a sentiment *means* when dictated by love and a deep and absorbing desire that you should appear in the eyes of others as a man of God. I was *not*, when I wrote, 'dreadfully put about' and harassed in my mind, but the spirit of God had been operating powerfully upon my heart and I felt afresh awakened to the superiority and importance of spiritual things and of course as I felt it for myself I felt it for you, but I think I spoke tenderly and carefully? As to *scolding* I never felt less like it than when I wrote that letter, for my whole soul was melted into tenderness and self-abasement. Do *read it again*... You could not possibly construe what I said as *against* revivals... but I see you are dreadfully harassed and most deeply do I sympathize with you. Indeed for me to be happy while I think you are not so is impossible, though I was *not unhappy* last week. I rejoiced with you in your prosperity, but at the same time I knew even that was dangerous and expressed the anxiety I felt, thinking you would rightly understand me. But I perceive you cannot bear it.

"Well, dearest, scold me if you like, blame me, or whatever else you will, but *faithful* as well as loving I must ever be. My conscience compels me and the more I love you the more I feel it a duty. If I could take your place I *know* I should value you the more for *such* anxiety. I should feel sure that I had at least *one* in this outside world who would be as far as he could an impartial, faithful, constant, enduring friend under all circumstances. Such I *will* be, my Love, as far as God permits. As to my estimate of you, surely you don't feel a fear that it is too low? While I am willing to give my happiness to so great an extent into your keeping, then don't call it scolding or seem hurt when I give you a gentle caution... I can only say I never dreamed of such a thing. I hope for perfect unity and fellowship in *all places* and least of all should I think of separation in the church of God... Your last two letters *did* please me. I thought I said so... they gave me unmingled pleasure. My anxiety had nothing to do with *them,* but only about your soul... I wish I could see you. My heart is as full as it can well contain... *I don't scold you.* Do not feel one painful feeling about it. I wish I could comfort you... I will continually pray for you. I have had some thoughts about writing to Mr. Shadford about your preaching so much and I certainly shall if you continue to do it. Nine sermons in one week—monstrous! I am sure you will not be able to do it neither ought you. They told you they did not wish for more than *five.* How very wrong of you to go beyond your strength, etc. and wrong yourself of time to study when they do not wish it. Is this scolding? If it is I really cannot help it, so forgive me, and if you were here I would *make* you forgive me. *I know how* I could do it, so do you, don't you dearest?"[75]

A few days later on the same subject Catherine writes "... one thing you said pierced my soul. It was this, 'if you cannot bear the hearty responses and Alleluias of *God's people* our fellowship will not be in prayer meetings', as though you excluded me entirely from their number... I cannot bear it, it *breaks my heart*... I have tried to recall what I wrote in that letter, and I think it was one of the most affectionate and spiritual I have ever written you. However I am sure no feeling but pure love dictated one word . . . Would that I could see you. My heart is almost bursting, but you think me extravagant, too extravagant for this world. Perhaps I am, but my Heavenly Father knows all about my heart . . . I thought you would understand me. I felt you loved me deeply and that I might say anything to *you* without restraint or fear of being misunderstood. Oh, my dearest William, let us be one, do not allow a cloud to pass over your brow, and angry feelings to rise in your heart when you peruse my letters. If you do where is the *foundation* on which to build our future happiness? Do not let *anything* come between your soul and mine—neither God's people, Methodism, nor anything else. We are one in all things . . . I hope, dearest, my soul will always be in tune not merely to hear 'a shout inspired *by* God and accompanied by His power', but to join in it. I never did shout, but *I have felt* enough of His power to have made me do so, if I had been in suitable circumstances, and though my constitutional temperament is opposed to noise, I think a note of praise will yet resound even from my unworthy lips. *Pray* that it may be so. Do not fear that anything of this kind will ever come between thee and me, if I can help it; where I do not, or cannot, exactly see with you I will at least acquiesce and try to help you. But in this particular case my views are quite in union with your own." There are well over 3,000 words in this letter which concludes with wishes for William's birthday: "If the poetic fire were not quite extinguished in my soul, I would try to fan it a little in honour of the day, but I fear it would be useless. I shall see whether the day itself brings any inspiration. I did wish you would send me a few lines on mine. It would have been easy to *you* . . . My dear mother is so much obliged for your kind remembrance of her garden. The dahlias are already set according to the milkman's directions."[76]

Their future of united service in the church of Christ might well have been in jeopardy if Catherine and William had not come into real harmony of mind about revivals *before* they married. The theme recurs ". . . You seem to doubt of a thorough sympathy of views and feelings with reference to the salvation of souls, and your own personal experience. This convinces me that you do not yet fully understand me, and when you talk of our 'views clashing' on such a subject, it pains me in *my soul*. No! They will never *clash* while you breathe such a spirit as this letter manifests. Clash! When it is the *highest ambition* of my soul that you should be a man of God and live only to save souls . . . Understand, however, that against *real revivals* I have not one objection . . . I believe the passions *are* to be moved. *Fear* is a right passion to appeal to in order to *arouse* from slumber, but a person *frightened* into a profession of faith in Christ without the judgment being enlightened as to the *costs* of a life of Godliness, and the soul made to apprehend the moral grandeur of holiness, will soon lose all relish for spiritual things ... These, dearest, are the views and feelings which have prompted my remarks on this subject, *fear* of what is *unreal* or superficial in so dreadfully important a work, rather than a depreciation of the real outpouring of the spirit. God knows how I long for it in my own soul and how rejoiced I should be to see it on the universal church, for I love all who love the Lord, I abhor sectarianism more and more."[77]

We may, I think, conclude that the following to William was written the next day, although again the page is not dated: "You doubtless received mine (posted yesterday) this morning. I hoped it would not cause you pain, yours today has done me good. I do sincerely praise the Lord for His goodness to you. I rejoice in the progress of the work and quite long to be with you. Don't imagine that 'confusion' would frighten me if it was the *consequence* of the shaking of dry bones. I hope never to resist God's own work, let Him adopt what means He may to accomplish it; indeed, the enthusiasm of my nature would sooner lead me to mistake feeling for grace than to oppose feeling the *effect* of grace. Perhaps it is this knowledge of *my own* danger which makes me apprehensive of it in others. However, I am sure we shall be *one* on this subject as well as others. *Don't forget* that in my anxiety to keep you from the *extremes* I have seen in some, I am apt to show you the most *cool* and abstract view of my heart and mind ... I am not without evidences that God *has* blessed others through even my instrumentality. Oh yes, I hope to be a 'nursing-mother in Israel', and after all my varied experiences perhaps I shall be better fitted for it than I should have been with less schooling of the heart; for after all it is a knowledge of human nature and of divine truth and influence which is most valuable in the Church."[78]

Both delighted in the beauty of nature. William writes: "I have been thinking about you during the week every day and every hour. The beautiful scenes by which I am every day surrounded, the blooming orchards, green fields, so beautifully green, the growing corn, the singing birds, and the frisking lambs, all bring *you* to my mind most forcibly as being things which I know you would be delighted to gaze on." And this of Catherine's in reply "... if the Lord should cast our lot amidst the beautiful in nature, I should praise Him. Your description of the fields, trees, etc. makes me long to gaze upon them. I love nature ... I shall never forget the feeling of buoyancy and delight I experienced after getting out of the train at Dovedale ... I hope some day to ride by *your* side over hill and dale and enjoy with you their beauty."[79] When the sight of Dovedale so delighted Catherine she was seven years old. Although William was brought up in a city he was one of those who was capable of responding to earth's beauty. He and Catherine understood the language and all their lives loveliness of land and sea had power to delight and refresh them.

5

In May 1853 William came to London for a few days. In her last letter before his arrival Catherine writes a happy medley of love and instructions, "Oh, I love to hear you say that you pray and yearn for perfect union of *act* and *word*. *That is it, William,* only let us cling to that, and storms may come, the wind may blow, and the rain descend, but the superstructure of our happiness and peace, so far as earth is concerned, will not give way if founded on *such* a rock. Let us have no secrets henceforth and forever. I trust we shall always be able to yield to the amount of 20/- on *either* side if Providence blesses us. At least I hope there will be no necessity to hide anything for peace's sake, God forbid. If I had not confidence in my own heart, and capacity to love enduringly, I would sacrifice my life rather than marry, so deep is my conviction of the evil results of such unions. But I fear not for myself provided I am loved ... Yes, I think you will be a tender, noble, generous, sympathizing, constant companion in this wide, wide world. I hope to be pretty well by the time you come, and able to go out, for though I do not care for company, I do long for the fresh air, and sweet, sweet country, and most heartily concur in your proposal to go a trip or two. I do not mind where it is, if we can only get away from smoke and people and bricks and mortar, for I am heartily sick of looking at them. We must study economy and go where it costs least ... I am sure I shall receive you with a heart full of affection and a soul full of feeling, but I think I shall not come to the door to let you in, though I shall not be far off." And we may be sure William made short work of whoever *did* open the door that day.

During his visit there was much talk of William's future. Friendly Mr. Rabbits entered into it. He had offered the young people an allowance of ten pounds a year to supplement their salary. There was talk, too, of the probable amalgamation of the Reformers with the Methodist New Connexion. Catherine and William approved this idea; and there were discussions with Mr. Rabbits and others including Dr. Cooke, a prominent minister in London, who evidently made a proposal that was declined at the time. Having to face four years on probation before marriage would be agreed was one objection. If the Reformers joined, the period of William's ministry with them would count. "If not we must wait and then decide on a course of action. I tell you *honestly* that I do not intend anything of the kind as doing four years probationist . . . remember, although I have declined this invitation of Mr. Cooke's, I have not shut the door. *Four years! Only think! . . ."*[80] Thus William soon after his return to Spalding.

Catherine sets herself to read the history of the New Connexion and feels, as she tells William, "I ought to have read it all before . . . I should have had a clearer view of the constitution . . . I feel deeply the importance of the thing, indeed I never before felt so deep an appreciation of the awful responsibilities of the minister as I do now. I see it is *men of God* the world wants and for lack of *these* and not of learning and machinery, thousands are sinking into hell." Before the close of her letter she comes back to the New Connexion again enquiring, "Where could I get a copy of the Rules? Would Mr. Rabbits have them? I want to read them very much. Do you know whether a young preacher has to travel any stated time before he can marry? If so, how long? If it is so, never mind, do not let that hinder you. We will in the interval work hard, and thus the better fit ourselves for the important position before us . . ."[81] Another May letter begins, *"My own dear Love,* Your precious, kind, cheering letter came before I was downstairs, so I lay down again in bed and read it, the first part roused all the tenderest feelings of my nature, and filled my soul with gushing gratitude to God, and tenderest affection for you. *Oh, my heart does thank you . . ."* She then refers to a spiritual conflict of which William had written, "Let me *know* of every such struggle and let me join you in praising God for every such glorious victory. For it is a victory of which angels take note; a far more important thing in the history of God's *moral* universe, than all the temporal victories of earthly things . . . You pain me by saying that perhaps I have more to do with your resolves and struggles than Christ; and perhaps it is so, but dearest . . . oh, think not more of me than you ought to think. I do want to be *next* to Christ in your affections . . . I do want to help you to serve and love Him, but I do *not* want to rob Him of His glory. Try, darling, to get Christ formed *in* you, and then I may be safely one with you."[82]

Whether or not to join the New Connexion is now a matter of grave import to them both . . . "It is an important question with me how far Connexionalism is really adapted to promote the *ultimate* prosperity of the Church . . . Christianity is self-propagating and aggressive and in my opinion will never fully triumph till disentangled from the gigantic systems of worldly policy which men have identified it with. The Kingdom of Christ is not of this world and how strikingly was this truth exemplified by the primitive churches. How gloriously successful were they in the propagation of the truth without any of the ponderous machinery of modern times . . . the amalgamation of the splits of Methodism must be desirable, but it wants deep consideration. Be cautious, my Love, that no personal benefits

107

weigh an atom with you. *First be fully persuaded in your own mind* that such a step would be for the good of man and the glory of God ... *then* consider whether you had better seek for *yourself alone* (leaving the Movement out of the question) admission among them. *Think* over their rules, and learn as much as possible about the way they are carried out, and lay the matter continually and earnestly before God, for it is an important matter to submit yourself to a *Conference* of any kind ... I only want to see you happy and useful and I care not where or how, provided it be according to God's will . . . Those thoughtfully expressed words about preferring to go back to business to staying with the Reformers, have made me feel anxious, not because I wish you to remain in your present position, *nor* because it may defer our union, *no*, only because I fear you should get wrong ... Do not take any *steps in order to marry* which you would not take if you did not know me. I love your description of the beauties of nature, and still more the expression of your desire for my company in their enjoyment. I should indeed like to gaze on the green fields and hedges, but most of all on the ocean, that enchanter of all my soul."[83]

Catherine's constant references to William's health should be linked with the times in which they lived. Cholera, for instance, persisted through all the period of the love-letters. Each is anxious for the other; and thought of losing the beloved by death is an ever-present dread. William's and her own chest troubles were thought important because so many died of "consumption". It was rampant all about them. Catherine had the perfectly sound notion that care of the general health helped the body's resistance to fatigue and infections. In an early letter she wrote, "My Love, *do* take care of your body! I beseech you don't act injudiciously. Remember you do God no acceptable service by killing yourself, you must try to live." And in another, "I was sorry to hear of your sore throat and headache and yet perceive you preached *three* times on Sunday; this really troubles me. I am satisfied you cannot do it without injuring yourself and especially when the weather gets warmer; no man ever did it with impunity, except blessed with the strength of a horse ... the evangelist is subject to all the natural laws of God and liable to the same suffering as other men if he transgresses them."[84]

Shortly after she and William had been engaged a year, Catherine wrote a letter more taken up with her own feelings than most and showing how necessary she thought it that she should be able to convince William that she was not perfect. "... Do not, my Love, call me meek, etc. I am not so. My will is impetuous and my temper irritable; with bitter tears I write it. These are my most trying besetments ... May the Lord smooth down all the inequalities of our nature and make us willing to yield love's sweet submission to each other. I will try to be patient . . . I fear this more than anything

108

else in myself. My temperament is ardent and my nervous system so weakened by past afflictions . . . I fear I shall be irritable and impatient; if I should be so, do you think you could bear it patiently? Do answer me this *once,* my dearest Love . . . Oh I wish I could see you and pour my soul into your bosom. My heart is too full to be *restrained* tonight . . . I will trust for strength according to my day and you will help me won't you dearest? You will bear with me and sustain me and defend me and *love* me even to the end of life. I will try to reward you for your kindness and count it my *highest* earthly joy to make you happy . . . *Tuesday afternoon.* Thank you *darling,* for the kind words contained in yours this morning. I had been thinking that I had written too passionately last night and that I ought to restrain the tide of feeling more than I do in writing to you, but no, now *you* write so affectionately I will let it roll on, and gush out, just as it will, without seeking to cool or restrain it, so that you may know of what I am made. Bless you. You have no reason to fear about true conjugal bliss if *your love* is only deep and fervent. I think I have a soul capable of enjoying and yielding as much as most; but remember, I have its almost invariable failings—capable of deepest feeling on one subject as well as another; therefore liable to anger as well as love . . . I will not fail to attend to your wishes respecting my health. Everything which Mr. Franks' wisdom, or my own prudence, suggests shall be faithfully attended to. I have had the shield altered again, which has made it worse to endure, and this warm weather it is almost more than I can bear. It is enough to have oneself to carry about in hot weather without a great heavy piece of wood on one's back! . . . My only recreation is walking in a field lately open, leading to the church, and *reading over* your letters . . . Write me all your heart, warm, loving and tender, as you feel, and forgive this disgraceful scrawl. I have written at express speed. My dear Mother's *kindest* love. You say you left my letter at *Spalding.* I hope it was locked up? Do take care no one sees them . . . Your own loving, loving Kate."[85]

We may, I think, conclude that a paragraph in an undated letter of William's was in response to this of Catherine's, "I do hope that you understood me to say in my last, bless you, that should I find in you any irritability more than I have discovered as yet, that I will bear with it and love you none the less; bless you; do not say any more on such a subject. I am more than ever satisfied with you—mentally, morally, and spiritually. Oh, it is *I* that am irritable, and will want bearing with, but, bless you, I will be all, all, all, you wish. Bless you I love you dearly."[86] This next letter of Catherine's is not dated to the day, merely June '53. It seems it might well have followed William's. ". . . You *will* bear with my weaknesses and faults, hush my fears, strengthen my hopes and efforts, and try to enter into the indefinable emotions of my sensitive heart. I shall at least have one being in the world able to sympathize with my *soul's* feelings and to *understand* the peculiarities of my mind and heart. Oh, how sweet! ...I think a great deal about your being out so much, and I do hope your present unsettled and whirlabout life will not beget a distaste for pure domestic *home* bliss, and oh I do trust that before we have a home Providence will make it possible for you to be more in it. Bless you, I feel indescribable things tonight, my soul is so full I cannot write at all collectedly. Oh, if I could but pour it into your ear; it does seem *hard just now* to be parted. I feel as though I could fly to you, my whole soul is drawn towards you, if I could explain *what* I feel, and *how* I feel, and *why* I feel, and *all* I feel, I am sure you would sympathize with me and clasp me more tenderly to your heart than ever you did before. I say this because I know that although perhaps I feel too deeply and too keenly, yet the class of feelings and their causes and objects *are* pleasing to God; they are not selfish but purest benevolence... *Pray for me.* I will not write thus, perhaps it grieves you, though I hope not. Do not call it sentimentalism dearest, it is the only reality of life... soul and spiritual things are the only realities we have to do with, and all relating to them are to us of paramount importance. Let us estimate everything according to its influence on each other's *mind* and *heart*... May the Lord give us grace to *study each other*, and love as He has enjoined. I often wonder whether others feel on these subjects as I do; if they did; surely there would be more happy unions? I scarce ever realize the happiness, for thinking of the duties and responsibilities of married life; I am so anxious to be a *good* wife and mother, and cannot think of the joy of being either. Never mind, dearest, my heart will not be the less sensible of the joy *when it comes*, and perhaps better prepared for it. Oh, for the grace to do my duty *to you* in all respects, and to those whom God may give us, and to the Church, and to the world, and to myself, and thus doing it in all the relations of life, to serve my God in serving His chosen ones, the service He Himself has required..."[87]

Catherine wrote a few days later, "...Respecting amalgamation I see no prospect at all in the movement as *such* and it would be a fearful thing for us to marry and cast ourselves and *our all* on it and in a few years to find ourselves without a means of support and I am sure the salary they will give will not enable us to save much, if anything, wherewith to meet an emergency. It would break my heart to have to look round on a young family... without the means to *educate* them and bring them up in comfort and happiness. And then to see your dear spirit oppressed and wounded by the same considerations, would increase my distress. And again, to behold mine would but increase yours. Then, it behoves *us*, my Love, to consider and be *wise*. I am glad you see the *importance of it*... You have often told me how you dreaded poverty."[88]

She then proposes a plan which would enable them to marry earlier. Health allowing, she will take a post as governess, being confident that she has mastered the music enough to enable her to "teach the rudiments . . . I have many qualifications for the schoolroom more important than mere learning which I doubt not would be appreciated. I speak thus to *you only*, it is not with the slightest feeling of vanity, but only as I should speak of any other fact, and I say it to *encourage* you. Then if I get about £20 per year I can save £10 of it, and if your salary were but £40 or £50 you could perhaps save £20 in two years? This *together* would be *abundance* . . . and we should only want a little furniture for two rooms for that time . . . and my dear mother says that *if she can* but get a lodger she can save us £10 towards a little furniture. So that all well, we might be united in *two* years— not so *very long* dearest—not like six years, is it? I think I see you smile . . . what do you say? Indulge me with an answer by return if you can . . . We could live on very little the first two years. I should want no clothes, and you very few . . . Keep your spirit up. Our hearts are one already."[89]

Three days later Catherine writes telling William she has felt a restraint in speaking to him of her spiritual experiences: " . . . But I will put all this away. With you I will be one. I will open my soul . . . the Spirit of God seems to lead me to such a *peculiar* work . . . I am the subject of such strange feelings. Many a time when passing a person in the street whom I had never seen before, I have felt as if I must speak to them . . . I have felt as if my heart would burst with feeling, as though I could kneel down in the street and pray for them . . . What am I to do? Do you think this *has* been the Spirit of God? I have tried to believe it was temptation, fanaticism, anything but the voice of God, but always when my soul has prospered and revived this extraordinary experience has revived also, and whenever I have been careless and cold this has subsided . . . But why should I have such singular and difficult work assigned me, and one for which nature has so unfitted me? I have obeyed in one case lately in writing to that poor woman a long, plain, full, simple account of the plan of salvation, with abundant Scripture references. May God own it. There is another case pressing on my mind constantly, and I *must, I will* obey in this also. It is a poor degraded sinking drunkard living in Russell Gardens. What I feel every time I see him I cannot describe, but I am *decided*, I will go and invite him here, not letting him know what I want him for till he comes, and then I will just tell him what is in my heart to say to him . . . I feel convinced if I must prosper in my soul this is the only way for *me*, and I *must* walk in it. *Do* pray that I may be *strengthened* to do so . . . Tell me what you think. *Advise* me. These are the secret feelings of my soul. I often wish I could have an hour's talk with Finney. I think he would be able to advise me. He would understand me.

I want to serve God as He requires, but I fear to err in my judgment and my nature shrinks from singularity and publicity. *Pray for me.* Bless you. I hope you will help me and teach me, and guide me and be my head in the Lord. Do answer this part of my letter. I have sat up too late. Good night once more. Forgive scrawl.

"*Monday 4 o'clock*. Your letter came to hand this morning . . . [it] gave an account of a driving accident. I must say I feel vexed as well as grieved. You doubtless *hurt* your back with falling, and then to go and risk your life a second time without any necessity displayed, I think, a sad want of prudence and a sad *forgetfulness of me* . . . Pray never ride behind *that horse* again, if you love me. I conjure you . . . What you say about the New Connexion has sunk into my heart. I know not what to say. My *opinion* is still the *same*, but your happiness stands *first*. I wish I could make you happy . . . Why do you not like the idea of my going out? [as a governess]. You did not say so before. I thought you approved it . . . But I will not urge it. I leave it. I have told you the secret verdict of my *judgment, not feelings* [on joining the New Connexion], in this case it was *judgment altogether*. As I said before, your well-being I will consider but do, my Love, think and pray much about it. I hope you do not think me *too* anxious about *means*. Remember, *they* had not, have not, never will have, anything to do with my *affection* . . . You have already told Mr. Cooke that but *for four years' probation* you should *immediately* offer . . . I have thought about little else than your going *again* with that *horse*. It was a wild trick. Do not say a word in justification of it. I cannot bear to read it if you do. Never ride with it again, I do beseech you . . . Bless you, I love you. Remember that and act as if you believed it, and as if you *loved* me. You know what I mean. I spell it most lovingly—receive it so. I do hope you are better, I rather expected a line this morning, but hope for one tomorrow. I do not intend ever writing such a long letter again, so this is the last of its kind."[90] Catherine was wrong about that.

Less than a month later William had another accident. He was thrown from a trap. Catherine writes in excited sympathy and horror: ". . . I should like to nurse you and press your poor bruised face to mine. These accidents make me feel very anxious; surely, surely, they are not going to be frequent?" She urges him to see a doctor, if he has not already done so, and then in answer to a question in William's letter Catherine goes on to write one of those powerful, self-illuminating letters, which to me seem remarkable as an expression of her own experience and faith, and to be notable for the unconscious authority, the sense of authenticity, that her words convey. As one reads them it is not easy to keep the writer's circumstances in mind or the fact that she is but a young woman of twenty-four dashing off an unpremeditated scribble to her lover. "I have thought much about the temptation you mention in the scrap on Saturday;

about the reality of spiritual things. You said it was something *more* than temptation. *No.* It is *not.* Neither is it peculiar to *you*: it is common to all. I have had it presented, as almost every other which Satan has in his hellish treasury. But I think he has plied that with as little effect as any. I always find it best to apply at once to my *consciousness.* I know the religion of Jesus *is* a reality just as I know I live and breathe and think, because my consciousness testifies it. And that is a more powerful thing than Satan's intellect or logic. It disarms him at once. On other subjects reasoning has been my bane, but on this I *never reason.* I refer him to time and things gone by, and my conscience says *that* was real . . . I know it was real for it bore me up on the threshold of eternity and made death my friend. There is nothing like the light of eternity to show us what is real and what is not . . . Oh, my Love, watch! Satan is a subtle foe. He knows just the temptations most suited to hinder your usefulness, and he knows that just in proportion to your *own personal* faith *in*, and experience of, the glorious Gospel will be your success in preaching it to others. He knows (none better) that it is the preachers who can say I testify that which *I do know* . . . Oh, dearest, be you one of them. Be the champion of real Godliness, cost what it may; know in your own soul the mighty power of the grace of God, and then you will preach it with awful influence and abundant success. It *is real,* more *real* than all beside—the mightiest power in this wonderful universe. True, the mystery of Godliness is great, but it is given to the real followers of Jesus 'to *know* the mysteries of the Kingdom', as far as is needful for them. But Satan makes so much ado about the mysteries of Grace, as though mystery were peculiar to *it*, when all nature is enveloped in mystery and what can be more mysterious than *thought?* What is thought, memory, emotion? How does thought arise? How does memory store up and hide and years after pour forth its awful or pleasing treasures? Who can *explain* these common operations of the mind? And what in the Bible is more mysterious? And yet I am as conscious that I *think* and remember, as that I live and breathe. All is mystery around me, above me, below me, within me, before me, but yet I believe, act, plan, live, according to what I *can* understand, and must be content to await the solutions of these mysteries at some future enlargement and enlightenment of my faculties.

"*All* men do this. As to the *natural* world, they acknowledge their ignorance, but yet *believe* in it and act upon it, as though they perfectly understood every law and operation and tendency. Then if mystery is so common in this natural world, how absurd of Satan to urge *it* as an objection to the reality of a system which proposes for its object the perfecting of what is confessedly in *itself* the most mysterious of all mysteries, viz. the human soul! If the Gospel were less mysterious, it would lack one of the characters of the Divine signature. If it were less simple and comprehensible it would lack adaptation to its great object. Oh then, let us hug it to our bosoms, and exult in its glorious simplicity in dealing with us; and reverence and bow down before its profundity in all that relates to its infinite Author. Let us, my Love, *experience* what it holds forth and though Satan may gnash upon us with his teeth he cannot hurt us. Let us get a firm footing on *this* rock and we shall have a *real* foundation to stand upon when all that is unreal is passing away. But I forget to whom I write. You know all this better than I do ... Nevertheless what *I* say may help you by 'stirring up your mind'. May the Lord own it to this end, if it be not beneath His notice. I should not have said that—nothing is too insignificant for His attention and blessing if prompted by a pure motive. Bless His holy name. He loved to use weak instruments to baffle the designs of His *proud* foe and perhaps He may deign to use this. I had no idea of writing thus when I began. I have been quite led off and all I intended to say is left unsaid. Well, it is bed time ... so I must retire and conclude tomorrow. My heart is unusually full of love toward you. I would give a great deal to see you, to be clasped in your arms and pressed to your bosom. Well, the time is coming. Oh, to be prepared to enjoy each other *in God*. What a blessed privilege it is that we *may* do so. Do you ever think how kind it was of God to make such a relationship a *holy* one, so that His own children may realize more bliss in it than any other? He instituted it in *Paradise*. He Himself performed the ceremony of marriage ... Good night once more, may the God of Jacob defend and bless you. May Jesus be your constant companion, and the Holy Ghost dwell in you richly ... I want you to *glorify God*. I want to glorify Him myself. We must and *we will*. Oh, answer me. We will, and we will begin now. *We do*. He will spare us to live in each other's love ..."

They had discussed the possibility of marriage at the end of the year, should William not be accepted by the New Connexion. The letter continues, Catherine's practical mind enquiring: "There is only *one* reason why I should like to know your serious thoughts on the subject ... and that is, because of course I shall have a great deal to do, and many things to buy and some of them, as for instance a dress and bonnet, and such like summer things, which we could purchase much cheaper this summer than to order them in the winter when all summer goods are out of sight. Mother thinks of buying a dress shortly [i.e. material], when we see one we like. I *think* father will buy me a black satin one. I don't know. If he does I shall have a real *good one*. You understand me. This is all I want to know for, as in winter everything must be *asked for* [ordered] ... I read over the Marriage Service the other day and wept over it. Because others go and swear in the presence of God to do certain things and fulfil certain duties, without even reflecting on their nature and extent, that is no reason why *I should do so. No,* I should go to the altar with a full sense of what *I am doing* and an awful view of its consequences through all time, nay, far beyond! And I should like you to do the same. I feel as though I should like to see you again before I give myself fully to you, but yet I feel it will be best for *some things* for it to be otherwise, but *you* shall decide that point . . . Dear me, how the sheets will fill. I must have done or it will be too heavy again . . ."[91] A letter a few days later ends with, "Do excuse this horrid rambling stuff . . . just pop it in the fire."

In August William paid the Mumfords another visit, probably to help recovery after the accident. There was evidently more discussion with Dr. Cooke and Mr. Rabbits. The lovers come closer than ever before, but William had not yet decided whether to stay in Spalding. After his return Catherine wrote, "*My dear Love* . . . I now want to give you my thoughts and conclusions. Listen to me and then act as your judgment dictates. First, then, it appears to me a matter of *pure policy.* If it could be resolved into a question of conscience or doctrine, it would be beyond *these* reasonings, but as it is, I consider it open to them all. First, then, you 'love the policy of the Connexion *very much*' . . . you hold it to be exactly *Scriptural* . . . In it you would have freedom from pecuniary anxiety . . . Mr. Cooke said £60 was the least, and I should think *you* would get *more*, but if not, surely, with a good stock of clothes to begin with, we could live, and well too, on less than £1 a week? Mother says we could on much less, and Mr. R's £10 would pay the rent, if you accept it. But I am sure we could do, even *without* that . . . I have no fears about our being as happy as princes on that salary, with a future *increase* and position and status to look to, but if we venture on the [Reform] Movement, all is *uncertainty.* Even if you stopped at Spalding, and they give you £90, or even £100, there is no security how long it will be, and it would be far worse to endure cramped means in three or four *years time* with a young family, than at first without one, or at least, not more than *one.* I think these are serious reasonings, I feel the importance of the thing, and I fear not for *your* acceptance wherever you go . . ."[92] That letter is followed by, "*My precious William,* Your loving letter this morning has made a deep impression on my heart . . . I am sure I only want to do right . . . I do want to be able to bring up our darlings in sunshine and comfort and mental development. This is the summit of my ambition. I care for nothing of this world beyond this . . . Well I leave it with you to decide as you think wisest and best and I will be happy either way . . . As I have often told you I consider *you first,* even when a second self comes to share our love. *No* being can come between us. I feel it so already. Don't you? *Tell me* whether in these matters you feel as I do, but I know you do . . ."[93]

Note in the letter she sent a few days later how unreservedly she

115

took the blame, she who always, in one phrase or another, told William that his happiness was her first concern. Note, too, there was to be a new "lovely bonnet"! If only she had told us what colour! Lastly, note that William at this stage was decided, or thought that he was, to join the New Connexion. In that event he would not be allowed to marry for two years. "... I am very sorry, dearest, that my letters have exercised a melancholy influence over your mind. I have not intended them to do so ... I love you and to be separated from you is a great trial, but the reasons for this separation are to my mind so important ... I rejoice in your determination to give yourself up to study. *Nothing in this world* could make me so happy ... I appreciate and admire Mr. Rabbits' character and kindness, and *fully approve* of the course he recommends, with the exception of getting you appointed in London the year we are married. I think country life for a year or two would be of great service to me, but of course I should not let such a consideration prevent you taking a good circuit ... I deeply sympathize with you in your loneliness, but, my Love, remember you will only have to live a day at a time. You seem to be taking the whole burden of two years' waiting and trial on to yourself at *once*, whereas it will pass by a day at a time, just as the past has done, and you will probably *never* again feel worse lonely or more desirous of my society than you *have done* ... Miss S. has got such a lovely bonnet, just what you would admire. Her sister, who is a milliner, made it, and I am going to let her make me one *like it*. It suits me first-rate. I look quite another being in it. Oh, William, this is your doing. Dress is a great evil. What is to be done?"[94]

Catherine now caught a chill and her chest was affected; her letter written while convalescent described her state and raised a point of some importance. "*My dear Love*, I have been trying to practise and to crochet, but I can do neither. I feel dreadfully restless and nervous, so I am going to divert myself from melancholy thoughts which will, somehow or other, thrust themselves into my mind, by writing to you a bit ... The pains in my side are very bad. Your cheering letter did me good. It does me good every time I read it. I do not want you to be anxious. *I believe you do love me*, and I should like to live to make you happy ... Have you thought any more about dress? Shall I dress plain, dearest? Will it not be a snare to us both, and to our precious little ones (if we have any) and perhaps to some of God's people? *Your position* will cause my example in *that respect*, as well as in all others, to be felt, and perhaps imitated. I will wear things as good as you wish, because I think it is the truest economy, nay I am sure it is, and you shall always choose as to colour etc., but let me have my things *made plain*. What do you say?"[95]

William was not sure that he agreed. Four days later Catherine wrote more on the subject: "... I will please you in my bridal dress

116

whenever the time may be. It is allowable for a bride to deck herself with ornaments I believe, is it not? But I referred to my dress when I became your *wife*. Your position makes me anxious about it. It is not so much for my own sake, but you will try and look *right at it* and settle it once and for ever, won't you? We cannot be two things at one time. We must either be Christians or worldlings. Let us set an example *worthy* of imitation or else we should not occupy such a responsible position, but think about it. You know my views. I do not wish to go to extremes. I dislike would-be sanctity in anything. I do not wish to be *conspicuous* either way, that is all ... I am so pleased with your love for little children. I think you are beginning to have some of my feelings on some subjects. God only knows what I often feel on beholding a sweet babe exposed to unholy and injurious influences. Many a wayside petition has been breathed from my soul to God in behalf of such precious gems ... Oh, yes, I love little children *dearly* and I understand your feelings perfectly and I am rejoiced that they exist ... Pray for me and may God mould our souls into glorious oneness, and give us the same thoughts, feelings, hopes, desires, motives and aims ..."[96]

In spite of talk and argument on paper, William was still torn between the two prospects: whether to stay in Spalding and marry, or to join the New Connexion and serve the required period before marriage. Just as when she would not consent to their betrothal until he was satisfied in *his own mind* that it was *right,* so now Catherine will not let him, if she can help it, allow any present advantage to influence him. See how she narrowed the field in this October letter, 'My dearest Love, Your two letters came to hand about an hour since ... Of course, dearest, *I* am subject to reasonings and controversy as well as yourself. I see how *nice* it would be to come to you at Christmas, and make a home with you, be received by a loving people, and enjoy all the pleasures of such a sphere of labour. *I feel* all this, no one would be more susceptible of such pleasure than I should but *my judgment* is, I cannot help it, in favour of the New Connexion. I do think the *future,* say ten to fifteen years hence,* when our children need educating so as to play an important part in this bad world, should influence our present course of action. Yes, I think it righteous and wise to make provision (not for luxury and display) but for the important purposes and end of life. Now, my Love, if I say anything, it must be the real feeling of my soul in the matter, and I *think* it would be your best and wisest plan to join, but if the *secret feeling of your soul* is the contrary, *act accordingly* and I will not say a word about it ... But I must notice one or two points which I think you look at in a false light. First, as to

* Twelve years after this date when there were six children William and Catherine choose a path without visible means of support.

leaving the people. If you were leaving them without any possible or even *probable* supply of their wants, of anyone to fill your place, then I should think it as serious as you seem to regard it, but is it any more than leaving one circuit to go to another? ... The next thing you seem perplexed about is the apparent solicitude about worldly things involved in the step, but the question is *why* do you consider them? ... If we were sure of having no family I would not care a bit, but oh, I do feel the importance of training children in all respects well and to this end there must be means ... But enough, I know you will do what *appears to you* to be right, and I desire only that. Bless you, my heart is so full of tenderness and emotion as it can well contain, and I long to see you."[97] Again on the same theme Catherine says, "I do not know what to say ... I had no idea of its being a matter of *controversy* between *us*. As to *what people will say!* I never take it into account. *Motive* is everything. Perhaps we are too anxious about the future. We must try to act as far as *we can see* and leave the future with the Lord ..."[98]

6

At last William acted. He wrote to Dr. Cooke offering himself as a candidate for the ministry in the New Connexion. No sooner done than he was again plunged into uncertainty. He wrote of "very bad cases of cholera down here near Holbeach", and went on to make a suggestion which later became fact: "If I do leave at Christmas I should very much like to have six months to myself and go into the house with some minister. I am gaining a little more love for study and feeling daily my own deficiency. But I know not what to do. If I thought the New Connexion was prosperous it would alter the matter ... I am one hour all but decided to go and then I think again I am decided the opposite."[99]

William's hesitancies derived in part, I think, from his past. We should not forget that he had offered himself for the ministry twice before, and it was only natural that the thought of going cap in hand, as it were, again, was the more distasteful now that he had proved himself to be a notable and acceptable preacher in the Reform Movement. It was no small thing to break away from all the warmth of popularity and success in winning souls, to face the prospect of two years or more of probation before full acceptance as a minister in the New Connexion. His congregations begged Booth to stay, and offered him every inducement. He liked the people, "my sort" he called them; and the lure of a home, to one who had hardly tasted home life since he was twelve, was overwhelming. There is a wealth of longing in these lines to Catherine: *"Home,* the word sounds sweetly to me now. I think I shall rightly prize one when I get it; at home with you; to have a home! And it is your presence only that makes it a home to me. Well, then, to some extent you reciprocate these feelings. You cannot entertain them to the same extent that I do. You have a sweet home now, and its quietude and solitude you enjoy and speak lovingly of. I have no home. Mine is a lodging, a study, that is all. I come into it tired and weary and, except there be some letters or news about my yet having a home, it seems a dreary and melancholy place...."[100] This letter's only date is 1853. One of Catherine's in the same year may very well have been her response to William: "It *makes me happy* to hear you speak as you do about home. Yes, if you will seek home, *love home,* be happy at home, I will spend my energies in trying to make it a more than ordinary one. It shall if my ability can do it, be a spot, bright, pure, and calm, refined and tender, a fit school in which to train immortal spirits for a holy and glorious heaven, a fit resting place for a spirit pressed and anxious about public duties, but oh, I know how easy it is to talk. I feel how liable I am to fall short but it is well to *purpose right* and to aim *high,* to hope much. Yes we will make home to *each other* the brightest spot on earth. We will be tender, thoughtful, loving and forbearing, will we not? Yes we will."[101]

William had to contend with an underlying lack of confidence in the quality of his preaching. He wrote, "The great doubt I have, which has staggered me for some time with regard to joining the New Connexion, is my being so superficial, but I must work harder."[102] There was no such lack in Catherine. Her prayers and her faith, her unshakeable confidence in him, compelled him to look beyond the *now* of life to its future; the far future she saw so clearly when she wrote, "Spalding will not be your final destination." Begbie wrote of the "immense influence" Catherine exerted on William; "so great and high indeed is this influence, that one may even doubt if his name had ever risen above the level of ordinary preachers but for the constant pressure, and the never-lifted consecration of Catherine Mumford's beautiful spirit."[103] Encouraging William she wrote "... As to your fears about coming often before the same people, if you do you will have a larger portion of time to *prepare for it;* you can *study more,* and surely you do not want to be a three-year stockman? ... in your *own circuit* you can be as energetic as you like and with all the peculiarities of Methodism at your command and sustaining a proper and influential position, you *can* infuse life and enthusiasm into the societies and excite them to as much zeal and effort as you please.

"Wednesday evening. My dearest William, I received your letter this morning just in time to take it with me to read in the omnibus on my way to Mr. Franks. It did my *heart good... I wish you could* spend the next six months as you intimate, in close study. Could you

119

not manage it? If so, it would be an inestimable blessing. The very fact of your being removed from so many distracting duties . . . with the feeling 'Well, I have nothing to do but study in order to fit myself for higher, holier and more effective efforts *for the salvation of souls'* . . . This feeling would, I should think, be sweet and encouraging and help you to *apply* yourself wholly to study. I wonder whether you seriously thought of such a plan when you mentioned it? There is a great difference between you and I in this respect. If I see a thing to be right and wise I never hesitate, but proceed at once, and I seldom repent. You speculate and dream . . ." She then wrote of the advantage that time for study would be to them both. "Music I *intend to learn*. I am practising four hours daily regularly . . . if you study any language besides your own, let it be *Latin*—I should think of *twice* the use to *you* which French would be . . ."[104]

Still encouraging William Catherine wrote: "I do hope *you will not allow your sense* of inability for the work to *influence you*. I am sure you need not fear . . ." This letter runs on to over three thousand words, and tells the reader a good deal about Catherine herself, "How I long to talk to you when my heart is all on fire . . . The first words of your Monday's letter sent the joy and gratitude bounding through my soul. Yes, the thought that you love me with a purer heart, that you love me so well now you love the Lord better, makes me rejoice, and I feel now that I may love you as much as I like and let my sympathies flow towards you without restraint. Don't fear now to let me see the best and brightest side of your heart and feelings. Let me know you as you know yourself. Tell me how you feel and what you think about our future, and what you hope, how much you purpose. Tell me all. It makes me happy and it does you good. Oh, Mr. Gough did make a large soul, and deep sympathies and broad views appear glorious things, and *so they are*. I feel thankful for them. I would not change them away for all the learning, polish and accomplishment in the world. I have often repined and murmured at the permissions of Providence with reference to my education and *bitterly wept* for the loss of advantages, but I thank God for what no education could have given me, and for what thousands who have possessed all its advantages *have not*. Oh, I *love* to feel my soul swell with unutterable feeling for all mankind, as it did on Monday night. I love to feel a deep, thrilling and intense interest in what concerns the good of my species. I love to weep tears of untold sympathy in secret before God for the sufferings and woes of all mankind and I love to pray for all great and good and glorious movements for the salvation of men . . . If, my dear, you are altogether given up to God, you cannot but be a soul-saving minister; holiness with a moderate degree of talent will produce far greater results than great talents without holiness, and I think you were never better fit for the work than now you feel your unfitness..."[105]

Winter was approaching when William read: "I was going to tell you last time but my letter was so long, to mind and take care in coming out of the hot meetings with these cold rimy frosts. If you have no flannel *drawers*, be *sure* and get a couple of pairs directly. Buy Welsh flannel at about 1/6 per yard; four yards and a half will make two pairs. *Now get it* and let that person make them who offered to make you shirts."[106] A little later Catherine wrote of an attack which sounds like influenza, "I never had it before in my *life*. Mr. U. [doctor] says it is in the air ... it is proving very fatal in London just now, as well as cholera and typhus."[107]

William was waiting for acceptance by the New Connexion and in the press of a revival of soul-saving in his circuit, when he received a letter as long as any. Extracts must suffice, *"My own dear William,* I experienced great pleasure in the perusal of your Saturday's letter, especially as you referred to my remark about my thoughts respecting our future oneness of sympathy and feeling. You cannot appreciate the pleasure it gives me after writing a sheet or two out of the fulness of my heart, to receive a response to the particular subject on which I write ... I was rejoiced to hear of the continued prosperity of the work, tho' sorry you were so worn out. I fear the effect of all this excitement and exertion upon your health, and though I would not hinder your usefulness, I would caution you against an injudicious prodigality of your strength. Remember, a long life of consistent holy labour will produce twice as much fruit as one shortened and destroyed by spasmodic and extravagant exertion. *Be careful,* and sparing of your strength *when* and *where* exertion is *unnecessary.* Now don't forget this. I am very glad you have decided not to do the walking from one preaching engagement to another ... I was truly sorry to hear of the ground which Satan has chosen from which to attack you. I appreciate your confidence in opening your heart to *me,* as I know you would not to another in the world ... You ask if such feelings as you refer to are not evidences of a bad heart. I answer, they are evidence of a partially unsanctified one, and, my Love, just in proportion to your satisfaction in the *simple fact* of God being glorified and souls being saved by *any instrumentality whatsoever, just so far* is your eye single ... Try yourself, dearest, by this standard rather than by your feelings in the excitement of a prayer meeting where *you* are the principal agent. I speak with all tenderness, and as the beloved of my soul I tell you that I see ambition to be your chief mental besetment; *not a besetment* if rightly directed and sanctified; but which, unsanctified ... will make your life a martyrdom ... but ambition simply to glorify God ... will take pleasure in infirmities (even such as want of talent) that the power of Christ may rest upon it, being willing to be thought a fool ...

121

This, dearest, is in my opinion full consecration to God; this is being *like Christ;* and religion in all its stages, I see more than ever to be assimilation to *Him* ... It is a soul spending itself simply for this one end, which God will honour, and which *He always has* honoured since He first spoke to man ... Talk of a stiff, formal people, a cold do-nothing people, a worldly-proud people, where there is a devoted, faithful, holy minister? I don't believe it. There never was such an anomaly lasted long. On the other hand, call up a faithful, devoted, holy man, who seeks only God's glory, and be he talented or not, there you find a prosperous, active, *living* Church. I feel that if God should ask me what shall I do for thee? I would answer without a moment's delay, give me grace to cry in all life's conflicts and changes and temptations, and in death's final struggle, as my Saviour did, 'Father, glorify *Thyself*' ... Oh, I shall never forget one season in my life when the divine glory eclipsed my spiritual vision and seemed to enrapture my soul with its lustre. Oh, how truly dignified did any employment appear, which could glorify God ... I felt it the highest privilege of my being to be *able* to do it, I wish I could make you feel just as I then felt, but Jesus can and He *will* if you ask Him. It was in secret communion with Him I realized the glorious vision, and if you wait for it, and cry as Moses did 'Show me Thy glory', He will come and then, oh, the comfort and the light which such a vision leaves ... I believe hell itself could not obliterate the view then given me ... let us give ourselves to the promotion of God's glory and let us ever remember that God is glorified in the full consecration of *what we have,* be it *small* or *great* ... I have often erred here. I will try to remember in future that *all I have* is all He wants. You remember it too, dearest ... hope that what I have said will be a blessing to you. If so, tell me."[108]

That a letter so imbued with the aspiration of pure religion and with tenderest solicitude for him should vex William is surprising. He fastens resentfully on a few exaggerating words. Perhaps he only read up to "spasmodic and extravagant exertion" before snatching up his pen to upbraid his Love. Note there was no sting in her retort. What she said really meant "You darling idiot, don't you know me yet?" If we had William's letter we might well find his own "extravagant" description of his exertions was responsible for Catherine's anxiety. He wrote pretty much as he felt at the moment, and she had to learn not to take his view of things too seriously. This was not easy because her love for him tended toward the very opposite. By the time he wrote "appetite good, digestion much better, pain in my side better", he had forgotten how violently he had described his ills a day or two, or even hours, before! Her letter gives an idea of what must have been the tenor of William's: "*My dearest William,* I don't know how you intended your letter this morning to affect me, but it produced a tumult ... if I said anything wrong in my last or in a wrong spirit, you should have *told me* ... the excited note I received on Tuesday morning indicating a state of health which my imagination perhaps exaggerated and which irritated me at the idea of your extravagant exertion, but how you could gather the idea that I was so 'little *pleased* with your success' I don't know. I have nothing to say in reply to a sentiment which has cut me to the heart, only that I am the *same* in view and feeling, and hope, and aim, as when I wrote ... perhaps I might not express myself so happily, but I fondly thought all danger of *misunderstanding* me was now over. I thought you had a *key* by which to interpret anything ambiguous ... I say again, I would *rather* you were instrumental in saving souls than in swaying sceptres. I only want you to spend a long life at it instead of a *short* one. Excuse me, but your views are too much bounded by the *present* ... The world is a large place, and human hearts *are* human hearts everywhere; and God, the Holy One, and Jesus, the Redeemer, are the same in wisdom and in power and in *love* towards all their creatures. The work you do at Caistor may be *re-done* a thousand times elsewhere and with tenfold increase. Don't forget all the future because the sun shines at Caistor ... but dearest, six weeks revival services has reduced you to the necessity of consulting a physician. What would six months or years do? ... God *guides us* into paths of safety if we will walk in them."[109]

Catherine liked to notice dates: there were special letters for special days, to William, to her mother, and later to her children. She began a letter to William, "*January 1st, 1854.* Quarter to one o'clock in the morning. A happy new year to you my dearest Love. May clearer light, deeper peace, and more extensive usefulness mark its flight than any which has preceded it and whether you live or die may you end it *with the Lord* ... I have given the future *all* up to God. *I am His* and He *will* guide me ... *We* are His and He *will* (because He is so merciful) bless us. I breathed your name on high as the clock struck the funeral knell of the old year, and I prayed that *our* union might be an eternal union, one that shall never, never, *never* end ... I have pictured you conducting the Watch Night Services and longed to be with you ... Jesus reads that deeper and inexpressible language of the soul which mortal eyes cannot scan. *He* knows how much I would say if I could find language, but poor, paltry *language* cannot convey the eloquence of soul which in heaven will need no such medium. Oh, to live as children of the skies ..."[110]

Through the maze of his perplexities William was sure of one thing —his *love for Catherine*. It was the home of his spirit. But when, in her absence, it came to expressing his feelings, he could only repeat the plain words. He would have liked to make them white hot in their intensity; he *felt* that, but in comparison what he said on paper often seemed flat. He warned her not to "expect me to say much, in fact I am tired of this mode of communication".[111] Here and there came patches that glowed for Catherine as, "Oh, how I wished yesterday evening that I had wings to fly to you to hide my head in your bosom and listen to your sweet comforting voice."[112] Often there was only a sentence sandwiched between accounts of his work and health, as *"My dearest and most precious Kate,* almost distracted with anxiety of one description or another, nervous beyond degree, I snatch a moment to tell you of continued and unclouded affection and love to you. Sunday morning I preached . . ." or "My darling, I am sure I love you and am prepared to make you happy . . . many a little laughing child sends me four or five years into the future with your company."

Catherine's exactitudes no doubt sometimes tried William. He says in one note, "My darling, you are rather pertinacious when you think you are right." I agree! Her craving for certainties raised fears that must have perplexed William. For example, when they had been engaged nearly two years she wrote, "If you are displeased with anything I say *tell me,* if there is *one* feeling in your heart other than love, *tell me.* Don't call this suspicion. It is not. I believe I have all your heart; but you say in your letter that you 'trust' your heart is fully and devotedly attached to me. *I* never speak doubtfully on this subject, but I think it is only a way you have of saying 'I trust', is it? If this grieves you I am very sorry . . . I have just glanced at your letter, and I see you assure me at the end that you are unchanged in all things, and *mine altogether.* Bless you, I believe it; I ought not to have thought anything about you saying 'I trust', but don't say it again. Good night."[113] And three days later, ". . . last evening about eleven o'clock, as I was undressing, I thought of your request for a few thoughts for a farewell sermon, and as I had earnestly asked the Lord at dinner-time to open some text to my mind, I took my Bible and looked at one or two passages and then turned again to the one you mention, when the train of thoughts pursued in the enclosed commenced. I took my pencil out of my watch-pocket, where I always keep it, and wrote a few of the leading thoughts sitting up in bed all of a shiver, when to my great disappointment my candle suddenly eclipsed, and compelled me to shut my eyes and go to sleep. I resumed the outline this afternoon . . . but I had no idea of writing half as much. However, I left my mind at liberty without considering whether it would be exactly what you want *now* . . .

"Monday morning. My precious William, I went to bed with my mind so active, and my soul so full of feeling that I did not get to sleep till very late or rather, early, and woke up again very early . . . Your envelope containing the beautiful piece of ribbon is to hand. I suppose it is to supplant those bonnet strings you dislike. Well, it is just the thing, for the black watered edge just matches the little bow. I *like it exceedingly,* you shall always choose for me. One of the

little things I want you to do for me when you come is to go with me to buy one of those favourite shawls of yours. Mother has promised me one. I have taken out those gay flowers. I think you will admire the bonnet now."[114]

Through all the "argument" about joining the New Connexion, Catherine's care was that William should decide on what *he* felt was *right*. Circumstances in the present must not be allowed to tip the balance, and thus sow seed of future regret. "I am very sorry to find that you are now perplexed and harassed about the change about to take place . . . even now it is not too late; stay at Spalding and risk all. Pray be satisfied in your *own mind* . . ."[115] William wrote in cheerful mood, *"My dearest and most precious Kate,* I write in great haste . . . I accidentally spied the ribbon at Mr. Handy's and thought it would make you a nice pair of strings to your black velvet bonnet; it just suited my taste and I thought you should see for once what my taste was . . . I received a note on Saturday from Mr. Rabbits stating it was agreed that I should go and live with Mr. Cooke according to my request. I know you will be pleased . . . It is probable I shall be in London about the third day of February . . . I sighed out your name in Spalding pulpit just as the clock struck the hour of midnight and prayed for your happiness . . . I have a strong faith that we shall yet be very happy. Oh I know I love you."[116] Catherine wrote, "Yesterday was my birthday, twenty-five years I have lived in the world, but oh, to how little purpose! 'God is love'; or I had mourned without hope, but as it is I hope for better things, my mind is solemnly impressed with the brevity of life—the flight of time and the vanity of everything which bears no relation to eternity. If we are not useful and happy while we do live, what a vain show is life; and if death were oblivion, what a sickening thing it would be to me. I should indeed feel disgusted with everything if I did not firmly believe in, and hope for, a future inheritance. It is this glorious prospect which gives value and importance to everything here . . ."[117]

However, even after all was arranged William again became doubtful. He received various offers giving him a good field to preach in, and making immediate marriage possible. We may well sympathize with him. This was his first taste of popularity. Since his father's financial failure life had been drab and laborious. His youthful efforts to help others into salvation had been frowned at. He never forgot his feelings when, having with prideful joy brought a group of converts from his meetings in Nottingham slums to a service in Wesley Chapel, he was told that in future he must bring them in by the back door and that they must sit on benches out of sight. He recorded that during the four years after his conversion "the leading men of the church to which I belonged . . . gave me plenty of caution . . . but never a word of encouragement."[118] When he came to London he was told that more ministers were not needed; but in Spalding all this had been changed. Barely a month before he was due at Dr. Cooke's he received the offer of a London circuit. His letter telling Catherine this disturbed her. He wrote, "I hesitate not to tell you that I fear, and fear very much, that I am going wrong. Yesterday I had a letter asking me if I would consent to come to Hinde Street Circuit, London; salary £100 a year . . . you see my dearest it is certainly enough to make a fellow think and tremble. Here I am at present in a circuit numbering 780 members, with an increase for the year of nearly 200. Am invited to another with near a thousand . . . I fear I shall regret it . . ."[119] Catherine replies emphasizing again her attitude to his future, and expressing the same tender solicitude for *him*. "*My dearest William* . . . as you seem so perplexed I will just put down one or two considerations which may *comfort* you . . . First then, you are not leaving the Movement *because* you fear not getting another circuit or not getting so good a salary as the Connexion can offer . . . Second, you are not leaving to secure present advantage, but for what you believe to be *on the whole* (*looking to the end*) most for God's glory and the good of souls, and the fact of Hinde Street offering £200 would not alter these reasons. If it is right in *principle* for you to leave the Movement and join the Connexion, no advantage in the former or disadvantages in the latter can possibly alter the thing, but mind, I do *not urge* you to do it, and I do not see even now that it is too late to retreat if your *conscience* is not satisfied . . . I wish we could meet for a few hours and talk all our hearts over. I cannot bear the idea of your being unhappy . . ."[120] This letter calmed William's excited frame of mind and plans as arranged were carried out.

About a fortnight before William came to London Catherine wrote, "*Bless you my precious one.* How I long to see you tonight. I have not been at all well since Friday evening, and the weather being very wet and foggy today, I have not been out, so have been deprived of the great pleasure and privilege of hearing Mr. T. However, I have not spent an unprofitable or useless day. I lay in bed till nearly twelve o'clock reading the blessed Bible, and some portions of the magazine and praying for *thee,* with special reference to the subject of my last letter. No doubt the exercises you mention were the result of temptation. I only wonder Satan does not harass you more in this way seeing what you are doing with his kingdom . . . I trust the Lord has delivered thee and that this has been a day of peace and success. Only mind that the people *understand* what religion *is* and thou need not fear their being excited—there is the most glorious precedent for such results. I *believe* in *revivalism with all my soul.* I believe that it is God's idea of the success of the Gospel. Of course, you know what I mean by revivalism. The genuine work of the Spirit and I believe these are such. *Go on,* do *all* thy duty and

leave results to God. This afternoon I have written the enclosed sketch
... I wanted to do something that would *live* beyond the hour and
remembering the text you named, I found it, prayed to the Lord for
help, and sat down to try. I send thee the result. It is *mine* and
therefore thine, if of any use, and if not preserve it and give it me
back as it has taken some writing and on reading it over, *I like it.*
And so thou thinkest sweetly and tenderly about me—when thou
enterest thy chamber at night. Bless thee. We shall enjoy communion
of soul *soon.* I will answer your letter tomorrow. I do wish I could
see you tonight. I feel tired and prostrate, and my spirit very very
tender. Thy sympathizing voice would be sweet indeed ... Good night
dearest. I sleep with thy loving letters in *my bosom,* and sometimes
dream about thee. God bless thee. I often think about that night
when thou wast so late home from the visiting at Mr. Rabbits. Thy
tenderness of manner to me when thou first came in has never passed
away, and my mind seems to go back to it as to a green spot in
our intercourse."[121]

7

William Booth began his stay with Dr. Cooke toward the end of
February 1854. Beghie says "that Booth did not make a good
theological student goes without saying. Into the speculations of
philosophy he never entered."[122] However there can be no question
but that the time with Dr. Cooke brought definite advantages and
both the lovers benefited. During the period spent as student William
conducted services in various parts of London, and it was of interest
to him and Catherine that at one of these a daughter of Dr. Cooke's
was converted. Of such a visit he wrote in his diary: "I felt much
sympathy for the poor neglected inhabitants of Wapping and its
neighbourhood, as I walked down the filthy streets and beheld the
wickedness and idleness of its people."[123] This impression was in
sharp contrast to the rich countryside of his Fenland ministry, and
one which never faded from his mind's eye. We may note in passing
that he named the two conditions of mankind that he came to believe
himself called by God to combat—wickedness and idleness.

Dr. Cooke watched William: heard him preach, recognized the
marks of native intelligence, sincerity and zeal. Soon the doctor
concluded that theoretical study would do little to improve the man
in relation to his vocation as a preacher. He gave him guidance as
to books he should read, encouraged him, and allowed him gradually
to do more preaching and farther afield, even when this meant curtail-
ing the time spent in the classroom. The doctor's perspicacity was
fully justified by Booth's subsequent history. Catherine herself said

127

in later years, "Perhaps I overestimated those literary and intellectual opportunities ... I think I did in view of what I have learned since."[124] Dr. Cooke's judgment of William Booth's character and talent was startlingly revealed when at the New Connexion Conference in June 1854 he proposed William as Superintendent of a large London Circuit. Was Rabbits concerned in this? Catherine said, "This amazing proposition staggered William", and it is not hard to imagine their excited discussions about it. That William's ambitions were not based on self-confidence is evident from the fact that he refused this sudden rise in status. He declared himself too young for such responsibilities, and suggested that he should act as assistant while an older minister be appointed Superintendent. Mr. Rabbits offered to pay the assistant's salary.

Another result of Dr. Cooke's report on Booth to the Conference was the decision that he should be given permission to marry in twelve months' time. Full of joy at this news from William, Catherine wrote, "Your letter this morning filled my heart with gratitude ... Far above and beyond all secondary agents or circumstances, I see clearly His hand. I know He heareth and answereth prayer, and though you may think me enthusiastic, I shall always believe this to be the Lord's doing ... after all our reasoning, praying, and perplexity, your position is now fixed and your security as a *minister* of Christ attained." Toward its end this letter gives one of Catherine's rare allusions to events of the time. In a vivid little word picture she told William, "The Queen opened the Palace* on Saturday. I got a sight of her for the first time. The procession came up from Stockwell Green just opposite Brixton Church. It was very pretty, but not in State carriages. There were great numbers of private carriages going all day—some of the most *beautiful* horses I ever saw. There was every conceivable vehicle from the kind of raft on two wheels drawn by a half-starved donkey, up to the Queen's own equipage. After a whole line of the most splendid carriages it formed quite a ludicrous contrast to see a well-filled dust cart creeping up the hill with a pocket handkerchief flying from the top in honour of Her Majesty!"[125]

The Superintendent under whom William worked was not very understanding; he was stiff and formal and William had not really enough to do. Calls to preach outside the circuit became frequent and he responded with alacrity. He went back for a visit to Lincolnshire. There he tasted the joy of finding converts, "most of them standing firm," as he wrote: "Enthusiasm ran very high ... a crashing prayer meeting, some splendid cases. I am more than ever attached to the people. *Just my sort* ... I love them dearly."[126] His fame as a preacher spread. Mr. Josiah Bates, an influential lay member of the

* Crystal Palace—originally the 1851 Exhibition Building in Hyde Park.

Preaching in the Dome, Brighton

The People's Mission Hall at Whitechapel

New Connexion in the circuit to which William was attached, wrote, "I regard the appointment of the Rev. W. Booth to this circuit as providential . . . Would to God we had a host of such men . . . I hope the next Conference will leave Mr. Booth without a circuit, so that he may go through the Connexion as an evangelist."[127] This was exactly what happened a few weeks later. After hearing of Booth's crowded services the Executive Committee, acting for Conference, appointed a substitute to take his place in the London Circuit and decided that for the next few months he should travel to hold evangelistic services.

During the study period at Dr. Cooke's the lovers met often. Letters ceased to be one of the necessities of life; but now they reappeared. Catherine, hoping she and William might go away together for a few days, wrote, "I always find a short sojourn in the country to be as beneficial to mind as to body . . . There is so much in nature to call up and strengthen the purest, most noble, God-like sentiments of our nature."[128] But this little hope died away, and William was soon engulfed in his new work. Cholera, in those days always a murmuring menace in London, rose to almost epidemic proportions in the summer of 1854. Catherine was rather ill again, and when recovering it was decided that she should go for a change of air to Burnham, where she had friends. She described the last lap of the journey there in a letter to William. I wish we knew what the carrier thought of his solitary passenger! At Chelmsford her train was met by her friend's sister and they walked together a little way out of the town "till the carrier overtook us, when I mounted a heavily loaded cart, and, behind a good horse with no other companion than the driver, started on a journey of twenty miles, which enormous distance we accomplished in the short space of four hours! This was truly having enough for my money . . . However the beauty of the country, together with sundry efforts to make my driver a teetotaller, the time passed more pleasantly than you might expect."[129] William wrote, "Cholera was bad in London—I was poorly, unable to go on with my work, and have gone off to Nottingham to my mother." Had he understood how deeply Catherine longed for a few days in the country *with him,* I feel sure he would have managed to fit in a visit to Burnham while she was there; as it was Catherine replied, *"My dearest Love,* Your letter arrived about an hour ago . . . I was surprised to find you gone without having dropped a line. I wish you had come to Burnham because I think the sea air and the country would have been far more beneficial than that of a crowded town and I could have amused you just as *I liked."*

The future envisaged by them both at this time was that after marriage William would be appointed to a circuit and that life together in a home of their own would begin. This was what they had so long desired, yet now that it was within reach William found

E

his particular work taking precedence. Catherine's letter went on "... I think much of your proposed plan of evangelizing; all within me seems to shrink from this continual separation ... nevertheless, *if it is His will* I dare not, I will not oppose it . . ."[130] In another letter she wrote, "Do I remember? Yes, I remember *all, all* that has brought us together; all the *bright* and *happy* as well as the clouded and sorrowful of our fellowship. *Nothing* relating to *you* can time or place erase from my memory. Your *words,* your *looks,* your actions, even the most trivial and incidental come up before me as fresh as life. If I see a child called William I feel more interested in him than in other children ... Oh, my Love, if you knew the ecstasy my spirit feels when resting in satisfied confidence on your affection, you would think [it] no mean work to kindle such a joy. My soul is capable of the most heroic devotion and when uncrushed and unalloyed by distrust can mount up as on the wings of an eagle far above the damps and fogs of melancholy and sadness and I doubt not will some day, when all restraints are removed, bear you with it to regions of purest bliss ... God bless us and crown our fellowship with *His* smile and let it approach as near the bliss of angels as mortals have on earth. You will think me extravagant. Well, bless God, He made me so and I love to feel like this ... If I get well, what a happy home we will have. It *should* be happy even if I were not well. I would not grieve you by complaining but oh, if I get well how sunny I will try to make it. How kind and cheerful I will be if we live in love, as *Christ hath loved us*—what a little heaven below—for I believe in training children Christians from babyhood ... I have made up my mind to dress as simply and elegantly as possible—to cut off all unnecessary trappings and to appear like a Christian—and then I am sure I shall always be lovely in your eyes, shall I not, dearest? And our sweet babes we will dress like children in all simplicity and loveliness. You smile, but I intend to *try.* Will you help me to be a pattern of whatsoever is lovely and of good report? I do yearn to be made a blessing in the world . . . I have omitted a lovely walk to write this ... I wish you were here—to go and gather me some blackberries. The hedges are full of them but the spiteful thorns and nettles neither eat them nor allow me to do so with impunity, but *your tall form* and long arm would overtop them ... God bless you. And now *just answer this* [or] I shall be discouraged from writing so many of my heart's feelings again. Burn it and believe me thy own loving Kate."[131]

A few days later she enthused on the beauty of the scene before her: "The sun is just setting, the western sky seems literally flooded with glory, which the placid waters reflect back again with redoubled splendour, while in the south appears the lovely moon veiled with a transparent mist as though reserving the full splendour of her silvery beams until the gorgeous hues of her consort's train have

130

faded into night ... all around is tranquil and serene. The boats and skiffs repose on the surface of the river as if weary with the day's engagements, except here and there a solitary sail flutters on the breeze ... altogether it is an enchanting scene reminding one of the land that is very far off. I wish you could see it just now. It would warm your soul with the fire of devotion, admiration and poetry, and *you* could do far more justice to its beauty than I can. I can *feel* far better than I can express. I don't know what effect the really sublime in nature would have upon you, but such a scene as this stirs strange feelings and touches chords which thrill and vibrate through my whole nature ... How sunk and sensualized a being must be, how earth-born and earth-bound, to whom nature speaks not of God: all unsophisticated souls *must* feel the power of its testimony to the being and goodness of Him whom we worship ... How strange that we can really be content about anything in comparison with the constant realization of His smile and blessing.

"*Wednesday afternoon* ... I am better pleased to hear you say you think much about our future—its happiness, its capacity for glorifying God, even than I should be with the most passionate and flowery declaration of present affection ... Oh, why should we not be fully and truly happy? Life is so short and so *uncertain*! Let us make it as sweet and as bright to each other as we can—if you were to die the thought of ever having spoken to you unkindly would be intolerable. I do see and feel more than ever the importance of *kindness*. If ever God gives us children their young hearts shall expand under its full and gentle influence ... If we truly love each other and feel perfect childlike confidence in each other's sincerity, integrity and fidelity, a oneness of sentiment, aim, and interest, a perfect transparency of soul, what a home ours may be!"[132]

Still from Burnham, Catherine to William: "*My dearest Love*. Your two kind short and sweet letters came duly to hand. Bless you. I am indeed thankful you are so much better ... Have you thought any more about vegetarianism? I am inclined towards it more than ever ... We will examine its claims. You want to hear more about myself —well ... I feel astonishingly better and *look* quite rosy and bright. Miss S. says you will be delighted ... I never received greater kindness in my life. Miss S. persists in it that I shall not come till you fetch me. She is going to write and tell you so. If you could come for a couple of days, you would certainly enjoy it and you could come to Southend by water for 3/6 or 2/6 and from there to the ferry for half a crown more or perhaps less, and there Mr. H. would meet you with his pony and chaise ... I think I had better stay a week or ten days longer, especially as I feel so much better and the cholera is so bad in London. We have had only one fatal case in Burnham and that was one of the finest men in the village taken and dead in twenty-four hours, and [in] the *house next to ours*! ... The Lord has

131

been blessing my soul the last few days. I went to the little Methodist Chapel on Sunday morning. There was a prayer meeting instead of the service, and would you believe it *I prayed,* to the no small astonishment of the natives ... I felt unusually happy riding home at night. Oh, the throbbing, swelling feelings of my soul as I gazed up into the deep blue sky, bestudded with so many worlds of light—I *did* indeed. It seemed just the time and place for love ... I am glad you were so happy too, and so successful. I love to be at work for God. I believe I should not have dwindled down to the dwarf I am if I had *worked* more. I think I shall rise superior to that timidity which has been such a curse!"[133]

8

William Booth was twenty-five, and had now begun the pattern which, save for a brief break, all his life would follow. The settled home, which he had pictured and which he and Catherine had so ardently desired, was allowed them for only three years during his appointment to two circuits in the North of England. Even when they "settled" in London, their house, as Catherine once said, was more like a railway station than a home. William was seldom there for more than a few consecutive days' stay. None will know the daily self-denial this kind of life imposed upon them both. In 1854, when William began his journeyings, travelling was a pretty strenuous affair. To be met at the station by a trap was the top notch of luxury. Sometimes his luggage must be left to be fetched. He wrote to Catherine once, "I had rather a dreary and tedious journey, and when I arrived at Stoke the last train was gone to Longton, so I had three miles to walk through wind, and I have not yet got my bag."[134] Few places had trams or buses; and trains were unheated, without corridors and with wooden seats. The length of his stay in a place varied, but was seldom for more than a fortnight. Dates were fixed and trains must be caught however tired the traveller. He often set out on a cold comfortless journey racked by indigestion, quivering from the excitement of the campaign just concluded, and burdened with the prospect of the new one at hand. His letters at this time are more hurried, but they express his love more freely. He has learned much about himself and Catherine while he was absent from her, and still more from the months he was at Dr. Cooke's when she was within reach. He has begun to count on her love for him and tells her all his heart. Begbie says: "... To his betrothed he shows himself with amazing candour in every word that surges through his mind; he never poses before her; he never pretends; he never acts; whatever his state of soul—there it is for her to see—the man of God seeking for God . . . the popular and pious young minister imploring the woman he loves to pray for him . . ."[135]

"My dearest and most precious Kate," he writes, ". . . I am yours, wilful, impulsive and fitful as I am, I am yours in an affection *enduring* and tender and *faithful."* And ". . . I hope you are very well and *very, very* happy. Bless you, I am more so . . . for two reasons, first, our union is more perfect . . . and my love for you more calm and tender. My thoughts stray to you much when alone, and after times of excitement and effort I fall back upon you in thought and imagination as I shall do in reality in the future, for repose and peace and happiness." The letter is then taken up with an account of his services until he breaks in abruptly, "I forgot to say that a second source of joy to me was that I have begun to live afresh [in God]. You will rejoice my dearest in this . . . If anything strikes you in the course of your reading or meditation likely to be useful to me, put it down on a paper kept on purpose, and then tell me about it when we meet."[136] A few days later he writes, ". . . I took the pulpit in this immense chapel. The congregation was very good, probably 2,500 people; at night the place was full. It was an imposing sight when we all rose up to sing. What a responsibility to have to preach to them . . . I will send you word if I want anything. I am in need of shirts. Now my own sweet Kate, *do* be happy. I shall see you again very soon, a month or five weeks . . ."[137]

This letter contained an enclosure from *The Staffordshire Sentinel* describing William's services: "The effect of the Revd. gentleman's preaching was truly astonishing; his view of the Christian religion was clear, his delivery powerful, melting his audience to tears . . . the happy result of his labours is an accession of about 150 members to the Church."[138] To which William adds a P.S. "Do not show or read this to anyone except your mother." But for the letters from Burnham there are none of Catherine's during the first six months of William's journeys. Probably she exacted a promise that he would destroy them. She felt horror at the thought they might be left at William's lodging and so come into other hands; but there are a number of William's, as, *"My dearest, my own precious Love . . .* I have this last day or two unceasingly carried thee with me, in my inmost thoughts and even when surrounded by crowds . . . I have seemed only to live for God and thee . . . I arrived here in Burslem about nine o'clock on Saturday after a very cold and wearisome journey . . . The chapel is very unique and comfortable, rather small, will hold about 800 persons. I never preached to a congregation so packed in my life as it was last night . . . all up the pulpit stairs, in the aisles, in the communion rails, in fact wherever there was standing room . . . Oh, my dearest, let us trust in God . . . I will love you as few are loved and watch over you as few are watched over, and we will

133

live for each other and every sinew and every nerve shall be strained to save *thousands* and tens of *thousands* of perishing souls . . . and when we meet I will look the love I cannot speak. Farewell; never more fondly did I press an epistle to my lips before posting than I do this . . . God bless you—remember me as *your own*."[139] A letter written the next day began, "*My own sweet and precious treasure* . . . You talk about my *popularity*; dearest, believe me, I care about pleasing *God* and *thee* and saving sinners. In seeking the salvation of souls popularity has come. It will not alter my future *course*; not an atom. *I mean to* do right, and to do my duty, *all my duty* . . . *Farewell*, my own sweet Love. Bless you, pray for *me*. You are lonely without me and I am lonely without *thee*. How I wanted thee last *night* to *go home to*. No one else can understand me, no one else can *sympathize* with me. Thy bosom is my earthly heaven. Next to the joy of my work and my heavenly *Master*, thou art my joy and thy smile is my paradise. Farewell! the 3rd of March will soon be here. P.S. I kiss this letter *many times*. Thou shalt have another pen when I come."[140]

And Catherine wrote, "The success of your efforts is truly encouraging . . . I am sorry to find that the 3rd of March is on a Saturday. If it is on the *next* Sunday you begin at Shoreditch—no rest between and a long journey on the Saturday—it is *monstrous*. I care not how you *feel* at present . . . why, you had need be a Hercules to keep up like this. I could not help smiling at Mr. Ridgway's remark, 'Mr. Booth being recruited by *two days* . . .' It won't do, and it *shall not be*; you *shall* rest; you *will* for my sake, dearest won't you? You *promised* me so faithfully you would . . . *Pray for me, my darling*. No one knows the efforts I make to feel calm."[141] The day following she wrote, "*My own dear Love* . . . The remarks in the paper exceed my expectation after what you said about them. *I* have no objection to your profile being considered Jewish. I rather like it and am inclined to second the opinion tho' it never struck me before; and as to 'elegance of attitude or gesture, swells and cadences of voice, oratorical climaxes', etc. . . . I think the highest encomium which could be passed on preaching is passed on yours, or rather on you, in the last clause 'the audience was rivetedly attentive. He talked with earnestness . . .'" Her letter continuing revealed that Catherine was reconciled to the probability that William will be asked by Conference to continue as a travelling evangelist—that is if she can travel with him—she was glad that his work was valued in the circuits "because they will be so glad to get your services that were I a very *incubus* they would gladly tolerate it". She goes on to ask "whether anything short of positive necessity shall separate thee and me? Death will separate us soon enough without forestalling it—life is awfully uncertain and very short . . . Do you see the papers sometimes? What do you think of political matters just now? Don't you

134

think we are in a pitiable fix before the nations of Europe? There has been a fine stir at the West End the last few days. On Sunday messengers and dispatches and noble lords were flying about in all directions. Her Majesty had interviews of an hour's length with four or five noblemen on that day and up to last night no evidence of the formation of a Ministry was forthcoming. I should so like you to see two or three articles by Kossuth which have appeared in the *Weekly Times*. They are indeed first rate. Oh, I do admire that man's spirit. I believe him to be a thorough patriot [Hungarian] and a lover of universal liberty—but perhaps you have seen them in some provincial paper. Christians had need to pray that our senators may be directed and our national privileges preserved."[142]

William wrote, "Do not fear about being separated. If you *can* go *I* shall not go without *you* . . . if spared we shall pass some happy, happy, happy hours *together*. By God's help I will calmly wait, and with His blessing I will enjoy the present . . . I have every earthly luxury and attention, and then I have thee, and a hope, a real and certain hope, of heaven."[143]

Catherine reverted to the question of William's proposed stay in London: "A week's *rest* will indeed be a boon to you, and yet what is a *week* after such prolonged excitement? *Preach on the Sunday* after your journey? *No*, that you *shall not* if I have any influence over you . . . if nobody else thinks about your body I must, and I declare I won't hear of such a thing . . . I think a week's sojourn in some country village about the beginning of April would do me a great deal of good . . ."[144] Poor Catherine was still hankering after a little spell in the country with her Love but this gentle hint fared no better than others. "*My very dear Love*," wrote William two days later, "Yesterday was a day of great anxiety. I knew expectation was very high and I had comparatively new and untried sermons to preach. At night the chapel was densely crowded, packed, I suppose 2,200 persons were present . . . A gentleman of the name of Bailey who keeps his carriage and pair, and who lives in a little paradise about two miles out of Longton, would very much like us to spend a month to rest at his house next summer; but I mean to visit Paris, Switzerland and the Rhine, if at all practicable—but we shall see."[145] Catherine was delighted and wrote, ". . . a trip to the Continent! There is nothing in *this world* I should enjoy so much, and it may be our only opportunity for such a pleasure . . . and how *much we shall learn*, what new visions of beauty and magnificence will burst upon us . . . Oh, I do hope we shall go."[146] Alas for her hopes! The idea was just another of William's dreams!

A week later William was in Oldham. He was not yet twenty-six. The thoughts stirring in him will take him out of Methodism to the godless masses in Whitechapel and to the birth of The Salvation Army. He confides to his Love, "*My dearest and most precious*

Catherine, Bless you, how I do wish for an interview—to see and love you. I am very low in spirits—very; the work does not progress to my satisfaction . . . My heart yearns for something more glorious and effective; here I am surrounded by a dense population of I should think 80,000 people, and yet our congregation last night was only about 300 . . . Pray for me, my dearest Love; oh, to live nearer God . . . My soul pants for something deeper, realler, more hallowed, in my soul's experience . . . I will try and serve God better, I want Him more in my heart's motives, in my soul's thinking and desires. To look at men and things and duties from a place close to His throne."[147] In reply comes this from Catherine, *"My own treasure,* and so thou art low and discouraged and dissatisfied with thyself. Bless thee. I wish I could come and cheer thy spirit, sympathize in thy trials, bear some of thy burdens, bow with thee at the mercy seat, and lay one hand on thy head and the other on thy heart, and my cheek to thine, and thus cause thee to forget everything but *love* for a season . . . Cherish as thy very life's blood those yearnings after a deeper and richer experience in the things of God . . .

"My health on the whole is most encouraging, I have been beyond Brixton church almost every day all this bitter weather, and today I walked to the gate and down the York Road to Mr. Franks', and *all* the way home without feeling at all over-fatigued. The palpitation of my heart has been much better the last month or so. I took the opportunity to tell Mr. Franks a little of what I anticipate in the future and to ask his opinion and advice. He seemed pleased and very *kindly* expressed his wishes for my happiness . . . He says I shall be quite prepared for the change before then and if I am *careful* in travelling and cautious not to sleep in damp beds, he thinks such a life will be *highly beneficial.* Is it not encouraging? Have we not cause to be thankful? Is not Mr. F's kindness remarkable? It is nearly twelve months since he took a fee . . . I do 'love thee with *satisfaction'.* I never was so happy since I knew you as I have been since you went away. Your letters have been quite a new series, their tender, extremely warm salutations and loving *heart*-breathing assurances have woke up a *trusting* love and a self satisfying affection to which I was before a stranger. I do love thee . . . a week tomorrow and we shall see each other face to face. Till then the Lord preserve us in health and peace."[148]

However, within a few days he was proposing to stay on at Oldham, thus cutting short the brief spell planned for rest. Catherine "boils over" with ". . . but William, are you set on self-destruction? Do you imagine that a being constituted as you are, can go on like this and retain *reason* and life? You tell me in every letter, and indeed your letters bear indirect testimony of your 'fearful nervousness', and yet you propose to prolong this toil and excitement till Monday, and then take a 200 mile journey, rest four or five days, then commence here and take all the burden and anxiety on yourself. Then, after a few days' flurry, take your leave for another two months' incessant excitement and fatigue . . . I can scarce write the monstrous idea for agitation. *God knows it is not* because I am not willing to give you up a day or two longer *now* that I write thus, but because I cannot endure the thought of ultimately giving you up to an *asylum* or the grave! I tell you, that I am *alarmed* at the state of your nervous system, and I see nothing but absolute and *unmolested rest* will restore it; and if you don't come before Monday, *no power* on earth shall compel you to preach here and go away again directly . . . Don't think I am angry. I am not, my precious, but I am *desperately determined* that you shall *have rest*, or I will write to Mr. Cooke, the President and every other man in the Connexion. Oh that you would act reasonably. You distract me. I have reasoned, begged, and implored, till I am thoroughly disheartened, but submit in silence to your being sacrificed, I *will not*. Leave here a week after the special services and preach at Brittannia, no! . . . I hope you have decided to come. Good night. It is because I *love you* I write thus . . . Your own anxious and loving Katie."[149]

It is tantalizing not to have William's reply to Catherine's "fury". We may conclude, I think, that he gave up the idea of prolonging his campaign and came to London early in March as originally planned. Even so the time for rest was cut short. He was announced for a series of services in London and, by March 24, was off again. The question of taking up a life insurance policy was gone into while William was in London. The snag was his health. He saw more than one doctor, but the verdict was not changed—he could only be accepted at a higher than normal premium. Kindly Mr. Bates wrote reams, appealed to the head office in Edinburgh on William's behalf but to no purpose, and at last told him that he must submit. "It is a shame," William comments to Catherine, "I don't care what any of them say, doctors or not, I believe I have a rational hope (without accident) of living thirty years longer."*[150] To which Catherine replied ". . . nonsense about thirty years if you go on as you have lately, you need not calculate on half as many . . . The weather is milder and I hope to get rid of my cough now. I am taking *homoeopathic* medicines and my throat is astonishingly better." This letter goes on to tell that in the moments before they parted, "I could not speak, but those few moments will never die, they are amongst those redeemed from oblivion and added to eternity." Catherine told too how after William had gone she thought about death ". . . till I felt as if I could get up and start by express train to come and throw my arms around your neck and vow that nothing but death should

* William lived until 1912—more than fifty years after this date.

137

ever part us again! I think I hear you say 'Oh, Katie, thy enthusiastic heart!' Yes, it is a foolish thing not quite cured yet . . ."[151]

On the eve of William's birthday Catherine wrote a special letter which she asks him to keep. Whether it were written by man or woman, it would surely rank as remarkable, but how much more so if one has in mind the times—1855—and the age and character of the writer. Reading it one realizes that William was being led to conclusions which would have a fundamental bearing on the form The Salvation Army will take. It is the only one of Catherine's love-letters to be given in full in this book. As she sat scribbling to her lover she had not the faintest premonition that her arguments might one day be applied to herself; in fact, she expressly excluded the possibility by saying to William ". . . you *know* nothing I have said is to be interpreted personally".

"*My own dear Love,* I am all alone, and not equal to much besides, so I will write a bit to *thee,* which generally makes me forget loneliness, and everything else for a time. I have been thinking that I did not notice a little information in one of your notes last week, although it gave me very great pleasure. I refer to your defence of those two subjects, not only dear to my heart, but in my estimation, of vast *importance* to the world. I am sure, had I been present, I should have regarded you with increased pride and affection, for there is nothing so inspires my admiration as a noble stand for *right* in opposition to paltry prejudice and lordly tyranny. I admire Mr. Thomas more for his *noble* nature than his splendid genius. I cannot bear a time-serving, truth-sacrificing spirit. I would not *falsify* my convictions on any subject to gain the plaudits of a *world*! and *proud* shall I be if my husband proves himself in this respect a man whom I can delight to honour.

"It is a great pity that in the *church,* at least, there should be so great a need for this fearless defence of what, but for enslaving prejudice and pitiable littleness, would *at once* commend itself to every man's conscience. But since it is so, God multiply the unflinching defenders of principles and rights of all kinds. I am thankful to my *heart's core* that you are a teetotaller, so deep is my conviction of the righteousness of the principle that *nothing* could buy my consent to your upholding and countenancing the drinking customs of society. I believe that God's deep curse is on them; and *never* till the church repents and washes her hands of them will she do much for the world. The convinced, convicted multitudes of her members *must* end the controversy by coming out on the side of *right,* or mere worldlings will put them to shame (as they are doing) and take the flag of this glorious conflict and final victory forever out of their hands. Oh, that God may send some mighty, rushing, moral influence to arouse them. I know you say Amen, and it is no little gratification

138

to me that you not only sympathize with my views, but defend them. It is sweet to see and feel alike, is it not?

"If on that *other* subject you mention, my views are *right,* how delighted I should be to see you as fully with me on it too. You know I feel no less deeply on the subject and perhaps you think that I take a rather prejudiced view of it, but I have searched the record of God through and through. I have tried to deal honestly with every passage on the subject, not forgetting to pray for light to perceive and grace to submit to the truth, however humiliating to my nature. But I solemnly assert that the more I think and read on the subject, the more satisfied I become of the true and *Scriptural* character of my own views. I am ready to admit that in the majority of cases the training of woman has made her man's inferior, as under the degrading slavery of heathen lands she is inferior to her own sex in Christian countries, but that *naturally* she is in any respect, except in physical strength and courage, inferior to man I cannot see cause to believe, and I am sure no-one can prove it from the *Word of God,* and it is on *this* foundation that professors of religion always try to establish it. Oh, prejudice, what will it not do? I would not alter woman's domestic position (when indeed it is Scriptural) because God has plainly fixed it. He has told her to obey her husband, and therefore she ought to do so, if she professes to serve God. Her husband's rule over her was part of the sentence for her disobedience, which would, by the by, have been no curse at all if he had ruled over her *before,* by dint of superiority—but God ordained her subjection as a punishment for sin and therefore I submit, but I cannot believe that inferiority was the ground of it. If it had [been], it *must have* existed prior to the curse, and thus have nullified it. Oh, I believe that volumes of light will yet be shed on the world on this subject. It will bear *examination* and abundantly repay it. We want a few mighty and generous spirits to go thoroughly into it, pen in hand, and I believe the time is not far distant when God will raise up such; but I believe woman is destined to assume her true position and exert her proper influence by the special exertions and attainments of *her own sex.* She has to struggle through *mighty* difficulties, too obvious to need mentioning, but they will eventually dwindle before the spell of her developed and cultivated mind. The heaving of society in America (that birthplace of so much that is great and *noble*) tho' throwing up, as all such movements do, much that is absurd and extravagant, and which I no more approve than you, yet it shows that principles are working and enquiry awakening. *May the Lord,* even the just and impartial One, over-rule all for the true emancipation of woman from the swaddling bands of prejudice, ignorance and custom which, almost the world over, have so long debased and wronged her. In appealing thus to the *Lord* I am deeply sincere, for I believe that one of the greatest boons to the race would

139

be woman's exaltation to her proper position, mentally and spiritually. Who can tell its consequences to posterity? If what writers on physiology say be true, and experience seems to render it unquestionable, what must be the effects of neglect of mental culture and the inculcation of frivolous, servile, and self-degrading notions into the minds of the *mothers* of humanity. Oh, that which *next* to the plan of salvation endears the Christian religion to my heart is what it *has done, and is destined* to do, for my own sex. And that which excites my indignation beyond anything else is to hear its sacred precepts dragged forward to favour degrading arguments. Oh, for a few more Adam Clarks to dispel the ignorance of the church. Then should we not hear very pigmies in Christianity reasoning against holy and intelligent women opening their mouths for the Lord in the presence of the church.

"Whenever you have to argue with such, just direct them to read the three following passages and Clark's comment on the first two: Exodus 15 c. 20-22 v; Judges 4 c. from the 4 v; and Second Chronicles 34 c. from the 21 v. On the first he says the same word in the original is used in reference to *Moses* and the other prophets, and therefore Miriam was as truly inspired, and that she was chosen and constituted joint *leader* of the people. We have the express word of God for it, viz. Micah 6 c. 4 v. 'For I brought thee up out of the land of Egypt . . . and I sent before thee Moses, Aaron and Miriam.' On the latter Clark says that Deborah seems to have been supreme as well in *civil* matters and spiritual. 'She *judged* Israel.' The same term is used to denote the functions of the regular judges. She *appointed* Barak as general of the armies as well as declared God's will for him, and Barak most unhesitatingly recognized her authority. But read carefully the whole account, as also that in 34th c. of Second Chronicles and say whether in any respect you can discover any difference between the exercise of the prophetic power, or the recognition of its reality and force in these cases, and those of Isaiah and Jeremiah. It is worthy of remark that there are no less than six prophetesses mentioned in the Old Testament, one of whom was unquestionably Judge as well as prophet, and these are not mentioned in a way which would lead one to suppose that the inspired Writer regarded them as anything very extraordinary. They are simply introduced to our notice like the other prophets.

"Now God having *once* spoken *directly by woman* and men having once recognized her divine commission and obeyed it, on what ground is Omnipotence to be restricted, or woman's spiritual labour ignored? Who shall dare to say unto the Lord 'What doest Thou?' when He 'pours out His Spirit upon His handmaidens', or when it is poured out shall render it null with impunity? If *indeed* there is in Christ Jesus 'neither male nor female', but in all touching His Kingdom 'they are one', who shall dare thrust woman out of the church's operations or presume to put any candle which God has lighted under a bushel? Why should the swaddling bands of blind custom, which in Wesley's days were so triumphantly broken, and with such glorious results thrown to the moles and bats, be again wrapped round the female disciples of the Lord, as if the natural, and in some cases distressing timidity of woman's nature, were not sufficient barrier to her obeying the dictates of the Spirit, whenever that Spirit calls her to any public testimony for her Lord. Oh, it is cruel for the church to foster prejudice so unscriptural and thus make the path of usefulness the path of untold suffering. Let me advise you, my Love, to get settled views on this subject, and be able to render a reason to every caviller; and then fearlessly incite all whom you believe the Lord has fitted, to help you in your Master's work, male or female. Christ has given them no single talent to be hid in a napkin, and yet, oh, what thousands are wrapped up and buried, which, used and informed, would yield some thirty, some sixty, and some an hundredfold.

"If God has given her the *ability* why should not woman persuade the vacillating, instruct and console the penitent, and pour out her soul in prayer for sinners? Will the plea of bashfulness or *custom* excuse her to Him who has put such honour upon her as to deign to become her Son in order to redeem her race? Will these pleas excuse her to Him who, last at the Cross and first at the sepulchre, was attended by women, who so far forgot bashfulness as to testify their love for Him before a taunting rabble, and who so far overcame *custom* that when *all* (even fellow disciples) forsook Him and fled, they remained faithful to the last, and even then lingered afar off, loth to lose sight of an object so precious.

"Oh, blessed Jesus! He is indeed 'the woman's conquering seed'. He has taken the bitterest part of her curse 'out of the way, nailing it to His cross', in Him she rises to the dignity of her nature. In Him her equality with her *earthly* lord is realized, for 'in Him there is neither male nor female', and while the outward semblance of her curse remains, in Him it is nullified by *love*, being made the law of marriage—'Husbands love your wives as Christ loves the Church, and gave Himself for it.' Who shall call subjection to such a husband a curse? Truly 'He who was made a curse for us' has beautifully extracted the venom; for what wife who *loves the Lord* can feel it a burden to reverence a husband thus like Him? And glory to His name, while His death *did this* and His precepts *are so tender* and so easy, His example is no less endearing. In her society He loved to spend His hours of repose and holy retirement, in the *lovely little home* at Bethany. To her at the roadside well, He made His only *positive* avowal of His Messiahship, and set aside the trammels of national custom to talk with her. For her He made a way of escape from her merciless, tho' no less guilty accusers, and while sending

141

them away conscience-smitten, to her He extended His tender mercy, 'Neither do I condemn thee, go in peace.' He never slighted her, overlooked her, or cast a more *severe construction* on sin in her than in man; no, He treated her in *all respects* the same. His last affectionate solicitude in the midst of expiring agony, was exercised for *her*. And, oh, best of all, His rising salutation, the first view of His glorified body, that pledge of His victory over her ancient enemy, was given to *her*; with a commission to go and *publish* to His disciples the fact of His resurrection. Methinks if some of our modern quibblers had been amongst them, they would have hesitated to receive such tidings from her; but not so Peter and John. They ran as swiftly at *her word* as if it had been a man's, and stooping down and looking in realized the glorious truth. Oh, that many Marys may yet tell of His wonderful salvation—but I must conclude. I had no idea of writing so much when I began, but I do not regret it. I have long wanted to put my thoughts on this subject on paper and I am sure thou wilt not value them the less because they are on such a subject.

"I have not written so much *to* thee as *for* thee. I want thee to feel as I do, if thou canst; but, if not, be as honest in thy opinion as I am and I will honour thee for this. If you gain anything by what I have written I *shall* praise God on learning it, otherwise I do not desire you to answer this. I have written it in much weariness [Catherine was still not fully recovered from her illness] and I should be pleased and gratified if thou wilt give it a second reading. Perhaps sometime, with thy permission (for I am going to promise to *obey* thee before I have any intention of entering on such a work), I may write something more extensive on this subject, and on reading over this letter I perceive it would, under such circumstances, be a help to you. Therefore I desire thee to take *special care* of it, for I can only write *thus* in certain frames of mind. Bless you, I know you will give some credit for true patriotism, for you *know* nothing I have said is to be interpreted personally. Alas, I feel that I am far inferior to many of my *own sex*. I, therefore, am the last to claim superiority, but such as I am I am *thine* in love's own bonds. Catherine. I have written it for a memorial in a letter instead of a book."[152]

To this fervent statement of her convictions William sent but a brief reply. Whether he wrote more fully later on the subject we do not know. Notice that even in this note, and one feels in contradiction to his judgment, he too makes a vital declaration. That he and Catherine have already discussed the question stands to reason; they talked about everything, and William makes it clear that she knows his views. "*My dearest and most precious Love* ... Thy remarks on woman's position I will read again before I answer. From the first reading I cannot *see* anything in them to lead me for one *moment* to think of altering my opinion. You *combat* a great deal that I hold as firmly as you do ... I would not stop a woman preaching on any account. I would not encourage one to begin. You should preach if you felt moved thereto; felt equal to the task. I would not stay *you* if I had the power to do so. Although *I should not like it.* I am for the world's *salvation*; I will quarrel with no means that promises help."[153] Thus he turned from the theoretical to the practical. This attitude of mind in William Booth was of enormous importance when he founded The Salvation Army. It cleared the way for the emergence of unorthodox methods. He swept all prejudice and criticism aside, holding fast to his life's purpose "the world's salvation". Does the innovation help to this end? That was the touchstone. If it helped men to turn from sin, let the innovators have a free hand. At this time Catherine may have grieved a little that in theory William did not take the matter of woman's right to preach very seriously, but she was fully content with him when the time came to *act*. Then he proved himself to be one of the "mighty and generous spirits".

Catherine was learning that it was part of his nature to be absorbed in the present. He had not had the letter she wrote for his birthday when he started his daily word to her, *"My dearest and darling Catherine,* In heading this letter I have just discovered that it is my birthday. I am today twenty-six. Oh, the importance of employing this fleeting *time*! Oh, my Catherine what must I *do*? I am almost in despair with *myself* ..." There is something lovable as well as revealing in these letters of William's dashed off in the mood of the moment. He tells of the small trials—how washerwomen spoil the cotton buttons; that he cannot wear the round collars; that he still sponges in cold water and has tried "with astonishing success" the horehound tea his Love recommended. Toward the end of April William began to feel the strain of his work. The question was shall this travelling-evangelist plan continue, or shall he apply to Conference for a circuit which would give him a settled home? He writes, *"My dear Kate, my own true Love* ... I have indeed this week been low. I should not like to continue this work if I am to be as I have for the last three weeks. My mental machinery has been a source of great anxiety ... If I had more *general* knowledge, love for study and *material for the pulpit,* I should not hesitate a moment ..."[154] Neither William nor Catherine realizes yet how much the physical as well as the nervous exhaustion of his life had to do with his inability to study. He was continuously short of sleep, yet the tension of constant preaching could only be countered by sleep and exercise, as doctors had already told him. In Manchester he was peculiarly lonely, but from Gateshead, where he had a triumphant fortnight, with 160 names taken, he wrote, "What can we say to this but that it is the Lord's doing ... with facts like these before our minds, retreat from this path seems impossible."[155] A week later he so longs to see Catherine that "had you been anywhere within reach, say fifty miles, this morning would certainly have found me by your side". He goes on to tell "... I have seen a tin box that will do capitally to hold your *bonnet* when travelling and that and a portmanteau, I should think, would serve you well."[156]

William's appointments for the next three weeks were now to be planned and the wedding must fit in with them. Hurriedly, in a matter of fact fashion he wrote, "I suppose we must be married as you say the week ending the 16th ... Do as you think best about everything."[157] A week later, "We will let Mr. Thomas marry us at his own chapel." This letter of William's included, "Write by return how much black silk you will want for a flounced dress ... I intend having a first rate one. If I buy without your letter I shall get black silk and sixteen yards."[158] To which Catherine responded "... as to the dress, *thy* choice is absolutely mine, just which you prefer, only I do think flounces will neither become our position nor profession ... Besides, if you wish people to form a *true* estimate of *my* character, you will let me dress plain, as *good* and *full* as you like, but don't insist on the flounces. Fourteen yards will make a handsome, full dress, plain skirt, twelve yards width, which it *should be*."[159] This put William off a little and two days later he wrote, "I am not sure whether I shall get the black silk. Without flounces I don't like them."[160] From Sheffield on June first came news that the New Connexion Conference had decided, "I am to have £100 for the year and my travelling; preachers and friends very cordial."[161] In the last letter of his we have before the wedding he says, "*My own darling Kate* ... You are to be mine. We are to be one. Yes. One. My whole soul must lie open before your gaze, and it will be. Yes! It shall be. And thou art to be my guardian watcher. And we are to commence our life together in one united, and I trust continued, sacrifice for God's glory and the welfare of our fellow-men. And yet in it I trust we shall be happy. Mutual forbearance, affection, heart-love will do all things, be a talisman which will turn all our domestic anxieties and trial into bonds of love and cause of mutual joy. You know me. I am fitful, *very*; I mourn over it, I hate myself on account of it. But there it is; a dark column on the inner life of my spirit. You know it, bless you; I will try; but suppose I fail to make myself better, thou wilt bear with me and I will try to be all that thou desirest. I pray for help from on high. Oh, yes, God will give it me."[162] One feels that as he nears the consummation of his joy he trembles a little—"suppose I fail". But he has the will to succeed.

9

On the morning of June 16, 1855, in the gloom of the big empty chapel,* Catherine lifted up the light of her sweet face to William, while trustfully, joyfully, her clear beautiful voice spoke her pledges; and William, looking down into her steadfast eyes, knew himself strong in the triumph of love's possession; knew, with an inner instinct of certainty, that Catherine's love would not fail him. And so, man and wife, they walked out of the chapel into the June sunshine (surely the sun was shining on that day?).

Only Catherine's father, a sister of William and the caretaker were present. Dr. Thomas, who married them, had no assistant. Catherine and William travelled forthwith to Ryde, Isle of Wight, for one week! No month in Mr. Bailey's "earthly paradise" for them! No journey to the Continent; but nevertheless they had one whole week to themselves with the "great and beautiful sea" at hand. When the week was up they embarked for Guernsey. William was known and welcome there from his previous preaching on the island. A crowd awaited them at the pier. This was surely a happy moment for the lovers, each feeling a happy pride in the other. William had written, "I long to show you to my friends," and at last he was able to do so. To her mother Catherine wrote, "William is preaching tonight . . . the doors were to be open at half past five to admit the seat holders *before the crush.*"[163] Before they leave Guernsey for Jersey where William is to conduct another series of meetings, young Mrs. Booth, wearing her thoughtful look, writes in an autograph album, "The woman who would serve her generation according to the will of God, must make moral and intellectual culture the chief business of life. Doing this she will rise to the true dignity of her nature, and find herself possessed of a wonderful capacity for turning the duties, joys and sorrows of domestic life to the highest advantage, both to herself and to all those within the sphere of her influence. July 20, 1855. Catherine Booth." Her thoughts, as she writes, are clearly of home life. She is content that her field of action should be the family.

Stormy seas beset them on the way home. Catherine proved a bad sailor and had a suffering time. In a letter to William afterwards she wrote, "I will try and reward thee for thy thoughtful care on board that packet, for thy sympathy at that hotel, for thy back-aching, limb-cramping attention in the train, and *all* thy other acts of kindness not one of which is or can be forgotten."[164] On arrival in London it was evident that Catherine was not fit to travel. Her treasured plan

* Stockwell New Chapel, South London.

145

to accompany her husband on his evangelistic tours was not for the moment practicable. It was perhaps a good discipline that the hindrance should lie at her door and not at his! She rebelled a little, but the happy cause helped her along; that, and William's letters. On the way to York where his campaign was to begin he wrote, "*My precious wife* (the first time I have written you that endearing appellation)... how often during my journey have I taken my eyes off the book I was reading to think about you... about our future, our home. Shall we not again commence a new life of devotion and by renewed consecration begin afresh the Christian race?"[165] William made all manner of happenings an occasion to "begin afresh". This trait in him, the impulse to dedicate anew, to part with the past, helped him incalculably through times of weariness and disappointment; and in moments when his spirit was elated by joy or angered by some new vision of iniquity, it helped him on occasions to take, as it were, a great leap forward. All through his life, making fresh resolves set his mind momentarily at rest and quelled his impatience at the unequal contrast between the need and the means to meet it.

And now little Mrs. Booth answers her *husband's* first letter, "*My precious husband,* A thousand thanks for your sweet kind letter this morning. I have read it over many, many times and it is still fresh and precious to my heart. I *cannot* answer it but be assured not a *word* is forgotten or overlooked. I will tell you all about myself in as few words as possible. On Saturday I was not sick once, as soon as you were out of sight the horrid stupor of which you heard me complain so much seemed to leave me and I felt as though I could have performed the journey with far less suffering than it cost me to stay behind. It was a supremely wretched day and long before night I had made up my mind to come to you, sick or well, on Wednesday or Thursday, and my dear mother, seeing the state of my mind, did not oppose it. You may say 'But Kate, how foolish! Why didst thou not think and reason?' I *did* my darling, I philosophized as soundly as you could desire, I argued with myself on the injustice of coming here and making my dear mother miserable, on the folly of making myself ill, on the selfishness of wishing to burden *thee* with the anxiety and care my presence would entail, etc., but in the very midst of such soliloquies the fact of your being gone beyond my reach, the possibility of something happening before we could meet again, the possible shortness of the time we may have to spend together, and such-like thoughts would start up, making rebellious nature rise and swell and scorn all restraints of reason, philosophy or religion... Yesterday I felt calmer, but was too ill to go out at all. Today I have been very bad since about ten o'clock... Take every care of thyself. I should indeed be a poor forlorn desolate being without thee, truly my destiny hangs on thy heart. I *do* pray for thee, I will try to begin afresh..."[166]

146

And two days later, "*My own precious Love,* I feel better this evening . . . I will write a bit now I feel able for fear I should be as bad as ever tomorrow. Well, what shall I say? Oh, just what comes bubbling up. Well, the first thing I feel is, *bless* you my own precious husband, and the next a few involuntary tears because I cannot throw my arms round your neck and tell you how dear you are to my heart . . . Bless you, that little study *shall* be a beauty, and thou shalt come out of it as often as thou wilt to greet little sunny faces and to bless thy loving wife with one of thy brightest smiles . . . I *am* as happy as I ever can be in thy absence. I have no other cause of sorrow and I can get everything necessary, so don't be anxious about me. I think everything concerning me is going on *right.* I have not been so sick today . . . Pray for me, darling, as I do for thee."[167] Feeling better Catherine started another letter on the same day. Her thoughts were of her love and of the home for which they both longed. "Mother says when I begin to mend I shall very likely be better than ever I was and able to go about with you for four or five months quite comfortably. Oh, if it please the Lord to let it be so, how happy we shall be. I find myself thinking more about a nice home than ever I did before. I should like to make it a neat, tasty, clean little place. I can just picture it to myself sometimes, the best bedroom—that room where our firstborn is to be ushered into the world. Oh my precious one let us pray about it. Bless thee. How I long to see thee . . ."[168] Two days later she spoke of her joy in a new portrait of William, "If I had known the superior comfort of having a small portable likeness to the one hung upon the wall, depend upon it I would have had one before now. I wish thou hadst one as good as this of me, but I shall never make a good picture. My face is of the wrong sort . . . Thy extravagant little wife has spent 1/6 in raisins since thou went, but they do me good and I cannot do without them. Mr. Franks told me to be sure and indulge all such fancies while they lasted . . . It is post time so goodbye my darling and remember me always as thy own faithful loving *thriving* joyful little wife, Catherine."[169]

William's next campaign was to be in Hull and there Catherine arrived with belongings intact in spite of an awkward snag of which she had written to him, ". . . thou hast the keys of both my boxes; I don't know how I shall fasten them!"[170] Friends had offered hospitality, and although this was not the home they had envisaged, they were together, and Catherine might fling her arms round William's neck and kiss him as often as she fancied. And find fault? Love is the only quite safe fault-finder. And those who have no one near enough to speak the truth to them in love walk in danger. These two greatly loving hearts maintained a habit of tender outspokenness between themselves which was a protection to both. Love was the master of life for Catherine, love to God, and love to William.

In her the instinct to correct was part of her love's hunger to see the beloved made perfect. It belonged to the image of God in which mankind is created. And always she had a wealth of love to spend in encouragement and comfort; she was no niggard with either. William had never before known cherishing. Memory caught hardly a glimpse of it in earliest childhood, and all too soon his father's poverty and death had pinned him down to being a money-getter. For one of his disposition it can well be understood that his former lack enhanced the comfort and joy of being the object of a love like Catherine's.

But it was William's love for Catherine as well as Catherine's love for William that was used by God to develop in them both that growing in grace which brings the soul to full stature in Christ. They exemplify in their own persons the beauty and strength of human love after the divine pattern. Catherine, dwelling in the Bible world of thought, guided by communion with God in prayer, early formed her ideals, her certainties about the manner of human behaviour which would please God and breed joy. She lived to prove these ideals true, and to discover, as so many lovers of Jesus Christ have, that life after this fashion, His fashion, was unbelievably happy. She brought her own ideal of love in her hand, as it were, and endowed William with its treasures, lavishing all on him and at the same time enticing him to respond in like measure. He showed himself to be an apt pupil. Catherine's notion of woman's place in creation gave her a conception of marriage differing widely from the examples she observed about her. The onlooker may see the joy of her relationships as wife and mother, and be entranced by a momentary vision of the wealth and beauty of human happiness that would fill the world today if Christian teaching and practice prevailed.

The happy abandon of Catherine's love in the early years of marriage went on growing throughout her life. In her first love-letter she told William, "If it is possible to love you more than I do now, the more shall I love you." And she might have repeated the words every day. Her love for William did not fade, was never fitful, and while they both kept love for God and for His kingdom first, their love for each other reigned in their home, from the least thing to the greatest. The people about them noticed it. They were said to meet and part "like lovers". Joy is the lot of all true lovers who are one in love, but never can it be so vivid, so enduring and satisfying as when both spirits know what it means to be joyful in God. For these two the *joy of loving* was not confined to any given moment, not tied to youth, nor at the mercy of circumstances; it was an ingredient of everyday life. In the future they will be refreshed by spells of delight in each other that amount to a kind of rapture, an access of joy and of hope in God and in their work for souls. The last of these timeless hours was one night they spent together when she lay dying. But the steady warmth of their love for each other blessed all their days.

In records we have of them Catherine's seriousness is emphasized in a manner that tends to overshadow the joyousness that was natural to her. But if we are to have a true picture of her, happiness must be in it. William and Catherine's capacity for joy and its expression in their lives had a bearing on The Salvation Army. William's unaffected happiness when sinners came to repentance in his meetings was visible to all present. At twenty-six he wrote, "No emotion that ever filled my heart were so rapturous, so pure, so heaven-like, as those that have swelled my heart while standing surrounded by penitent souls . . ." He closed a letter to Catherine once with ". . . may the blessing of Israel's God be on thy waking and sleeping hours and *mercifully work out for us a highway in the world wherein we may journey together spreading light, life and gladness all around.*" (The italics are mine.) Surely The Salvation Army with its joyful expression of Christianity was a hundredfold answer to the prayer? The Salvation Army has sung its way round the world, emphasizing the joy which true religion brings. Almost every kind of instrument has been used to make music in Salvation Army meetings, from tambourines, drums and home-made flutes to silver-plated brass bands playing on their "home ground" outside the pub, and by invitation outside palaces.

Wherever the flag flies there is music. It became "correct" in The Salvation Army to be "happy in Jesus" and to show it. The Army's early history, and especially its songs, demonstrated how vigorously joy broke forth. A natural manifestation of the heart's feelings was accepted by converts as one of their new freedoms. The Salvation Army rejoiced by families; all sang together the happy songs of salvation, often with clapping of hands. Catherine once said, "Nothing seems to puzzle the unsaved more, with respect to The Salvation Army, than the happiness of our people." This joy, not all divine, that would be unnatural; not all human, *that* would be incomplete; but a mingling in the heart of both, has been a possession of believers in all ages. David knew about it when he wrote, "O, come let us sing unto the Lord . . . and show ourselves glad in Him." Bunyan tells how he was "glad and lightsome, and said with a merry heart, He hath given me rest . . . then Christian gave three leaps for joy and went on his way singing." There was certainly something of this heavenly radiance to be seen on the faces of old and young when, in Salvation Army meetings, the soldiers and converts sang; sang and shouted, and sometimes, like Christian, leaped for joy. They sang songs like this:

> *Gone is my burden—He rolled it away,*
> *Opened my eyes to the light of the day;*

149

> *Now in the fulness of joy I can say—*
> *I'm happy, I'm happy in Jesus.*[171]

or:

> *A robe of white, a crown of gold,*
> *A harp, a home, a mansion fair,*
> *A victor's palm, a joy untold*
> *Are mine when I get there.*
> *For Jesus is my Saviour,*
> *He's washed my sins away,*
> *Died for me on Calvary's mountain;*
> *I'm happy in His wondrous love,*
> *Singing all the day.*
> *I'm living, yes, I'm living in the fountain.*[172]

The prototype, if not the actual translation, of such refrains as this are to be found in scores of languages wherever Salvationists gather. It is something of an experience to hear a great crowd in, say Berlin, singing and clapping hands in accompaniment,

> *O es ist so schön, gerettet zu sein!*
> *Es ist ein Leben voller Glück und Sonnenschein!*[173]

roughly translated, O, it is so lovely to be saved. It is a life full of joy and sunshine. Having The Salvation Army in mind, it is significant that William and Catherine Booth believed a sense of joy in God to be consistent with deep piety. They considered happiness to be an integral part of the experience of living in harmony with the will of God. They believed, too, that such joy should be freely expressed, and the methods of their Army allowed for, and encouraged such expression.

10

Catherine's puritanism has been stressed, and rightly. It was part of her direct logical way of thought. The reality of her own convictions, the pure fount of joy in God from which her soul drank, made her scornful, perhaps too scornful, of trivial or selfish pleasures. But she was certainly not a long-faced Puritan! The Booths had a sense of humour and an eye for the comical, which brought them lots of fun. William's was a buoyant nature. It was normal for him to be cheerful, often he sang about the house; laughter came to him swiftly and he could make others laugh with him. But, as often for such spirits, he was given to sudden gloom and then was inclined to exaggerate his feelings and the difficulties of the moment. Catherine knew how to change the atmosphere of his thought. Her exuberant nature could sweep him back into hopefulness and happiness. Long before her engagement she had made her code of laws to promote happiness in the home.

The first was, "never to have any secrets from my husband in anything that affected our mutual relationship, or the interests of the family".

The second rule "was never to have two purses".

"*My third* principle was that, in matters where there was any difference of opinion, I would show my husband my views and the reasons on which they were based, and try to convince him in favour of my way of looking at the subject. This generally resulted either in his being converted to my views, or my being converted to his.

"*My fourth* rule was, in cases of difference of opinion, never to argue in the presence of the children."[174] Of these resolves she said nearly forty years afterwards, "I have carried them out ever since my wedding day."

While William was preaching in Hull where, Catherine told her mother, they were "lodged in a very close part of the town", they took Friday and Saturday to rest with friends of William's Spalding days. Catherine was persuaded to stay until William fetched her back a week later. A letter to him has somehow remained intact. Reading it I can see her perched on the hedge bank, looking about her with a smile, her thoughts a mixture of love and prayer. She was very near to God in the sunshine of her joy. Here are some of the pencilled lines, "*My own sweet Husband,* Here I sit under a hedge in that beautiful lane you pointed out to me, it is one of the loveliest days old earth ever basked in, no human being is within sight or sound, all nature, vegetable and animal, seems to be exulting in existence; and your ruralizing little wife is much better in health and in a mind to enjoy all these beauties and advantages to the utmost. I have had a vegetarian breakfast, one of the most sweet and refreshing dabbles in cold water I ever had in my life and now, after a brisk walk and reading your kind letter, I feel more pleasure in writing to you than anything else under heaven (except a personal interview) could give me. Bless you my darling (I love that word) . . . I am reading Muller's* Life. It is giving me a *shaking*. Oh, what dwarfs and cowards the generality of Christians are, the Lord help us to trust in Him and Him only.

"I feel exactly at home here, and experience just that free, sweet, wholesome kind of smell which I have so long been panting for, my

* George Muller, born in Prussia 1805, came to England in 1829, was Minister in Bristol. Established his Scriptural Knowledge Institution 1834. Founded Orphanages in 1836. Died 1898.

natural spirits are in a high key this morning...My soul also rises to the great and benevolent Creator of us all and I feel stronger desires than for a long time past to be a Christian after His model, even Christ Jesus...The bells are ringing and guns firing on account of the news that Sebastopol is taken, but I should think it is a delusion...

"*Afternoon.* Got home just in time for dinner, which I relished well and now I am lying down and wishing thou wast here, thy night-cap is under my head, where I keep it airing every night, it will be quite ready by Friday...I hope thou art reading that homoeopathic book and also a little on vegetarianism."[175]

Catherine had been advised to consult a homoeopathic doctor and after her zealous fashion she enquires into the system and writes to Mrs. Mumford who was not well, "Go at once to the homoeopathic dispensary of Dr. Crowning's. I believe in it more than ever... William has given sixteen shillings for a book for me to study, on the subject...Well, experience is the best proof of efficiency of anything, and I am happy to tell you that I am very much better than when I wrote last, and have taken homoeopathic medicines every three hours and adopted the prescribed regime ever since I had the doctor and I am nearly well again."[176] A few weeks later, "The more I read on homoeopathy the more deeply am I convinced of the importance of simplicity and regularity in diet. My views are very much changed in many respects. I don't think half as highly of *meat* (animal food I mean) as I used to do. I rarely touch it more than once a day and then I don't eat as much as I used. Another thing I take very little of is coffee—the homoeopathists speak strongly against taking much of it and I believe I am much better without it at *supper*...A halfpenny worth of milk warmed, or half a pint of thin gruel for drink to your supper would be far better for you, and you would soon get used to it. I take milk every night..."[177] The homoeopathic doctor advised her not to take any laxative drug. "He said, 'Do as I advise and I will venture to say you will not need it.' He ordered me to take a little creed white wheat* to my supper with a little treacle. Tell father to get some and try it. It wants creeing in a jar in the oven fourteen or fifteen hours; it is very nice and exceedingly nourishing."[178] Catherine made a thorough study of homoeopathy, including *Hahnemann's Organon*, and practised it all the rest of her life. She became strongly opposed to the prevailing custom of giving large doses of medicine, black draught and the like, especially to children. It was during these early years of William's ministry in the North that they learned something of hydropathy. As

* A hundred years after the advice given in this letter, some of Catherine's descendants were eating creed wheat. During World War Two they were allowed a sack at a time by special permit of Lord Woolton, then Minister of Food.

a result of her opinion and experience in treating her own family, advice on health, and instruction on how to apply hydropathic treatment, was, until 1950, included in *The Salvation Army Orders and Regulations,* as also in the handbook on *The Training of Children.*

From Hull the Booths went to Sheffield. Catherine was delighted to find their host's house overlooked "splendid scenery" and that they were not to live "in the town, which for *smoke* I thought as we entered it, must rival the infernal region itself". William was "posted on the walls in monster bills". Begbie called William's Sheffield campaign "perhaps his first whirlwind triumph". And in the midst of it all Catherine told her mother, "I never was so happy before. My precious William grows every day more to my mind and heart..."[179]

Through all the letters to her mother during these months there trickled a stream of happy interest in the preparations for her child's arrival, as in this one: "... Then I want you to get enough corded muslin such as they use for baby's day gowns, to make three. A lady whose opinion I asked thinks seven yards will make three, but consult with Mrs. Brown. Then I want you to buy a nice fine long cloth for four nightgowns and give them all, both day and night gowns, to Miss Tasker to make ... I think Scotch cambric will do for frills for the nightgowns."[180]

Begbie says, "The coming of the first baby was no longer an inspiration for theological ... discourses. Catherine Booth is now concerned only with the little clothes which she commissions her mother to get made for her, issuing minutest commands in the matter of style and trimming."[181] But here Mr. Begbie altogether misunderstands Catherine. She is not "now concerned *only* with the little clothes"; being God's child she felt that all her concerns were God's too. There were no compartments in her life from which God was excluded. Her eldest son said, "her own home was never neglected for what some would call—I doubt whether she would have so described it—the larger sphere. Both alike had been opened to her by God. She saw His purposes in both. In the humble duties of the kitchen table, her hands busy with the food, or in the nursery when the children were going to bed, or at the bedside of a sick child, she was working for God's glory."[182] Certainly neither her first baby, nor any of the seven that followed him, engrossed her to the exclusion of thought about God and His Kingdom on earth; rather the responsibility of the children increased her need for God's help. The very letters that contained the instructions to which Begbie refers, told too of the meetings, of William's sermons and of her own aspirations.

While they were in Sheffield William's mother came to visit them. Catherine writing to her parents said, "I anticipated seeing my new mother with much pleasure and some anxiety, but on our first interview the latter vanished and I felt that I could both admire and love her. She is a very nice-looking old lady . . . We have all. been out riding in Mr. Firth's phaeton this morning, a splendid ride . . . I am very very happy . . ."[183] And again, *"My very dear Parents,* I am at home alone this evening having had rather a fatiguing day yesterday . . . We had a mighty day at the chapel [Sunday] a tremendous crowd jammed together like sheep in a pen, one of the mightiest sermons at night I ever listened to . . . The chapel continued crowded during the prayer meeting and before half past ten o'clock seventy-six names were taken. All glory to God. My dearest Wm. has been very prostrate today but he is preaching tonight. They had collections to defray the incidental expenses of the services yesterday. They got £25—far beyond anybody's expectations. The farewell sermon is to be on Wednesday night when he will finish up five weeks' services preaching twice on Sunday and four nights per week in the same chapel."[184]

And two days later, *"My precious mother* . . . I am sorry you were disappointed of a letter . . . it sometimes happens so that I cannot help it . . . Don't imagine that because I am happy in my husband and have so many things to take my attention that I think or care less about you. I don't think I ever loved or *valued* you so much and I am sure I never longed to see you more . . . Now don't worrit."[185]

As the end of the Sheffield campaign drew near, they planned for a few days' rest. Rooms were taken at a lodge of Chatsworth Park and Catherine's first letter from there explained the situation. "I am sorry it is too late to post this today, but we did not come yesterday according to arrangement, in consequence of my being taken very ill in the morning. I was but poorly when I got up, but went out with Wm. to get a few things and was taken very sick, was sick three times in the public street! And about a dozen times during the day, which I spent in bed. My dearest Love was very anxious as to the cause and went to Mr. Smith, my homoeopathic doctor, he said it was a bilious attack and sent directions for my infinitesimal doses which were to relieve me in two hours. I was only sick once after taking the first dose and was sufficiently restored to come here by the half past nine o'clock coach this morning . . . When Wm. asked Mr. S. for his bill, he told him that he had served him quite as much as he (Dr. Smith) had served us, by coming to Sheffield to do good and that he should charge us nothing . . .

"I thought and talked much of you on the journey here, as I rode over those Derbyshire hills and witnessed its wild and romantic scenery. It is a splendid spot where we are located, right inside the park, where we can see the deer gambolling. I feel a peculiar interest in the scenes around, doubtless owing to its being my native county . . . It has been raining ever since we came, but we have sunshine inside." The P.S. in William's hand runs, "Bless you. We have had some first-rate tea—cream and butter."[186] Next day—Sunday—*"My very dear Mother* ... my dear Wm. has gone to the Reform Chapel not far off. We went to the village church this morning, there being no service elsewhere. It was a dry affair but we worshipped God ... This afternoon we walked through the park right up to the Duke of Devonshire's residence. It is one of the most splendid spots I ever was in, it is all hill and dale, beautifully wooded ... This first day has been a very happy one indeed. I could not tell you *how* happy we both are, notwithstanding my delicate health and our constant migrations, we do indeed find our earthly heaven in each other ... I am having a new velvet bonnet made, a green one, for best, but am having it *plain and neat* and in these matters we are both determined to be more circumspect."[187]

They had only one week, and the weather was a trial. "... Monday, Tuesday and Wednesday were wet and boisterous in the extreme so that we were glad to keep close by our fireside and found enough to do to keep warm there. Yesterday, Thursday, was a splendid, fine frosty day of which we took due advantage, and directly after breakfast started for a walk of four miles to see the rocks of Middleton Dale. The scenery all the way was enchanting. I could scarce get along for stopping to admire and exclaim; the dark frowning cliffs on the one hand, the splendid autumnal tints of rich foliage on the other, and the ever-varying views of hill and dale before us, all as it were, tinged with glory from a radiant sky, filled us with unutterable emotions of admiration, exhilaration and joy ... I wish I could describe the wild grandeur of the place, but I have neither time nor ability. We walked about half a mile up by the dale and then I rested and got a little refreshment at a very ancient and comical kind of inn while Wm. walked half a mile further, during which time I had a very cosy and amusing chat in rich Derbyshire brogue, with an old chap over his pipe and mug of ale ...

"This morning we were just preparing to visit Chatsworth House and to explore a part of the park we had not seen, when to our surprise Mr. Fenton and Mr. Mark Firth (brother of the gentleman named in my last) came to the door. They and Mrs. F. had driven over in their phaeton to spend the day with us, so we set off to climb some tremendous hills in order to reach a tower built on the highest part of the park grounds. I got about half-way up and then my physical strength failed me and I begged to be allowed to sit down and wait while the rest of the party completed the ascent. After much persuasion I carried my point and was left alone, sitting on a stone, my eyes resting on one of the loveliest scenes I ever expect to witness in this world. I enjoyed my meditation exceedingly. I was on an elevation about as high as St. Paul's with a waterfall on one side of me and the most romantic scenery you can imagine above and below. The old Duke ought to be a happy man if worldly possessions can give felicity ... Sir Joseph Paxton's* residence is between the lodge and the Duke's residence. It is a fine building, quite a gentleman's seat, and it is only eighteen years since he came here on an equal footing with the man who keeps the lodge where we are staying, and who still works as a plodding gardener. They both came on to the estate together at equal wages which were very low, and now one is Sir Joseph, known all over the world, and the other is the keeper of the lodge still ... Well, we enjoyed our morning's ramble very much and then went with Mr. F. to dine at the head inn in the village, and to such a dinner I never sat down before, nor would I wish often. First we had trout, second fowl, third grouse and mushroom sauce, fourth plum and cranberry pie, and Bakewell pudding, etc., rich in the extreme, fifth cheese ... I would not like to fare sumptuously every day! I did wish father had a bit of the trout and mother a bit of the fowl which was splendidly cooked ... We have to pack this evening and are going to Sheffield by the half past eight coach in the morning, and from Sheffield to Dewsbury by the two o'clock train."[188]

Soon after arriving in Dewsbury Catherine fell ill, rather seriously, with congestion of the lungs. She ascribed her rapid recovery to following homoeopathic remedies and to William's devotion. I admire his courage in treating Catherine by the new fangled methods. No doubt he faced a good deal of solemn head-shaking when he refused well-meant advice. To her parents Catherine wrote: "There is no nurse like a mother, however kind, except a *husband* ... You will readily conceive that being ill in another person's home and here only for *a time* has been a cause of much anxiety to my apprehensive heart, but amidst all my fears I have not forgotten how many things I have to be grateful for. In the first place it is a great mercy it did not happen just when we were wanting to leave for Leeds. Secondly the constant presence and care of my dear William has been an unspeakable blessing. Thirdly the superiority of homoeopathic treatment, by which I have been spared the misery of blisters, purgatives and nauseous doses, and the tedious weeks of convalescence attendant on them, fourthly the kind and hospitable entertainment I have received from Mrs. Ward, she has been very kind. As to my dearest Love, I can only say that he has so far exceeded all calculations in patience, watchfulness and sympathy that I shall never fear any future emergency ..."[189] And in a later letter, "... I am very thankful to be once more downstairs. Depend upon it I shall be careful, for I fear this attack will leave me very susceptible of cold for the winter; and a constant change of houses, rooms, etc., is not very congenial; ... I am making some little ducky shirts. I wish you could see one.

* Sir Joseph Paxton (1801-1865), gardener and architect. Designed the Crystal Palace for the Great Exhibition 1851.

Oh, how many times I do long for my dearest Mother . . . If we don't meet before March [when the baby is expected] what a deal we shall have to tell each other . . . What does my dear Father say to sparing you for three weeks or a month? How will he manage? But I do hope he will make up his mind to it and try what he can do, for Wm. says there is nobody else in the world *capable* of taking care of me but my Mother and himself, and he thinks it will take *both of them*. Bless him, we get happier in each other every day . . ."[190]

Letters to her parents give us the thoughts of the moment, caught on paper, and preserved there. They tell a great deal about the writer and show her growing joy in William and his work. See this extract: ". . . The work here is progressing gloriously, though we found a people *frozen* and formal and quite unprepared and although several of the nobs stand aloof at present (if they don't actually ridicule the work) the excitement is taking hold of the town and sinners are being converted every night. Yesterday was a precious day. The chapel was full in the morning and by night . . . at five past six o'clock [Sunday night] William had to request the friends to lock the gates in order to prevent any more from crushing in . . . I never heard him preach with such liberty and power . . . I often wish you could see how happy we are, and how much I have to be thankful for . . . I hope you find no difficulty about the things I sent directions for in my last. Buy the corded muslin *good*. I am getting on but slowly with my work. I have a very nice loose jacket made out of the old one, which I am wearing in the house. It is like one Mrs. Firth of Sheffield wore; both William and I like it much. I have made a skirt of Scotch woollen plaid to wear with it which looks very nice. You will remember these plaids are favourites with William, he often tells me how beautiful I look and says he wishes you could see me . . ."[191]

As to a home of their own, "We have quite given up the idea of having one; even after I have a baby, we intend to travel together and carry it with us and take apartments with attendance in every place. This is one thing which has made me so much happier of late, the dark cloud of separation which has always hung over the future having been dissipated. It was at Caister the idea first struck us and we were not long in deciding it."[192] Catherine was well enough to attend one of William's services and wrote, "The crowds for the last Sunday's meetings at Dewsbury could not be accommodated even in the Wesleyan Chapel seating two thousand, lent for the occasion. The doors closed on hundreds outside. On Sunday night they did not leave the chapel till quarter past eleven . . ." Of the tea meeting on Monday, "I did wish you could have heard William's speech, it was a 'stunner', a regular out and out one. I ventured there, enveloped in a mountain of clothes, and feel no worse for it except it be worse to feel a little prouder of my husband, which I certainly do."[193]

William's campaign in Leeds began the day after their arrival and lasted eight weeks. They were met at the station and driven, Catherine told her parents, "in a cab to our host's ... we have a nice bedroom with a four-post bed of gigantic dimensions—quite a luxury to my beloved after sleeping in fashionable beds with footboards ... Altogether we are really snug and at home."[194]

And, oh joy, *the house was warm*. Another letter home gives a picture of William among his converts that shows his friendliness toward them and how quick he was to ignore conventions; shows, too, their enthusiasm for him. "Between twenty and thirty of the young converts came from Dewsbury to spend the day at the chapel. They had walked a distance of eight miles that bitter morning. They beset us like a swarm of bees as we were leaving the chapel. We went into the vestry with them [I seem to see the excited group, all eyes on Booth as they crowd in] William started one of his favourite hymns and they sang like larks."[195] Catherine found it very affecting.

A later letter is more about baby clothes than anything. She wants "work" (embroidery) for one of the muslin gowns, "let it be good and handsome", and the paragraph closes with, "I am having some fun with William as I am writing. He is talking about the money, and I am telling him if he will have babies he must provide for them."[196] She and William have their fun, and laugh together. They were both quick to see the humorous side of things, and Catherine enjoyed the rarer delightful capacity of being able to laugh at herself. I see in a letter of this time to her parents, "I am glad you find some satisfaction and amusement in thinking and talking about us, be assured if you picture us and sometimes laugh at the remembrance of past scenes and sayings, we as often do so in reference to you. William often says 'Your Mother would say so and so', and then we laugh and wish we could see you. William has got lots of funny things to tell you, he is hoarding up lots of tales about me and my doings to be made the topics of future conversation and a bit of fun."[197]

Of Christmas Day Catherine wrote, "... William had three sermons, and was full of anxiety and discouragement. Nevertheless, it was not an unhappy day by any means. No, thank God, I know nothing of *real* unhappiness now, underneath all temporary and surface trials there is a deep calm flow of satisfaction and comfort ... The friends begin to manifest a strong affection as usual!"[198] And three days later, "I am glad you thought about us on Watch Night. It was a fine night here, and I spent the afternoon at one of the friends and went with them to the chapel ... I cannot tell you the nature of my feelings on again mingling with the great congregation on such an occasion and under such new, interesting and happy circumstances. It was a thrilling hour to my soul. You know what an enthusiastic excitable nature mine is, and can easily imagine the rush of emotion

I should experience at such a season, while meditating on the past, rejoicing in the present, and anticipating the future . . ."[199] On New Year's Day they went to breakfast with a friend who had a fortune and a beautiful house. The next day William went for a private talk "with him about his soul, and we think he is sure to be brought in". Ten days afterwards "the finish at Hunslet was grand. Three hundred names were taken in all. The gentleman I mentioned in my last two letters gave in his name on the last night, making glad the heart of a devoted wife, who had been praying for him for a long time."[200] This is an example of the interest Catherine and William took in *individuals* who came to their services. They prayed for, spoke to and planned how to get into contact with individuals. It was characteristic of them both and formed a pattern for Salvation Army officers, especially in the early years of the Army.

The campaign on the other side of Leeds started well; people came over from Hunslet, wrote Catherine, "night after night with as much eagerness as strangers, though they have been hearing him now almost eight weeks. Some of them almost idolize him, so great is their love toward him, but amidst it all he is kept humble . . . I only attended once on Sunday, in the morning, and returned home with a full heart. William was so poorly and yet exerted himself so much that I could scarce bear it . . . However I am thankful to say he is going to rest a week prior to going to Halifax. It will be *thirteen* weeks on Saturday since we left Chatsworth and he has had no rest since."[201] Through all their time together Catherine found her fear for William's health a fierce assault upon her faith. She never seems to have worried seriously lest her own strength should fail; but where those she loved were concerned her anxiety was acute.

William took a hand in a letter Catherine wrote during their few days rest, ". . . The finish up at Leeds was glorious, triumphant! My precious William excelled himself, and *electrified* the people. You would indeed have participated in my joy and pride could you have seen and heard what I did. (W.B.) I have just come into the room where my dear little wife is writing this precious document, and snatching the paper have read the above eulogistic sentiments. I just want to say that the very same night when snug and cosy in a certain place she gave me a curtain lecture on my 'block-headism' stupidity, etc., and lo! she writes unto you after this fashion. However, she is a *precious*, increasingly a precious treasure to me with all her eccentricities and oddities. (C.B.) I have had a scuffle over the above, but I must let it come for I have not time to write another having an engagement at two o'clock and it is now near one and I have to dine, but I must say in self-defence that it was not about the speech or anything *important* that the said curtain lecture was given, but only on a point which [in] no way invalidates my eulogies. We came here on Saturday where we are treated in the most kind and hospitable manner and where I hope William's strength will get recruited. We go to Halifax on Saturday ..." William closes with, "Kate has not time to write more this time so I must conclude for her and put it into the post. I hope you are both better. Kate keeps up delightfully all things considered and is better looking than ever she was in her life. Farewell. Believe us, dear Parents to remain Your affectionate son and daughter William and Catherine."[202]

11

On Saturday, February 9, 1856, after a week's rest, Catherine and William arrived in Halifax. William's services, planned to last four weeks, were to be held, Catherine tells, in "a very nice chapel, the largest in the circuit". Its minister, the Rev. J. Stacey, reports at the close of the mission that 640 names were taken, and of those nearly 400 became members of his church. The membership of other chapels was also increased. Catherine is predisposed to be happy in Halifax. No sooner arrived "all safe and comfortable", than she unknowingly draws us, all these years afterwards, into her family affairs by writing to her parents, "I wish you could just peep in and see us. We are for the first time in a home of our own, with a servant of our own engaging. I feel so happy and at liberty, you cannot think ... While we stay here we have the house to ourselves. It is nearly a new house, *very nicely* fitted up with gas and every convenience in a beautiful and healthy locality. They proposed providing us a servant, but I objected to have a girl of whom I knew nothing, and so William wrote to say we would bring a domestic with us. She is an elderly woman ... who goes out as a monthly nurse ... if you knew her and knew as much about her as I do, you would feel rejoiced that I have such a person with me. She bears a first-rate character as a religious, kind, industrious, clever body ... we have engaged her for five weeks at a guinea a month. If she nurses me her terms are two guineas ... I should not mind if it happened here. I feel so comfortable in a home to myself ... I like Halifax ... It looks so clean and clear."[203] Across the years my heart warms to the "kind, industrious, clever body". How different Catherine's story would have been without the help of such women.

Another letter home tells: "... I should like you to send the parcel as soon as you can now, as I want to get everything ready ... Send the rose ointment you made for me, and the marking ink out of William's dressing case; also the small soft brush out of his case. If I think of anything else between now and Wednesday, I will write again. Pay the carriage and put it down to our account."[204] The recipe

160

Mother of The Salvation Army

Katie, "La Maréchale",
on her departure for France in 1881

Bramwell as Chief of Staff in 1882,
the year of his marriage

for the rose ointment Mrs. Mumford made for Catherine has vanished for ever; so has the first part of a letter of which a stray page numbered "five" somehow survived. I like the picture it gives of Catherine and her thoughts: "I possess every comfort and am as happy as the day is long. Nurse has been washing my little shirts and things today. I felt strangely as I saw the [clothes] horse. Oh, it seems scarcely possible that I am about to fulfil a relationship which I have always regarded as so sacred and responsible. Surely I shall have the needful wisdom and grace vouchsafed to me? . . . I am better today than I have been for two or three days . . . We have been a beautiful walk this morning without going up hills and in the summer it must be very picturesque and beautiful, but I suppose summer will find me far away somewhere else. Well, I can bear this incessant change outside, while all within is satisfaction and contentment."[205]

Catherine's letters, especially since Christmas, show that she longs that her mother should come to her for the babe's birth. They had not met since August, and letters were their only means of communication. Quick to sense her mother's reluctance and to reassure her, Catherine stifles her own disappointment as she writes, "I am sorry you should still be perplexed about coming. Be assured that I enter fully into the circumstances of the case, and though I do feel disappointed I do not for a moment think you should act differently. It is not as though I had no one with me, or lacked for anything necessary . . . I am happy to say I continue as well as can be expected. I cannot but feel some anxiety lest I should break-down before we leave here, which would involve great inconvenience, as the Chester people [William was to preach there next] will have the advertisements and bills out . . . We have been thinking of nurse and me going on first, on Tuesday. It would be safer, but Wm. seems to prefer going with me . . . we shall get off early on Thursday. I suppose we have to change stations and wait an hour on the road . . . One of us will write again before we go and as soon as we get there, so don't be anxious. You may feel very comfortable about nurse. She is one in a thousand. I feel the fullest confidence in her, and in several respects she will be a special comfort to me. I believe her to be a real Christian, and she feels a deep interest in this work and consequently sympathizes with my dear Wm. in his toil [this of course endears her to Catherine!] and will take care of his comfort when I am laid by. This will be a great comfort to me . . . Be of good cheer. I trust the Lord will bring me safe through."[206]

It was on March 7, 1856, that William's little wife sat scribbling away to her parents of arrangements for the move to Chester. She had seen the little shirts hanging before the fire, felt "happy as the day is long"; but tomorrow she would be happier still, for on the evening of March 8, 1856, Catherine's first child was born. As soon as she was able his mother held him in her arms while his father prayed,

F

and together they dedicated their son to God, especially desiring that he should become a preacher of holiness. In this hope he was named William Bramwell. In a pencilled scrap to Mrs. Mumford Catherine said, "Now I know what it is to be a mother, and I feel I never loved you half as well as I ought to have done. Forgive all my short-comings . . . My precious babe is a beauty."[207]

That "home to ourselves", the first they had known, lasted just long enough to be their son's birthplace. William's visit to Chester was post-poned and the family remained in Halifax until he was due in Macclesfield. Here there was much excitement. Crowds, Catherine said, were more than she had yet seen. Women from the silk factories, who attended the meetings with their shawls over their heads, "were specially kind to me and the baby. Sometimes they would come in troops and sing in front of my window."[208] It was in Macclesfield that the baby was baptized by his father, being one of over thirty infants in the ceremony. This was arranged in case a separate service should imply that the evangelist's child was in any way "special".

From Yarmouth, where the Booths went after Macclesfield, Mrs. Mumford got a letter telling her, "Your little darling is growing like a willow . . . we have bought him a doll which pleases him vastly. He laughs and talks to it in great style!"[209] No doubt of it, the little mother is in love with her baby. The east coast is bracing and the landscape restful; and *there is the sea*! To Catherine (from the vantage of dry land) the sea was ever entrancing. "The great and beautiful sea," she called it, and ". . . the ocean that enchanter of all my soul!" All too soon she found herself in the "smoke" of Sheffield, where a year before William had had such a great work. On this second visit 645 names were taken during the six weeks of his meet-ings. From there Catherine wrote, ". . . it is a cause of great rejoicing to us to find such numbers who turned to the Lord when we were in Sheffield before . . ."[210] Of the Farewell "I never saw an assembly so completely enthralled and enchanted as this one was while my beloved was speaking. He spoke for near two hours never for one moment losing the most perfect control . . . over the audience." William was presented with a lithograph portrait and of this Catherine wrote, "I like it much although I do not think it flatters my beloved in the least."[211] There was good news of converts elsewhere too. In some chapels, they had been "received into fellowship" by hundreds. Catherine wishes they could be better looked after; her mothering instinct deplored "the heartless manner in which the preachers let the work down after we are gone. Oh, for a church of earnest, con-sistent, soul-saving men!" Of meetings in Birmingham, where they went next, the minister of the chapel wrote of the whole place being packed, and hundreds left outside, of the preaching "earnest, terrible, melting", and that this went on for nearly six weeks. "And oh, what scenes have we beheld! Penitent sinners have come up the aisle so overcome with emotion as to be hardly able to reach the rail. Fathers and sons, mothers and daughters, have knelt side by side at the communion rail ... What a glorious sight this was, such as I had never seen before."[212]

From Birmingham to Nottingham, where Grandmother Booth took her son's firstborn in her arms. "This handsome woman," Begbie called her; "a sombre, sad, silent, tragic figure." A friend of one of William's sisters described her as a "tall, proud woman, very proud and austere". Surely the proud old heart must have quickened in its beat with joy at her son's triumph? After all, he was only twenty-seven, and all Nottingham was astir with his name: the Mayor and his family attended the services. And here was William's lovely little son laughing into her eyes. I think we may be certain that the period of William's preaching in his native place was a time of great happiness for William's mother. Of the meetings Catherine wrote to Mrs. Mumford, "Yesterday the chapel . . . [seating 1,200] was so packed that all the windows and doors had to be set wide open [and this in December] ... The Mayor and Mayoress, with a family of fine young men, are regular attendants and stayed to the prayer meeting the other night."[213] One of the stewards wrote, "The services were kept up with thrilling interest night after night." In these six weeks 740 persons came forward giving their names and addresses. From Nottingham the three happy people came to the Mumford home in London. Arriving on Saturday, both William and Catherine, with characteristic energy, went on Sunday to hear Spurgeon.* William records in his diary, "A truly simple, faithful and earnest sermon. I doubt not that he is doing a very great work."[214] They had a fortnight with Catherine's parents, and then William went off to Chester for that postponed visit. Catherine and the baby, now ten months old, remained in London.

In this book we see William for the most part through Catherine's eyes, but sometimes a sentence from one of his letters is illuminating, showing the child-like heart of the man with its surface fluctuations of feeling and beneath the rock-like obstinacy of purpose which dominated his whole being "to live for Christ on earth" and "do something for this perishing world". I judge he wrote to her every day while he was in Chester, but I find none of Catherine's letters to him. The fantastic success of his preaching in Nottingham had already faded from his mind when he wrote, "I have not been in very good spirits today. I have been looking at the dark side of myself. In fact, I can find no other side. I seem to be all dark, mentally, physically and spiritually. The Lord have mercy on me! I feel I am

* Rev. Charles Haddon Spurgeon (1834-1892), popular Baptist minister. The Tabernacle in South-East London (destroyed by German bombs) was built for him.

indeed so thoroughly unworthy the notice of either God or man. My preaching is more than ever, or even as much as ever, at a discount in my own estimation. Continue to love me. Aye, let us love as God would have us love one another ... Let us be one. I am quite sure that we do now realize far more of this blissful union, this *oneness*, than very many around. I meet with but ... very few who realize as much domestic and conjugal felicity. And yet there are many things in me that want mending. God help me ...".[215] or, *"My dearest, my darling, my own Love* ... how lost and lonesome I am without you. Life loses half, nay all its charms! ... I am oppressed with the thought and feeling of my unworthiness of the devotion you manifest for me." Again, "I am glad little Sunshine is better. I am anxious to hear more about him. He is a joy to me. I often bless God for bestowing such a treasure upon us. Let us regard him as a loan from heaven."[216] And in the same vein, "How is baby? ... Oh Kate ours is a solemn and important vocation, the training of that boy. I often think about him and imagine him lifting up his little arms to me ... May God bless you with every earthly and heavenly blessing and shelter you under His spreading wings from all evil! So most devoutly prays the father of your darling boy, and the beloved of your soul ... I love you. And the love I bear you and my sweet little son is a constant joy to me."[217] In another strain he wrote of indisposition: "If it does not get better I shall go to the homoeopathic doctor. Chester is either blessed or cursed with three of them. But as *you* deem it a blessing I am fain in this, as in many other respects, to pin my faith to your sleeve, and with me there the controversy ends! So I throw up my cap and shout 'Hurrah for homoeopathy!' with its infinite quantity of infinitesimal doses, in whatever society I may be where the question is mooted. All because I have such a blessed little *wife*, in whose judgment I can confide ..."[218]

On William's return from Chester they set forth together once more, this time to Bristol whence, after three weeks of preaching, they went on to Truro and St. Agnes in Cornwall. They travelled by train to Plymouth and from there, for lack of rail, by road. Kindliness made room for Catherine inside the already full coach. In three months her second child would be born, and on this journey she was too poorly to hold the baby who, with his nurse, that same "kind, industrious, clever body" and his father, travelled outside in torrents of rain. Water dripping from the nurse's bonnet strings dyed the baby's face blue. Catherine wrote home of the journey, "Babs seems to have stood it the best of any of us. Bless him! He was as good as a little angel ... He has just accomplished the feat of saying 'Papa'. It is his first intelligible word."[219] At first the Cornish people were unresponsive. Then came a break. Catherine said, "It was Good Friday, April 10, the anniversary of our engagement ... we found ourselves in a perfect hurricane of excitement." To the Mumfords the next day William wrote, "It was a glorious stir last night . . . I am happy but weary. I have had nine public services this week; have to attend a meeting tonight and have three more tomorrow."[220]

From Cornwall, Catherine, baby Bramwell and the luggage followed William to Stafford, where his next campaign was to be held. He had gone on ahead to make preparations for her arrival; Ballington, her second son, was born five weeks later. Of the journey she told her mother, "We arrived safely here at about half-past twelve last night after one of the most harassing and fatiguing journeys I ever experienced. In consequence of it being Whit Saturday there were great numbers travelling, and great confusion amongst the trains; we had once to change stations and three or four times carriages and having all the luggage to see to you may imagine what it was, I felt ready to lay down on the road by [the time] we got to Wolverhampton within 20 miles of the end of our journey. In this state of feeling you can imagine how I felt when informed that we were too late for the train to Stafford and must wait three and a half hours for the next. I did not know what to do. However I resolved to bear it as patiently as I could, so first of all dispatching a telegram message to Wm. informing him of the cause of our non-appearance and telling him to meet us at the next train, we got a cup of tea and some refreshments. I packed myself up with rugs and lay down in one corner of the waiting-room. Willie [now fifteen months] ran about the room like a little kitten until ten o'clock and then went to sleep, Eliza nursing him with great tenderness and self-forgetfulness although very much knocked up. At quarter past eleven o'clock we set off for Stafford. We had not gone two miles before we had to change carriages again heaving all the luggage out in the dark, etc.! However through mercy we got here at last."[221] And on Whit Sunday William opened his campaign.

Conference, meeting in Nottingham early in June, 1857, by a vote of forty to forty-four against, unexpectedly terminated William's work as travelling evangelist and appointed him to Brighouse. Letters from friends who were present make it clear that there was determined opposition to Booth on the part of some of the leading ministers. Begbie says, "many felt that he was too young for such perpetual prominence; others were unquestionably jealous of his powers."[222] To Catherine the attitude of Conference came as a shock. "I have felt it far more keenly than I thought I should," she told her mother. What hurt her was "the manner in which our mission has been put down". Most of all she grieved at the resulting curtailment of soul-saving. Writing home: "Great interests are involved, far more than are seen at first sight but it is God's cause. I believe He will order all for the best. I have no fears for the future. I have confidence in my husband's devotion and capacity for something greater yet."[223] When the decision came she was in bed rather ill and while lying there alone she was given what was for her a rare, illuminating moment which was to be remembered by her all her life. Toward the end of it, she said, "That morning as I lay in bed, for I was too ill to leave the room, there dawned upon me a vision of success, which has been marvellously realized in later years. And I could have risen from my couch, bid good-bye to the Connexion, and walked out with my husband into the wide world without a fear."[224]

The house in Brighouse was in what Catherine called a close part of the "low smoky town", and was larger than she had expected. It was quite a task to get all cleaned up and arranged as she wished "before it happens". Her parents were told "... it is very nice to be in a home of one's own and I think we shall be very happy and useful in the Circuit tho' I shall never alter my opinion with reference to the spirit and motives which brought us here yet I do recognize the hand of God in it and am determined to reap the advantages it offers ... My precious husband is kinder and more thoughtful for my comfort than ever, he seems willing to go to the utmost of his income rather than let me do more than I am equal to. He says it seems very sweet to him to have a home with me as its *mistress*. He had a society meeting last night. He told the leader that his wife would commence a class and a maternal meeting as soon as she got out again. So you see I am in for it! You need pray that I may be fitted for such undertaking. Alas, I feel how much I come short of that inner life which alone can qualify for such work ... Willie [Bramwell] is quite well, and is joy and sunshine in our dwelling. I wish you could see him just now; he looks beautiful in his white frock ... I wish you could come and take tea with me in my new home. I would make you a 'right good cup'."[225]

12

The marriage of Catherine and William brought joys to each that did not wane. They became engulfed in work for others but in a curiously intimate way their love for the work enriched their love for each other and their love for one another added a glow to all their doings. The eagerness of young lovers to share everything is not uncommon, but these two went on being interested in each other's doings and wanting to know "your secret heart", as Catherine so often put it, until death parted them. But her pre-marriage resolve that they should have no secrets from one another would not have held good, as Stead wrote, "if the married pair did not take sufficient interest in each other ... it is no use trying to share secrets, if the other one feels bored by their communications. Sympathy is the key to secrets. . . . If Mrs. Booth told her husband everything, it is because he was interested in everything, and vice versa."[226] To them their betrothal meant that they were to be "henceforth *one*". When, except for the joy of seeing souls brought to Christ, all was discouraging; when the attitude of fellow-religionists was even hostile; this sense of their unity was balm. It made them feel equal to anything. It was a miracle all their own. Some time after their marriage William wrote, "*Let us be one* . . . few think and love and hate and admire and desire alike to the same extent that we do . . . How strange is the feeling that binds us together, and makes us single each other out from the wide, wide world and make our hearts fly to each other like two magnets."[227] Near the close of her life Catherine said, "From the moment of our engagement we had become one; and from that hour to this, I don't think there has ever been any question of importance concerning either principles or practice in which we have not acted in perfect harmony."[228] "Perfect harmony," but this did not mean mere acquiescence of one or the other on matters of opinion. The vigour of their love gave them freedom to argue a point. Catherine and William never bored each other. Their love touched life's trifles making them into things that mattered. Thirty years after their marriage William wrote from America, ". . . send me love-letters . . . Tell me about yourself. To know what you wear and eat and how you go out, indeed, anything about *yourself*, your dear self . . . You must go on thinking about me; I reckon on this."[229]

When Begbie was preparing to write the Life of William Booth he visited Miss Jane Short and spent some time talking to her. He says of her that her "memory is as perfect as the most exacting biographer could wish". This lady was helped spiritually through Catherine's preaching and their acquaintance rapidly grew to friendship. For a while she lived in the Booth home and gave a vivid account of their doings. Miss Jane Short said of William, "His love for his wife was the most beautiful thing I have ever known. It really was an exquisite thing . . . The least noise on some occasions would almost distract her. [This after a long and grave illness.] Well, it was at such times as these that the love of the General shone out most beautifully. Never once did he say a harsh word, never once did he try rallying her with rough encouragement; no, he would be more courteous and chivalrous than ever; he would make love to her as tenderly and sweetly as if she were his sweetheart; and he would wait upon her, soothe her, and nurse her with a devotion that I have never seen equalled . . . his love for his wife, well, that was quite perfect; and when I look back now I can see very clearly that it was this wonderful and beautiful love for Mrs. Booth which made the greatest impression on my mind. I may forget many other things about them, but I shall never forget the General's love for his wife."[230]

Bramwell wrote of his mother and father "... in my boyhood I have sometimes known her exceedingly harassed by the cares of a house full of children ... and by her own bodily weakness. I have seen him come into the house, put his hat down in the hall and, entering the room, find it all out in a moment. Taking her hand, he would say, 'Kate, let me pray with you', and he would turn us out while they knelt together. Then a little while after it was evident that the skies were blue again. Although he was at times irascible, and when displeased had great liberty of speech, I never heard him in all those long years, many of them years of intense strain upon them both, with all the demands which poverty and sickness make upon patience and kindness in the home, *say one harsh word to her*. There were times when he would arrive at the house like a hurricane, blowing, as it were, the children right and left ... but to her he would be like a lover of twenty come to visit his girl!"[231] The burden and the glory of loving William was Catherine's portion from the day they met till the day they parted. Griefs were keener and delights deeper because of William. News of any kind was estimated from its probable effect upon William. Catherine could not only keep up with him but even anticipate his reactions. She had the capacity to enter into his plans in such a manner that he always found her in the mood to listen. She wrote to her mother in the early years of her marriage, "William ... I see the constant need he has for my presence, care and sympathy." He said when she died, "she was to me never failing sympathy. On no single question of any importance have we ever acted independently of each other's view."

It is impossible to separate their love for each other from their love to God. Before they met both were possessed by it and by the longing to be doing something "to save this poor world". The Salvation Army grew out of that attitude of heart. They were ready to sacrifice *everything* for *the work's sake* and their dedication to it infused a heaven-like quality into their earthly relationship. If Catherine had a triumph in some great preaching effort, William would clasp her in his arms on meeting, with "Darling, you were magnificent" or its equivalent. His emotions at such moments warmed his whole being and made him feel how precious she was. But he felt also an impulse to praise God! It was just the same the other way round. Catherine never loved her William better than when he was pleading with sinners. In her first love-letter she had said, "The nearer our assimilation to Jesus the more perfect and heavenly our union", and in an early letter of William's he said, "Let us love Him better for the love we bear each other." They felt like this to the end of earthly life. God and man, sin and sorrow, death and judgment were part of life itself; but *that* did not make life sombre, on the contrary, the joy that sprang from loving God and loving souls was often so intense

168

that it was akin to ecstasy. It brought a deep flow of joy that could not be quelled by sacrifice or grief. There were certainly griefs, what Paul called the care of the churches was sometimes crushing, but the burden and the glory fed their love for God and for one another. The habit of telling "all my heart" prevailed, and came to include what concerned their work. News of some success such as a gift of money for the funds, the acquisition of a property, good "cases" at the penitent-form in their meetings were personal joys. True, these were shared with those about them but that did not lessen the happiness William and Catherine felt. Their delight was keener because over and above the thing itself was the joy of seeing one another's joy. And sharing sorrow was as real. Building The Salvation Army cost them many tears! While they lived they comforted each other with exquisite tenderness. In middle life as in youth their love was a shelter always within reach and when Catherine came to dying it was still true for them both that "we do indeed find our earthly heaven in each other".

When in 1886 William was touring Canada and the U.S.A. Catherine wrote, "I cannot tell you how much I want to talk to you about so many things . . ." During this visit across the Atlantic William wrote letters full of details of the work, of the opportunity for extension, of his impression of candidates for officership, and for her encouragement. "Mr. G. my host, said last night . . . that you were the most eloquent speaker he had ever listened to . . ."[232] Catherine in turn wrote of her delight at the success of his meetings and tells of her own, as from Castleford: "I have had a grand time here—they are a dear lot of soldiers . . ." The same letter tells of their own children, and their Salvation Army work, of slanderous attacks necessitating "a letter to *The Times* . . ." on, and on, flies her pen, "you need make no apologies either as to the number or character of your letters; in the former you have exceeded my *hopes,* and as to the latter, you are no *judge.* I think they are beautiful." Campaigning in the North she finds that in some places "we are getting quite chapelly . . . This packing takes up so much time, so I write you generally in a hurry . . . I think of you continually and wish, oh, so much! But wishing is fruitless work. I must save up all till you return . . . If I am able, after a fortnight at home, another tour will be best for the Army."[233]

What is best for the Army is the dominating factor in both their lives, but there are words from lover to lover in the letters full of Army matters as these sentences from William while on his American campaigns: ". . . I must scribble a few lines to my beloved. My thoughts have been with you through the night. When I awake I can safely say my heart comes over to you, and I embrace you in my arms and clasp you to my heart and bless you with my lips and pray God to keep you from *all* harm and bring me safely to meet you again on earth. The time is flying. The third week has passed

169

since I gave you that hurried farewell..."[234] In reply Catherine said, "It is over five weeks since you left us...I got home from my last tour and saw your clothes hanging up, I felt *awful*. I thought what it must be when the occupant is gone for ever—at least for time! *I long for you daily*..."[235] And from William, "I am sure my heart feels just the same as when I wrote to you from Lincolnshire or came rushing up Brixton Road to hold you in my arms and embrace you with my young love."[236] That was thirty years ago and Catherine we find has not changed her mind about letter-writing! "...You can't realize the sense of *danger* I feel about you in so much travelling, etc., and the thoughts of the voyage home already jump on me in the night...This hateful writing one can't express what one wants."[237] William wrote, "I long for your smile and voice, and to lay my head on your bosom once more. I am just the same, your husband, lover, friend, as in the earliest days. My heart can know no change."[238]

Their eldest son Bramwell knew and loved them both better than any other being. He wrote of their love to each other: "...That love became a kind of element remote from the world, purer than the common air, in which they acted and re-acted on one another to the comfort and joy of both. She brought to him, and ever rendered to him, the utmost tenderness of a woman completely yielded to the man of her choice. The bonds between them were continually strengthened over that long stretch of years by the loving surrender of each to the other. They both saw, she especially, that the real value of true love is not merely that it sanctifies the endearments and tender intimacies of a complete union, or that it produces transient ecstasies, *whether of body or soul, but that it permeates* and transfigures commonplace life and everyday service. This it did for them." For "in their love they were equals."[239]

BOOK THREE

Catherine's Love for Souls: "Mother in Israel"

"I am not without evidence that God *has* blessed others through even my instrumentality. Oh, yes, I hope to be a 'nursing-mother in Isreal'."*

"It is a glorious work in any way to be instrumental in winning souls. Oh for *wisdom* and *grace* to do it the best way and, having done all, to feel in our inmost souls our insignificance, and adore the condescending love which deigns to use *such* instruments for the accomplishment of so great a purpose."*

"Let us make up our minds to win souls whatever else we leave undone."*

"Oh, I cannot tell you how I feel . . . the poor sinners, the poor lost sheep for whom my Saviour died! How few truly care for their souls."
                                        —In a letter to her parents.

"I see as I never saw before that all God wants with us, in order to fill us with His Spirit and make us flames of fire, is for us to be honest and whole-hearted with Himself."
                                        —In a letter to a daughter.

"I see it is my business to make the most of the present and *trust Him* to direct and provide for the future."*

"I believe it is possible to live without grieving the Holy Spirit in anything. Though I see this to be a very high state."
                                        —From her Journal.

"I feel a sweet consciousness of having given myself in an everlasting covenant to the Lord. Pray for me that I may be able to endure every consequence of that consecration."
                                        —In a letter to her parents.

"I believe that one of the greatest boons to the race would be woman's exaltation to her proper position, mentally and spiritually. Who can tell its consequences to posterity."
                                        —In a letter to her parents.

*In a letter to William Booth.

1

Catherine as a girl dreamed of her future; set up her ideals; conjured up that unknown William who should be tall, dark and perhaps a minister? Thinks Catherine, as a minister's wife, 'I could occupy the highest possible sphere of Christian usefulness.' But even in relation to the world of her dreams Catherine acted in a common sense manner. She got ready, so far as she knew how, and when at twenty-three she met William, she was already versed, not only in theology and church history, but also in the home-making arts; could cook, bake and sew. Catherine knew that a minister's wife would certainly need to know how to make little go far. When she and William became engaged, she resolved, as she tells, "with all my might to prepare". Her thoughts dwelt much on William; what he was to be. She saw herself at his side, to encourage, advise and help him. She turned to books with renewed avidity; criticized and copied out sermons, responded with alacrity to William's calls for suggestions of new matter for his talks. Her whole being, alight with the joy of loving, and of being loved, was quickened into new vigour. Her thoughts reached out to include the strangers with whom, as the minister's wife, she would soon come into contact but to be William's companion intellectually and spiritually continued to be the height of her aim. When the children were given she added to this, or rather she included in it, the practice of her ideals of motherhood.

Of herself as preacher she had no dream, no premonition. She had written to William before they were married, "I do want to be useful but it must be in retirement and quietness." When at seventeen she had prayed "Lord prepare me for all," what was included in the "all" God alone knew. To strangers Catherine appeared a small, almost girlish figure. When they knew her, people soon forgot that first impression. The dignity of her bearing, especially the way she carried her head, somehow made her seem not little; but most of all, it was the force of her glowing personality that eclipsed the small frame. William was once shocked to find that he did not immediately recognize her. It was when they had been parted for that fortnight on their return from the wedding-preaching trip to the Channel Isles, and she had been too poorly to accompany him to Hull. He came to meet her at a railway junction. It was a happy little joke for Catherine to put in her letter to her mother, "My precious husband met me at Milford and was delighted to see me. He did not know me in the distance, he said I looked such a *little, young* thing when I went towards him."[1] And William was not the only one who, seeing

173

Catherine Booth coming on to a platform (though not a railway platform), thought her "such a little, young thing". Her son Bramwell says, "To many who did know her by sight, but only by reputation, her first appearance was a complete surprise. 'What a slip of a thing!' they would exclaim."[2]

Catherine's marriage was supremely happy; but her convictions were in no degree confused or weakened by the felicity of her love; on the contrary, the early years of married life proved that joy is a wholesome atmosphere for religion. She prayed for William as never before and they went on praying together. She prayed for individuals among his hearers and singled out those toward whom her heart was drawn, pleading with God for their salvation. She *cared* whether those who came weeping to the front really found what they sought; and began speaking to them herself, knelt there, with the young especially; and often prayed with some of the older men, seeing, we may be certain, in each grey head bowing there, one who might be her father. Though neither she nor William realized it, here was the beginning of that partnership in their ministry for souls that was to make them the prototype of thousands of Salvationists of many nationalities. In The Salvation Army, husband *and* wife* share in all spiritual ministrations. Catherine, talking to penitents, learned of the burden of sin, of the struggles and needs of individual hearts. But in 1855 William's little wife, moving quietly among the penitents, her grave eyes often brimming with tears, was intent only on helping someone to yield fully to Christ. The miracle of the moment was enough for her. She had, as yet, heard no faintest call to *preach*, but here was her school for preaching. The importance to her of these private conversations with individuals can hardly be exaggerated. They taught her, by the Holy Spirit's light, how to establish intimate relationship with the congregations that awaited her. She was already learned in the Scriptures; now she became learned in the human heart; familiar with its fears and foibles, sins and secrets. And all the time, in every fresh vibration of her own emotions of sympathy, indignation or compassion, her conception of God's work for man's distracted spirit was growing clearer. She applied the Bible truths, drew comparisons, saw in the men groaning at the communion rail the Abrahams, Jacobs and Davids of her own time. She ministered to them with utter unselfconsciousness. She did not think of herself as the minister's wife filling a sphere (nor indeed was such work as this undertaken by ministers' wives, so far as she knew); she did not even think of herself as William's wife helping her beloved with his task. She does not think of herself at all. She is oblivious to everything but

* Officers wives receive the same training as do single women officers. They deal with souls, visit people's homes, lead meetings and conduct marriage, funeral and other ceremonies.

the wondrous truth: here are men and women in need, and she, "poor creature that I am", is able to help them. This praying with people and hearing their confessions, waiting with them until the assurance of forgiveness is given, increased the need she felt to be nearer to God in her own spirit. She has much to learn yet about God and His will for her and about her own heart and its needs. The theories she had so well thought out, the conclusions so logical, so inevitable whilst they dwelt in her mind, will become a plumb-line for her own experience. She, who had such clear light about God's will for *others,* will be searching her own heart for assurance that she herself was walking in it.

William loved Catherine with an adoring passion and did to the last, but that did not blind him to her skill in his own field of action. It was a most endearing thing about him, I think, that in the midst of his own phenomenal success as a preacher, he retained a humble admiring reverence for her judgment and ability. They always discussed his sermons together and it was he who, while they were at Brighouse, insisted that she should take more part in chapel doings. When she demurred, he kept on saying in his blunt, obstinate way, "I know you can do it, Kate." No sooner was Ballington safely arrived than William announced to his office bearers that "Mrs. Booth will take the leadership of a class of female members" and that she would teach in the Sunday School. When it came to it Catherine found that she could not breathe in the Sunday School room, crowded as it was. To Mrs. Mumford she wrote, "I commenced teaching a class of girls on Sunday afternoon in our own back parlour ... So you may picture me ... surrounded by thirteen girls, striving to sow the seeds of eternal truth in their hearts and minds. Pray for my success. I feel as though I am doing a little now, but oh, I want more grace. *Gifts are not graces* ... I got on well, the children seemed very pleased."[3] As to the class of adults, there were twenty-nine members, many of them elderly, "it is against my judgment ... I wanted a new one consisting of young people." In the presence of these older women she felt small and young and somehow at a disadvantage; good for her this, perhaps? William introduced her and presided on the first occasion. "I spoke and prayed," wrote Catherine, "and felt it good ... I don't fear anything but lack of spiritual power." And then she leaps on in thought to: "Perhaps I shall gain in confidence and undertake something more important in another circuit."[4] Of her attempt without William she wrote to her mother, "I met my class yesterday for the first time and got on better than I expected ... I felt very tremulous at first but gained confidence and freedom as I went on."[5]

A week or so later William writes to Mrs. Mumford, "Kate had a very good class yesterday afternoon, twenty-three present and all full of glory. The people speak highly of her. She seems to be far more successful in pleasing the folk than poor me!"[6] After this William urges her to lecture and they laugh over the word. The upshot was a decision to experiment with a temperance talk to the Band of Hope at the chapel. Catherine set herself to prepare; roped in her father to help her. Since her engagement to William, Mr. Mumford had again become a teetotaller. "Thank you for your hints for my meeting," she wrote to him. "If I get on well and find I really possess any ability for public speaking, I don't intend to finish with juveniles ... I only wish I had begun years ago ... Had I been fortunate enough to have been brought up among the Primitives I believe I should have been preaching now! You laugh! But I believe it. The cares of a family and the bother of a house now preclude any kind of labour that requires much study, but I don't think lecturing on temperance would need much."[7] She got on well. "Indeed I felt quite at home on the platform, far more so than I do in the kitchen! There were a few adults present ... But I must not be too sanguine. Perhaps I may lose my confidence next time."[8] She began to be very busy now. The first week in 1858 there was a function nearly every night and life at this pace proved too much for her. Twice she had to be carried out of chapel faint. Here was Satan in his old guise to torment her. "It is the Band of Hope meeting tonight," she wrote to her mother, "but I dare not go. I have not been able to attend it for six weeks. So are my plans frustrated with a sick body! It is much harder to suffer than to labour, especially when you have so many calls on your attention ..."[9]

Catherine was well enough to go with William to hear Mr. Caughey, the evangelist, preach at Sheffield. They dined with him the day after at his host's home, and Catherine wrote to her parents of Caughey, "He is a sweet fellow, one of the most gentle, loving, humble spirits you can conceive of. He treated me with the greatest consideration and kindness; conversed with William on his present and future position like a brother, and prayed for us most fervently." The next day Mr. Caughey called on the Booths where they were staying and baptized Ballington in the presence of a few friends. "He wrote me an inscription for my Bible and took leave of us most affectionately, expressing the deepest interest in our future ... I heard him preach ... this did not in the least discourage me as to William's future career, I believe him to be adapted for quite as much usefulness ... He [Caughey] is free to visit any denomination where there is an open door, and is not handcuffed or shackled by Conference or Annual Committees. I believe our path will be made plain if we are willing to follow the light. I think we are. God forbid that I should stand in the way of such a work ... No, I will, if needs be, trust in God alone for my daily bread, rather than hold my dear husband back from the work his heart is set on, and in which he has been so gloriously useful ... You smile at my enthusiasm and say to yourself 'Silly Kate'. Well, I have prophesied correctly in several instances about his future, and we shall see if I am not right this time also."[10]

Catherine's thoughts of the settled home, with its study for William, seem less important to her now. Memories of the hundreds brought to Christ in his meetings during their first year of marriage loomed large; surely to win souls was what mattered most? We should keep this letter and others like it in mind as we watch them go their way. They make it evident that William's action in walking out of the 1861 Conference, as he did, was neither precipitate nor unpremeditated as some have thought. In fact they prove that the question of his return to the post of travelling evangelist had occupied their thoughts ever since Conference abruptly decided to terminate it in 1857.

As the date of the 1858 Conference approached, the vital question for the Booths was whether now that William had served the required year in a circuit he would be re-appointed travelling evangelist. This had been the arrangement. But, "Dr. Cooke ... called to see us yesterday. We were rather disappointed with him. He does not seem so thorough on the subject of William's work as we expected."[11] Thus Catherine to her mother. And a little later, "We don't anticipate William's re-appointment to the evangelistic work. All the whispers we hear on the subject seem to predict the contrary ... We are endeavouring to consecrate ourselves freshly to God, promising that if He but clearly shows us *His* will in the matter we will walk in it at any cost."[12] William, backed by the unanimous request of a number of circuits, asked Conference to re-appoint him as evangelist and was refused; but a resolution *that he should spend one more year in a circuit and at its close be recalled to revival work was passed.* On these terms he accepted the Gateshead Circuit. Catherine felt it an injustice that Conference had failed to honour the arrangement made when they went to Brighouse, and she feared the same thing might happen again but she accepted the decision as God's will for them.

"The chapel is a beautiful building and seats 1,250 they say," Catherine wrote home. At the close of his sermon on the first Sunday night William called on his wife to pray, and the "unheard of novelty" increased the interest associated with the new minister. Catherine was at once asked to become a class leader and consented on condition that the class should meet in her home. Walking to and from the chapel involved going up a steep hill and she was not up to doing that too often just then. Three months after arriving in Gateshead on September 18, 1858, a daughter, Catherine (Katie), was born. William's work at Gateshead thrived. He introduced new methods; for example, on Whit Monday, toward the close of his first year there, he opened a fresh series of revival services by a day of "fasting and prayer" lasting from seven in the morning until ten at night. Ten weeks of special *daily* services followed. The whole town was canvassed beforehand with bills. Little Mrs. Booth set the women members an example: she undertook a district and went from door to door talking to the people and personally inviting them to the services. There were open-air meetings, and groups of converts and others went singing from these to the chapel. A list of the names of people for whom prayer would be made had been prepared. At the close of the special services it was found that nearly all these persons had been to the meetings and become converted, notorious sinners amongst them. One, the chairman of a public house "Free and Easy", was carried round the shipyard where he worked, on the shoulders of his mates, to celebrate his conversion! He became a staunch chapel member. This hurly-burly was to become typical of The Salvation Army two decades later. As she moved among them Catherine absorbed a knowledge of people, their lives and thoughts; took impressions of their circumstances that dwelt in her mind and coloured her thoughts in years to come. It was not merely that she noticed more than some might do, but that her over-mastering craving to put people right impressed things upon her. She hated the sight of children, especially girls, trooping into the factories; "this horrible system" she called it, when writing to her mother, "... they begin work as half-timers when they are seven or eight years old and after a little while are able to earn eight or nine shillings a week ... I never met with such 'pounds, shillings and pence' people in my life. They seem to have lost sight of every consideration ... for the 'brass' as they call it ... parents seem to lose sight altogether of the demoralizing unwomanizing influence of the system ... I wish someone would begin to agitate the subject in the newspapers."[13] In the spring of 1859 a change in William took place. Catherine announced it to her mother thus. "William is better and in my eyes very much improved since you saw him. You will scarcely know him I think. He wears his beard and it is a beauty, it makes him look much more manly and interesting, though that is not the reason he wears it but as a protection to his throat. I can tell you that I am much more proud of him than ever I thought I should be, both physically and mentally, of course this is to your eye only ..."

While in Gateshead Catherine took a very important step. On her way to chapel one Sunday evening, she recounts, "I chanced to look up at the thick rows of small windows above me, where numbers of women were sitting, peering through at the passers-by, or listlessly gossiping with each other. It was suggested to my mind with great power, 'Would you not be doing God more service, and acting more like your Redeemer, by turning into some of these houses, speaking to these careless sinners, and inviting *them* to the service, than by going to enjoy it yourself?' I was startled; it was a new thought ... I felt greatly agitated and trembling with a sense of my utter weakness, I stood still for a moment, looked up to Heaven and said, 'Lord, if Thou wilt help me I will try'; ... I spoke first to a group of women sitting on a doorstep; and oh, what that effort cost me, words cannot describe! . . . I went on to the next group standing at the entrance to a low dirty court . . . I began to realize that my Master's feet went before me, smoothing my path and preparing my way. This . . . so increased my courage and enkindled my hope, that I ventured to knock at the door of the next house, and when it was opened to go in and speak to the inmates of Jesus . . . I was thinking where I should go next, when I observed a woman standing on an adjoining doorstep, with a jug in her hand. My Divine Teacher said 'Speak to that woman'. Satan suggested 'Perhaps she is intoxicated'; but after a momentary struggle I introduced myself to her by saying 'Are the people out who live on this floor?' observing that the lower part of the house was closed. 'Yes,' she said, 'they are gone to chapel.' I said, 'Oh, I am so glad to hear that; how is it that *you* are not gone to a place of worship?' 'Me!' she said, looking down upon her forlorn appearance; 'I can't go to chapel; I am kept at home by a drunken husband.' I expressed my sorrow for her and asked if I might come in and see her husband. 'No,' she said, 'he is drunk; you could do nothing with him now.' I replied, 'I do not mind his being drunk, if you will let me come in; I am not afraid.' . . . 'Well,' said the woman, 'you can come in if you like but he will only abuse you.' The woman led me to a small room on the first floor, where I found a fine intelligent man, about forty, sitting almost double in a chair, with a jug by his side . . . As I began to talk to him, with my heart full of sympathy, he gradually raised himself in his chair and listened with a surprised and half vacant stare. I spoke to him . . . until he was thoroughly waked up, and roused from the stupor in which I found him. His wife wept bitterly and told that although her husband earned good money, he drank it nearly all and the family were often without food. I read to him the parable of the prodigal son, while the tears ran down his face like rain. I then prayed with him . . . I now felt that my work was done . . ." Catherine arrived in chapel just in time "to lend a helping hand in the prayer meeting . . . On the following day I visited this man again . . . He listened attentively to all I said. Full of hope I left him to find others . . . From that time I commenced a systematic course of house to house visitation, devoting two evenings a week to the work . . . I was obliged to go in the evenings, because it was the only part of the day when I could have found the men at home . . . I used to ask one drunkard's wife where another lived. They always knew . . . I remember in one case finding a poor woman lying on a heap of rags. She had just given birth to twins, and there was nobody of any sort to look after her. I can never forget the desolation of that room. By her side was a crust of bread and a small lump of lard. 'I fancied a bit o' booter,' the woman remarked apologetically, 'and my mon . . . he couldna git me iny booter, so he fitched me this bit o' lard. Have *you* iver tried lard istead o' booter? It's *rare* good.'

179

... I was soon busy trying to make her a little more comfortable. The babies I washed in a broken pie dish."[14]

These visits to their homes made Catherine familiar with those whom Salvationists learned to call "our people", and her experiences among them proved vital when instructing Salvation Army officers in their work. The insistence on the *need* for "house to house" visitation contained in the *Regulations for Officers* issued by William Booth, when General of The Salvation Army, was inspired by Catherine's own experiences. Toward the end of her life she said "... I esteem this work of *house to house visitation* next in importance to the preaching of the Gospel itself ... This is the work that most needs doing of any work in the vineyard. There are teeming thousands who never cross the threshold of church, chapel, or mission hall, to whom all connected with religion is as an old song, a byword, and a reproach. They need to be brought into contact with a living Christ in the characters and persons of His people."[15] The knowledge she gained of them in their own homes enabled Catherine to make people feel that she understood them; a definite advantage this, when later she preached to rough and rowdy congregations. St. John Ervine says, "In this manner was begun what was to be an important part of The Salvation Army's work ... this ill woman went alone into slums ... where, by her grace and sweetness and sincerity, she soon made herself welcome. She was the first of thousands of Salvation Army lassies who were to do the same."[16]

2

Sensing that the views of Conference had not materially changed, William consented to the unanimous appeal of the Gateshead Circuit Quarterly Meeting that he should remain for a second year as Superintendent. He and Catherine were most influenced by the plea that they should stay to care for converts and to consolidate the work. Chapel membership in William's first year there had risen from thirty-nine to three hundred. All debts had been cleared and the circuit was in a position financially to engage three ministers instead of two. William, attending Conference, found it a monotonous affair. "Conference drags its weary length along," he wrote to his wife. He was glad to be home and back at work.

Their first baby girl was just over twelve months old, and Catherine was looking to the birth of her fourth child, when a significant paragraph appeared in one of her weekly letters home. "... Received a unanimous invitation from our Leaders' Meeting the other night to give an address at the special prayer meeting this week. Of course I declined. I don't know what they can be thinking of!"[17] Thus tossing the matter aside, her letter runs its course of family and chapel news. But Catherine's thoughts sprang back to that "unanimous invitation". She asked herself if she ought to have been quite so certain, quite so quick to decline? William, she knew, agreed with the inviters. She was always trying to convince him that whatever might have been possible once, now, with three beauties, as she often called her babes, she cannot possibly tackle anything of the sort; at any rate not anything requiring preparation. Besides, she is now finding it taxing to carry on with the chapel duties already undertaken. For the moment she is not strong enough to continue visiting drunkards, and there is such a difficulty in getting trustworthy maids. So her thoughts run on . . .

In the late autumn of 1859 Dr. and Mrs. Palmer came to Newcastle for a series of meetings. Catherine was keenly interested. She knew these American evangelists well by repute, had read Mrs. Palmer's books; knew that Mrs. Palmer was "the principal figure in the meetings . . ." Ballington had been unwell and was taken by his mother to the sea at Sunderland for a change of air which benefited them both. It was from Sunderland that she wrote that she had "hoped to go and hear" Mrs. Palmer, but was not well enough to do so. In a sermon directed against Mrs. Palmer, and twice repeated to his congregation in Sunderland, the Rev. Arthur Rees attacked woman's right to preach. Later he issued his speech as a pamphlet. When Catherine read it she was roused into a whirlwind of indignation. She devoured the replies to Mr. Rees which appeared in the local newspapers and told her mother that they "do not deal with the question at all to my satisfaction. They make so many uncalled for *admissions* that I would almost as soon answer her *defenders* as her opponents." As to Mr. Rees' "notable production, would you believe that a congregation half composed of ladies could sit and hear such self-depreciatory rubbish? . . ."

Mr. Rees talked of publishing another pamphlet. "I hope he will wait a bit till I am stronger," Catherine was dashing off another letter home, "if he does bring out any more in the same style, I rather think of going to Sunderland and delivering an address in answer to him. William says I should get a crowded house. I really think I shall try . . . William is always pestering me to begin giving lectures and certainly this would be a good subject to start with. I am determined it shall not go unanswered."[18]

Her husband was away visiting another part of the circuit when Catherine decided in favour of not waiting till she should be able to reply by a lecture, but to do it in writing. Her letter home tells: "This pamphlet has been a great undertaking for me and is much longer than I at first intended being thirty-two pages. But when William came home and heard what I had written he was very pleased with

181

it, and urged me to proceed and not tie myself for space, but to deal thoroughly with the subject, and make it a tract on the subject of female teaching which would survive this controversy . . . You must send me your honest and unbiased criticism . . . Whatever it is, it is my own . . . for I could get no help from any quarter . . . William has done nothing but copy for me . . . I did above half of it while he was away."[19] She had two good maids now and finds mornings and evenings most free from interruptions. The baby is due to arrive in a couple of weeks or so.

Catherine now has her first taste of men in the guise of printers. Her enthusiastic nature, and the pressure under which she has worked at the "tract", made delay the more intolerable. "You will be disappointed at not getting my pamphlet. But 'I am sold into the hands of a man', a printer, and if this is a specimen of printers I hope to keep out of their hands in the future. He got the first sheets for press on Monday evening and the finishing stroke on Friday, and they were to have been out *yesterday* and in the hands of reviewers and publishers, but alas they had to stand still for want of steam, and so they won't be out till *tomorrow*. I feel very vexed, but its of no use. However, it is pretty well known that a lady has tackled him [Rees] and there is much speculation and curiosity abroad, it seems."[20] Catherine's pamphlet *Female Ministry* is the basis of Salvation Army teaching on the subject. Nothing has yet been written to supersede it. St. John Ervine says, ". . . Catherine Booth had all the qualities of an exceptionally able pamphleteer: clearness, concision, sense and sincerity; and the cause which she advocated was one which was very dear to her."[21]

There is space here for but a paragraph or so of the treatise. Catherine deals first with common objections, the power of custom. "Making allowance for the novelty of the thing we cannot discover anything either unnatural or immodest in a Christian woman, becomingly attired, appearing on a platform or in a pulpit. By *nature* she seems fitted to grace either. God has given to woman a graceful form and attitude, winning manners, persuasive speech, and above all, a finely-toned emotional nature, all of which appear to us eminently *natural* qualifications for public speaking." She then goes on to admit the lack of "mental culture, the trammels of custom, the face of prejudice and the one-sided interpretation of Scripture" as "handicaps"; and she warms to a smiling irony in asking, "Why should woman be confined exclusively to the kitchen and the distaff, any more than man to the field and workshop? Did not God, and has not nature, assigned to man *his* sphere of labour, 'to till the ground and to dress it'? And, if exemption from this kind of toil is claimed for a portion of the male sex, on the ground of their possessing ability for intellectual and moral pursuits, we must be allowed to claim the same privilege for woman! Nor can we see the exception more *unnatural* in the one case than in the other, or why God in this solitary instance has endowed a being with powers which He never intended her to employ."

Further on, the supposed Scriptural prohibitions are dealt with in detail; and she passes on to give proofs from the Scriptures that women did, in fact, preach and were recognized as preachers and deacons in the early church. In Catherine Booth's opinion "whether the church will allow women to speak in *her* assemblies can only be a question of time; common sense and public opinion and the blessed results of female agency will force her to give us an honest and impartial rendering of the solitary text on which she grounds her prohibitions. When the true light shines and God's words take the place of man's traditions, the Doctor of Divinity who shall teach that Paul commands woman to be silent when God's Spirit urges her to speak, will be regarded much the same as we should regard an astronomer who should teach us that the sun is the earth's satellite." After more argument, she declares, "we sincerely believe that woman has a *right* to teach. Here the whole question hinges. If she has the *right,* she has it independently of any man-made restrictions which do not equally apply to the opposite sex. If she has the right, and possesses the necessary qualifications, we maintain that, where the law of expediency does not prevent, she is at liberty to exercise it without any further pretensions to inspiration than those put forth by the male sex."

Catherine draws attention to the opening chapters of *The Acts of the Apostles* as the basis of her contentions. "These passages expressly told that the women were assembled with the disciples on the day of Pentecost and ... that the cloven tongues sat upon them *each,* and the Holy Ghost filled them *all,* and they spake as the Spirit gave them utterance ... We think it a matter worthy of ... consideration whether ... the circumscribed sphere of woman's religious labours may not have something to do with the comparative non-success of the Gospel in these latter days."

When answering Mr. Rees, as when writing to her lover on the subject, Catherine does *not* apply her argument to herself. She is not claiming her *own* right to preach. She argues that all women are not required to do so any more than are all men. She is probably the more confidently didactic because she is concerned with establishing woman's right and fitness in general, and not with any particular woman in mind. But for the babe's impending birth it is likely that Catherine would have made her first appearance in public as an exponent of woman's right to preach the Gospel. It would have been an able lecture. But looking at her life as a completed picture, it seems to me fitting that when she stepped into public life it should be as a preacher, Bible in hand, and not as a lecturer, however worthy the subject. The power that moved her to open her lips was

183

not a surge of indignation liable to die down when the provocative circumstance was passed or dealt with. No, rather it should be, as it was, an inner voice, commanding in the name of the Lord and in spite of her own feelings at the moment.

Hardly were the printed pages of her pamphlet, under the title *Female Teaching*, in her hands, than on January 8, 1860, baby Emma* was born. In a few days' time Catherine was to celebrate her thirty-first birthday. The baby's birth brings a spell of rest. The nurse engaged for a month had been with her when Katie was born; and was known and trusted. This time, more than on previous occasions, Catherine is able to relax, to "let tired nature drink in rest" as she put it in a letter home. All that excitement over the pamphlet certainly had taken it out of her. Lying restfully in her pleasant bedroom, her thoughts wander about in the past, the happy past of her married life. She writes home, "William never was more tender or more loving and attentive than now. He often tells me I grow more beautiful in his sight and more precious to his heart day by day . . ."[22] Her thoughts roam in the future too: William's future. She dwells with joy on his growing power in the pulpit. Surely Conference will now appoint him as evangelist? She is ready, and has been ever since she saw him struggling with the small congregations in the Brighouse Circuit. She had written to her mother before the 1859 Conference, "I have fully and formally consented to let William go forth as an evangelist on condition that he concentrates on one district at a time, making his home in some central town . . . so that I shall see him at least once a week."[23]

As she lies nursing her little child, she feels her joy to be almost perfect. She is happy in a deep, thrilling way, and again, as often before when she has been conscious of special joy, there comes welling up in her heart a sense of her own unworthiness. Oh, that she had more grace! Oh, that she could *do* more for God; do more to bring men to salvation. She thinks of the converts who were witnessing for God; *they* would spread the Word. But had *she* done what she could? Of course her pamphlet would do good. She had proclaimed the truth. But was that enough? What if women, as convinced as she herself was that they had the right to speak for Christ, *did not act on it*? Was she right to have said "no" so swiftly, when that unanimous invitation to speak to the class leaders had been given? She had thought of it often since, and of William's pleading, and of his certainty that she could have done it. Looking back it seems to her as if in the first joy of assurance about her conversion, when she was seventeen, she was more ready to obey every inner prompting and to witness for God than she is now as a minister's wife! Of her

* Emma Moss Booth.

184

experience in the days after Emma's birth she said, "I could not sleep at night with thinking of the state of those who die unsaved . . . Oh, it was this view of the case that led me to open my mouth first in public for God . . . Perhaps some of you would hardly credit that I was one of the most timid and bashful disciples the Lord Jesus ever saved . . . I used to make up my mind I would, and resolve and intend, and then, when the hour came, I used to fail for want of courage . . I was brought to very severe heart-searchings at this time . . . One day it seemed as if the Lord revealed it all to me by His Spirit. I had no vision, but a revelation to my mind . . . I promised Him there in the sick-room, 'Lord, if Thou wilt return unto me, as in the days of old and revisit me with those urgings of Thy Spirit which I used to have, *I will obey*, if I die in the attempt!"[24] Nearly six years before, Catherine had written to William, "I think I shall rise superior to that timidity which has been such a curse, if God spares me . . ."[25] She had been spared and now she cast the responsibility on God. *If the Holy Spirit prompted she would obey.* This was a vow.

Spring approached, Easter passed, baby Emma was becoming the pet of the family. William was more than ever in demand. He could have spent all his time outside his own circuit. As it was he was working very hard, too hard. But sinners were being saved. Would Catherine, William asked, undertake a cottage meeting? He and a chapel member tried to persuade her to do so. All who rejoice in Catherine's power and influence as a preacher should honour William that he would not give up inciting her to begin. But she felt no compelling impulse and again refused. Whit Sunday came. Had the day been fine there was to have been a great meeting out of doors at a place called *Windmill Hill*. The weather proved unsuitable and the company of over a thousand, including visiting ministers who took part in the service, assembled in the chapel. What happened can best be told in Catherine's own words. "I was in the minister's pew with my eldest boy, then four years old . . . and not expecting anything particular . . . I felt the Spirit come upon me. You alone who have felt it know what it means. It cannot be described . . . It seemed as if a voice said to me 'Now, if you were to go and testify, you know I would bless it to your own soul as well as to the souls of the people.' I gasped again and I said in my soul '. . . I cannot do it.' *I had forgotten my vow!* It did not occur to me at all. All in a moment after I had said that to the Lord, I seemed to see the bedroom where I had lain, and to see myself . . . and then the Voice seemed to say to me, 'Is this consistent with that promise?' And I almost jumped up and said, 'No, Lord, it is the old thing over again, but I cannot do it.' . . . And then the devil said, 'Besides, you are not prepared to speak. You will look like a fool and have nothing to say.' He made a mistake! He overdid himself for once! It was that word that settled it. I said, 'Ah! This is just the point. I have never yet been willing to be a fool for Christ, *now I will be one.'* And without stopping for another moment, I rose up in the seat, and walked up the chapel. My dear husband was just going to conclude. He thought something had happened to me, and so did the people. We had been there two years, and they knew my timid bashful nature. He stepped down from the pulpit to ask me, 'What is the matter, my dear?' I said, 'I want to say a word.' He was so taken by surprise, he could only say, 'My dear wife wants to say a word', and sat down ... I got up—God only knows how—and if any mortal ever did hang on the arm of Omnipotence, I did. I just told the people how it came about. I said, 'I daresay many of you have been looking upon me as a very devoted woman, and one who has been living faithfully to God, but I have come to know that I have been living in disobedience ... but I promised the Lord three or four months ago, and I dare not disobey.' "[26]

Years later Catherine commented, "That honest confession did what twenty years of preaching could not have done." Petri says, "Her letters and writings about woman's right to preach were all preliminary victories. Now the decisive battle was won. Mrs. Booth's first proclamation was typical of herself and the people whose prophetess she was to become ... Her first prophetic act was quite simply to go to the 'penitent form'! She stepped before the people and 'confessed' ... After that, her proclamation was ever a personal testimony."[27] Stead was right when he said of her, "She preached out of the fulness of her heart. As she had lived, so she preached. It was her own experience which she served out to seeking souls ... she guided the footsteps of the penitent along the road which she herself had trodden."[28]

The congregation was much moved by the time little Mrs. Booth finished speaking. Many were weeping audibly and only this sound broke the hush as she went back to her place. In a moment William was on his feet: wise, loving heart that he was, announcing that *his wife would preach at the evening service!* We may be certain that he embraced her directly they reached home, and that they knelt together, as they did continually, hand in hand, to thank God and to ask His help for her. The cook, who had been at the service, rushed down to her semi-basement kitchen and danced round and round the table saying, "The mistress has spoken, the mistress has spoken," homely evidence of the place Catherine had won in her heart.

Pause to ponder for a moment what might have been the effect on both their lives—on The Salvation Army and all its works—had William reacted differently at this crucial moment. If his little wife making her confession to the Sunday morning congregation was having in mind the times in which she lived, a dramatic figure, so, as he sat listening, was William! His face must have been a study! To try to persuade Catherine to speak at a cottage meeting was one thing, but to see her in the pulpit ... ? Did he still feel as when he wrote the words, "You should preach if you felt moved thereto ...

Although I should not like it?"[29] No, I think not, for William would have no doubt but that in rising to speak Catherine had acted in obedience to what she felt to be the prompting of the Holy Spirit; and he was ready, without cavil, to respond on the instant and to ratify her new status in the presence of them all. The moment was of immense significance for them both. It was necessary in God's providence for them and for His purpose through them in the world, that these two should, at that instant of time, be of one mind.

3

Catherine Booth stands halfway on her life's earthly journey. Behind her the thirty-one years of her past, before her the thirty years of her future on earth. Thus, at the centre of her time, she opens her lips to preach "righteousness in the great congregation". On that Whit Sunday evening Bethesda Chapel in Gateshead is thronged. People stand all along the aisles and crowd about the pulpit spaces and stairs. Young persons are precariously perched on the window ledges; and in front, with the chapel elders, sits William Booth. From the pulpit Catherine announces her text, *"Be ye filled with the Spirit"*. In this first essay there may have been but a faint foretaste of that "genuine gift of oratory"[30] for which she became famed, but there was already about her for all to see and feel "a certain winsomeness which drew, touched, melted, fascinated".[31] Most powerful of all, there shines in what she says on this first occasion, as on every one to follow, "the earnest sincerity which was one of her greatest characteristics".[32] Her eldest son, Bramwell, gives a picture in words which presents his mother to the mind's eye of those who will never see her on earth. Thus she appears to the people of Gateshead as she stands before them on that Sunday evening. "A slightly built woman ... extremely gentle and refined in appearance, suggesting even timidity ... and in her countenance such strength and intensity as made it, especially when animated, almost mesmeric in its power to hold the attention even of the indifferent and casual ... Her head, which was small, was well set on her shoulders, its poise and movement conveying great personal force and dignity ... Her eyes were wide open, rather than large ..." "in the pulpit [she] arrested attention ... by the modesty and simplicity of her manner."[33]

On Whit Sunday 1860 in Gateshead Catherine entered another phase of her life. From then on she was, in a most literal sense, at the disposal of others. She gathered about her children after the Spirit. The news of her preaching ran through the North, where she was already known over a wide area from having accompanied

187

William on his revival campaigns. Wherever she had been with him she had made friends. There was something appealing about her, people fell in love with her at first sight. The idea that shy little Mrs. Booth had stood in a pulpit caused quite an excitement. Invitations to preach reached her from many quarters. On the first Sunday in June she went to the nearby circuit of Newcastle. The *Leaders' Meeting* there, June 6, 1860, thanked her unanimously "for the addresses delivered in the chapel on Sunday last . . . and earnestly hopes that she may continue in the course thus begun."[34] Thus she is accepted as a preacher outside her husband's circuit.

In a way all her early life led to this consummation. Through those Bible-reading days of youth; through those years of wrestling with theories and with Satan; through the study of early Church history and doctrine; through the high rapture of her loves; through the repeated experience of leading individuals from repentance into faith; through her growing love for souls and a deepening perception of the desperate spiritual state of many; she came prepared to be a messenger of the Gospel. She said of this first period, "Whenever I spoke the chapel used to be crowded, and numbers were converted . . . It was not I that did this but the Holy Spirit of God . . . with four little children, the eldest then four years and three months old. It looked an inopportune time, did it not, to begin to preach? . . . While I was nursing my baby [at the breast], many a time I was thinking of what I was going to say next Sunday; and between times noted down with a pencil the thoughts as they struck me."[35] "But oh, how little did I realize how much was involved! I never imagined the life of publicity and trial it would lead me to . . . All I did was to take the first step." Only a few weeks after that first step, something she had often feared suddenly became a horrible fact. William fell ill. And without hesitation Catherine stepped into his place in the circuit and was accepted there by his colleagues and congregations alike.

The first hint we have of William's illness is in a letter to her parents, ". . . Wm. has been confined to the house for a fortnight with a bad throat attack. I have consequently had extra care and work . . . I hope when Mary [Kirton]* comes to be able to get some study and some matter prepared for future use . . . I went to Bethesda last night to supply for Wm., the bottom of the chapel was crowded, forms round the communion [rail] and aisles; I spoke for an hour and five minutes. I got on very well and had three sweet cases and from all accounts today the people were very much pleased. I cannot tell you how I felt all day about it; I never felt in such a state in my life. I could neither eat nor sleep. I was pressed into it against my will and when I saw the congregation I felt almost like melting away . . . Wm. is of course very pleased and says he felt quite comfortable at home

* Mary Kirton remained in the Booths' service until her death in 1876.

minding the bairns, knowing who was supplying his place!" I break in at this point to say that I think we can hardly overestimate the good effect on Catherine of knowing that "William is very pleased". At the beginning of her public work and through the years afterwards he never failed to give the encouragement which was so necessary to her, and this gave him a share in all her success as a preacher. The letter continues, "Of course I only say this to you. If I had only time to study and write I should not fear now, but I must be content to do what I can consistently with my home duties and leave the future to the Lord . . ." In these words we hear a note that will sound on throughout her life; *"if I had only time"*. Another thing we should mark is that though the labours of her public work were prodigious, she was resolved "to do what I can consistently with my home duties". The Mother in Israel did not oust the Mother in the Home. And as if she had not enough on her hands now, "I continue my visitations among the men [drunkards]. Our first weekly meeting is to be on Thursday evening at eight o'clock . . . I can only devote one evening per week to it."[36]

Things at home were by no means all plain sailing as a letter to her parents three weeks later tells: ". . . you are aware that I expected to be left with only one girl and little Polly Scott for a fortnight but this arrangement only lasted a week, when Bella, notwithstanding a promise of reward and a day at home when Mary came, turned so disagreeable and abominably ill-tempered that I bundled her off home . . . of course we were all done up when Mary arrived on Tuesday night . . . I like Mary so far . . . You will see by the accompanying bill that I have some work before me. I am requested to take the night service all myself at least as far as the speaking goes . . . They put me on the bill for the tea meeting on Monday night without my consent, and in spite of my protestations. Pray for me. William continues very poorly; if he is not soon better I think he will have to go away for a fortnight . . ."[37] A week later, "Wm. is still very poorly, not able to work and so by the advice of many friends and two doctors he is going to Smedley's Hydropathic establishment at Matlock in Derbyshire. He thinks of staying three weeks or a month, the expense will be heavy unless he gets some favour, but he *must* get better . . . If you can borrow at one of the newspaper offices a book entitled *Smedley's Practical Hydropathy* it will give you an account of the institution and the treatment. If it should restore Wm., I tell him, I shall want to go when he comes back when I have weaned baby, and I think if there is anything in the world that would do me good it is that, but we shall see."[38] A deputation of leading officials waited on her with the request that she would take *all* her husband's preaching appointments while he was away. At first she felt this to be impossible, but when the request was renewed by a second deputation, she agreed to preach on Sunday nights. This she did for the *nine weeks* to which William's absence unexpectedly extended. In addition she held other services within the circuit and supervised its affairs; thus, from the force of circumstances, she had become *Mother in Israel,* at least in the Gateshead Circuit.

Extracts from her scribbled letters tell, as nothing else could, how she now lived. These are not accounts tinted, lighter or darker in retrospect, but the unpremeditated chatterings about the moment they describe. We learn from them how the sermons, that held the people's attention for an hour or more, had to be prepared in the odd moments available in the home. With all this Catherine's "extravagant heart" was engrossed and that "poor body" must keep pace as best it might! In the letters to William as elsewhere, Catherine used "meek" in its old-fashioned way, meaning piously humble. I do not think she qualified for it in any other sense! To William, "The chapel was very full upstairs and down, with forms round the communion rail. It was a wonderful congregation especially considering that no bills had been printed. The Lord helped me, and I spoke for an hour with great confidence, liberty, and I think some power. They listened as for eternity and a deep solemnity seemed to rest on every countenance. I am conscious that mentally and for delivery it was by far my best effort. Oh, how I yearned for more *divine influence* . . . Many are under conviction, but we had only three cases, I think all are good ones. I kept the prayer meeting on until ten. The people did not seem to want to go. The man I told you about as having been brought in a month ago prayed last night with power. Mr. Firbank, Thompson, and Crow were talking in the vestry afterwards, and they said that I must prepare myself to preach at night very often. I told them it was easy talking, etc., they little knew what it cost me, nor anybody else either, except the Lord. You see I cannot get rid of the care and management of things at home, and this sadly interferes with the quiet necessary for preparation . . . I told you I had refused an application from Salem [chapel, Newcastle] for the afternoon of the 26th. Well, on Saturday another gentleman waited on me, and begged me to reconsider my decision. He evidently came determined to make me yield. He was most doggedly obtuse to all my reasons and persevering in his entreaties. I thought to myself you have got your match this time! But after half an hour's arguing, in which he assured me that every office-bearer had been consulted and that all were anxious for me to come, I said, there was only one way it could be done. If Mr. Williams would take afternoon and night, I would serve them in the morning. The people are saying some very extravagant things. I hear a stray report now and then. But I think I feel as meek as ever, and more my own helplessness and dependence on divine assistance. Don't forget to pray for me. I have borne the weight of circuit matters to an extent I could not have believed possible and have been literally the 'Superintendent'. . ."[39]

To her mother, "... I was truly sorry to hear that father was so ill ... Instead of mustard plasters try cold water bandages—wet afresh as soon as it gets dry ... I have scarce time to write today [but still the scribbled lines multiply] I have to go out directly to visit and I have been writing all the morning, preparing for Sunday. I am published for anniversary sermons at Felling Shore morning and night. I shall take Miss Newbery and baby with me. On Sunday week I am at the Teams anniversary morning and night, and the Sunday after they want me to take Bethesda again, and the Sunday after that they want me at Sherriff Hill for their anniversary, and then they want me at Gateshead Well ... I find the preparation is the great difficulty. I am subject to such constant interruptions and noise that I am often almost bewildered."[40]

In spite of all this work Catherine went on visiting drunkards; she tells her mother, "... I have been quite as successful as I expected and have met with nothing but the greatest civility and attention. I have visited two evenings *this* week and attended two cottage prayer meetings at which I have given addresses and had four penitents. The rooms were very full and hot, and of course I felt rather knocked up the next day, but by lying down in the afternoons I don't think I am any worse. We give baby [now seven months] a little sago. She takes it better than the bottle, and it seems to agree with her very well, so I can leave her for the evening very comfortably ... Miss Scott helped me to make my dress skirt so I can wear it to speak in with the jacket till I get the body made. I intend to have a dressmaker in the house, so please send me the pattern of your bertha [shoulder cape]. I have kept the silk like yours ... While my feeble efforts seem so acceptable to the people and owned of God, I feel as though *I must do what I can*. If I could only get a stronger body I would not mind ..."[41] Soon word came that William was not doing well. Catherine cannot suppress the cry, "Oh, *what shall I do* if he is not soon better?" Humanly speaking her situation could hardly had been more precarious. She and William possessed no reserve funds to speak of. Both her own parents and William's mother have been receiving, and needing, financial help from their son and daughter. The Mumfords began now to be in better case; but there was no hint of security for the Booths and their four babies should William's health really fail. It seems to me that Catherine's own letters now show the fibre of her spirit better than any descriptive words could do. It is consistent with the character we have come to know that she lived in those she loved. I can find no suggestion that having obeyed God in the matter of speaking in public she thought her way might have been made easier. Would she have undertaken the preaching had she known how sickness was to dog their steps? There is no sign that she ever asked herself the question. There was no repining. Her hand was in her Heavenly Father's: He will

191

order all things for them. She was still, with simple forthrightness, *taking God at His word.* But read this letter to her parents and the one to William following, written when her fears for him were at their height. Note the courage and common sense pervading them.

"My dearest parents, I fear you will think me unkind, but I have had so much on my hands and have been so very unwell that I have not found a minute to write you. I am better today and somewhat relieved from anxiety being prepared for Sunday, but I had a letter this morning from William which put me about very much. I fear he is very little better and Mr. Smedley has ordered him away from the Establishment to the seaside. He complains of great oppression on his chest and difficulty of breathing. This is, of course, a very unfavourable symptom and I have written to insist on it that he goes to some fully competent doctor and gets sounded before he goes to the sea. As, if his lungs are in the least affected, he has no business near the sea, and if he does, and the doctor pronounces his lungs unsound, I shall propose that we leave here at once and go south. I feel exceedingly anxious. It is what I have long feared, but I could not persuade him to be careful. I am trying to leave him in the hands of the Lord, but oh, *what shall I do* if he is not soon better. Pray for me.

"I was at Teams on Sunday, had a very good day—at night the chapel was packed and many went away unable to get in ... I spoke an hour and a quarter with liberty and effect; the attention and interest never appeared to flag for a moment and nobody seemed aware that I had spoken anything like as long ... If William does not get better I shall insist on making a change with some preacher in the south and leaving here before winter sets in ..."[42]

"My precious William ... I have let you proceed with the hydropathic treatment quietly and trustingly, although I have had many fears about its suiting you. The difficulty in breathing of which you speak distresses and alarms me. And now that you have left Mr. Smedley's I shall expect to have some jurisdiction over you. And I do hope you will prove the love for me, of which you speak, by at once attending to my advice. Your health is too important a matter to be trifled with ... Oh my dearest, what shall I do if you don't get better? I dare not think about it. The Lord help me. I feel as though I must come to you. I can scarce restrain myself at all. Write by return ... neither expense nor any human means must be left untried to bring about your restoration, and if our means fail I can get some money I am sure. I will get up some lectures and charge so much to come in and with such an object in view I could do far beyond anything I have yet done, and the people would come to hear me I know."[43] A few days later she told William of circuit affairs and described the Sunday night service at which she spoke "an hour all but five minutes with liberty and strength of voice exceeding any time

before. We had a good prayer meeting ... and good praying, many strangers but only *one* case ... There were several under conviction ... We lack a general. [Is Catherine, then, the first to give William his title?] If you had been there we should have had several cases I have no doubt ... I gave them some solemn truth last night; a few extemporaneous thoughts on the *justice* of God."[44] Her reference to "a few extemporaneous thoughts" shows her as feeling her way to the freedom of thinking on her feet. Later some of Catherine's most powerful utterances were given in this manner. It would not be correct to think of such addresses as unprepared, for her mind was diligently furnished beforehand, but the capacity to marshal thoughts for the moment's opportunity greatly added to her ability to deal with a particular congregation. In a second letter on the same day, "... next Sunday is the day for Salem anniversary [Newcastle]. They have got tremendous bills out advertising for Mr. Love in the morning and Mr. Cooke of London in the evening. It appears that Mr. Love cannot come, and Mr. Proctor has been to Mr. Firbank to ask him if he thinks I could be got to take his place. They are going to have a meeting of trustees and leaders tonight on the subject ... They propose getting my name printed to correspond with the bill and sending a man round to stick it over Mr. Love, and they will fetch me and take me to Sheriff Hill at night. What do you think? Write by return. I should not like to give an answer until I hear from you ... Mr. Cooke would be one of my hearers! If so, I shan't forget that bit about the women; the Spirit sat upon them 'each and all', and 'they spake as the Spirit', etc. But I almost shrink from it. What am I to do? You know I must 'obey my husband' if I do preach?"[45]

In spite of having a cab on Sunday night, Catherine was obliged to go to bed with a chest cold and "almost total loss of voice". Also baby is "cutting two more teeth which meant two bad nights", but she hastens to add, "I am better today and hope to be more so tomorrow" which William will know means don't worry on my account. This letter tells him, "I was very much surprised to hear of your being in London ... I thought you were going to Wales ... I shall be bitterly grieved if you go and knock yourself up by tracking about to see this body or the other. Remember what an effort I am making at home to let you *rest happily* and in order to secure your strength ... I have been reading *Arthur's Tongue of Fire* and I should very much like you to get it and read it in your retirement, it is some time since I enjoyed a book so much ... I don't get on with my work to my mind and my back is so bad it nearly racks me to sit to write. Oh, for more patience, what a glorious deliverance will it be to me to get rid of this body! ... Kindest love to father and mother."[46]

In letters at this time there were signs that Catherine's concern for individuals was growing. She prayed now for persons in her own congregation, claimed this one, that one; that "he shall be given me".

193

From now on she would carry upon her heart the burden of the "ones". Few preachers have commanded such large companies of hearers so continuously as did she, but increasingly her thoughts were with individuals in her meetings over whom she yearns. To her parents she wrote, "... I believe we shall get two very interesting young gentlemen who were among the number [who stayed to the prayer meeting]. Oh, how my heart felt for them last night. They were two such fine young men, one just about to be married to a nice young lady, one of my *spiritual* children, the fruit of my last service at Bethesda. Pray for me ..."

Echoes of Catherine's fame, notoriety *almost,* began to reach her. As light on her character her lack of interest in the published reports of her doings is illuminating. She neither feared nor courted publicity, it was simply unimportant, it had no bearing on what she was doing. On first seeing her name "on the walls", she was startled, for she had not realized that preaching would mean *that* kind of thing. William asked her if, when she gave herself up to do God's will, she had not given her name also? To this, for once, Catherine had no answer. This letter continues, "My name is getting trumpeted round the world, I suppose. Mr. Crow informs me that it is getting into the foreign papers now, and in one of them I am represented as having my husband's clothes on! They would require to be considerably *shortened* before such a phenomenon could occur, would they not? Well, notwithstanding all I have heard about the papers, I have never had sufficient curiosity to buy one, nor have I ever seen my name in print except on the bills on the walls, and then I had some difficulty to believe that it really meant *me.* However, I suppose it did, and now I think I shall never deem anything impossible any more ..." Her letter reverts to things more important than notices in the Press at home or abroad: "Willie [Bramwell] is very large about his Grandpa coming. He is going to show him all round and get a cab to take him I don't know where! Bless him, he gets more engaging every day and so does Ballington. He improves very fast and Katie is a perfect *gem.* She looks so well and jaunts about like a little queen, everybody falls in love with her at once, but like *one* of her maternal ancestors she has the facility of keeping them at arm's length! Baby grows like a rabbit. She has now three teeth and is cutting a fourth—*wonderful,* is it not? Well, I suppose such wonders occur in every mother's history?"[47]

William had gone to Guernsey to continue his rest and Catherine poked a little fun to make him smile; what she told conjures up a picture of her, driving through Newcastle, that makes me smile too. I fancy the proposal to give up tea came to nothing! "*My precious Husband* ... I am quite willing to join you in giving up tea, and in every respect to co-operate with you for our mutual improvement ... On Monday Mr. Thompson brought his pony and a phaeton to take me a drive. The back seat was very narrow and uncomfortable and Mrs. T. was by his side in front, so he said I should have his place and drive when we got out to even ground. I thought to myself I could easily drive as well as *him* but I did not say much, only I used to drive very well but it was a long time since. You would have been amused at our brother's nervousness and anxiety to put me right, but he soon discovered that I needed no instructions . . . When we got home he said he thought he dare trust me with the pony without him, so yesterday being a beautiful day and we never having been to Tynemouth since you went, I thought I would put his confidence to the test and wrote a note asking him to lend me the pony and hire a phaeton (3/-) and send it down by ten o'clock. I wanted to drive to Tynemouth. Much to my surprise he *did*, and I drove Miss Scott from Sunderland, who has been staying with me since Saturday night, Mary and your two sons to Tynemouth and back without mishap or accident. We had a beautiful day and a most pleasant outing. We took plenty with us for our dinner, took tea with Mrs. Kimpston at their lodgings. What do you think of that! I never had a day's pleasure with so little fatigue for a long time. I drove right through Newcastle amidst a good deal of bustle and apparently to the astonishment of the natives . . . Mr. Buston happened to see us on the high level and looked as if he was going to be petrified!"[48]

Her letter, a few days later, *Friday, October 1, 1860*, is unique so far as I can discover, in that she *reproaches William*, pleading her *own* trials. Catherine was counting on his return on ". . . the 12th or 19th. According to your intimation you will then have been away *seven* weeks and unless there is some very great advantage to be realized I think you should come. I think there are more difficulties in the way of your prolonged absence than you seem to think. In the first place you were announced yesterday for Bethesda for the 14th. In the second place there is the Quarterly Meeting on the 15th which you seem quite to have overlooked. I don't see that you need forgo the voyage. You can stay in Guernsey till the 8th and then leave by the first packet for London and take the whole week to the journey, the same as the next week, and as to preparing for Bethesda, surely you can do a little bit of studying to get *one* sermon for night? And if you cannot get two, I will take the morning . . . I have found one of the manuscripts. I will send it by this post. Do you think it is wise to preach? . . . If you are really fit to preach [in Guernsey], you are ready to come home, and if *not* then it is absolutely wrong to attempt it. You must reconsider the matter of your return and let me know at once as I don't receive your decision as final. I think before you *decided* you should have consulted *me*. It seems a very long time for *me* to look forward to three weeks longer and especially as the distance is so great and I can only get a letter three times per week. I have said as little as possible about your absence and have written as cheerfully as I could with one exception in order to make you contented and happy about me, but you must not suppose that I don't feel it and all the additional anxiety that it involves and I do think you speak rather coolly about staying another week. I may be mistaken but I have shed some bitter tears about it, I assure you, however I will not urge any personal consideration; be guided by your *best* judgment in the matter..."[49] Three days later and *before* William had had time to reply she wrote, "I have got over the disappointment of your not coming...but you must write me longer letters now I get so few."[50] This was because of limited postal facilities from Guernsey.

At last after nine weeks' absence (twelve weeks since he had been able to preach) William was home. But alas, there is no little spell of "recreation" for Catherine! "All the children have whooping cough," her letter home tells, "I shall not undertake any fresh work until they are better"; but being "published" for the next Sunday morning she must fulfil the engagement, as also at St. Peter's, Newcastle, on the Tuesday evening, "but I go and come in a cab". She has promised to be careful and to be "in a cab" was her notion of extreme carefulness. Ordinarily visiting at a distance for services meant, as she wrote once, "having to come home in an open conveyance, as I will not let them go to the expense of hiring cabs".

The fact that William's throat in spite of treatment and twelve weeks' rest was still not right, hung like a dark cloud in the background of Catherine's thoughts; and for both of them the children's condition was a tax, for even with homoeopathic and water treatment, whooping cough went its leisurely way. Small wonder that by the middle of November she was telling her mother, "I am but very poorly myself and almost bewildered with work...I am making them [the children] flannel petticoats, etc., and their winter frocks are waiting to be done ...I cannot afford to put the work out. We shall be sadly behind this quarter. I regret now having my shawl. We cannot afford it, although I like it very much."[51] I, for one, am glad she had the pleasure of that shawl. However, in spite of whooping cough, and sewing, and being so poorly, and so poor, another letter tells, "I was at St. Peter's last Tuesday night and at Windy Nook last night, chapel crowded." Cold water treatment, we note from another letter, was still in vogue, "I wish you could be induced to try the cold sheet in a morning. I believe it is doing Wm. a deal of good; he is nothing like so susceptible to cold as he used to be. I have it tepid, but only just the chill off, so that it feels cold enough to me."[52] Knowing them, and having often endured a full sheet pack, the thought of my grandparents lying side by side, wrapped in cold wet sheets and rolled in blankets, like cocoons, is irresistibly funny. It was no mean discipline before breakfast!

A fortnight later: "The children are all better," and perhaps more

196

important still for Catherine's well-being, "I continue to like Mary as well as ever. I have received more kindness and attention from her during this time I have been so poorly than ever I did from all the others put together and she is very kind to the children." Kind, faithful Mary Kirton; in heaven she surely shares Catherine's reward? Scribbling on, Catherine tells of another matter about which something *ought* to be done. "I want to know if my dear father can get me a letter into *The Times* newspaper, if I write one and if not what paper he can get it into of next *importance*. I should like to write a letter on one phase of the employment of women question, viz. that of midwifery* and in doing so I am prepared with some good material on the evils, nay *horrors* and monstrosities of man-midwifery—my very soul burns with indignation against the infernal imposture on the ignorance, credulity and fears of my sex, and if I can only get a hearing I think I can excite enquiry on the subject."[53] This was one of the things she did *not* get done. But she continued to hanker after the amelioration of woman's lot at childbirth. I find a letter to her daughter Katie written nearly thirty years later which shows that Catherine's vehemence on the subject had hardly softened through the years. Here of nurses and their ways: "It always seems to be their first great aim to hush the fears of everybody about rather than to create sympathy for their patients! Never mind what anyone *suffers* if only they are not going to *die*! It was just the same with the old machine I had for my first, which if I had known then what I have learned since, I would have kicked up the chimney! I believe the great *sufferers* amongst women would do far better with some ordinarily sharp, tender, sympathetic, country mother than with the majority of trained (as they are called) Nurses. The absurd idea that when people are in agony of any kind, sympathy hurts them, is born of heartlessness . . ."[54] On the last day of the year 1860 Catherine wrote her customary letter home. William was at the Watch Night Service, the cold was intense. "I never felt so cold in my life." The Society meeting wanted her to preach more often, "but I shall not consent. I cannot give the time to preparation unless I could afford to put my sewing out and it never seems to occur to any of them that I cannot do two things at once, or that I want *means* to relieve me of one thing while I do the other . . . I wish that they would remember our temporalities a little more than they do."[55] The new year will bring bigger problems than that of how to get the sewing and preaching both accomplished without any increase of means and there will not be even the small stipend of the Gateshead Circuit to fall back on.

* The Midwives Act, requiring the training and registration of women acting as midwives, was passed in 1902.

Catherine was well informed on the Wesleyan teaching of the doctrine of holiness. The many names by which it has been known are but different definitions of the experience: nevertheless those very names give to an enquiring mind a good idea of what it means. For example, sanctification; full salvation; a clean heart; perfect love. Couched in the language of prayer and praise, the hymns of John and Charles Wesley alone form a commentary on the commands and promises of the Bible on this subject. The Salvation Army Articles of War summarize the doctrine in the words, "We believe that it is the privilege of all God's people to be 'wholly sanctified', and that their 'whole spirit and soul and body' may 'be preserved blameless unto the coming of our Lord Jesus Christ'."[56]

It is strangely incongruous that teaching this doctrine aroused bitter criticism of the Booths and their Army by religious leaders, for the experience is daily defined and prayed for in the Church of England. As, among many similar phrases,

"O God make clean our hearts within us."

"Vouchsafe, O Lord; to keep us this day without sin."

"Grant that this day we fall into no sin . . . but that all our doings may be ordered by Thy governance to do always that is righteous in Thy sight."

"Let us beseech Him to grant us true repentance and His Holy Spirit, that those things may please Him which we do at this present; and that the rest of our life hereafter may be pure and holy."[57]

Unless God be able and willing to grant these petitions, is not their constant repetition a mockery of man and God? For Catherine Booth, as for many sincere disciples of Jesus Christ, it was from lack of clear teaching, in their own circle, that the experience was not sooner enjoyed. Even so it is unexpected to find that she had not claimed it until she was thirty-two; and after she had taken her place in the pulpit. In fact it would seem that searching out the truth for her sermons aroused a new sense of her own need. Twice before in her life she had felt it. She was eighteen when she confided to her Journal, "I have received a letter from Mr. West today who took so kind an interest in my welfare while at Brighton. He writes very kindly and urges me to press after a full salvation. Oh, that I could believe for it! I feel convinced it is unbelief that keeps me out of the possession . . ."[58] After reading the life of William Carvosso her Journal recorded, "Oh, what a man of faith and prayer he was! . . .

My desires after holiness have been much increased. This day I have sometimes seemed on the verge of the good land ... and yet there seems something in the way to prevent me fully entering in ... *I want a clean heart.*"[59] Her argumentative mind, that "tyrant reason", as she called it, was an obstacle to her faith. The longing to obtain *evidence* made faith's committal the harder. Her natural instinct was to *act* on conviction; no lack of courage then, but she must first *have* the conviction. Her craving for reason's assent made walking by faith a kind of antithesis. But let reason judge *God's will* to be the highest possible good, *reason* may then admit that the only real test of this conclusion is to trust God and to act on the assumption that it is true. "Faith is an experiment that ends in an experience."[60] Yes, and the experience of holiness can only come by faith in God's will and power to sanctify. Only when man's spirit is emptied of self-trust is it safe for God to begin and go on to perform His perfect will in the heart. The active, practical element in Catherine Booth's nature warred against the experimental renouncing that was essential to this life of submission and faith. She was yet to learn that complete surrender to God restores to man's will its full power. When he cries "not my will, but Thine be done" man's own will takes on new strength and authority. The "I will" of a sanctified heart has not been silenced, it has been brought into partnership with God. The power of the Holy Ghost is not manifested in man independently of his own will.

Those aspirations for a "sanctified heart" which had agitated Catherine's spirit at eighteen had subsided. Interest in the possibility tended to take the place of crying to God for the possession. She asked herself whether for one of her temperament, described by herself in a letter to her mother as "an evil heart of unbelief", might it not, after all, be impossible to reach the heights of which she read? For of course she went on reading! When William Booth first awakened her love and drew its beauty forth, Catherine's whole being was quickened. Love brought a new flowering of emotion, of hunger and thirst for righteousness. Love to God was already a real part of her life, and it was a quite natural result of the new life of love for her lover, that she should be moved to desire with deeper ardour to please God, to *be* what He willed. In one of her love-letters she wrote, "The desires of a whole life to be consecrated to the service of God seem revived in my soul. I feel sometimes as though I could do or suffer anything to glorify Him who has been so wondrously merciful to me ..."[61] "I must get more religion, and then all will be well. I must get self destroyed,"[62] she declared in another of her love-letters. But can she? If at this time Catherine could have heard *holiness* preached, she would, I feel certain, have claimed the experience. But holiness teaching from the pulpit had much declined in Methodism. Dr. Thomas's sermons—he was a Congregationalist—were more an intellectual treat than a call for holy living, and though she and William discussed the experience, neither of them claimed it.

Whilst awaiting the birth of her first child, her soul was again deeply stirred. Writing to William when she was in the country for a few days, she says, "I feel stronger desires than for a long time past to be a Christian after His model, even Jesus Christ. Oh, to be able to receive the Kingdom of Heaven as a little child." And to her mother, "Oh, for grace to surrender our whole selves up to do His will." *"To do His will."* This is the crux. The stronger the character, the more intense the nature, the greater will be the conflict before the human heart is brought into complete submission to God. And especially will this apply to man's right to choose. To bind the will, by the free choice of that will, to the will of another, is the final surrender. When this is consummated the poorest heart comes into a relationship with Almighty God which enables it to say, "Not my will, but Thine be done."

The tendency with nearly all seekers for this experience is to renounce piece-meal; reserving the citadel of the will to the last. So it was with Catherine. When anything specific was in question, she would "give God the benefit of the doubt", as she used to say in later life. She was ready, a step at a time, to "do violence" to her own feelings, or at any rate to silence argument by some valid reason for not doing so; as, when on that matter of beginning to speak in public, she told herself that whatever she might have done in the past, *now* with an armful of babies it was impossible! A little later on she saw clearly enough that it was not the babies that had prevented obedience to the call, but her own timidity. So then obedience was pledged, "if I die in the attempt" she had said. But though she won that victory she had not yet surrendered *her whole self*. To William, while he was away ill, she had already confided, "Oh, why could I not believe for the blessing of holiness? I *tried* but I have not yet learned to take the naked word as a sufficient warrant for my faith. *I am looking for signs.* Oh, pray for me. I have solemnly pledged myself to the Lord to seek till I do find ... Oh, my Love, I cannot tell you how bitterly I regret that I have not been a greater help to you in spiritual things. I see how I might have stimulated you to fuller consecration ... but if God spares us to meet again, by His *help* I will do better."[63]

The continuous preaching she undertook in William's absence had been a strain and then, before she could get a rest, whooping cough had seized upon the children. Irritability broke out at unexpected moments. When things would not get themselves going her way, the passionate in her surged to the surface and challenged control. The end of 1860 was at hand. Baby Emma, now nearly twelve months old, "is as fat as ever and a very big child. I forgot to tell you she was weaned about a fortnight ago; she was not the least trouble about it. She has eight teeth and can stand by a chair." Thus Catherine to her parents shortly before Christmas and in the same paragraph, "I am absorbed in my subject for Sunday night: I want to get it done by Thursday and then I have to get a speech for the tea meeting and I have some little preparation to make for Xmas, and withal but very poorly. I think my back is as bad as ever it was in my life. I could often roll on the floor with it, but I have about given up all hope of ever being any better than I am and so I must try and make the best of it and suffer as a Christian."[64] A little time before she had written, "It is far easier to labour than to suffer, but I suppose perfect Christianity would enable us to do both?" Another letter shows her discontent with her own spiritual state: "I have been for some time past in a very low miserable state of mind, partly perhaps arising from physical causes but chiefly from unbelief and unfaithfulness. I seemed to reach a climax on Thursday. I felt as if the devil was in personal contact with me. I was almost driven to despair on Friday morning. However William tried to encourage me, and after a long and agonizing struggle together at the Throne of Grace I was enabled afresh to cast myself on Jesus ... I have pledged myself to seek till I find *holiness of heart.* I see what an enemy unbelief has been to me all the way through my religious life. It is *faith* that brings power, not merely praying and weeping and struggling, but *believing,* daring to believe the written word with or without feeling ..."[65]

Strange as it may seem, Catherine's poor health, the children's whooping cough, and such homespun difficulties as are familiar to all mothers, helped her to find full repose in Christ. Many, who have experienced how the Holy Spirit takes of the day's insignificant straws to show the way the soul must go, will understand. Delicate, harassed, though not unhappy, little Mrs. Booth learned from the very trials she suffered that there was a "better way". William was still not really well. Here was a grave threat to their future; a new obstacle to that "experiment in faith". If lack of faith had hindered in the past, how now, when demands on faith were so much greater? For her, as for many another, delay in trusting revealed more mountains that faith must move! She wrote to her parents, "My soul has been much called out of late on the doctrines of holiness. I feel that hitherto we have not put it in a sufficiently definite and tangible manner before the people—I mean as a specific and attainable experience. Oh, that I had entered into the fulness and enjoyment of it myself."[66] A long and remarkable letter recorded one more step toward complete surrender. The question agitating her mind was, would William be parted from her to become a travelling revivalist again? In some new way she felt that God required this. But that she might be *with* her beloved was the *one* condition she had asked of her Heavenly Father. She was prepared to renounce all else. She anticipated poverty, so love was not disturbed to find poverty companioning them. She liked the country but was ready to live anywhere. Her love sank all lesser longings in this very life of longing that, come what may, she and William should be *together*. It meant a kind of maiming of life for her to contemplate separation. Must she now forgo love's one proviso?

William had not asked her to free him for this roaming work. He understood better now the strength of her love. He could not ask for more than she could give. And besides there are the children; "my precious children" as he so often called them in his letters. Yet, in his heart, he knew himself called to go forth as an evangelist. Not even his love for Catherine could obscure that. He looked at her and looked into the future. There seemed to be no more trace of a way for him than on the water of the North Sea they sometimes viewed from Tynemouth. No, he dared not, for love's sake, tell his Beloved! But God told her. Let any student of her character thoughtfully read the extracts from this letter to her mother. It has much to reveal of the writer.

"I spoke a fortnight since at Bethesda on holiness, and a precious time we had. William has preached on it twice, and there is a glorious quickening amongst the people. I am to speak again next Friday night and on Sunday afternoon. Pray for me. I only want perfect consecration and Christ as my *all*, and then I might be very useful, not of myself, the most unworthy of all, but of His great and boundless love . . . I have much to be thankful for in my dearest husband. The Lord has been dealing graciously with him for some time past . . . He is now on full stretch for holiness. You would be amazed at the change in him. It would take me all night to detail all . . . As has always been the case with every quickening we have experienced in our own souls, there has been a renewal of the evangelistic question, especially in my mind. I felt as though *that* was the point of controversy between me and God. Indeed I knew it was . . . I determined to bring it to a point before the Lord, trusting in Him for strength to suffer, as well as to do His will, if he should call me to it. *I did so* . . . since that hour, however, although I have been tempted, I have not taken back the sacrifice from the altar . . . Such an unexpected surrender on *my* part of course revived William's yearnings towards the evangelistic work, though in quite another spirit to that in which he used to long for it. In fact, now, I think the sacrifice will be almost as great to him as to me. He has got so much more settled in his habits, and so fond of home. But he feels as though the Lord calls him to it. So we are going to make it a matter of daily prayer for a week, and then decide, leaving all consequences with the Lord. He says that we shall not lack any good thing if we do His will, and if He puts us to the test we are going to trust Him with each other—life, health, salary, and all. Will you not pray that He may reveal unto us His will so clearly that we cannot err?"

Was Catherine still "looking for signs"? Considering what was to be risked, how blame her? Was this wanting to see *"so clearly that we cannot err"* essentially the reasoning mind recoiling from commitment by *faith alone*? The letter continued, and, as often in her letters, she was talking to herself as much as to the one she addressed, "Oh, for faith in the simple word! The curse, of this age especially, is *unbelief,* frittering the real meaning of God's Word away, and making it all figure and fiction. Nothing but the Holy Ghost can so apply the words of God to the soul that they shall be what Jesus declared they were 'spirit and life'... The Lord will order all things if we only do His will and trust Him with the consequences... Oh, what a fool I have been! How slow, how backward, how blind, how hindered by unbelief! And even now some bolts and bars are round me, which my foolish heart will not consent to have *broken* down..."[67] Once more she was on the verge of the promised land. Will she step out into the seeming void *against* reason? Argument will not help her now. The moment must come, the very instant, when her *will* bids faith make the "experiment".

The letter in which Catherine told her mother of the seeking and finding is beautiful in its unreserved simplicity. Here are extracts: "My mind has been absorbed in the pursuit of holiness, which I feel involves this and every other blessing... when I made the surrender referred to in my last, I was made to feel that in order to carry out my vow in the true spirit of consecration I must have a... perfect Saviour and *that* every moment. I therefore resolved to seek till I found that pearl of great price, 'the white stone which no man knoweth save him that receiveth it'. In reading that precious book *The Higher Life* I perceived that I had been in some degree of error with reference to the nature, or rather the manner of sanctification, regarding it rather as a great and mighty work to be wrought in me *through* Christ, than the simple reception of Christ as an all-sufficient Saviour, dwelling in my heart... on Thursday and Friday I was totally absorbed in the subject and laid aside almost everything else and spent the chief part of the day in reading and prayer, and in trying to believe for it. On Thursday afternoon at tea-time I was wellnigh discouraged and felt my old besetment, irritability; and the devil told me I should *never* get it, and so I might as well give it up at once. However, I knew him of old as a liar... On Friday I struggled through the day until a little after six in the evening, when William joined me in prayer. We had a blessed season and while he was saying 'Lord, we open our hearts to receive Thee', that word was spoken to my soul 'Behold I stand at the door and knock. If any man hear My voice, and open unto Me, I will come in and sup with him'... William said, 'Don't you lay all on the altar?' I said, 'I am sure I do...' Immediately the word was given to me to confirm my faith, 'Now ye are clean through the word which I have spoken unto you.' And I took hold—true with a trembling hand, and not unmolested by the tempter—but I held fast the beginning of my confidence and it grew stronger ... I did not feel much rapturous joy, but perfect peace."[68]

Catherine Booth, in common with all who in sincerity come near to God, felt the accusing past the more keenly as her soul became more sensible of Christ's presence. From the moment that Catherine had received the Saviour in that secret fellowship that made Him her "perfect Saviour" no words were too strong to tell how she despised herself that she had not yielded and trusted *before*. The seed of all sin was in that, she felt. The principle of all evil springs from the roots of *self-will* and *unbelief*. Now that she *was* sanctified by Christ's indwelling, she looked back upon the old state of fearing and doubting, and suddenly realized how far below her present experience it was. William and she now enjoyed each other and their work together in Gateshead with a new freedom. A sense of deeper unity pervaded all. Catherine was at rest, by faith, about their future, trusting God "with each other, life, health, salary and all". Her love for her beloved flowed out to him like a river renewed in spring. William, too, was happy, though not so aboundingly confident about the future as was Catherine, which was fitting. She was ready for risks, but, after all, it was on him must come the responsibility for letting her take them.

They were now both willing to resume the wandering life of a travelling preacher; the question was ought they to take any action in the matter? Make another appeal to Conference, perhaps? Ten days after that letter home telling of her new experience of Christ's indwelling Catherine wrote, "... In reply to your enquiries about our decision, I cannot say that we have arrived at any, save that we will follow the light as we get it. Wm. has written to Mr. Caughey and another friend and neither of them seem disposed to risk any advice. Mr. C. is evidently afraid, but our trust is not in man, and if we take the step it will be solely trusting in the Lord. Wm. is going to write to the President in a day or two and then in about three weeks Wm. is going to preach in Birmingham, and he will call at Sheffield and see Mr. Stacey, and I rather think Wm. will come on to London for a couple of days and then he will tell you all our thoughts ... I feel a sweet consciousness of having given myself in an everlasting covenant to the Lord. Pray for me that I may be able to endure every consequence of that consecration. The children are all nicely and I am middling, my back is bad but my dear husband has been seeking all round Newcastle for a chair to suit me better than any one I ever sat in. We shall carry it with us ... "[69]

Catherine had no illusions about the attitude of Conference and anticipated no change. Now that she was ready to let William go, she saw with unmistaking clarity that he would! God had prepared him and God would open the way. They agreed on sending a letter stating William's position to Mr. Stacey, President of the New Connexion

Conference for 1861. The letter shows signs of joint authorship and was a plain statement of William's case. He wrote of his sense of his vocation; and of his success in winning souls while working as an evangelist. He explained that: "My soul has lately been brought into a higher walk of Christian experience" and suggests that Conference should employ him either working from a centre under the direction of the President, receiving the same salary as other ministers, or, that while recognizing him as a regular minister, he should be free to visit wherever invited and be responsible to raise his own expenses. This letter was sent on *March 5, but there was no acknowledgment of it until the beginning of May.* Then Booth was informed that the Annual Committee had referred the matter to Conference. There was no word of cheer or advice in the letter giving this information, and if anything had been needed to confirm Catherine's view that Conference would reject William's proposal, this reply gave it. But she was not cast down. She was strong in faith. It was upon her, at times, that William leaned for comfort. Her faith and courage took him by the hand, as it were, to run almost joyously up the steep hill of their difficulties.

They received an invitation to conduct services at Hartlepool for Easter. Thus, for the first time, they shared a pulpit outside their own district. They arrived on Thursday. On Good Friday morning Catherine preached to a full chapel. William preached afternoon and night. On Sunday he took the morning and night services, and Catherine the afternoon. On Monday William left in order to lead the Easter Monday tea meeting at Gateshead. Catherine stayed at Hartlepool by special request to hold a service on Monday night. "Shall return, all well, tomorrow night," she wrote to her parents. "There were many under conviction last night whom I hope to see converted tonight."[70] Another letter close on the heels of this one recounts, "You will be surprised to find I am still here, but so it is. I told you I had to stay Monday evening. Well, the Lord came down amongst the people so gloriously that I dare not leave, so the friends telegraphed to William and I stayed . . . I preached again on Tuesday evening. I gave an invitation and the communion rail was filled with penitents again and again during the evening . . . I preached again on the Wednesday and Friday nights, and also gave two addresses in the morning and afternoon on holiness. Above a hundred names were taken during the week . . . Oh, if I had time to particularize some of the precious cases we have had I could fill sheets. But I have not . . . The friends tell me that I get numbers every night who never before put their heads inside a place of worship. Nearly a hundred pamphlets have been sold by a notice put up in the lobby. I am expecting several people to call upon me this morning who have expressed a desire to see me before I go. I give an address principally to the new converts tonight and tomorrow morning I return."

Reading this letter, and others like it, we can judge how radical has been the change in Catherine since she entered into full salvation. It cost her many tears and prayers to come to the place of willingness to let William be away from home; and now, without a word to mark it, she herself is the one to be away first. The letter goes on, "I know what you are thinking, viz. that I shall be knocked up. If you could know how I have laboured, talking to penitents as hard as I could talk for two hours every night after preaching, you would not believe that it could be me. I scarcely can believe it myself . . . Oh, I cannot tell you how I feel in view of the state of the church; the poor sinners, the poor lost sheep for whom my Saviour died! How few truly care for their souls . . . The children were all pretty well when I heard last. My precious children! Oh, how I long to inspire them with truly benevolent and self-sacrificing principles! The Lord help me, and early take their hearts under His training. William says that Mary and Tilly are most kind and attentive to the children and that he does not think that they are suffering from my absence, neither do I believe the Lord will allow them to suffer."[71]

On her return to Gateshead Catherine wrote home and William added his word, "She came home much exhausted . . . I was very lonely without her, very much so indeed." Poor William! It was good for him, I think, that he should taste what must, in the future, so often be Catherine's portion. She had preached twelve times in the ten days at Hartlepool; a tremendous physical effort, the greater when we recall the hours spent kneeling with seekers in the after-meetings. Both William and her mother remonstrated with her on the length of her sermons, they feared for her health. "I do take notice of your kind advice . . . but I really cannot preach shorter. I do try, but I always fail, and even *then* I have to leave out much that I would like to say . . . However, I don't think it hurts me, as I speak very naturally, and they say my voice is so adapted for it, and my utterances are so distinct, that I don't need to raise my voice beyond its ordinary compass. It is the prayer-meeting work that exhausts me the most."[72] For those who listened to her time flew. When she stopped they wondered why, and could not believe that it was over an hour since she began. As Catherine wrote once, "The attention did not flag for a moment and no one seemed aware that I had spoken so long."

Conference met in Liverpool that year, 1861, and William told Catherine he wished her to accompany him there. "My heart almost fails me," she told her parents, "in going to the Conference and leaving the children behind. But William would like me to be there, to advise with in case he is brought into a perplexing position. I shall be in the gallery while the discussion goes on, so that I can hear all that is said . . . Pray for me." Some ministers of the Methodist New Connexion were as opposed as ever to Booth's appointment as an evangelist; and this party was strengthened by the appointment of

Dr. Crofts as President. It was he who, when in that office before, had refused William's request to be allowed to return to evangelistic work. Arrived in Liverpool William and Catherine were invited to dinner with Mr. Love. "I am to prepare him a bit," says Catherine. "I have great influence with him just now ... I may as well use his esteem to good purpose if I can."[73] This Mr. Love—a reputed millionaire—was an influential lay member of the Conference, as was also our old friend Rabbits, and they both worked to further William's hopes.

Catherine was much disappointed in the Conference proceedings. "... Its deliberations did not tend to raise the debating system of government in my estimation. Hours were wasted in discussing trifling details, in exchanging empty compliments, in speechifying, in proposing alternate resolutions and amendments. From beginning to end there was nothing to inflame the zeal, or deepen the devotion, or heighten the aspirations of the members."[74] This was an object lesson neither she nor her husband forgot when it came to establishing The Salvation Army. Looking back Catherine said, "... Nothing surprised me more than the half-hearted and hesitating manner in which some spoke, who had in private assured us most emphatically of their sympathy and support. I believe that *cowardice* is one of the most prevailing and subtle sins of the day. People are so *pusillanimous* that they dare not say 'No', and are afraid to go contrary to the opinion of others, or to find themselves in a minority."[75]

William Booth was invited to read the letter he had addressed to Mr. Stacey, after which it seemed the debate was moving in his favour, when a compromise was put forward by Dr. Cooke. Let Mr. Booth take another circuit, but, by arrangement with his office bearers, carry on a certain amount of revival work outside in addition. Being a member of the Conference, William was seated on the floor of the chapel, but where he could easily look up and see Catherine in the public gallery. As the decision was announced William looked into that loving face above. Was there a question in his eyes? Catherine thought so and was instantly on her feet, her clear voice answered him "Never". She made her way to the exit, William met her at the foot of the stairs, where they embraced and walked out. No sooner had the Booths arrived at the house where they were staying than Dr. Cooke and another minister drove up. Already three times William Booth had been persuaded to accept the decision of Conference that for twelve months he should not resume the work of a travelling evangelist, and it was hoped that the worthy doctor might persuade him to do so once again. But William knew that it would be impossible to raise a soul-saving work in a circuit and then to leave it for revival tours away. Dr. Cooke, however, persuaded William to attend Conference deliberations the following Monday and explain his objections. After taking Sunday's services in Chester, he did so. But before he was given an opportunity to speak, his appointment to the Newcastle Circuit was announced, and only *after* that was he asked to express his views! He simply reiterated his conviction of a call to evangelistic work, and explained from experience he had found that to combine this with circuit responsibilities was impracticable.

Conference did not look upon his refusal as a resignation, and William asked the Newcastle Circuit to grant him leave of absence, arranging for a colleague to carry on in the circuit. It was suggested that the preacher's house in Newcastle should be at William's disposal for six to eight weeks, but that he would draw no salary. This was unanimously agreed by the circuit officers, and Catherine and the children moved in. Expecting that it would be easy to find a suitable house within the time stipulated, the Booths had sold their piano and left the greater part of their luggage in Gateshead. Catherine scribbled another of her long letters home. "William has been out every day since we came seeking a house, he has walked miles and miles and I have been with him two or three times, and we have found nothing yet that will do under £27. We don't want to give so much, neither will the circuit next year ... Our position altogether here is about as trying as it well could be. We have reason to fear that the Annual Executive Committee will not allow even this arrangement with the circuit to be carried out and, if not, I do not see any honourable course open but to resign at once and risk all, if trusting in the Lord for our bread in order to do what we believe to be His will, ought to be called a *risk* ... The President has written to know the nature of the arrangements come to with the Newcastle Circuit. William will send them, and if they object I shall urge him with all my might to resign ... I am but poorly and almost bewildered with fatigue and anxiety. We don't know what to do. We only want to do right. If I thought it was right to stop here in the ordinary work I would be glad to do it. But I cannot believe it would be right for my husband to spend another year in plodding round this wreck of a circuit, preaching to twenty, thirty, and forty people, when, with the same amount of cost to himself, he might be preaching to thousands ... And none of our *friends would think it right* if we only had an *income*! Then, I ask, does the securing of our bread and cheese make that right which would otherwise be wrong, when *God* has promised to feed and clothe us? I think not. And I am willing to trust Him ..."

William hesitates. "He thinks of *me and the children,* and I appreciate his love and care, but I tell him God will provide if he will only go straight on in the path of duty. It is strange that I, who have always shrunk from sacrifice, should be first in making it! But when I made the surrender I did it whole-heartedly, and ever since I have been like another being. Oh, pray for us yet more and more ...

We are very much obliged for your sympathy and kindness and counsel. With reference to any upbraiding, I have often told Wm. that if he takes the step and it should bring me to the Union [workhouse] I would never say an upbraiding word. To upbraid anyone for taking a step for God and conscience sake, I think would be worse than *devilish*. No, whatever be the result I shall make up my mind to endure it patiently, looking to the Lord for grace and strength ... We have nothing coming in now from any quarter."[76]

The Mumfords look with alarm on the turn things have taken. They are more prosperous now but decidedly not in a position to support Catherine and her children, gladly though they would have done so. Her parents have tasted the bitterness of being without resources and when Catherine wrote, as in her last "we have nothing coming in now", the fatherly heart felt a pang of remorse as well as apprehension. If only he had managed better with his business—but at least his dear daughter must be advised, above all, not to act rashly. But how? They wrote and anxiously awaited her reply. In a few days it came. We can imagine how the eager fingers fumbled to open it. Of this letter St. John Ervine says, "There is a Franciscan sanctity in that letter which makes it one of the great documents of religion."[77] For me it is enhanced by the knowledge that it is the spontaneous outflow of her thought, caught for us at the very instant of expression; a snapshot as it were of her mind at the moment.

Here is the important part of it: "Your kind letter came to hand this morning. I am sincerely grateful for all your concern and kindness. I am only sorry to be the occasion of so much anxiety to you ... I hope neither you nor my dear father think that I want to run precipitately into the position we contemplate. I have thought about it long and much. It has cost me many a struggle to bring my mind to it, but once having done so, I have never *swerved* from what I believed to be the *right* course, neither dare I but I am quite willing to listen to argument ... I have no hope that God will ever assure us that we shall lose nothing in seeking to do His will. I don't think this is God's plan. I think he sets before us our duty, and then demands its performance, trusting solely in Him for consequences. If He had promised beforehand to give Abraham his son back again, where had been that illustrious display of faith and love which has served to encourage and cheer God's people in all ages? If we could always *see* our way, we should not have to walk by faith, but by sight ... The Lord help me to be found faithful. I don't believe in any religion apart from *doing the will of God*. Faith is the uniting link between it and the soul, but if we don't *do* the will of our Father it will then be broken. If my dear husband can find a sphere where he can preach the Gospel to the masses I shall want no further evidence as to the will of God concerning him. If he cannot find a sphere I shall conclude that we are mistaken and be willing to wait until one opens up. But I cannot believe that we ought to wait until God guarantees us as much salary as we now receive. I think we ought to do His will and trust Him to send us the supply of our need . . . but I am willing to go with my dear husband either way and do all I can to help him which ever way he decides upon."[78]

These two letters seem to me to be among the bravest in the world. They declare the foundation upon which Catherine's life was building. She will not shift her ground. These scribbled lines define what religion means to her. There will be twenty-eight years more of life on earth for her and she will live through them holding fast the beliefs expressed in these lines. She was walking by faith, and the experiment was becoming experience. Circumstances were never more hostile; reasons would only pronounce it folly to step out penniless. Yet, intense, logic-ridden little Catherine Booth was ready to do just that. This attitude of mind emphasized the change marked in her by complete submission to God and child-like faith in His word.

5

It was soon plain that the policy of Conference, known of course to all its ministers, had effectually doused the desires even of his friends to invite William Booth to their churches for revival missions. Four years before these same men and their circuit officials were disputing as to who should have him first. While invitations then could have filled his days five and six times over, there were now but one or two proposals. William decided to go to London to meet certain independent evangelists there. Hand in hand, he and Catherine knelt in prayer and dedicated their future afresh to God. "My dearest is starting for London. Pray for him. I have promised him to keep a brave heart. At times it appeared to me God may have something very glorious in store for us." Something very glorious! Surely this is seeing the invisible? How else could a prospect so different from present realities "appear" to her? The letter goes on, "Of course some would brand us as fanatics . . . but the same integrity of purpose which would enable me to enjoy honour, will likewise sustain me under reproach."[79]

Arrived in London Booth met several persons who were interested in special missions. To Catherine describing one of these he wrote, "The interview was such a contrast to the discouraging looks and desponding words of everybody I have come in contact with for the last two months, save one (my Kate), that it quite cheered me— I shall not of course decide on any plan until I see you . . ." He concludes characteristically, "Well, whatever comes we must live to God, close to God. Oh, let us give ourselves afresh to Him . . ."[80]

William also saw Mr. George Pearse. He was a member of, and a large contributor to, the undenominational Garrick Theatre Mission. To Catherine William recounts, "I went to dine with Mr. Pearse. After dinner we had a long conversation on the work of God, my own position, you, etc. Mrs. Pearse is a very amiable lady, so free, and both appeared much interested in all soul-saving work. Mr. Pearse had attended a meeting of the *Garrick Theatre Committee* that afternoon, and my name had been brought before them. They were very much interested in me and wished me to take part in the service at the Theatre tomorrow [Sunday] night. To this I consented. He said they were but humble people, and the work there was but of a humble character, and they thought that if I offered myself it should be in dependence upon God alone. Still, if I did so, they would, as far as they were able, open me halls and render me pecuniary assistance. I said to Mr. Pearse, in the best way I could, that all I desired at present was a sphere to which I was adapted, and then I hesitated and stammered. 'Still,' I said, 'for the first few months I should need a friend or two who would look in and say, Children have you any bread?' He, and Mrs. Pearse too, laughed aloud at this, and on my commencing to explain, he said, 'I laughed that you should think Christian love should be so low as not to do that much!' We prayed together and then parted."[81]

William came home from that London visit, having decided against binding himself to work in this particular Mission. Booth Tucker says the chief reason was "the lingering hope that it might yet be possible to retain his position [as minister] in the *New Connexion*."[82] He and Catherine were announced to lead anniversary celebrations at a centre established in Nottingham by converts of William's revival campaign in that city. Whilst there he received a letter from Dr. Crofts, President of the New Connexion, calling upon him to take up duties in the Newcastle Circuit. Catherine wrote to her mother, "William received another letter from the President yesterday, objecting to the present arrangement, and after a day's deep anxiety and fervent prayer, we decided on our knees to send in our resignation ... We both attended the tea meeting last night, William made a thrilling speech ... At the close of it he announced the step he had taken ... Much to our surprise, Mr. Clifton, who occupied the chair, instead of getting up to defend the Connexion, said that while he deeply regretted the step Mr. Booth had taken nevertheless he could not but honour him for acting out his conviction ... this was very cheering under the circumstances. The people were most affectionate at parting, and sang with us all up the road on the way home." The letter told of Catherine's preference for Derby as a centre to work from and went on, "My scheme is this, for you to let Mary [Kirton] and the children come to Brixton and my dear mother to come and stay with us in apartments for a few weeks ... perfect quiet and *rest* as we shall have the work done for us and you could attend our services and see the work and get a deeper interest in it in your own heart ... By this plan you need only just remove the furniture out of the front sitting-room and make it the nursery ... You could lock the parlour up, putting into it everything you were afraid might get injured ... you could take up the stair-carpets if you like, they will do as well without as with. If you knew Mary you would not be afraid of leaving two girls with *her* ... You will see I presume on my dear father's willingness to be left ... Write by return as Wm. will have to go back to Newcastle and get them out of the house as soon as possible and bring them by the earliest boat. I shall most likely not return to Newcastle but stay here and meet Wm. wherever we commence labour as we must save all the expense we can and Mary will manage the packing ... I feel happier this morning than I have done for three months past ... We have thought and reasoned and prayed and drawn lots,[!] and done *all* we could ... so now the step is taken! We both intend to brace ourselves for all its consequences!"[83]

So now that they no longer have a roof over their heads, that the bridge back to security in the shape of a circuit is blown sky-high; that they are cut off from all official recognition; now, in these threatening circumstances, Catherine is "happier than for three months past." She was walking by faith and faith sustained her. Speaking of this time she said, "We gave up home, income, every friend we had in the world, save my parents, with four little children, to trust only in God, as truly as Abraham did when he left his native land ... We had no more idea ... what God was going to do with us."[84]

Plans for beginning in Derby fell through and from Nottingham Catherine went straight to London by rail. The children and luggage went by sea for cheapness. Before the Booths went to Newcastle, Mary Kirton had been told that they could not afford to keep her but she had refused to leave them. Wages did not matter to her, she said, and she was ready to go with them anywhere. So Mary, with William's help, packed their personal belongings, children's toys and the precious books into boxes; and all were got safely aboard. The children were excited and gay, from five-year-old Bramwell to Emma, now eighteen months. The sun was setting at the close of a warm summer's day when William and the family arrived at the Mumford home. Before the children went to bed they all knelt down together to thank God for a safe journey. What a tender moment for the Mumfords. It is always moving to see a child kneeling to pray and these little ones were their grandchildren. What was to become of them?

Catherine felt a sense of relief in being free from the unfriendly supervision of Conference. She had none of the sorrow that still brooded in William at having to break from the New Connexion. However, the breathing space was not for long. Before there had been time even to formulate plans, guidance came in the shape of a letter which William read aloud at the breakfast table. It was from a young circuit minister in Cornwall, one of William's own converts, begging him and Catherine to visit Hayle. He had not much to offer. The chapel was small; no remuneration could be guaranteed; in fact nothing was certain except a sincere welcome. The Mumfords did not think much of the proposal! Surely it might be wiser to wait a little and find something better? But William was impatient to start. He argued that nothing would be more likely to bring invitations than making a beginning. Mrs. Mumford, quietly ignoring the invitation to Catherine, suggested that William might go, and she would see that Catherine had a real rest while he was away. At this lively argument broke out. One can picture handsome, vehement Mr. Mumford and black-headed vehement William; with Catherine inclined to look demure, and Mrs. Mumford looking vexed, as William maintained that, since Catherine had shared in the battle for their freedom to be evangelists, she should now share in the first fruits of their liberty. Remembering the scene, Catherine herself says, "My feelings could be better imagined than described during this conversation. The earnest way in which I had been included in the invitation ... appeared to prelude the opening of a way by which we could travel *together*."[85] Finally the Mumfords consented to take charge of the children, and William and Catherine immediately prepared to go. They set forth "in excellent spirits and full of high enthusiasm". It was almost a honeymoon journey over again, only that they were infinitely more precious to one another now. To be with William and able to help in the burden of the preaching was a kind of heaven on earth to Catherine.

On arrival at Hayle a plan was made, pretty generally followed throughout the Cornish visit, which from the proposed six weeks stretched to eighteen months. William would preach Sunday morning and evening and four nights in the week. Catherine on Sunday afternoon and Friday evening, with afternoon and other meetings on occasion. Saturday was to be for rest and preparation. August 11, 1861, was the date of the first Sunday of their independent evangelistic effort. The chapel was gorged, but there was no response in the prayer meetings that followed the preachings. On the Thursday, however, Catherine was able to report to her parents: "The work has commenced in earnest. We have had three very good nights. William preached Monday and Tuesday and I last night. I never saw people cry and shout as they do here. I can do nothing in the way of invitation in the prayer meetings, the noise is so great. I occupy myself with going to the people in the pews* ... I think the way is opening in Cornwall for a much longer stay than we first contemplated.

* Talking to individuals during the prayer meeting in Salvation Army services was called "fishing" by William Booth — meaning to seek out hesitant souls in the congregation.

William went by invitation to see the Rev. Samuel Dunn at Camborne, four miles from here, the other day, and he wants us to go there. He will be away from his chapel next Sunday, and I am to preach for him, and to stay for two or three evenings, as my strength serves."[86] Neighbouring places now began to press for visits. By September 2: "St. Ives is most impatient for us to go," Catherine wrote home. "On Saturday night the Wesleyan Superintendent sent one of the circuit stewards offering the *loan* of their chapel for Sunday and Wednesday evenings. We accepted it, and accordingly William preached last night in the Wesleyan chapel, crammed to suffocation, and I in the New Connexion, *well filled*, even though I was not announced to preach. We had a glorious prayer meeting in both chapels, about thirty cases in the Wesleyan and twenty with us."[87] A few days later, "On Wednesday night William preached in the largest Wesleyan chapel, about half a mile from the other. It was crammed out into the street. I should think there were 1,800 people inside, and I never witnessed such a scene in my life as the prayer meeting presented. The rail was filled in a few minutes with strong men, who cried aloud for mercy. Oh, it was a scene!"[88]

The whole neighbourhood was stirred. People walked ten, twenty miles to the meetings, and the influence of the converts changed the character of some places for long afterwards. In St. Ives the Booths held services in all the principal places of worship in the town except the Church of England, although its members joined with them. More than a thousand persons over fourteen years of age professed conversion there, including twenty-eight captains of vessels. Whilst at St. Ives Catherine held morning week-day meetings in addition to others "well attended and much blessed". The children were now sent for, and all were comfortably fixed up in a furnished house, adding to their mother's work, but to her joys too. She writes home, "The revival here is rolling on with much power ... We have also the pamphlet [*Female Teaching*] on the go. I have finished the emendations for the new edition ... With all these things to do, together with morning meetings one day, children's meetings another, and the services at night, you will see we have enough on hand. I never was so busy in my life. I have to help Mary with the children, in dressing and undressing them to go out twice a day; in washing them and putting them to bed at night."[89]

From Cornwall William made a report in diary form for a friend, part of which was published in the *Wesleyan Times*. He wrote, "By nine o'clock in the morning souls in distress have found their way to the schoolroom. [Mine agents repeatedly gave men permission to leave the mines for this purpose.] One morning nine men came out of one mine, and seven from another, unable to work for anguish of spirit ... When I say that the whole place is moved, I mean that nearly every individual in the neighbourhood is more or less

214

interested in the subject of religion . . . Some of the vilest characters in the town are being saved. . . . The public houses are deserted."[90]

St. Just was next visited. Catherine preached there with great power. The people came in companies to her Sunday afternoon meetings, bringing their food with them and sometimes walking throughout the night to be present at that one meeting, having to set off at its conclusion to walk back in time for work early Monday morning. Whilst at St. Just she began meetings on week-day afternoons for women only. Mr. Chenhalls, a leading Wesleyan of St. Just, was on his way home to tea, when, as he wrote, "My wife met me saying, 'Oh, Alfred, we *have* had a time! There never was such a sight seen in St. Just before. Mrs. Booth talked with such divine power that it seemed to me as if every person in the chapel who was not right with God must at once consecrate themselves to His service . . .' "[91]

A Salvationist visiting Sir Edward Hain*, a few days before his death, heard from him the story of his conversion when a small boy. It happened while the Booths were preaching in Cornwall. Mrs. Catherine Booth, he said, was coming home alone from one of her meetings when she met the child. They walked a little way together and she explained what it meant to give himself to God; then she said, "I should like to pray with you, my dear boy, just here and now if you will kneel with me." She took his small hand in hers and they both knelt while she prayed. She then asked the child to pray as well, and he remembered saying a few words from The Lord's Prayer. Sir Edward said that for him "the grass verge on the roadside was made for ever sacred by Mrs. Booth's action." He looked upon the happening as the beginning of his spiritual life.

Meantime officialdom, in the shape of the New Connexion Annual Conference 1862, was taking action. Ignoring the glowing account given by the circuit ministers from Cornwall, of the revival at St. Ives, it accepted Booth's resignation, and defeated a motion that this should be accompanied by an expression of regret. William and Catherine were so engrossed in their work that this last rebuff from their former friends had little power to hurt them. Later, Dr. Cooke expressed his regret and made an effort to bridge a way back but it was by then too late. The Booths did not realize that the effect of this decision of Conference would be to deny them the use of the New Connexion chapels. The Primitive Methodists followed suit, and passed a resolution the same year, instructing their ministers to "avoid the employment of revivalists". The Annual Conference of Wesleyans met about the same time and passed a resolution prohibiting the use of their buildings to Mr. and Mrs. Booth, whose work in Cornwall was queerly described as "the perambulations of the male and female".[92] Thus, in spite of the blessed results of their preaching, antagonism to

* Sir Edward Hain, M.P., Methodist; shipping magnate; High Sheriff, Cornwall.

215

William and Catherine from Methodist bodies became official and final. It was hoped that the prohibitions would not be enforced in Penzance, where arrangements for a visit had already been made and where they were installed in a house. But Conference decision prevailed and the announced services were cancelled. This was a serious blow. Awaiting the birth of her fifth child, Catherine and the children remained in Penzance and in spite of all she was in a mood of calm confidence. She wrote to her mother, "There is a very strong and universal desire for us to labour here. Mary cannot go into a shop, or speak to an individual, but they want to know when we begin meetings in Penzance ... In the meantime William is holding meetings in Mousehole, population one thousand five hundred ... I do not know what doubts and fears William has been expressing to you ... but I do not participate in them in the least and have no fear about the future, if only his health holds out."[93] A few weeks after the baby, named Herbert Howard, arrived, a free Methodist chapel in Redruth invited them and the campaign there proved to be equal in power to any preceding it. William recounted, "The work has spread throughout the entire neighbourhood. ... At the recent quarterly meeting of the Wesleyans it was reported that an addition of about 400 members had been made during the quarter to their societies in the Redruth Circuit."[94]

The Cornish revival helped Catherine Booth. The development of her skill in leadership was hastened, her authority to preach confirmed. The holiness experience into which she and William had entered before leaving Gateshead brought power to speak the Word. Her natural timidity which in a love-letter she told William had "been such a curse" was mastered. She wrote to her mother from St. Just, "I am wonderfully delivered from all fear once I get my mouth open." And it was here among the demonstrative, unsophisticated Cornish people that Catherine came to understand and value freedom of expression and method in religious assemblies. She learned the importance of not confining testimony and public prayer to the old and experienced, and recognized the immense influence of a convert's witness on his former companions. She saw the good effect on congregations when William began his service "with several testimonies from the newly saved". In Cornwall they witnessed for the first time the less controlled expression of joy and conviction of sin in the meetings. William was nervous of these ebullitions. When one night at St. Agnes a woman sprang to her feet and began to jump up and down in time to the hymn, shouting "Glory" at each jump, he was shocked. As she could not be quietened, he caused her to be taken out. This changed the feeling of the meeting. Later William regretted his action. He and Catherine discussed the whole question and it is noteworthy that Catherine who, in the early days of their acquaintance, seemed not to go far enough with William on revivals, was now able

216

to help him to accept a wider tolerance of expression of feeling, *if people were but sincere*. Freedom to express their feelings in a manner natural to them became a part of the privilege of Salvation Army congregations. Catherine argued, "We feel so about temporal things. People drop down dead with joy! . . . The manifestation will be according to your nature. One will . . . weep in quietness, and the other will get up and shout and jump. You cannot help it. When He [the Master] comes, you won't be ashamed who knows it . . ."[95]

Perhaps most important of all for the future was the *success* of Catherine's ministry. It had been vital that, in William's eyes and in the public view, there should be no difference between the visible results attending *her* preaching and his own. Control of the crowd, reverence for the message, conviction and surrender of souls, all obtained when she preached. Not that William needed convincing, but it is certain that, had Catherine not proved her ability to do a preacher's work without male assistance, William would have had a different conception of the part women might play in the service of religion. When he saw her successful, sometimes more successful than he was himself, he rejoiced as only love can in the triumph of the beloved. A niggard soul, a self-centred mind, might have reacted very differently. The more we get to know them the clearer it becomes that both William and Catherine were essential to the creation of The Salvation Army.

6

The fame of the Cornish revival spread. More than 7,000 persons over fourteen years of age had professed conversion: and the great majority of these joined established denominations. Even after eighteen months the Booths were reluctant to leave. They had invitations for visits that would have kept them in Cornwall for much longer. But now requests for their services came from many parts of the country. A group of their own converts, sailors, were responsible for the decision to visit Cardiff. These men had brought such accounts of the meetings, and themselves showed such zeal, that a group of Christian leaders joined to invite Mr. and Mrs. Booth. The brothers John and Richard Cory were among these. Both of them became fast friends of the Booths. It may be said that John Cory came to love Catherine as a daughter, and until his death he and Richard gave generously to the funds of The Salvation Army. Their complete confidence was won during the first Cardiff visit, when they recognized in William and Catherine children of God without guile. Interesting to note that after this visit, the firm Cory Brothers, shipping and

217

colliery owners, named one of their newly built ships the *William Booth*.

When they began the work in Cardiff the Booths used various places of worship for their services where Conference vetoes did not operate. Catherine preached in a large Baptist chapel. In a letter home she tells of some of the difficulties and that the friends who had invited them were anxious to find some "neutral ground" for the meetings. "But the music hall is an unwieldy ugly place and the circus not much better." On the next day she writes of a venture which was to prove important to The Salvation Army. "It was decided last night for us to commence in the circus on Sunday. It has been taken for a fortnight at seven pounds a week ... The Wesleyans, who are very revivalistic here, will not come and help us in a Baptist chapel! But we have reason to believe they will come to the circus."

Catherine and William were learning new things about the difficulties that throng the path of soul-winners; learning how many human prejudices there are to be placated, or held at bay, if the precious work is to go on. In the midst of these perplexities and the threat they constituted to their future, Catherine's faith feeds the strength of both. Picture her presiding over her household, her infant son at her breast, the four lively "beauties" threatening the life of "other people's carpets", her husband taut under the strain of responsibility for her and the children and the tremendous physical and emotional exertion of his continuous preaching. All look to her. *She* must never fail of skill to soothe, to encourage, to manage and command. And added to all this came the claims of her own public work: she too must prepare sermons and preach them. Yet with all its demands upon her, *she is in love with life*. See how she puts it as she fills sheet after sheet of her letter home, "William is very anxious— I think unnecessarily so. I don't know what he would do these times without me. However, amidst all the unsettledness anxiety and trials peculiar to the work, I love it as much as ever, nay, more, and I never look back on the step we have taken with a single regret. I believe we shall have strength according to our day and shall be instrumental yet in bringing tens of thousands to the Saviour ... We have got work enough for a lifetime, and whilst God stands by us, it matters not who are against us."[96] Certainly material conditions are as precarious as when they left Gateshead, yet Catherine is full of joy. But of William she wrote, "I think I never knew him lower than last week."

In imagination I see him as he rushes in and out of their "new" home, telling Catherine of the latest arrangements while he gets a bite. She must have had to be very careful about his food just then for indigestion was still a menace where he was concerned. I see them as they talk. Talking always did William good, Catherine too. They discussed every detail of the circus venture, the personalities involved, how to justify the spending of that enormous sum of money, one pound a day! And of how to raise it and live themselves. His beautiful hands are never still; one could almost tell his mood by watching his fingers. He ruffles his hair till it stands on end; is one minute elated at the prospect of the success of the plan, at the next despondent, decrying his chosen sermon and finding his very love of Catherine adding to his fears for the future. She encourages, suggests a new point, reminds him of some incident that makes them both laugh, and now it is time he were off to meet someone or other, and they fall on their knees, hand in hand, to pray. Oh, how they pray, in simplicity imploring help; and then she puts her arms round his neck and draws him down to kiss and William, not waiting for any answer, asks what he would do without her and is gone again.

The tension increased; Catherine wrote, "Humanly speaking, a failure here would have been deplorable." The letter went on to tell of the first Sunday's meetings. "The Circus answers much better than we expected. William had a good attendance in the morning. I had it full in the afternoon. The sight of the building almost overwhelmed me at first. It looks an immense place. I spoke from the stage, on which there were a good many people sitting around. The ring in front of us was filled with seats. Then commences a gallery in the amphitheatre style, rising from the floor to the ceiling; this, when full, forms a most imposing scene. The side galleries and those behind the stage were likewise well filled. It was a great effort for me to compass the place with my voice, but I believe I was heard distinctly, so that I intend to exert myself less next time ... William had it crowded again at night—a mighty service, and fifty-six names taken in the prayer meeting."[97] A few days later it gave her a flash of fun to write, "I am to have a chapel for Wednesday mornings. The Wesleyans have offered theirs. So, all well, I shall be in it next Wednesday. If the reverend gentleman who talked about 'the perambulations of the male and female' hears of it, he will think that the said 'female' has been one too many for him and his resolutions! ... My time now is never my own. I am subject to so many callers and if I had the strength for it, and no other claims upon me, I might almost be engaged in dealing with the anxious. I could tell you some very interesting incidents that have transpired here ... a physician and his wife are coming from Lanport today on purpose to get some spiritual counsel."[98]

From now on Catherine recognized her correspondence and conversations with individuals as being part of her opportunity to help people. To men and women who confided in her she wrote with the same decisive clarity as she wrote to her parents. She laid down the law; quoting her own experience in support. These letters carried her influence still further afield, and those who talked with her in her home, or kneeling at the communion rail in one of the meetings, were

219

bound to her with a sense of intimate understanding seldom lost. This brought with it freedom to write to her, as children to a mother. The heart's most carefully guarded secrets were confided. Perhaps the fact that she kept these entrusted sorrows and problems to herself emphasized them to her, in any case it was her nature to feel intensely; and it was partly her capacity for entering into the sorrows of others that made her so dear a confidant and help. Her husband, her children, her parents, the servants in her own household, increasing numbers of people in distress, all turned to her for comfort, for guidance, teaching, advice and fun. And all who looked to her found her love equal to their demands. Her whole life was a triumph of loving.

While the campaign in Cardiff proceeded, William held additional meetings in the neighbourhood; and when he was away Catherine undertook full duties at the circus. Her morning week-day meetings also continued. She was overworking, but she was more than ever in love with soul-saving. She wrote to her mother, "William has gone to Pontypridd...he has been fearfully low, partly the result of physical exhaustion. But I cannot convince him of it...I have had the best morning meetings I ever had anywhere, and about 130 have come forward. The attendance has been excellent. The last for women only, being the best of all. I have every reason to think that the people receive me gladly everywhere, and that prejudice against female ministry melts away before me like snow in the sun. I believe I have never been so popular anywhere as here. Everybody treats me with the greatest consideration and affection. I sometimes feel quite overcome. *Burn this at once.* I should not mention it to anyone but to you."[99]

At the conclusion of the circus mission they went to Newport. The campaign was hampered because available chapels were too small and at the close William was overtired and discouraged. The family was invited to take a rest at Weston-super-Mare with a Mr. and Mrs. Billups. These friends were among several made in Cardiff, and their admiration and affection for William and Catherine came as a special gift of God's love at a time of isolation and need. Mrs. Billups became Catherine's closest friend, the one to whom some of her most revealing letters were written. She was an intelligent motherly woman, and her love for Catherine, who had been enabled to help Mrs. Billups spiritually, was a mixture of a mother's and a disciple's. Mr. Billups' affection for the Booths was second only to his wife's. He was a contractor, builder of roads and railways; a self-made man, a hearty admirer of his wife and proud of her education. A handsome open-browed face looks out from the old-fashioned portrait of him. To these two friends, Catherine and William and The Salvation Army owe much, though the Billups never felt like that about it. They counted themselves honoured to be intimate with the "heavenly ones" as Mrs. Billups sometimes called them. Mrs. Billups, whose own children were grown-up, took Catherine's babes to her heart. She fell in love with Bramwell, who remained her favourite. It was to the Billups' house at Barry, twenty years later, that he used to go to meet his betrothed.

Walsall was next visited. Here a band of Caughey's converts had built a large chapel and carried on a thriving work. This visit was noted for several happenings important to the Booths and to The Salvation Army. Here, in one of Catherine's services for children, her eldest son, William Bramwell, then aged seven, gave himself to Christ. Here, to attract their friends, William announced that "converted pugilists, horse racers, poachers and others" would speak. "They say a Hindoo for Hindoos, an African for the Africans, and so a working man for working men."[100] It was at Walsall that evening street meetings, preceding the chapel services, were held. I quote from William's diary. "At night a useful open-air service ... I was afraid it might fail, I had but few supporters ... however a crowd gathered ... I was relying entirely upon the inspiration of the moment ... at the close of an hour and a quarter address [!] during which we sang twice, I invited the people to accompany me to the chapel. Then jumping off the chair, I linked my arm in that of a navvy with a white slop on, and we marched off arm-in-arm."[101] A crowd followed. This should be remembered as the prototype of The Salvation Army procession.

A few days after this entry in his diary William put his foot into a hole made by workmen altering the gas fittings in the chapel. As a result he was laid up for a fortnight, and the whole work of the campaign came upon his wife. To her parents Catherine wrote, "I have conducted the service every night since William was hurt, and have only been very poorly myself. The weather and the smoky atmosphere of this place seem quite to overpower me ... William's ankle is wonderful, considering what a serious sprain it was. You would have been frightened had you seen it. The leg was black and blue almost from the knee to the toes, and the joint was very much swollen. We have given Mr. Smedley's hydropathic treatment a fair trial. William has had a steam bath for the limb twice and three times daily [what a scene, this, for an imaginative caricaturist!] and it has answered so well as to astonish all who have seen it."[102] After eight weeks the Walsall visit ends. Good in many respects, there were great crowds and many converts, but it yielded the labourers *less than the cost of travelling and rent*! The smoke, or too much speaking in the open air, had adversely affected William's throat, and the old trouble threatened. But they were now not without friends who were able and willing to help and they both went to Smedley's Hydro for a week's rest and treatment.

Home was next set up in Birmingham. Catherine was not able to

221

do much public work at first. In the early months of this pregnancy she was troubled by much sickness, but by December (the baby was to be born in the following May) she was helping William, travelling to and from Birmingham. We have a letter that tells us something of the difficulties at this time. "I have returned this afternoon from Lye. I was too much exhausted after my service yesterday [Monday] morning to return that day... But the preachers have created an opposition at Brierley Hill, so *that* door is shut. It does seem incomprehensible, when William has consecrated life and all to the work of saving men, that we should be opposed and thwarted by those who *ought* to be the first to encourage and help us! Nevertheless, we have great encouragements. I don't like this mode of living at all. William has now been away from home, except on Friday and Saturday, for twelve weeks. I long to get fixed together once more. The going backwards and forwards and being in other people's houses does not suit William. Nor do I like leaving home for the Sabbaths. I am much tempted to look gloomily towards the future. But 'my heart is fixed'. 'I will trust and not be afraid'. Pray for me! I sometimes feel as though I had taken a path which is too hard for me..."[103] William's absence, it is clear, is *the* privation for her. Together they can endure almost anything. A stranger's description of those morning meetings of Catherine's brings them to life for us today. She wrote, the chapel "was crowded morning after morning, and never shall I forget the memorable scenes... The women left their work and in all sorts of odd costumes flocked to the meetings, some with bonnets, some with a shawl fastened over their head, others with little children clinging to their necks.... And when the invitation was given, what a scene ensued! It baffles all description..."[104] "William," Catherine tells, "came back fearfully exhausted. It is a perfect mystery to me how he stands it night after night, first the long sermon, and then the tiring and protracted prayer meeting. It is killing work—although an infinitely blessed one."[105]

But above the discord of their circumstances Catherine hears the clear note of conviction about their main aim, to *"get at the masses"*. The Booths are being prepared to raise up The Salvation Army. "If the work promises well we shall seek a house immediately and get the children here. I must have a home now soon, somewhere, for I feel very unsafe and very different to what I have felt before. If this place disappoints us I shall be quite tired of tugging with the churches and insist on William taking some hall, or theatre somewhere, and trying that. I believe the Lord will thrust him into that sphere yet. *We can't get at the masses in the chapels*. They are so awfully prejudiced against all connected with the sects, that they won't come unless under some mighty excitement."[106] And a little later she is writing, "...I found William looking ill in the extreme poor fellow, he has gone through untold anxiety and fatigue with one thing or another and I fear my presence won't alleviate it much at present, and yet he *says* it *does.* Well, we feel as though we were literally walking on the waters with nothing but the promises of God to depend on. Faith says, well is not that *enough?* The Lord help us to feel it so."[107] William suffered not only the constant strain of taking services in inadequate buildings, often without the help of church members, but also from frustration at being cold shouldered by former colleagues. Yet even this "wilderness" experience was afterwards seen to be God's purpose. "He was not to serve one church, but all the churches; he was not to labour in one country, but in all countries."[108]

Leeds was decided upon as the next centre from which the Booths would work. Here a house was rented and furnished. All economy was practised. William grudged himself the price of a book. It is moving to me to come across such sentences in his letters to Catherine as "I bought two books from him [bookseller] for 2/6. One by Calvin Cotton on revivals, and a good *School History of Greece* for Willie and the children in turns. He has two volumes of Macaulay's History of England . . . offers them for 5/-. Should I have them? I suppose not. They are good reading for a leisure hour."[109] However, denying themselves books, and much else as they do, will hardly make up for running revival services that do not even cover rent and travelling! Household expenses must be met if the children are to be fed. Catherine thinks things over while she lies up with her baby daughter,* and decides on a course she has more than once discussed with William. *She will undertake her own evangelistic missions in future.* This should come near to doubling their income, with but small increase of expense; and, sweet thought, more people will be helped. When baby Marian was five weeks old Mrs. Booth began work on this plan. Keeping Leeds as their home, she and William each undertook an almost continuous series of services. In the course of Catherine's meetings at Batley, Pudsey, and Woodhouse Carr, more than 500 adults came forward to seek God. Financially this running two sets of services was a success, most necessary now that a competent governess was needed for the elder children's education.

Letters make it plain that the real hardship for Catherine and William was the separation from each other. Writing from Sheffield William tried to comfort himself with dwelling on the possibility of bringing his wife and children there. He says, "I want no company but yours," he longed to "be at home" but then began to set out costs. "Ten pounds at least to move, and the dentist must be paid, and assurance due. So we must look before we leap. Still I think there is a sphere here . . . and we will all live together again . . ." The letter goes on, "How very much I should like to see you today; to hold you in

* Marian Billups Booth, born May 4, 1864.

223

my arms and look at you, right through your eyes into your heart, the warm living beautiful heart that throbs so full of sympathy and truth for me and mine, and then to press you to my heart, and hold you there and cover you with kisses . . . Kiss the children for me . . ."[110]

Of Catherine's letters to him at this time no trace is left. At her wish William burnt them. But he would ask her to send him "a little love talk" to keep in his purse. When she found such scraps preserved, she destroyed them and he would write to complain '. . . you robbed my purse of the bit you sent me. Oh, we won't be afraid of loving one another. We will not hold in and bind up our hearts. Let us be grateful for all our mercies. We have *many, many* more than many around, and there may be gloomy hours in the future . . . separation made by the grave . . . Now you are away but I am feasting on you, and on the hour when again *I hold you*, and look at you and kiss you, and have the delicious rapture of hearing you say you love me and reciprocate all my feelings."[111]

In another letter that helps us to picture their lives William writes optimistically, ". . . I am really concerned about this sleeplessness. You must rest next week . . . If the Lord *does* open the way with the Independents, or if He does continue to open our way to labour and to secure the income we have had the last two months, I will have a house in which you can have some quiet, if I pay £50 rent for it. And we will have a governess too, with some heart and conscience, if we go on changing one per month for ten years . . . But look up. I think you err by not diverting your attention by reading. Here is the difference between us and it may have something to do with my standing the wear and tear. I suffer my mind to be diverted, for a season at least, by papers or books. You must always be at *work*. A change of mental occupation is rest for the mind. When *I* come home, I divert *your* attention. Could you not let some book do the same? I send you the W. T. Read the article on Disraeli's speech . . . With care we can earn all the money we *need*."[112] And from another letter, "Our children are in health. We are saved, so far, from those gloomy visits to the churchyard which so many other families have to pay . . . and we have that which is most precious of all that is human, *our own warm, sympathetic, thorough, intelligent, well-grounded, confidence in and affection for each other*."[113] And "what folly in you to do without a fire. It is not in these little things that our cash goes, but if it were surely you can afford a bit of fire while you are at home?"[114] A few days later, ". . . I am going to study economy with all my might! I have those new kid gloves on the mantelpiece to be ever before my eyes, as a standing rebuke to my extravagance."[115] What was the story that led to the kid gloves? I wish we knew! The next extract touches on the core of the hardship, "It is no use talking to me about my rebellion of heart against this separation. I must submit . . . As I turned into my lonely lodgings last night a young gentleman with a lady on his arm knocked at the door of the house opposite mine. I could not help asking why I was parted from my young and precious wife . . ."[116] This extract expresses his longing, ". . . to spend the evening with you alone, far away from all excitement and disturbance, where we could commune with each other's hearts and be still."[117]

Once Catherine called London a "dreary waste", but that was when William was there without her. Now after her years of journeying, London took on an air of permanence very attractive to one who still longed for a "settled" home. And there are other reasons. She wrote, "My very dear Parents . . . Well, it is of no use making excuses, or I could fill a sheet, but the fact is I have been so poorly, and so overdone, that I have had the greatest difficulty to write a line to William! I never sent him such scrawls in my life. Last week I came backwards and forwards to Pudsey, but the trains were so late I did not get home till nearly twelve o'clock, which knocked me up so that I resolved to stop this week, which I have done; on Thursday night all well I shall return.

"I had a very good week. Chapel which seats 800 nearly full every night . . . I suppose I am immensely popular with the people, but that is no comfort unless they will be saved . . . I hear from Mary this morning that the children are all right, and all is well at home . . . My precious husband is so perplexed it seems as though everything was against him. Perhaps I could get some services in London, and if I was once going, I think I should succeed, but we shall see."[118] William was diffident about this last idea. He thought London standards of preaching were too high for him. Catherine said "Nonsense" in her most decided manner, and I think with a smile and kiss. When early in the new year she received an invitation to conduct a series of services in a Free Methodist Church in Rotherhithe, it was at once accepted. The children stayed in the Leeds home under faithful Mary Kirton's care, aided by another maid and the governess in charge of lessons. It gave Catherine great pleasure to be with her parents. The plan was that when the meetings were over she should stay with them and have "a good rest". William would come for a rest also as soon as he had finished his engagement in the North.

The idea that eventually grew into The Salvation Army was already alive in Catherine's mind as she turned towards London. Not that the notion of raising a special force had occurred to her or William at this time, but the conception of themselves as shepherds seeking *lost* sheep, "the masses" far from the sectarian folds was, as through a mist, becoming clearer. How could the idea be translated into action without money, without friends, without a roof to shelter "the masses" they would preach to? That was the question. On February 26, 1865, Mrs. Booth preached for the first time in London. The services continued Sundays and week-days until March 19. There

225

were remarkable conversions. Some of the converts became members of Spurgeon's Tabernacle; others of the Rotherhithe chapel. Many years afterwards there were still names on the chapel register of more than a hundred members who were converted during Catherine Booth's first London preaching. A number of these had had no interest whatever in religion before but had been attracted by handbills inscribed "Come and hear a woman preach".

While these services were going on, Mr. Morgan, editor of *The Revival,* later to become *The Christian,* wrote a friendly note to William Booth, whom he addressed as "Beloved Brother". Mr. Morgan said he hoped to hear Mrs. Booth preach, and to mention her meetings in *The Revival,* but that he had a word to say on the "subject of female preaching". Mr. Morgan thought perhaps it could be defended "in principle", but in practice "ought mothers to be away from their home duties on any account, not excepting this most important work? Furthermore ... it appears questionable on Scriptural grounds."[119] I cannot find William's reply to this letter but I am sure it was convincing! When this good man heard Catherine preach, his scruples about women in the role of preacher melted away, and he became a friend and supporter, often presiding at her meetings. Not that he agreed with all the methods that the Booths later employed. The nearer in friendship the more wounding to meet unexpected yet sincere censure; and Catherine and William bore many such wounds. Mr. Morgan, for example, after ten years of fellowship, suddenly felt he must break with them because of their holiness teaching. One senses the hurt was deep from the fact that William did not let Catherine see Morgan's letter until her Sunday's meetings were over. Then she wrote a long reply quoting Scripture in support of the teaching to which he objected. And near its conclusion came this paragraph: "Will you, my dear brother, define for us what standard we shall put before the people if we are not to tell them to seek and believe to be saved from all sin? If it were a fact that no man had ever yet attained it (though I doubt not thousands have, glory be to the God of all Grace) yet, if I saw a provision and a promise of it in the Word, I would follow it in the face of earth and hell. How do I know that man's faith has ever reached God's uttermost?"[120]

But this letter was not written until 1875. It was in March 1865 that Catherine's Rotherhithe meetings were concluded. Their success won William to her mind about London. He came up. A suitable house was found in Hammersmith. In his whirlwind way he soon had all in readiness and was off to Leeds to bring the household to town, again by boat. The time of rest with her parents, to which she had looked forward, was not Catherine's portion after all. William went off to preach at Ripon, and Catherine began another campaign in a larger chapel than the one in Rotherhithe, belonging to the same group, this time in Bermondsey. A stranger who attended some of those services wrote a description of her. "In dress nothing could be neater. A plain black straw bonnet, slightly relieved by a pair of dark violet strings; a black velvet, loose-fitting jacket, with tight sleeves ... and a black silk dress ... A prepossessing countenance, with at first an exceedingly quiet manner, enlists the sympathies and rivets the attention of the audience ... Her delivery is calm, precise and clear, without the least approach to formality or tediousness."[121] The family was now almost entirely dependent on the financial results of Catherine's meetings and the sale of her pamphlet. Invitations to William were to comparatively small chapels. The Methodists' buildings were still closed to him. Catherine decided to arrange services in a neighbourhood where, she hoped, returns in funds would be better. It was quite a venture. She said of it afterwards, "I felt the responsibility of this opportunity very strongly. It was expected that a number of very respectable people, so called, would attend the meetings. To preach to such a class is always supposed to be a more important and difficult task than to preach to people in a lower society ... I believe I was somewhat influenced by such feelings when I was about to commence. But on entering the hall, as my eyes glanced over row upon row of intelligent expectant countenances, I realized that they above all others needed the plainest utterances of truth, and this had inspired me with confidence."[122]

Just about the time that Catherine was occupied with this first campaign among the "upper classes", the way opened for William to preach to the "lower". One Sunday he took the place of a minister who had fallen sick. It was a small chapel, the congregation numbering only a score or so. But on his way from and back to Hammersmith he must walk through Whitechapel. *Here were the masses!* Here too was the devil! What William Booth saw on that Sunday never faded from his mind. Its ugliness obsessed him. His waking moments, and they were the more from its haunting, were hardly ever free from its presence. It was as though the crowd of devil-possessed humanity had taken up its dwelling in his heart. When he was asked by the East London Special Service Committee to undertake one week's services (which lengthened to six) in a tent on an old Quaker burial ground in Whitechapel, there could be only one answer. Before the meetings William, as at Walsall, preached in the open air, generally on Mile End Waste, used as a market, and for boxing, dog fights, gambling and worse.

One night after the meeting, arriving home between eleven and twelve o'clock as usual, he found Catherine, who had returned from her meeting by cab, also "as usual" awaiting him. She was sitting by the fire, and William, greeting her in an absent-minded way—not at all "as usual"—flung himself into the arm-chair opposite her and burst out with, "Oh, Kate, as I passed the flaming gin palaces tonight, I seemed to hear a voice sounding in my ears 'where can you go

227

and find heathen such as these?' . . . I feel I ought at every cost, to stop and preach to these East End multitudes." There was a pause. Catherine tells, "I sat gazing into the fire. The devil whispered 'this means another new departure, another start in life' . . . the question of our support constituted a serious difficulty. Hitherto we had been able to meet our expenses by collections from respectable audiences. It was impossible to suppose that we could do so among the poverty stricken East-Enders."[123]

I see William his hair rumpled, his long fingers restless about the arms of the chair, the grey eyes in the lean face set on Catherine. He can read her thoughts. This is the moment when *he* puts *her* on the altar; as she had long before put him. The firelight leaps between them. How comely she is; as she sits thoughtful, with the gentle look that he loves only less than the light of her eyes when she lifts them, as she never failed to do, shining with her love for him. And she lifts them now, and speaks. "Well, if you feel you ought to stay, we have trusted the Lord once for our support, and we can trust Him again!"[124] St. John Ervine says, "The answer was, perhaps, not as stimulating as it might have been, but it was heroic, none the less. In her state of health, with six children already and with another soon to come, only a very brave and a very religious woman could have made the answer that she did, to that momentous question."[125]

I cannot prove the date of this vital decision, but what I know convinces me that it was towards the end of July, 1865, perhaps on the very day that William met Peter Monk, an Irish prize fighter, whom Begbie interviewed when he was writing Booth's life. This man said, "I was walking toward the public house, but on the opposite side of the way, just strolling along with my hands in my pockets, when I came across General Booth for the first time in my life. I met him promiscuously. That was on July 26, 1865." The Irishman's account continues: " . . . Something in the man's external appearance took hold of me then and there. I stopped dead in the street, looking at him; and he stopped too, looking at me . . . after he had looked at me a long while, says he very sadly, 'I'm looking for work'. I was taken aback . . . I got hold of some coins in my pocket, and was just going to offer them to him, when he pointed to 'the boys' outside the public house just opposite, a great crowd of them, and, says he, 'Look at those men! . . . Why should I be looking for work? There's my work, over there, looking for me. But I've got no place,' says he, 'where I can put my head in.' "[126]

Was it during that strange pause when he and the Irishman stood staring at each other a "long while", that William recognized his sphere? Did he see it in the Irishman's eyes, in the crowd of ruffianly men outside the pub? In that moment, I believe, he had a revelation, and the Irishman was the first to be told. "There is my work." The "but" which followed was the devil's last throw, as it were. "How can this be your work?" ran the Satanic argument. "You have no place to carry it on in." Note the obstacle was not Catherine and the children, not his poverty, it was lack of means to do the work itself. I do not think that William would have said, "I'm looking for work", if in fact he had already decided to stay and preach in the East End. To me it seems clear that something happened to him that made him burst out with, "Why should I be looking for work? There's my work looking for me." He had recognized his destiny, and that night he told Catherine.

7

William Booth had found his sphere. From now on he worked with a kind of elated energy. Miss Short said, "The force of his nature would drive him furiously through the day's work. He was always facing in one direction. The day could never be too long for what he had to do. And nobody, I'm afraid, could ever be quick enough . . . to keep up with him. . . . Mrs. Booth herself warned me on several occasions that if I let him he would kill me."[127] The Irishman's comment was, "If he worked other people hard, he worked harder himself. All day long he was at it. . . there was never a man like him for that."

Six weeks after the first meetings began, the tent, on the old burial ground, collapsed. Some said that it was blown down, others, among them our Irish friend, said the guy ropes were cut by the "roughs". For William, then, the most pressing need was still a place to preach in. A dance hall was hired for Sunday. William organized the help of converts to clean it after dancing had stopped at midnight on Saturday. Seats for 350 were then carried in. Various holes and corners were found for week-night services. In the years that followed converts eager for meetings in their own neighbourhood on Sunday sought out available "shelter". In Poplar between a stable and pigsties, "the stench which oozed through the open cracks was enough to have poisoned us all"; in Old Ford a carpenter's shop, in Whitechapel a covered *skittle alley* "where they bowled and gambled and drank on week-days, while we preached and prayed and sang on Sunday". Many sinners sought salvation in a room twenty feet square in the yard at the back of "a pigeon shop", through which the congregation must pass. All manner of birds and animals in cages lined the walls, and the owner and his family ate and slept there. Perhaps some came to the meetings who were glad that they could slip into the shop from the street and so camouflage their real destination? From a stable which, after whitewash and the erection of a platform, promised well, Booth was evicted in only a week because the singing disturbed the boxers next door! Visiting converts, which often included getting them work; finding meeting-places; wrestling with people in interviews and doing "paper work" in his "office" at home; all day, every day, he worked. In the dance hall there were often four meetings on Sunday, three of them prefaced by a "preaching" in the open air. William said, "The bulk of the speaking in all these services fell on me. But the power and happiness of the work carried me along."[128] In a way this last sentence described all the rest of their lives, his and Catherine's.

William said of this time: "I saw multitudes of my fellow creatures not only without God and hope, but sunk in the most desperate forms of wickedness and misery . . . these crowds had a fascination for me." He saw, and as Begbie said, "He had no rest until he gave himself to the work of rescue."[129] There was one lack. He had no friend to look in and say, "Children, have you any bread?" Somehow there must be bread at home and the sinews of war for his East End campaign. He sent an account of his work and intentions to *The Christian*. Brief extracts from this show how The Salvation Army began. William Booth wrote, "More than two thirds of the working classes never cross the threshold of church or chapel . . . It is evident that if they are to be reached extraordinary means must be employed . . ." He goes on, "we propose, God helping us, to devote our little time and energy to this part of London . . . We have no very definite plans . . . At present we desire to hold consecutive services . . . every night all the year round. We propose to hold these meetings in halls, theatres, chapels, tents, open air, and elsewhere . . . We propose to watch over and visit personally those brought to Christ . . . In order to carry on this work we intend to establish a 'Christian Revival Association'."[130] William Booth concluded with an appeal for funds from those "The Lord has entrusted with means." The editor in his notes for the number of *The Christian* containing the article, wrote, "The condition of East London is more appalling than of any other spot of the same extent . . . The dregs of sin and misery . . . from all quarters of the world are precipitated there . . . We cordially welcome Mr. Booth and no less his good and useful wife, to the labour field of the East of London, and earnestly hope and pray that God's people may prove that they agree with God, that the labourer is worthy of his reward."[131]

There was not much response to this appeal in the way of money, but God had not forgotten the family bread bill. We do not know if Catherine's preaching was the instrument, or some account of William's work, but a few weeks after he began, a Christian with means at his disposal asked Booth to come and see him. Mr. Samuel Morley* then enquired all about what was being done in Whitechapel; and was told of the open-air meetings, processions of singing converts (well

* Samuel Morley (1809-1886), M.P., wealthy Christian philanthropist.

pelted the while with garbage), the penitent-form filled with kneeling men and women, and the testimonies of the converts to their companions. Morley listened with expressions of sympathy, and then took the role of questioner. What had the Booths to live on? How many children had they? And so on. Computing what he thought would be necessary to maintain them suitably for one year, he handed a cheque for nearly the whole sum to William Booth, suggesting that he should ask friends to contribute the balance. William was elated! At least for a few months now he had money to give Catherine for necessities. She was at her meeting in Kennington, where she was conducting a series, but such news could not wait. Off he dashed, and driving home in the cab to Hammersmith they rejoiced together. Mr. Morley proved a good friend to Catherine and William until his death, describing himself as "a sleeping partner" in their work.

The Kennington meetings were held in October 1865. The next month the Booths moved to Hackney in order to be within easy reach of Whitechapel. Here, on Christmas Day, their seventh child, a daughter, was born. She was named Evelyn Cory, after the Cardiff friends, and called Eva. By the middle of February, 1866, when the baby was six weeks old, Catherine Booth began another series of meetings. These were to last for *ten weeks* without a break, and were held in the Assembly Rooms at Peckham, at that time a very "select" neighbourhood. This Peckham effort was the longest campaign in one place that she had yet conducted. She preached twice on Sundays and several times during the week. Usually she arrived at the hall unaccompanied, and took the whole of the service, including the prayers, unless she saw a minister in the audience upon whom she could call for help. At the close of her sermon she gave an invitation to any, not at peace, to come and seek God. And then for an hour or more, she would talk and pray with individuals kneeling at the front. The physical strain was enormous, and the emotional even greater.

Soon after these meetings were concluded, Catherine began to suffer from symptoms of dysentery that did not yield to treatment. She lost weight to an alarming extent, and doctors prescribed country air and the "life of a tree". Accommodation was found near Tunbridge Wells, and there she went. This visit would hardly be mentioned here, but that a matter of importance came of it. Catherine was better, though not cured, when William came down on the last of periodical visits, intending to bring her home with him. Walking together they chanced to notice that the Reverend W. Haslem, one for whom they both felt a sincere regard, was speaking at a gathering in the grounds of Dunorlan, a large house in the neighbourhood. They decided to go. Arriving after the meeting had begun, they sat at the back on the fringe of the company. Mr. Haslem hurried to them at the close of the service, and introduced them to Mr. Reed, the owner of Dunorlan from whom they learned that he had built a hall where meetings were held for the people on his estate and their friends. Would Mr. Booth come over and preach for them on Sunday afternoon? No, Mr. Booth was announced to preach in Whitechapel, but it was agreed that Mrs. Booth should come to stay with Mr. and Mrs. Reed for the week-end and speak on Sunday afternoon.

As the party walked through the lovely leafiness of Kent's July to the hall on the edge of the park, Mr. Reed told Catherine that the meeting always closed *promptly at four,* and asked that she be sure to finish speaking just before that hour. Catherine explained that she could not promise, saying with a smile, "You must be my time-keeper, for when once I am started I am apt to forget myself."[132] The hall was full, and with Catherine's opening phrases there came a sense of awe upon the little company. Mr. Reed and all of them were caught up with her to ponder eternal things. Time had ceased to matter. But Catherine, suddenly recollecting the strict injunction to finish by four, paused, and turning to Mr. Reed, asked, "Ought I to stop now?" Mr. Reed, tears on his cheeks, raised his hand as to wave onward, saying, "Go on, go on. Never mind the time." And Catherine, turning again to the people, went on until nearly five, when, asking Mr. Reed's permission, she invited seeking souls to come forward. With these Catherine, as usual, knelt in prayer and counsel. Mr. and Mrs. Reed were won to loving admiration of her from that day; their beautiful home was open as a place of rest and recovery for the Booths and their family.

A native of Doncaster, Mr. Reed had made his fortune in Tasmania. He was an energetic, warm-hearted, hard-headed man; a type well understood by William, who had much in common with him. Reed did not agree with all William's methods. Paying for use of a theatre, for instance, even if it were a good place for getting a crowd of sinners on Sunday, put money, he said, into the owner's pocket, and to that extent helped the bad effects of week-day performances. But Mr. Reed had been enthralled by the work of the Mission and he propounded a proposal to spend ten or twelve thousand pounds in building a proper hall and centre for the Mission in the East End. A further sum for the support of their family was to be settled on Mrs. Booth. This offer must have seemed heaven-sent! Catherine liked these dear friends and could have received a gift at their hands with gratitude. But it was too good to be true, and proved a test to single-heartedness, rather than a reward. Mr. Reed was quite as masterful in his way as old friend Rabbits. He stipulated that William Booth *must agree to confine himself to this work in the East End.* Also, Reed reserved the right to withdraw the use of the hall if the Mission were not carried on in a manner he approved. At the moment the Booths looked upon the East End as their chosen field, but they—and especially Catherine—were resolved never to accept bonds that might hold William back from seeking sinners anywhere, or that might block an as yet unknown future opportunity for reaching the masses. Looking back now, with the international Salvation Army a familiar fact, it is easy to agree the wisdom of the Booths' decision to refuse Reed's conditions. But at the time, for Catherine and William, with their need of a good centre for the Mission, and of some regular income for their own support, it was a courageous act of faith, if not of folly. Generous well-meaning Mr. Reed was flabbergasted to find his offer firmly rejected. But he did not yield on the matter of conditions. And so his vision of the fine hall he would build for the Mission faded away although his interest in the work continued.

Catherine's health improved while in Kent, but on her return home the complaint revived with virulence. Booth-Tucker says "she was reduced to a shadow". In bed, sorting a packet of letters, she came across a pamphlet advocating a preparation of charcoal. She tried it and was soon cured. But for a time her nerves were shattered and she developed acute sensitivity to noise. A sparrow chirping was enough to waken her and the building of a church nearby drove her almost frantic. Recovery was slow, it was months before she was able to resume public work, and her nervous system was never fully restored. To add to the difficulty of her situation Catherine was expecting the birth of her eighth child in the spring. One day she was taking a walk with some of the children when she noticed a house for sale overlooking Victoria Park, between Bethnal Green and Hackney. Here would be quiet, she thought, room, and the park at their doorstep for the children. Enquiries were made. William said it was too expensive, but Catherine said she would take lodgers rather than miss a house so well suited to them. She used her own need, for once, to overcome William's scruples at increasing financial claims; said—her eyes smiling, I think, to balance the words—that unless she could get quiet, she would soon be "beyond needing a house of any sort". She had her way. The family moved into their Gore Road home, where there was room for them when the nursery was outgrown. When the direction of an Army made a Headquarters a necessity, almost every room in the house was used at some time or other as office including bedrooms. Bramwell passed at fourteen from being his mother's right-hand in the home to being his father's right-hand man for the already multifarious activities of the Mission—"the Concern", "our Concern"—as father and son affectionately called it. Bramwell was the first to fix up a bedroom-cum-office in the Gore Road house. Catherine said later that it became more like a hotel than a home, from attic to kitchen every available space occupied with papers and secretaries. "Of course," she said, looking back, "we might have refused ... to allow the privacy of our home to be invaded ... but then The Salvation Army would never have been what it is today, and my husband and children would have had to be made of different

233

material . . . I sometimes think that if our critics could have seen the drudgery and toil . . . they would have been less ready to add to our sorrows . . . by their unkind reflections. When we established a regular headquarters the greater part of the business was transacted there . . . but the fact that we have been accustomed to discuss among ourselves any important step . . . has led to much of the most important work being transacted at home."[133]

Even after the move to Gore Road Catherine regained strength but slowly and was not well enough to do public work beyond meetings at Mission posts until early in 1867. She then began a series of meetings, lasting three months, held in the Eyre Arms Assembly Rooms, St. John's Wood, on Sundays, and in the schoolrooms of a nearby Baptist and other chapels on week-days. On the first Sunday a heavy snow storm thinned the congregation and Catherine only reached the hall with difficulty, but a fortnight later notices were posted outside announcing that the hall was full. To these congregations (more than three parts, it is recorded, were men) she poured out her thoughts, reasoned, denounced, pleaded. "Mrs. Booth set forth God's truth without passion or eccentricity but with profound earnestness and was to multitudes of educated people like a messenger from God," thus one who heard her. Catherine began telling her listeners something of the work going on in Whitechapel, and so entered upon what was later described as "the most striking peculiarity of Mrs. Booth's life—her ambassadorial position, between the richer and poorer classes. The intensity of her sympathy for all who were in any sort of spiritual or temporal distress and the simplicity and directness of her appeals to the hearts of her hearers to—whatever class they might belong— peculiarly qualified her to promote practical charity as between all sorts and conditions of men. In the morning she would be denouncing the extravagant waste of life and money in the drawing-room . . . in the evening she would be demanding, with no less energy, from some huge audience of the working classes, an abandonment at once of low, sensual indulgences and of all bitter feelings against wealthier neighbours."[134]

The St. John's Wood meetings resulted in substantial help for the Mission. A young man, whose brother was converted at the services, was greatly blessed and what Catherine had said about the work took him to some of the East End meetings. He gave an account of what he found to the Committee of the Evangelization Society of which he was a member. As a result William's work was further looked into, and the Committee agreed to give a weekly grant towards the cost of renting the Effingham Theatre, then a low resort, for Sunday night services. Peter Monk, the former Irish prize-fighter convert and Mission member, often drove Catherine to and from her meetings in the East End of London. He recalled, "She'd look at you in a queer way, smiling out of her eyes, and talk to you as if you were something of a child. I'd drive her to meetings, hand the horse and carriage over and go inside with her. 'Brother Monk,' she'd say to me, 'remember I want you to keep the devil out of this meeting.' And many times the only way I could keep the devil out was by throwing him out, for Mrs. Booth would go to some queer blackguard places, same as the General . . ." At the close of the St. John's Wood meetings "a deputation of gentlemen waited on Mrs. Booth, offering to build her a church larger than Mr. Spurgeon's Tabernacle."[135] I wish we had a description of the scene, and I should like to know what Catherine said when declining such a munificent proposal. These meetings were concluded towards the end of March, and on April 28, 1868, her eighth child, Lucy Milward, was born.

It had been suggested to Catherine that some people were reluctant to attend religious services other than those held in the church with which their family was associated. If, it was averred, Mrs. Booth could hold a series of meetings at some fashionable summer resort, being away from home, people would feel free to come. This idea was thought to be worth testing. In early summer Catherine herself went to Ramsgate, engaged a hall and began another series of meetings. Crowds overfilled the place hired and when an opportunity came to take the Royal Assembly Rooms in Margate the meetings were transferred there. Seeing prospect of good results, Catherine decided to preach on Sundays throughout the season. The plan had been that she should travel to and from London each week but she soon realized the tax on her strength would be too heavy, yet she felt she could not be absent from home altogether. Why not bring the children to the sea? No one encouraged the notion. "It will cost too much." "Margate is fashionable and crowded, you'll never find a house." But Catherine held on her way and expounded her hopes to the lively group in the nursery. She always bathed the baby herself when she was at home, and no doubt it was at this evening "ritual" that she told her plan. We may picture her rocking gently as baby Lucy drank her supper. The bright-eyed group around her eagerly putting their questions about the sea and castle-building, and—oh, bliss— riding on donkeys! There was a new concentration of thought as kneeling they prayed together as usual and, speaking the words after their mother, asked that God would show her where to find a house. On leaving them for the next journey to Margate she told them to go on asking God to "find us a house".

Back in Margate, Catherine looked around expectantly, and saw a house to let, about which she felt at once that it must be the one for her need. Immediate enquiry elicited the fact that the owner had already been much blessed in her meetings. He was sympathetically interested in her predicament; *he* did not need money, and would be happy to let the house at a much reduced rent. So the delighted little mother told the news on her return home! No need to ask God again,

235

but to thank Him now, and get ready for the journey. Happy pandemonium held sway until the exit of the youngsters. There must have been two "growlers" to take the eight, their mother, Mary, a friend, and all the luggage to the station? William, with cook and housemaid, waved them off. We are not told what he thought of the plan. One advantage was a quiet house, in the brief time he had there, and Catherine did not leave him for long without running up for a day or two. He came down sometimes and joined the children on the sands. A fine frolic with them always did him good, especially if in the open air.

Catherine's meetings were most successful. People came to hear her from many parts of Britain. Ministers, journalists, business men, and those who had no particular interest in religion. For many, a quickening of their spiritual life resulted. Mr. Knight, member of a publishing firm, made himself known to Catherine and said that he felt that her messages were of such importance that there ought to be a record of them. He offered to "undertake the entire responsibility of reporting and publishing her sermons" and to give Mrs. Booth any profit from their sale. But Catherine told Mr. Knight that she felt he overestimated her powers, and that her words were hardly worth printing. Perhaps she told William of the offer, but somehow I think not. She, though not he, was sensitive to the impression that her preaching was more praised than his. She never wished to emphasize that. In the latter years a professional shorthand writer was employed and several volumes of her addresses were published.

These Margate meetings tired Catherine more than previous efforts of the kind. They lasted longer, for one thing, and she was quite alone for the whole period. It was some weeks before she could rely on any one even to start the hymns! She was not musical and could not be sure of striking the right pitch. This was a great trial to her; opening a meeting was at times a nerve-racking affair. She stood literally alone before the crowd, acquainted with none, had to announce the hymn and then appeal that someone in the congregation should begin to sing. One feels a certain sympathy with the audience, and it is not surprising that there was often a considerable pause before the meeting could even get started! Catherine said, "The more respectable the audience, the greater was my difficulty." And remember that after the nervous tension of getting a start with the hymn, she must offer prayer as well as preach, and then undertake what was perhaps the most arduous of all, to kneel and pray with penitents. Hundreds came to Christ in these gatherings, many new friends were made for the East End work, and substantial financial aid resulted for the Mission and for their own family needs. Two persons were influenced to be active helpers in the Mission. One was a daughter of Mr. and Mrs. Billups. Booth-Tucker described her as "a gay, fashionable worldling, a brilliant musician". She had taken a great fancy to Catherine and persuaded her parents to allow her to live with the Booths that she might study at the London School of Music. She had announced that she "hated revivals" but when the family moved to Margate, in order to be near their mother, Miss Billups went with them for a holiday. She was persuaded to go and hear Mrs. Booth and was converted. She renounced her former ambitions, became a preacher herself, and was William's chief helper in producing the first tune book for the Mission. The other person was Jane Short, whose friendship was to be so helpful to the Booths at home and in the Mission. She said, "You can never say 'no' to William Booth. It was he who decided, not I, that I was to live with them." Miss Short worked herself, or rather the Booths worked her, to a standstill and she was obliged to take a sea voyage for recovery. But this was after five years of devoted service. Her presence in the home enabled Catherine and William to be away with a more quiet mind. In their absence "Sister Jane", as they called her, carried on. She and Mary Kirton have their not unimportant part in the making of The Salvation Army.

Catherine came back from Margate fatigued but full of eager enthusiasm about the work. William had found his sphere—no doubt of that; and they were working together. They incited each other to new ventures, and at the same time rested in each other's companionship. An atmosphere of special joy filled the Gore Road house. Their parents decided that the children should have a "thoroughly happy" Christmas celebration. Great preparations were made, excitement was soaring. When William returned from preaching on Christmas Day morning, according to Miss Short, he was not in his usual "boisterous" spirits with the children. "He was pale, haggard and morose. He did his best to enter into the ... fun and frolic but it was no use; he kept relapsing into silence and gloom. He looked dreadfully white and drawn ... then suddenly he burst out, 'I'll never have a Christmas Day like this again!' and, getting on his feet and walking up and down the room like a caged lion, he told us of the sights he had seen that morning in Whitechapel ..."[136] This was Miss Short's first Christmas with the Booths. Her account of it goes on, "Well, he was true to his word. That Christmas Day was the last Christmas Day the Booth family ever spent together." On the next they were scattered, distributing Christmas fare—including 150 Christmas puddings "many of them made in the kitchen at Gore Road". It was the beginning of The Salvation Army Christmas feasts in which hundreds of thousands of lonely, poor or homeless people have taken part all over the world ever since.

The work grew. Only three years after the decision by the Hammersmith fireside, there were thirteen "preaching stations" in East London. In September 1868 a report of the Mission was published, incorporating the first balance sheet,* and announcing that 140 services were held weekly. The list of means employed to help those with whom the Mission was in touch is of more than passing interest when we consider the Mission as the nursery of The Salvation Army. Preaching was carried on in the open air, in theatre, shop and shed; there was visiting from house to house; a Bible carriage was in use for the sale of Bibles and "soul-saving literature"; there were temperance meetings, evening classes for teaching converts and children to read and write; there were reading rooms, penny banks, soup kitchens, relief by distribution of food and small sums of money. William Booth reported, "The workers in this Mission have, for the most part, been brought to God in the Movement . . . Since the commencement there have been 4,000 anxious enquirers at the different stations . . . Situations have been obtained for numbers, while others have been assisted to emigrate.[137] The resolve to do what was needed for individual converts—even to emigrating them—was thus early in evidence. William Booth's view was that once converted everyone must be encouraged, helped, if need be, to earn an honest living, and set to work to help others. Then, as now, converts soon changed their environment—one reason why large corps of Salvationists are not found in the slums: many salvation soldiers today travel to and from their homes to the bad districts to carry on the attack against evil; they do not live there.

An important development the following year was the issue of the Mission Magazine in October 1868. A monthly, its title was *The East London Evangelist*; but in January 1870, the Mission having spread beyond London, it became *The Christian Mission Magazine*, and was published until the end of 1879. Having had one year's issue under the title of *The Salvationist*, it gave place to a bi-weekly *The War Cry*, later published weekly. Catherine, jubilant, shared with William the joy of preparing the first copy. They corrected the proofs together. The editorial "we" of the first number is unmistakably Catherine's as well as his. It states the policy as "twofold"; first the publication of revival intelligence "so that, hearing of the Lord's marvellous doings in one place, Christians at a distance may be stirred to desire, pray and labour for similar manifestations of His saving power in their own churches and neighbourhoods . . ." and secondly to devote "a large portion of our space to the topic of personal holiness. Practical Godliness is the great want of the age."[138] Secondary hopes about the magazine were that by putting the needs of the Mission before sympathizers, financial support would be increased. This hope was realized to some degree. One may smile, if a little wryly, that in the first number readers were told that "all our funds are exhausted". In the second that, unless help comes there "will not be money to pay

* A yearly Balance Sheet has been published ever since.

the workers". The first words of the first copy were in the form of a dedication. ". . . to all those who, obedient to the Master's command, are simply, lovingly, and strenuously, seeking to rescue souls . . ." and trying to "clothe the religion of Jesus with its primitive simplicity, fervour and energy. To such, belonging to whatever division of the Church of God . . . we dedicate *The East London Evangelist* . . . in the Master's Name."[139]

Shortage of funds tended to damp William's joy in what was already being accomplished. Catherine, who knew so well how his spirits flagged under that kind of strain, set herself to gather help. Every conceivable economy was practised. Friends and strangers who came, often from a distance, to look into the Booths' work expressed their "surprise that so extensive an organization can be sustained with so little". Catherine tackled the writing of begging letters. For the Mission she was eloquent and moving, her heart was in it, but she loathed it when she must plead personal needs. These were sometimes acute when ill-health prevented her from undertaking long series of preaching. She confides to Mrs. Billups, "I hope it is not pride; if it is I am afraid it is incurable. If it were possible to alter our mode of living I would be willing to go into a white-washed cottage, and live on potatoes and cabbage . . . and we have almost come to that! My precious husband is careworn and overwrought with his great work; the tug to get money for that is bad enough, but to have to think of self is worse than all."[140] In the spring of 1869 Catherine campaigned in Croydon. She preached there twice on twelve consecutive Sundays and on at least one other evening each week. These meetings resulted in the establishment of a Mission post. Dowdle, a fiddle-playing ex-railway guard, was in charge of the station and it is a matter of interest and importance that his assistant was a Sister Coates, who preached on the second Sunday with "blessed results in the conversion of souls". Giving women equal opportunity with men to preach had become a *fact* before The Salvation Army had either its constitution or its name.

Before the Croydon campaign had finished, a visit to Scotland was under consideration. Mr. P. Ross, an Edinburgh businessman, had started a mission in the capital. He attended some of the Booths' meetings in East London and was greatly stirred. He returned to Edinburgh desiring to set his own Mission on the same lines. The work grew, became too much for him, and he invited William and Catherine to come down and look into the possibility of taking it over. They went in late July and Bramwell went with them. Of this visit Catherine wrote, "We both felt not only that a little rest was necessary for us, but that we had earned it. We had never been to Scotland so we thought we might combine a little recreation and change of scene with this stroke of business for the Kingdom."[141] Reading the account of the visit in the Mission Magazine, it seems more than doubtful whether either recreation or rest had a place in the programme! Sunday, July 25, 1869, found 400 assembled for a free breakfast, at which William preached. Many remained to the meetings that followed and twenty sought the Saviour. In the afternoon William preached again. In the evening hundreds were turned away; the old galleried chapel was crammed. The Magazine records that "Mrs. Booth preached a heart-searching sermon". Thirty came to the penitent-form. The meetings continued on Monday, Tuesday and Wednesday. The Booths stayed longer than originally intended "in order to make all the necessary arrangements for working the Mission". August 15 was the last of the *three Sundays* on which they led the services. Again there were crowds and penitents. On Monday at a great tea meeting the amalgamation of the Edinburgh work with the East London Mission was announced thus outmoding its name, though this was not noticed until later, when it became The Christian Mission. Catherine rejoiced in this enlarging of William's sphere, but neither of them yet saw, much less planned, that going forth to preach *in all the world* which had in fact already begun. Begun in suitable sequence surely, London, Edinburgh?

For Catherine, on her return from the rest that was not a rest, there lay only a matter of *days* before another of those long preaching efforts which included the slow, jolting journeys to and from the London terminus to the coast and back. Brighton, on a proposal from the Evangelization Society, was the selected ground. The first two Sundays (she began on August 29) brought crowds to the Grand Concert Hall. Noting, perhaps surprised at, her popularity, the owner thereupon demanded increased rent, far above that agreed upon. How little he knew the woman he was dealing with! Catherine thought his demand unjust and unreasonable, and before the next Sunday it had been arranged to transfer her meetings to The Dome, at that time one of the finest halls in the land. She said, "The first sight of it appalled me. It was indeed a Dome! As I looked upward there appeared space enough to swallow any amount of sound that my poor voice could put into it. To make any considerable number of people hear me seemed impossible. On this point, however, I was greatly encouraged to learn at the conclusion of the first meeting that I had been distinctly heard in every portion of it ... I can never forget my feelings as I stood on the platform and looked upon the people, realizing that among them all there was no one to help me ... The Lord was better to me than my fears, for ten or twelve of them came forward ... The way was led by two old gentlemen of seventy or more years of age. One of them said that he had sinned for many years against the light ... asking the Lord to save him with all the simplicity of a little child."[142] Later one or two rallied to her help.

Probably it was during this Brighton campaign that Father Ignatius*
heard Catherine Booth preach; at any rate it was while she was
conducting meetings there, where he also was holding services, that
he wrote to her. We have her reply though not his letter to her.
With rare exceptions she destroyed letters from members of her congregations. She wrote, "I return your kind and Christian greeting with
all sincerity and Christian affection, and I pray most earnestly that your
desires for me may be fully realized, that I may be led into 'all
truth'. From a child I have loved and studied the Scriptures, and I
bless God that He has given me His Holy Spirit thus revealing to
me that 'the Kingdom of God is not meat and drink, or anything
outward', but 'righteousness and peace, and joy in the Holy Ghost'.
And this is to be realized only by a living faith in Jesus. I pray that
whatever other revelation you may hold, above or beyond this, that
you may not fail of this, but that our gracious God lead you to its
full realization and enjoyment, and enable you to lead hundreds of
poor deluded souls, who are seeking rest in 'washings and carnal rites',
to find this blest inward kingdom. I trust that we shall meet when the
fogs of time will be dispersed, and all the saints will see eye to eye.
My heart burns in anticipation of that glorious oneness with all His
real Israel."[143] His view of her comes to us clear cut in the words
he wrote to a friend at her death, "What a glorious woman! What 'a
mother' of giants 'in Israel'! What an astounding *Fact* is The Salvation
Army! What a shame, and what a glory to the churches! ... New-
man, Liddon, Booth—true saints 'promoted' almost together!"[144] By
the use of surnames here Father Ignatius deliberately marks the
Christian declaration "there is neither male nor female, for ye are one
in Christ Jesus."

The Brighton effort was concluded on November 30. Throughout
this strenuous campaign Catherine bore the strain of watching at her
mother's death-bed. Doctors had pronounced Mrs. Mumford incurably
ill more than twelve months before, and the Mumfords were persuaded
to give up the house at Brixton and come to live near their daughter's
home. Mrs. Mumford suffered much. Catherine was constantly at her
mother's side, helping to nurse in the intervals of her public work.
Miss Jane Short tells, "This was the first experience either the General
or his wife had had of death in their own immediate circle. They
were both deeply affected." Mrs. Mumford's "death was remarkable.
Mrs. Booth was kneeling at her side, holding her hand, and quite
suddenly Mrs. Mumford regained consciousness, opened her eyes wide,
and with a light on her face that was unearthly, exclaimed 'Kate—
Jesus!' and was gone in that moment."[145] Catherine said, "Such a

* Father Ignatius revived the Benedictine Order in the Church of England, died 1908.

241

heavenly look of peace and victory and glory passed over her face as we had never witnessed before. It was indeed a transfiguration."[146]

The four years since she and William had accepted the East End masses as their sphere had imposed immense effort on Catherine. The scope of her public work was greatly increased, and the uncertainty of the financial situation remained a burden on her, the more so since William must not suspect how heavily it weighed. The tax on her strength of the "lone" responsibility for great meetings and what they entailed was not all. Her family and her own undiminished sense of her love's duty to them, including always her beloved William, was perhaps the most exacting of all. The more tired he, the more excited by the forward rush of the Mission, the more insistent was his need of her. Her love was a never-failing well of sympathy, encouragement and cherishing. But love's riches do not always consist of gifts without cost to the giver. And added to this there were her spiritual children. "My mother in Christ," "My spiritual mother," they call her; men and women "anxious" about their own problems whose letters need replies that only she can give. To these were added the actual and urgent claims of the Mission; its finances, properties and most of all the men and women who carried on the work of the stations. Her own evangelistic efforts, including hiring halls and arranging for public announcements, all came upon her. Once the meetings began, the sins, sorrows and difficulties of the converts were carried in her heart. She and William had almost no leisure, their time together or apart was devoured in meeting the demands of the Mission in relation to which William once said, "Time is so precious that unless it can be spent in sleeping or working every minute of it is begrudged." Have in mind too, her own family of youngsters. This over-crowded period of public life coincided with the most vital years in their development. Few mothers I think bore the burden of love and delight in her children as did Catherine Booth.

The Salvation Army had not yet received its name, but in essentials it was formed and fighting. Doctrine and methods exemplified in the work of William and Catherine Booth were, in the main, followed by the "Missioners", paid and voluntary, whom William Booth engaged. Accepted methods included open-air preaching and processioning; the use of secular halls; public testimony of men and women converts; women as well as men preachers; children's meetings in which the children themselves took part; material help of sick and poor; sensational methods to mark events. At funerals, for example, ". . . Around the house very soon the footpath and streets were blocked with people."

". . . A procession followed the hearse to the cemetery, singing hymns all the way . . . Some 2,000 people crowded closely round the grave . . ." Later brass bands led such processions and often sinners knelt in penitence at the grave side. All this, which would be characteristic of The Salvation Army, was building and spreading in The Christian Mission. Unconventional challenging of sinners by Mission members had begun. One started remonstrating with gamblers under a railway arch in Bethnal Green, another opened his shop front and Mission members within shouted the Gospel message in competition with raucous salesmen of the Limehouse Sunday morning market. There was freedom for Mission members—as there still is for Salvation Army officers and soldiers—to attack the devil's strongholds in any way they thought might be effective.

One of her letters to Mrs. Billups seems to me like a light illuminating Catherine's inmost soul. Through its mixture of comment on preaching, money-raising, the mystery of sickness, the need of faith and on God's immanence, this letter shows me Catherine as the same intense and loving spirit I have learned to know. When she writes this letter she is in her forty-fifth year; the youngest of her eight children is six; Bramwell, her firstborn, seventeen. The Gospel is being preached to "the Masses". This is still her life's goal and it contents her. She herself is a famous public figure; she has seen thousands of people kneel in submission to God in her own meetings, but I find the same humble-minded, aspiring, tender heart, possessed by the same passionate sincerity. She has experience now of God, of man, of Satan too, but Catherine, wife and mother, lover of souls, swift-writing to her sisterly confidant, is intrinsically unchanged. Unlike many of her letters this one is dated so that we know exactly when it was that alone in the railway carriage, she felt as she here tells:

"*My dearest Friend,* I have been at Wellingborough and Kettering over a week. I went against my will, but had been long promised, so was obliged. The Lord went with me and mightily stood by me. I was at the Independent chapels in both places and had crowds of people at the services and rich blessing. The friends told me that on Friday night the oldest ministers in both Independent and Baptist bodies were present. The Rev. Mr. Toller opened for me very appropriately . . . He is a sweet-spirited man, took leave of me on Sunday morning after service, weeping so that he could hardly speak. Oh, for more men of like mind!

"Well, the Lord works in His own way, and it is marvellous in our eyes. We got £175 promised while I was there toward a new hall, making in all £250 for Wellingborough. *I think* they are thoroughly shaken up. All praise to Him who worketh all in all. Many thanks to you, my dear friend, for all your love and care of my dear Willie [Bramwell]. I know the difficulties relating to his health of which you speak, but pray that you may be able to avert the spasmodic attacks of his heart which are so alarming. I grieve to find he is not so well. He is kept much too anxious. I know it all to my sorrow, but what can I do? I can only try to rest and hope in God. I would like you to see two or three of his letters written from Cardiff, they made my heart leap for joy. He has chosen God for his portion, come prosperity or adversity, and I know the Lord will take care of His own. Is it not strange these freaks of disease? How are they to be accounted for in natural principles? I am persuaded they cannot. Let us get back through second causes to God. Oh, what a deal of unbelief is mixed with our small measure of faith. We need the Spirit to sound in our heart of hearts, 'Have faith in God'. O Holy Spirit, sound it in my soul and keep it sounding!

"I am truly sorry to hear that dear Mr. Billups continues ill ... We *have* a little faith, let us use it on his behalf. I am trying. Are you? ... The Lord knows the end from the beginning, and if it be for His glory and kingdom He will hear us and do it for us." And then comes a passage telling how in spite of her anxieties, alone in the railway carriage God gave her, as Rutherford* put it, a "look over beyond ... to the laughing side of the world," made her feel, "I triumph and ride upon the high places of Jacob."[147] "I had such a view of His love and faithfulness on the journey from Wellingborough that I thought I would never doubt again about anything. I had the carriage to myself and such a precious season with the Lord that the time seemed to fly. As the lightning gleamed around I felt ready to shout 'The chariots of Israel and the horsemen thereof!' Oh, how precious it is when we see as well as believe, but yet more blessed to *believe* and *not see*! Lord, work this determined, obstinate, blind, unquestioning, unanswering faith in me and my beloved friend, and let us two dare to trust Thee in the midst of our peculiar trials. As I looked at the waving fields, the grazing sheep, the flashing sky, a voice said in my soul, 'Of what oughtest thou to be afraid? Am I not God? Cannot I supply thy little tiny needs?' My heart replied, 'It is enough, Lord, I will trust Thee; forgive my unbelief.'

"My dear Friend, you *do* trust a little; oh, be encouraged to trust *altogether*! Sickness in our loved ones, weakness in ourselves, perplexity in our circumstances, even the workhouse in the distance are 'light afflictions' compared with what many of His dear ones have had to bear, and 'All things work together for good' while we love Him and do His will. Lord help us.

"I shall rejoice to hear that you are comforted by an improvement in Mr. B. Give my kindest regards to him, and tell him I am pleading the Lord to remember all his kindness to His servants, and to add a few more years to his life for His kingdom's sake. From your ever loving friend. C. Booth."[148]

* Samuel Rutherford, Scottish divine (1600-1661).

BOOK FOUR

Catherine's Love for The Salvation Army: The Army Mother

"If my dear husband can find a sphere where he can preach the Gospel *to the masses*, I shall want no further evidence as to the Will of God concerning him."

—In a letter to her mother.

"We want men who are set on soul-saving; who are not ashamed to let every one know that this is the one aim and object of their life and that they make everything secondary to this."

—In a letter to her son Ballington.

"Here is the principle ... adapt your measures to the necessity of the people to whom you minister. You are to take the Gospel to them in such modes ... and circumstances as will gain for it from them a hearing."*

"We shall go on trying to make men right, and when they fall down we shall pick them up again, and nurse them and prepare them for everlasting righteousness and heaven."*

"He may not be able to put together two sentences of the Queen's English, but if he can say that he has been born again, if he can say 'I once was blind but now I see', he will do for The Salvation Army."*

"What can be a more fatal cause of religious declension than inactivity? Yet there are multitudes ... professing to be Christians who do *absolutely nothing* for the salvation of souls."

—Treatise on the care of converts.

"Oh, to help in some small degree to revive and enforce a *practical* Christlike Christianity."

—In a love-letter to William.

"... the drinking customs of society. I believe that God's deep curse is on them; and never till the church repents and washes her hands of them will she do much for the world."

—In a love-letter to William.

"Religion is doing the will of God with a heart full of love."

—In a love-letter to William.

"The curse, of this age especially, is *unbelief*, frittering the real meaning of God's word away, and making it all figure and fiction."

—In a letter to her parents.

* From public addresses.

1

"A sweet lady, rose colour in her cheeks, gentle voice, a *mother*. I saw her on the platform afterwards. She was sedate in speaking, but mighty convincing."[1] Thus Elijah Cadman,* one-time boy chimney-sweep, drinker and pugilist, saw Catherine Booth. He was one of the first to call her "The Army Mother". All who had to do with her felt in some measure as did William Stead who wrote, "She was as kind, as sympathetic, as patient, and as helpful to me, as if she had been my own mother."[2] His personal acquaintance with her and her time gave Stead a certain authority to say of her that "of those who, in the last quarter of the nineteenth century, have most notably influenced the religious life of England, there are few who can be compared with Mrs. Booth . . . To begin with, she was a woman, and no woman before her exercised so direct an influence upon the religious life of her time. Her work was not the mere carrying on of an existing organization. She and her husband built up out of recruits gathered in the highways and byways of the land, what is to all intents and purposes a vast world-wide Church . . . The Salvation Army is a miracle of our time."[3]

By 1870, in almost all save name, The Salvation Army was in being. In the spring of this year the *People's Market* in Whitechapel was bought, to become the People's Mission Hall, and the first property owned by Booth's Mission. Raising the money was a terrific task. *The Christian Mission Magazine* tells, "We have a large airy hall, class rooms, book shop and soup kitchen, in the heart of Whitechapel."[4] The Booths had a very clear idea of what they wanted for their Army. William, when he first came to London, was horrified by the number of public houses and noted of churches that "very few of them were open more than one evening a week . . ."[5] From the first beginnings of the work of the Mission the importance of having the halls *open and in use every night* was constantly emphasized. In later years Catherine defended William's "daring" in the matter of buildings, saying, "We think that the same enterprise which actuates business men with respect to their buildings should be incorporated into religion. What care and sagacity are exercised as to the situation and suitability of business premises . . . opening the theatres, dancing hells . . . and gin palaces every day, and making them attractive every night by flaring gas, music and other attractions . . . God's buildings ought to be open

* Elijah Cadman, born 1843; became a Commissioner in The Salvation Army.

247

every night, and every innocent means used to draw the people into them."[6] These words were almost revolutionary when spoken.

Those first Whitechapel premises were used as chief centre for meetings, and as headquarters of The Salvation Army until 1881. Here mid-day meetings were held daily in the roomy portico. Here Bramwell Booth began a week-night holiness meeting that drew people from Europe and America. Here people brought their friends to see what a Salvation Army meeting was like. Stead tells that Canon Liddon, then Dean of St. Paul's, "had often talked about The Salvation Army, and he had expressed his curiosity ... I offered to take him to a holiness meeting, which was then being held at Whitechapel, one Friday night. It was late in the year, I think, of 1881, and it was quite dark when I got him into a hansom at Amen Court ... Canon Liddon had no sooner seated himself in the hansom, than he began to take off the white collar which is the distinguishing badge of the cleric. 'I hope you will not think ... that this savours of a lack of moral courage but,' he added, 'if I were not to change, I should be sure to be recognized and all next week I should be bothered by ... letters I could not ignore, either protesting against my attending a service of The Salvation Army, or enquiring why ...' In order to minimize the possibility of being recognized, we took up our seats in a remote corner beneath the gallery. What was our consternation ... to see a clergyman of the Church of England clambering over the forms towards us! When he reached us he said, 'Oh, Canon Liddon, I am delighted to see you here!' ...

"The meeting was of the ordinary type; there were testimonies, prayers, and lively singing. Among others who testified was a girl in a Salvation Army bonnet and the regulation dress, and a stoker, fresh from some steamer in the London docks, whose grimy face did not prevent him taking part in the service ... When we left, we walked back through the City. Canon Liddon was deeply impressed. He was at first somewhat silent, but after a time he said, 'It fills me with shame. I feel guilty when I think of myself.' He continued musingly, 'To think of these poor people, with their imperfect grasp of the truth! ... Of course,' said he, 'I did not like the women speaking, although I was prepared for it.'" As they walked they argued woman's liberty to witness in public for Christ. "The chief point, however," Stead records, "round which discussion raged, was his [Liddon's] stout assertion that The Salvation Army had only a small part of the truth. I agreed, for all human beings only know in part; but I said 'Surely you must admit that they have got the essential truth?' He replied, 'I no more recognize essential truth, than I do an essential horse.' ... And thus it went on until we came to Amen Court, where we stood in the cold night air, arguing ... When we at last parted, Canon Liddon had caught such a cold that next day he could not use his voice."[7]

At the opening of the People's Mission Hall 250 persons gathered at seven o'clock on Sunday morning for prayer and praise. This meeting was followed by "A public breakfast". William Booth was present in the afternoon, but very unwell, and to his bitter disappointment too ill to preach at night, as announced. This illness was finally diagnosed as typhoid fever. He suffered several serious relapses before he was sufficiently recovered to be back at the controls. In the meantime Catherine and the boy Bramwell carried on the work of the Mission. She took William's place at night on the opening Sunday. The hall was thronged. "The outer gates had to be closed to keep out the crowd eager to press in." A hundred and fifty came to the penitent form, and others knelt and prayed at their seats. "It was . . . a matter of exultation that the service could not be abruptly closed, as at the theatre [previously hired for us on Sundays] by the punctual turning out of the lights."[8]

Catherine's joy is clouded only by William's illness. She moves among kneeling seekers during the prayer meeting with a richer responsibility. These penitents are their *own* people, William's and hers, and Catherine is ready to take her place as their spiritual mother, naturally, unquestioningly; and, as unquestioningly, naturally the people accept her. "Our Mother," they call her, and look to her as to one whose love and wisdom will not fail them. Stead said, "She undertook in all seriousness the spiritual direction of the souls of her converts . . . These converts, whom, until they had come within the range of her voice, she had never seen, were straightway adopted into her family. As members of that family they were entitled to carry to her, their mother, all their troubles, difficulties, doubts and temptations."[9]

The instinct to care for converts, strangely absent in some preachers, was highly developed in both William and Catherine even before they met. According to the notions of these two there must be personal contact that could convince a new convert that he was *someone's care*. When he began his East London Mission, William made after-care of converts a recognized part of the organization. In the plan of work he set forth in *The Christian* he said, "*We propose to watch over and visit personally those brought to Christ.*" In the early days William Booth did a great deal of this himself. He made it a principle of the Mission that when converts had wronged others there must be confession and restitution. A number of people went to prison as a result. Jane Short tells that during the time she worked in the Mission "many had to put things right with employers", William himself often going with them. In The Salvation Army leaders of "posts" (corps) were made responsible for visiting converts in their homes or on their way to and from work; and for arranging weekly meetings for the instruction of converts and soldiers.

Some time before their marriage Catherine had set forth her ideas on the care of converts. In this treatise* she compared the needs of an infant with those of the new convert, who, she insisted, above all must be nourished on the Bible and "taught how to apply the principles of action laid down in God's Word to the daily occurrences of life". An atmosphere of love in the Church was essential; when this was lacking "far from its being a matter of surprise that so many converts relapse into spiritual death, it appears to me a far greater wonder that so many survive!" The new convert, she declared, needs the "tender watchfulness of fathers and mothers in Christ; and freedom to exercise faculties". Catherine asked, "What can be a more fatal cause of religious declension than inactivity?"[10]

When she had become the Army Mother, she maintained that "the very first aspiration of a newly-born soul is after some other soul ... father, mother, child, brother, sister, friend ... If Christians were only true to the promptings of this blessed Spirit, it would be the prevailing impulse, the first desire and effort all the way through life ... Jesus Christ has nobody else to represent Him here but Christians—His real people; nobody else to work for Him. These poor people of the world, who are in darkness and ignorance, have nobody else to show them the way of mercy. If we do not go to them with loving earnestness and determination to rescue them from the grasp of the great enemy ... who is to do it? God has devolved it upon us."[11] These words were matched by William's when he defined his aim for the Mission, "Every man saved . . . and every man at work, always at work, to save other people."[12] This sense of responsibility for "saving" others was the quintessence of Salvationism. Without it The Salvation Army would not have survived, still less spread; and if it should decline, it will be because eager self-denying *love for sinners* has dwindled in the hearts of Salvationists.

Easter in 1870 fell the week after the opening of the People's Hall and on Easter Monday more than 800 Mission members assembled at the new centre. Several open-air meetings were held and then the company, in procession and singing "above the revelling" of the bank holiday crowd, "came rejoicing to the hall". Here 800 sat down to tea, after which came a public meeting. William was too ill to be present. The Mission Magazine tells: "Mrs. Booth was listened to with breathless attention ... We all blessed dear Mr. Pennefather† in our hearts, as with his open, loving spirit, he told us that the great delight with which he looked upon the beautiful hall was only surpassed by the pleasure with which he looked upon the faces of the

* Published in *The Methodist New Connexion Magazine*, June 1855.

† Rev. William Pennefather, died 1873. Originated interdenominational work in 1856 when vicar of Barnet. Became vicar of St. Jude, Mildmay. Founded Mildmay Medical Mission. Friendly supporter of William and Catherine Booth.

people gathered in it, and then fell upon his knees and implored the benediction of Heaven on . . . the Mission."[13] This bird's eye view of the proceedings shows how free from formality the meetings had already become. The service went on with prayer and testimony and penitents until midnight. Public houses did not close until midnight in those days, and many in the congregation had been drinking until that hour on the Easter bank holiday a year ago.

During William's illness Catherine went from his bedside to London Mission stations and, while he was convalescing, she led a campaign of several weeks in Stoke Newington where a Mission station was afterwards opened. After William resumed control of Mission affairs, Catherine went to Hastings where she held a series of three months meetings. William was able to lead the 1871 Easter celebrations at the People's Hall. Miss Billups, who had become a Mission worker and preacher, reported, "Our greatest cause for gratitude is that our beloved Superintendent is with us. Last year his serious illness cast a gloom over all." Tea for a thousand was provided by Mr. Reed. On past occasions Mission folk had spent a day on his estate. In 1869 at 8.30 in the morning 1,420 persons had left London in two special trains and Cannon Street Station had resounded to the sound of singing. Numbers so increased that this kind of coming together had to be given up and Reed contributed instead to the jollifications in the People's Hall where all was "carefully prepared and tastefully set out". There were pots of flowers in "luxuriant bloom" given by a lady in Walthamstow, "adding to the happiness of those who rarely see anything of the beautiful". Gatherings on public holidays were part of William's programme to keep converts together and away from old companions. The occasions were made as attractive as possible, from the substantial quantity of the meal, to the free and easy style of music, song and testimony in the meeting that followed. This was no doubt a development of the Wesleyan tea meeting and it played a happy part in Salvation Army methods. Bringing large companies together, for anniversary and other meetings, also helped to enthuse Mission members and many returned to the comparatively small congregation of their local station feeling themselves to be part of a "conquering host". Besides this, many saw William and Catherine for the first time on these occasions and from that moment were knit into closer unity with the aim of the Movement. At this 1871 Easter "tea party" meeting they heard William declare, "Glory be to God! Our cry is still, souls, souls, souls! We are still a penitent-form people; we believe in getting sinners to the penitent-form. For every new attack of Satan against our work, I feel the only answer to give him is to *open a new Mission station*! People say we must wait for an open door. The devil will not open the door for us, nor the publican, nor the infidel! We must go and open it for ourselves. So we say, wherever there is a dark, evil-ridden neighbourhood, *go there*

251

... and soon someone will ask you to hold a meeting in his house."[14] *The Christian* reported, "addresses of several working men were really remarkable". A gipsy testified, "Now eight of my family are on their way to heaven. Though I can't read my Bible, I can read my title to heaven . . . My heart is so full that, instead of crying out in the street, 'Chairs to mend' . . . I have called out 'Souls to mend'!"[15]

Catherine's path at this time was a continual trial of faith and strength. William had of course returned to work too soon after the typhoid. His efforts to make up for lost time aggravated his condition. It was in this period that he attempted to combine helping the poor with augmenting income for the support of his family by cheap food shops. And just before Christmas, Miss Short, who had done so well as preacher in the Mission and helper in their home, broke down from over-work, and by Easter 1872 had sailed away to Australia. William was again too ill to be at the People's Hall for Easter Sunday as announced, and again Catherine took his place. To a tense congregation she declared that *even if her husband were to die* "the Mission should, by God's help,"[16] be carried forward. Doctors found William's condition grave, "caused by overwork". Catherine felt that she did not need a doctor to tell her that! One prescribed at least a year's complete rest away from all anxiety. Another declared William would never again be able to resume charge of the Mission. Once more there were fears for his life. "Love adds horribly to the strain of nursing the sick," Catherine wrote to Mrs. Billups. Directly he was well enough William went to Mr. Smedley's Hydro at Matlock and was induced to stay away from work for over six months. Everything was left to Catherine and sixteen-year-old Bramwell. What a tumult of heart pangs and prayer must have seethed in her, as the cab rattled on its journeys to take her to and from the London meetings. Her energy and courage at this time, her faith for her husband's recovery and for the progress of the Mission, seem to me to be a kind of continuing miracle.

It was while Booth was ill that Lord Shaftesbury invited him to attend a conference called to consider the amalgamation of undenominational religious organizations in London. Catherine Booth went in her husband's place and spoke on behalf of The Christian Mission. Lord Shaftesbury* listened with "evident interest and appreciation". The proposed amalgamation was not carried into effect, but the glimpse we have of Catherine, representing the authorized head of a religious body, gives an idea of the place she had already won in Christian circles. William was absent for rest and treatment until October 1872. Catherine visited him and at such times Bramwell managed home, Mission, and food shops. Letters show how his parents

* Lord Shaftesbury (1801-1885), philanthropist, celebrated for reform of Lunacy Acts and Factory Acts.

relied on him. Miss Short said that "with the other children, his influence was more like that of a parent than of a brother". The Mission workers accepted him in much the same manner. Money was frightfully short, both for the Mission and for support of the family. Hopes that the cheap food shops (several had been opened) would contribute to the family funds faded. The food was too cheap and the managers not always trustworthy. While away William wrote instructions, advice, and admonition to the sixteen-year-old boy in Whitechapel. Catherine was with William when news of further loss on the food shops came from Bramwell and the sick man wrote to his son, "My dear Boy, Mama has just told me the substance of your letter. I am very sorry for your sake and dear Mama's. Bless you for all your thoughtfulness for me and all the burden you have borne . . . now is the time for us to *trust*. We will do our duty and leave events calmly to God. If there is no other way, I must have a salary from the Mission, and Mama must earn some money by preaching. But some other way may be opened. *I have confidence in God*. Look up. Rest and hope in infinite Love."[17] It throws light on the characters of William and Catherine that at this time of extreme need, they looked upon drawing a salary from the Mission as a last resort. What a strength this proved when a few years later William was accused of having made a "good heave for himself and his family out of The Salvation Army—the pence of the poor". To my mind there is something stoical in their steady adherence to the self-imposed resolve only to give to and never to take from its funds. The family was still largely supported by money raised in Catherine's campaigns, which were independent of the Mission, and by the sale of her pamphlets, and of Song Books compiled by William Booth. While he was away Catherine could not undertake series of meetings, time available was taken up with visits to Mission stations, and family income suffered.

When at last William came home and was safely through the winter Catherine made plans to visit Portsmouth. As usual she went alone. She writes to Mrs. Billups, "I never was so hampered for help . . . the most able man I have keeps a milkman's shop, and one that opens [the service] for me generally, is overseer of about 500 men in the dockyard . . ."[18] A hall seating a thousand proved quite inadequate, and Catherine took a Music Hall for Sundays. She insisted on this, in spite of objections that low entertainment was carried on there during the week and that it was in a bad neighbourhood. On the way there one had to pass "drinking dens and brothels". Catherine did not mind. She wanted to gather in the worst of sinners. Warnings that there might be rowdyism did not alarm her either, "the godless masses" in Whitechapel had inured her to much. Two policemen did prove necessary, but only to deal with the crowd shut out after the building was full. A letter to Mrs. Billups told of crowded meetings and continued, "...Pray for me. No one knows how I feel. I think I never realized my responsibility as I did on Sunday night. I felt really awful ... The sight almost overwhelmed me. There are two galleries ... and when full of people it looks most imposing ... It seems to me God's time to visit this place, and whoever had been the instrument He had sent He would have blessed it. I adore Him for sending me. It seems like a new commission with which I have received new power ... Pray for me. I never needed your prayers so much. This is a dreadfully wicked place." The letter closes with mention of the children who were with her in apartments at Southsea. "I shall not be able to keep them here long however. It is so expensive and funds are low ... My beloved writes me that he is better. I hope it is not imagination,"[19] which tells that William was not yet so well that he might not be better.

In Portsmouth hundreds of notorious sinners were converted in her meetings. The prayer meeting sometimes lasted longer than the first part. The Sunday morning services were devoted to Christians who did, after all, brave the "low locality". Catherine gave twelve consecutive Sunday morning addresses on the words, "Go work today in my vineyard." After preaching for an hour, she would announce that the subject would be continued on the following Sunday morning, God willing, but whether to conclude or not was more than she could say. There is no record of these sermons, which would have made a unique treatise on Christian duty. A good deal has been said by her biographers about Catherine's delicate health, but she must have had a sound constitution as well as the *will to do,* or she could not have directed the Mission in her husband's absences or sustained these prolonged spells of preaching. The Portsmouth meetings lasted for seventeen weeks.

There ought now to have been a breathing space for her. Instead Catherine set off for campaigns in London, Wellingborough and Kettering. She would not like William to be blamed, but surely he ought to have realized that she was overtaxing her strength? Chatham was then decided on for her next effort. An enlightening account of her method to inaugurate a campaign was given in *The Chatham News,* in which her reading of the Bible with running comments is remarked upon. This method was soon to be used throughout The Salvation Army to help apply Bible teaching to everyday living. On the first Sunday morning, reported the paper, "Mrs. Booth read the second chapter of Nehemiah, at various times making remarks of her own upon the events of the sacred narrative ... She can rise to the height of a great argument with an impassioned force and fervour that will thrill many a hearer."[20]

How to reach the Masses with the Gospel was the title Booth gave to the Annual Report for 1872. Morgan wrote the preface, and the pamphlet was advertised for sale in the Magazine. It came into the hands of a profoundly religious young enthusiast, George Scott Railton. What he read convinced him that "these were the people for me". Unconventional, even eccentric, he felt an affinity with William Booth and his methods. After a visit to see the work, he wrote to William offering his help, addressing him as "My dear General" and signing himself "Your loving Lieutenant". (This anticipated the use of Booth's title by six years.) He described the Whitechapel work as "the nearest I know to Heaven below". In March 1873, after certain business commitments had been concluded, he arrived to make one more in the Gore Road home, where he was treated as a son by Catherine. "Both determined and tractable, original and simple, aggressive and tender, able to take blows and insults like a lamb . . . he was a fascinating and unexpected personality."[21] Thus Bramwell described him. His literary gifts were increasingly important as The Salvation Army developed and hymns he wrote are still sung by Salvationists. Railton lived in the Booth home until his marriage eleven years later. His friendship with Bramwell continued till death parted them. "For the first time in my life I am blessed with a companion—a friend who can greatly help me . . . we have a great affinity of disposition and enjoy each other's society . . ."[22] Railton wrote of Bramwell to Mrs. Booth. His help whether in the office or preaching gave Bramwell more freedom to be absent from the centre.

What a mercy for Catherine that her son was with her and that she was *not* alone when on the third Sunday of her campaign in Chatham, just as she had finished her address in the night meeting, she fell in a faint. Bramwell gathered her up in his arms and carried her into an ante-room, realizing with something of a shock what a "light little thing" his indomitable mother was. She was very ill, and suffered an anguish of pain, but in three weeks was back in Chatham to carry the campaign to a victorious finish. William took her place on the two intervening Sundays when for the first time in her preaching years Catherine was not able to fulfil a public engagement.

On June 20, 1874, leaders of the Mission stations gathered in greater force than ever before to attend the annual conference in Whitechapel. This conference is worth marking in that *for the first time women* were present and *took part as delegates*. Among other matters it was resolved that all converts "should be taught to speak publicly to their fellow men about Christ", and that "bands for missioning in the street, and for house to house visitation" should be formed; that "special effort for the rescue of drunkards should be organized at each station". Catherine rejoiced at these decisions, in particular the last, which she had inspired on the lines of her own efforts in Gateshead. She made a stirring plea at the public meeting concluding the conference; speaking with bitter compassion that set a kind of spell on the congregation. Even in the few selected sentences I feel it: "Drunkards? . . . they are generally looked upon as disgusting good-for-nothings, the refuse of mankind—hopeless, unredeemable slaves of the devil. The very publicans, who have fattened on their ruin, spurn them from their doors the moment their last penny is spent, lest the sight of them should bring disgrace upon an 'honest trade'! The public regard the drunkard in his intoxicated state as an object of ridicule, when not a just cause of fear ... Despised by everyone ... with a fearful craving, to endure which is agony, and to satisfy which is to be drunk again; no wonder that the poor wretch comes to look upon himself ... as hopeless. *But is it true?* ... Can our Christianity do nothing for such a one? Is this man possessed by a legion which Jesus of Nazareth cannot cast out? Shame on us! Should we not rather ask, '*Can Jesus do anything with such miserable unbelieving agents as we are?*' ... The poor drunkard ... is still a *man* ... in many instances a man possessed of the highest susceptibilities and capabilities of human nature; only these have been smothered, blasted or prostituted by the demon drink. Let this devil be cast out and the drunkard, like the man among the tombs, will be ready to take his seat, clothed and in his right mind, at the feet of Jesus. *Yes, the drunkard can be saved.*"[23] The report of the work for the year 1874 was entitled *The Masses Reached*, and it stated that out of 100 typical converts of the Mission, *eighty* had been drunkards.

William Booth announced to the anniversary meeting that "during the twelve months, halls had been built or purchased at Plaistow, Portsmouth, and Bethnal Green". The owning of property brought new responsibilities. The Booths had long discussions, in which Railton joined, as to how the position might be safeguarded. During the ensuing year William decided. He told the Mission members and friends at the 1875 Conference, "... We have at length completed and enrolled in Chancery, a Deed (1875) which will, we think, render the use of our halls for other than purely evangelistic purposes utterly impossible."[24] Mr. Samuel Gurney Sheppard, who presided at the public anniversary meeting that year, said, "I expected I was coming to a little tea meeting and should, perhaps, be asked to address a few workers; but now that I see before me this large and enthusiastic gathering ... Your enthusiasm is catching."

Catherine's subject at the meeting was the *"Righteousness of enthusiasm in the cause of Christ".*[25] She spoke with characteristic intensity. Never were her words more moving than when she was speaking to "our own people". "Apostle she was and prophetess, but she was a mother first of all and last of all,"[26] Stead had said, and it is on occasions like this that the loving solicitude of the mother shines out. The congregation in the People's Hall is made up for the most part of Mission converts; the majority are East-Enders, ignorant, but not by any means stupid. They sit, tightly packed together, with their friends and families. The meeting has been going on some time when Catherine begins to speak. She is listened to with breathless attention. I find this quite as much a testimony to the intelligence of the congregation as to her eloquence. She is not talking down to them, "entertaining" them, tells no anecdotes, but dwells on the need for zeal, for minding doctrine, for caring for converts. She leads them to think of a responsibility for the *world*. Ex-drunkards, former prostitutes, and what William called "the submerged tenth" of the great city are made to feel that they themselves have a part to play, a duty toward "the utmost parts of the earth". And Catherine Booth has this effect on them, in part at least, because of the relation already established between them and her. They *feel* she has a mother's heart towards them. They can take anything from her. When she talks about love for souls they feel that they know what she means. They have seen her tears and heard the tenderness in her words; they know that it is something real in her and when she tells them that the Holy Spirit of Love is for all and each of them, they believe her. While she speaks all eyes are on her. "Mr. Sheppard said that he liked us for our enthusiasm; and I have very often ... had to defend this characteristic of our workers; so many people seem to take exception to this! ... When the life-boat goes out to the stranded ship and brings some of the shipwrecked crew safe to shore, no one complains of the enthusiasm! ... I maintain that it is *right* to be enthusiastic in such circumstances; and, if so, how much more right have we to be enthusiastic when we have such a Gospel to preach and such results to rejoice over ... [Of] the future of our work I say now, as I have said again and again before, let us prefer quality to quantity. Let us care what Gospel we preach. Let us mind our doctrine. Let us ever set forth the atonement for sin, together with the conditions upon which alone the benefits of the atonement can be participated in by any sinner.

"Work to be worth much must be husbanded ... It is of the highest importance *to maintain the spirit of the Mission* ... The converts cannot be quiet. They cannot help going out and pushing their religion upon others, while the Mission spirit is kept up. There are hundreds of them scattered all over the world, and nothing encourages me more than the letters which we receive from them ... telling of their efforts *to save souls*. Those who are born in the Mission cannot be quiet; they are sure to shout; and this is nothing more than Christianity, for Christianity is necessarily aggressive always . . . The true light cannot be hid; it cannot shine for itself; it must go *out* and *out* and out, to the end—it must go on to the ends of the world."[27]

Before the 1875 Conference had dispersed, Catherine was seized with an attack similar to the one she suffered in Chatham. Doctors diagnosed acute angina pectoris. William was aghast. Her state was serious. *She* wanted hydropathy tried, but was too ill to be moved any distance, so to go to Mr. Smedley at Matlock was out of the question. A practising hydropathist, a Mr. Richard Metcalf, was recommended. He had an establishment in the then countrified Paddington Green. He became a friend of the Booths and many Salvation Army officers benefited by his skill. There William drove with his little wife and wondered if he would get her to the place alive. More than once the cab had to be stopped, the shaking was too much for her even when supported by William's arm. Death seemed to be at hand. Both of them, Catherine we are certain, must have thought of that *first* drive together, when the path to heaven had seemed so shining clear. William held her close. She wanted to live, but thought she might be dying. On arrival she was carried straight into a Turkish bath. Relief from pain, and a spell of quiet sleep followed. There is a pencilled note written to Bramwell while she was at the hydro. It is about love: about the anxieties that spring from love: about William, and how Bramwell may best help him if she should die. She is very ill and weak, but her love reaches eagerly for life...

"My dearest Boy," the letter begins, "I have been thinking very much about you the last day or two. Since my heart has been bad, I have thought and felt more about you than ever before. I am so troubled..." Not for herself, but for William, for Bramwell, for all the "children" and the task that consumes them. Then, with a sudden flash of her loving peremptoriness, "Mind! I have no supernatural impression that I shall not get better...I wanted you to know my wishes...Forgive me for all my defects and shortcomings as a mother. I have always had too much on me of care and work or I should have been more helpful to you all than I have been..." concluding, "you have my tenderest and never-dying love, now and ever."[28]

She stayed at Metcalf's for some weeks. Strength gradually returned; the distressing heart symptoms subsided. Catherine went for rest and convalescence to friends at Hardres, near Canterbury. There William visited her. He had not intended to stay long, but an accident kept him at Catherine's side for more than five months! They were out driving together, as they loved to do. Having come up a hill, they drew up to enjoy the view, and to please Catherine as well as the pony gave it a wayside nibble of grass. Suddenly the bridle slipped off its head, and at that very instant, startled, the pony bolted. William jumped out of the chaise in an effort to get at the creature's head, and was dragged a few yards before he fell with a badly sprained knee. The frightened animal galloped on but finally came to a standstill at a miller's yard. Willing hands soon put things right and Catherine insisted on driving back *at once* to William. The kindly miller went with her, and William was found sitting by the roadside. During his enforced stay he compiled his first book of revival songs and music with the help of Miss Billups, while Catherine nursed his injured leg. It was the best real rest she and William ever had. Bramwell, with Railton as companion, directed the Mission.

258

At the 1876 Conference the important decision was made to appoint women evangelists *in charge* of stations; before this they had been assistants only. The Minutes record, "Miss Booth (Katie at the time eighteen) reserved for general evangelistic tours." Catherine's children were taking their place in the Mission family, Bramwell was recognized as his father's second in command, and next year Ballington would be a recognized Mission worker. At this Conference the Booths proposed another innovation, but this time without success. Bramwell recorded in his diary, "... On the 6th [of June 1876] we met again, hard day, very; ten to one, two to five, six to ten—and committees in between. I brought on my motion 'That no persons shall be hereafter received as members who do not abstain from the use of intoxicating drinks, except under medical advice.' There was a long discussion. I replied with some little effect; it was lost."[29] This happening had an important bearing on William's decision, given effect the following year, to take the direction of the Mission into his own hands.

When she first knew William he was not a total abstainer nor entirely convinced that he ought to be. His "little Love" soon won him over. Catherine's convictions on the subject were stronger than ever. Confessions to which she had listened from both rich and poor had laid bare such ghastly wounds, such ruin of family life, such sorrows caused by the "great destroyer" that her soul was filled with loathing of it. It was in order to help drunkards, and for the sake of converted drunkards already in the Mission that, in 1878 when William was in full control, *all members were required to abjure strong drink.* Tobacco was also prohibited to all who would take any active part in the work. Both abstentions were *for the same reason;* that is, for love of those to whom smoking was a step toward drinking, and a little drinking, a step toward drunkenness. Literally hundreds of thousands of working people have denied themselves "for love's sake" of this kind of self-indulgence. And it was the Army Mother's love for the weaker brother, and her hatred of the enslaver, that set the standard for Salvationists. Challenged to prove the use of tobacco sinful she once replied, "That depends on a man's light; but it must be a higher degree of devotion for a man to abandon it for the good of others, than to smoke for his own indulgence."[30] The force of her feeling about the drink showed itself in two ways; first, by the bold call to drunkards to rise and be made free. She proclaimed God's power to deliver with a faith so fearless that the most helpless felt hope revive as they listened to her. Catherine declared that there was only one way to reclaim drunkards: By "... *the power of the Holy Ghost.* We have had a great deal of experience, and we find that drunkards who sign the pledge, if they do not get the grace of God, soon fall back again." And the other side of her attack was denunciation of the evil when she addressed believers; as, "We might adduce overwhelming evidence that strong drink is the natural

259

ally of all wickedness ... How shall we deal with the drink? We answer, in the name of Christ and humanity ... wash your hands of it at once and forever ... The time has come for Christians to denounce the use of intoxicating drinks as irreligious and immoral."[31]

2

Catherine Booth was a fervent spirit, yet not a creature of changing moods, as those of highly emotional natures often are. Intensity of feeling about things that moved her was not so much a tide rising and falling, as that of a river flowing on and on in greater volume and power. There was something tough, unquenchable in her zeals. The love of God dwelling in her complemented and directed what might, of itself, have become a weakness and led to an intolerant even contemptuous frame of mind. As time went on, her capacity to feel and to make others feel was seen to be one of the most powerful instruments she wielded. She was able to infuse something of her passionate loves and hates into people who came under her influence. Those who recalled her when thought of this book first came to life in my mind were necessarily old but, on each, the mention of her name had the same almost magically vivifying effect. Said one to me, "How she *cared* about their sins! I saw, in her, what love for souls meant. She made me feel Christ's dying. It was at Colchester, while she was preaching, I saw her tears! It was a revelation to me." Throughout the years of development, the Army Mother's teaching and example was an element of fusion in the ranks. To unite the soldiers *"in the loves and hates of their hearts"*, she said was her aim. "Then, you have real union, and they will do and dare, suffer and die for their principles."[32] Catherine indoctrinated early day Salvationists just as surely as some mothers implant in their children enthusiasms that remain lifelong.

The Booths continued their habit of talking everything over. William called Catherine "a counsellor who in hours of perplexity and amazement" never failed. She lavished her sympathy on him while she comforted and stimulated his mind. Bramwell was in all their counsels and now often Railton too. In that company more than in any other Catherine showed herself a being "of persuasive charm, with a rare gift of seeing the essential".[33] Bramwell said of her, "In the early days of the ... Movement her hand was upon many matters to an extent unknown to anyone outside the inner circle ... Her insight and what I have sometimes called her unfolding power were really wonderful ... she would at once discern and fasten on the potentialities of a situation and carry us all to the future outcome of the thing proposed . . . She had the analytical mind . . . and further, she enhanced the reasonableness and beauty and value of the work we were doing in our own eyes."[34] This was her role through the years when The Salvation Army was being shaped.

Altogether 1876 was a good year for the mission. Catherine was able to re-visit several Mission centres, and to conduct a two months' campaign in Leicester where a new branch of the Mission was established. A letter to Mrs. Billups gives an idea of the trials and triumphs of this effort ". . . I have got some valuable lessons and illustrations here! I have secured the theatre, after great perseverance and prayer. The first service on Sunday night was packed to the ceiling, and they tell me hundreds were shut out. The Lord was with me, but the effort prostrated me, so that I could not leave my bed until yesterday, and I am so poorly that I can only just sit up now. I am almost sorry that I began here, but I trust the Lord will help me through, and then I shall have to seek rest and quiet again. I have no kind friend like you to take me out a bit. I have been here a month and never been outside the town but once, though there are several attend the services who keep their carriage. There is not a bath-chair to be got in the town, except an old one, like a child's large perambulator, all open and exposed, in which I have to go in sight of hundreds of people to my service, and I am so nervous that it quite upsets me. And yet, what are all these little things compared with souls? Pray for me that I may have strength to go through triumphantly. I have Emma here. She is not at all well, but her presence is a comfort to me."[35]

At the very least the Army Mother ought now to have had the help of a good secretary with authority to protect her from unnecessary strains. She used to say that it was absurd that good sense should be called "common"; in her view common sense was one of the rarest gifts. That she possessed it is clear from her dealings with all manner of people and situations. When, however, it came to looking after herself she often ignored its monitions! Whether the emotional strain of her life contributed to the development of the cancer that killed her or whether its incipience weakened her nervous system I do not know. What is certain is that many unimportant trials cost her much. To throw off the effect of uncomfortable lodgings, loneliness when on tour, the cold, or noise, or spoiled children became more difficult. She wrote to Bramwell, "I think my preaching days are about ended. I am too low to be sufficiently enthusiastic to raise the people, and it is of no good without. You young ones must take up the flag and win the battle, of course I feel spent as I generally do on a Monday . . . Give my love to them all." But there is energy left to remark, "I see a good improvement in your writing, still your long letters are too short."[36]

But William fell ill again! Even Catherine could not hold him in.

261

It was not only that he overworked, but that he was carried away with excitement at any fresh prospect of getting more *done*. He still suffered the alternating extremes of elation and depression so inimical to good digestion. So now, though but poorly herself, Catherine is once more nursing him. A pencilled note goes to Mrs. Billups, "I must snatch a moment to tell you that my dearest continues very ill . . . we are following Smedley's treatment as far as our patient's strength will allow. We have one of the best homoeopathic doctors within reach of us . . . a friend of Dr. Kidd's. He seems clever and approves of the water treatment . . ." The patient "takes nothing but rice water . . . I need not tell you how I feel. My soul seems dumb before the Lord—a horror of great darkness comes over me at times, but in the midst of it all I believe He will do all things well."[37]

William came back to life after several relapses of "gastric fever" which lasted months. Another undated letter to Mrs. Billups seems to link up. "My dearest continues very poorly. He had quite a relapse of the fever yesterday . . . I wish there was some means of restraining people when they are not fit to govern their actions . . . If you knew just how he is you would not wonder at my fears . . . he is thinner than ever I knew him . . . Do pray for him dear . . . I wish you would write him about his health. It may have a *little* effect." The fact is William was a very difficult patient! Even when he was well, as Stead said, "He was a man imperious enough in his way, but Mrs. Booth knew how to manage him and never forgot that he needed managing." She was in no danger of forgetting, as this disagreeable illness dragged on. "He is *so foolish*, he will not have a bit of game or anything out of the common, though game is easier to digest and suits him better than meat. He says he cannot eat such expensive things when so many are starving! I tell him for their sake he ought . . ." And then the letter gives news of the work and future plans and "I would like you to get to Merthyr just to look at the work there. I wish the Corys would go, seeing is so different to hearing about things. Excuse a hasty finish . . ."[38] Small wonder that Catherine felt the strain and that her heart was troublesome again. At last they went to Deal for convalescence taking Katie, who had been far from well, with them.

Smallpox in London disrupted the plan. William rushed up to town and was with some difficulty turned out of the Gore Road home, where their youngest child Lucy lay stricken, and where Railton, already ill, was soon to be almost at death's door. The rest of the children were packed off to the country. Bramwell wrote to his mother, "I had such a job as you never saw last night to persuade Papa to let the children go, but I was sure what you would have done, and therefore I went on with all my might and did it . . . *He has no apprehension* . . . Mrs. Hoey is with the children—they have their books and are very comfortable. Cook is with them . . . And now

I want Papa away. While he was out of the room a minute last night I said to the doctor, 'Ought my father to be away from the house?' and he leaned over to me and said quietly, 'Most certainly and *at once.*' ... Now I hope you have telegraphed to him; if not, do so tonight, saying unless he leaves the house, you will come home and *make* him."[39] Bramwell is in league with his mother to manage their headstrong beloved. They had their way this time. William took up his quarters with Bramwell at Whitechapel, and was soon off for a tour of meetings in the North out of harm's way. Railton was long ill. Bramwell, with the help of a nurse and instructed by his mother, gave him and Lucy hydropathic treatment. Both recovered unmarked by the scourge. But, to the grief of every member of the family, faithful Mary Kirton died. She was the first to be stricken and at her own request was taken to hospital; doubtless she hoped that if she left the house the infection might not spread. Other helpers were found but none took the place Mary Kirton had held for the sixteen hectic years that she was with the Booths. All in the home felt her loss but none so deeply as Catherine, who had come to trust her completely and felt at rest about the children and the household while she was there.

Meanwhile William had reached a decision. His enforced absence from "the work" had given him time to think and talk, the terms were almost synonymous for him if there were anyone to talk to! He and Catherine now saw clearly that unless he had full control of the Mission the pace would not be fast enough. Majorities are seldom in the van when sacrifice and zeal are concerned. The leader must needs spend the first freshness of his inspiration in persuading or goading a majority in committee to support him, and sometimes having done both fail. In January 1877 the Evangelists were brought together, and to them William, as he himself told, "frankly and fully expressed the feelings of my heart and my intentions as to the future, and my explanations appeared to be as frankly and cordially received."[40] At this conference it was decided at the *unanimous* recommendation of its members that the East London Mission should come under the direct control of the "General Superintendent, William Booth". One resignation was announced. Evangelist Abram Lamb had written that he could not tolerate the decision that women be given charge of Mission posts. The main points of disagreement had been the position of women, the "drink" question, and the teaching of the doctrine of holiness. If William Booth's views on these matters had *not* prevailed, could The Salvation Army have been raised up? Contemplating its past, the answer is emphatically no!

William had announced in January that the annual conference was to be known as a "Council of War". In June 1877 it met for the first time under the new title and decisions reached in January were unanimously confirmed. William's opening address began with serious words. "We have been called by the arrangement of Divine Providence to be Officers and leaders in His Army." Prophetic words, soon to be accepted as Mission parlance. He concluded by saying, "We give up the Conference Committee . . . a Committee is far too slow for us . . ." Catherine was not well enough to be present. She was staying with Mrs. Billups, and sent a letter. "My dear Brethren and Sisters in the Lord, I cannot express how deeply I feel my forced absence . . . on this most interesting and joyous occasion . . . Cast off all bonds of prejudice and custom, and let the love of Christ which is in you have free course to run out in all conceivable schemes and methods of labour for the souls of men. Let your sympathies go *out, out, out,* unrestrained, free as air, fresh as the dew, and all encircling as the light of the sun. Acknowledge no bounds, no limits to your obligations and responsibilities, but those of capacity and opportunity . . ."[41]

In the first year under William's direct leadership, the Mission took a leap forward. A new freedom to become "all things to all men" ran through it. The Evangelists followed their General Superintendent's example. They *wanted* to do things his way. And he went among them with fresh liberty to counsel and encourage, to find fault and so improve them, or to finish off the unsatisfactory. This year he began taking Katie, then aged eighteen, with him. She sang solos, spoke in the meetings, dealt with the anxious, and delighted her father. At Stockton immense crowds heard William preach at the Market Cross. Here he went in for mid-day meetings. Catherine wrote to Mrs. Billups, "Katie plays the harmonium out of doors at noon every day, and crowds stand round to hear her sing . . . Doubtless the Pharisees think us enthusiasts or mad to allow her to do such a thing . . . Pray for her, dear friend . . . that she may be deaf alike to the voice of flattery and of condemnation."[42] It is in Stockton that William Booth observes "many spots where . . . the women and men too, lounge about . . ." He was always on the look out for such spots. How to reach the masses was still the paramount problem. To a magistrate who offered a field in which to hold open-air meetings, Catherine replied, "But the men are not in the field! We are after the people, and we must go *where the people are*."[43] William reported a novelty on the Sunday march, which apparently worked well. "Among the converts . . . one plays a cornet and to utilize him *at once* [he was put] with his cornet in the front rank of the procession . . . He certainly improved the singing, and brought crowds all along the line of march . . ."[44] William Booth believed that every convert should be utilized *at once.* It helped to establish him (or her) in the new life and draw others in. This principle was accepted throughout The Salvation Army.

Catherine joined William at Stockton for a few days on purpose to have a meeting with converts. Writing to Mrs. Billups she says, "William is utterly amazed at Katie: he had no idea she could preach as she does. He says that she is a born leader and will, if she keeps right, see thousands saved. He is delighted, and her health is improving. Dear friend, join me in praying that she may be kept humble and simple, and that all that the Lord has given her may be used only for Him. Praise His name that she can stand in my stead to bear His message."[45] Again to Mrs. Billups, "Pa and Katie had a blessed beginning yesterday. Theatre crowded at night, and fifteen cases. I heard Katie for the first time since we were at Cardiff. I was astonished at the advance she had made. I wish you had been there . . . It was sweet, tender, forcible and divine. I could only adore and weep. She looked like an angel, and the people were melted and spell-bound like children . . . Katie had a meeting for women only, and had seventy forward, most of them married women . . . Papa says he felt very proud of her the other day as she walked by his side at the head of the procession with an immense crowd at their heels."[46]

While William is making this Northern visit, Bramwell and Railton are here and there visiting London and nearby stations. Almost unnoticed the Mission takes on the shape of The Salvation Army. The single cornet leading the procession in Stockton is forerunner of its host of bandsmen. The Magazine reported the use of "banners" thus, "Well Bill, on my word this *is* a licker," shouts a great fellow, as braces tied about his waist, and newly awakened from the Saturday night's debauch, he watched 120 Missioners, headed by banners, pass his doorstep at 6.30 on Sunday morning, singing with all their might,

Oh, I'm happy all the day
Since He washed my sins away,
And I never mean to grieve Him any more.

These banners were flying in Leicester. At Whitby handbills announced "War on Whitby, 2,000 men and women wanted at once to join the Hallelujah Army . . . led by Captain Cadman from London." Cadman was thinking of the captain of a ship, nevertheless his handbill presaged the time when Missioners would bear such titles. It was at Whitby a few weeks later that for the first time in public William Booth was announced as "General".[47] Cadman reports, "We had a review at 7 p.m. marching through the streets in good order, singing . . . We halted in the Market Place . . . and listened to a powerful address by the General." *The Salvation Army is ready for its name.*

The Christian Mission Report and Appeal (1878) is being prepared. Early in the morning, in a room at the Booths' home in Gore Road, Bramwell and Railton sit at a paper-strewn table, while William, attired in dressing gown, paces up and down, throwing out suggestions. "What is the Christian Mission?" is the agreed headline and Railton, reading aloud from the draft gives the answer, "We are a volunteer army." Bramwell, looking across at his father, exclaims, "Volunteer?

Here, I'm not a volunteer. I'm a regular or nothing."[48] William stands still; stares a moment into space; gives Bramwell a flashing look; takes Railton's pen, and leaning over him, crosses through the word "Volunteer" and writes in its place "Salvation". "We are a Salvation Army," then ran the script. Bramwell and Railton instantly recognize the significance of the moment. Both stand up. William looks happy; he likes to startle the youngsters! He too feels that this marriage of words is by good inspiration and to be useful and blessed. Gradually the new title came into use. At first it was added to the old Mission title with an "or", and presently the places were reversed and one read, "The Salvation Army, commonly called the Christian Mission". In August 1878, a War Congress met. The new Deed of Constitution, incorporating the decisions made at the 1877 Conference, had been prepared with the help of Mr. Cozens-Hardy, later to be Master of the Rolls. The General spoke soberly to the assembled leaders: "We are sent to war. We are not sent to minister to a congregation and be content if we keep things going. We are sent to make war ... and to stop short of nothing but the subjugation of the world to the sway of the Lord Jesus. We must bear that in mind in all our plans ... Our aim is to put down the kingdom of the devil ... This Mission is going to be what its officers make it. *Here* is *your* responsibility ..."[49] The statistical state of the Movement was announced. During the year in which William had had full control, the number of stations had risen to fifty, an increase of twenty-one. The number of penitents whose names had been recorded was more than doubled, and stood at 10,762. The War Congress included a "Musical Service". All who could play instruments had been instructed to bring them. Advertisements of the Congress meetings included this announcement, "Processions led by a band of musical instruments will march to and from Fieldgate."

The Salvation Army was nearly ready. The flag and crest and a uniform were accepted "weapons of warfare" before this notable year closed. Writing to Mrs. Billups in October Catherine said, "We have changed the name of the Mission into The Salvation Army, and truly it is fast assuming the force and spirit of an army of the living God. I see no bounds to its extension, and if God will own and use such simple men and women (we have over thirty women in the Field) as we are sending out now, we can compass the whole country ... And it is truly wonderful what is being done by the instrumentality of quite young girls. I could not have believed it if I had not seen it ... In one small town where we have two girls labouring, a man, quite an outsider, told another that if they went on much longer all the publics would have to be shut up, for he went to every one in the town and he found only four men in them all. The whole population, he said, had gone to 'the Hallelujah lassies'! ... *Pray for our officers.*"[50]

As a wholly independent testimony to the work of the "quite young girls", we have Stead's account of the Army in Darlington. He wrote, "As there is nothing like personal testimony as to one's own experience, I may as well set down here how it was I came to believe in the Salvationists ... My farm-lad Dick used to attend regularly. 'It's as good as a "theayter",' he told me. 'You can go in when you like, and if you want a drop or a smoke in the middle, why, out you come, just as you please. But there's some of the biggest blackguards turned converters now.' By 'converters' he meant converts; but his word was true, for all The Salvation Army converts are converters ... At last I went to see the girls who had turned Darlington upside down. I was amazed. I found two delicate girls [aged twenty-two and eighteen] ... ministering to a crowded congregation, which they had themselves collected out of the street, and building up an aggressive church militant out of the human refuse which other churches regarded with blank despair. They had come to the town without a friend, without an introduction, with hardly a penny in their purses. They had to provide for maintaining services regularly every week-night, and nearly all day Sunday, in the largest hall in the town; they had to raise the funds to pay the rent, meet the gas bill, clean the hall, repair broken windows and broken forms, and provide themselves with food and lodging. And they did it ... these girls raised a new cause out of the ground, in the poorest part of the town, and made it self-supporting by the coppers of their collections. Judged by the most material standard, this was a great result. In the first six months, a thousand persons had been down to the penitent-form, many of whom had joined various religious organizations in the town, and a corps or church was formed of nearly 200 members, each of whom was pledged to speak, pray, sing, visit, march in procession, and take a collection, or do anything that wanted doing. [And what perhaps Stead did not know, to renounce the use of intoxicants and tobacco.] 'It will not last,' said many, and dismissed the miracle as if it were less miraculous because it was not capable of endless repetition. I sat next a young mechanic one night in the meeting, and asked him what he thought about the business.

" 'Dunno,' he said, 'they're a queer lot.'

" 'Do any good?'

" 'Mebbe. There's Knacker Jack—I know him.'

" 'Well, has it been good for his wife and bairns?'

" 'Dunno, but I work in the same place as him, and it has been good for his hosses. He used to strike 'em and knock 'em about dreadful. But since the lasses got hold of him, he's never laid a hand on 'em.'

"Suppose that it did not last, and the converts only stood so long and then fell away; then, for so long as they stand, a great and beneficent change has been effected, in which all surroundings share—

from the police to the horses . . . If Salvationists had rendered no other service to humanity and civilization than that which is involved in revealing to the world the latent capacities and enormous possibilities of usefulness that lie in womankind, they would have deserved well of their generation. This, however, which seems to be one of the crowning glories of the Army, has been a stone of stumbling and a rock of offence to many."[51]

Catherine Booth's campaigns were never again to be of such length as the seventeen weeks at Portsmouth, partly because her strength did not suffice, partly because she was needed at the Mission stations. Many of those outside London were established as a result of her meetings. Her spiritual children all over the country longed to see her and were ready to receive her commands and teaching. She was called the *Mother of The Salvation Army* by its people, because in all those early formative years she lived among them, behaving as a mother, and above all as a *loving* mother. She knew what she wanted to say to her children, and what they needed to hear. For the purpose of telling them, she held special gatherings for converts when she dealt with everyday living. "What sort of person ought you to be now that you are converted?" was a question she often asked and answered at such meetings. It is on record that at one meeting when she dealt with the bad effect nagging had on family life more than 300 women came to the penitent-form. The Army Mother made the nurture of converts her special care. William Booth was the warrior, leading his troops in battle. At the Army's beginning, it was as natural that Catherine should be called "Mother" as that William should be called "General". And she is called so to this day. This husband and wife were in a beautiful way complementary to each other. In a vivid fashion, like founding a family, The Salvation Army grew up around them. It is important to realize that these two felt like that about it. Their love for their people was not by measure. There was never the faintest claim to "credit" for their unstinted labour and sacrifice; nor a remnant left of "rights" of their own. Their time, strength, gifts, children, their *life*, was bestowed upon this new family in God's household. This man and woman were perfectly united by love to God and to each other. One searches in vain for disagreement. Letters, sermons, methods, the testimony of those who knew them, *all* reveal harmony of mind between them. Stead said, "Mrs. Booth, by the warmth of her love and the wealth of her prudence, supplemented the genius of her husband in such a way as to enable him, with her, to do a work for which there is no parallel in our times."[52] The Booths did not at first realize what was developing in their hands. Catherine said, "My dear husband . . . commenced in the East of London without any idea beyond that of a local work . . . God so wonderfully blessed him that the work soon began to grow of its own aggressive and expansive force . . . It grew because of the divine life that was in it . . . We had no idea . . . What God was going to do with us; but we both had the inward conviction . . . that He wanted to use us to the masses."[53]

3

By the Deed Poll of 1878 William Booth's authority was established. A lot of nonsense has been talked about his autocracy. The word is misapplied in relation to him and his Army. Autocracy can only be exercised when supported by force or fear. In considering the rise of The Salvation Army, one must remember that it was built on a foundation of *voluntary adherence*. Announcing the 1878 Constitution Booth said, "Let no one come to, or stay with us, whose heart is not one with our heart." Defending his position, Catherine said, "Nearly all the folly that has been talked on this point is exploded by *one consideration*, namely, that this General assumes no *jurisdiction over the conscience* . . . Nobody is bound either to join the Army or stay in it after they have joined. Nobody is un-christianized or anathematized merely for leaving it. Many who have left it are now happily working for God in other spheres . . . by our recommendation . . . You see, God has trained us by a very peculiar discipline for this work. He has delivered us to a great extent from the trammels of conventionalism, and used us to make this Movement out of the untaught masses . . . We do not intend this Movement ever to settle down into a sect, if prayer and faith or prudence and foresight can prevent it. We desire that it should continue an *ever-aggressive force*, going to the regions beyond while there are any sinners left unsaved . . . and all the praise, honour, and thanksgiving unto God."[54] Observing critically the use William Booth made of his authority, it must be conceded that he increased rather than diminished both the difficulty of joining and of continuing in the ranks! He decreed that anyone accepted as a soldier, i.e. member of The Salvation Army, must give clear testimony to, and evidence of, conversion through faith in the Saviour Jesus Christ, and *be ready to testify to that experience*. He must declare his belief in the doctrines set forth in the Deed of Constitution, and promise to do all in his power to win others to salvation. In the world, but no longer of it, worldly amusements, companionships, dress, and indulgences must end. He must forswear intoxicating drinks, drugs (except on doctor's orders) and gambling; and, if he aspire to play in a band, or take part in activity for the young, or hold any office whatsoever (all unpaid services), he must also forgo tobacco smoking and taking snuff; wear uniform when on duty; and hold himself ready to speak and pray in public. This high standard is a strength, but does

269

not tend to swell the ranks! Contemplate the result if similar conditions and qualifications of membership were instantly imposed upon Christian Churches and associations. What proportion of members would pass muster? The Salvation Army standards of faith and behaviour are high, and these are owed under God to William and Catherine Booth.

Now that Headquarters was set up in Whitechapel, Catherine must surely have looked to home as a place where she and William might get a little rest and quiet between campaigns? But no! The din of battle was still there. Bramwell, Ballington, Katie, Railton all dashed in and out, overflowing with enthusiasm about their experiences. If Catherine were at home they wanted to share their "adventures" with her and she wanted to hear about everything. All of them still looked to Catherine for whatever at the moment they needed. Katie, now an "officer" in the Army, was snatching a few days' rest with friends when her mother wrote, "It would be useless your coming here at present, all is rush and drive . . . and tribes of Captains coming and meetings! *Cooking bad* and meals all irregular—Army life. No place for you."[55] Alas! Poor Catherine with her clear notions about proper food and regularity and a neat well ordered house! Still "poorer" cook, who must somehow manage to have meals ready for eighteen hours in the twenty-four! My Aunt Katie told me that when she *was* at home, she was often called upon by her father to make tea at midnight and after, when he and Bramwell and Railton were wrestling with problems. Sometimes she looked in, in her dressing gown, to hint that it was time to "close down" for what was left of the night, and then her father might call on her to sing (she had a sweet clear voice) and all would join in the chorus! A few minutes singing was more reviving than tea, she said.

Many things troubled the Army Mother at this period. She, woman's champion, who had convinced William of woman's equal right with man to preach, was sometimes aghast at the result. It was frightening that women, or men either for that matter, with so brief an experience of spiritual life, without education, almost without knowledge of the Bible (some indeed could not even read), should be preachers; responsible for converts and for raising funds and spending them judiciously. At home, in Gore Road, or at Headquarters, dealing with plans on paper, discussing methods, dangers, needs, lack of men, lack of money, she tended to be oppressed. What of the future? What pitfalls had the devil in readiness for them and their "Army"? But on the field, *with* the people, listening to the crudely expressed testimonies, looking on the marred yet illuminated countenances of saved drunkards, her faith revived, fears evaporated. These miracles of salvation were the work of the Holy Spirit. If *He* chose these uncultivated minds to be His messengers and win their fellows to God, would she question? Doubt? Here once more was a demand on her faith.

270

Faith, her faith, must prevail. And it did. She saw that there were dangers, but it became certain to her that *this Army was of God. And she loved it as it was.* She liked the language of its rough and ready people, their ebullience, the laughter and tears in the meetings. The "Army spirit" that was ready to dare anything to reach and win souls. Toward the end of her life she said, "... it has always been a cause of amazement to me how it is that intelligent people can fail to perceive the connection between feeling and demonstration. How utterly unphilosophical is the prevailing notion that persons can be deeply moved on religious subjects, any more than on worldly ones, without manifesting their emotions ... The cold formal services of the Protestant church have done more to shut out from it the sympathy and adhesion of the masses than any other cause, or indeed than all other causes put together ... Had I my time over again I would not only be far more indulgent toward the natural manifestation of feeling but would do more to encourage it than I have done before."[56]

No one can read her words in defence of the Army's methods without recognizing the voice of her love. She was middle-aged now. Love toward God was still the living force in her and was still growing. Her love for William and the children was still warm and tender. Her love for the sinful and weak burned in her with deeper intensity, and there was a sense in which her love for the Army was linked with all these. And she loved her Army children for Christ's sake which, as she told Stead, "is quite different from loving the brethren for their own sakes". Familiarity with men's failings did not breed contempt in her but simply *more love.* She did not get disillusioned by the sinful, nor, what was more remarkable, was she disheartened by the faults of the saved. Less censorious than in youth, she was more ready to find extenuating circumstances; she pleaded for patience and understanding in dealing with people but she never lowered the standard, nor wavered in her certainty that the Holy Spirit could transform men's lives. Her conception of the holiness and love of God was not *dimmed* by life's vicissitudes, rather it shone through all her thoughts of men and things to inspire her even when her physical strength was at its lowest ebb. She felt with something beyond faith —with a kind of revelation of love—the truth that the Army is God's and that He condescended to use it. To her daughter Emma she wrote, "Hundreds of the greatest roughs have been converted, and all through the instrumentality of such young women, humble, simple souls, full of love and zeal ... It is not to the clever, or talented, or educated that these things are given, but to *the whole-hearted and spiritual.* It was so in Christ's day and it is so now ... I feel as though I had been wrong in criticizing some of our folk and measures to you. I see that we cannot have a great movement among such a class of people without a lot of defects and weaknesses. But then, God knows it all. And we are as weak in His sight in *some* things, as they are

271

in others. He has to make the best of *us,* and we must do the same in regard to others. You will see it better when you get more among the people."[57]

William, with joyous, almost superhuman energy, swept on. The advance of his Army was never fast enough for him. And Catherine defended his rush tactics to the critics. "The Salvation Army," she said, "has thousands of people in its ranks who have been picked up from the lowest depths of social and moral degradation, [and who are] now good fathers and mothers, good husbands and wives, and good citizens. Having positive demonstration of such results, why should we be accused of ambition or fanaticism, because we are burning with anxiety to press the Gospel on the attention of all men? ... All the slander, persecution, toil and anxiety that this Movement has brought upon me ... God only knows how great these have been ... I can bear all this easier than the maudlin half-and-half view of the situation which leads these men to say, 'Why attempt so much? You are going too fast. What will this grow to?' I say, I don't care what it grows to, so that it grows in holiness and devotion, as it grows in size ..."[58]

Banners bearing texts, questions, warnings, and admonitions had come into use with processions, and the idea of a flag to be carried at the head had been discussed by the Booths. Four years before the War Congress of 1878, William wrote to his son Bramwell, "A flag also should be settled, colour and character—and device—this must wait however."[59] Bramwell tells that the flag adopted was designed by his mother. As usual there were people who objected to the innovation. The Army Mother said, "We are marching on. Some of our friends say, 'Well, but could you not march without a flag?' Yes, we could ... and we have marched a long time and a long way without one; but we can march better *with* one, and that is the reason we have one ... All armies have banners and we are an Army; we grew into one, and then we found it out, and called ourselves one. Every soldier of this Army is pledged to carry the standard of the Cross into every part of the world, as far as he has opportunity. Our motto is 'The world for Jesus'. We have all sworn fealty to the Lord Jesus Christ, and faithfulness to the Army, because it represents our highest conception of the work which He wants us to do."[60] The flag is red, for the blood of saving, bordered with blue, for the purity of a holy life, having for the fire of the Holy Spirit a centre star of yellow, bearing the motto 'Blood and Fire'.

In September 1878, the adoption of a flag and motto was announced, and Catherine set out with William to visit the Northern stations, corps as they were designated henceforth. During their eight weeks' tour, colours were presented at twenty-five places. At Coventry, a disused factory was opened as premises for the six months' old corps. The *Coventry Times* recounted: "In anticipation of the arrival of

Mr. Booth and his friends, great crowds assembled near the railway station . . . Great excitement was caused in the city . . . It is estimated that the number of people in the Pool Meadow between eleven and twelve o'clock, [on Sunday morning] was no less than three or four thousand."[61] Beginning with a great testimony and prayer meeting out of doors on Sunday morning at 6.30, the attack on Coventry continued throughout the day. A crowd had to be shut out at night, even after hundreds had been let in to stand, packed together in the basement "where many knelt on the sawdust floor to give themselves to God". The new hall held seats for 1,500. The building also provided quarters for the officers and a number of rooms. "The main portion of the basement is a room where 400 at a time can comfortably sit down to tea [700 had tea there at 9d a head on Monday] . . . in short, one of the completest and largest buildings for our use we ever got, all at a total cost of £660, or thereabouts, freehold."[62] To William and Catherine the scenes and sounds spoke of future opportunities, and the need to prepare for them. Wrote William to Bramwell, "The opening services here at Coventry have fully determined me to have the General Orders out as soon as possible . . ."[63] The whirlwind of the Northern tour concluded with "War Councils" for the officers in the various centres. In Sunderland a snowstorm threatened the programme. William sprained his ankle. He enjoyed sharing the "fun" of his predicament with the Magazine readers. "Through that storm I had to go to Sunderland. No cab, nor conveyance could be had . . . I commenced the journey on the stalwart shoulders of a brother, then was glad to rest on some straw on the bottom of a milk cart, and before I reached my quarters . . . that night, I was thankful to accept the service of a wheelbarrow."[64]

Home for a brief respite at Christmas, Catherine was almost at once away again. Her three elder children were travelling and preaching now. Katie's campaigns continued. When she was at Whitby "the hall was packed to suffocation on Sunday night (it seated 3,000) and numbers were unable to get in. People all over the town are seeking God,"[65] thus Catherine to Mrs. Billups. Ballington took his fiddle and flung himself into the work in his father's helter-skelter style. Bramwell toiled all day at Headquarters, in addition to Sunday preachings. From a letter of his we read, "The last fortnight has been an incessant whirl. Sunday week I got to Wellingborough at three in the morning, preached twice, and then walked ten miles or more to Northampton, and preached again, and was in London by ten the next morning."[66]

Of a visit this year to Newcastle and Gateshead, Mrs. Booth wrote, "I am having a glorious time here . . . I am to preach next Sunday at the circus; it holds nearly 4,000 . . . Pray that God may fill me with His spirit and power, that they may forget the poor little instrument in the great and awful message. God helping me I will sound an

273

alarm to them in their sins."[67] On the Saturday afternoon, May 17, 1879 she presented flags to nine newly formed corps in the district; the circus was crammed for the occasion. Uniform now everywhere making its appearance was in evidence. The red jersey, worn by many, often bore a text or legend in yellow describing the owner as "converted dustman". Failing red jerseys, red arm bands, or red handkerchiefs, with a crest in yellow at the corners, knotted at the throat, and for all happy faces. Before she handed over the flags, the Army Mother spoke: "The flag," she said, "is a symbol of our devotion to our great Captain ... and to the great purpose for which He ... shed His blood, that He might redeem men and women from sin and death and hell ... This flag is emblematical of our *faithfulness to our great trust*. Jesuu only wants faithful soldiers in order to win ... the uttermost parts of the earth for His possession. If Christian soldiers had been faithful in the past, the world would have been won for Christ long ago. Why not? ... When the Holy Ghost has fair play, and is allowed to use men and women as He likes, what are hours or weeks to Him?" Now her voice is ringing passionately. Impossible to explain, say those who heard—and people of very differing temperament agree on this—impossible to describe the intensity of conviction she was able to convey. Salvation soldiers received what she said as if from heaven itself, and prepared to pledge their faithfulness to God and to the flag. Her concluding words rallied all. "If God works," she asked, "what does it signify about the instruments? ... This flag is ... an emblem of victory ... By what power is this victory going to be achieved? By fire! The Holy Ghost ... this fire of the Spirit can transform us as it did Peter ... Let all go that occupies the room which the Holy Ghost might fill in your souls ... charge on the hosts of hell, and see whether they will not turn and flee!"[68]

The flags were presented, and fidelity to God and the Army pledged with fervour. The next day, Sunday, various buildings in the district were packed. On Sunday night, more than 12,000 were present in the audiences. The series of meetings concluded with an all-night of prayer on Monday. The testimony of the police and of the magistrates in Gateshead was conclusive: "... The Salvation Army has reduced the charge list in Gateshead by one half, and effected a startling reformation in the personal habits of ... the worst characters in the lowest slums on Tyneside."[69] Old debts were paid. Commenting on this result of conversion Catherine, speaking at the Cannon Street Hotel, in London, said, "If you can only resuscitate and energize the moral sense in a man, he will soon rectify himself in all the relations of life." On the same occasion she spoke of the self improvement that sets in with salvation. "When in Darlington, one of the Fry family took the chair for me at a select meeting at Livingstone Hotel, and told us that he had been drawn to look at the work in consequence of thirty men having applied to be admitted into their [Fry's] evening school to be taught to read, within a few months, who had been converted in the Army meetings." And most precious of all to Catherine is that, "The devil cast out ... the man is willing to make any sacrifice for the good of his family ... his children are properly fed" and "clothed ... and at least loved [and] prayed with ... Who can estimate the results of such altered conditions of tens of thousands of children?"[70]

The Army Mother travelled continuously throughout 1879. She visited fifty-nine towns; presented colours, and, in private meetings, talked to soldiers and converts about living a holy life. She counselled officers, listened to their account of their work, and noticed, with a mother's eye, their living conditions, health and happiness, scribbled off long letters to Bramwell, gave her views about properties and the importance of finding suitable lodgings for women officers: "It is miserable for them to come in to a fireless place, worn out as they often are, and alas, the most valuable ones are often the most delicate." She tells of talks with them; as of one: "Have dragged out piecemeal that she feels she can't go on, I believe she is godly. She wants a few days rest and must have it." And finally, "I have spotted two chaps who will make Captains, I think—stunners—in time ... send this on to Pa! I cannot write things twice over. I sent him word that you will send it."[71]

Another letter of the type to Bramwell about the problems of the "lassies" shows from its first phrase that while on her tour she reckoned to write on current business daily. "I was so very sorry last night that my letter was late. I am a mile and a half from General Post, and expected someone to come to post it, who did not, and I could not get *anyone* so, much to my mortification, yours and Pa's and others were late ... The girls at Jarrow are with a nice old woman who does all for them except make their beds, for 7/6 per week the two; has a cup of something hot for them when they go in, and is quite a mother ... I am off to look at the circus, but it is such a storm, bitter cold with snow! I am obliged to have a cab ... Ballington writes me, place full at night, nine souls and £9 including £2 book money ... I give them a part of a service tonight in the Alexandria, and on Thursday night Bethesda ... you should prepare a list of questions for lassies who are candidates ..." On and on rushed her pen finishing, "Oh, I forgot to say that I read Katie's article and I like it. With a little of the quotations taken out, it will take with a lot of our folk better than mine ... Put it in and encourage the lass a bit. Have you heard of a man yet for office? Your loving Mother, C.B."[72] Sometimes her advice was in more forceful terms, as this: "I do hope you will not throw a lot of money away in trying him just for want of courage to tell him at once that he will not do ... It is the *nature* of the man that is at fault, and not his circumstances. He is a *drone* and nothing, no change of place or position, can ever make him into a bee ... He never ought to have left his trade; he never would if he had thought Missioning was harder work! ..."[73] Glasgow was visited, three corps in that city. Catherine said she had never spoken at such uproarious meetings. People blame The Salvation Army, but, she said, "This is not my town; this is your town. I have not created this mass of heathenism and ruffianism ... What have you been doing, you genteel people? When I show you your wares you come down upon me! ... I only gather them together for you; *there they are!*"[74]

Towards the end of this year, at Darlington, Stead met her. They took to each other at once. Stead was an important ally in one of Catherine's toughest campaigns and came to know all the family, especially Bramwell. At one time he considered joining The Salvation Army. He was a great talker; William found him a bit bombastic but Catherine, who treated him as she did her sons, took him seriously and was ready to listen to him. On his part he relished what he called "her shrewd mother-wit and intense fervour of spirit". He said she "possessed more than average of that saving gift of humour which is the indispensable lubricant of human intercourse", from which I gather that she sometimes made him laugh! Part of a letter she wrote to him gives a notion of discussions between them. "Christ must be the best expounder of His own system, and He declares over and over again that His first and highest work in this world was to glorify His Father and to reveal God to man. He further taught that there was no other way of doing this than by the revelation of, and reception of, Himself. Christianity is as much a spirit as a practice, and herein it differs from all other religions and ethical systems, inasmuch as the practice of it is impossible without the infusion of the living spirit of the Author. A man must live, by Christ and in Christ, a supernatural life before he can exemplify the principles or practise the precepts of Christianity; they are too high *for unrenewed human nature*, it cannot attain unto them ... Praise up humanitarianism as much as you like, but don't confound it with Christianity, nor suppose that it will ultimately lead its followers to Christ. This is confounding things that differ ..."[75]

4

The "field" was now so large that Catherine and William must, with few exceptions, fight separate "battles"; they seldom had the joy of being together for meetings, and new problems arose. One shrinks from saying new enemies, though William and Catherine felt far more keenly the opposition of certain sections of the religious world than anything suffered in the war with sinners and the devil. The publicity inevitable from their huge unorthodox form of gatherings; from the sensational methods employed by local zealots, especially in the streets; and from the innovation of a military style brought a storm of criticism. Many religious people were as horrified, and almost as antagonistic, as the publicans, if for different reasons. The Army's "methods are to many minds simply revolting".[76] The exuberance of some of the Salvationists was a problem. Wrote William to Bramwell, "I wish we did not do so many *silly* things. I think I see a great difference between manly, natural, bold, daring action and *weak, frivolous,* childish *comicality*."[77] He was right. But the Booths understood human nature. They believed that mere exhibitionists would wilt if left to go on exhibiting. To quench erratic wild-fire would not be difficult but in the process genuine expression of zeal for the salvation of souls might be extinguished. They knew that spirited innovators were often sensitive "critters"; a light hand on the reins was indispensable if courage and self-sacrifice were at all levels to be preserved in potential leaders. And the Army desperately needed leaders possessing those precious qualities. Said Catherine, "You object to the noise and *éclat* connected with our measures; but if you look into the subject, you will see that these are indispensable, because we seek those who cannot be reached without . . . they will have nothing to do with your quiet and genteel methods . . . Why should we not attract their attention by some novel or startling announcement, so that the terms be innocent? What does it signify that they are strange and unconventional?"[78]

Mr. Samuel Morley, that staunch friend, found himself embroiled in controversy about the Army's doings. He once said to William, "Tell your wife that I love and esteem her, but that she has got me into a deal of trouble!" Morley now felt that he must do something to clear the air. He told William, who chanced to call, of his proposal to convene private meetings for interested and influential people, to which he would invite the Booths to tell about the work of The Salvation Army and answer objections. William approved the idea. Walking down the street on his way home from this interview he met Sir Arthur Blackwood and found that he disliked the military style of the Army processions. William, in his impulsive way, said, "I'm going to Coventry on Saturday, come with me and see for yourself." They travelled down together. At the station (it was during the Coventry Fair) the Army corps had assembled in force to welcome their General. The flag-bearer, prominent in the foreground, was instantly recognized by Sir Arthur as a one-time blackguard of the regiment in which he had served in the Crimea. A greengrocer's cart owned and driven by another recently saved notorious sinner carried the General and Sir Arthur at the head of the procession, followed by some fifty officers ordered in from nearby corps, and the confused ranks of hundreds of men and women soldiers. "Dear me, Mr. Booth, that was a remarkable procession!" said Sir Arthur. Later he explained that what had struck him most was seeing the colour-sergeant in his new state of heart. If *he* were a sample of the converts, why then . . . !

Mr. Morley took the chair at the first of the explanatory meetings, which was held at his city offices. Sir Arthur Blackwood spoke, and told of what he had seen and heard. Catherine wrote to Mrs. Billups, "We have had two meetings at Samuel Morley's. At the first there were twenty present, mostly wealthy . . . We heard all they had to say, and then I spoke on the general principles, and the meeting was adjourned until Thursday at two. On this occasion my dearest husband opened [the meeting], and answered the objections previously raised, one by one, triumphantly. He made it clear that while he sympathized with the wish of our friends not to bring sacred things into less regard . . . yet, poor as we are, and God only knows what a struggle we have financially, he would not give up one jot or tittle of anything essential, no, not for all the wealth of the West End! Some others spoke for and against, but kindly . . . Then I followed and the Lord helped me. Mr. Morley assured me, with tears in his eyes, that I 'carried them, every one . . .' I finished by telling them that we had fought thirteen years for this principle of adaptation to the needs of the people . . . and that whether they helped us or not, we should not abandon it. We dared not. And we should not, if we ended in the workhouse . . . Mr. Denny* spoke like a brave and true-hearted man . . . The excitement made me worse than I have been for two years. My heart was really alarming . . . This has disheartened me again as to my condition. But God reigns and He will keep me alive as long as He needs me."[79] Typical of Catherine that meetings in halls crammed to suffocation and lasting three or even four hours should not tell on her as did dealing with a score of wealthy "critics"! And she was to have much more of it to do; defending the Army, defending William. He wrote to his youngest son Herbert, naming some of those present at one of these meetings. "We had quite a fight. Your mother did magnificently, and we came off with flying colours."

The year 1879 closed with one more major victory. The first issue of *The War Cry*, official gazette of The Salvation Army, bore the date December 27, 1879. William Booth defined its purpose, "To inspire and educate, and bind together our people all over the world." In twelve months the circulation had risen to 110,000 a week, without a penny from advertisements and including no fiction. At one of the anniversary meetings Catherine Booth spoke of her joy in letters from converts who had travelled to other shores, and were there striving to work on Army lines for the conversion of their neighbours.

* Mr. T. A. Denny, wealthy London merchant. Gave generously to the work. Became personal friend of William Booth. Died 1909.

For want of leadership none of these efforts in the U.S.A. had long prospered. Now the General decided to send Railton to take over work begun in Philadelphia by a silk weaver, Amos Shirley, and his wife and daughter: all converted in Army meetings in Coventry. The Army Mother presented two flags at the God-speed meeting in Whitechapel Hall, on February 12, 1880, one for the first New York, and one for the first Philadelphia corps. "You look young," she said, turning to the small group of seven women officers. "To some people you may appear insignificant, *but so are we all;* so did those women who stood grouped round the cross of Christ appear to the proud Pharisees, who walked mocking past . . . I present you with this flag in the name of our great King, who bought all sinners with His blood, and Who bids us go forth . . . Pray that God will give you, young as you are, strength to fight under this banner, and that tens of thousands may be saved!"[80] To be noted, at this meeting the women officers wore the first "military style" uniform, including hats with crimson bands, inscribed in gold, *The Salvation Army.** Two days later Railton and his party sailed. Writing to Mrs. Billups Catherine said of this departure, "We have been in a perfect whirl of excitement and rush . . . the getting off of dear Railton and the sisters was a scene. Hundreds of people walked in procession to Fenchurch Street. They sang all the way, and omnibuses, waggons and vehicles of all kinds stopped and lined the roads to see them pass. They then marched on from Tidal Basin station to the ship. We had half an hour in the Basin, in which a large ring was formed and a meeting held. All the crew and passengers on the ship seemed quite struck, standing on the deck in the rain to listen . . . it was a grand sight. The women's hats looked capital . . . Three of our flags were flying on board . . . Dear devoted Railton looked well in his uniform, and appeared as happy as an angel. Bless him! I love him as a son. Oh, to win millions for our Saviour King."[81]

"Happy" Railton had had twelve months leading the forces in the U.S.A. when he was peremptorily recalled to help with problems arising from opposition at home. Mutterings of the coming storm of persecution had been heard even before the triumphant eight weeks' tour of the Northern stations. Some Salvationists had gone to prison for preaching in the open air. Catherine and William had been pelted in the streets of Newcastle. Salvation Army street meetings evoked a certain amount of rowdy opposition almost everywhere. In some districts it might truthfully be described as *ruffianly.* "Skeleton Armies',† often subsidized by publicans, made continual and organized

* Later women wore bonnets.
† Skeleton Armies were bands of people organized to disturb the Army meetings. Many members of these armies became converted and joined The Salvation Army.

attacks on the "Hallelujahs". Baiting the "Sally Army" became a popular recreation for young "roughs". Edward Joy* describes his experience as a youthful soldier. "One night I had a new cap and a new overcoat; an epoch in my life I can assure you! I was in the back row of the regiment, and when I returned to the hall it was minus the cap and with my new overcoat ripped up the back seam and half way round to the front, and many a kick and clout I had received from the 'roughs'... One Sunday the hall was surrounded, back and front, by a roaring raging mob of several hundreds. Every remaining window was smashed, and the soldiers who had come to knee-drill remained on the premises until past ten o'clock at night, without food or drink, sheltering as best they might, between the various window places, while across the hall floor were heaps of stones and other missiles with which the mob had maintained a constant fusillade..."[82] This in Folkestone.

The peak of persecution was reached in the twelve months 1881-1882, when over 660 Salvationists were injured, many seriously; eighty-six, including fifteen women, were sent to prison, and fifty or sixty buildings were attacked. This kind of persecution did not hinder The Salvation Army. John Bright† was right when he wrote to Catherine in a note of sympathy, "I suspect that your work will not suffer materially from the ill treatment you are meeting with. The people who mob you would doubtless have mobbed the Apostles. Your faith and patience will prevail..."[83] The Booths knew who were the trouble makers. "We have thousands of converted drunkards in our ranks," Catherine Booth declared, "who for years spent the chief of their earnings at the public house... We know as a fact that numbers of houses which used to do a roaring business are now on the verge of ruin; and we know also that their masters attribute this state of things to the influence of The Salvation Army... and... they vent their wrath on our poor people, by pressing and bribing their drunken dupes to create disturbances, so that our officers may be taken into custody for the uproar..."[84] In a letter to Mrs. Billups from Hull: "There are fourteen public houses to let, for which they give us the credit, and one publican openly says he is losing £80 per week through us. Another was at the penitent-form the other night, and has shut up his 'house'. A town councillor said to me after the lecture that we had influenced the entire population and stirred up every church in it. *Oh, it is glory.*"[85]

But there was another side to this. Before the Hull visit Catherine had written, "We have been much harassed by the recent rioting at

* Colonel Edward Joy, officer in The Salvation Army. Author of books and many popular songs and music.

† Rt. Hon. John Bright (1811-1889), M.P. for Birmingham. Statesman and orator. Promoted reforms leading to abolition of Corn Laws and to free trade.

Whitechapel. We have several people seriously injured, one dear woman lying delirious and others much hurt. The police are against us and the publicans and their friends are in Co. The General has had to go about seeing lawyers and M.P.s, etc. . . . We have now got things into line however for going to the Home Secretary, and if that is not sufficient to the Prime Minister. We shall win, but it is all an increase of work and wear."[86] Yes, *that* is the snag, "increase of work and wear"!

Among the rank and file the wave of persecution, riding the rising tide of salvation, far from subduing their zeal, helped to carry enthusiasm still higher. Converts, who might have wavered in faith and slipped easily back into their old ways, were helped to stand their ground when forced to pray and testify in the very streets where past sinning was so close a memory to themselves and to their neighbours. In that atmosphere of hostility converts must step very literally from darkness into light. None could hide his side. The puncher of yesterday became the punched of tomorrow. The Booths' chief anxiety in all this was that their people should come through the ordeal as befitted followers of Jesus Christ. All the influence of their authority was bent to inspire soldiers to endure *without retaliation*, and to pray for the salvation of their persecutors. Many of those who saw the courageous gentleness of the molested men and women in the streets were won to believe their testimony. The Mayor of Bath wrote to the Home Secretary, "We find that even when struck, assailed with foul and abusive language, and their property broken and destroyed, the Salvationists do not retaliate."[87] This did not prevent His Worship from asking the Home Secretary for powers to forbid Salvationists holding street meetings! Ballington, Catherine's second son, was among the first to suffer imprisonment. He was in charge of the work in Manchester, where many bad characters had been saved. With common felons in Belle Vue Gaol he lived on a few ounces of bread and a little "skilly", and slept on a plank. He was not at all pleased when a sympathizer paid his fine, thus cutting short his imprisonment! Catherine was with William in Sheffield when the 'Blades'* attacked the Army march. She sat in the carriage in which he stood. Stones and bricks were aimed at them all the way, miraculously neither was hurt. The few policemen present were helpless, and no reinforcements were sent. One of the soldiers was an ex-wrestler, well known to the mob, riding a horse in the procession; he was so plastered with mud and muck as to make his face and coat indistinguishable. At last he was seriously injured, and had to be supported on either side in order to be got alive to the hall. He was in great pain, but before becoming insensible he was heard repeating, "I hope they'll get saved." When the procession arrived at

* Blades—the Sheffield "Skeleton Army".

the hall and the General saw the group of battered officers at the door where the soldiers were holding back the crowd, he called out with a smile, "Now is the time to get photographs taken." He was always able to poke fun when in a tight corner. From Sheffield Catherine wrote to Mrs. Billups, "... I have just been to the hospital to see the wrestler and found him utterly prostrate and unable to speak more than a whisper and shaking from head to foot—concussion of the brain. We are going to get him out as soon as the doctors will permit. We have another man who was kicked, in a dangerous part, at Reading a week ago—said to be sinking fast! The state of the people is truly awful ... The language used yesterday was fearful in many instances. I only got a botch of mortar on my bonnet. I felt quite sorry to wash it off this morning and would not if I could have explained to everybody how it came there. I lecture in the Albert Hall, Sheffield, tomorrow night—pray for me. I fear that the fear of the mob will deter timid people."[88]

Describing an Army meeting of this period *The Saturday Review* reported, "Those must have been very dull or unsympathetic persons who could resist the pious jollity of the meeting." The refrain of the song at the beginning "was sung, or rather roared, again and again ... Those ... who blame the apathy and cold-bloodedness of the English character can never have attended a Hallelujah meeting ... the sight of many hundred pairs of radiant eyes and waving arms ... the manifest affection of all these rough people for one another, the absence of anything like hypocrisy or self-seeking in the whole affair, were not to be overlooked by any candid spectator. That the nature of the prayers and speeches was oddly boisterous, and that shouts of laughter pervaded what was intended to be a serious divine service, interfered not in the least with the sincerity of the worshippers."[89] It was this freedom in the Army meetings to laugh as well as weep, to shout and sing, that shocked many quite good persons. The Army Mother defended it as something precious. She was certain that joy was part of the heritage of the saved and she encouraged her Army children to expect it and to express it. William Booth once said, "It was heavenly music to hear the new converts tell of deliverance . . ." Letting their feelings shine out for all to see was part of the example William and Catherine set their Army children.

It is perhaps difficult to realize the barrier the Booths raised between themselves and much of the religious world, by allowing converts, especially when they were women, this freedom to testify. How Catherine laboured to remove it! I find nothing more valiant in her than the patient meekness with which she reasoned, pleaded with, and almost we may say cajoled the indignant objectors. It would have been so much more to her taste to let them think what they liked, and to forget the shadow of criticism, in the reality of winning and rearing "our people". But love compelled her as their Mother to defend her Army children; and besides, these carpers were often the rich whose support the Army desperately needed. If it could help the Army there was nothing she was not ready to do; but trying to make people see the truth, who would not even open their eyes, exasperated her to a degree heaven only knew. She said once, "The obtuseness, indifference and heartlessness of professing Christians is the greatest trial of my life, especially their obtuseness." For one thing, amidst her multifarious activities, how could she find the actual time it took to write such letters, and she wrote scores, all by hand. And when it came to writing to friends the task was all the more exacting. See this to Frank Crossley* for whom Catherine had come to feel real affection. I quote less than a third, "If all our friends were of your spirit, it would be so different, but you can never know quite what it has been to fight the battle we have fought with conventionalism and prejudice ... You see this whole question of demonstration depends so entirely on the spirit which prompts it, that whilst the things of the Spirit remain to the natural men foolishness, it would be impossible to find any demonstration at all which would be agreeable to him. You see, dear friend, all men are by nature *ashamed of God* and His claims on their hearts ... this is the crowning triumph of the devil; not only to separate men from God, but to make them ashamed to own allegiance to Him in any way offensive to the world! ... The whole history of the Christian Church shows that Satan has always raised the loudest and most determined opposition towards any demonstration of real feeling in religious exercises, such as men naturally allow and practise in regard to all other subjects ...

"This being the case, we have seen—I believe the Spirit has revealed to us—that we must set ourselves at all costs against this false shame, and allow the people to 'shout with a great shout', or to cry 'Hosanna' in the open-air ... or to have a wave-offering of kerchiefs instead of palm leaves when they feel like it, and when their hearts are full of holy enthusiasm; or to have music and merry-making when they are glad in the Father's house, whatever the elder brother may say or feel ... Let us not be more careful for the ark than God is; better have the ark shaken by oxen, with the divine blessing and glory in it, than ever so steady and genteel—*empty*! I believe the Church has suffered as much from the interference of Uzziahs as from Judases ... Our critics would have smitten David, not Uzziah! ... You must help us—because you are a David at heart, and all Davids are enthusiastic for God!"[90] Of the strictures of a prominent minister

* Francis (Frank) William Crossley (1839-1897). Religious leader and benefactor. Drawn to The Salvation Army by the Booths' teaching of Holiness. His generous gifts, amounting to well over £100,000, enabled William Booth to extend the Army's missionary work.

Catherine wrote to Mrs. Billups, "These things cut us to the heart, but they do not and shall not move us from our purpose; I wrote him a letter of twenty pages . . ." On one occasion she said, "If we find that processions and music will draw the people together better than any other means to listen to our message, why should we not use them? Who so worthy of a banner as our King? And to whom does the music of earth and heaven belong, if not to Him? *I contend that the devil has no right to a single note* . . . We find that music not only draws the people but it begets friendly feeling and secures attention from the very lowest and worst."[91]

Catherine Booth set forth her husband's aims and methods with some pungency at a meeting where she protested against strictures made on Salvationists by Dr. Harvey Goodwin, Bishop of Carlisle, when preaching in the Cathedral. She declared, "I have no desire to retaliate . . . though I might do so! All I shall say in respect to the Bishop is that I feel quite certain that if his Lordship . . . had himself attended those meetings on which he founded his remarks, he would have come to very different conclusions . . . *I wish he were here!* . . . for tonight I shall appeal to reason and understanding—that the measures of The Salvation Army are neither foolish nor unscriptural, nor irrational."[92] Her meeting was held in the Theatre Royal, Carlisle, on Tuesday evening, September 29, 1880. It was said that there were as many people shut out as had filled it. She appealed to reporters present, "Please deal fairly with me, and do not divide sentences, and give consequently a wrong interpretation . . . I hope your gallantry will lead you to do this much for a lady . . ." And went on to ask "every Christian to let me premise one or two things; first, that whatever success or blessing I may attribute to the efforts and measures of The Salvation Army, I *always* pre-suppose a pre-existing qualification—*Equipment of the Holy Ghost* . . . We deem it a great mistake to suppose that any human learning, any human eloquence, any human qualification whatever, fits a man or woman for ministering God's word or dealing with souls. Whatever else there is or is not, there *must be the equipment of the Holy Ghost,* for without Him all qualifications . . . are utterly powerless for the regeneration of mankind . . .

"Secondly, you will bear in mind, that while I am speaking directly upon The Salvation Army and its measures, my views of the result of this meeting are not bound by my own little horizon. I do not want to tell merely about The Salvation Army . . . but I want to make the intelligence [i.e. information] the means of enlightening you Christians, and stirring you up to more vivid responsibilities toward the degraded un-christian, uncivilized masses of this country. I want you to go to work, if not in my way, then in your way. I do not care how genteelly, how quietly, how respectably, so that you *do it* . . . Statistics not of our taking (I believe that of the Church of England)

... ascertained ... only ten out of every hundred of the working class population ever entered your churches and chapels. Think of that, and then think if it is not time something should be *done*! ... A lady came to one meeting, and she said, 'I was perfectly disgusted ... the way some behaved outside was scandalous!' She seemed to reflect upon The Salvation Army as if it were our fault ... Ask yourselves, do *we* create this mass of heathenism? ... You have let them grow up at your very doors, under your church steeples. Here they are, essentially heathen, not caring about God ... you Christians—Independents and Churchpeople—have let them grow up so, and when we try to gather them together you turn about and slap us in the face! ... I don't want to cast any unkind reflection on anybody, but things are as they are ... Only one thing can save us, and that is a revival of pure and undefiled religion, a fear of God, and a respect for man ... Go to them as men ... talk with them face to face, and make them feel that somebody *cares* for their souls, and you may bring them by hundreds. We have thousands in the land who are as good as any Bishop before God! I do not mean any particular Bishop!" I am sure that here she looked round with a smile. "They have as good hearts, and some as good heads! ... they only want picking up and washing and putting at the feet of Jesus, and educating and developing and leading outwards and upwards, and God will not be ashamed to have them one day beside His throne."

There is only room here for a fragment of her address. She went on to say that the agency employed must be adapted to the exigencies of the case. "When my dear husband resigned his position as an ordinary minister, and gave himself to evangelistic work, he saw that the churches had gone above the heads of the common people ... Years after this when he took his stand in the East of London, it flashed upon him, as an inspiration from heaven, that if they were to be reached it must be *by people of their own class,* who would go after them in their own resorts, who would speak to them in a language they understood, and reach them by measures suited to their tastes ... I speak of adaptation ... with respect to modes and measures of bringing the Gospel to bear on the people ... *I teach no adaptation of the Gospel.* I will keep the blessed Gospel *whole,* as it is. You may send the Gospel through a leaden trump as well as through a golden one—as well through a poor man who cannot read, as through a Bishop! He may not be able to put together two sentences of the Queen's English, but if he can say that he has been born again, if he can say 'I once was blind but now I see', he will do for The Salvation Army ... God looks at the *heart.* What does He care about our difference of expression? How do you know that your latest version of English grammar will be the language spoken in heaven? What are words for but to express ideas? It is the idea that is wanted." Suddenly her heart is heavy. She thinks of the ex-drunkards, the one

285

time thieves and prostitutes, and the odds they must face. What do Bishops know about the struggles of those once darkened minds striving to walk in the light with their Saviour? What is the use of answering objections that have been answered as she once said "150 times"? She realizes, as she has done before, and will do again, that "religious prejudice is perhaps the most inveterate of all".

The meeting in the Carlisle theatre is nearly over. The Army Mother in conclusion declares that Salvationists "do believe in hell and heaven, in right and wrong, and in the *Voice,* that has come down through the ages ... from the Throne of God ... We shall go on trying to make men right, and when they fall down we shall pick them up again, and nurse them, and prepare them for everlasting righteousness and heaven." Here spoke the Mother of The Salvation Army. None knew better than she that men were not made into saints in the twinkling of an eye! These Army children will not all run well. *That* is why they need mothers and fathers in God who will *"go on trying to make men right,* and *when they fall down ... pick them up again, and nurse them and prepare them for everlasting righteousness and heaven."*[93] This was Catherine Booth's conception of The Salvation Army's business in the world.

But not all ecclesiastical voices were condemnatory. Cardinal Manning said, "Let any man stand on the high northern ridge which commands London from West to East and ask himself how many in this teeming, seething whirlpool of men ... have never been taught the Christian faith, never set foot in a church ... what sins of every kind and dye and beyond all count are committed day and night ... If this be so, then at once we can see how and why The Salvation Army exists."[94]

Throughout the early eighties animadversion and contumely assailed the Booths and their Army from many quarters, but the very fury of the onslaught moved some noble souls to swift words of sympathy and praise. The Salvation Army owes them much, because such messages heartened William and Catherine and loomed far larger than did the abuse; shone perhaps the brighter in the contrasting dark of general disfavour. Lasting friendship with some followed. This was so with Canon and Mrs. Josephine Butler.* In particular, Mrs. Butler and Catherine were kindred spirits. Courageous, sensitive, and of boundless compassion, Mrs. Butler's influence and help made her an effective ally in the "purity campaign" which was soon to raise another howl against the Booths. Mrs. Butler's first letter to them— she addressed them both—reveals the writer's quick perception and sympathy. Mrs. Butler had herself faced bitter criticism, and was rich

* Mrs. Josephine Butler (1828-1907). Wife of Canon George Butler (Winchester). Leader in women's movements. Was instrumental in repeal of the Contagious Diseases Acts.

in wisdom born of experience. "I ought not perhaps," she said, "to give you the trouble here of reading a letter from me, in the midst of your arduous and blessed work, but I cannot any longer refrain from writing you a line to express—first my joy in the advance being made by The Salvation Army; and secondly, my sympathy with you in the numberless criticisms and strictures passed upon you, your teaching and your practice. I am sure your burden is already heavy enough without anyone's adding to it by fault-finding. The attacks of enemies are comparatively easy to bear, but the fault-finding and misunderstanding of Christian people, these are what grieve and hurt. I do so feel for you, and with you. I can truly say there is not a day, scarcely an hour, in which I do not think of you and your fellow-workers, and rejoice in the tide of blessing which our eyes are privileged to see. My own duties, domestic and public, keep me from being among you as often as I would, but I doubt if there is anyone living who is more with you in spirit . . . I think there are many others who now rejoice as I rejoice. I am sure that you are sustained under the fire of criticism."[95]

5

For all the Army Mother's uncompromising belief in the privilege of every one of His disciples to be Jesus Christ's witness irrespective of sex, education and talent, she perceived from the first the importance of *training* those who were to be leaders in The Salvation Army. I find this sentence in a letter to Bramwell written when Catherine was campaigning in the North. "We must have some training of some kind for lassies but what can I do?" And again, "The mad haste will ruin us. If Pa would but wait till we have reliable people." Bramwell, so like his mother in outlook on life, was concerned about the risks of sending untried, untrained and often illiterate converts to be marked before the crowds as "officers". True, the needs of the advancing Army forced their hands, but the Booths could not escape accountability and particularly for the women, whose position was vulnerable because beset by new dangers. Bramwell, frantically striving to keep pace with demands on the "field", wrote to his mother, "If this ship is going to live out the storms, ought not the whole strength and skill of everyone on board to be concentrated on the one great want, organization of the rank and file, and training of officers? . . . I beg you to consider this. Here is no plan for training these women . . . We are daily taking out girls without any previous training or education whatever."[96]

Money, lack of it that is, was one of the difficulties in the way of a training scheme. But Catherine felt there must somewhere be money to be got for so vital a need, and anyway, she was still beggar in chief. Just a year after Bramwell's letter, a Training Home for women cadets was set up under the Booths' second daughter, Emma. Here was accommodation of sorts, simple in the extreme, for about thirty cadets in the house in Gore Road; the family had moved to Clapton Common. A little later a similar establishment was opened for men, under Ballington. Thus the first training of Salvation Army officers was very closely under the Army Mother's influence, through her daughter and son. She and Bramwell visited the Training Homes regularly. Catherine's talks to cadets remained a vivid memory, lasting through life for some of them. It was so for Harriet Lawrance, one among the first company of cadets to be trained at the Congress Hall, Clapton, where there was room for men and women. A Yorkshire woman, almost illiterate, taught to write whilst a cadet, Lawrance had a keen perceptive intelligence. Catherine's dealing with her illustrates beautifully her care for her Army children and her belief in her own dictum that "God's gifts are far more generously and impartially distributed than we are apt to imagine. Polish is not power; education is not intellect."[97] Lawrance, who first saw the Army Mother when she came to lecture, said, "I shall never forget. We were all assembled in the big schoolroom. It was nine o'clock in the morning. [The hour gives an idea of Catherine's energy!] There was something wonderful about her ... when she came on to the platform, I felt as if God walked on with her. I can hear her voice now as she spoke her first words 'God said let there be light'. I understood everything differently after that. Mrs. Booth generally spoke for about an hour; there was no singing, just her talk."

Years later Lawrance sometimes accompanied Mrs. Booth to her meetings. Once "in a bone-shaker, just as we got to the turning into Whitechapel Road, an old cod's head came through the window, and I threw it out. Mrs. Booth said, 'Never mind, Lawrance, poor things they don't know any better; that's why I am going to preach to them.' She had her Bible in her hand and a concordance on her knee; she was preparing her sermon. When speaking she began low, put her head a little on one side, moved her hands a little, would point her finger and put a question, 'Do you see what I mean?' Another way she had was to hold her hands together, fingers crossed, and rest them on the reading desk before her; or when reasoning, strike the fingers of one hand on the palm of the other. In public meetings she wore black kid gloves, but always took off one glove before she stood up to talk. She was very particular and neat, and she wore white frilling in her neck and sleeves always." As she was telling me this of Catherine's gestures when speaking, Lawrance suddenly paused, as if remembering something, and, dreamily, she said, "Beautiful hands. Mrs. Booth had beautiful hands; soft and strong; it was a lovely feeling when she put her hands on you."

Whilst she was a cadet Lawrance had been badly injured in an open-air meeting when she was knocked down by roughs and her knee jumped on. The Army Mother visited her in the Training Home "cubicle" and found her in great pain. Perhaps it was then that Lawrance first noticed that Catherine's hand was soft and strong? Not satisfied with the cadet's condition she arranged to meet the doctor attending, and insisted that a specialist should be called. The report was serious. Eventually three doctors came and the Army Mother with them. After they had examined the injured knee, they retired down the corridor, but Lawrance overheard them say that the leg must come off, above the knee, without delay; and they enquired for the young woman's parents. "Then they walked away, but Mrs. Booth came back and said to me, 'Now Lawrance, the doctors think your leg ought to come off, but I don't believe in the knife, will you leave your leg to me?' When Mrs. Booth looked at you, you felt you could trust her with your life, with everything, so I said 'yes'." The Army Mother gave orders that Lawrance was to be carried at once to sit in a hot bath, this treatment to be continued at intervals daily, with cold water packs between whiles. Catherine often applied these herself. The leg was saved and Lawrance lived to give brilliant and fruitful service as a Training Officer, and for many years as Head of the Women's Side of the International Training College. She recalled being sent for by the Army Mother and told, "Lawrance, you've a brain like Railton. I want to send you to Switzerland for two years to be educated. 'Oh, no, Mrs. Booth, if God had wanted that He'd have done it before I began my work.' Then she looked at me a moment with her wonderful eyes, 'Very well, Lawrance, if you feel like that you shall go on with the Training Work.' Not long afterwards Mrs. Booth spoke to me again, 'Lawrance, I'm giving you someone to help you to do the things you can't do, and you will help her to do the things *she* can't do.'" Aggie Jones, an educated young Quaker lady, was appointed as secretary to help Lawrance with all that side of things. Catherine knew how to match people for their work. It was Catherine who encouraged the "Staff" on training work to "mother" the cadets, as well as train and instruct them. For some time Emma Booth was called "Training Home Mother". The mode passed, but it had served to establish the relation between the cadets and their Training Home Leader on the lines of personal affection which Catherine Booth deemed the most helpful atmosphere in which to mould character.

A letter to Mrs. Billups gives us a concept of Catherine's sense of personal responsibility for the young people in the Army's care. Observe her calm, assured exercise of the "right" to act, this time for a sick lad. It may be worth noting too, how ready, herself so hard driven, she yet is to do Emma's work, so that Emma may rest. There was never a hint of "highmightiness" about her. Just as in her own home she would don her apron and take over the cooking if need arose, so as Army Mother her concern was to get things done that needed doing. Thus the letter. "I came home to do Emma's work in order to let her have a week's rest, little thinking what an undertaking the Lord had in store for me. I had only just arrived when I was told that one of our most devoted cadets was raving mad. He had flown at Ballington, of whom he was most fond, and it took eight men to master him. They had a doctor, and he stated that it was a case of hopeless insanity, and ordered him to be taken to an Asylum, as their lives were in danger. I came in just as they were negotiating this, and said he should not go! I felt sure it was a case of inflammation of the membrane of the brain. I sent the Commissioner of Lunacy off when he came, and dismissed the doctor, taking charge myself. They had him tied with ropes, hands and feet, and four men to watch him. I instructed them to take the ropes off one hand at a time, substituting strips of wet linen, leaving ends for them to hold, let them undress him, got a wet sheet ready, and we had him in the pack and *asleep* in three quarters of an hour. He had not slept for three nights and days. I have had him 'packed' morning and night, and a hot mustard blanket up to the loins at noon . . . he has got the turn and will be well in eight or ten days. We have given him nothing but milk and fruit. I sent for Dr. Metcalf [the hydropathist] yesterday to confirm our people in the course I had taken, and he says I am quite right."[98] Catherine was as ready at fifty as she was at fifteen to rush in and *act*. Courage and strength kindled in her to match the occasion. She might pay for it afterwards, but in the hour of need the impulse toward action was irrepressible.

In the matter of training officers criticism was to be expected, but the "contrariness" of critics was bitterly clear. First they made an outcry against using young, *untrained* lads and lassies to "preach"; and then when a course of training *is* begun, expressed themselves as being "afraid that we are in danger of departing from the simplicity of the Movement and going off on to college lines!" From each set of objectors *some* subscriptions would be withdrawn. Catherine wrote, "You caution us, dear Mr. Reed, against aiming at anything great in our place for training. So far from this, we are so convinced of the necessity of keeping our evangelists down to the level of the people amongst whom they labour that we shall aim at the greatest possible simplicity both in the abode, food, dress, and habits."[99] William retorted that the critics "must come and see". How often "come and see" was his only answer to detractors. Catherine tried to make people understand what this training amounted to. She defined its aims, and what she said is, in the main, apt today. "All our training is to fit our officers for the work they have to do . . . teach a shoemaker to make shoes, and a soul-winner *to win souls*." Do you ask how?

"Well we begin with the heart . . . True, we receive no candidates but such as we have good reason, after careful enquiry, to believe are truly converted. Nevertheless, we find many of them are not sanctified; that is, not having fully renounced the flesh or the world, and not thoroughly given up to God . . . which we regard as indispensable to the fullness of the Holy Spirit and success in winning souls. In addition to meetings and lectures devoted to heart-searching truths, every cadet is seen privately, talked and prayed with, and counselled according to his or her individual necessities . . . each being allowed opportunity to state difficulties . . . We take it to be a fundamental principle that if the soul is not right, the service cannot be right, and therefore we make the *soul first and chief care.* Next, instruct the candidates in principles, discipline and methods of The Salvation Army through which they are to act upon the people. Not only is this done in theory in the lecture room, but they are led into actual contact with the ignorance, sins and woes of the people."[100]

The same year, 1880, that saw the training of officers begun, opened a door for Catherine to preach in the West End. Mr. Denny, his own soul refreshed and warmed by her enthusiasm and clear doctrine, wrote to William: "Your blessed wife will affect the West [End] of London and do more good to the cause than any other machinery that I know of. God is with her, of a truth."[101] Catherine saw this as simply another opportunity to lift up the name of Jesus. Congregations were not large, mere hundreds, but they inspired her and she poured out her messages with glowing intensity. "I feel it is the Spirit," she says in a letter to Mrs. Billups. "The Lord has very graciously stood by me . . . Last Sunday we had the Hall crowded and a large proportion of gentlemen . . . thirty-one came forward for both blessings. Some of them were most blessed cases of full surrender. We did not get away till nearly six, and we began at three. Everybody amazed at this for West End. Pray much, dear friend, that God may do a deep and permanent work in this Babylon. It seems as though He gave me words of fire for them, and they sit spellbound. Nearly all I say is extemporaneous and new."[102]

In certain particulars the several series of West End meetings, beginning with these in 1880, were the most influential of Catherine Booth's public efforts. These congregations, and others of the same type, spread her fame, establishing her as "perhaps the most conspicuous and the most successful preacher of righteousness this generation has heard. Some preach ritual; others dogma. She preached righteousness."[103] Of converts at the gatherings some became leaders in The Salvation Army, others in the Churches. For the first time verbatim reports of Catherine's words were taken and form several slim volumes, some of which were translated and published in Europe. Together with reports of speeches and open letters printed in *The War Cry,* these are all that is preserved of her lifetime of preaching and teaching. Pale is the printed word in contrast with the vibrant expression of the living speaker, as a brilliant bloom is when lying flaccid and faded between the pages of a book. Allowing for this loss it is still possible to sense the urgency that lay behind her recorded words. The feeling becomes cumulative as one turns page after page, her exquisite longing to convince her listeners, to *compel* acceptance of the truth, shines through the text. It was surely the bright flame of this desire that illumined the truths she uttered. "You may think that you are only neglecting the entreaties of a little woman . . . I don't care what people say of *me*; I will never speak to sinners so that one man or woman in my audience can stand up and say, 'You might have warned me more faithfully' . . . I would rather die than that should be the case."[104]

It was never more true of any than of Catherine Booth that she spoke from her heart. "What was the touchstone which she applied to the sinners who knelt at her feet? The answer is written at large in all her writings. She preached out of the fullness of her heart."[105] Yet, it is equally true that she spoke from altogether outside herself, "beside herself" as the old-fashioned expression has it. Her own feelings, fears, preferences, *herself*, was lost. She forgot all save the message and those to whom the message was sent. It is important to our understanding of her, and of the influence she wielded, that we accept the survival in her of the capacity for complete unself-consciousness, lost to most people as they emerge from infancy; it brought an impression of "other world" authority to her words and, at least in some measure, explains the general acceptance of the authoritative cast of her speech as though in verity she were but the mouthpiece. This she herself believed: and that faith gave her confidence, not in herself but in the validity of her message, gave her, too, courage to utter the "hard saying". Some have adjudged her as being too often "cutting". But one needs to know what leads up to the thrust; and to note that the hardest things are said to those who profess but do not perform. Stead said, "She was Carlylean in her intense hatred and scorn for humbug and humbugs. A religious sham was for her the worst of shams, and she was ever on the war-path against sanctimonious hypocrites of all kinds."[106] To these she could be scathing. As when she declared, "In this so-called Christian country . . . look at the state of the nation. Look at the godlessness, the injustice, the falseness, blasphemy, the uncleanness and the debauchery everywhere. Do you ever look at the condition of things close to your . . . churches? The worse-than-heathen beastliness into which thousands of our neglected neighbours, rich and poor alike, have sunk? . . . All the legislation, education, or provision of better dwellings . . . won't touch the moral cancer, the spring of all this wickedness and misery; nothing will do it until the *Christians rise up to do their Master's bidding*. But *they* do not see any *need* for it . . . *They* have no heart for the fight! *They* do not *feel* these things . . . *They* want to be quiet and comfortable, and to have their religion in a snug back-parlour fashion!' And again, "Many of these latter day Christians are most zealous in building the sepulchres of the prophets . . . They are often great at lectures on . . . Luther, George Fox, Wesley and others, and they will listen most interestedly to a dissertation on their heroism . . . but as to imitating their deeds of valour, it never enters their minds! . . . They go home and live the coming week exactly as they lived the week that preceded it . . ."[107] Sometimes she was less inclined to expostulate, or perhaps felt it to be useless? As when she exclaimed, "When people object to us, I say, 'Are you doing the work? And if not, for Christ's sake let us alone, for we are'."

To one of her West End audiences she had been speaking of the alleged "brutal tastes of the *lower* orders", and when contrasting these with those of the "upper classes" her scorn may still be felt in her words about the hunting of carted deer.* "Here is . . . half the aristocracy of a county, male and female mounted on horses worth hundreds of pounds each, and which have been bred and trained at hundreds more, and what for? 'This splendid field' is waiting whilst a poor timid animal is let loose from confinement and permitted to fly in terror from its strange surroundings. Observe the delight of all the gentlemen and noble ladies when a whole pack of strong dogs is let loose in pursuit, and then, behold the noble chase! The regiment of well-mounted cavalry and the pack of hounds all charge at full gallop after the poor frightened creature. It will be a great disappointment if by any means it should escape or be killed within so short a time as an hour! The sport will be excellent in proportion to the time during which the poor thing's agony is prolonged, and the number of miles it is able to run in terror of its life. Brutality! I tell you, that in my judgment at any rate, you can find nothing in the vilest back slums, more utterly, more deliberately, more savagely cruel . . ."[108]

From the West End select gatherings in the afternoon, the Army Mother often went to a hall in one of London's unfashionable neighbourhoods. J. C. Carlile† wrote as a youth he sat in a room over a shop in Whitechapel listening to Catherine Booth's "sweet penetrating voice . . . her searching eyes seemed to look right into the soul . . ."[109] Through that encounter with her there came to him what he called the greatest happiness of his life. As the rich and educated had sat spellbound on the Sunday afternoon, so on Sunday

* The practice of carted stag hunting has not been abolished by law but discontinued since 1963 on economic ground. The secretary of the R.S.P.C.A. wrote to me that the Society intends to press for legislation making such a form of hunting illegal.

* J. C. Carlile, C.H., became president of the Baptist Union.

night the ignorant and poor sat wedged tightly together, hanging upon her every word. I have been told that after the hurly burly of the singing, the hush that fell when Catherine stepped to the front of the stage or platform was beyond explanation. Bramwell said, "One of the most attractive qualities of her utterances was their naturalness. She dealt with themes as old as human life itself, yet she managed to give a freshness and informality to her addresses which made them seem new to her hearers ... She had a gift of lucid statement, and few even in the roughest crowds could fail to see the idea she was seeking to enforce.[110] It was said that after hearing her preach Archbishop Randall Davidson's father told his son, "If ever I am charged with a crime, don't bother to engage any of the great lawyers to defend me; get that woman."[111] Of one of the West End meetings Catherine wrote to Mrs. Billups, "We had a wonderful time, even in my experience at the West End on Sunday afternoon ... between forty and fifty came out [to the penitent-form] ... I cannot tell you a tithe of what the Lord is doing ..."[112]

And what comfort came to hearts long oppressed. Bramwell Booth said, "In the smaller after-meetings, which followed most of her public services, it was not at all uncommon to find penitents confessing to lifelong frauds or other hidden wrongs. Men put into her hands cheques, sometimes for considerable sums, on behalf of those they had deceived or injured in years gone by, and others made confessions and entreaties to her to help them in restoring unions which had been shattered by cruelty and unfaithfulness."[113] Naturally private interviews and still more letter-writing resulted. This being confided in by "thousands of English men and women", as Stead put it, "brought her into more or less vitalizing contact with all phases of human life from the highest to the lowest ... She became the supreme mother-confessor of our time."[114] "These West End services have landed me in heaps of work, correspondence, etc. ..." Catherine told Mrs. Billups. Her letters sometimes touch on her own feelings, as in these: "On Sunday I thought it would be impossible to preach. I *could not* resist an uncontrollable fit of depression all day. I could not hide it from the strangers round about me, which to me is dreadful. I have no very sympathetic soul here, so I am very much alone. I went however, feeling well I will try and if I fail I shall fail *trying to do His work.* He again stood by me ... lifting me completely out of myself and giving me power to hold every eye and heart. But afterwards I went down just as low; all day Monday could scarcely lift my head. Perhaps there is *no other way* by which He could lead me. He knows best. He knows best in *your* case, dearest friend. Will you trust Him?"[115] Near Christmas she recounts, "I tried to get an opportunity to write before leaving home, but it was impossible. I cannot tell you the many worries and duties I had, neither would I if I could, for you have plenty of your own ... Life is a mystery, darkness and clouds are round us, but light will break by-and-by. David said 'All Thy billows and Thy waves have gone over me'. Bless the Lord for these Psalms . . . I go to Kidderminster tomorrow for Sunday and Monday, and then home on Tuesday. Shall not have much time to make puddings."[116] And again, "Just a line though I have to leave at three o'clock for the drawing-room meeting at the West End and don't know a bit what I am to say. Pa has gone off to the North, and I have had a perfect drive all the morning. I have been dreadfully down since you left, worse than usual, it is of no use reasoning. I *cannot* help it. Nothing cheers me when these fits of despondency are on me and I feel only fit for the—I won't write it because I know the devil would like to see it in ink! If I dared give up working I should a hundred times over, but I dare not. I got letters yesterday telling me of *five* precious cases of long-standing professors getting the peace and power—one, a wine merchant, is giving up his business."[117] Later in the same year she confides to Mrs. Billups, "I am much tried just now by perplexities of every kind, uncertainty humanly looked at hedges me in on every side. Satan says it is useless trying to steer straight through such a labyrinth but I am determined to hold on to the promises, come what will. Will you join me dearest Friend? Shall we two dare to go all lengths with God in everything. Our God is the living God. He sees me, knows me, loves me, wants to have me with Him in Glory as much as He did Abraham or Paul or John. If this is true what have I to fear? Because all the world have broken off from Him, forgotten Him, is that any reason why I should? Lord help us to be witnesses for Jesus as a living ever-present almighty Saviour, help me and my beloved friend. Amen. Yours weak, but believing C. Booth."[118]

Catherine herself was working at the same high speed she so much deplored for her dear ones. The over-fatigue, I judge, at any rate in part, produced the spells of depression which tended to increase in her last years but chiefly they were the result of the emotional strain of her life. All her activities involved her emotions. Emotional fatigue can be more exhausting than physical. After all, the "poor old body" can be made to lie down, but an overburdened heart is a much more awkward customer! In fact, Catherine suffered from too much loving, she had too many loves. I think also that she saw further into the future than either William or Bramwell—saw ahead of them as it were—what they came to see later. The beloved "work" had developed to an astounding degree. It was only fifteen years since William began his Mission in Whitechapel in 1865. Now Salvationists numbered tens of thousands; Catherine's insight showed her how the very success of the "concern" multiplied the demands and dangers of its future. Lawrance said to me, "You see she was always so anxious for the future of the Army, so earnest about building the Army right, about the character and religion of those who were to be officers in the Army, and preach Jesus Christ. She was always talking about helping the people to be better, better homes, better wives and children. Oh, how she carried *children* on her heart . . ."

There began at times to creep over her spirit a new oppression; a vast discouragement and fatigue of mind at seeing so clearly what *ought* to be done for her Army children, while at the same time she must face the incontrovertible fact that for her, as she wrote to Mrs. Billups once, "the bounds of possibility are reached". Knowledge of the moral degradation of the people spread like a dark shadow over her mind, making what had been accomplished for them seem small, and emphasizing, perhaps magnifying the vastness of their need. Sometimes Catherine shared her anxiety and grief with her congregation as: "The state of the masses in our country is to me a cause of daily, hourly grief and apprehension. Since coming more in contact with them I have found their condition to be so much worse than anything I had previously conceived, that I have often felt confounded, disheartened, and almost paralyzed . . . Is it possible that these are our fellow-countrymen in this end of the nineteenth century, in this so-called Christian country? [I have seen] hundreds of men in *one crowd* . . . bearing in their persons . . . and behaviour all the marks of heathenism and debauchery . . . I am often received by friends living at a distance from the halls used for our services on Sunday, so that on my way to them I have to pass through many streets. This gives me an opportunity of observing the character of the population . . . I have met thousands of the youth of both sexes, ranging say from fourteen to twenty years of age, rushing away to seek their Sunday evening's enjoyment . . . screaming at the top of their voices, pushing one another off and on the pavement, frequently using most offensive, if not positively blasphemous and obscene language. In our large gatherings . . . it is quite a common thing for these boys and girls to say to our officers . . . 'what do I care' and to laugh in their faces, saying, 'I don't believe in your God' . . . There are thousands who . . . are squandering their opportunities and abusing their capacities in all manner of debauchery and sin . . ."[119] Before their marriage Catherine wrote to her lover, "I never look at a little child but I feel unutterable things; what is he? What will he become?" And she has not changed! After thirty years, to see the *young* in peril moved her more deeply rather than less. When her great meetings were over, and the elation had ebbed away, it was of the young she thought, of the young among the multitude *who did not know Christ*. Her grief for the godless continued to be a living and at times an overwhelming emotion. She wrote to Bramwell, "It drinks up my spirit when I look upon the multitudes as sheep having no shepherd."[120]

There was more commendation than contumely now for Catherine Booth. She was praised in the religious press, in the secular too. But there is no whit of change in her demeanour. She had no "thunder" reserved for the simpler, or if you prefer, sinfuller sinners, and a milder version for the respectable educated. It was said of her, "She would never admit that one kind of sin was more respectable than another." And observe, the effect of her presence was the same whether on the small intellectual congregation, or on the large untutored crowd. She compelled from both the acknowledgment "God is in this place." Stead said, "She could smite . . . but for the individual sinner, when once he showed signs of turning from his evil ways, no one could be more compassionate or tenderly kind."[121] Lord X was "desired" for God with the same untiring solicitude as some wreck of a rapscallion. *She coveted them equally for Christ.* Speaking at a meeting in Whitechapel one night she particularly noticed a woman in the congregation. When the preaching was over Catherine told, "I went to her and besought her. She said, 'Yes, I know it's all true . . . I can't speak of it tonight. I will come another time.' I followed her right into the draught of the door, for I felt my heart go out after her . . ."[122] Catherine had felt like that about people in William's services before she began to preach herself and her feelings never got blunted.

Had Catherine been given to reverie, what fantastic experiences she might have conjured up from the fifteen years that had passed since that moment of silence fell between her and William after he had told her that he wanted to stay to work in the East End. Then she had asked herself what the future would hold for their children? The Salvation Army came into being. Catherine had linked each of them by prayer and desire with the "glorious" war in which she and William were engaged. To her daughter Emma she wrote of a soul-saving campaign, "Oh, my dear child, it makes me long to see you all at it in some way or other." It is hard to grasp that in these turbulent years she found time and strength to win every one of her eight children to her Saviour and to His cause. And that is the story I tell next.

BOOK FIVE

Catherine's Love for her Children

"I intend to make myself fit to become a mother and, being that in every sense, I shall be fit for any destiny which God may impose upon me."*

"I do see and feel more than ever the importance of kindness. If ever God gives me children their young hearts shall expand under its full and gentle influence."*

"Children brought up without love are like plants brought up without the sun."†

"The first important matter for a parent to settle in her own mind is this: to whom does this child belong? Is it mine or is it the Lord's?"†

"I believe in training children [to be] Christians from babyhood."*

"I am convinced that the Spirit of God works mightily on little children long before grown-up people think they are able to understand."*

"My precious children! Oh, how I long to inspire them with truly bene- volent and self-sacrificing principles! The Lord help me."
— In a letter to her parents.

"Conversion from the animal to the spiritual nature comes naturally to those whose parents have really—not nominally—dedicated them to God in infancy and earnestly claimed the divine influence of the Holy Spirit to guide them in teaching and to open out the soul of the child to receive what it is taught."

— In a pencilled scrap.

"... authoritative ... I maintain that this is the *only* proper form of government for young minds and so far from its dwarfing and stinting, it is the only safeguard from that animalism and lawlessness which destroys the very germ and bud of true greatness."

— In a letter to Bramwell.

"Just let me say to you who are parents ... train your children in moral courage. Teach them from five years old to be bold enough to say 'No' to the tempter. Teach them to despise the man who can't bear to be laughed at."†

*In love-letters to William Booth.
†From public addresses.

1

The capacity to take responsibility has been called the key to Catherine Booth's nature. She said of herself, "If I were asked for the main characteristics that have helped me through life, I should give a high place among them to the sense of responsibility which I have felt from my earliest days to everybody who came in any way under my influence. The fact that I was not *held* responsible was no relief at all! 'Why trouble? It is not your affair!' friends constantly say to me even now.' But how can I help troubling,' I reply, 'when I see people going wrong!' "[1] This sense of responsibility for others ran through Catherine's life like a strong bright thread, and it shone with a new lustre when she became a mother. She was happy beyond any former conception of happiness, almost too happy? Could one be too happy? If there came a hint of anxiety lest she and William might not be wise enough to train their son, she was instantly reassured by the certainty that she loved him enough for anything—for everything —and that God would help her. So soon as she had strength, she and William held him up to God and dedicated the babe to be a preacher. When the children were grown men and women and she was nearing the close of her earthly life, Catherine said to Emma, "With all my children I have sought *first* Christ . . . First, not *among* other things, but *first*. Since the hour that I first kissed Bramwell as he lay a little babe on my bosom, I said to the Lord, 'In all my ambitions for this child and for any others that may follow, in all my dealings with them and in the education that I may be able to give them, Thy Kingdom shall be first."[2]

Soon after her engagement to William she had written in one of her love-letters, 'I never look at a little child but I feel unutterable things. *What is he?* What will he become? What might he be? What eternal destiny awaits the jewel lodged in that beautiful little casket? What influences will gather round it in this life's prilgrimage? What friends will aid it? What foes try to ruin it? are questions my soul shrinks from answering even to itself."[3] These undefined emotions and questionings were intensified and concentrated on her little son as she suckled him. She felt "infinite yearnings" for him. Were not she and his father *responsible to God* for preparing this new being for life on earth and in heaven? She embraced the responsibility with the full force of her nature. William and Catherine were disposed, by their views of life and religion, to regard the child born to them as one for whom noble possibilities were already purposed in the mind of God. They believed parenthood to be a God-given vocation. Stead said of Catherine, "She was a modern woman in many things, but there never was a woman of woman born who regarded with more absolute loathing and disgust distaste of maternity."[4]

Bramwell was a happy baby, soon nicknamed "Sunshine" by his father. Writing to her mother when the child was a few months old she said, "The baby is a real beauty, everybody exclaims when they see him. 'What a sweet child'; 'O, what a lovely baby'. His eyes are bright as stars and yet get darker every day ... everybody says he is the picture of his mother, but I have not the vanity to believe it."[5] Catherine's letters home, and to some extent her public words in after years, show how her delight in her children was joined in her mind to the belief that she and their father must answer to God for the nascent spirits entrusted to their care. She once said, "The first question for a parent is 'To whom does this child belong? *Is it mine or is it the Lord's?*' Surely this question should not need any discussion, at least by Christian parents ... We are *able* to train our children in the way they should go, or God would not have enjoined it upon us ... the training God requires is a moral training, the inspiring of the child with the love of goodness, truth and righteousness ... mere teaching, informing the head without interesting or influencing the heart, frequently drives children off from God and goodness ..."[6]

For her own children Catherine began this training early. When there was a suggestion that Bramwell, then fourteen months old, should be left for a time with his grandmother, Catherine wrote that she could not part with him: "First because I know the child's affections would inevitably be weaned from us, and secondly because the next year will be the most important of his life, with reference to managing his will, and in this I cannot but distrust you. I know, my darling Mother, you would not wage war with his self-will so resolutely as to subdue it. And then my child would be ruined, for he must be taught implicit, uncompromising obedience."[7] She spoke from her own experience when she said, "God has laid it on parents to begin the work of bringing the will into subjection in childhood; and to help us in doing it He has put in all children a *tendency to obey*. Watch any young child and you will find that, as a rule, his instincts lead him to submit. Insubordination is the exception, until this tendency has been trifled with by those who have the care of him ... I am sometimes asked, 'What do you consider the secret of successful training?' I answer, 'Beginning *soon enough*' ... That is the secret of success. There is a way of speaking to and handling an infant, compatible with the utmost love and tenderness, which teaches it that mother is not to be trifled with; that, although she loves and caresses, she is to be obeyed ... Take an illustration ... We will suppose that your son of six months old is in a fractious mood, and indisposed to take his morning nap; nurse has put him in his cot and struggled with him ... At last you come and take the baby ... lay him down with a firm hand, saying with a firm voice, 'Baby must lie still and go to sleep', putting your hand on him at the same time to prevent him rising in the cot or turning over after you have spoken. Now, if this child for the previous three months has been trained in this line . . . he will, as a natural consequence, lie still and go to sleep; but if he has not been accustomed to this kind of handling, he will perhaps become boisterous and resist you; if so, you must *persevere*. You must on no account give up, no, not if you stop till night . . . But you say 'it is so hard'. Not half so hard as the other way, for when the child finds that the mother is not to be got over, he will yield as a matter of course. I have proved it, I think, with some as strong-willed children as ever came into the world. I conquered them at six and ten months old, and seldom had to contend with any direct opposition after."

One almost sees the young mother placing her firm little hand on Bramwell in such a manner as she describes. ". . . What has God given you authority for, if He did not intend you to use it? If your child can do as well without it? He has sent your child to you to be guided and restrained by your authority, as much as to be inspired and encouraged by your love."[8] Catherine's children were trained to obey from infancy, and it was the *love* that lay behind her words that ruled them. ". . . One of the worst signs of our times," she said, "is the little respect which children seem to have for their parents. There are numbers of boys and girls from twelve to seventeen years of age, over whom their parents have little or no control. But how has this come to pass? Did these children leap all at once from the restraints and barriers of parental affection and authority? Oh, no! It has been the result of the imperceptible growth of years of insubordination and want of proper discipline . . ."[9]

I think it is evidence of her sound mother-sense in rearing them that all but one of her eight (Emma was killed in a rail accident, in 1903) lived to be old. Each was welcomed as God's gift and from earliest days cherished by her love. Each was subject to that gentle but firm hand in babyhood. Early Catherine appealed to the child's own love. This was part of the training too. She always smiled on any manifestation of a child's instinctive delight in doing something for someone else, the delight of being relied on, of being needed. See this letter to her mother written soon after the birth of her second child and notice how she had already begun to foster the love of the two babes for each other and especially the love of the elder—he was under two—for the younger. "The children are well, they are two beauties. Oh, I often feel as though they cannot be mine! It seems too much to be true, that they are so healthy when I am such a poor thing. Willie gets every day more lovable and engaging, and affectionate . . . You would love to see him hug Ballington and offer him a bit of everything he has. He never manifests the slightest jealousy or selfishness towards him, but on the contrary, he laughs

303

and dances when we caress the baby, and when it cries he is quite distressed. I have used him to bring me the footstool when I nurse baby, and now he runs with it to me as soon as he sees me take him up without waiting to be asked."[10]

In one of her love-letters to William, Catherine said, "I believe in training children [to be] Christians from babyhood," and she acted on this belief when it came to her own. She wanted her children to be early acquainted with God, and who better able to introduce Him to them than their mother? She recalled, "I used to take my eldest boy on my knee from the time when he was about two years old and tell him the [Bible] stories ... in baby language and adapted to baby comprehension, one at a time, so that he thoroughly drank them in."[11] Clearly to my mind's eye, I see her seated on a low rocking-chair by the nursery fire, the little head at rest on her breast, her encircling arms about him, bringing God and eternal truths into the orbit of the nursery. Perhaps it was towards bedtime, when this child's ceaseless energy ebbed a little. Her voice is music to him, though he does not know that until a long time afterwards. His imagination is awake. He listens. His mother gives a comforting squeeze at the thrilling parts of the story. "You will be very much pleased with Willie," she writes, "He loves to listen to stories about Joseph, Moses, Daniel and the Saviour."[12] She recalled of Bramwell, "I remember once going into the nursery and finding him mounted on his rocking-horse, in a high state of excitement, finishing the story of Joseph to his nurse and baby brother, showing them how Joseph galloped on his live 'gee-gee' when he went to fetch his father to show him to Pharoah."[13]

The Booths were still in Gateshead when their fourth child, Emma, was born. She was a most attractive infant with curly brown hair and lovely eyes. If Bramwell, as his mother said, "was a sort of father to the younger children", Emma was like a "mother". This baby was six months old when Catherine began to preach, and was the first to accompany her on a day of public services in order to obtain nourishment. Catherine and William continued lovers in growing capacity for love and joy in one another, and that love and joy were increased by their almost extravagant love for their children. In turn their love for the children beautified and intensified their love for each other. It was a vivifying circle! See these scribbled lines to Mrs. Mumford, "They are all fine, healthy, lovable children, and as sharp as needles and amidst all the toil and anxiety they occasion I am cheered and sustained by the love and sympathy of their father. William was never kinder or more loving and attentive than now."[14] These personal loves, to God, to husband, and to children, taught Catherine how to deal with the strangers who, from the time of her first preaching, came into her life seeking her help; what she learned in her own home was immensely important to her as a "Mother in Israel".

From Cornwall, where after leaving the Methodist New Connexion the Booths began their independent evangelistic work, Catherine wrote her first letter to Bramwell. I think it gives an idea of her way with children. It was enclosed in one to her mother, with whom the children had been left, asking her to "read it to him two or three times, just before he goes to bed at night so that it may affect his heart the more. Bless him." And here is part of what she wrote to her five-year-old son, "My dearest Willie, I promised to write you a letter all to yourself, and so the first thing I do this morning shall be to write it ... I do hope you are praying to the Lord every day to help you, and are trying to do as Grandmama and Mary tell you. If you are, I know this letter will find you happy and joyous, because when little children are *good* they are always *happy*. But I never knew a naughty child to be happy in my life, and I daresay Grandmama never did. Just ask her if she ever did. I often wish you were here with us. It is a beautiful place; such nice fields and lanes, where you could run about and play and romp and sing and shout, without troubling anybody, and such nice places to fly kites without trees about to catch them ... Try every day to do exactly as you are bid and then you will get to do it quickly and easily ..."[15]

And see how she encouraged their love for each other in a second letter to Bramwell, "... I fear you begin to think it is a long time before Papa comes to fetch you ... You see, my dear boy, your Papa and I came down here to do the Lord's work, and although we have worked very hard we have not got it all done yet ... so our dear little ones have to wait a long time. But, oh, what a good thing it is that you have a kind Grandma to take care of you and find you a home! The Lord does not let you want for any good thing. He sends you plenty of food to eat and nice clean clothes to put on, and a nice bed to sleep in, just the same as though you were with me. Do you ever think about this and thank Him for all His kindness? I hope you do, and that you try to please Him by being a very good boy ... When you get here Papa and I will take you with us on to the cliffs and show you the great and beautiful sea. In fact you will perhaps live just opposite to it, where you can see the ships and boats out of your nursery window. Won't that be nice? You can show them to Ballington, Katie, and baby, and tell the names of the ships as they sail past. I often wish very much that you were here ... By the by this is Katie's birthday; *dear* little girl! It is just three years today since the Lord sent her to us, a dear little tiny baby! I wish I could give her a birthday kiss. But as I am so far away you must give her one for me—a real bumper, right on her sweet little cheek, and tell her how much her mama loves her, and that she must be a very good little girl. I hope, too, that you do not quarrel with Ballington now, about the play things. You must try to remember that he is much younger than you [one year!] and always give way to him and try to teach him to be good. Tell him all about what I have told you in this letter and about the great water and the ships. I wonder how dear baby is getting on. Do you think she has forgotten me? I hope not. You must talk to her every day about Papa and Mama and try to make her understand that she is coming to see us. Bless her little heart! I hope her brother Willie is very kind and gentle with her, now she has no mama there to love her. Give my kind love to Grandma, Grandpa, and Mary, and always remember me as your loving Mama."[16]

When the Booths went to St. Ives they rented a furnished house and the family was reunited. From there letters tell of the children, "... It is such lovely weather that they are out most of their time. They go off directly after breakfast and stop till eleven o'clock on the sands and then again from two till five. They each have a spade with which they dig mountains, brooks, etc., they never had such fun in their lives. You would be delighted to see them running away from the waves and then back..."[17] "Willie has commenced to write you a grand letter... He is so tender and tries hard to be good and obedient. Everybody says what a sharp boy he is ... Emma is the pet of the family and has a sweet happy disposition..."[18] A week or two after this letter Catherine's fifth child, Herbert Howard, was born. His music and songs were to be an example of Salvation Army style and hold a permanent place in Christian hymnology.

Thus happily for the children began perhaps the most strenuous time for their mother. During the first two years of her marriage she had known what it was to be constantly moving; but now, with five "beauties" in the nursery, she began that spell of life when she "endured torture always treading on other people's carpets, and using other people's furniture". To mitigate this trial for the children she "carried a nursery carpet, chose a room for a nursery, put in some plain furniture and turned the children in with their nurse".[19] Here they could romp and shout, "gallop" on the rocking-horse, enjoy all manner of imaginary adventures and "let off steam". Catherine was a great believer in the salutariness of this last. She never coddled her children but encouraged sturdiness in everyday things, as in the use of cold water and exercise in the fresh air. She believed too in plenty of toys and all kinds of games that spelled occupation for the children. She said, "I never stinted them in toys, I thought them as needful as food. I used to teach them to count with raisins and apples and always let them have rice or any sort of dry stuff to weigh up. It was a never ending treat and many a pair of scales was broken in the doing."[20] Another dodge for providing occupation was to empty her workbasket on to a sheet of newspaper, and set the little girls to "tidy" it for her as she sat mending. As for the mending and sewing, there was no end to it. Bramwell said, "Before everything else she was a mother, and a mother in the most domestic and practical sense. For example, she made our clothes until we were ten or twelve. She could not only sew, but cut out and plan ... she was a most economical woman."[21] There were very few ready-made clothes in those days. Soon after she began her public work she wrote to her mother, "I cannot give the time to preparation unless I can afford to put my sewing out." And after the birth of her sixth child, Marian Billups, when she was preaching nearly every week-day as well as on Sunday, she told her mother, "My time is almost wholly taken up in mending, turning and attending to the clothes ... I cannot bear to see them 'go out a figure'."[22] She liked the children to look nice and made their clothes of good material but these were not elaborately decorated as was often the fashion of the time. She wrote to William before they were married, "Our sweet babes we will dress in all simplicity and loveliness."[23] What she and her husband felt to be harmful was extravagance and display for display's sake; ostentation in dress and behaviour did not in their view fit a sincere Christian. Mrs. Mumford, who was an expert needlewoman, enjoyed making things for her grandchildren. Several of Catherine's letters to her mother find them too grand. "What will you say when I tell you that the beautiful frock you brought Willie has never been on him yet! I am now altering it a little to make it less showy ... You see dear Mother, William speaks so plainly on the subject of dress that it would be the most glaring inconsistency if I were to deck out my children as the worldlings do."[24] And later, "Accept my warmest thanks for the little frock you sent. We like it very much. There is only one difficulty, namely it is too smart ..."[25]

When William decided to work in Whitechapel there was a new reason for restraint in dress. Mission people were poor. Converts were tempted to spend on "making a good show" in dress what ought to be used for food and other necessities or for paying debts. Miss Short said of William, "It used to make him furious when he saw the way in which poor people wasted precious money on stupid finery." But she thought the Booths "carried this too far" when it came to their children. To dress simply without jewellery or ornaments was characteristic of Salvationists in the early years. A real desire to be *separate* from the world in dress and behaviour actuated them. It was not merely conformity to rules but something deeper arising from desire to be dedicated to the service of God. Often those who knelt at the penitent-form discarded jewels, pipes, flowers and feathers on the spot and *before* receiving any teaching on the matter.

Catherine's popularity as a preacher increased but at home, for William, for the children, and for the servants, she was as truly the centre of attraction as she was in the pulpit. She drew them all like a magnet. "The challenge in her laughter,"[26] the tenderness in her eyes, the sense of elation at being alive which belonged to her presence was never more vivid than when she was in her own home with those she loved. Sir Winston Churchill said, "My mother . . . shone for me like the evening star. I loved her dearly but at a distance."[27] Catherine's children loved her dearly but close at hand in joyous intimacy which was the basis for them of all happiness, and of unhappiness sometimes because naughtiness always made her unhappy as well as the culprit. In her nursery realm her feelings were not allowed to warp judgment. Justice, she knew, is love's throne, and love's rule can never be fully beneficent unless love be based on justice. In a letter to Mrs. Mumford William wrote, "Kate says we must have no distinctions, such as forty kisses for Willie and only twenty for Babs. No coat of many colours. You must love both alike."[28] This held good for them all. And what was almost as important, she knew how to *show her love*: her children all grew up in the sunshine of it, and relied on it so long as she lived. Her plan of making the older children in some degree responsible for the younger ones was good for them, added to their happiness and hers. The youngest was always "the pet of the family" otherwise there were no favourites in Catherine's nursery. Each in turn learned from her to lend a protecting helpfulness to the "little ones", and her boys and girls grew up in equality of self-expression. To counteract anything they might see or hear outside their own home to the contrary, their mother, as she put it, "ground into my boys that their sisters were just as intelligent and capable as themselves".[29] Her eldest son Bramwell amplified this with, "One thing hammered into her children from their tenderest years was the need for good manners, courtesy, and, in boys especially, courtesy to women . . . we learned from her . . . the absolute equality in every obligation and privilege of boys and girls."[30] This upbringing was a preparation for the new situation which was to arise when The Salvation Army came into being. The boys and girls growing up in the Booth home in common with young people in the homes of their converts, up and down the land, were to find an open door set before them. Boys and girls alike would hear a call to go into all the world and preach the Gospel.

2

Catherine's children could not remember a time when they did not know that more than anything, their mother *wanted* them to be good, to be God's. Bramwell wrote, "Her main care was of her children's souls, and she set herself to win them for Christ. She had the joy of seeing all her children converted."[31] "The great end of Christian training," she once said, "is to lead children to realize the fact that they belong to God, and are under a solemn obligation to do everything in a way which they think will please Him. Parents cannot begin too early, nor labour too continuously, to keep this fact before the minds of their children."[32] "... I am convinced that the Spirit of God works mightily on little children long before grown people think they are able to understand."[33] Catherine had proved this in her own childhood and counted on the Holy Spirit's help in dealing with each of her boys and girls.

Writing about his own conversion Bramwell gave a vivid picture of his mother, of himself too. He was seven. Services for children, led by his parents, were being held in a circus in Cardiff. During the after-meeting in one of these his mother came to where he sat in the congregation; he wrote, "She said to me with great tenderness, 'You are very unhappy'. When I replied 'yes', she added, 'You know the reason?' And again I had to say 'yes'. Then came the clear question as to giving myself to God, and I said, 'No'. She put her hands suddenly to her face, and I can never forget my feelings on seeing the tears fall through them on to the sawdust..."[34] His mother recorded, "I had been anxious on his behalf ... and one night at the circus I had urged him very earnestly to decide for Christ. For a long time he would not speak but ... I shall never forget the feeling ... when my darling boy, only seven years old ... deliberately looked me in the face and answered 'No'."[35] His mother knew that to be valid the decision must be the boy's own; she declared, "God will not invade the freedom of the will even of a child of seven years old. No one can decide for him, no one, in heaven, earth or hell, but himself."[36] Bramwell's account continues, "My parents treated me with loving patience. They did not say much to me ... I remember however how my father's prayers at family worship seemed to take on a new meaning for me."[37] Three months later, at one of the services for children led by his mother, the decision was made. Catherine "discovered him kneeling at the communion rail among a crowd of little penitents. He had come out of his own accord from the middle of the hall."[38] Soon his mother was kneeling beside him; she put her hand lovingly upon his head, prayed with him, and as he tells "led me to cast myself with faith in His promise upon my Saviour ... Great joy overcame me. My heart was filled with love ... Along the street as I walked with my dear mother I could hardly feel the ground we trod upon ... After reaching what was then our home, my dear mother joined her tears of joy with mine, and the beloved father gave me his own blessing."[39] To Mrs. Mumford Catherine sent the news, "Willie has begun to serve God, of course as a child ... I feel a great increase of responsibility ... Oh, to cherish the tender plant of grace aright."[40]

On the subject of conversion in childhood Catherine enquired, "What is conversion but the renewal of the mind by the Holy Ghost through faith in a crucified Saviour? ... Why may not the minds of children be renewed very early? Why may they not be led to choose Christ and

His yoke at seven or eight years old as well as at seventeen? If the will of a child be sincerely yielded to God, cannot the blessed Spirit as easily and as effectually renew and actuate its heart and affections as those of an adult? ... Because in the case of some ... conversion is necessarily sudden and followed by a great outward change, is that any reason why in the case of a child carefully trained in the 'nurture and admonition of the Lord', the Holy Spirit should not work together with such training, adapting His operations to the capacity and requirements of the little ones?"[41] As to how religious teaching should be given Catherine expressed her views clearly and forcibly. "... I have not a doubt that many an impetuous, earnest, high-spirited child is driven to hate the Bible ... and religious exercises in general, by the cold, spiritless, insipid, canting manner in which he hears them ... Now if you want your child to ... love and read his Bible, you must tell him its stories ... so as to make it *interesting* to him. If you want him to love prayer you must so pray as to interest and draw his mind and heart with your own; and teach him to go to God, as he comes to you, in his own natural voice and manner, to tell Him his wants and to express his joys or sorrows."[41]

She described her methods with her own children when they were small, having "a Noah's ark which was kept for Sabbath use; making the ark itself the foundation of one lesson, Noah and his family of another, and the gathering of the animals of a third, and so on ... when my family increased it was my custom before these Sabbath lessons to have a short lively tune; a short prayer which I let them all repeat after me, sentence by sentence ... and after the lesson another short prayer, and then another tune or two."[41] Katie, eldest daughter of the Booth family, remembers that one Noah's ark lesson had an exciting interruption. A confused noise of shouting and laughter was heard from the street; looking out of the window Catherine saw that "a tall youth lurching ridiculously and muttering nonsense" was the centre of an amused crowd. In a moment she had left the children and was in the midst of the mockers ... She rebuked the crowd and brought the young man into the sitting-room. Tea and toast had a sobering effect and were followed by a motherly talk and prayer. He went home in someone's charge, not named, but I fancy it might have been Miss Short who was told to get him "safely past every public house" and bring back news of his family and circumstances. Emma, Catherine's fourth child said, "I remember how she would gather us round her and pray with us. I used to wear a low frock and her hot tears would often drop upon my neck, sending a thrill through me I can never forget. Often she would pray aloud, making us repeat the words after her."[42] These prayers were not vague mild repetitions but colloquial and sometimes startling. She used to pray in the very presence of her children that she would rather lay them in a grave than have to mourn over one who turned away from Christ; and the children felt that it was true. During her last illness, when some of her family were gathered in her room, she said, *"The Lord knew I could not live with wicked children.* I gave you all to Him before I had any of you, or any prospect of you, so far as that goes. I said, 'God, they shall be Thine own, down to the third and fourth generation.' I remember . . . the covenant I made with the Lord long *before I was married."*[43]

Family prayers on week-days in which the household joined went forward in a free matter-of-fact fashion. Individual needs were named in everyday language. Advising parents Catherine said, "Father or mother or whoever conducts prayers should bring the children specially before the Lord, asking Him to give them grace *this day* to be obedient to those who have the care of them; to be diligent at their lessons."[44] As her children grew out of babyhood, praying became part of living just as games and lessons were. Once, when having moved to a house on their journeyings where paper-hanging was not finished, the family had breakfast in the kitchen. They were about to begin prayers when the sweep called to know if he would be wanted. "Yes," said Mrs. Booth, "so come in now and have prayers with us." A few days later William learned that at one of the meetings the sweep and his wife had sought salvation and thus morning prayers were linked for the children with what went on in father's "big meetings". All of them had piano lessons and soon one or another was able to accompany the singing. Later other instruments came into favour, adding to the interest of family prayers; violin, flute, guitar, concertina, were all played at one time or another in that house of singing.

Their mother educated her children in the joys and beauties as well as in the responsibilities of life, this life on earth, which was the prelude to life in heaven. All of them learned from her to wonder and rejoice at God's purpose for mankind, at the nobility of soul God wills for the individual, and to look with reverence and delight on the beauty of God's works; the heavens, the fields and flowers; the inexhaustible contrivances, intricacies, comicalities in which God clothes life. She was enamoured of the earth's beauty herself and knew how to lead her little ones into happy companionship with the Creator and His creation. One of Bramwell's earliest recollections was being lifted by his mother to peep at a thrush upon her nest. Catherine's childhood pre-occupation with God and things eternal enhanced rather than dimmed the glory of the universe. In a measure all her children learned to look at things through her eyes, to enjoy the beauty of the earth, and to approach with admiration and understanding the innocent creatures, man's companions and helpers. Their mother's passionate love for animals and hatred of any cruelty became in turn the standard for each. A natural sequence was to have a pet of their own to love. A dog, a canary, mice and others were added to the household as the children grew older. One cannot pretend that the animal denizens of her home did not add to Catherine's anxieties about "other people's carpets", but I love her for taking it for granted that animals added to her children's joys, and that therefore it was natural and proper that the creaturely companions should have their place, and travel here, there, and everywhere with their small owners. It helps me, too, to see that Catherine with all her high standards and firmness was not in the least a prim and finnicky sort of mother; for while she revelled in a neat and spotless house, the happiness and health of her children always had first place, except of course that of William's comfort.

Before they settled in London their father was constantly away preaching, while the children lived with their mother at or near the centre where she herself was holding meetings. This mode of life Catherine detested. She and William were such good companions that apart they felt only half alive. Catherine told her mother, "... William had now been away from home, except on Friday and Saturday, for twelve weeks. I long to get fixed together again once more." William's letters show how his thoughts turned to her and the children and give a whiff of what the atmosphere of their home was. "Bless my darlings for me ... put your hand on their heads and bless them for their Papa. In passing a shop this morning I saw a large wooden horse, I exclaimed, 'That is the thing for my little Bertie'."[45] Ballington is encouraged to "be good" by a happiness in prospect: "Tell him I am going about the white mice." And when their father is to be home for a couple of days, "If they are good and *obedient* they shall have a party again on the Friday evening ... and we will have a great many more nuts and have some nice games."[46] One of these "nice games" was "fox and geese", a favourite with William. Bramwell told Begbie that his father generally played the fox. The most uproarious game of all started with their father prone upon the floor and all the children pulling and pushing to get him to sit up. Excitement reached its height when on the verge of success the "giant" would sway from side to side and fall back suddenly with most of the children on top of him when, amidst shouts and laughter, the operation would begin again. "Snap" was a game in which their mother joined, though it too tended to be noisy. But the best of all recreations was to go into the country. Miss Short tells that when she lived with them excursions to Epping Forest were a favourite delight for parents and children. On such occasions William drove the wagonette or landau which held Catherine, the children, provisions, Miss Short, a dog, toys, and a Bible. William always carried a Bible and often stopped to talk and read to the gipsies they came across. Miss Short, who went with them, said William "was like a schoolboy directly he got away from London; laughing, singing and joking!"[47] If this were his mood, it may be imagined how his excitable flock danced to his tune! After a romp with them William would lie with his head on Catherine's lap, as she sat leaning against a tree, her fingers moving gently in his hair while they talked. As likely as not the outing ended in singing, in praying too. All the children inherited William's musical ear, and he and they delighted in singing. Miss Short said he sang going up and down stairs, or wherever he might be in the house. So in Epping Forest, or at home around the fire, they sang. There were many "favourites", but probably William seldom missed striking up the refrain that he used to sing in the Mumfords' house when he first knew Catherine. The children of course loved it. Katie and Emma could sing it together when aged only three and two, with d's for g's to the amusement of their parents, "I'm doin' home to Dory". It sounds well when they were old enough to make a volume of melody, and sing in parts, "I'm going home to Glory where pleasures never die." The fire flickers, their eyes sparkle, the light plays about their hair. Catherine looks from one to another, most of all her eyes dwell on William, sitting, a child on each knee, and singing with all his heart. They believe it. They all grow up believing it; grow up to preach the Gospel that includes man's dwelling-place with God, and pleasures there for evermore.

Sunday was planned for happiness. "The Sabbath," their mother said, "was made a day of pleasure . . . I deemed it an evil to make a child sit still for an hour and a half, dangling its legs on a high seat, listening to what it could neither understand nor appreciate." And further, "Children need to be taught how to behave *now*, in the little duties, trials and enjoyments of their daily life . . . a deal of so-called teaching is right away above their heads . . . instead of coming down to such everyday matters as obedience to parents and teachers, the learning of their lessons, their treatment of brothers, sisters, and servants; their companionships; their amusements; the spending and giving of their pocket-money; their dealings with the poor; their treatment of animals—in short everything embraced in their daily life . . ."[48] For the Booth children religion was all mixed up like that with lessons and playtimes, and not reserved for the awesome part of their lives. They felt that it was wonderful, exciting, comforting, that they all belonged to God and that, in a sense, God belonged to them. He was Holy, Almighty, but loving and friendly and He wanted to help them to be good; they knew that *to be good was the main business of life*. Stead wrote of Catherine, "Whatever her teaching did or did not do, it did not make religion hateful to her youngsters. On the contrary they grew up to regard religion as the chief joy and luxury of their lives."[49] In spite of this outlook, or more likely because of it, the Booth children were a happy, even boisterously happy crew. The whole family did things with zest, whether laughter, argument, romps or family prayers. Miss Short said William Booth was a born actor; so were all the children. They could enter into the part when telling

313

a story or indulge in mimicry that made onlookers helpless with laughter.

Their mother treated each child as an individual and never as if she expected or desired that they should be alike, except that they should all be good. Each felt he was "special" to her, knew himself cherished with "special" love. None felt impoverished by her love for another because each was loved for what he was himself alone not for attainments or appearances. Escapades did not ruffle her, she could enter into the fun of things. She was herself so "alive" that no one could be dull when she was there, least of all her own family. She was a superb story-teller and talking to her and hearing her talk was entrancing. Stead went to see her several times when she lay dying and records that "it was a privilege to hear her cheery, confident, defiant, conversation".[50] And this when at death's door! What must it have been like to share her "defiant" talk when she was young and surrounded by her loved ones? They stimulated her argumentative mind and she theirs. Conversation was the livelier that the Booth parents and children had a sturdy sense of humour; laughter helped many an argument to its conclusion. Bramwell said her countenance "especially when animated was almost mesmeric". She made that impression on them all. To be with her was the children's delight, when they were good that is!

There were few "rules" but what there were, were enforced. Miss Short told, ".. . there was a steady sense of orderliness in this household. Meals, for instance, were served to the moment, and woe betide the child who came in five minutes late." She went on to describe that William "never sat at the head of his table, when Mrs. Booth was present, but always beside her. She carved at dinner, or poured out the tea."[51] Meal time was by no means a glum affair. His parents, Bramwell said, were "remarkably tolerant of different opinions over the family table. In all our discussions at home, whether on historical, political, social, or religious questions, we were permitted great freedom of expression."[52] On occasions there were dramatic interruptions. Miss Short recounted of William Booth, "I've known him suddenly kneel down in the middle of breakfast and give thanks to God because a letter he had opened contained money for the Mission."[53] Of course all at the table knelt down too and, when William had prayed, joyful chatterification was resumed with even greater vigour. It was good for the children to be drawn into their parents' anxieties and joys about the work, it meant sharing in real life. Laughter came easily. William was often laughing. He would change from "dejection to a contagious hilarity that carried everything before it".[54]

In Catherine's day severity, even cruelty to children, was horribly prevalent in institutions and schools as well as in some families, whilst at the other extreme children, especially of the new rich, were often pampered and indulged to an incredible degree. During the first year

314

of her marriage she wrote to her parents about the behaviour of children in the homes where she and William were entertained, ". . . I hope if I have not both sense and grace to train mine so that they shall not be a nuisance to everybody near them, that God will in mercy taken them to heaven in infancy but I trust I shall have and I am learning a few useful lessons from *observation*."[55] There is a dateless quality in her view of the way children should be treated. Even those who dislike her didactic style must admit that she talked sense on this subject. For instance take these words of hers about the care of children.

"*Children* brought up without love are like plants brought up without the sun."

"*Happiness* is a condition of health."

"*Food* should be ample to satisfy appetite, to consist chiefly of fresh vegetables, fruit, milk, eggs and cereals, no gormandizing on rich food."

"*Fresh air* day and night."

"*Clothes* should be comfortable and warm enough in winter."

"*In sickness* no strong drugs, keep warm; little food but plenty to drink. Simple hydropathic applications." (This in the days of purgings, blisterings, blood-letting and the like.)

"*Punishment*. Never threaten unless you intend to carry out: never do so in anger; never in a state of irritation; never by exciting a child's fears." Catherine and William favoured brief chastisement for small children; what in their book on the *Training of Children* is called "a little whipping". It is soon over and happiness may be quickly restored by gathering the culprit into its mother's or father's arms, kisses and promises are exchanged and love's sun is shining again. Older children, at an age to be reasoned with, should be deprived of privilege; a task set; or a solitary sojourn in a room, "but be careful to provide occupation. A child should never be made to look silly."

"*Courtesy* and consideration for others, including all dumb creatures, must be instilled from the child's earliest years."

"*Children* should be kept occupied, taught a pride in doing things well, and to enjoy being busy. Occupation should be considered an essential of happiness."[56]

Catherine believed that the influence of parents over their children "is irresistible until parents by their own injudicious conduct fritter it away. A little child . . . has unbounded, unquestioning confidence in its parents; what father or mother says is to it an end of all controversy, it never seeks further proof. This influence wisely used will never wear out, but will spread like an atmosphere around the child's moral nature."[57] As mother, Catherine exerted that kind of influence on her children. Bramwell said, "Natural gifts, high intelligence, notable achievements, social position and wealth, dwindled into nothing as we listened to her words . . . And first among her

315

principles was *love*; love for God, and therefore love for each other; love for the outcast and the wicked, the poor and the oppressed, love for animals and birds, love even for the characters of history."[58] Her own love for God and for her children was the life of her teaching. It was the inexhaustible treasure in her store. It was her love for them and their certainty of it that enabled her to enforce that "implicit uncompromising obedience" without which she felt their lives would be spoiled. When I said to my Aunt Katie, "But wasn't Grandmama rather a strict mother?" she bristled with a kind of pitying scorn as she replied, "You didn't know her, Cath, you don't understand, she loved us so much and we all loved her and *wanted* to please her." Catherine was not a disciplinarian in the ordinary sense, but she believed that obedience was a foundation for the happiness and safety of a child. The *habit* of obedience, she maintained, might very well save a child's life in emergency, and certainly be a protection from many evils. All her children knew that "to disobey, however small the matter involved, was to incur her highest displeasure."[59] Both parents were agreed on this. When their eldest son was eight William wrote to Catherine that "he must set his brothers and sisters an example in obedience or be prepared to lose his dog."[60] But as Bramwell wrote years later, "Hers was not that insistence upon obedience observed in many grown-ups, which is derived from the fact that obedience in children is more comfortable for the grown-up; it was her appreciation of the fact that obedience is a necessary principle in education, growth, and development."[61] Concluding a letter to her mother Catherine wrote, "The Lord help me to be faithful and firm as a rock in the path of duty to my children."[62] What she meant by "duty to my children" was defined in a letter to Bramwell when he was twenty-one, ". . . I am quite prepared to recognize your maturity, and am glad for you to have convictions and to act upon them; still, I feel that I have a right to try and form right and true ones for you or rather to lead you to form them for yourself, whenever I think you are in error. This right no age or intelligence on your part can ever destroy . . . Government founded on *right* and guided by benevolence can never be despotic in the true sense, but if you mean authoritative, I maintain that this is the *only* proper form of government for young minds and, so far from its dwarfing or stinting, it is the only safeguard from that animalism and lawlessness which destroys the very germ and bud of true greatness. God's form of government *must* be the highest, and the greatest development must be attainable on the lines He laid down. The difficulty is that so few are unselfish enough to children to train them wholly on His line, hence the failure . . . God's plan is tutors and governors until trained so as to be *able* to go alone, *then* 'Go ahead leaning on Him'."[63]

Petri considered that Catherine Booth was "something of a tyrant"; perhaps, but even so, Miss Short averred that it was "quite certain the children adored their parents. They thought there were no two people in the world who could compare with their father and mother."[64] Even when strangers were concerned there was something disarming about Catherine that disguised the "tyrant". Florence Soper, who later became Bramwell's wife, told that on speaking to Mrs. Booth for the first time and before she had seen any other member of the family "our eyes met, I felt that she was one whom I could love. It was easy to talk to her." And Florence was very reserved. Catherine lived for eight years after her eldest son's marriage, and her daughter-in-law had an unique opportunity of knowing her intimately without having grown up under her spell. She wrote, "Mrs. Booth's nature was tender and sympathetic, yet there were times when her wishes were exacting. When we moved, our second daughter Mary was about six weeks old. The move was for me very trying in view of my inexperience. I had just laid down the carpet in the dining-room when dear Mrs. Booth came in after lunch to see how I was getting on. She noticed at once that a width of the carpet was much worn, while the one that had been under the table was good. I was instructed that the shabby width must change places with the better. To my dismay she showed me how to unpick the seam and, providing me with a carpet needle and thread, taught me how to sew a carpet seam. I was very tired when the job was accomplished."[65] When hearing this about the carpet recounted, one of Florence's daughters protested, "But it was cruel of her; she *must* have been hard to make you do it." Her mother replied, "No, no, you think so only because you can't *imagine* what she was like. *You couldn't help wanting to do what she wanted.* It wasn't only that I felt she was so wise and right and seemed always to know how a thing ought to be done; it was that *wanting to please her* seemed more important than the thing itself." Being able to make people feel like that was an asset, and sweetened Catherine's masterfulness when she took people's affairs in hand. She was not always pleased with the way things were done but even in reproof she was always comforting and inspiring about the future, whether for the child or maid. There was often difficulty in finding suitable servants, and any who proved untrustworthy were sent away "for the sake of the children", but there is no record of anyone giving Catherine notice. Miss Short said, "The servants loved, I was going to say idolized, the Booths . . . They considered themselves members of the family."[66]

Catherine the mother ruled her realm in the home with the same transparent naturalness that was revealed in her love-letters and that made her so unselfconsciously "herself" on the public platform. When the Booths were in the midst of a revival campaign, dignitaries from the chapel, arriving one evening to discuss plans for the services Catherine was to address, were surprised to find her ironing—such tasks in those days were left to the servants. She went on ironing. She was entirely unembarrassed. One of the visitors recorded that she was

317

ironing "with all the dexterity and confidence of an experienced hand", and found himself "much affected".[67] Watching her patch his trousers one day, her first-born suddenly exclaimed, "But Mama, the boys will think we're poor!" And his mother answered in her direct way, "So we are!" He said of her, "She not only patched our clothes, but made us proud of the patches."[68] Her children early felt the reality of her love for them and that her displeasures were real too. Bramwell said, "We learned from her the necessity of sincerity." "Mother, if you want your child to be truthful and sincere," she once said, "you must not only *teach* it to be so, you must be so yourself."[69] Catherine was. There were no pretences about her, nothing merely for show. She wore no masks. No unaccountable changes of mood or manner perplexed those about her. Servants, children, William, all felt that they knew and understood her. They could count on her consistency. If something vexed her today, one could be sure that the same thing would vex her tomorrow. She did not condone behaviour at one moment and come down upon it like a load of bricks the next.

From the time the Booths left Gateshead to be travelling evangelists Catherine had to cope with a horrible uncertainty about their income. There was no hint of future security. The present seldom held more than enough to meet the day's bread bill. Shortage of money became a nasty, nagging part of life's practical problems. To make little go far was one of Catherine's skills, and the children never went hungry, but "the meals", as Miss Short said, "were of an extreme simplicity. A generous rice pudding appeared on the table with every dinner ... Mrs. Booth held that no child need leave the table hungry, however meagre the joint, so long as this rice pudding completed the feast. There were currants in it on special occasions."[70] Of this pudding the children could always have a "little more". Catherine liked what used to be called plain cooking; the kind that went well with a good fire in the kitchen range and a big hot oven. It had to be big, for bread takes room, and baking bread "to my liking" was one of the first things little Mrs. Booth would teach a cook. The smell of new bread made any place they happened to be living in home-like to them all. Fruit was more valued than in most middle class families of the day, especially apples and dried fruits. Catherine always got the freshest food available. Dry goods she bought in bulk, thus saving a little on the price and ensuring a supply to fall back on at need. But, in spite of all her economies and contrivings, poverty persisted; it put a spoke in the wheel when home affairs should have been running smoothly. Until they came to London there were lesser trials too to cope with, for instance, the ever recurring threat of packing. Often the stay in one place was a matter of mere weeks, seldom more than two months. The children enjoyed the commotion of moving but this repeated arrival and departure of a family of five or six youngsters, maids, governess and entire household stores including pets, toys and some furniture, was a major operation in life's campaign for their mother. It was at these times that Mary Kirton proved so reliable and "comfortable" for all of them. The Booths and their children owe a lot to the servants who helped with household chores. Mary Kirton was queen among them, cooks and housemaids changed from time to time. Mary stayed until her death.

In spite of their poverty Catherine and William agreed that somehow they would afford a competent governess. They were resolved that the children should have a good education and they denied themselves of much in order to make this possible. Day schools were tried for Bramwell in several places, but as Catherine wrote to Mrs. Mumford, "Nobody cares to take any pains with him when they know he is going in a few weeks. The last school we thought was a first-rate one, but the master ... put him into babyish spelling which he learned three years ago, and let him sit doing nothing."[71] On education, as on almost everything, Catherine knew her own mind. She would not have lessons made a "misery". "I am glad to hear that Willie does not feel happy unless he knows his spelling," she wrote to her mother when the children were staying with their grandparents, "but I would not have the book made a *bore* to him for a hundred pounds ... If his governess scolds him, I would rather he did not learn anything at all ... let him do a little at a time and he will like it better ..."[72] In her view the one great rule to be observed in all teaching was to make the lesson *interesting*. The problem was to find a governess who could do just that. While still in their wandering life, when Bramwell was eight, his mother wrote he "is getting on nicely with his lessons ... The Free Church Minister here, a nice educated man, is teaching him Latin, he gives him two lessons per week."[73] William shared Catherine's anxiety that a reliable governess should be found. Once he wrote to her that he was "heartily and honestly glad Miss C. is going. She was not born for such a service as we require." To her mother Catherine wrote, "If I were not afraid of evil contamination I would send Willie and Ballington to boarding-school, but I feel as though I dare not think of it."[74] And she felt the same twenty years or so later when she spoke "against the practice ... of sending children to boarding-schools before their principles are formed or their characters developed ... A school is a little world where all the elements of unrenewed human nature are at work with as great variety, subtlety and power as in the world outside."[75] Booth-Tucker included in his book a letter without date or clue to recipient, the manuscript of which I have not found. In this Catherine alluded to the problem of dealing with young people on standards of purity. "I believe few people have any conception of the foul condition of our schools of all classes; it is simply awful. Well do I understand your feelings of discouragement ... I agree with your remarks as far as adults and young people arrived at maturity are concerned ... It seems

319

to me that there are ways of warning and forearming children without enlightening them so far as to let in temptation. I brought up my own children in ... ignorance on these subjects ... I believe that I succeeded in inspiring them with a positive dread and hatred of anything rude or immodest, and this without their knowing my reasons, and I consider they were thus spared much unnecessary conflict till they were sufficiently established in the fear and love of God to enable them to bear it."[76] Her way with the children was, as she said, to be "beforehand with the devil! I have not allowed my children to become pre-occupied with the things of the world before I have got the seed of the Kingdom well in."[77]

3

As the children grew older Catherine developed her method of enlisting the elder ones to watch over the younger. She fostered the sense of responsibility in them each in turn. To Bramwell when he was but five she wrote, "I have been thinking a great deal about you, my dear boy, and about Ballington, Katie and the baby too; but most about you, because you are the eldest and biggest, and I know if you are good and do as you are told, they will most likely be the same."[78] Bramwell was soon able to "manage" the nursery. Miss Short said, "He was an unmixed blessing in the home with the other children and a jolly lively lot they were."[79] He could order the household in practical matters by the time he was ten. He was a favourite with the servants. He knew that his parents expected him to help the others, and he went on doing so long after they were all grown-up. We get a glimpse of Bramwell in the nursery from a letter of his to his then eighteen-year-old sister Eva, Catherine's seventh child, who was born when he was nine. "I feel today about you as though you were grown little again, as in the days that are gone, and I want to lift you in my arms and sing to you till you rest."[80] I picture the small boy pacing the nursery in his mother's absence, singing in his clear boyish treble one of the happy hymns his father liked, and feeling a quiver of love for the infant he holds in his arms with a mounting sense of joy that what he is doing will "please Mama, darling Mama". When Marie fell ill with smallpox all the other children were packed off to Billups's country house at Lydney; Bramwell, fifteen, was in charge of them. His mother, in a letter that indirectly revealed much about her own method of managing the children, wrote, "Your somewhat graphic epistle cheered me a good deal this morning. I am glad to find you in such good spirits. What a pity you lost your hat! However, it was better than losing your head, which would not at all have surprised me, seeing you are so fond of poking it where it ought not to be . . . Very much depends on you as to the ease and comfort of managing Ballington and Herbert. Do all you can; be forbearing where only your own feelings or comfort are concerned, and don't raise unnecessary controversies; but where their obedience to us, or health is at stake, be firm and unflinching in trying to put them right. Mind Emma's medicine—two teaspoonsful twice a day—and her feet kept warm. I will send the overboots for her in the house . . . The Lord bless you all. Pray for us. Your loving anxious Mother. P.S. You need not fear the letters as I lay them between blotting sheets saturated with Condy's fluid after writing and envelopes, too."[81]

It was about this time that Catherine wrote to Mrs. Billups about vaccinaton for smallpox. "I send by this post a pamphlet on vaccination. Do read it, if only for the exhibition it gives of the prejudice of the 'profession'. It seems as though all advance in the right treatment of the disease has to be in the first instance largely in spite of the doctors, instead of their leading the way . . . I should sooner pawn my watch to pay the fines, and my bed too, for the matter of that, than have any more children vaccinated. The monstrous system is as surely doomed as blood-letting was. This is one of the boons we shall get by waiting and enlightening. Who knows how much some of us have suffered through life owing to the 'immortal Jenner'*? . . . There is nothing worse in this pamphlet than several cases I have come across personally. But these were direct effects. It is the indirect I dread most. The latent seeds of all manner of diseases are doubtless sown in thousands of healthy children. It has only been the stupid treatment which has made smallpox so fatal. Mrs. Smedley (of the Hydropathic Institute) says in her last manual, that they have nursed numbers of bad cases, and never lost one."[82] One must have in mind the method of vaccination practised in Catherine's day, i.e. taking pus from one child and injecting it into the blood stream of another. Such a practice would I think, horrify doctors today as much as it did Catherine a hundred years ago. She came to feel an utter abhorrence of it, having herself observed most grievous results. When later The Salvation Army opened maternity homes for unmarried mothers they were helped by visiting magistrates to claim exemption for their infants and advised not to have them vaccinated until they were at least twelve months old, if at all.

Love for their parents and the desire to please them affected the children's care for each other. Emma said that when she was in charge of the younger children she "used to imagine that Mama was in the room all the time and could see everything that was done."[83] Catherine had been ill, and was resting in the country when she

* Edward Jenner (1749-1828), physician, discoverer of vaccination with cowpox prophylactic to smallpox.

321

L

wrote, "My dear Emma ... I thought so much about you yesterday. I hope your party went off without any serious disappointment. I was very pleased to hear by Katie that all was going on well. Be sure and do not let the children take cold; it would be a great trial to me to have any of them ill while I am away ... I hope Katie is not neglecting Marie's and Lucy's music; it is important now and especially Marie's. Tell Mary not to neglect the windows, and cook must join in cleaning them while we are away; I was so pleased to hear that Mary was in such good trim ..." A phrase gives me a view of William in a new role. Herbert was staying with his parents and the letter continues, "Papa is helping him with his sums ... You will be pleased to hear that I feel better today than I have since I left and though I had an attack yesterday I was not so faint as before ... I like the place ... it is beautifully quiet ... I must have first one and then another of you with me a week or two at a time. Tell Annie to see that the top closet is kept sweet and that the windows are open a little bit at the top at night. Bless you all I love you very dearly." It was one of the characteristics of Catherine's letters to the children that she always commended one of them, or the servants, on some score. This letter concludes, "My love to Annie, and tell her she packed my box very nicely, and did well to remember my directions so well. Love to cook and Mary and love and kisses to the little ones."[84]

Illness, which had prevented Catherine from undertaking long preaching campaigns, had had a bad effect on family finances. To Herbert, then fifteen, his mother wrote, "I am sorry that I am away now that you are returning [he had been away ill] but I hope you will be a very good boy and render to Emma the same respect and obedience that you would to me. There are not many such sisters, she loves you all nearly as much as I do and is willing to make any sacrifices for your good." One glimpses his mother's anxiety about him and expenses as her letter continues, "You must have set hours for study, and if the children have school in the nursery, which I think they have, you must be in the dining-room, so one fire will serve, and you must do with as little as you can. We have been much put about, Pa and I, to find that our money matters are in a worse condition than we thought, so you must try to be careful in every way ... if you are going to be a preacher, spelling, grammar and composition are of the first importance. All these you can improve yourself in with Emma's help, just as well as with anyone else, and we cannot pay anyone till after Xmas ..."[85]

Exchange of confidences between a mother and her children were, Catherine felt, part of the "opportunity which parents possess, and especially mothers," of "being acquainted with all their peculiarities of disposition, and entering into all their joys and sorrows ..."[86] She considered that talking together about anything and everything was one of love's sweet occasions, which often invited an expression of that love of mother to child that was "special" to that one. She believed that expressing love strengthened it. From their infancy Catherine encouraged her children to confide in her. She listened to them—she was a good listener—and discussed things with them. There was a kind of individual wavelength between her and each. She appealed freely and unaffectedly to her love for them and to their love of her and their "dear precious Papa". In a letter to Ballington she wrote, "Listen to these counsels because they are from your mother, and are given in love and desire."[87] To Bramwell about taking proper rest, "Tell me that you will for *my* comfort." In her conversation with them she dealt as readily and naturally with spiritual needs and prospects as with practical matters and often passed from one to the other in almost the same breath. As to "talking religion" she asked, "Why is it that when speaking about religion a stilted and unnatural style should be so commonly in vogue? The stirring tones, the flashing eye, the eager gesture which emphasizes conversation on every important theme—why should these be banished?" These were certainly not banished from Catherine Booth's conversations with her children! She believed that *talking* to them was one of the best ways of maintaining that sense of knowing one another which made it easy for each, as they grew older, to continue to confide in her. Constant exchange of thought with their mother became a very powerful influence in their lives. Bramwell said that "in the nursery when we were yet small children and later on in her room kneeling beside her bed—she gave us wonderful counsel."[88] Catherine made a habit of talking and praying with her children *one by one*. These private confabs kept a two-way means of communication open between mother and child and strengthened her influence on each. It is a noteworthy fact that their mother continued to be her children's confidant throughout the unstable teens and on into man- and womanhood. They continued desiring to please her. Her approbation was a kind of treasure that adorned homely happenings. It added a savour to any plan or public event. To find that "Mama was pleased" was more than praise from any quarter.

That Bramwell's education had not suffered as a result of his peripatetic life is shown by the fact that he won a place at the City of London School by competitive examination, and was the youngest boy in his form. Miss Short recounted how one day he came home looking pale, he did not make any complaint but after a time became very ill, spitting blood. A doctor made an examination and questioned him carefully, at last getting out of him that the boys had caught him hands and legs, and bashed him against a tree to "bang Salvation out of him". Pleurisy and rheumatic fever followed and from being a lively healthy child the boy was a complete invalid for two years and for many longer suffered with heart trouble. Formal education came to an end for him. This happening hardened

Catherine's aversion to schools. The fact is that she was out of tune with the educational trends of her day. "All the mischief," she thought, "comes from upsetting God's order—cultivating the intellect at the expense of the heart; being at more pains to make our youth *clever* than to make them *good*! For what is the highest destiny of man? ... making every faculty of the being subservient to the highest purpose— the service of humanity and the service of God! And all education that falls short of *this* seems to me one-sided, unphilosophical, and irreligious. And *that is my quarrel with modern education.*"[89]

Catherine's idea was to safeguard her boys and girls until they were mature enough to distinguish between good and evil for themselves. They should not, if their mother could prevent it, be caught in the meshes of wrong thinking and desire until they were familiar with the beauty of truth and goodness, and able to recognize the shabby mean- ness and ugliness of evil. Speaking to parents from her own experience she once said, "If you want your boy to" become "a man of righteous principle, integrity and honour, superior to all the doubleness, chicanery and devilry of the world, you must train him to look upon all the world's prizes as dross, compared with the joy of a pure conscience and a life of usefulness to his fellow-men ... Labour to wake up your children's souls to the realization of the fact that *they belong to God* and that He has sent them into the world, not to look after their own little petty personal interests, but to devote themselves to the promotion of His, and that, in doing this, they will find happiness."[90] The Booths succeeded in convincing all their children that this was true. Catherine's objection to sensational types of fiction was because she was convinced that they gave a false, unnatural view of life and tended "to create in the minds of young people ... discontent with their surroundings, impatience of parental restraint and a premature forcing of the social and sexual instincts, such as must do untold harm ..."[91] She added that she did not include all novels in these stric- tures. Worldly dress, worldly amusements, indulgence in things harm- ful or frivolous were taboo in the Booth household. Not that her child- ren were sheltered from a knowledge of what is called the seamy side of life. When William Booth began to preach in Whitechapel his eldest son was nine. Late one Sunday evening they were walking home together after a meeting when William paused, took the child by the hand and pushing open a door of a public house pressed into the bar where men, women and children in all stages of intoxication stood crowded together. Stooping towards his son William said eagerly, "Willie, these are *our* people, these are the people I want you to live for and bring to Christ."[92] Bramwell never forgot that moment. He began then to look at "our people" through his father's eyes and so, as they grew older, did all William's sons and daughters. William wrote with evident joy to Cory, "My children are just beginning to work. The four eldest take a service among the young people and are very useful. Willie conducts the meeting."[93] Before they reached their twenties all, except Marie, who was an invalid, were dedicated to the task of helping "people" to be good.

From Catherine's letters to her children I have chosen extracts that seem to me to reveal something of herself, rather than the character of the recipient. Most of the letters coincide with the years when the Mission was becoming The Salvation Army, and when her preaching was incessant. How she found time and energy for all the letter-writing I cannot imagine. Those letters are surely the fruit of countless small self-denials. Her time is taken up with doings that cannot be postponed, other people's claims clamour incessantly, yet she wrote without a hint of what it cost her in time alone. I fancy she enjoyed writing letters! I hope so, for if not she must have suffered a martyrdom. True, she learned to write in bed. When preaching at night she often rested in the morning. Even so, members of the household rushed in and out. Her accessibility at home was one of the facts of life for them all. Writing to Katie, then fourteen, who was staying with friends her mother advised, "Above all, my darling girl, keep close to Jesus, run to Him in every difficulty. Tell Him all, just as you would me if you were at home."[94]

Few of the children's letters remain. One from Ballington soon after his arrival at school, where with the help of a friend he was sent at fifteen, may serve as an introduction to Catherine's letters to her second son. He wrote, "I know you will like to hear how I am getting on. All right! On, on I must go till I reach home again ... We have an observatory at the end of the grounds and I go sometimes and sit there; it looks right over for miles. I sit there and pray and talk with God ... The grounds are beautifully kept. The college looks splendid, much better than the picture, and I like the school very much; in fact I have not a fault to find with it. Still, I should like to see you again very much. I have just been in to breakfast and received your letters. I feel fit to cry. They are worth more to me than gold. I *will* get on. No, you shan't lose heart about me, Ma ..." The letters from home may be "more than gold" but the lack of it impinges upon every situation. Ballington concluded, "I will make 3d do, I can go without eggs. I know what it costs very well."[95] Was this 3d to last a week? Here is part of his mother's reply to this letter, "I do hope you are industrious ... Remember Satan steals his marches on us little by little. A minute now and a minute then. Your time is flying, one quarter will soon be gone. Do, my boy, work as hard as your health will allow you. One egg at eleven o'clock you may have. I will send you a few stamps for extra letters, but you must do without any other extras ... All your little trials will soon be over, so far as school life is concerned, and every one of them, if borne with patience, will make you a better man. Never forget my advice about listening to *secrets*. Don't hear anything that needs to be whispered, it is *sure to be* bad...I enclose you six stamps for extra letters. Papa is nearly killed with work; pray for him...Katie is a dear girl; she loves you very much, so do they all, and so does your own Mother."[96]

And again, "...We are all delighted to find that you have made up your mind to improve...what is better still that you are doing it. That is what I like...Let me caution you against giving any *unnecessary offence.* Don't parade your religion. I don't mean that you are not to confess Christ on all proper occasions and to reprove evil, but don't be sanctimonious, or *talk about it* when it can do *no good.* Ask the Lord to give you *wisdom.* Try to live and act and talk that they may *see* your good *works!* your respect for the rules of the school, for the authority of your masters, your diligence in improving your time, your kindness to everybody, even to those who persecute you. **Remember that in all probability this is the last time in your life when you will have to *live* amongst unconverted people and therefore is the finest opportunity for you to be a witness for Jesus...Above all things labour to be *real* and *true* in everything. Neither be held back by fear nor lured by favour. Don't put anything on, that you don't feel,** nor fear to confess what you *do* feel and know, when it is proper to do so. I pray earnestly for you and so do we all."[97] And from another letter to Ballington, "...the past is gone for ever. You could not recall *one day* if it would purchase you a kingdom. Now is your only time. I trust you have begun afresh to do a little reading and seeking the meaning of words...Read Fletcher a bit every evening and find every word you don't understand. I used to do this without any prospect of it ever being of much use to me. Surely *you* ought to do it, for the sake of such a future as you hope the Lord has called you to?"[98]

For the sake of such a future! But there is nothing glamorous about the future Catherine sets before her children. She depicts it as a life of poverty, persecution and fatigue yet glorious none the less like their father's! The children had a realistic view of his Christian Mission and the kind of people he was taken up with; they knew his love for the sinful and the poor. Their mother inspired them to feel that to help bad people to be good was the noblest, joyfullest purpose in the whole of life and worth the dedication of every gift they possessed. See this to Ballington at nineteen, "...If I know my own heart, I would rather that you should work for the salvation of souls, making bad hearts good and miserable homes happy, and preparing joy and gladness for men at the judgment bar, if you only got bread and cheese all your life, than that you should fill any other capacity with £10,000 per year."[99] Sometimes to stimulate study, she emphasized William's need of help with the Mission, as in this written to Ballington when his mother was campaigning, "Do not let your thoughts be so absorbed even in study as to lead you to forget your Bible and to neglect prayer. I am sure the Lord will help you to learn and understand if you constantly look to Him and trust Him. I am as certain that God gives mental light as that He gives natural light, if we only seek it from Him and watch against those things which tend to darken the mind . . . I had a good time in the theatre on Sunday night. It was packed, and hundreds, they tell me, were unable to get in . . . The man they sent me here is a perfect sell neither soul nor sense . . . Poor Papa! It is very trying for him. Make haste, get on so that you may help us."[100] And again, ". . . we want men who are set on soul-saving; who are not ashamed to let everyone know that this is the one aim and object of their life, and that they make everything secondary to this . . . Your Father is a man of this spirit; the Lord make all his children such, and you among them the first."[101]

Four years later his brother Herbert joined Ballington. I choose a paragraph or so from a rambling kind of letter, which shows Catherine still occupied with the children's clothes. Thus to Ballington when the delivery of a parcel was delayed, "I am afraid you will have needed your trousers badly. I bestowed a good deal of trouble on those trousers in the parcel for you, altering them all down the legs . . . I should like you to hear Mr. Gange sometime. He is a clever man . . . Mind and do not receive any new doctrines until you have talked them over with me. Things that you cannot understand jot them down to be talked over when you come." And from doctrines to nightshirts, "Your nightshirts were both marked—at least Annis says so. She says she brought you one down into the dining-room to mark for yourself, and she supposed you did it? . . . I should have thought you would know your own by the length; very few people make them as long as I do. I shall be vexed if that new one is lost; it was a double milled calico, 1/4 a yard. Send me word if you find it . . . Take notice of the make and quality of your things, and then you will come to know your own at a glance . . . if you see anything unmarked, get a 6d bottle of marking ink and a quillpen, and mark them yourself. You had better *also mark* the sheets at the other end, *the bottom* I mean, about twelve inches from the hem. Mark them W. C. Booth, and the year underneath, nicely, then when they come back I will have the bottom hem torn off and a wide one put on and make that the top, for Annie marked them without consulting me disgracefully. Do this, then if anyone does get them in exchange, they will have 'Booth' at both ends! . . . We expected a letter from Bertie before this. He *must* have time to write home . . ."[102]

Towards the end of his stay Ballington was helping in the school while continuing his studies and his mother wrote, "I am pleased that Mr. W. feels such confidence in you but do not be puffed up by it; remember how weak you are and ask the Lord to save you from conceit and self-sufficiency. Try to be fair and just in all your dealings with the boys. Do not be hard on a boy whom you do not happen to like so well as another, but be fair and treat all alike when left in charge . . . My dear boy walk consistently . . . Mind and observe all laws, keep you own counsel. Never allow any boy to approach you with a secret which you would not like me to hear. Then you are safe. I am in haste now so good bye."[103] And here is another word on having courage to confess Christ, "Think of the joy when the Judge shall say, 'Ballington Booth, you confessed me in that school, where it was quite as hard and harder than in the streets of Whitechapel' . . . At the same time be gentle and pitiful. Think how lately you were overtaken in a fault and how dark it made you for a bit. Think how many little inconsistencies people see in us, which we cannot see in ourselves and let this make you gentle and tender."[104]

Ballington went for a time to a theological college; he sent his mother copies of his sermons. She was pleased and in spite of the rush wrote, "I am very busy . . . go to Hastings tomorrow and K. [Katie] to Leicester [to preach] so you may guess I am very full. But I have left everything, carefully to read your sermon . . . it is very good, and it is for the most part *your own*. It gives evidence of marvellous improvement . . ." and then she went on to show how he might develop the theme. As to spelling she told him in another letter that it helped her to read over again a book she did not care for "so that my mind would not get occupied with the *subject*, and so keep my mind and eye on the *words* noticing the spelling only. Try this."[105] And in a different vein, ". . . Never be ashamed of a threadbare coat if it is the best your means can afford, or if you wear it in order to do good with your money. Railton's self-forgetfulness in this respect is very beautiful (tho' he does go to an extreme) it is far nobler than a foppish care which spends all it can get on self . . . I want you to be above being *troubled* by a shabby coat."[106] Thus to Ballington at nineteen. Bramwell at twenty must be handled differently. Whilst with her mother on campaign Emma wrote, "Mama tells me to tell you that . . . she can do better with the help of Mr. Cobley than with you in your old trousers! Ma did *not* tell me to say this last but I know she means it."[107] A day or so later his mother wrote peremptorily, "*Get the clothes, get black*. A serge for the trousers. Get as good a cloth as he can give you for £3, for a coat. And get a hat. *I will not* have you with me a sight. I do not think it helps our cause."[108]

Days of study were near their end when Ballington received this word from her, "I hope you feel that you are getting ready for the work which lies before you. You have only to master that one weakness we talked over at Hastings, and in everything else you will do, and improve rapidly. *Grace*, and effort, and self-control will accomplish it . . . Every day makes your future in the Mission more important. It is growing so rapidly and will grow. It will need superintendents of districts almost immediately, and Pa says it will be impossible to go on doing all the management from London. It is getting awful. Pa is now in Wales. B. [Bramwell] in the North, and R. [Railton] begins at Leeds in a tremendous circus next Sunday. Poor R. is at home writing for his life all day today. Pa is after another man for the office."[109] And in an undated note, ". . . I hope you are getting on in your studies and not allowing them to draw you from God. There is no illuminator like the Holy Ghost. He is promised on purpose to lead us into *all truth*, consequently to guard us from error. Seek His light on all you read, and His help in all you do, and your progress will be real and rapid. I was talking with a young minister the other day, who has spent a deal of time in studying science! Knows a great deal I doubt not, but alas, by his own confession, and by the miserable results of his ministry, he knows *not* how to win souls. I saw in talking to him more clearly than ever, that the main qualification for preaching is not gifts, nor learning, but *Spirit*. 'Ye know not what *spirit* ye are of' might be sounded in the ears of thousands of minds now-a-days. They are a scientific, a philosophical, a metaphysical, an astronomical, or any other kind of spirit."[110] And on the use of notes when preaching, Catherine advised him, "Get out of them! They don't fit our work. When you get on you do not want them and when you don't they are no good! At first, if your memory won't serve you, just jot on a small bit of paper, the size of a ticket, your main divisions in large writing, but no more."[111]

Petri is critical of Catherine's attitude to her children. She wrote that to their mother's "admiring devotion they were princes" and brought up as "heirs to The Salvation Army Kingdom".[112] But Catherine's letters to her children do not, I think, support this opinion. Petri ignores the fact that "The Salvation Army Kingdom" hardly existed until after the four eldest were in their twenties and had chosen their vocation. Their mother's ambition for them was that they should become preachers of the Gospel, devoting all their energies to helping *bad people to be good.* She prepared them to be "heirs" to poverty and persecution, certainly not to power and popularity. There was little of either at the time her children made their choice. True the needs and opportunities of the "work" thrust the young Booths into places of responsibility, but the same thing happened to scores of converts. Kate Shepherd, who led the Welsh revival, was seventeen years of age. Miss Ouchterlony was appointed to pioneer Salvation Army work in Sweden and Norway after a visit of only a few months to England to "see" the work. James Barker, a convert of Bethnal Green, was put in charge of Australia and sailed with his wife the day after their wedding. George Pollard was not twenty-one and his Lieutenant but nineteen when appointed to begin The Salvation Army in New Zealand. And there was another side to it; L.C leadership meant not the preaching alone but close contact with individuals. In a letter Catherine gave a glimpse of Ballington, when in charge in Manchester. "A dear man had signed the pledge twenty-one times, and fallen each time. After this he sank into despair . . . my second son visited him . . . and making the man get out

329

of bed at ten o'clock at night, in a half drunken condition, he got him on to his knees and prayed with him in faith, encouraging him to believe and expect that God would that hour deliver him from the appetite . . . For six years he has been one of our most devoted and successful officers."[113] In their youth her children were "at home" in the poorest districts, visiting converts and praying with the sick, going to see people in prison. From their experiences what was afterwards called the "slum" work of The Salvation Army grew and spread to other lands.

Catherine was aware of the dangers for young people in occupying posts of great responsibility. Today it is difficult to imagine the privations joyfully undertaken by officers and the courage needed to face the scorn showered on Salvationists. She dreaded the strain the work imposed and warned her sons and daughters of the spiritual perils. She wrote to Emma of Katie, who was preaching with great success, "God grant that she may be kept humble and childlike and grow in grace. You have need to pray for her. *She* is an object worthy of your sympathy and prayers—not because she is your sister merely, but because of the immense opportunity she has for winning *souls*. Plead with God for her, dear, that the dangers may be averted, and the blessings secured. He can supply *all* her need."[114] And again when Emma, then in charge of training for women, was grieving that one of her cadets had deserted her post, "We must make a new generation. And oh, don't let us be in too big a hurry to get people to say they believe. We will go in more and more for *righteousness*. I wish we could incorporate the word somehow in the Army's name. Well . . . my children must stop at the war, whoever runs away . . . I suppose that salvation work must always be in the teeth of the devil, and that if he did not oppose, it would not be salvation work, but only sham . . . You are very dear to me . . . 'Courage' our Captain cries. Let us march on and fear nothing . . . I think about you more than usual, and praise God for you . . . God is going to give me the great absorbing desire of my soul from the time all of you were thought of: that you might be of use to poor, dark, erring, suffering humanity. God knows this has been my highest, almost my only, ambition, for any of you. Oh, my dear, learn from His faithfulness to your own poor mother to trust Him with a 'great faith'. I wish I had always trusted and never been afraid. The Lord bless and keep and comfort you with His own presence, prays your ever loving mother."[115]

To Ballington while he was still at the theological college she wrote a warning word, ". . . Papa was at the prayer meeting in Aldersgate Street . . . Mrs. McPherson prayed for our 'wonderful family' . . . Now this is of no consequence in itself, only it shows how the tide has turned and what is before us. Now shall we *fail* and let a bit of popularity and prosperity spoil us? Shall we get vain and puffed up and think *we* are able of ourselves to do any good thing? NO, NO, surely the Lord will find us true where so many have proved false! Shall we? Can you keep down at His feet? If so, I shall truly have a wonderful family! Oh, my dear boy don't disappoint me."[116] Just as for William, when he and she were first lovers, she dreaded the dangers of popularity, so now she is anxious for the son who was so like his father. A colourful, clever young man, Ballington's gifts compared favourably with other young workers in the Army. He was versatile, musical, a tall handsome figure, easily able to command the crowds. He preached dramatically as did his father, and played a "fiddle" to the delight of the "roughs". He had a good voice and he sang solos in the style his mother liked, "with unction", moving the hearts of the congregation. Sometimes words and melody were of his own composition, and thus his voice is still heard through songs he wrote which are sung by Salvationists.

4

Catherine Booth was convinced of woman's equal right with men to preach. She was herself a preacher. Yet, she was taken aback when her son Bramwell told her that his sister Katie, then aged fourteen, had accompanied him to open-air meetings held outside the *Cat and Mutton* public house in Hackney and that he had persuaded her to speak to the crowd of men congregated there on Sunday morning. Bramwell had urged Katie's evident gifts and her power to hold attention. His mother objected that at any rate her daughter was far too young for such publicity. Catherine recalled, "It was not until I was holding some services at Ryde that I fairly faced the question, as to whether I should give her up to speak in public for Jesus." Katie had accompanied her mother to Ryde and whilst they were there, Catherine began to feel "I had held her back; for though so largely engaged in public life myself, somehow or other I did not realize that God would call my girls to this work and I felt all the same shrinking which any other half-enlightened Christian mother might feel. While we were there my eldest son came over to see us for two or three days. He held meetings in the open air, and on one occasion my daughter accompanied him with two or three other friends, only, as I supposed, to help them to sing. My son at that meeting was led, as now we see, by the Holy Spirit to put her up to speak to a large crowd . . . When they came home he told this and of the result. I rebuked him for having done it, and felt, as perhaps some of you would feel, on account of her tender years and other considerations. In our conversation he fixed his eyes upon me and said, 'Mama dear, you will have to face this question alone with God, for God has as assuredly called Katie and inspired her for this work as ever He called you, and you must mind how you hold her back.' I felt proud and thankful to have a son through whom God could send me such a message, and as soon as dinner was over I rushed up to my room, shut myself in and faced the question. I faced it alone with God . . . I promised God in that hour that I would never hold any of my children back from what seemed to be His way for them."[117]

"From that hour," Bramwell wrote, "my sister's path was clear. Continuing her education . . . she gradually undertook more and more public work. In nearly all these expeditions, by an arrangement of our mother, I accompanied her . . . after a few months, my sister began to conduct evangelistic campaigns which sometimes lasted for three weeks or a month . . . People were greatly prejudiced until they saw and felt for themselves that God was with her." When Katie was sixteen Bramwell wrote describing one of her meetings. "Rows of men sat smoking and spitting . . . while many with hats on were standing in aisles and passages bandying jokes. This went on throughout the first part of the service; then my sister rose and standing before the little table just behind the footlights commenced to sing with such feeling as it is impossible to describe

> The rocks and the mountains will all flee away
> And you will need a hiding-place at that day
> Oh, may we be ready.

There was an instantaneous silence over the whole house. After singing two or three stanzas she stopped and announced her text: 'Let me die the death of the righteous and let my last end be like his'. While she did so nearly every head was uncovered. In moments the fourteen or fifteen hundred present, and the young preacher herself, were completely absorbed in her subject. For forty minutes her clear young voice rang through the building. No one stirred, and when concluding she called for volunteers to begin the new life . . . a man rose up in the midst of the throng in the gallery and exclaimed, 'I'll make one!' There were thirty others that night."[118]

Her mother still felt that Katie was too young to undertake the burden of a preacher's life, and most of all that she needed a deeper spiritual equipment for the task. Catherine opened her mind about the blessing of full salvation to each of her children and sought to lead them into the experience. Can anyone read this letter to Katie on her sixteenth birthday without sensing her mother's tenderness, and her yearning that this beloved child might yield herself up fully to be led by God? "My very dear Katie, I am very pleased with your letter. It is the Spirit of God that is showing you your own heart and leading you to seek that peace and satisfaction in Him, which is not to be found anywhere else. I rejoice, my dear child, that the Lord is so gracious as to condescend thus to draw you after Himself. I can truly say that it delights me more than any earthly good possibly could. But while I rejoice, I tremble, because I know that many are thus drawn who never do give themselves fully to God. It is in the yielding ourselves up, my dear child, to be led by the Spirit in everything, that the peace and victory come. This requires us to crucify nature—that is, not to let nature have its own way; but when inclination, or temper, or pride, or desire would lead us one way, and conscience and the Spirit another, we must follow conscience and the Spirit, and put down and trample upon nature. This is walking in the light. The Spirit is teaching you this . . . We learn in the divine life much as we learn in the temporal, by experience. A step at a time. Yield yourself up to obey, and though you sometimes fail and slip do not be discouraged, but yield yourself again and plead more fervently with God to keep you. Fourteen years ago you were learning to walk, and in the process you got many a tumble. But now you can not only walk yourself but teach others. So, spiritually, if you will only let God lead you He will perfect that which is lacking in you and bring you to the stature of a woman in Christ Jesus. Praise Him that you feel you are His child, though but a babe. It is a *great* thing to be a child of God at all. Don't forget to praise Him for this . . . I did not forget your birthday. I think I gave you afresh to God more fully and determinately than ever before. I laid you on His altar, for Him to glorify Himself in you in any way He sees best. You must say Amen to the contract, and then it will be sealed in heaven. Your loving Mother."[119]

Katie was a clever, intelligent girl, very keen to study. Her ability to hold the attention of the crowd and to influence people stirred her own mind to a realization of her need for knowledge; and after Ballington was sent to school, she expressed her desire for the same kind of opportunity. Her mother was anxious that nothing should happen that might spoil her daughter's sincerity and simple faith. There were discussions at home and a divergence of opinion which might have led to a rift between mother and daughter. Catherine went to give an address to the pupils of a highly recommended girls' school, but was horrified at their worldly get-up. The tone of a letter from her mother, when Katie was seventeen, gives a clue of her feelings and fears. "I have written at least three times that you *might* go to school. I did not think it needful to say it again. For the first time in my life I consent to a step (on so important a matter) on which my judgment is not satisfied. We shall see how it ends! I see that you are all set on the fruit that is to make you wise, eat it my child and God grant that it may not turn bitter in your belly. Your Papa is dead against the school—he says it will ruin you! but it is of no use *us* talking because you think you know better than we do! You think also that we do not understand you! How I wish I did not, so well

333

as I do! One of the greatest writers on mental philosophy says 'self-knowledge is the most difficult of all knowledge to attain', but then he did not know you or he might have altered his opinion! You think you know yourself perfectly and that we are all either mistaken or prejudiced or unkind or foolish. You think we do not rightly value education and are too indifferent to it; whereas we have denied ourselves the common necessaries of life to give you the best in our power. Being so many of you, even if I had sent you to schools they could only have been common schools . . . I think we *do* put a right value on education in making God and righteousness first, and it second. If I had life to come over again I should be still more particular . . . Ballington went to Clarks one term and came home and ridiculed the name of Jesus! Suppose I had let him go on in such associations?

"You talk, my darling girl, about Herbert becoming a mighty man in God's Israel . . . Mightier youths than he have fallen. Besides *where* did he get the principles you have such faith in? Under his mother's thumb and eye, not at a preparatory school for little boys getting ready for college! where deception and lying and infidelity are the order of the day; where the lazy or over-taxed mistress has no time to ferret out sin, and expose and correct it, and weep over and pray with her poor little motherless charges as you remember I used to do with you when you told a story! . . . Then you will say 'You don't want me to learn any more'. Yes I do, a great deal more . . . I would like you to learn to put your thoughts together forcibly and well, to *think* logically and clearly, to speak powerfully, i.e. with good but simple language, and to *write* legibly and well, which will have more to do with your usefulness than two languages . . ."[120] Katie had done well with French under a governess and was all agog to learn German. And the next day having received another letter from Katie Catherine added, "My dearest Katie, I have not changed about the school at all . . I do not think your desire to learn sinful if it be subordinated and rendered helpful to your serving God . . . your letter seems as though education was first in your mind and righteousness and the Spirit only thrown in as an adjunct. I am sure I do not want to misjudge you or to think one unjust or unkind thought of you for I never felt to love you so deeply, but oh, *I do so want you and all my children to live for God* . . . I see as I never saw before that all God wants with us in order to fill us with His Spirit and make us flames of fire, is for us to be honest and wholehearted with Himself, and I want you to begin life by being so . . . You see the whole question with me is not whether you shall have some more teaching, but whether this is of the right kind. Perhaps if we pray and wait a bit the Lord will show us and open a way as He has done for Ballington. Still if Papa is willing, I will waive my fears and you shall try it for one term, then I will be guided by what I see. I am writing Papa to send you a definite word."[121]

A significant sentence found its way into a letter from his mother to Bramwell, "...I don't know what to do about her [Katie] she is so poorly. I think twelve months *away from the work* [i.e. the preaching] in some country place would help...If it were not for the infernal worldliness of all the schools—*Pray about it*."[122] Later that year, Katie, then eighteen, and Emma, sixteen, went to the sea for a rest and a course of special treatment. "My dearest girls," wrote their mother, "...do all that you possibly can for your health. *Tell* Mrs. Simons *all*. Katie, do not go on making out that there is nothing much the matter with you...Remember you are gone at all this expense on purpose to get good and your mother is doing without many things...in order to spend the money for this end. I don't mind it in the least, nay, I shall enjoy doing it *if you get good*, but if you go and defeat my purpose I shall be bitterly grieved. This is to you both mind...Cheer and comfort one another. Don't be tart or snappish...You may never be thrown as much together again as long as you live, and there may come in your lives days when you would give a great deal for one of these hours back again. Make much of them as they fly and use your time and influence with one another to help each Godward...pray together. Seek to *enjoy* God."[123] And a few days later their mother was sending more advice, "I wish you would be more explicit about your health; I want to know particulars ...I am more than ever satisfied that indigestion aggravates every other malady. Do you get nice fish? The less meat Emma takes the better, if she can get fish and eggs. Try Cadbury's cocoa essence for a drink; it agrees with me...watch what you find agrees with you and stick to it; but I am certain that both tea and coffee are bad for you. One cup of tea in an afternoon is all you ought to take...it rains here without ceasing, but you must put on your oldest things and get out between the showers. You *have* something to look at...the beautiful sea!"[124]

In 1877 Katie went to a school in Penzance which was under the direction of a religious woman. The letters flowed on with advice fitting school circumstances as, "My very dear Katie...are you sure it is wise to absent yourself from many of the lessons in school? You see you may not know as thoroughly as you should some things which younger children may know, who have been more regularly taught. Geography for instance...I am glad Miss H. helps you at arithmetic, perhaps she can help you to do a little Euclid—worth all the German in the world for mental improvement. You want mental discipline and *method*...To learn to systematize your thoughts...As to health it troubles me to hear that your back is so bad. I *know* nothing but lying down in the day will save it. You might try a compress worn at night and the back washed over with cold water in the

335

morning, and a bit of flannel worn down it. I believe there is no accounting for the benefit of *warmth* to the spine . . . *Have you got a mock desk?* [For use to write at when standing] Once more I ask! Miss H. is sure to know a carpenter who could put you a bit of deal together . . ."[125]

And again, " . . . very glad that you think your back is better—stick to the callisthenics and all the other measures which you find helpful to your *health* . . . I hope you are not wearing your stays at all tight [tight lacing was the fashion in those days]; I am more than ever convinced that they are a curse . . . Ballington is here. I am very pleased with him. He is much improved . . . I am disappointed in what he tells me about his school. I shall not let Bertie stop after Ballington leaves. Pa is only poorly . . . Midsummer will soon be here, and then you will come and see us all and I trust we shall have some of the happiest times in our lives . . ."[126]

The last page of one of her letters to Katie shows that Catherine is still fearful of the harmful effect being at school might have on this dearly loved child. "It is dangerous for you to mingle with the worldly, the gay and the ambitious; and I see that my responsibility is very great in allowing you to do so. I see that God has given you a rare gift of influencing others for good, and I tremble lest the abuse of it should sink you into hell! Oh, my dear child, my heart is full of tenderness towards you. I would give all I have to make you see as I see. To make you know *yourself* and *realize* that your besetment is to be ambitious and vain of superior attainments. Will you go to the Lord and ask Him to search your heart as with a lighted candle? Will you be *willing* to know the worst of yourself and put away this desire to be learned and wise and great as an *end,* and only desire *anything* in order that you may be *holy* and useful . . . ? Do not think that I do not sympathize with you. I believe it was my own snare when I was young."[127]

Katie was perhaps a bit homesick when her mother wrote this enlightening note, "My very dear Katie, You *know* how I always answer Papa when he asks me if I love him! It seems such a superfluous question! I feel much the same to you! However, if it is a comfort to you to be *told* it, I just snatch a moment this awfully busy morning to tell you. *Yes,* a thousand times more than you know . . . I am sorry my letter discouraged you, but *why* should it? *Supposing* that you are in yourself of a restless and discontented nature, are we bound always to remain what we were at the beginning? . . . By watchfulness on our part, and discipline and succour on His, what may we not become? It is not of nature's tree the fruit of the Spirit springs. It is of the tree of the Lord's own right-hand planting . . . Here is encouragement for you and for me . . . Beware of letting the enemy take occasion to discourage and depress you by the *greatness* of the work to be done, either in yourself or for others. Remember He who reveals the need, can supply it ... My dear child let nothing frighten you or lure you from your trust. This is all the difference between a conqueror and a coward."[128]

On her return home from school Katie became officially an evangelist in the Mission and was one of the first women officers in the newly formed Salvation Army. I choose one more extract from Catherine Booth's letters to her eldest daughter. This was written when she was conducting a campaign in Leicester. It moves me to read it even now; how powerful it must have been to the nineteen-year-old girl to whom it came illumined by her mother's example and love: " ... And now just divest your mind of any and every other concern for the present and live for God and Leicester! I want you to gather every convicted soul in the place. Next Sunday you will feel more at home and have a better hold of the people. Only pray and believe and keep near the Lord, and Leicester will be your first great victory for Jesus and eternity. Oh, it seems to me that if I were in your place—young— no cares or anxieties—with such a start, such influence, and such a prospect, I should not be able to contain myself for joy ... I pray the Lord to show it to you, and so to enamour you of Himself that you may see and feel it to be your chief joy to win sinners for Him. I say I pray for this; yes ... and if ever you tell me it is so I shall be overjoyed.

"I don't want you to make any vows (unless, indeed, the Spirit leads you to do so) but I want you to set your heart and mind on winning souls, and to leave everything else with the Lord. When you do this you will be happy—oh, so happy! Your soul will then find perfect rest. The Lord grant it to you, my dear child ... I am sorry to hear there was such a paucity of help. We must *make* workers. There are few who know how to deal with souls. *You* must make some by God's grace and help. You must now take the flag and hold it firmer and steadier, and hoist it higher than ever your mother has done ... Look onward, my child, into eternity—*on and on and on*. You are to live *for ever*. This is only the infancy of existence, the schooldays, the seed-time. *Then* is the grand, great, glorious, eternal harvest."[129] To Mrs. Billups goes a letter clearly showing Catherine's joy at Katie's success, this time at Whitby. "She is having one of the most mighty moves I ever knew of, so great that we are letting her stop another week. The proprietor of the hall is converted ... all *Whitby* is moved about religion. The hall was packed to suffocation on Sunday night (seats 3,000) and numbers unable to get in. People all over the town seeking God, going to their ministers asking what they must do to be saved. Join us in praying that she may be *kept*. At present she is humble and teachable as a child. Ask God to keep her from any distracting circumstances for Himself alone."[130]

The meetings and the converts, and most of all the need she saw among sinful people, tore at Catherine's heart. In a letter to Emma

337

telling that hundreds of "roughs" had been saved she burst out with, "Oh my dear child it makes me long to see you all at it in some way or other! Tell Eva and Lucy . . . to get ready . . ."[131] As her own strength began to fail her hopes of what her sons and daughters would accomplish shone brighter. They would do better and do *more* than their mother had done. Such thoughts comforted her. In large measure her sons and daughters justified her hopes, especially in that they really *cared* for the people and by their free unaffected style on and off the platform were able to convince those for whom they worked that they cared. This was a gift and memory of it even today sometimes calls forth comment about "the Booth way".

Only one or two letters from the children to their mother survive. One from Emma indirectly gives a picture of Catherine in the home and her attitude toward William, as seen by her fifteen-year-old daughter: " . . . Sometimes I think there never was another heart like mine. You see it is so *full—what of—* is quite another question, and what is more I cannot tell you. Perhaps you do not need telling? You remember when you were fifteen yourself. That is what most mothers *forget*. And no wonder. They have no *time* to make castles in the air . . . There is Tommy wants a new pair of breeches, and Bessie a new hat, and most of all, Papa's tea wants getting ready, and she must get a smiling face and sparkling eye ready to meet *him*. Of course she must. As if she had nothing but golden futures and castles in the air to think about since she saw him last!"[132] Love of their parents for each other was easily recognized by the children. It was an ordinary part of life like breathing, an invariable atmosphere to which plans and doings could be related. "Look after Mama," "take care of Papa," "your precious Papa," "your darling Mother," this type of phrase slips into the letters as part of everyday usage, they all meant the same thing. Both father and mother talked about each other to the children, drawing out sympathy, or delight in their achievement, according to the circumstances and enhancing the beauty of being loved by such a parent. Catherine and William were at one about shielding the little ones from the perplexing effects of diverging opinions of parents. Catherine said, "It was agreed . . . in cases of difference of opinion never to argue in the presence of the children. I thought it better even to submit at the time to what I might consider as mistaken judgment rather than have a controversy before them." On the other hand the knowledge that there was free expression of thought between their parents encouraged the young people to open their minds to father or mother whose love they knew was the premise to every command.

Emma was nearly sixteen when her mother wrote, "Yes, I know all about it, more than you think I do. But this is only the infancy of our being, and it is better to possess these capacities of loving, even if they are never filled in this world, because there is a grand realization

338

for them in the next ... We are made for larger ends than earth can compass ... 'Do I love you as much as ever?' What a superfluous question. I cannot measure my love for you by degrees. It is of the sort that knows nothing of decrease or increase. *It is always full.* I repose in you the most sacred trust, and this is the highest proof of love and confidence."[133] The "sacred trust" was giving Emma the charge of the home during Catherine's absences. How well she could match her word to the child's mood one may judge from this: "... I hope that you are recovering from the fit of dumps into which you had fallen when you wrote me. I note all you say, and am quite willing to admit that most girls of fifteen would feel very much as you did about Katie coming, my being away, etc., but then *my Emma* is *not* one of these *'most girls'*. She has more sense, more dignity of character, and above all, *more religion.* She only got into the dumps, and for once felt and spoke like 'one of the foolish women'! Well, that is all over now, and I doubt not she is herself again, acting as my representative, taking all manner of responsibility and interest in her brothers and sisters—tired often with them but never tired of them— acting the daughter to her precious Papa, the mother and sister to Ballington and the faithful, watchful friend to the whole household ..."[134]

As they grew up Catherine sometimes confided her own disappointments to one or other of the children. Following meetings in Whitby, she found comfortable lodgings and stayed on for a short rest. Here William joined her. The joy in prospect of having him to herself for a brief spell and the enchantment of the sea revived her spirits, she was ready to be gay! This letter to Emma tells how the bubble burst, "I was very glad to think that Papa's coming was a comfort to you. That atones for the disappointment it was to me! We had just got comfortably fixed up as I *hoped* for a few days comparative quiet and communion when lo! a combination of things makes it important for the work's sake that he should rush off again; and so it has ever been, and so I suppose will be to the end. Well, a good soldier ought to be ready for sudden moves as well as for hard fighting, though even a soldier may rest *sometimes*! Well, I hope his presence has helped you—then I don't mind so much.

"Perhaps you wonder why I did not come with him. The chief reason was that I was getting good, and I am so *anxious* to come home to you really better that I feel I can submit to anything for this end ... for your sakes I feel I ought to use every means to get better. When I am free from care and strain *I am like another creature.* Well, praise the Lord I *am* much better ... I have some thought of trying to get a furnished house cheap at Hastings for the Xmas holidays and taking you all after Xmas Day is turned. We shall see. It is lovely here, almost as nice as summer. I wrote Pa yesterday about you going to see Grandpa. If you do go, try to interest him all you can and pray with him and do him good. I shall soon be home now ... Tell Annie to get all her work done if she can by I come, as I shall want a few things doing. Give my love to her. I hope you mind that gas in the bathroom—I suffer many a worry about it. Tell Annie to hang up a saucepan lid over it to keep it off the ceiling— Bertie can drive a nail in the wall or something long enough to hang it on. My hand is so painful I can scarcely hold the pen."[135]

Emma had a deeply affectionate, sensitive nature. To Bramwell who was encouraging her to begin speaking in the meetings, she once wrote, "I want to work for God and souls. But I am afraid I shall not be able to do it in the way Katie does ..." And again, "No I am afraid I was not born for a parson, much as I should like to be one for *your* sake." Her parents were becoming reconciled to the thought that Emma was not suited by temperament for public work. When her mother heard that Emma, then sixteen, had given the address in a Sunday night meeting at St. Leonards, Catherine wrote a jubilant account to Mrs. Billups finishing with, "Does it not seem as if the Lord was going to take me at my word and use them *all* in His work?"[136] In another letter she writes of "the honour God is putting on me that all the children should be preachers". Her love dwells on them each with "infinite yearnings", with tenderness beyond words; she rejoices with a joy deeper than any earthly joy, with a rapture of happiness, that her sons and daughters have chosen the path of self-denial and poverty. This was what she hoped for them before she bore them.

5

As Catherine's responsibilities and anxieties increased, it was to Bramwell that she turned. Not, certainly not, that she turned in any sense away from William, but once the work in Whitechapel had begun William was, as it were, riding an unbroken horse. The untutored, and often unstable, excitable throng of converts became a power in the fight against evil but they were unpredictable, a "pretty handful" as he sometimes called them. William needed cheering and cherishing and all the more so when depressed by sickness. He must not be troubled with knowledge of any burden Catherine could carry without him. So, in her anxieties about the children, the lack of money, her own ill-health, the beloved work, and William himself, *she leaned on Bramwell.* An intimacy of thought developed between mother and son both beautiful and rare. There never seems to have been a shadow between them since that resolute "no" in the Cardiff circus. The lively intelligent child who was Catherine's first-born had developed into a studious, self-effacing youth. In many ways he resembled his mother. He had the same tenacious will and the same logical turn of mind. From his early teens he had acted, under William Booth, as manager of all the affairs of the Mission. The boy worked fantastically hard and delighted in serving his adored father. He asked nothing better than to go on doing so.

Bramwell at seventeen, still confided in his mother; there was no restraint between them and confidence in their mutual love allowed great freedom of speech. Another element had knit their hearts closer through the years—that was their love for William. For want of space there is not enough of him in this story of Catherine's loves. In fact, he dominated her life and the children's. He was attractive to children. "The children laugh and dance and sing at my coming," he told Catherine in one of his loveletters, and his own flock felt the same. Between Bramwell and his father a wealth of affection developed in boyhood and enriched all their relationships. Years after Catherine's death William wrote to him, "I know you care for me, and the knowledge is one of the chief human sustaining influences of my life. My love for you is more than I can tell."[137] When in 1876 Bramwell was ordered a complete rest, and went to stay with a friend of his parents in Scotland, his mother wrote, "Poor Papa seemed dreadfully restless and unsettled after you were gone. I don't think there are many fathers that have the same kind of feeling towards their boys— it is more like the love of woman."[138]

Bramwell had encouraged Ballington, Katie and Emma to begin preaching, helped them with "sermons", was made glad by their successes. In a letter to Catherine William said, "Willie, or rather Bramwell, as I like to call him now, has just left me. He is a good lad ... I have no fault worth calling a fault to find with him ... Were he only stronger I should rejoice in contemplating his future ..." but his "voice and chest are so weak that I don't see how he is going to make a preacher."[139] From Portsmouth while campaigning there, Catherine wrote to Bramwell, then seventeen, "I differ with you about speaking. I think that it is your vocation, if the Lord enables you to do it without hurting your body ... You see, you can talk to three or four hundred in the same time and nearly as easily as you can talk to one ... Are you coming here on Saturday? I think you would enjoy your Sabbath and be useful."[140] Hearing from Railton that in William's absence Bramwell had spoken for thirty minutes at a tea meeting in Whitechapel, Catherine wrote to Mrs. Billups, "Perhaps the Lord is going to cure his heart ... What an honour to give our children to such a work! I would rather my boy should do it than be the greatest merchant or professional man in England ..."[141] But at eighteen Bramwell stood irresolute, doubting; at times even antagonistic to his mother's conception of his future.

I dwell on this because her son's attitude to public work was one more challenge to Catherine's faith. If from weariness or disappointment, or for very love of the son whose happiness she longed for, she had for a moment questioned the validity of her covenant with God that he should become a preacher, The Christian Mission would not have become The Salvation Army as we know it today. She did not realize it at the time, but when she wrestled and reasoned with Bramwell, pleading for him in prayer, she was helping to prepare the instrument that God would use to translate into action the fresh ideas of reaching and harnessing the masses in the cause of Christ, exemplified in her own and William's life and teaching. Catherine's letters to Bramwell during the period of this hesitancy in him show the urgency of her desires for him. He once said of her, "Her reasoning was really persuasive . . . it was no mere cunning of words . . . through which she gained her influence and swayed assemblies. It was rather her own intense conviction of the truth of what she had to say."[142] This was as true of her conversations as of any sermon she preached.

Catherine's love for William and the Army increased her anguish of desire for Bramwell. She prayed much, with such love as hers was, one must pray or faint! Bramwell was told how she grieved for him, "Your sadness about preaching is like a standing sore underneath all my other matters." She wrote to him on the eve of his nineteenth birthday, "I have thought very much about you . . . your future harasses me considerably; it seems 10,000 pities that with the crying need for preachers, *you* with your *views*, capacity and opportunities should be lying dormant. If you can preach without injury to your heart, it seems to me that you are throwing away a splendid opportunity of serving your generation . . . *you* cannot judge of your ability . . . Your birthday is on Monday. Suppose you were to make it a matter of unceasing prayer between that and the following Monday and then decide as you perceive the Lord's will. I will join you, and I am sure Papa and Railton will . . . May the Lord show you *His* mind. I only want you to serve your generation *according to His will*."[143]

In response to his mother's letter, among other things, Bramwell said, "I hardly know how to thank you for all your loving wishes . . . Anyway, my dearest Mother, if in the days to come I find I *should* have been a preacher, I shall remember that in the tenderest words you told me what you wished and what you 'asked' of God for me, and come what may, I can never forget to thank the Lord that He gave you to me for a mother."[144] His mother reasoned with him, rallied him, pleaded and poked fun by turns. "Your name ought to have been 'Bramble' instead of Bramwell, for you are all contradictions,"[145] she wrote. There was no fun in her mind, she was in dead earnest when she wrote, "I wonder it does not make your blood boil to do something to rescue the people; I hope the Lord will make you so miserable everywhere and at everything else, that you will be compelled to preach . . . Oh, my boy, the Lord wants *such as you*, just such, to go out amongst the people, seeking nothing but the things that are Jesus Christ's. You are free to do it; able by His grace ... Will you not rise to your destiny? You *must* preach."[146] In different mood, "Don't be discouraged about your preaching. The devil withstands you of course, *he* does not want you to preach ... what is preaching? Paul says it is 'speaking to edification ... and comfort'. *Not*, mind, speaking to one's *own* satisfaction with fluency, eloquence and demonstration! Judged by Paul's rule, I contend that you *can* preach and that you *ought* to preach."[147]

Time flowed on. Bramwell was nearly twenty-one. In all but name The Salvation Army had come into being, the flags were flying and thousands were being won from sin to the Saviour. Bramwell in spite of physical weakness was working fanatically; all day and far into the night, if not in the "office" in Whitechapel, in his bedroom-cum-office in the Gore Road home. *But he had not yet admitted that he was called to preach.* When they were apart, mother and son precipitated their talk on to paper as it were, and for all that the letters are so many they represent but a fragment of the discussions between the two. "My dearest Boy," she wrote, "I am sorry to find you so desponding, and it seems to me without adequate cause ... this miserable foolish underestimating of yourself ..."[148] And to reassure and convince, "My very dear Boy, it has not been because I have not thought about you that I have not written, more likely because I have thought so much. I truly smpathize with you in your feeling of want of liberty, but it is simply want of *confidence*. Some of the grandest spiritual men since the days of Moses and Jeremiah have been those who had the greatest conflict at first with themselves and the devil ... Do you think your *circumstances* are the result of chance? Were we, your earthly proprietors, *sincere* when by the side of your natal bed we held you up in our arms to God and gave you to Him for an *evangelist*? Yes, if any act of my life was thorough and real, *that* was. Did not God regard it? Is the name you bear and its associations a chance? The circumstances you have been placed in have given you such a practical knowledge of *men* as other people are a lifetime in acquiring! You *start* where most men finish. Your whole life may have been shaped for this very work. I tremble to think of all this being thwarted by the fear of man! For this is the real difficulty ... My boy, you once made my heart leap by telling me that now you were 'willing to be one of God's damnation fools'! Are you true to that assertion?"[149]

When at Whitby for a campaign his mother wrote to Ballington, "Bramwell spent a few days with me here last week; we had a nice time together, but he was poorly and down. *Pray for him.* He spoke and preached *beautifully*, and yet he thinks he is out of his sphere; surely the devil is a cunning adversary ..."[150] And to Bramwell, "My dearest Boy, I can only send a line or two. I am *so* tired, but I

343

must send one. How can you be so foolish as to talk of 'winding up'?
... Go on, boy, *go on*! What on earth do you want? By your own
account, in between the grumbles, you are moulding a new concern ...
let the sermonizing go to the devil ... now I beseech you, don't throw
away your freedom, and because you cannot do after a certain fashion
conclude that you cannot do it at all. *You can.* I am certain you can
talk more for the good of souls than almost anyone I ever knew ...
Mrs. Shepherd is here cleaning. She asks, 'How is Mr. Bramwell, bless
him?' and goes off into ecstacies about the blessings she gets when he
speaks, etc., etc. She does not know that he is in the dumps because
he cannot do the grandiloquent!"[151]

On Bramwell's twenty-first birthday his mother wrote, "I need not
say how much I am thinking about you today. My son is a *man* in
the eye of the law today, but oh how much more I rejoice over the
fact that he is a *man of God*. I gave you to God twenty-one years ago
tonight and now on your arriving at maturity I praise Him for having
accepted the offering and ratified the covenant. I think in *this* I have
been *true* to my vow and made it the leading purpose of my soul in
all my dealings with you to train you for God and for His work.
Your letter rejoices me because I see what influence and power the
Lord has given you, that you have been able to work such a change
in A. and G. in so short a time. Only hold on living and working,
and it must tell on all around. I am concerned about your health ...
Strive consistently with the laws of your *physical* nature ... now you
are a man act as a man ... Emma is in low spirits. Write her a line
when you have time, also Bertie and spur him on ... Good bye my boy.
The Lord bless you and from this day forth and for ever be more
to you than father and mother and all earthly good, prays and will
pray, your ever loving Mother."[152]

Bramwell wrote a desponding letter in reply. "I do thank you for all
your kind words ... I have had such teaching and training and
example as no other young man in these kingdoms ... I could not
but feel awfully abashed at the miserable failure I seem likely to
prove."[153] To which his mother's response was, "... Now about your
'failure'—and all that stuff. Even *supposing* that you cannot sustain
protracted preaching services, do you call the results of this visit
North a 'failure'? ... I think it is casting a reproach on the Holy
Spirit to talk thus ... Pray in faith for deliverance from the fear of
man and get that amount of rest needful to recruit your nervous system,
for if your body is down it requires a physical miracle to give you
energy and animal spirits both of which are necessary."[154] To which
Bramwell's rejoinder, "My dearest Mother ... You do not know how
precious you are to us all, a very part, and Heaven knows the *better*
part, of us ... If I can only get rid of the *burden*, physical, mental
and spiritual, that preaching is ... but this intolerable weight and
darkness which seems to settle over me the moment I begin either to

make a sermon or to preach it, clogs everything, destroys my quiet of mind . . ."[155] "I used to feel just as you describe at first—*awful*," Catherine told him, "would rather have gone 100 miles many a time than have got up (to reach). God will, I feel sure, give you the victory and as soon as He can trust you. Success is a dangerous good; perhaps a thorough, emptying is indispensable first. Keep praying and believing."[156] And a week or so later, ". . . I regard your present state at the result of low physical health and spirits combined with Satanic agency . . . You see, I believe the obligation is universal to preach where there is the ability to talk to people's hearts, and the opportunity."[157] That Bramwell had this ability was increasingly evident as he preached more often. The demands on the "field" compelled him to. He left the "office" in time for a meeting with soldiers and converts on Saturday and after three or four services on Sunday and the hurly-burly of the open-air meetings, travelled back by night to be at Headquarters first thing Monday morning.

Catherine's letters showed her delight that the children were all engrossed in "the work" but she had her qualms. The headlong pace at times appalled her, but it could not be denied that she and William had themselves set that pace! "You see now we are more and more engulfed and enthralled and enslaved by the *Concern*, every one of us . . ." Bramwell wrote to Emma. Their mother pleaded for a little common sense for love's sake; as in this to Bramwell, "I do wish you would give one evening a week to take Emma somewhere to hear Parker, or anywhere you like for a change both for yourself and for her. You say you have had a heavy pull since you came home. Of course I know what *that* means, and no matter what I *say* I cannot *believe* that you care about me as you ought till you are willing to yield a little to meet my wishes on this question of work. When you will take one day per week for rest and recreation I shall *know* then how much you love me."[158]

After one more extract I shall put away these letters from Catherine Booth to her children. I wonder whether any mother who had so little time to call her own has managed to write such letters to her sons and daughters? Such ingenuous, eager, humble-minded letters; breathing out her love for her children and her love for God and showing those loves inextricably mingled; letters expressing motherly solicitude about diet, clothes, health, behaviour, books; with advice on everything, almost, under the sun. I can well imagine the explosive "Really, Mama . . ." that broke out now and again as they were read. Yet these sometimes irritating admonitions were what brought the writer so vividly to mind, they were "just like her". Her written word was an echo of her speech, and recalled her eager manner and merry eyes which in absence were almost unbearably sweet. At one time or another on reading a letter from their mother all her children must have agreed with Ballington, "I feel fit to cry" with longing to see her.

345

In their discursiveness and intensity they remind me of her love-letters to William, and of course they *are* love-letters, but this time to William's children. Here then to Bramwell my last choice from Catherine's words to her children in their youth. ". . . I believe it was the Lord who led us to *begin* the work, and it seems to me He has 'grown' you up on purpose to carry it on, for certainly no one else could have given you *such a heart for it* but He. I used to think when you were about twelve, when you used to go off to the chapels round about, that your tastes would lead you off from our sort of work and that you would never feel at home in it, but how wonderfully the Lord has led you by a way you knew not. By rheumatic fever, He put His veto on your being a doctor and saved you from a vortex which has swamped the religion of thousands of promising religiously trained young men . . . step by step He has led you on to your present position and absorption in spiritual work, and now bless His name He is showing you that *with Him* you can do all things. Oh, my boy go on to follow the Lord fully, and I feel sure He will make you a mighty man of valour in His Army . . . If you would read Finney, it would do more for you than anything I know of, and you could understand and appreciate him. This and your *Bible,* the longer I live the more I believe in the study of the Bible, with the Spirit; it is dead without the Spirit.

"Be assured that you were never so dear to my heart as now. The first time I clasped you to my bosom I am sure I was not conscious of so great a joy as I have felt in hearing of your enjoyment of, and dedication to God. I rejoice over you with singing (inside at any rate) and love you with a love above that of earth altogether . . . Don't be discouraged at difficulties. Those who are to lead in the *fight must* be prepared to see their comrades fall *and run* as well as the enemy, and must be willing to stand alone, if need be, grasping the standard even in death. All men will go on seeking their own, more or less, to the *end* but *you* are to be a Paul who *seeks* nothing but Christ and *Him* crucified . . ."[159]

His mother would have rejoiced beyond her hopes to have seen the influence of Bramwell's preaching on The Salvation Army. He developed a style that won an attentive hearing from vast crowds yet that enabled him to appeal to the individual conscience. There was a charm, an intimacy, an unconventionality about his preaching, above all a genuine gift of communication never more brilliantly used than when talking in private meetings to classified groups of Salvationists, officers, bandsmen, young people. His mastery of his subject and of his hearers made each occasion unique. Everywhere to the few or to the many, his word was with power.

In 1880 the Booths celebrated their silver wedding. A scribble from Catherine to Mrs. Billups, ". . . We also are to have a great meeting at Whitechapel on June 16 which will be our silver wedding.

346

Pa pledged himself to it the last great meeting, so we must go through with it. All the children are to be there to sing and the elder ones to speak."[160] The London Corps crowded the Whitechapel Hall. Singing and laughter and loud Hallelujahs had their part in the meeting. Speakers included William and Catherine and four of their children but perhaps "the most heart-appealing feature of the meeting was when the family rose to their feet and sang together,

> *We all belong to Jesus,*
> *Bless the Lord!*

As the clear young voices rang through the hall, a practical illustration in full consecration was taught which was more eloquent than any of the burning addresses given."[161] The youngest of the group of eight was Lucy, then aged thirteen; the eldest, Bramwell, twenty-four, was his father's right-hand man, "prophet and teacher" as his mother had foretold. Stead wrote, "The Army itself is grouped around the family. The most novel and instructive feature of this religious army, not of celibates but of married folk, is the extent to which the institution of matrimony ministers to the success of the organization . . . General Booth has made marriage one of the corner-stones of The Salvation Army."[162] The silver wedding celebration emphasized the unity of the family in the Army and helped to set a standard for Salvationists in many lands. "We're all in the Army," became a joyful form of family boasting and is common to this day. A large proportion of Salvation Army officers are the children of Salvationists, some representing the dedication of their whole family to the service. At one of the talks Catherine gave about the work of The Salvation Army, she said, 'People say, 'They have put their children into the Movement too!' Yes, bless God! and if we had twenty, we would do so. But . . . it is all from the same motive and for the same end, the *seeking and saving the lost.*" And she asked, "How comes it to pass that these children all grow up with this one ambition and desire? . . . Could all the powers of earth give these young men and women the *spirit* of this work, apart from God? Some of you know the life of toil, self-sacrifice and devotion this work entails. What would induce our children to embrace it? Surely God hath fashioned their souls for the work He wants them to do."[163]

Before she fell fatally ill, all Catherine's children, except Marie, an unassuming, sincere Christian, were officers and preachers in The Salvation Army. Bramwell was his father's Chief of Staff, Ballington was in charge of the thriving Army work in the U.S.A. Katie, with her husband, led the forces in France and Switzerland. Emma, after having charge of the Training of women cadets, went to India to help expand the work lately pioneered there by her husband. Herbert, Eva, and Lucy held posts in the homeland. Their mother's love for each was so strong and tender, her faith for them so high, that had she lived, she would, it is thought by some, have been able to dispel the misunderstandings which after her death caused her lonely William such grief, and led, while they were serving overseas, to the withdrawal on different scores of three of their children from The Salvation Army. But even so, *all* of them continued to be preachers of the Gospel, caring about the sinful and winning souls to Christ. Thus her highest hope for each was fulfilled.

6

Memory holds for me a gentle picture of Catherine as grandmother. I am nearly four years old. I am perched on a cushion to raise me high enough to sit at table. Grandmama is at its head, her back to the big bay window. I sit at her right hand. Uncle Herbert is on my right; there are aunts present, too. Auntie Emma comes and, standing behind me, ties an enormous white napkin loosely round me and the folds touch my cheek at the side as I feel her fingers fumbling at the nape of my neck. I am shy, silent, it seems difficult to raise my eyes *except to Grandmama*. I seem to know her quite well. I feel completely content because she is there. When she will not allow Uncle Herbert, who carves, to give me a piece of meat,* I hear her speak distinctly, "No, Herbert, she shall not have anything in this house that her mother would not wish her to have," and suddenly I have lifted my eyes to find her face turned to me and we smile at each other, as if we knew something nice that the others did not understand about. I feel a wave of happiness as if I had somehow escaped a danger. I like Uncle Herbert, though I am a little afraid of what he may do next, he teases sometimes; but I am sure that Grandmama knows *everything* and will let nothing harmful happen to me.

Later I am six and I go to stay at the house at Clacton-on-Sea where she lies ill. I am still shy, more shy than at three. I am not very happy for I do not like being away from home. There seem to be many strangers in the big house. I feel safest in the garden to which I can go by the side door near the housekeeper's room where I have my meals. My Aunt Emma is in the house and always very kind when I see her, but I am silent, uncomfortable, wishing I were going home. But the moment I am beside Grandmama's bed, that feeling of being strange and shy is gone. She and I talk and talk. Would that I could remember anything she said! I have a small doll in a pale blue woollen frock. Grandmama talks to my doll and perches

* My parents were vegetarians at the time, and all their children were brought up so except for occasional fish and poultry.

it on the bedclothes, and we keep on talking. I am completely comforted and happy, and there is still lots more to say when Captain Carr or Auntie Emma comes to take me away saying, "Grandmama is tired now." I am lifted up to kiss her as she lies propped up by pillows.

I read that when some time after this visit I was taken with my sisters Mary and Miriam to see her, I burst into tears when I was told that Grandmama was going to heaven. I am told that she said to me, 'Well, ducky, I am going to heaven . . . you know how to get there? You must pray to Jesus to take all the naughty out of your heart . . . He will, ducky, He will." Her hand is on my hand, and those about her hear her voice, clear and eager, as if her strength had rallied, she is praying for me. "Bless the child. *My* blessings are nothing, Jesus will bless the child . . . Jesus, Father, I ask You as I did for her father to keep her from the evil that is in the world . . ." My sisters and I are lifted up to kiss her and we are led away. Of all this, except that my tears fall very fast, I remember almost nothing. I am glad that it is so. What memory keeps for me is lovely to me, with a sense of delicious happiness in being with Grandmama, especially in being alone with her. Now that I dwell upon her life, pry into her secret thoughts, read even her love-letters, I see the faces of those she loved and made happy gradually increase in number and gather about her, and I am glad that I too am there. As I look back into the far-off past we smile into each other's eyes, and I am once again her "little Cath" and she is my darling Grandmama.

BOOK SIX

Catherine's love for Mankind:
"Mother of Nations"

"Oh, I love to feel my soul swell with unutterable feeling for all mankind . . . and I love to pray for all great and good and glorious movements for the salvation of men."*

"I love all who love the Lord, I abhor sectarianism more and more."*

"A man must live by Christ and in Christ a supernatural life before he can exemplify the principles or practise the precepts of Christianity; they are too high for unrenewed human nature, it cannot attain unto them."
—In a letter to W. T. Stead.

"I see it is men of God the world wants and for lack of these and not of learning or machinery thousands are sinking into hell."*

"We must go out and save them. We must not stand arguing and parleying as to whether we ought to go, or what it will cost us, or what we shall suffer . . ."
—From a speech at Farewell of officers for Service Overseas.

"Praise up humanitarianism as much as you like, but don't confound it with Christianity, nor suppose that it will ultimately lead its followers to Christ. This is confounding things that differ."
—In a letter to T. W. Stead.

"This is the great distinguishing work of Christ—to save His people from their sins . . . Without a Divine Christ Christianity sinks into a mere system of philosophy and becomes as powerless for the renovation and salvation of mankind as any of the philosophies that have preceded it."
—From a public address.

"I want the world to be saved. I don't care how it is done. My heart is set on the Kingdom, and I don't care how it is propagated."
—In spech at Farwell of officers, Exeter Hall.

"Cast off all bonds of prejudice and custom, and let the love of Christ, which is in you, have free course to run out in all conceivable schemes and methods of labour for the souls of men."
—Message to last Christian Mission Congress.

". . . there *must be the equipment of the Holy Ghost*, for without Him all qualifications . . . are utterly powerless for the regeneration of mankind."
—From public address.

"Do not expect people to speak Greek who have never learned that language."
—Family tradition.

* In love-letters to William Booth.

Katie speaking in a café in Paris. From a painting by Gustav Olof
Cederström now in the Gothenburg Art Museum

Exeter Hall, scene of many great Salvation Army rallies

1

"When it was first mentioned about my daughter going to France, it seemed as if a fresh difficulty arose. I had never thought of a *foreign* land! That seemed to bring a little controversy and shrinking. I faced the matter, and I remembered the promise of the Lord, 'I will make thee a mother of nations', which promise I hid away and thought too great and that it could not be." Catherine was speaking at a gathering held in St. James's Hall, London, February 4, 1881, at which her eldest daughter was dedicated to raise The Salvation Army flag in France. Persistent requests to begin the work there had been received from Christian friends in Paris who had seen something of The Salvation Army in England. The Booths hesitated. This field would present problems different from the lately occupied U.S.A. and Australia; the language for one thing. I do not know who proposed that Katie should command the operation; her brother Bramwell, I surmise. She was twenty-two years of age at the time and had a fair knowledge of French. Unexpectedly Catherine shrank from sending her daughter. We are told by an eye-witness that even during the farewell meeting she was observed to be deeply agitated. In those days "foreign" still had a menacing sound to the ordinary person. Travelling, except for the rich, was a much more isolating experience than it is today. The bloody scenes of the Paris Communes were barely ten years away, and French ferocity and lawlessness got exaggerated in the atmosphere that hung over France like dust from the explosion of the first revolution eighty years before. Catherine certainly believed that a great part of French society was monstrously wicked. She wrote to Mrs. Billups before Katie's departure, that accounts of conditions in Paris "make me shudder". But I do not believe that this was what oppressed her as she sat on the platform of the St. James's Hall on that February evening. I think she knew that she had lost her children to the Salvation War—to the world. Mother of Nations she was, and would be, people of many nations were to become her spiritual children, but her own children must leave her in the process; she would have them no more in the old mothering way.

Catherine sat in that crowded hall listening to Sir Arthur Blackwood praising the work of the Army. She agreed with him when he said, "I believe the Gospel of Christ preached through the lips of His dear servant, who is about to be sent to France, is as well calculated to do its work there as anywhere else,"[1] but to her Katie's going brought home starkly the *fact* 'that she has gone from me for ever".[2] Once Catherine was on her feet and speaking, her self-forgetting

M

courage asserted itself. She declared, "All our confidence is in the Holy Spirit. We should not be so foolish as to send so frail an instrumentality if we believed it depended on human might or strength, but we do so because we know that it depends on divine strength and because we believe that our dear child is thoroughly and fully given up to God . . . Some friends may perhaps think that it does not cost us what it would them to give up their children so fully for such a work. They do not know us. I do not think that any mother in this hall could have felt and realized more the difficulties and dangers connected with this work, than I have . . . but as it was when I first gave her up to preaching, so it is now . . . I have offered her for France, and I believe the Lord will take care of her; though I shall feel very much the parting because I shall feel that she has *gone from me for ever* . . ." The Army Mother then turned and called to her daughter. She and the two young women Lieutenants* who were going with her stood forward on the platform. All three were inexperienced, but each dedicated, and ready to live or die for Jesus' sake in France. While the assembly stood the Army flag,† which was the first to fly in France, was handed by mother to daughter with the charge, "Carry it into the slums and alleys everywhere where there are lost and perishing souls, and preach under its shadow the ever-lasting Gospel of Jesus Christ."[3]

After the little party had left the country Catherine sent Mrs. Billups, "Just a line to let you know our precious one has gone. She went off as bravely as could be expected, but it was a hard task—the parting. What I feel the Lord only knows; but He *does* know all, and the why and the wherefore. Satan says it will kill her—or worse —she will come back a helpless invalid for life. The doctor told me this on Thursday and Satan has repeated it night and day ever since. I can only say 'Lord, I have given her to Thee' . . . It is not so much the parting as the toil and burden which I know must come; and she is so frail!"[4] Two years before, Katie was treated for spinal trouble. As her brother Bramwell put it in a teasing letter, she had been "hanged up by the neck and then done up in cement!" In an undated letter to Katie Catherine swiftly scribbles a note filling the page without pause or paragraph and running down the narrow margin: "My darling Girl, I cannot tell you what I felt after you left but my heart found relief in pouring out its desires for you to the Lord, the God of all the Nations of the earth. I have given you to *Him* for the salvation

* One of them was the slight, fair haired ninteen-year-old, Florence Soper, who would be like a sister to Katie through the first hard year in Paris, and later Bramwell's wife. The other was Adelaide Cox, who became a Commissioner.

† Made by Catherine's own hands. The flag is still used for important Salvation Army events in France and all cadets there are commissioned to be officers beneath its folds.

of the souls for whom He gave *His* Son . . . Now let us hush our grief even at being parted and look onward to the recompense of the *reward*. God will be your strength and reward. Never allow the thought that you can ever be in any degree less to me than you ever have been, oh no not less but *more,* a thousand times. I am proud to have such a daughter to give to Him who gave Himself for me and tho' my mother's heart *bleeds* to part, my Christian heart rejoices to suffer. The Lord bless you. My dear *little Katie* you shall ever be. Write me all your heart and never think I shall worry if you will only tell me the whole truth. The Lord bless and keep you. *He will.* Give my mother's love to Florrie. I will write her tomorrow. Your own ever loving Mother C. Booth."

The pioneering campaign in France proved hazardous. To prosecute it was a keener test of faith than to launch it. The roughs who came to the meetings were even more obstreperous than those in England. In fact the advance into France began to look like a retreat. Katie came home for counsel. Mrs. Booth, lecturing at the Cannon Street Hotel, said, "I wish some of our detractors could have been behind the door this morning, when my precious daughter should have (returned to) Paris. Through an accumulation of disappointment and perplexity, some of it occasioned by the most cruel treatment . . . she broke down . . . If you could have seen the agony of nature that we all endured, you might comprehend that it is not so easy a thing after all to send your child to a foreign land, to bear the responsibility and anxiety and toil of propagating a spiritual work amongst infidels and socialists, with all the malice and spleen of the Pharisees arrayed against you!"[5] Katie and her youthful helpers had been visiting the low cafés and drinking shops, singing, speaking and praying there. Sometimes maudlin tears were shed by the onlookers, often the praying girls wept in pity and horror for the dissolute and depraved men and women who sat drinking and scoffing. One of the early converts was moved to decision in the prayer meeting, when Katie had sat down beside her, and putting her arms round the poor creature had *wept* as she told the love of Christ. In after years the woman always testified that it was Katie's tears that had melted her heart. As a Sergeant of Police said with "half the cut-throats of Paris" crowded together in the alley-way hall, it is not surprising that the meetings were often very rowdy, nor that there were difficulties with the authorities. For a time the hall was closed and all meetings forbidden. This was a grievous blow. Nineteen-year-old Herbert was sent to Paris to reinforce Katie's "staff". His mother wrote to him, "Keep your mind quiet. Lean back on God and don't worry. It is His affair, and if you have done what you could, that is enough! There are plenty of other countries to save besides France, and if God's time has not yet come you cannot help it . . . Let us learn to trust in the dark, to stand still."[6]

Meanwhile, at home, Catherine persuaded the Lord Mayor of London to join in an appeal to the French authorities. She and William had lunch with him on the day he signed a document taking the form of a guarantee of the Army's "reputableness". There were other signatures—Lord Cairns and the City Chamberlain among them. This, with other appeals, proved successful. The Salvation Army was allowed to resume its activities in Paris and hooligans in that city resumed their attacks on the Army!

2

Shortly before Katie left for France the Booths unexpectedly came into a new phase of their lives. Apparently without giving any preliminary hint of his intention, Mr. Reed, who had returned to Tasmania, wrote to say that he was giving them £5,000 for their own support. Catherine's "extravagant heart" overflowed with relief and joy. Before details had been received she had dashed off a letter in her exuberant confiding style which must have brought her vividly to mind for her old friends. Signing herself, "Your ever loving and grateful Catherine Booth," her letter begins, "My dear Mr. and Mrs. Reed, I must put in a few lines expressive of at least a little of what I feel on hearing of your great kindness, though pen and ink seem but a cold and poor medium. I feel something like the man who, when he got saved, could only fill his paper with hallelujahs! I am so thankful to be delivered so largely from dependence on comparative strangers and those who only partially sympathize with our views. Oh, it is kind of you and of the Lord ... your kindness will stimulate us afresh to go on seeking the Kingdom of God *only*, bless His Holy Name for giving us grace to hold on in past times of darkness and trial known only to Himself ... Pray for us, dear friends. I know you do. I only wish we could meet again down here. How I would like to show you some of our noble regiments, your souls would leap for joy. I often picture dear Mr. Reed's joy at that little meeting at Dunorlan when the penitents began to come up! What would you feel now to see them by forty and fifty ... Oh, it is grand, and then to hear them testify the next night! Praise the Lord for ever."[7]

When fuller particulars of Mr. Reed's gift reached her, Catherine wrote again. The letter ran to close on 2,500 words and contained explicit directions for treating Mr. Reed's illness by hydropathy, as well as news of the Salvation War. "My dear Mr. and Mrs. Reed, We had only an indefinite idea of the purpose of your last when we wrote ... Since, we have realized the extent of your munificent kind-

356

ness, the Lord alone knows our feelings of gratitude to you . . . Your letters woke up very deep and tender feelings in our hearts, indeed we were just starting on a journey when they reached us and I could not help weeping most of the way. It seemed so painful to realize that just as dear Mr. Reed had given us such proof of his love and confidence, that he appeared likely to leave us. For though you are so far away, we feel as if he were a *father* in a sense that no one else can ever be . . . We are delighted to hear of your dear Walter beginning to preach. May the Lord make him a valiant soldier of Christ and also the younger ones . . . What a change a few years makes in the children! Well they *must*, they shall, by the help of God stand in our places and rout the foe more fearlessly and faithfully than we have done! It seems as though God were going to fulfil a promise He once gave me, 'I will make thee a mother of nations', in a way I little dreamed of." There follows a full account of the purchase of the Booths' home on Clapton Common, offered cheaply by the mortgagee "although there is a ground rent of £25 per year. I fear you will not like this, neither do we; but the neighbourhood is improving and all think it will be a good investment." William will consult the lawyers "about the investment of the other money, and will abide by your wish in every respect. Accept my heartfelt thanks, dear Mr. Reed, for your generous kindness in allowing this to be done now so that we may have the comfort of it for the remainder of our days. And thank you dear Mr. Reed for wishing it to be tied so that it cannot be spent. To show you how wholly my dearest is given up to the work, I will tell you one of the first things he said after he got the news, *before he had seen your letter*: 'Now I can buy a printing machine for *The War Cry!*' . . . I would rather not have our affairs mixed up with the Army's. Your way is best and as you have thus so kindly cared for us, I would like to feel *sure* of it and that my precious Marie (and Emma if need be, which is very likely if she goes on with this work and continues so delicate) may have a little provision. The Lord bless and reward you. He will. You see, dear friend, you have *always* been independent and do not know the trial of always feeling *uncertain* as to what you have, nor of having to receive help from those who only partially sympathize with your views."[8] Henry Reed died soon after making this gift, which was the fulfilment of the kindly impulse to settle a fund on Catherine Booth made ten years before on conditions which neither she nor William could accept. I am glad to think that he had the joy of giving and she the joy of receiving this bounty as from friend to friend; mutual affection made the giving a happiness for both.

Petri wrote, "Mrs. Booth was a teacher and above all a teacher. William Booth on the contrary was not a teacher. He was at his best in the conduct of big business, in leading men in the mass. He was a demagogue. But Catherine Booth was a born teacher, and remained a teacher to the end. In her less happy moments she was typically the governess . . . the strong masterful trait in her character sometimes made her a hard taskmaster."[9] This is, I think, a fair judgment of Catherine but as I see it her aptitude for teaching, backed by that "strong masterful trait", fitted her exactly for her role as teacher of the newly grouped heterogeneous company which was The Salvation Army. Catherine's instinct to instruct thrust itself into all intercourse with her fellow beings, whether public or private. True, she was always ready to explain and to quote her authorities, which included her own experience, but whatever the subject might be she could not resist laying down the law. She never seems to have questioned the validity of the advice she gave to those who came to her with their spiritual and family problems. To the individual or to the crowd there was a logical, scriptural simplicity in her words that could not be misunderstood. One might not agree with her but it must be admitted that what she said was never ambiguous. There was nothing nebulous about her teaching; it was practical and applicable to daily living.

At first neither Catherine nor William had any idea of what would result from the preachings in Whitechapel. As Catherine told, "During the first ten years we were groping our way out of the conventionalism in which we had been trained." Their converts needed help to follow the same path, no easy task, for the ignorant are often the most bigoted when it comes to breaking with convention. Not that early day Salvationists were all uneducated. There was a growing company of converts from the middle and upper classes, and from them came some of the leaders who were to have a part in welding the comradeship and organization essential to the Army's growth. All must be helped to accept innovations and be inspired with love of a free and joyous expression of religious experience.

Catherine looked upon the education of converts as her special sphere. Long before she opened her lips to preach she had written to William that she would share in his work "by taking under my care, to enlighten and guard and feed the lambs brought in under your ministry".[10] Her ambition was that for the newly-converted she might become a "nursing-mother", and it was certainly fulfilled. From the time of her first preaching Catherine convened meetings for converts only. These gatherings were the precursors of the holiness and soldiers' meetings which later became obligatory in every Army corps. She was able to show the ideal of the "mother in Christ" in such a manner that thousands of men and women saw what she meant, and set themselves to be like her in the mothering. To Salvationists she said, "If anybody were to ask me the one most powerful quality for dealing with souls—that on which success in dealing depends more than on any other quality of the human heart and mind, *I should say sympathy*. That is, the capacity to enter into the circumstances and difficulties and feelings of the individual with whom you are dealing . . . Don't you think sinners feel? At the penitent-form, in the barracks, in the street? Don't they know when they have got a fellow-heart, a brother or sister, who really enters into their circumstances . . . who suffers with them? That is what sinners want."[11] To an extraordinary degree she and William inspired and fostered a sense of family feeling in the Army. By their teaching and example they gave their converts a fresh interpretation of the truth that all men are brothers, and in particular succeeded in inspiring them with the conviction that every Salvationist must be his "brother's keeper".

My friend George Hurren* wrote to me, "The unanswered questions about Catherine Booth are many. What were the influences which made this genteelly nurtured and sensitive girl one of the leading figures among that body of great Victorian women who fought for female emancipation? A partial explanation could be that there was much in Catherine Booth's early reading which convinced her that in the Christian Church women should exercise an equal ministry with men. But perhaps her greatest achievement was in establishing herself as the 'Mother' of the Salvationists . . .

"In this capacity, achieved by sheer force of personality, she ruled not only her own family, but also legislated for the world-wide family of Salvationists. In imposing the idea of the family upon The Salvation Army and its parish, which like Wesley's was the whole world, a rigid Victorian family discipline was established over the officers and soldiers, who to a large extent cared for one another as well as for the unregenerate, as members of a family should. The sinner, until converted, was the object of compassion and care equalled only in the great days of Christian belief. But once he had repented and been converted he came under the family rod. Any lapse from a state of grace brought shame on the family, and compassion was tempered by family chagrin. It is doubtful, however, if this was resented. Rather it was accepted as evidence that one really belonged to the family. Of course there were those who could not stand such a discipline . . . Is it too far-fetched to see The Salvation Army as an extension of the Victorian family, but, exceptionally, as

* George Hurren, Salvationist, son of Commissioner Samuel Hurren.

dominated by the mother? This is no reflection upon William Booth whose devotion to his wife and his Army was unequalled."

That the Army people were willing to be mothered by Catherine was abundantly evidenced. They felt her love and there was something about her that drew love in return. And one of the lovely things about her was her ability to make her compassion acceptable even to those who rejected her message. In the early years the freedom with which the Booths expressed their sympathy became a pattern of behaviour for their officers. People who remembered an individual link passed on an aura of it to their children. William became "My General", "Our dear General". Sometimes a trivial action gave a sense of intimacy. Railton recounts that a poor woman told him years afterwards, "The first time I and my sister were in the hall after we had lost our mother, the General came down off the platform and knelt beside us, to pray for us, and Mr. Bramwell who was then a boy . . . came and stood in front of us and sang, 'Earth has many a scene of sorrow'."[12] Memories of such informal incidents were treasured for generations.

The Bible was the foundation of all that Catherine taught. "I love this Word and regard it as the standard of all faith and practice, and our guide to live by."[13] At every stage any new effort or method was justified only if in harmony with the Bible. "No person," she said, "who followed us carefully can imagine for a moment that we would hold or teach any adaptation of the Gospel itself."[14] Salvationists were taught to proclaim "the unadulterated Gospel of Jesus Christ". She wrote to a friend, "We must stick to the form of sound words, for there is more in it than appears on the surface. 'Glory be to the Father, and to the Son, and to the Holy Ghost' was the theology of our forefathers, and I am suspicious of all attempts to mend it."[15] Catherine was not afraid of using Bible language. By example and precept she taught Salvationists to use the idiom of the day in order to make the Gospel known, but that did not mean abandoning the phraseology of the apostles. Her words in public abound with it. In one address she said, "But people say, 'a good deal of the language is figurative . . .' But supposing that some of the language were figurative, what then? What do you gain by making it out to be figurative? What are figures for? Surely no one will argue that the judgment as prefigured in the words of Jesus Christ and His apostles, will be less thorough, less scrutinizing, less terrible than the figures used to set it forth! Therefore it does not matter whether these be figurative expressions or no, seeing that they are calculated to convey the most awful and tremendous ideas . . . which any figures could convey, which the wisdom of God could select."[16]

Overwhelmingly persuaded of the truth of Christianity herself, the fire of that conviction burned in all she said of Christ. She declared that by His Holy Spirit "Christ Who appeared in Judea is now abroad in the earth just as much as He was then and that He presents to humanity all that it needs. He is indeed, as He represents Himself to be, the Bread of Life . . . I stand and make my boast, that the Christ of God, my Christ, the Christ of The Salvation Army, *does* meet the crying need of the soul . . . He promises pardon and He does pardon . . . He promises to purify and He does purify. He is a real, living, present Saviour to those who really receive and put their trust in Him." And contemplating Christ's Divinity she said, "If you take it out of His teachings, you reduce them to a jumble of inconsistencies. His Divinity is the central fact around which all His doctrines and teachings revolve . . . Take this mystery out of Christianity, and the whole system utterly collapses. Without a Divine Christ Christianity sinks into a mere system of philosophy, and becomes as powerless for the renovation . . . of mankind as any of the philosophies that have preceded it."[17]

Whether to her children in the nursery or to the great congregations Catherine declared, "I know Whom I have believed." For her, as for Thomas, Jesus Christ was "My Lord and my God". Everywhere she exalted Christ as God and Saviour. This stupendous fact was the life of her teaching. From that foundation her faith reached out to embrace mysteries beyond man's understanding and to glory in the measureless scope of God's creative activity, confident that what was known by revelation about God was in harmony with the unknown. She taught that everyone might exercise this comprehensive living faith independently of circumstances. Salvationists learned that ". . . Christianity is intended to sanctify human nature, letting it still be human," but that Christ did not mean that His followers should continue insin, ". . . what I call an Oh-wretched-man-that-I-am religion . . . Jesus Christ Himself established in this Book, the Bible, a standard, not only to be aimed at, but to be attained unto—a standard of victory over sin, the world, the flesh and the devil: *real, living, reigning, triumphing* Christianity!"[18] "We teach the old-fashioned Gospel of repentance, faith and holiness, not daring to separate what God has joined together . . . we teach that a man cannot be right with God while he is doing wrong to men—in short, that holiness means being saved from sin . . . and filled with love to God and man . . ."[19] Catherine pressed home to the hearts of the people that religion meant being submitted to God, keeping His law by His grace and being right with their fellow-men. Had there been a cheating? Restitution must be made. Disputes must end in reconciliations. "We have numberless instances of long-standing quarrels and animosities being healed . . . We teach the fear of God as the basis of regard for man . . . When the fear of God departs from a people, the fear of man is not long in following, and we all know what happens when every man feels free to do that which his own evil and inflamed passions excite him to do . . . Do you say, 'But we are educating the masses'? I answer . . . the more educated, the more dangerous, unless you also make them good . . . You cannot reform man morally by his intellect . . . man is fallen, and cannot of himself obey even his own enlightened intelligence. There must be extraneous power brought into the soul. God must come to man."[20] She once said, "Everyone who deals with souls should have a clear and definite understanding of the conditions on which alone God pardons and receives repenting sinners. These conditions always have been and ever must remain the same . . . God's unalterable condition of pardon is the forsaking of evil; . . . let us beware of a theoretical or sentimental faith, which leaves the heart unwashed, unrenewed, unsanctified. (This is) . . . the faith of devils, which is like the body without the spirit—dead."[21] That holiness of heart was within reach of the weakest by the power of the Holy Spirit, was fundamental to her teaching. Thousands of people, young and old, among the educated and the ignorant, undisciplined and self-indulgent, were helped by her to accept for themselves Christ's standard of integrity. She taught that in the home, in the factory, honesty, kindness and self-denial were concomitants of true Christianity. "It means sincerity and thoroughness . . . Give me a man sincere and thorough in his love (to God) and that is all I want; that will stretch through all the ramifications of his existence; it will go to the ends of his fingers and his toes, through his eyes and through his tongue, to his wife and to his family, to his shop and to his business, to his circle in the world. That is what I mean by holiness . . . It means that a man is wholehearted in love, and thorough out-and-out in service."[22]

Bramwell said that his mother was "intensely aware of evil". At seventeen she wrote in her journal, "I have this day taken up my cross in reproving sin." It was a cross that she carried all her days. She believed it to be the duty of all disciples of Christ to teach in plain words that sin must be renounced and forgiven. Likeness to the Master in her opinion, included this power to reprove. "He would eat with sinners, talk familiarly and tenderly with the worst on earth and lay His hands (in healing) upon the most loathsome, but He was incapable of dealing lightly with their sin."[23] Catherine taught her Army children that with this implacable attitude toward sin could go, must go, a tender compassion for the sinner, a coming near to souls; not in a stooping-down-to-you manner, but in going lower and lower for love of the lowest. Speaking of Jesus as the example of those who are His, she said, "Christ's compassion stands out in its *spiritual fellowship*. The King of kings makes eternal friends of the fishermen. He did not 'visit the poor', did not 'elevate their sad lot' . . . having His fellowship, His joys, His sorrows apart from them; but He shared His life with them in a holy comradeship . . . He had faith in the possibilities of these people, which possibilities would not have been apparent to any other eye. He believed in the transforming power of the Spirit which He could send them. *His* hope was not chilled by stupidity or foolishness or non-comprehension on the part of disciples ... Many a fine scheme of modern benevolence dies and goes out when the people who are to be benefited get to be known! ... So ungrateful, so presuming, so hopeless! But Christ hoped all things, believed all things, until the Peter who was afraid of a servant-girl stood triumphant before the three thousand converts! ... Christ went up to Calvary undismayed by His perfect knowledge of sinful, perverse, opposing men, to die for the whole ungrateful race ... The whole work of Christ was aimed at the salvation of men's *souls*. And this is not less true because He also benefited their bodies by healing their diseases and sympathizing with their sorrows ... He was too merciful to men to spare them the bitter truths of hell ..."[23]

Catherine magnified the work and power of the Holy Spirit. Quoting the words, "Be filled with the Spirit," she said, "I believe that this injunction is given broadly to all believers everywhere, and in all times, and it is as much the privilege of the youngest ... believer here to be filled with the Spirit, as it is of the most advanced; if the believer will comply with the conditions and conform to the injunctions of the Saviour on which He has promised this gift ... Oh, it is the most precious gift ... to be filled with the Spirit, filled with Himself, taken possession of by God ..."[24] She constantly told of her own experience for the encouragement of the faltering. The weakest might be made strong by the Holy Spirit, as she had been, *if they would but be obedient to Him*. "It is not the greatness or smallness of the matter in itself, but the principle of obedience which is involved ...Christ Jesus is too much in love with His Father's will to dwell with those who will not obey."[25] Salvationists were called upon to accept the Bible's teaching, to obey Christ's commands and prove the power of the Holy Spirit in their own experience. Then they were required to testify of it. This was a duty laid upon men and women alike. "It is a great strength and joy to the convert to testify ... and it is the bounden duty of the church to give him the opportunity to do so."[26] "We say the world is dying. What for? Sermons? No ... For fine spun theories? No ... What is it dying for? Downright, straight-forward, honest, loving, earnest testimony about *what God can do for souls* ... for people who can say, 'He has broken my fetters and set me free and I am the Lord's free man; He has saved me and He can save you.' That is what the world wants—*testimony—witnessing*." "The living testimony of living men.'" This was the standard set for Army soldiers.

The Army Mother constantly warned her "children" that forms and ceremonies are nothing save as they embody and express spiritual life and truth. "All through the New Testament," she said, "no truth is taught with greater force and frequency than this, that without a vital union of the soul with Christ, all ceremonies, creeds, beliefs, professions, church ordinances, are sounding brass and a tinkling cymbal . . . everything else falls short of our need and the purpose and end of the Gospel of Christ.[27] Is it not manifestly necessary that we should go back to the simplicity and *spirituality* of the Gospel, and to the early modes of propagating it amongst men? " . . . We cannot get the *order* of a single service from the New Testament, nor can we get the form of a single church government . . . Do you think God had no purpose in this omission? The form, modes, and measures are not laid down as in the Old Testament dispensation. There is nothing of this stereotyped routinism in the whole of the New Testament . . . and when I have brought my reluctance and all my own conventional notions, in which I was brought up like other people, face to face with the naked bare principles of the New Testament, I have found nothing to stand upon . . .' Here is the principle laid down that you are to adapt your measures to the necessity of the people to whom you minister . . . what beautiful scope and freedom from all set forms and formula . . . what scope for the different manifestations of the same Spirit . . ."[28]

The Salvation Army probably issues more "Orders and Regulations" for the guidance of its people than any other Christian body except perhaps the great religious houses, but within those rules utmost freedom of method is allowed to all ranks to "propagate salvation". The Army Mother continued to reiterate, "Let us keep the message itself unadulterated . . . but in our modes of bringing it to bear on men, we are left free as air and sunlight." An idle Christian Catherine felt to be a contradiction in terms. "What is our work?" she asked. "To go and subjugate the world to Jesus." On one occasion she quoted Dr. Lightfoot, at the time Bishop of Durham, as saying, " . . .'The Salvation Army has at least recalled us to the lost ideal of the work of the Church—the universal compulsion of the souls of men.' Yes, we have been teaching our own people . . . that we are to compel men to come in, that we are to seek by our own individual power and by the power of the Holy Ghost in us, to persuade men . . . This is our great characteristic—pressing the Gospel upon the attention of men . . ."[29] On another occasion, speaking of her own experience of talking with people in their own homes, she said, "I esteem this work of house to house visitation *next in importance* to the preaching of the Gospel itself. Who can tell the amount of influence . . . on our whole nation if all real Christians would only do a little of this kind of work . . . this is the work that most needs doing of any work in the vineyard. There are teeming thousands who never cross the threshold of church, chapel or mission hall to whom all connected with religion is an old song, a byword and a reproach. They need to be brought into contact with a living Christ in the characters and persons of His people." Even in the marriage service Salvationists declare, "We also promise that we will use all our influence with each other to promote our constant and entire self-sacrifice in fighting in the ranks of the Army for the salvation of the world."[30] For the salvation of the world! Do the words seem pretentious? They were spoken in dead earnest by William and Catherine Booth, and inspired deeds of valour and sacrifice in a multitude of men and women. Catherine declared, 'Christ's soldiers must be imbued with the *spirit* of war. Love to the King and concern for His interests must be the master passion of the soul . . . If the *hearts* of the Christians of this generation were inspired with this spirit and set on winning the world for God, we should soon see nations shaken to their centre, and millions of souls translated into the Kingdom . . . The soldiers of Christ must *believe in victory* . . . He knows it is only a question of time, and *time is nothing to love*."[31] At the Cannon Street Hotel Catherine gave an address entitled "The Salvation Army and its relation to the Churches", in which she expressed with clarity what Salvationists were taught. "We do not attack either organizations or individuals. It is not your business to go and find fault with other people. Rejoice in all the good done, by whomsoever it is done. Be glad whenever you find a good man or woman at work for God, and for the salvation of the people. Never try to find a hole in their coat, or pull them to pieces. Mind your own business which is seeking and saving the lost."

Having in mind the standard of living in the first fifty years of The Salvation Army, the contribution of officers and soldiers entailing deeds of individual sacrifice is almost incredible. And the persistence and pluck of the lad or lass shaking the collection box on the street corner prepared the way for the "Flag Days" of our own time. There was urgency, there was zeal, in raising funds. *"The war must go on.* Money must be found. The Booths made no secret of the sometimes desperate need. They pleaded for funds in big meetings, asked for promises and made special collections. Once £10,000 was raised at a gathering in Exeter Hall.[32] Catherine begged for money in small drawing-room meetings, wrote numberless letters setting forth the need. Often it was her own enthusiasm that touched the heart of those to whom she appealed. On her last visit to Samuel Morley not long before his death she persuaded him to double his offer of £1,000 toward rescue work for women and children. She wrote to Mr. Denny, "I feel as though I could beg from door to door and go without my necessary food to get money for that notorious hell trap the Eagle." Salvationists knew how William and Catherine felt, and while they were encouraged and taught to give what money cannot buy—sympathy and friendship toward their fellows—they were constantly admonished to exercise self-denial and to help swell the funds out of their own pockets. Converts early learned to scorn the false shame that shrank from asking for money. Enthusiasm in raising money was part of the zeal for the extension of the work itself. The burden of what Catherine called the "financial struggle" was shared by officers and soldiers alike. She made them feel that success in raising money was something to pray for, to work for and to rejoice about. Meetings, in which the results of special money-raising efforts were announced, were often hilariously exciting, young and old taking part in an atmosphere of joyful rivalry and thanksgiving when it seemed pence were as precious as pounds in the sight of heaven. Within a few days of her death Catherine reminded her Army children throughout the world of their responsibility to help the Annual Self-Denial Fund, "My dear children and friends, I have loved you much, and in God's strength have helped you a little. Now at His call I am going away from you. The war must go on. Self-denial will prove your love to Christ. All must do something. I send you my blessing. Fight on and God will be with you. Victory comes at last. I will meet you in heaven."[33]

Another aspect of Catherine's teaching must be noticed—her bold insistence that Salvationist parents should inspire their children to dedicate themselves to God for the salvation war. Speaking to friends about the Army, "We have hundreds ... all over the land with no other ambition than to train their children so that they shall be saviours of men ... These poor and untrained people, who perhaps never read a chapter in their Bibles until they were converted, are training their children, inspiring them from their very infancy with the highest ideas of moral heroism and self-sacrifice for the good of the race."[34] In almost her last public address she said that she wanted her words "to inspire every father and mother here to present their children to God ... to spread that divine love and that brotherhood of mankind that we have proclaimed all these years".[35] The influence of her preaching prevails today and a high proportion of children in Army families become preachers whether in the Army or outside. It was said at her death that, "The result of Mrs. Booth's training and example in her own home is only a striking exemplification of the effect of her ministry in the homes of thousands of the people ... many are in danger of losing sight of the extraordinary educational effect of The Salvation Army's work ... considering how strong were Mrs. Booth's views upon the training of children, and how deeply they have been impressed upon all the members of The Salvation Army, who can measure the after-result of her labours in this direction."[36]

Concluding his book *Twenty-one Years Salvation Army*, Railton, referring to temptations and difficulties to which Salvationists were exposed, wrote, "The Salvation Army has found its unfailing remedy in prayer. It has been by faithful prayer more than anything else, that each little handful, from the first onwards, has been enabled to stand ..."[37] The example and teaching of William and Catherine had much to do with the place of prayer in the lives of Salvationists. She talked freely to her "spiritual" children of her own experience, told how sometimes she must pray aloud, how she prayed pacing her room, how she made covenants with God when praying. She laid stress on the immeasurable influence exercised by parents when they prayed with son or daughter and encouraged the child to pray in the presence of father or mother.

In all she taught about prayer Catherine maintained: that man possesses an inalienable right to speak to his Maker without recourse to any intermediary.

That "God never pays any attention to people's words; it is what they mean and feel that He pays attention to".

That it is the duty and privilege of all who belong to Christ to pray for others, and in particular for and with members of their own families. A promise to do this on their return home from the meeting was often made by persons whilst they knelt at the penitent-form. Mrs. Shepherd, from Wales, became a drunkard in Poplar, was known throughout the district "to be capable of fighting on any provocation". She went to the penitent-form in the first Army meeting she attended. On reaching home and seeing her three little girls asleep "although it was eleven o'clock she insisted on their getting up at once to begin to pray."[38] Mrs. Shepherd and her daughters eventually became officers. Many families were won to Christ as a result of prayer made by converts in their own homes. To lead family prayers, however brief, was imperative for salvation soldiers.

That prayer should be made in private and public for the unsaved. Prayer times dubbed "knee drill" were organized at every Army centre. Children prayed in children's meetings. There were early morning prayer meetings, mid-day prayer meetings, half-nights and all-nights of prayer. In Sunday evening meetings "praying bands" mustered near the penitent-form to "pray souls into the Kingdom". Sometimes a "prayer ring" was formed about a hesitating sinner. The prayers of his former companions often proved more powerful to help than was the Captain's preaching earlier in the service. Notorious sinners were prayed for by name and sometimes the potency of these petitions was feared by the subject of them, who came storming to the hall, swearing and threatening to invoke the help of the police if the praying did not stop. Soldiers were expected to be ready to pray aloud whenever called upon to do so. Prayer was made by Salvationists, often kneeling, in back streets and alleys for people in the locality.

That prayer can be made in any place and in everyday language. William Booth spoke of the open air as the Army's cathedral. Certainly thousands were converted kneeling in the dust (or mud) at the drumhead in street meetings.

That Jesus Christ's words about sparrows and hairs and His command that men should pray for "daily bread" must mean that man's communion with God was concerned with the whole of life, with things temporal and spiritual.

That man's consciousness of the mystery of prayer does not detract from its efficacy. Catherine Booth taught her Army children that about everything, everywhere, as Christ commanded, "men ought always to pray".

4

Catherine was now at the height of her influence. Begbie said of her this "beautiful spirit impressed itself alike upon the most exacting of her intellectual contemporaries and upon vast masses of the poor . . . the growth of her spiritual powers seems to me like one of the miracles of religious history. In her frail body the spirit of womanhood manifested its power and the Spirit of God its beauty. It is a tribute to the age in which she lived that this power and beauty were acknowledged by the world during her lifetime. She exercised a spell over many nations."[39] In spite of persecution the salvation soldiery grew by tens of thousands. Everywhere among them affectionate reverence prepared the way for the Army Mother's words. Always her messages called forth a breathless attention. Katie had gone to Paris in February. At Easter that year there was a new development. Exeter Hall,* a fine spacious place, was engaged for holiness meetings all day on the Bank Holiday Monday. Admission was by ticket. Criticism of the Army's teaching, of holiness in particular, was vocal on all sides at this time. Rowdyism in the provinces and in the East End continued. Catherine wrote to Mrs. Billups, "We have now 4,000 tickets out, and they are being sent for from Scotland, Ireland, Spain, and France. We shall have an overflow meeting in the small hall and are hoping for a wonderful day. Satan has done his best to upset it by every possible means . . . The authorities charge £50 for the day! The devil thought we should be frightened at that, but he is mistaken. Think of it! We shall have five thousand people to a holiness meeting in Exeter Hall! That speaks for itself. Pray for much of the Holy Ghost."[40]

* Bramwell Booth writes in his book *These Fifty Years*, "When we first applied for the use of Exeter Hall of which the London Y.M.C.A. had lately come into possession, it was refused. Various reasons were given; fear of damage from riot, fear of injury to the Y.M.C.A. reputation from any connexion with The Salvation Army, doubts as to the 'teaching' we should advance . . . We fell back on the trustees of whom Morley was one. I met him at the hall with Mr. Hind Smith . . . he concluded that the hall might be let to us. His attitude that day settled for good and all the question of future lettings . . . The opening to us of the doors of Exeter Hall—which was not only an auditorium but a symbol—opened the doors of many public buildings throughout the country which had hitherto been closed."

The great hall was filled three times, and at night crowds unable to get in were turned away. Officers came straight from scenes of violence, a lassie Captain hobbling from a sprained ankle who had been "knocked down and trampled on"; a young lad Captain who had his wrist broken in one riot and a "piece bitten out of his arm" in another. Cornets led the singing and were considered helpful. One report says, "'Bayonets' in the middle of a song of praise to God might sound strange, and yet, behold in a moment, the exact effect of 'fixed bayonets'* is produced as the thousands raise their hands high above their heads." Hundreds yielded full consecration to God during the day. The meetings were such a success that another "Day" was announced for 27 May. The crowds were still greater. Mrs. Booth "combined straight truth with a beseeching tenderness". A third holiness "all Day" was held on September 19. Thousands of tickets applied for had to be refused for lack of space. The lower hall was used as an overflow, but still thousands were turned away; many offered high sums for reserved seat tickets.

The meetings proved something of a sensation. Catherine Booth's speeches were discussed in the daily press. "Although I did not say what the *Chronicle* imputed to me, as our report in '*The War Cry* shows, what I did say has done good . . . Everybody knows it is true, and to find anyone who dare speak the truth in these days is striking to the infidels! . . . You will have heard that even the *Telegraph* is coming round, and there were two pieces in *The Times* yesterday! Wait a bit and we will astonish the world, in the strength of the God of Israel. Pray for us. Our poor weak bodies are the great drawback."[41]

What Catherine said, to which objection was taken, seems to me plain and practical, Scriptural too! "We believe in a living God! We have done with a *dead* God . . . I say we believe in this living God . . . He wants to be in fellowship with us . . . God created all the intelligences of the universe to be fellow spirits with Himself, to commune with Him, to walk and talk with Him . . . Oh, what monstrosities we have taught to us in these days! And one is that we have no right to expect this living God to speak to us! and that we have no right to speak to Him, or at least no right to expect answers when we do! There is a mongrel system of Christianity abroad. I wish they would not call it Christianity, call it anything else; but for Christ's sake, don't talk of Christianity that shuts me out from personal intercourse with a living personal God! What better am I for a God who cannot speak to me? . . . What better am I for a 'conquering Saviour' if He cannot deliver *me* in the intricacies of my individual life

* The term "fix bayonets" became a commonplace of Salvation Army nomenclature. The gesture, raising the right arm above the head, in witness emphasized the theme of a chorus or refrain of congregational singing.

and experience? Away with such a notion! He is a 'Horn of Salvation' not only for David, and Elizabeth, and Mary, but for *ME*, and for my husband, and for my children, and for each one of us. He *is* a living God. He speaks living words to living souls ... *He will speak to us*, and we shall *consciously speak to Him*. Why not? Tell me, why not? Whence comes this lifeless, voiceless system of divinity? Give me Scripture for it, give me reason, philosophy if you can! I defy you! It is a solar system without a sun! A mouth without a voice! A socket without an eye! A body without a soul! That is the sort of God they offer us in these days. *That is not the God of The Salvation Army!* We have the God Who made man's ear, and shall He not hear? The God who created man's mouth, and shall He not speak? The God who launched those starry worlds into space, is He not able to direct and over-rule, and lead and deliver a poor little mortal like me? Why is it that *all* do not hold this living fellowship? What hinders? ... What hinders you in London, on a foggy morning, from seeing the sun? You say, the fog! To be sure the fog. It is not because there is no sun, but because there is a fog! What hinders you from seeing and hearing God? Your sins and your iniquities ... Your souls will rise spontaneously, as the rivers seek the sea, *to God*, when sin is out of the way."[42] This day's meetings were followed by an all-night of prayer at the old Mission Hall in Whitechapel, but Mrs. Booth was not present.

The Salvation Army was now thrusting far into "enemy country", although it was but seventeen years since William Booth began preaching in Whitechapel and only four since its Deed of Constitution. Important bases were established in 1882. The flag was raised in India, Sweden, Canada and Switzerland. It had been flying in Australia since January 1881. In London three large properties were converted to the Army's use. A skating rink in Oxford Street (Regent Hall); the Grecian Theatre with Eagle Tavern attached in City Road; and third the London Orphanage, Clapton, which provided premises for training men and women cadets. Roofing the quadrangle made an oblong amphitheatre with seating for 6,000 to be known as the Congress Hall. Corps numbering 251 at the beginning of the year had risen to 442 at its close. Officers, including 164 cadets in the new Training Home, numbered 1,067. A year earlier Headquarters had moved from Whitechapel to 101 Queen Victoria Street, where bold letters across the front proclaimed *The Salvation Army International Headquarters*. The devil counter-attacked by fiercer rioting and much smashing of doors and windows in Army Halls.

For some time Catherine had wanted to see her eldest son married. Bramwell, in her view, needed the understanding companionship that only a wife could give. In her natural, forthright manner, she told what was in her thoughts. To Bramwell she had written, "You want a wife, *one* with you in soul, with whom you

370

could commune and in whom you could find companionship and solace . . . God will find you one, and I shall help Him."[43] It was a joy to her son that his choice of Florence Soper had the full approval of both his parents. Bramwell wrote, "Dearest Mother, I feel quite sure that this matter is all the Lord's arranging . . ."[44] But Florence Soper's father was without the happy assurance that to give his daughter to Bramwell Booth of The Salvation Army was "the Lord's arranging"! He raised vehement objections, and insisted upon delay. His attitude was a fair example of the feeling in many quarters and especially among churchmen toward The Salvation Army. In February 1882, Catherine entered the lists for the young people. Her letter to Dr. Soper is long and reasoned. He found it hard to answer. Here is part of what she wrote: "Dear Dr. Soper, I have purposed writing you ever since my son's first visit . . . my dear sir, as the Providence of God has settled it beyond our will and control that we *must* come in contact, at any rate through those we both love . . . will it not be the wisest . . . and happiest course for yourself to face the facts and act accordingly? Is it of any avail to fight against what God has ordered?

"Perhaps you will say what right have you to assume that this matter is of God? First, I believe this to be of God because for years I have prayed in faith that God would save my boy from being influenced in such a choice by any secondary consideration . . . and that He would prepare and send the right person at the right time . . . Now I know that this is no boyish fancy, but the supreme choice of his soul, and I know further that what attracted him in the *first instance* was dear Florrie's devotion to God and His Kingdom.

"Secondly, I judge this matter to be of God because He has evidently *prepared* her for the important position she must occupy in the future, uniting in her, capacity, simplicity and devotion . . .

"Thirdly, I judge this because of the mutual affection begotten in their hearts simultaneously and spontaneously. I believe real holy love to be one of God's choicest gifts, and I would rather one of my daughters should marry a man with only a brain and five fingers with *this*, than a man with £10,000 per year without . . . Believing that both our dear ones have conceived this love for each other, ought we not, as desiring their highest happiness, to embrace it and try to make them as happy as God intends them to be? Will not even the happiest life have enough of trial and sorrow without our embittering the morning with clouds and tears?"[45] This letter and visits from Bramwell and Katie won the doctor's consent to his daughter's marriage after her twenty-first birthday.

The friendship between Katie (the Maréchale as Bramwell had dubbed her) and her Lieutenant had given Florence the place of a daughter in the Booth home before her engagement to Bramwell. Now that it was settled Catherine took her altogether under her wing, and presently set about furnishing the little home near the house on Clapton Common to which the Booths had lately moved. How far it was necessary, for the sake of the Army, that the mirrors should be taken out from the wardrobes destined for Bramwell's home, as being too ostentatious, is hardly for us to judge, nor does it matter, since the Army Mother believed that it was! She passionately desired to set up and maintain a standard of simplicity for Salvationists. Crowds of them, since conversion, were coming into a better way of life materially, and temptation to display and extravagance in their homes and dress was a real obstacle to progress in the way of holiness and self-denial. William Booth's instructions on this point to soldiers and officers alike are clear and definite. I quote from *Orders and Regulations for Soldiers*: "The spirit of unworldliness, which is the spirit of The Salvation Army, should reign in every home ... All who come inside its doors should see that Salvationists live there."[46]

Florence owned that she thought some of Mrs. Booth's prohibitions rather hard, but there could be no doubt that "Mama" felt them to be important. "Mama" was always right, or so the family felt, and Florence was in the family now, and besides, she herself loved her mother-in-law devotedly. Everything to do with the home and the children God gave to it was ordered as nearly as possible as Bramwell's mother desired. Catherine's condemnation of showy things was balanced by her dislike of anything shoddy. One of her dicta was that "good things are always more economical". In spite of the rush in which she lived, she was at trouble to search out bargains and she felt a prideful happiness in a many-leaved mahogany table with rounded ends—telling Florence "no corners for the babies to knock their heads on"—which she bought very cheaply. It had been made to order for a customer who had not approved of it. Round that same table Bramwell's family still gathers. The saving on the table went toward the expense, insisted upon by Catherine, of a bed made to special measurements. It was long enough for Bramwell "to stretch in" and was fitted with separate springs and mattresses to grant the sleepers the minimum disturbance from collateral restlessness. The monster, six feet six inches in length and six feet wide, took up a substantial part of the front bedroom, but proved worth its houseroom in comfort.

The wedding was celebrated at the lately opened Congress Hall. *The Daily Chronicle* of the day reported, "To General Booth is due the initiative in showing that even a marriage can be made profitable to the cause of religion. Excepting officers, nearly 6,000 persons, who filled the Congress Hall yesterday on the occasion of the marriage celebration, paid for admission, at the rate of a shilling a head. The funds so raised, together with the offertory, are destined to help in the liquidation of the balance of £8,000 that still remains unsettled in connection with the purchase for salvation purposes of the Grecian Theatre and Eagle Tavern in the City Road."[47] William and

Catherine's idea, in making a public event of the wedding, was that it should be a *blessing* to the people; it was their way to turn everything to account.

The bride and bridegroom spoke, so did Katie. Catherine's love for her son, and the love between her and her "Army" children gave her words a validity, a sense of authority, that can hardly be understood or even imagined by those who know nothing of the strange, half mystical, half human bond existing between Salvationists and the Army's founders. It was a relationship unmatched before in religious history. The Booths "belonged" to Salvationists everywhere. People from distant places sometimes burst into tears when they first set eyes on William or Bramwell. We find Emanuel Hellberg, one of the early Army officers in Sweden, referring to "my precious General", when he wrote to William Booth who had, at that time, only visited Sweden once, and then as a complete stranger to young Hellberg.

On her son's wedding day, Catherine, happy herself, spoke with affectionate freedom. It was a family occasion in which her Army children shared. Said an old officer to me, "You only needed to see the General hand Mrs. Booth to her seat when they came on to the platform together, to recognize how he adored her. That was so good for our rough people, especially the young ones." And this was even more than usually evident as William took Catherine's hand and led her forward to speak. They stood together for a moment, smiling at each other, and then William said it reminded him of their own wedding day, and asked, "You are as fond of me as ever, are you not?" Catherine replied to the delighted crowd, "Well, I can say this much, that the highest happiness I can wish to my beloved children is that they may realize as thorough a union in heart and mind, and as much blessing in their married life, as the Lord has vouchsafed to us in ours." And she went on to say, "I covet for them that, where I have been the mother of hundreds of spiritual children, she may be the mother of thousands, and I covet for my son that, whereas the Lord has blessed his father to the salvation of thousands, He may bless him to tens of thousands! I gave him when he was born to the Lord. If you want to know how to get your children saved and to make the God of Abraham, Isaac and Jacob the God of your *families,* I can only recommend the way that has succeeded with mine ... I covenanted that I would, as far as my light and ability went, train my son for God alone; that I would ignore this world's prizes and this world's praises, and this world's glory and that he should be, as far as I could make him, *a man of God.* And, what is remarkable, I consecrated him to God for a *holiness preacher.* We called him William Bramwell, after the most distinguished man of holiness we knew ... I set him in my heart to be a teacher of this glorious doctrine and experience. And you see how God has honoured my choice. *I* could not have made him this; I could only give him to God for it, and do my best to train him." Catherine then appealed to parents. "The principle of successful training is that you acknowledge God's entire ownership of your children ... He says choose My Kingdom first. Give them wholly and solely to Me, and train them for Me, and leave Me to choose their inheritance ... and I will give you the power of My Spirit and you shall have 'every hoof of them'. I have every hoof of mine, for God and this glorious work ... May God help us as Salvation Army soldiers thus to consecrate every power of body and soul, and all the *precious children* He has given us, to this great war and then He will multiply us a hundred fold. He will give us thousands of such children who will begin to chant our songs as soon as they can lisp, and who, from very infancy, will learn to love the good with all their heart and who will grow up to be valiant soldiers of the Army, and carry salvation to the ends of the earth ... I cannot say that I feel that I am gaining a daughter today, for this dear one is my own spiritual child, and has been from the first so united with us in spirit that I realize the earthly relationship is only secondary to the heavenly. May this marriage propagate salvation through all its generations. Amen."[48]

5

A few days after Bramwell's wedding the Army Mother went to Paris for the opening of a new and larger hall. There were afternoon meetings in "salons". Of these she said, "I tried to scrape together all my patience to meet and answer the old time-worn objections to our measures ... to a respectable audience of Christians."[49] Katie recounted, "My mother defended the Army measures and explained our work in such a manner as to remove a great deal of prejudice and misunderstanding."[50] Mrs. Booth visited a number of friends, in particular Pastor Theodore Monod, who was like a brother to Salvationists throughout the period of opposition and until his death. He translated in the meetings for her. She found the method "extremely trying". But she was listened to with rapt attention, and there were fourteen at the penitent-form in the new hall on Sunday night. At her meetings in the old hall, attention was decidedly not rapt! In her own words to Mrs. Billups, "I would have given a trifle for you to have been with us yesterday ... at night, in the midst of an excited audience, who grinned and groaned and hooted so that anybody but Salvation Army soldiers would have given in and been beaten. We had a splendid congregation, however, of just *our sort*, mostly men, many of them young, full of the 'blood and fire' of hell ... The uproar was terrible, but, just at the worst, the Maréchale [Katie] advanced into the middle of the hall and, standing right in the midst of them, she mounted a form and pleaded like an apostle. Oh, it was a sublime sight, worth coming from England to see! There were a few desperados, ringleaders who said awful things. One, with a face full of the devil, hissed in rage inconceivable; baring his arm and holding it aloft as he shrieked, 'We will hear you if you will talk to us about anything else but God, but we hate *Him*: *we will not have Him*. I wish I had Him here. I would pour a pail of cabbage water over His head!' When we put our French converts up [i.e. to testify] they shouted 'Ah, paid to figure there!' Nevertheless we got some truth into them between the outbursts, and sang it into them too. It was a veritable meeting of the hosts of hell and heaven, and I feel sure that some rays of light entered into many a poor darkened soul ... I consider that we won the victory with the majority of our audience, and shall get scores of them for salvation soldiers yet! ... As the meeting dispersed, however, some few spiteful ones handled him [Clibborn*] very roughly, giving him two or three blows in the face ... Also two or three of our French soldiers, Emile, Carlo, Hodler, and a railway porter, were badly wounded ... not one of them flinched or ran, and it was a trying ordeal for French blood not to strike back." Catherine must have been smiling as she scribbled on, "I thought how I would have liked those Christians who were at the afternoon meeting to have been there, especially one good pastor who had been talking to us about reading more Bible in our meetings! I should have liked to see him try! They would have torn his Bible to ribbons, and perhaps him too! So little do these people understand the things they talk about ... We go again tonight ... pray for us. I never saw so deeply into the enmity of the human heart against God as last night."[51]

Of her sally into the middle of the hall, Katie recounted, "I felt particularly calm. I knew that my mother and a little group of officers on the platform were praying for me ... for some minutes there was a lull, though we could hear the mob thundering outside the gates ... It was almost as bad inside as out. Some of the men cleared away the seats in order to have a wild *can-can* dance ... How we got home I can scarcely tell. It was a terrible time. They flourished their knives in our faces ... They followed us with cries of 'There is Jesus Christ! It is He! It is He!' My mother was deeply moved." Katie said her mother's visit was "like that of an angel, and inspired me with fresh courage and determination in our difficulties".[52] Sinners did not repel Catherine. With that steadfast gaze of hers she looked into the faces distorted with rage and scorn and received a new vision of "the enmity of the human heart against God". But she did not doubt God's power

* Arthur Sydney Clibborn, member of the Society of Friends. Became Salvation Army officer, married Catherine Booth's eldest daughter Katie.

to cast evil out and to remake the worst of men in His likeness. She returned home from Paris, heart pent up with a new intensity of desire to make Christ known, her love endowed with clearer insight went out afresh to all mankind.

On November 28, 1882, Exeter Hall was nearly full before eleven in the morning, and crowded afternoon and night for the dedication of 101* officers for home and foreign fields. The morning was mainly taken up with Catherine's address on *Our responsibility for letting the world know about salvation.* When she stood up to speak the congregation gave "volley after volley",† and volleys more than once broke in upon her words. "The Salvation Army is of God's making," she declared. " . . . We bless God that He makes us realize that we are led by Him . . . No one in this hall feels more—no little child, no weak-kneed, trembling believer—realizes more fully than the General and I do, that without *Him,* this work would go to pieces. We believe it to be God's doing from beginning to end. We dare not for a moment take the credit to ourselves of having made this Movement . . . He found us suitable instruments to His hand, in the sense of being ready . . . and, if He had not found us, He would have found somebody else . . . This Salvation Army did not spring out of the brain, or even the heart of one man, God simply used that brain and heart to bring into operation *His idea* . . . to raise a people out of those who were not a people . . . He has inspired The Salvation Army and kept it going, and is going to send it all over the world! . . . And if this Movement is not enough to compass His ends I hope He will go on making new ones! *I want the world to be saved.* I don't care how it is done. My heart is set on the Kingdom and I don't care how it is propagated . . ." Then with rising power she spoke of the wicked, of those she had seen with her own eyes; the ignorant, debased and ruined. "How are they to know God? There is but one way and that is for those who *do* know Him to go and . . . reveal Him to them by God's Spirit, taking His message and thrusting it upon their attention. Because *they do not want God* . . . we Salvation Army people are called to the rescue and salvation of those outlying multitudes, millions of whom every other instrumentality has confessedly failed to touch. *We must go out and save them.* We must not stand arguing and parleying as to whether we ought to go, or what it will cost us, or what we shall suffer . . . You need no other argument than that the whole generation if rushing down to hell and God has empowered you to do something towards stopping them. *That* is the argument, surely you can need no other?"

Presently she said, "I see my time has gone." From all over the

* This number must have been linked with the I.H.Q. address—101 Queen Victoria Street—but I can find no evidence to support this idea.

† "Fire a volley", The Salvation Army term for "Cheers".

building came loud cries of, "Go on. Go on." And she did. Concluding "... I am so tired of hearing the words 'I can't' ... Mark me, God does not call me to do what I can in my own strength, but He calls me to do what *He has commanded in His strength.* Will you think of that next time you are tempted to say 'I can't' ... Oh, friends, have you ever really and fully placed yourselves at the divine disposal and said 'Lord, I am quite willing to be a fool' ...? Have you ever said 'I don't care what Mr. So-and-So says, or what Mrs. So-and-So, smirking in the next pew, thinks. Lord, floor me to the bottom of the pew; *only fill me!*' Did you ever come to that? No! You are too proud ... when you come to *that* the Lord will use you."[53]

The climax of the day came in the evening meeting when at the call of the General each detachment advanced to the front of the platform to the strains of:

> *We're marching on to war,*
> *We are, we are, we are,*
> *We care not what the people say*
> *Nor what they think we are.*
> *We mean to fight for Jesus*
> *And His salvation bring,*
> *We're Hallelujah soldiers*
> *And we're fighting for the King.*

Representatives spoke from each group. Captain George Arthur Pollard farewelled to "open" New Zealand. Bramwell presented his own convert to the Army, Miss Hannah Ouchterlony, with Sweden's first Salvation Army flag. Both these pioneers were to become Commissioners in the Army. Hannah Ouchterlony was the first woman to reach that rank. The Army Mother gave colours to the Indian party and to Major Rose Clapham* and her assistants who were to establish the work in South Africa. "... I give you this flag," said Catherine, "to carry to a land where we have not yet been. My comrades, my children, my beloved in the Lord—this *flag represents war.* It means fighting *with all evil* ... Preach repentance towards God and faith in the Lord Jesus Christ, that the people may receive forgiveness of sins ... May God help you and give you great and lasting victory through Jesus Christ our Lord." The exuberant volleys of the day had died away. A hush was over all as the Army Mother made the last appeal. She spoke of the dedication of the hundred and one young officers, "... You have heard the testimonies of God's little ones, and if they can do such great things through the Lord, how much could such intellectual, and cultivated and learned people as

* As Captain she started the Army in Darlington where Stead received his first impression of the work.

377

some of you are do, if you were to put your shoulders to the wheel with equal devotion, self-sacrifice and zeal. My friends, will you begin? Oh, we want to be done with a mere selfish religion, a religion of saving our own souls, which is very good as a first step; but we want . . . a determined consecration for the salvation of the world . . . this is what God demands of us all . . . These 101 . . . are going, many of them, to be kicked and cuffed, and hustled, and perhaps put in prison, and they know it. They are going to face stones and oyster shells, rotten eggs and cabbage stumps. They are going to struggle with lapsed and fallen populations who care nothing either for God or man, who neither respect themselves nor anybody else . . . They go . . . to take hold of them in love and pity, to weep the Gospel of Christ into them . . . and to *make everybody face God and salvation* . . ."[54] When her voice ceased, one by one men and women in all parts of the hall stood to their feet in token of a fresh dedication to seek the salvation of their fellows, whether at home or abroad, and after singing *"All hail the power of Jesus Name"* the "101" and the thousands that made up the congregation dispersed into the cold November night. One more day at Exeter Hall was over.

Often now after the exaltation of the meetings Catherine was swept by anxiety. In Paris Katie "pleading like an apostle" with a crowd of cut-throats "was a sublime sight worth coming from England to see" but at home in the wakeful nights, that for her now always followed the extreme exertion of preaching, her heart sank. In these last years of her life fears for those she loved brought a new test of faith. They were all given to God, could she still trust them to Him, now that she saw what was entailed? She had rejoiced when her children had dedicated themselves to the Army but she had not contemplated their living at such high pressure. The flying pen catches for Mrs. Billups, and for us, her mood as she thinks about Katie, "My soul shall not draw back; though He slay me, and her too, yet will I trust Him." She will not draw back. But the excess of effort that devotion to the Army generates will, she fears, in the end destroy them all. For the beloved William it was the hardest to be calm and trustful. Up to the time when she knew that her course was run, she had not grown accustomed, or should I say hardened, to seeing him exhaust his strength. And now the children were working at the same headlong speed. The frantic stress of their lives was an affront to her reason. What Bramwell called "the ingrained feeling that whatever happens the work must be done" seemed to her to denote a lack of balance, anyway of common sense. And was it really God's will? I came on a sentence in a letter from her mother to Katie shortly before she went to France, "It rejoices my heart to see the blessed results . . . but I suffer a crucifixion every time to see the blood and sweat it costs those dear to me. Of course Pa and Bramwell are simply exhausted, and some of these times the last feather will break their

378

backs. I don't think God requires *life* as a sacrifice?"[55] And in the same strain to Emma, "I suppose we must go on to the end, always living at the utmost tension of every power."[56]

Her refuge is prayer. She renews her covenants to God. Is not this ever Love's response to the Beloved whether human or Divine? To speak *again* the old vows? And love to God is still Catherine's master passion. She will take back nothing that she has dedicated to Him. In age as in youth she will *"trust Him for all"*. Trust Him for these her beloveds, whom she loves with far deeper yearning than when they were infants. She knows now how much harder it is to trust God for the objects of one's love as they travel a path of suffering and sacrifice, than to suffer and sacrifice one's self, *how much harder.* Now that she knows so much of men's sins and sorrows, it is more than ever true that Catherine Booth is a lover of mankind, but that does not dilute her love for individuals, and she is still the Mother of The Salvation Army concerned with the needs of her "Army" children, young officers especially. She takes pains to understand their side of circumstances and feels a mother's responsibility for them: as for example in writing to Bramwell as Chief of the Staff. Her letter makes it plain that she disapproved the manner in which a lassie officer had been dealt with by her immediate superior. "Tell him I think he is hard upon her ... if she loves the man, and she does, it was no joke to let her go for twelve months without seeing him. I do not say it was *wise* or expedient for her to go *to him,* but after all it was only human and *not wicked* ... Deal gently with her ... We must *deal with children as children,* and the mass of the people are only children, *morally and intellectually,* swayed any way by their *interests and their feelings.*"[57]

6

The Salvation Army's war of aggression against the devil and his works has pressed on with tremendous energy, and simultaneously the Army must be on the defensive. Catherine is still defender-in-chief. She must refute misrepresentations by publicans, by the press, and by the churches, not once but over and over again. She must, as she put it, "scrape together all my patience" to answer the old objections in Paris; she summoned a more fiery virtue for London! There was "lightning" if not thunder in her addresses* at the Cannon Street Hotel in that city. Her words were vibrant with the mingled pride

* Published under the title *The Salvation Army in relation to Church and State.*

and indignation that possessed her. Salvationists may well find her words a plumb-line for testing their works today.

Curious how similar the devil's tactics proved. Rowdyism in the East End of London spread strangely far to Calcutta, to Uppsala, to obscure Swiss towns. "Curiouser and curiouser" that authority in these far separated places yet conformed to condemn the praying Salvationists and *not* their assailants! From France to Switzerland was not a far cry, even in those days. In December 1882 the Maiden Maréchale, judging her forces well engaged in France, led a handful across the border. They did not attempt the sensational methods used elsewhere, which, some have averred, were the original cause of disturbances. In Switzerland there were no processions down the streets, no flaring posters on the walls. Everything that might be misunderstood or cause irritation was avoided. But to no purpose. Hooligansim broke out, meeting-places were besieged, broken open, and literally pillaged. The authorities sided with the mob; closed halls, forbade the meetings, and expelled the officers. New decrees were hastily issued. In their anxiety to get rid of The Salvation Army, the authorities violated the provisions of the Swiss Constitution by forbidding Salvationists to sing and pray *in their own homes*! Driven from one Canton, the Maréchale and her few helpers went to another. Several times she was conveyed across the frontier back into France. In spite of this opposition by the Government, friends and converts opened their houses for meetings, and risked having them smashed up and themselves arrested. Captain Kate Patrick, "in charge" of Neuchâtel Corps, describes what happened at a private meeting: "On Wednesday evening the house of one of our friends was besieged by a handful of roughs, who hurled against it a torrent of stones, even tearing up the pavement to furnish missiles."[58] The police ignored the whole operation! Gatherings continued to be held in kitchens and parlours; souls were saved. "Born in the firing line" had already become a description for converts won in the midst of persecution. Many Swiss were of this company.

Appeals to the Federal Swiss and British Governments had so far failed; and for a time it seemed that the "Army" in Switzerland was to be smothered at birth. Catherine shared in all the anxious consultations at International Headquarters, and in the still more vehement examination of pros and cons round the supper-table at home. She or William would be one of those who prayed when they fell on their knees before Bramwell left for his home nearby. Railton was still living with the Booths, so that in fact their discussions were a continuation of talks at Headquarters. It must now be decided whether Katie should be advised to return to France and stay there. Would not that be tantamount to ordering retreat? So far as I can discover no one had the temerity to hint at such a course! No. Let there be the wisdom of serpents, but let the harmless doves remain. And further, there were converts to be considered. Many remarkable cases of conversion had occurred. Life-long drunkards and wild young people had been changed into practising Christians full of the joy of the Lord. These could not be deserted.

In the opinion of some in Switzerland the persecution of The Salvation Army had become "a plain question of religious liberty of the elementary kind".[59] The only logical step, the Booths felt, was to challenge the illegal orders. And since appeals to authority brought no redress, how better set about it than by deliberately infringing these hastily conceived enactments? Lawyers were consulted, plans made that would compel judicial action. For although halls had been closed and officers expelled by the police, neither Katie nor any Salvationist in Switzerland had yet been brought before a tribunal on any charge. A number of Swiss friends and converts were found ready to suffer the consequences. The Booths, and especially the indomitable Maréchale Katie, thought that Swiss comrades must not be the only ones to suffer. She herself would lead the band of law-breakers. All was arranged so as to give the least possible pretext for action by the authorities. Invitations to a special meeting were issued privately. There was no public announcement. The gathering was held in woods five miles from Neuchâtel. "The Prefect of Police, with the Chief of the Gendarmerie and fifteen gendarmes" turned up but did not interfere with the progress of the meeting which lasted from 2 to 6 p.m. Among the converts testifying some appealed to the police as witnesses of the change of heart they had experienced. When Katie prayed, the police "stood with heads uncovered and faces bent . . . she prayed for the Prefect of Police* asking for him blessings, temporal and spiritual, with such sincerity and simplicity that he wept. She prayed also for the Government and nation of Switzerland."[60] The Prefect—he had never attended an Army meeting before—owned that he had been misled about The Salvation Army, but—yes—the praying and singing were good; nevertheless—, politely but firmly he declared, at the meeting's close, that it was his hard duty to arrest Miss Booth and Captain Becquet.

The Maréchale was allowed bail in order to conduct the funeral

---

* In 1883 *Punch* published a set of doggerel verse entitled "The march of the Salvationists" which included these lines about Katie:

> *"Hey for our Catherine, blushing so feminine,*
> *Rousing the Swiss to conviction of sin;*
> *Out on their 'beak' who, the tide of grace stemmin', in-*
> *Sisted on brutally running her in!*
>
> *List to dear Catherine's fervent beseeching,*
> *Even for prefects, policemen, and all;*
> *Poor old St. Paul rated women for preaching,*
> *Catherine knows rather more than St. Paul."*

of a convert in Geneva. About 300 Salvationists and friends, some from France and Italy, gathered at the dead boy's home a mile outside Geneva. Mrs. Josephine Butler was there and described the scene in her book *The Salvation Army in Switzerland*. "A circle was formed in front of the house of M. Wyssa, in the bright sunshine. The coffin was placed in the centre of the group, the father, mother, sisters and brothers of the deceased being gathered round it. The Salvation Army flag was spread upon the coffin surmounted by a branch of palm."[61] During the simple service the "Mayor of the Commune appeared at the outer edge of the circle. He declared that this was a 'reunion' of The Salvation Army, and pronounced it to be dissolved, ordering us to disperse ... Colonel Clibborn explained, 'We are about to bury a friend,' to which the Mayor replied, in tones which must have grated harshly on the ears of the weeping mother, 'Bury him then.' ... The Mayor withdrew, saying as he left that he would bring armed force unless the singing was discontinued ... The service over we moved on in a line very quietly from the house to the cemetery along the open high road ... Before reaching the gate of the cemetery a police officer ran to meet us and when we entered the Mayor again appeared, and stood during the proceedings opposite to Miss Booth and her group of friends at the other side of the open grave. The coffin was lowered, while all stood around in perfect silence. Miss Booth then spoke on the beautiful words from Revelation, 'Who are these which are arrayed in white robes, and whence came they?' John Wyssa, the younger brother of Charles, then came forward to the edge of the open grave, and in a loud voice, trembling with emotion said, 'I give Charles's dying message to all his fellow workmen, *that they choose the better part*, and meet him in heaven. It was through his prayers that I was won to choose that better part' ... It was just at that moment ... that the Mayor with his Marshal approached and arrested Miss Booth and Miss Charlesworth,* there in the presence of the dead."[62] They were conducted to the carriage in which they had come, and driven to the Hôtel de Ville where they were questioned at length. Finally they were conveyed to the frontier under escort.

Mrs. Butler went with her when Katie surrendered to her bail in Neuchâtel. Because of Katie's delicate health Captain Kate Patrick, though not charged, was allowed to share her imprisonment. The three were led to the cell which, Mrs. Butler tells us, contained two iron beds with straw mattresses, a couple of wooden chairs and a table. The walls and furniture, she noticed, were filthy but as a great favour the jailer told that he had provided clean straw to stuff pillows and mattresses. The cell was fourteen by seven feet and there were

*Maud Charlesworth, daughter of Rev. Samuel Charlesworth, later married Ballington Booth.

two minute barred windows high up in one wall. If she stood on a chair, Katie could look up and see the sky. For a moment they stood in silence, looking round, then Mrs. Butler recounts "... 'let us pray', suddenly said Miss Booth. We all kneeled down." In a letter she wrote to Mrs. Butler from prison Katie said, "It was the Lord Jesus Who prompted you to write as you did. It was such a comfort ... Yesterday I was in great sadness ... All at once I heard singing. It was our people! The singing sounded glorious in the silent night and the burden fell from my heart as I listened ... Your sympathy and help and above all your mother's heart toward me are a great consolation ... Pray for me during the trial. God will teach me what to speak."[63] The night after the Salvationists had stood singing on the terrace below the prison, roughs gathered there shouting threats and curses. It went on for hours. The sound was so hideously ferocious that it gave Katie a trembling fit. But the police did not interfere, and no names were taken.

The Army in the homeland was kept informed by *The War Cry*, under bold headlines, *Maréchal Booth in Neuchâtel Prison*. Katie telegraphed: "No need for anxiety about me; Jesus here."

Exeter Hall was crowded at a few days' notice for prayer for Salvationists in Switzerland and in particular for those in prison. The Army Mother sent a message; she could not be present, having meetings in the North. "My prayers will ascend with yours on behalf of my precious child and for Switzerland." William spoke briefly because most of the time was to be spent in prayer. "People ask why The Salvation Army is in Switzerland? Because [the words] 'Go ye into all the world and preach the Gospel' ... are the marching orders of The Salvation Army." Mr. T. A. Denny, just returned from Switzerland, recounted interviews with leading Christian men in Geneva, "They want to see what our Foreign Office is going to do." At this point he is interrupted by cheers. Mrs. Josephine Butler rose to cheers. She described the legal position and her feelings when she saw Katie arrested at Wyssa's grave side ... "As for dear Miss Booth she is full of peace, joy and love for souls."[64] Katie spent twelve days in Neuchâtel prison, awaiting trial.

Catherine wrote to Mr. Gladstone, then Prime Minister. "Sir, Allow me to intrude on your valuable time for a moment in order to call your attention to the perils of my daughter, Miss Booth, and her companions in Switzerland, which may not have been fully presented to you. Six months ago, after this illegal and groundless persecution commenced, Earl Granville* promised my husband that he would interfere, but although we have made two or three applications to his Lordship through parliamentary friends since then, so

* Earl Granville (1815-1891), M.P. for Morpeth, Foreign Secretary at time of Swiss imprisonment of Katie.

far as we can see *nothing has been done!*" She referred to her daughter's delicate state of health and "fearing that even a short imprisonment would cause a serious illness . . . I beg, with a mother's importunity, your timely interference . . ."[65]

"Nothing done." Exclamation mark and under-scoring but feebly indicate the fury Catherine felt at this supineness. Meanwhile, she is comforted, as so often before she has been, by attending to details in her practical way. Thus she has at least the illusion that *something* is getting "done". To Katie, "My precious Child, words cannot convey what I have suffered about you during the last twenty-four hours, only hearing that you were in prison and not knowing whether anyone was with you, or how you were being treated. This is a test of one's consecration certainly; still I can say my soul does not draw back, and *I know yours* does not . . . Be sure to insist on having comfortable food and *bedding* . . . Even if your imprisonment was legal you have a right to be treated as a State prisoner *before trial.* Take care you insist on your right, and don't suffer unnecessarily, because of *your health* . . . There are times when it is as needful to claim our rights as it is at others to sacrifice them. The Lord wants you to fight another day, and perhaps for other nations besides Switzerland; so take all the care *you can.* It is an unspeakable comfort to me to know that Patty is with you; give her my tender love . . . Saviours must be sufferers, and sufferers just to the extent in which they are given up to be saviours . . . It is hard work to flesh and blood, especially when our bodies are so weak; but dearest girl, His grace is sufficient, and it shall be sufficient both for you in prison and for me lying awake in the night *imagining* what you are passing through, which latter I sometimes think is the hardest of the two. Do let me know particulars. Instruct someone outside to write me daily; I cannot endure suspense if it is possible to avoid it. Be sure we are all praying for you, and doing all we can also. Your darling father is much harassed in many ways, but he talks about you continually when he is at home. He says he fears nothing but your health; if you can only be calm and confident, he is sure that God means to work out great results from all this. He comforts me . . . Dear Mrs. Butler! How remarkable that God should send her to you just then! If she is near you, give her my tenderest love, and tell her that I admit her claim to be mother No 2."[66] And in another, "Mind, and keep it prominent in all your letters that you dispute the lawfulness of your expulsion *by Swiss law!* . . . The attitude of some of the professing Christians here, and their journals, is simply shameful. If it had been an infidel or a Turk that had been treated in the same manner they would all have been up in arms . . . My darling child, hold on to God, the living God, and don't doubt for one moment that if He permits the worst to happen, He will cause it to work for the spread of salvation to the

384

A pastel portrait by Frank Shields, 1887

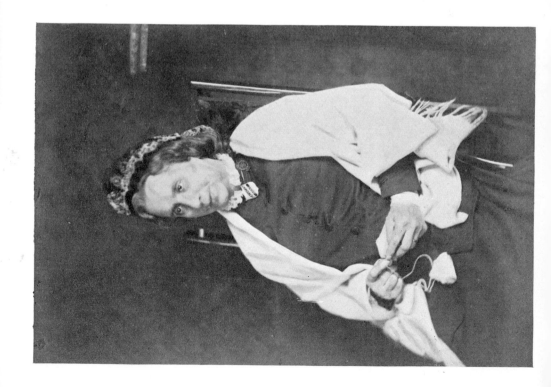

ends of the earth. There is much prayer being made for you. Fear not, be strong and very courageous for He is with you. With tenderest love to dear Mrs. Butler."[67]

News of the trouble in Switzerland, and of the arrest and imprisonment of Miss Booth, was telegraphed to continental capitals. Thousands heard of The Salvation Army for the first time from these press comments, and thus news of its doings was spread. Two members of the Neuchâtel Bar, friends of The Salvation Army, represented the Army at the trial, and the accused spoke in their own defence. The Public Prosecutor, an unbeliever, declared himself against all religious associations, and religious fanatics in particular. The little court at Boudry was crowded. In the middle of the Public Prosecutor's peroration a window suddenly flew open and a gust of wind scattered his papers in all directions. A voice was heard to say, "It is from Heaven!" The Maréchale addressed the Court toward the end of the second day. Her manner was calm, but intense, so that she seemed possessed by secret power. As to "why The Salvation Army should come to Switzerland" she declared: "Our aim is to bring people to the feet of Him Who alone can change them . . . the Saviour of the world. Our only message has been 'Repent and turn ye to the Lord that your sins may be blotted out.' We want to see the drunkards, the thieves, the outcast, washed in the precious blood of Jesus . . . If to preach the Gospel, to denounce sin, and to pray over the masses is a scandal, then we are guilty . . . The Prosecutor General has avowed that he has never attended a single meeting . . . he cannot therefore be considered capable of judging since he has never seen them!" Here there was laughter. After dealing with groundless charges made by the Prosecutor, she asks and answers, "But what are our proceedings? (1) We have sung hymns in the hall that we have hired. Everybody can procure a little book of the hymns we use and judge of it themselves. (2) We read the Bible. Switzerland has not waited till The Salvation Army came to read the Bible. You know this Book already. (3) We pray and (4) we persuade men to leave the road of sin and death and to give their hearts and lives to the Saviour. And God is our witness that *we have done nothing more.*" As she goes on the Maréchale is a little less calm, a little more "out of herself". She demands, "Is that a scandal? It is not *we* that throw stones, that break windows, that howl and hoot after respectable people in the streets. It is not *we* who violate domiciles. It is again illogical to say that we are the scandal of your country . . . We have submitted again and again until you have taken away from us the right to meet and pray . . . We are not here to plead 'not guilty'." She commented that the godless were permitted to drink, shout, sing and dance, and make what noise they liked "without the least interruption on the part of the authorities, while we are made prisoners for praying in a wood!

N

... You can punish us, you can imprison us, you can persecute us (as long as you are permitted) but what you cannot do is to stop this work."[68]

On their return to the court room the jury gave the verdict on the three points submitted:

(1) Did the accused take part in a meeting? Yes.
(2) Was the meeting in violation of the decree? Yes.
(3) Have they acted with culpable intention? No.

The judge then pronounced the acquittal of the accused. There was a mob outside. Police had been withdrawn and Salvationists were roughly handled; but cuffs, kicks and stones were hardly noticed, they were all so happy. It was a victory! *The Times* commented, "Miss Booth may claim to have come off with a very good measure of success. The authorities have done what they could to repress her, and they have found her irrepressible."[69]

On October 23, 1883, three meetings of thanksgiving and consecration were held in Exeter Hall to celebrate the result of the trial at Boudry. The press gave full and friendly reports. *The Times* noted that "Miss Booth spoke at each meeting and sang a song of deliverance in the morning which was written by her in prison at Neuchâtel."[70] The Army Mother emphasized that "the grand purpose of The Salvation Army is to bring all men *back to God and goodness...*" Better laws, better houses, better education are all to the good but these will not succeed in making better men. She went on, take "the greatest moral wreck you can find and if he be really restored by the grace of God he will soon get himself a decent covering, find a place of decency and cleanliness in which to lay his head." Volley—there were many that day—the crowd was in a cheering mood. Catherine challenged, "Go and talk to our converts. Ask their wives. They don't want anybody's charity. They can earn sufficient money to keep themselves, their wives and their children comfortably." At this point a loud cheerful voice from the body of the hall shouted, "Ask my old gal about that!" When the laughter subsided Catherine added, "Yes, and something to put in the collection as well." She pleaded for freedom of the streets. "I claim the streets and the market-places... in God's name and for God's work. Here is our Commissioner Railton... with a black eye and a swollen nose and a bruised knee, got in the streets..."[71]

Katie and her comrades had been acquitted at Boudry but persecution in Switzerland continued. Six years later Captain Charlotte Stirling, an English lady working in Switzerland, was sentenced on a trumped-up charge to 100 days in the prison of Chillon. Converts were stoned, many suffered serious injury, one was killed. But The Salvation Army went on conquering in Switzerland and today is marching without protest with banners, bands and drums.

Before the close of this year Catherine lost her dearest friend. Mrs. Billups died after a long illness and much suffering. From the time when she and Catherine first met in 1863, their mutual love never waned. Catherine's letters to her friend are more revealing than any she wrote, excepting always those long letters to William before their marriage. William and Catherine visited her during her illness. Catherine had a knack of encouraging those who were cast down and her love for her friend brought tenderness as well as authority to her aid.

Contingents of the Cardiff Corps gathered from time to time in the garden near the sick-room, to sing Mrs. Billups' favourite hymns and to pray. Mr. Billups sometimes stood at the open window in the warm autumn days and relayed a message from the sufferer within and gave her the greetings from her friends. At other times a few gathered in the sick-room for singing and prayer. A change for the worse brought Catherine hurrying to her friend's side. She desired very much to be with her when she died, but this time Mrs. Billups rallied. Catherine wrote home, "I wish I could stop to the end, she so clings to me for comfort, and the Lord is very good in enabling me to lift her spiritually . . . Her loss will never be made up to me."[72] The last change came suddenly. Word did not reach Catherine in time; merciful perhaps for her. By her own wish Mrs. Billups was given an Army funeral. The service was conducted by William Booth. In spite of inclement weather, thousands gathered in the cemetery and a great sound of singing filled the wintry air. The Salvation Army had lost a loyal supporter and Catherine the only confidential friend of her life.

7

"I never saw so deeply into the enmity of the human heart against God," said Catherine Booth after her experience of Parisian sinners. But she is to see deeper yet. In Switzerland, as Mrs. Josephine Butler tells in her book, some of the mobs were first set on Salvationists by persons who had an interest in brothels. Girls from these hellish places were among the early converts. Of course they were helped to escape; outcry and riots resulted. Katie, writing from prison, said, "I have learned much lately which throws light on this persecution. It is wicked men who are resisting . . . because it touches their own interests. Oh, there is an awful state of things here[73] . . ." And things more awful are shortly to be laid bare nearer home.

In the Whitechapel Corps meetings, there were from time to time, among those who came to the penitent-form, some who had no shelter but a house of ill-fame. Temporary lodging of one sort or another must be found while employment was sought. The penitent-form sergeant, Mrs. Cottrill, so often took home for the night one of these "poor ones" who had knelt to pray, that she and her husband, at considerable sacrifice to themselves, decided to use their front parlour as a shelter for them. Soon it became clear that more accommodation was needed, and Mrs. Cottrill told "Mr. Bramwell" what she and her husband had been doing. He arranged that the Cottrills should be helped to rent a larger cottage, but still the number of homeless girls increased, and Mrs. Cottrill felt that more oversight than she could give was needed. Again she went to "Mr. Bramwell". He talked with his mother. Should The Salvation Army carry on this "operation" officially? So far the work of the Army had consisted only of corps, i.e. preaching posts, cadets' training centres, and headquarters. To care for sinners in a dwelling set apart for them would be a new development. It would entail heavier financial responsibility. Yet how could one preach salvation and not hold out a helping hand to those who wanted to come out from their sins? In the 'eighties prostitutes were a class apart in a manner hard to realize today. A girl in this way of death found it extremely difficult to escape from it or to find employment once she had done so.

For once William Booth shrank from undertaking a new burden. He "fratched" about *debts*. Borrowing he thought almost a sin. Where was the money for such a venture to be found? Talk went on and always there lurked in the talkers' thoughts the beautiful but awkward fact that Brother and Sister Cottrill's little house was actually overfull of these pitiful ones. Catherine recalled speaking at the Midnight Movement meetings in 1865 when she first came to London. Her heart had gone out to the women, and she had felt ruffled to find the would-be rescuers treating them with suspicion and condescension rather than with love. Of one of these meetings the *Wesleyan Times* had reported, "The address of Mrs. Booth was inimitable . . . and delivered in a most earnest sympathetic manner bringing tears from many and securing the closest attention of all. She identified herself with them as a fellow sinner, showing that if they supposed her better than themselves it was a mistake, since all had sinned against God. *This*, she explained, was the main point, and not the particular sin which they might be guilty of."[74] Now in 1884 she remembered those meetings and what she had seen in Paris; remembered too what Katie had told her of the state of affairs in Switzerland. As the question was debated, Catherine in imagination saw the youthful figures kneeling at the penitent-form. How was a girl to escape from the evil in which she was enmeshed unless there were a place of safety within reach? Love wins the day! Love for the lost, in William's heart as well as in Catherine's. His reluctance was routed, money or no money, he decided that the Cottrills' little house in Hanbury Street, Whitechapel, should be taken over by the Army as a home for girls. The next question was who should look after this new flock? There was none among officers

388

experienced in this kind of job. William suddenly said, "What about Florrie? ... let her have charge."[75] And so it came about that Bramwell's young wife, with a Lieutenant to assist her, began the new work. Daily, with her baby and bag, Mrs. Bramwell set out for the little "Rescue" home. There were only two rooms on the ground floor, the larger kitchen-cum-dining-room, and the small front room with its window flush with the pavement.

One day, a few weeks after the work had begun, to Mrs. Bramwell's surprise a cab drew up at the door, and through the window she saw Mrs. Booth and her daughter Emma getting out! At first she felt a kind of panic at the thought that they were come to see how she was getting on with this new sort of "saving" work. Florence soon recovered from her first fears and all her life remembered how she and Emma and Mrs. Booth went through into the kitchen, remembered too that the ceiling was full of washing hanging up to dry (it had been a wet day). Here, as they sat round the tea-table, Catherine talked to the girls. After that first visit she came several times. Mother of Nations now, she drew immense congregations, was famous and beloved of multitudes, yet in the midst of this popularity she chose to spend an evening in the small house in Hanbury Street. I love to picture her there, the beautiful eyes searching the faces of that small company, the beautiful voice soft in the little kitchen explaining, pleading, striving to win those dark young hearts to Christ. I should like to paint the scene, that it might witness today of her eagerness to *tell sinners about the Saviour.* Her free evenings were all too rare; her fragile health clamant for rest. Time was needed for the preparation of her sermons; time to answer the endless letters; time for a little leisure; but she *chooses*, insists even, on jolting over the cobble stones in the almost springless "growlers" of the day, all the way from Clapton to Whitechapel and back, just to talk to a handful of the most ignorant and degraded women and children.

Children? Yes, it was in the little house in Hanbury Street that the hideous truth came to light. It made a wound in young Mrs. Bramwell's heart that would not heal. Some of the "prostitutes" to whom she talked individually in the small front room were *mere children.* Oh! dark depth of horror, to be *old* in depravity at fifteen, at thirteen, at eleven! The seventeen-year-olds had a lifetime of vice behind them! She went home to cry herself to sleep, or, as often as not, to stare into the darker than night's dark, all night long. The tender sympathetic Bramwell thought that from inexperience and excess of pity his young wife must be exaggerating. But he could not pacify her. Well—he would find out. Not saying anything to anyone he went, incognito, to certain neighbourhoods, and into certain houses to "see things for myself". What he saw he said "filled me with horror ... astonishment ... pity."[76] So Florence was not exaggerating! After seeing for himself, the way was clear for going to his mother with *the facts*. She listened. She did not weep. Hot indignation mounted in her; her lips were firm. Her son knew the signs! Before she spoke her decision was taken. The only question for her was how best to set about doing what must be done. How stood the law? Could no protection for these innocents be invoked? She wrote to Mrs. Josephine Butler about holding popular meetings. "If people *knew* . . ." Mrs. Butler replied, "We *have* the votes of the people . . . we need to reach the upper classes and Government."[77]

Bramwell went on gathering information by entering brothels and other dens of evil. A mass of facts was accumulated. But how to use it effectively? A House of Lords Committee had sat for ten months enquiring on this very subject, and included the traffic in young girls from this country. Lord Shaftesbury, a member, had said, "Anything more horrible, or anything approaching the wickedness and cruelty perpetrated in these dens of infamy in Brussels, it was impossible to imagine."[78] The committee stated that "upward of twenty procurers had been at work in England, to the knowledge of the police, since 1875." These revelations had been made public, *but nothing had happened!* The press? But would any paper of sufficient influence touch it? Particularly if invited to do so by the notorious Booths! And the General did not want a Salvation Army agitation. This was politics, or soon would be, and his Army must have nothing to do with politics. However, let something be done without public outcry. Sir William Harcourt,* then Home Secretary, was approached, and certain facts from Bramwell's "mass" put before him. He at once set about putting a Bill, which had already passed the Lords, for the third time, on the Orders of the House of Commons. But it fared no better this time than on two former presentations, and was talked out on the second reading. This was in May 1885. So now there was no alternative but to "go to the people". Catherine was still confident that "if the people knew . . ." Well, they should know!

There were further conferences in particular with Mr. Benjamin Scott, Recorder of the City of London, and Mrs. Josephine Butler. To them Bramwell Booth unveiled the horror which his eyes had seen. Catherine's son, so like her in his unselfconscious zeal, revealed himself to Mrs. Butler; she said of him, "Amongst all my fellow workers during the last seven years of this crusade against vice and injustice, I never met any man who, more than Mr. Bramwell Booth, combines the exquisite pity and refinement of a woman with the decision, the keen intellect and the courage of the bravest of men."[79]

It was Bramwell's zeal that brought Stead in. Bramwell says that

* Sir William Harcourt (1827-1904), prominent statesman. Held many posts in the Government.

390

he "told him the facts of child enslavement and prostitution . . . I said that I and Mrs. Booth [Florence] had looked into them . . . I asked him to give publicity to the business so that the Government should become aware of the pressure of public opinion. At first Stead hesitated . . ."[80] However, Bramwell won the first round when Stead agreed to come to Headquarters where, by arrangement, he met Mr. Benjamin Scott who "explained the legal situation, also the continental traffic . . ." When that interview was over, Stead talked individually with four children under sixteen and with a converted brothel keeper. The conversation over, Bramwell and he were alone together. There was a brief silence. I can so well imagine Bramwell, his questioning eyes fixed on Stead as he sat brooding, and when Stead brought his fist down on the office table with a thump that made the inkpots jump and let out a loud "damn", Bramwell knew that the publicity campaign was launched! They talked plans and prayed before parting, vowing as they knelt to expose the shame and compel a remedy. *The Maiden Tribute** was there engendered. There is another picture I should like to paint! The two young men, Bramwell twenty-nine, Stead thirty-five, kneeling together in the shabby gas-lit office *praying*.

Stead with Bramwell and others continued investigations, went into dark places to gather evidence. Mrs. Butler recounted the effect of all this on Stead: "To my mind the memory is ever present of a dark night on which I entered his office . . . We stumbled up the narrow dark stairs; the lights were out, not a soul was there, it was midnight. I scarcely recognized the haggard face before me as that of Mr. Stead. He threw himself across his desk with a cry like that of a bereaved or outraged mother rather than that of an indignant man, and sobbed out the words, 'Oh, Mrs. Butler, let me weep, let me weep, or my heart will break.' He then told me in broken sentences of the little girls he had seen that day sold in the fashionable West End brothels . . . to whom he had spoken of his own little girls."[81] And Catherine? She plunged into a series of immense meetings inaugurating the Purity Crusade. To some of these William accompanied her and took his share of the talking. Although he did not hide his preference for "my peculiar and special business of saving souls", still, once at it, there was no doubt about his heart for the fight. At the Congress Hall to a huge and excited crowd he said, "I should like us to go on thundering and lightning until the atmosphere is cleared . . . but one voice at least shall speak, *the voice of The Salvation Army!* We are asking the Government tonight to protect, to put a guard, a hedge, round young and ignorant girls . . . We must let the Houses of Parlia-

* This was the title under which Stead, in *The Pall Mall Gazette*, revealed the facts of child enslavement.

ment know that when we got the light it was given to a people not afraid to hold up the torch."[82]

A full platform of supporters at the first of these meetings to be held in Exeter Hall made an imposing array. There were many speakers and much applause. In his opening words, the General said, "The Salvation Army reckons to take its religion wherever it goes." Mrs. Josephine Butler, introduced by him as a "true and tried friend of The Salvation Army", said, "I was called by God to a strange and terrible work eighteen years ago and I knew all these horrors." Many members of both Houses of Parliament, to whom she revealed what she knew, found it impossible to believe her and "thought I was an insane woman ... I thank God ... for this wave of public opinion, and thank Him that He has spared me to live to see this day ... I, as a woman, am jealous and afraid that this noble agitation, which is now beginning through the land, should be left too much in the hands of men. Women must be by your side everywhere. I call upon the women of the land through this meeting to raise a great army of women to prosecute this noble work. God will be with them."[83] Catherine Booth was "satisfied nothing but public exposure would have answered the end. We thought it was necessary that there should be a loud and long blast to awaken public opinion on the question ... As a woman and a mother," she said, "my pity is with these girls ... but I do not know whether we ought not to be as much concerned for our little boys as for our little girls. Legislation is needed to prevent our little boys being fetched away from the streets of London ... for equally diabolical purposes."[84]

Meetings were held in the largest halls obtainable: the Free Trade Hall, Manchester; City Hall, Leeds; Albert Hall, Sheffield; and in the Exeter Hall repeatedly. Afternoon meetings, evening meetings, meetings for women only, but for the most part public and open to men and women. At every one of these Catherine spoke, excepting only in those held at the same time elsewhere by her husband. She poured out her mother-heart. In the heat of her zeal her words were often vitriolic. At one of the Exeter Hall meetings, she said, "I question whether any face has burned with fiercer shame than mine ... Three years ago a committee of the House of Lords sat to consider these very things and they recommended improved legislation for the protection of young girls ... and yet *nothing has been done.* I would like to ask those responsible for this state of things how many thousands of innocent victims have been sacrificed during those three years? ... They have found time to legislate on the preservation of game, and the diseases of cattle!

* It was computed at the time of the investigation that of some 50,000 prostitutes in London, between four and five thousand were under sixteen years of age. *The War Cry,* 29.7.1885.

...time to legislate for British interests in far-off corners of the earth, surely they might have found time to legislate for the protection of the children of their own country! ... The wretches who cater for the child-destroying monsters perfectly well know the present state of the law ... Hence their anxiety to get children who are turned thirteen even if only by a day!"[85] Catherine wrote to Queen Victoria "on behalf of tens of thousands of the most pitiable and helpless of your Majestey's subjects". In particular Her Majesty was prayed to "cause the Bill to be re-introduced during the present session of Parliament," concluding, "If I could only convey to Your Majesty an idea of the tenth part of the demoralization, shame and suffering entailed on thousands of the children of the poor by the present state of the law on this subject, I feel sure that your womanly feelings would be roused to indignation, and that Your Majesty would make the remaining years of your glorious reign (which I fervently pray may be many) even more illustrious than those that are past, by going off merely conventional lines in order to save the female children of your people from a fate worse than that of slaves or savages. Yours on behalf of the innocents,"[86] Catherine signed herself. But queens cannot, at least not openly, go off "conventional lines", although in the reply on the Queen's behalf by the Dowager Duchess of Roxburgh, we read of "Her Majesty fully sympathizing with Mrs. Booth on the painful subject."[87]

Catherine next addressed Mr. Gladstone, Prime Minister, and later his successor, Lord Salisbury. William spoke of the responses to these and other letters of the kind as "a few crumbs of comfort". Part of her letter to Mr. Gladstone may serve as a sample of others. This letter-writing was part of Catherine's effort to "get something *done*". "Dear Mr. Gladstone, My heart has been so oppressed of late with the awful disclosures forced upon us ... that I feel constrained to write to you to implore that you will insist upon the re-introduction of the Criminal Law Amendment Bill during this session. I think I may thoughtfully say that I represent hundreds of thousands of the working classes ... I would also entreat you to use your great influence in order to raise the age of the responsibility of girls to seventeen, and further, that the Bill shall confer power to search any premises where there is reasonable ground to suspect that any girl under age is detained for immoral purposes; or for any woman so detained against her will. I feel sure that if you knew of the fearful crimes that are being daily perpetrated in this city, the numbers of helpless children who are being literally bought and sold ... you would deem this question of so great importance that you would take steps for the immediate alteration of the law in the direction suggested. Dear Mr. Gladstone, you have done much for the helpless and oppressed in this and other lands; let me implore you to turn your attention to this question."[88] The "crumb" in reply informed Mrs. Booth that Mr. Gladstone had "passed your communication to the Home Secretary".

We have a private view of Catherine's state of mind from letters she wrote at the time to Emma who, with Lucy, was resting in Switzerland, as, "... Oh, how wicked the world is. Bramwell and Stead have been engaged on some investigations about the child prostitution of London and their discoveries are awful. Pray for us. I have never known anything take such a hold of Bramwell for years. I told him I never felt so proud of him in my life. But all this on the top of our other work is killing. However I have felt better the last few days ... How I should like to spend a week with you. What a boon 'air' travelling would be if they could only perfect it."[89] Which shows how alert and ready for new things Catherine's mind still is! And a week or so later, "The first article is coming out in the *Pall Mall* tomorrow. My word it will cause a shaking! And time it did! ... It has made me feel awful sometimes while the investigations have been going on. We have got some of the children in our keeping. Pray that we may be able to burst up this machinery of hell. I am going to hold some meetings with Mrs. Butler on the [word unintelligible] in the West End. Pray for me. Oh, if I were only—but it is no use wishing. You young ones must take my place and do better ... We are determined to have the law altered. Poor Bramwell has been sadly overdone, but I trust the worst is now over. I hope there will be a line tomorrow saying how you are ... How is your appetite and do you want more brown flour ..."[90] I like to think of Catherine fussing about Emma's appetite and posting whole meal to Switzerland whilst in the midst of that welter of horror. This letter comes to an end abruptly with "Pa has come in."

And again, "I am delighted to hear of your improvement. It has been the ointment to my heart this morning in the midst of a deluge of distressing feelings aroused by these dreadful disclosures, which I do hope you know nothing about. I told Bramwell not to send the *Pall Mall* and I hope you won't ask for it. You see, you can do nothing away there, and you could not possibly read it without harrowing every feeling of your nature and upsetting your nights for a week at least. Therefore do be persuaded, and be willing to remain in ignorance till you return. We are doing all that mortals can. Poor Papa is dreadfully harassed and I am more distressed than I can say at being just now so helpless physically. However, I am mending, and hope to be able to address two meetings on the subject, one at the Prince's Hall, Piccadilly, the other at St. James's in which Mrs. Butler and others are going to help me. Mr. Samuel Morley is to take the chair on Tuesday. The excitement in the City and in the House of Commons yesterday was unparalleled for many years gone by ... Of course the rascals who are in this iniquity are raging, and our one fear is that it may make it worse for our poor people*; however, we see no way to mend the evil but by fighting it out. . ."[91] And later, ". . . I miss you tremendously in this fray, the only comfort I have being that you are out of the horror and anguish which it would have inevitably brought upon you, and that you are laying in strength to fight evil in coming days . . . What all this has cost me I will not attempt to write. I had four bad nights in succession, with the dreadful subject burning into my heart and brain. I felt as though I must go and walk the streets and besiege the dens where these hellish iniquities are going on. To keep quiet seemed like being a traitor to humanity. Oh, it has been a fearful time. However God has helped me to speak. The reports are very poor, I was too rapid for anyone to report me, but the truth I uttered electrified the people till they could hardly sit on their seats. They shouted and clapped and wept in all directions. I have rested better the last two nights. Pray for me . . ."[92]

At one meeting Catherine said that bad as were the facts revealed, worse were kept back "for very shame of our humanity". Her chief cry in all this crying aloud and not sparing is "protect our children". It was hardly credible that if a child of thirteen years old was taken advantage of by any base man, the violated child's mother had no redress . . . What sort of men must they be who have passed this law! . . . The legislature took care that such a child should not be empowered to dispose of her *money* or *property* until she attained the age of twenty-one; how came it that they gave her power to dispose of her virtue when she was too young to know the value of it? . . . Is there anything worse than that, think you, in hell? . . . I say it is time we women had some sort of voice in choosing our law-makers!"†[93] More than once Mrs. Booth declared that if the Bill were not passed, she would "turn away from the fathers to the mothers . . . and would march at the head of 50,000 mothers to Buckingham Palace to petition the Queen, The Mother of the Nation."[94] These Purity Crusade meetings helped to rouse the whole country. *The War Cry*, with a circulation of 216,000 issued *twice* weekly at a halfpenny, gave reports of meetings and speeches to millions. Stead's sensational articles in the *Pall Mall Gazette* were like a scream for help. Many bookstalls refused to sell the paper, but it was on sale at Army centres, including the International Headquarters. Eva, in charge of the training for women in Emma's absence, led cadets and training officers in special raids on the city streets, selling *The War Cry* giving The Salvation Army news of these events.

* Salvationists were being attacked and sent to prison for holding meetings in the streets.

† Women had not the right to vote at Parliamentary elections in England until 1918.

The Salvation Army demanded that the Bill be passed forthwith, and that four provisions be included. These were:

1. Protection for children, boys and girls, to the end of their seventeenth year.
2. That it be made a criminal act to procure young persons for immoral purposes.
3. That parents or guardians be given the right of a search-warrant to recover children from brothels.
4. Equality of men and women before the law, that is, that it should be an offence for men to solicit women.[95]

In *The War Cry* of July 18, 1885, a petition was printed which people were asked to sign. Copies were displayed in every corps. In only *seventeen days* 393,000 signatures were received. These were made into a gigantic roll which was taken to Westminster, housed under a Noah's ark-like roof on a dray drawn by four white horses. This contraption, accompanied by marching Salvationists, set out from the Congress Hall, Clapton, and proceeded to Trafalgar Square whence, in order to comply with the law forbidding processions within a mile of Westminster, the marchers started on their return journey. Officers in charge of the procession were mounted. The march was headed by a brass band of fifty men playing well-known hymns. A hundred and fifty uniformed Salvation Army "Life Guards" marched in close formation, with a number of less marshalled Salvationists, including "ranks of English Mothers". In Cheapside they were loudly cheered. The dray was driven on to Westminster. There, eight Salvation Life Guards in red jerseys and white helmets carried the petition into the House of Commons, across the floor, and deposited it by the table near the mace. Members stood to get a view of the unique apparition. Professor Stuart, M.P. for Hackney, presented the petition. The police were helpful and friendly, in particular the Chief of Police at the House of Commons.

The Bill, the Criminal Law Amendment Act, passed the House of Commons early in August with the Army's demand for the age of protection reduced from seventeen to the end of the fifteenth year, and the law has since remained unchanged. Thanksgiving meetings were held in Exeter Hall, amid much enthusiasm. The General said that although they had not got all they wanted, they were there to "sound the note of triumph". The Army Mother declared, "I look upon the Bill as a first instalment of a long and heavy debt of justice due to women. The age of sixteen to eighteen years is the most dangerous for our girls and boys and the law must be altered further yet."[96] Had she lived it is possible, one feels, that young girls might not still be destroyed with impunity in these vital years.

But there has yet to be an abortive skirmish on the enemies' part. It makes a story of its own. Here I can only touch upon it. Hardly were the meetings of thanksgiving concluded, than on Monday, September 7, 1885, summonses were served on Bramwell Booth, William Stead, and others for being concerned in the abduction of a child and conveying her to the Continent. In order to prove how easily such a thing might be done, Stead had, with the help of Rebecca Jarrett, an Army convert and ex-brothel keeper who knew the ropes, bought a child from her mother. Eliza was taken to France in the care of Salvation Army officers. Stead, while on bail, spoke at some Army gatherings, where he was loudly cheered; at others cheers were raised for him and Bramwell Booth in their absence. Mrs. Josephine Butler wrote to *The Christian*, "For many years past English girls have been carried off to ruin and death in evil houses on the Continent. We ourselves [Mr. Scott's Committee] exposed this traffic ... a committee of the House of Lords endorsed all the horrors we had proclaimed, but, sir, is it not painfully significant that among the multitudes of children so ruined, in not one single instance have the police ever brought one of these girls back, nor has the Government ever instituted any proceedings against their abductors, although these persons are perfectly well known to Scotland Yard! The one girl produced by the police is little Eliza Armstrong for whose pretended abduction our friends are now on their trial."[97]

The Army Mother was writing too: to the Home Secretary, protesting that no bail was granted to Rebecca Jarrett, whom she herself had visited in prison and who was "in a stone cell with only a mat to lie on"; to Lady Cairns (expecting through her to reach the Queen) of the "burning sense of injustice driven into my soul by the present action of the Government. What a sight it must be to God and angels to see the power of the Government of this great country exerted to crush those who, at great personal risk and suffering, have dared to attack the enormities which are destroying the very vitals of our national life ..."[98] Later Mrs. Booth telegraphed to the Queen. Regilious opinion was roused. A half-night of prayer was held throughout The Salvation Army at home and abroad on Monday October 19, to pray for the accused. William Booth was in command at the Congress Hall. "Let us begin by offering God our ... undivided heart ... When your hearts are thus given ... He will answer your prayers ... Let us ask for such a deliverance as shall be for the glory of God, for our way may not be God's ..."[99] The General's way, he told them, would have been to call the whole thing off! But that prayer was not granted. The accused were committed for trial at the Old Bailey from the Bow Street Magistrates' Court. The trial lasted twelve days. Bramwell was acquitted, Stead sentenced to three months' imprisonment.

His mother, leading meetings in Glasgow when Bramwell was

making his defence in court, told the people that she had never felt more proud of her son than that day when he stood with Stead in the dock. She telegraphed to him, "Keep up your spirits. Your defence is in *The Times* and is worth a thousand prosecutions because be read by hundreds of thousands persons." The sensation of the trial revived mob attacks on Salvationists. Bramwell came home bleeding from rough handling on his way to and from the court, and later was given the protection of a "Black Maria"* as a conveyance. On the whole the Purity Crusade and its queer sequel did The Salvation Army good and not harm; 1885 proved one of the most successful years in its history.

In November of that year six consecutive days of special meetings were held at the Congress and Exeter Halls. These were designed to strengthen and inspire Salvationists and other Christians in their task of winning men to God. In Exeter Hall the meetings began at ten-thirty a.m. and continued with but short breaks until ten p.m. The announced subject was *How to save souls*. Catherine spoke with vigour, with "boundless enthusiasm and irresistible eloquence" (the words are from an outsider's account of her at these meetings). But the prolonged excitement, and all that "boiling over" of indignation and pity during the Purity Crusade had told on her. Directly these six days of meetings in London were over heart trouble once more prostrated her, and it was months before she was able to resume preaching. William had to go to four days of meetings in Norwich without her. She could not be at the Congress Hall when Salvationists gave Stead an uproarious welcome on his release from prison.

Stead described Catherine as he saw her at the time of the Purity Crusade. "In the great campaign against the criminal vice of London I had always the immense support of her indomitable courage and her fiery energy. Mrs. Booth was a splendid fighter. She was pre-eminently one of those whom you would choose to have at your back in a fight. There was in her a whole-hearted zeal, a thorough-going earnestness, a flaming passion of indignation, that cheered one like the sound of trumpet ... No wonder I learned in that trying and testing time to know her and to love her ... The Salvation Army has a noble record in the work of the protection of women and children. It is, so far as I know, the only religious body which makes this subject a matter for a special article in its creed. Article 13 in the Salvation pledge runs thus: 'I do here declare that I will never treat any woman, child, or other person, whose life, comfort, or happiness may be placed within my power, in an oppressive, cruel, or cowardly manner, but that I will protect such from evil and danger, so far

* Black Maria—slang name for van used for carrying prisoners to the court and prison.

as I can, and promote, to the utmost of my ability, their present welfare and eternal salvation.' The hand of Mrs. Booth is visible in every line of that article ... This sympathy for women, as women, knew no limitation of race or colour."[100]

8

To William before their marriage Catherine had written: "Oh, I love to feel my soul swell with unutterable feeling for all mankind ..." She had been conscious of such upsurges of benevolence from her youth. The responsibility she felt for people came in part from this sense of *caring* about them. It was an impulse of imaginative sympathy when a mere child that took her at a bound to the side of the drunken lout in the hands of the police. His misery mattered to her. This keen edge of feeling for others was never blunted. As she came to know God more fully she experienced what Mrs. Butler beautifully expressed when she wrote, "God ... did not deny me my request that He would show me of His own heart's love for sinners ... and when He makes this revelation He does more, He makes the enquiring soul a *partaker* of His own heart's love for the world."[101] Of this love Catherine and William Booth partook. Even when they were young it was the over-riding passion of their lives. All their other loves were in subjection to it. Soon after they first met Catherine wrote to William, "Oh, for a Christlike sympathy for souls ... let us make up our minds to win souls whatever else we leave undone." William is just as emphatic. He tells Catherine, "My resolutions are unbroken, to live and die only for the salvation of souls ..."

This was their frame of mind before they married and it did not change, but as they grew older it became more all-embracing; it was the mainspring of their every activity. Impossible to understand the inner energy of these two and of the early Salvationists whom their example fired, unless we accept that they were actuated by pure love to God and genuine benevolence toward their fellows. They *cared* for sinners. The state of the people festered in their minds. Of William Miss Short remembered "how he had once stopped me at every public house in the Mile End Road, pointing to the young men and women who crowded the different bars, exclaiming, 'Look at that! Look at it! enough to make the angels weep.' Sights of this kind ... seemed to stab him to the heart."[102] Years later Catherine declared, "We consecrate ourselves, our whole being, our children, influence, time, life, and, if need be, death, to the pressing of this salvation on the attention and acceptance of our fellow men. We make all things bow down before this unbending resolution, *to seek and to save the lost.*"[103] She despised a profession of Christianity that did not include spreading the Gospel and caring for sinners. Catherine was able to receive God revealed as Love. She took literally as God's word to man, "I have loved thee with an everlasting love." Christ's command "Love one another, as I have loved you" was to her not merely picturesque language, it was stark reality for everyday practice. She felt that she had proved, and that all men might prove, the power of the Holy Spirit to kindle and to sustain love of this nature. To a friend she wrote, "It is a standing mystery to me that thoughtful Christian men can contemplate the existing state of the world without perceiving the desperate need for some more effective and aggressive agency on the side of God and righteousness."[104] Stead wrote, "The regeneration of society seemed to her only possible by increasing love between man and man."[105] Of Salvationists Catherine said, "The precepts of Jesus as to all men being our brethren and having a claim on our sympathy and benevolence, irrespective of their condition, are resuscitated and clothed in living acts . . ."[106] Not that she idealized sinners or dramatized sin. She said once, "We must give up sentimentalizing. Sentimentalizing is of no more use in religion than in business, and we must set to real, practical, common-sense scheming, and downright hard work. If ever the Gospel is to make headway against the rush of evil passions, worldly ambition, and devilish animosity . . ."[107] She had no illusions about sinners. Dr. Petri wrote of her, "She knew the secret labyrinths and dark chambers of the human heart. She knew the sins of the slums and the sins of society. She knew the sins of scribes, and the sins of businessmen . . . She knew the sins of this world's children, and she knew the sins of the so-called children of God. She was most merciless against the latter."[108] But always, whether among the rich or the poor, Catherine *identified herself with the sinner*; she felt herself to be one of them, only that she was reconciled to God, and *she* believed that all sinners might be—ought to be! To talk of "the criminal classes" she declared was "another of the cant phrases of modern Christianity" and she denounced as "bastard Christianity" the spirit that "set about in a helpless, patronizing sort of way . . . to try to help 'such men' as though they were of different flesh and blood to themselves! Verily such Christianity is of different blood from Him who preferred talking to a thief in His last moments . . ."[109] "Oh, the Lord fill us with the pity of Jesus Christ, Who, when He saw the multitudes, wept over them."

This caring for the people's salvation was not something that belonged to her preaching only, it welled up in her on all manner of occasions. Catherine had been gravely ill with a bad heart and was taking treatment at Metcalf's Hydro when she sent a pencilled note to Mrs. Billups which gives an enlightening glimpse of her behind the scenes: "I felt so much better Friday and Saturday that I got permission to meet the servants, so we had them here in the evening.

400

The Lord was with us. We all got a blessing. Miss Noel prayed for the first [time] before anyone, and got blessed. I believe three of the young women were convicted of sin. After I had got into bed at night a gentle tap came at my door, and X. asked if she might come and tell me something. My words had made her feel dreadful about her past life. Of course I let her pour out her heart to me, counselled and prayed with her, and I believe we shall get her saved. Inevitably a sleepless night followed this emotional effort." At Whitby for a few days' much needed rest she could not restrain her longing to help, and tells Mrs. Billups, "... I was very much occupied in doing ... a bit of benevolent work for the family with whom we lodged; reduced from wealth to almost beggary by a villain of a manager, who made off with £19,000 about two years ago. Then to add to their sorrows, the father and husband drinks and seems to have given up all effort. Seven interesting children the eldest only fifteen; accustomed to three servants and a governess, and now scrubbing and cleaning boots and waiting on lodgers, etc. Friends all forsaken them in their adversity, the wife heartbroken. I went to the ex-Mayor, who used to be on familiar terms with them, and to two or three others amongst the leading men in the town, and I trust have been instrumental in putting things in train for some permanent help. I fixed an interview with the father and pleaded with him for more than half an hour for his soul and his family's sake to give up the drink and start afresh, but he was the *hardest* specimen of humanity I ever tried at in my life, high or low. Still, I trust the Spirit was with me, and if I might judge from his change of colour, there was *some* impression produced. May the Lord save him."[110] One day as Catherine left home to catch a train for meetings in the North, she met a teenager on the doorstep, who said she wanted to speak to Mrs. Booth. Catherine took the girl by the hand and turned back into the house. The cab was kept waiting, the train missed, while the Army Mother talked to the little scallywag from Whitechapel. This story had a happy ending, or it might not have been recorded, but it is Catherine's attitude, not the result, that brings it into this book. Sometimes she had a sort of second sight, and would suddenly see what "that one" might become if touched by God. She knew the pain of striving to bring people to take a definite step; to be explaining, pleading, praying and yet to fail at the last. "One feels how far they come," she said once, "... and how they falter and draw back. None but those who travail for souls can ever understand the agony of feeling that souls are drawing back when you have brought them on the road so far."[111]

Although she spent her life preaching, Catherine never approached it lightheartedly. Often she was almost prostrated by a sense of her own insufficiency; and suffered an anguish of desire for the salvation of sinners. An unexpected gleam of light shone on a corner of the past

401

for me when an old Army comrade of mine told me of an incident which had been recounted to him by a friend who had entertained Catherine and one of her daughters when they visited King's Lynn. This friend recalled, "We talked late that evening and, following prayers, retired to rest. Somewhere about one o'clock in the morning my wife woke me and said, 'I'm afraid one of those ladies is unwell.' Making careful investigations on the landing, I returned and said, 'Those ladies are actually praying for the sinners of King's Lynn' ... Such fervour for the souls of the people was to us, even as Methodists, a very great surprise." Sometimes Catherine's motherliness paved the way for a religious appeal; she had a really remarkable aptitude for winning the confidence of antagonistic spirits. One day she was journeying from the North of England; a young man was suddenly thrust into the compartment (no corridor carriages then) as the train was leaving York. His travelling kit was thrown in after him. On seeing Catherine alone he sat down and exclaimed under his breath, "Damn the women!" After a little while she spoke to him about the influence of good women, and gradually drew from him a story of disappointment and failure. Before they reached King's Cross he knelt with her to pray. He became a friend of Catherine and kept in touch with her for many years.

If Catherine Booth were a fanatic this craving to see men and women saved was the focus of her fanaticism. Had it not been for her sound judgment, her logical common-sense turn of mind, it might have produced a serious unbalance in her life. Stead said that it "was in her case kept in check by a sincere personal humility, an abiding sense of her own unworthiness and an absolute dependence upon the grace of the Infinite".[112] But even so it would be easy to criticize her concentration on this aspect of Christian experience. She certainly went to extremes in her own efforts, and schooled her children in the theory until they, too, saw the same vision: the *world for Christ*. To those fervent hearts it did not seem far-fetched. A genuine enthusiasm for soul-saving, for leading men into holy living that they in their turn might become saviours was, they felt, something worth spending life for. When her children got married she could think of nothing higher to wish for them than that they "might be blessed to the winning of thousands of souls", and her wish for them came true. I believe that the white heat of love for God and man that consumed William and Catherine was necessary to forge The Salvation Army, to weld men and women of different race, language and background into an integrated force with one aim—to *win souls to Christ*. Wherever the flag was unfurled, praying Salvationists sent up a heart cry, singing in different languages and melodies what came to be the same song, "Jesus Thou Lover of souls, O let me drink Thy Spirit, make me a

402

lover of souls"; or "Love I ask for, love I claim, a dying love like Thine, a love that feels for all the world; Saviour, give me a love like Thine." Catherine's first-born, Bramwell, spoke for his own generation when he said, "The Salvation Army is love for souls."

9

In June 1886 the first International Congress was held, and Catherine was sufficiently recovered to take part. "What was best for the Army" was still the plumb-line for every decision. Neither she nor those about her had any inkling that the coming months would be her last "at the battle's front". If any change in her were detected it was that her words in public were more urgent in calling men to repentance, more tender in understanding as she reasoned with the timid and the doubting. Exeter Hall was engaged for five days for the Congress meetings. Officers of sixteen nations were present. Public meetings were held simultaneously in London's largest halls. The Army Mother drove with the General in a procession from Broad Street Station to Exeter Hall. Her sons and others were mounted. Groups from overseas posed on drays. There were bands and drums and flags. Assisted by city police, over 2,000 Army officers marched through the crowded streets. On the whole the reception was friendly, although one officer was felled by a well-aimed block of wood.

Catherine's words at one of the meetings held in the Congress Hall show us how clear was her concept of the Army's role. "Twenty-one years ago," she said, "we stepped right out in the name of God, single-handed, with the one all-absorbing desire and determination that at all costs *we would reach the people with the Gospel* . . . As I rode through the crowded streets in that procession the other day and saw some hundred thousand people, in thousands of instances with smiling faces, and heard their 'God bless you', I could not help rejoicing that God had given us, to so large an extent, the desire of our hearts . . . that He has not only helped us to reach the masses of the people in this country, but He is helping us in other countries . . . I thought as I looked round upon the platform of Exeter Hall yesterday . . . how can any thoughtful man help seeing that we have reached the true cosmopolitan idea of the Gospel? . . . We have found the true idea, Jesus Christ's idea, of fraternity, the fraternity of all men, irrespective of difference of colour, customs or speech. We have not only one spirit, one song, one language, one Saviour, one heaven, but we shall be all of one colour! I don't know whether it will be black or white, and I don't care. I would just as soon be black as white, so that the King admires me . . . 'By this shall men *know* that ye are My disciples, if ye love one another.' That poor fellow in America about whom we have just heard knew, by the spirit the Captain showed, that he *loved* him. Not only have we got this love, but we go on propagating it; we are getting lower and lower, freer and freer [and here she poked fun at Bramwell] ... You see that my son—the Chief of Staff—could not help having a little bit of a jig tonight. I don't know whether that may not be regarded as one of the ... triumphs of this Congress! ... so precious do I feel this spirit of family freedom to be ... Who has the right to say that we shall not be joyful in the presence of our Father? If it is so sweet to realize this blessed union and freedom down here, what will it be to enjoy it up yonder? There, there will be no enemies ... no elder brothers to criticize or condemn us."[113]

A little later the Army Mother was at the Congress Hall again, and this time to dedicate tandem tricycles on which a specially trained force of Salvationists was to ride forth. Typical, this, of the swift laying hold of novelties to lure people to *listen* to the Army's message that characterized Salvation Army tactics in the early years. On her feet, facing the crowd, Catherine's energy seemed limitless. But in truth there was no longer the same spring of renewing strength; the old resilience was gone. At Norwich a *War Cry* report recorded that after she had been speaking an hour, one of the accompanying officers "pulled Mrs. Booth's jacket", fearing that she would over-tax her strength. She took no notice and went on another half hour, holding the crowd tense to the last word. Next morning, how-ever, she was not well enough to go to the officers' meetings as arranged. "Pulling Mrs. Booth's jacket" was, in her latter years, a duty entrusted to an accompanying officer or daughter in an attempt to prevent Catherine exhausting herself. Marianne Asdell tells that she went to the Clapton house to help Mrs. Booth with correspon-dence. On one occasion "the Chief [Bramwell] came to me and said: 'My mother is really ill but she insists on going to the *Grecian* for her meeting tonight. Take her and bring her back in Balls's cab.'" [Balls! The name conjures up the picture of him remembered by me. He was always affixed (How?) to the box of a squarish closed cab, always tightly swathed to the armpits in a blanket of nondescript grey-brown colour, and wearing a huge beard to match. His high bowler hat wedged low on his head left only just enough room for the eyes between rim and beard, out of which the snub nose rose like a small bald promontory. His figure persistently suggested to my child mind something uncanny about the hidden legs; yet it could not be true, could it, that they had no power to get Mr. Balls down from the box?]"Take her and bring her back in Ball's cab," Bramwell instructed Miss Asdell. "She has promised to speak only so long, and if she doesn't stop then you are to pull her coat." Marianne Asdell, then but a young recruit, asked, "But what shall I do if Mrs. Booth

doesn't stop?" Answer, "Pull again." Miss Asdell, "And if she doesn't
stop the second time?" Answer, "Pull again, and then get up and
make her sit down." Miss Asdell added, "I had to pull three times.
... In the cab going home to Clapton, Mrs. Booth put her hand on
mine and said, 'My dear, you were quite right to pull my jacket,
I should have stopped. I could have, but I had so much on my
heart to say.' Mrs. Booth smiled at me; she could pay you for any
trouble by a *complete look of love.*"[114]

"I had so much on my heart to say..." She possessed rare energy
of mind and could multiply ideas on a subject in a moment. When
in the early years of their marriage William burst into the kitchen
and sitting on a corner of the table where she was kneading bread
or making a pudding told her his idea for a new sermon, she caught
the thread of his thought and on the instant could give him twice
as much matter as was needed to develop the theme. It was one
of the precious things she brought to him that her exuberance had
the effect of kindling his own thought, she enhanced his ideas in
his own eyes. As the years went by he counted increasingly on her
judgment. When in conference he had heard what Bramwell and
Railton thought, he was sure to turn to her with "what do you say
Ma?" If she were critical, as some have said, it was the kind of
criticism William *wanted* to hear. When their home comprised Headquarters, he would send a shout through the house, "Kate, come
and tell me what you think of this," and she would drop her sewing
or her pen to run to him, first to listen and then to give her view of
the matter. These two could convey their thoughts to one another,
always with comprehension. She knew how to encourage him and
he how to calm her. The fact that her agitation was on account
of others made it none the less taxing on herself and those about
her. Things "on her heart" tended to get exaggerated, small matters
got out of proportion and caused her undue anxieties and exertions.
To Ballington she wrote from Shields, "Now I hear that fevers are
raging all over! Have you got the plumbers for those closets?...
Do get the man to go at once. There were eighteen cases of typhoid
in one street in one town, all traced to an untrapped drain." After
dealing with other matters she comes back to the drains, "Will you
get the closets done... for the sake of a few shillings, *don't* run any
risk, I beseech you. If there is anything wrong at Whitechapel, just
get a plumber in without consulting anybody, and if anybody says
anything, say I authorized you...[115] Catherine's insistence when
anything got "on her heart" could be exasperating but it was of the
sort that finished with a kiss and not by slamming the door!
Absolute sincerity was characteristic of her concerns whether for
trifles or on great themes; no one doubted *that*. It was very disarming! and gave weight to anything she said, emphasizing the naturalness of her manner when she was preaching. "What was she like when

on the platform?" I have asked those who heard her in the later years. All reply in different ways, but to the same effect: she was "like herself". "She talked on the platform just as she talked to you if you were the only person in the room."

Mrs. Hugh Price Hughes* first heard Catherine Booth at a meeting in the Corn Exchange in Oxford, where they were then living. She wrote, "This was a great occasion for the undergraduates to let off the exuberance of their spirits. As soon as Mrs. Booth began to speak, they began their antics, but something in her manner and personality entirely quelled them. In simple words she told them ... of the love of Christ for humanity, and in a few minutes you could have heard a pin drop."[116] I think it was this speaking out what was on her heart, her simplicity and sincerity that attracted young people. Parties of undergraduates often came up from Oxford to attend her West End meetings; from among these several became Salvationists. Many young men came at first for the novelty of the thing and then went time after time. Frederic Sheilds, the artist, was one. He was an agnostic and told that he paid no attention to what she was saying but went just for the pleasure of watching her, drawn by he knew not what. Then one day he found himself noticing her message and suddenly felt that she was talking to him. He knelt at the penitent-form and was converted. He joined the family of Catherine's spiritual children, and not long afterwards he asked William if he might make a portrait of her. She sat to him several times after the nature of her last illness was known and the pastel he drew is reproduced here. I think it shows the shadow of her secret grief.

Catherine went with the General to Glasgow for three days of meetings. Railton reports to *The War Cry*, "Mrs. Booth so over-exhausted herself on Sunday as to be hardly able to speak; yet she made the effort in the Monday morning holiness meeting and spoke also at a soldiers' gathering in the afternoon, and at night held the great crowd for her message."[117] On September 17 Ballington, her second son, was married at the Congress Hall, to Miss Maud Charlesworth, who had served the Army for four years in Switzerland, Sweden and England. The bride wore her Army uniform and a white sash on which the words "United for the War" were embroidered in red. Catherine gave them her blessing. Soon after his marriage Ballington was appointed in charge of the Army's work in the U.S.A.

The General left London for meetings in the U.S.A. and Canada on the day after his son's wedding. Catherine, anxious at the thought

* Mrs. Price Hughes, wife of Hugh Price Hughes (1847-1902), Wesleyan Minister. (Founded the *Methodist Times*. Famed for fearless utterances in the cause of social reform.)

of three months' separation from him, wrote to Mr. Denny, "There is laid out for him ten thousand miles of travel and much exhausting work before he returns, but prayer is being offered for strength and grace equal to the emergency. I am glad that you are pleased with, though my heart aches for the necessity for, our resolution to abstain for the present from incurring further expenditure ... I don't think I was ever so nearly heart-broken as on hearing a discussion as to ways and means just before the General left. The devil said 'You are beaten at last!'"[118] Funds at Headquarters were so low at the moment that even money for stamps had to be borrowed. Few can appreciate the feats of faith and toil needed to raise funds for the Army's expansion.

William away, Catherine, often accompanied by Emma, toured the country. Before the end of the year she had held meetings at nearly all the London Corps and a number in the provinces. She spoke at stone-laying ceremonies. At one such she said: "Poverty often prevents people attending respectable places of worship ... This building is to be a poor man's place ... It will be opened every night and noonday ..." In her practical way she told, when laying a stone, "I give five pounds out of my own pocket, and five pounds sent by a friend." She knows what an Army Hall *ought* to be; note this paragraph in a letter: "You see, they are not churches, or chapels, nor, in many instances, halls or theatres, but comprise every imaginable class of building from a church to a pig-sty.* In addressing three or four hundred of our soldiers the other day I explained to them that 'barracks' [Army Corps buildings were called barracks in the early years] meant a place where *real* soldiers were to be fed, taught, and equipped for war, not a place to settle down in as a comfortable snuggery in which to enjoy themselves, and that I hoped if ever they did settle down God would burn their new barracks over their heads!"[119] Ten years before, Catherine had written to Bramwell, "I see our principal danger is in our very best agents settling down in Army measures just as Churches settle down in Church measures. They constantly want stirring up and *setting on in fresh tracts*. The Lord help us."[120]

William Booth returned from America on Christmas Day and went straight from Euston Station, where a company of his forces met him, to meetings at Exeter Hall. On February 8, 1887, Catherine's eldest daughter Katie was married to Colonel Arthur

* Commissioner Hugh Sladen told me that when he, then a lad of seventeen, and his mother the Lady Sarah Sladen were "sworn in" as soldiers of The Salvation Army, the meeting was held in a shed used as a slaughter house on week-days. The Captain-in-charge carried in benches and covered the walls with red bunting to hide the blood stains. The place was crammed with people and to judge from Hugh Sladen's evident delight in describing the scene to me the ceremony was a happy and enthusiastic occasion.

Sydney Clibborn at the Congress Hall, Clapton. With her husband she continued in charge of the Army's forces in France and Switzerland. At the wedding Catherine spoke as both mother and preacher, revealing that the claims of these two vocations might be in conflict and that the demands of her own physical strength had seemed, at times, too heavy to be borne. Katie was frail but so evidently gifted to reach the people with the message of the Gospel that her mother had already, in imagination, set her eldest daughter apart for that "glorious calling". This marriage seemed to mar the vision. It is said that as the service went on Catherine sat weeping. When she addressed the gathering she told in her homely intimate manner about her hopes and fears, "I have only a very few words to say dear friends on this occasion. In fact I begged to be left at home that I might have spent the time in prayer, but my dear husband and children insisted on my coming and, lest an appearance of sadness in me might be misunderstood, I feel I ought to say a word for their sakes. I think I need not say even that word to the mothers present. Mothers will understand how I have realized, as I have been sitting here, and many times before while this question has been on the carpet, a side of life to which my child is yet a stranger. Having experienced the weight of public work for twenty-six years, also the weight of a large family continually hanging on my heart, having striven very hard to fulfil the obligation on both sides, and having realized what a very hard struggle it has been, the mother's heart in me has shrunk in some measure from offering her up to the same kind of warfare. It was a cherished wish for many years that she might be permitted to have the one side without the other, but our ways are not God's ways. The consecration which I made on the morning of her birth, and consummated on the day that I gave her first to public work, I have finished this morning in laying her again on this altar . . . God is my witness how sincerely I coveted to give to the world men and women who should have no other consideration, no other aim or object in life but to win its inhabitants for Him. *That* has been the highest ambition of my soul, from the day I became a mother until this. And if, in carrying that out, sometimes God has led me by a way I could not see, a way my natural heart shrank from, a way in which I have many times said 'Lord, if it be possible let this cup pass from me' nevertheless, I have not, as far as I know, rejected that way. I have accepted that way this morning because it has seemed to me that it is the Lord's way."[121]

To celebrate Queen Victoria's Jubilee in 1887 fifty officers were dedicated for the work in India. In July more than 20,000 people went to the Alexandra Palace for the Army's twenty-second anniversary meeting; 1,000 brass instruments and 100 drums made a joyful sound, if not always a musical one. Past the saluting point, where the Army Mother stood beside the General, marched something over 11,000 Army troops, including the Jubilee Fifty for India. These, in Indian dress, marched barefoot! Men and women of many nations mingled with British Salvationists now. *The War Cry,* reporting the day's events, named the countries represented in the march past, commenting, "their Salvation Brigades go down with a swing". The whole day from 10 a.m. to 10 p.m. went with a swing. One press report gave an impression of the crowd, "Such a genuine low-class mob can rarely be seen ... yet the order and true courtesy which prevailed were astonishing. Very astonishing, too, was the general beaming happiness. Never have I seen such a mass of people more thoroughly enjoying themselves."[122] It was in this year that William came running down the steep stairs of the Army's Headquarters, giving instructions all the way to a following officer, and dashing across the pavement dived into a waiting cab with a shout of, "Where am I going?" He and all the family went their hectic ways. None of them appeared to have noticed any serious decline in Catherine's strength. Granted she tired more quickly, from sheer exhaustion must more often be carried to the cab at the close of the meeting, but she was still the centre of all their lives, the inspirer at every conference, the one whose love never burned low.

A series of meetings in various cities led by General and Mrs. Booth was described for the first time as *Two Days with God.* The first was held in December in Exeter Hall. Contemporary accounts agree that these meetings were marked by a sense of urgency and solemnity "impossible to describe". Thrusts from the platform brought eager response from the crowds. Speakers, including members of the Booth family, caught the mood of the moment. In Manchester Catherine spoke in three of the six meetings. There the opening song on Monday morning was Herbert Booth's hymn of prayer beginning, "Lord, through the Blood of the Lamb that was slain, cleansing for me"[123] and singing it seemed to transport the congregation into the very presence of God. People told one another afterwards that they had never before had such an experience as during these meetings. It was something special, unique, to be remembered to the end of life. Near the close of the second day Catherine scribbled off a letter to Emma; only a stray page remains. Probably ever since Mrs. Mumford's suffering death and more insistently since the loss of her friend Mrs. Billups, the fear that she might develop cancer had ebbed and flowed in Catherine. Did Emma know of this? Or was this word in her letter about "submission" designed to sow a seed in Emma's mind that might grow into a little balm for her heart should her mother's fear become fact? We do not know. Perhaps Catherine wrote on impulse as she might have done to Mrs. Billups in the old days, to confide this new act of faith and set the seal of testimony to the inner submission? Former surrenders had meant venturing the future by faith, putting the claims of God and the people before all earthly loves and joys (and how her loves and joys had been multiplied as a result!). But acquiescence in *this* meant being *willing* to sacrifice the very opportunity to sacrifice, being *willing* to accept a command to sheathe her sword, to relinquish life itself. Was her own surrender linked with the closing words of her address in the first meeting when she said, "Oh, Lord help these people who cannot manage their own hearts, to choose Thy will and then Thou wilt enable them to do everything else."[124]

Characteristically catching her thoughts on to paper just as they arose Catherine wrote that last page of her letter to Emma. Here is part, "P.S. We have had wonderful meetings. Free Trade Hall crowded afternoon and night and this morning almost full tho' it snowed hard at the time of the gathering. I got on well I think this morning. I got a blessing yesterday. I *accepted* if the Lord's will for me, the disease I have so dreaded in my life, against which I fear my heart has rebelled, and this has helped me as submission always helps us! This won't bring the disease if it is not to come but it will make it much easier if it should come . . . We are at Mr. Crossley's; he is a dear fellow. I do think you should write him, he would be so pleased and you need not be a bit nervous, just thank him for his interest . . . He has asked so often and so kindly about you . . . I have just had a talk with Pa, and he thinks with me that you should come home as soon as this present fit of cold weather is over . . . Your loving mother. C."[125]

At Bristol in early February 1888 in spite of a heavy snowfall *The War Cry* reports that the Colston Hall was crowded to its farthest gallery when Mrs. Booth rose to speak on the evening of the second of the two days' meetings. It is almost certain, from what she said to Bramwell afterwards, that Catherine carried in her heart the conviction that she was fatally stricken. But there is no hint of her personal pain as she came to grips with her audience. Easy to say *after* the event that she spoke as never before, but it seems that it was felt at the time that her address in this meeting manifested transcending power. At its conclusion at least 800 men and women answered the call, dedicating themselves to a life of holiness and service to God. Following her husband's reading of the Scripture, Catherine had taken as her text "Advise and see what answer I shall return to Him that sent us" and swiftly, straight to the heart of her listeners, she pressed home the fact that "*God wants the answer*. What is the response which you, individually, will make to the *Voice* which has been sounding in your ears during the last two days . . . you *know* it is the Voice of God. It matters not what human instrument it has come through. If God had used a sparrow or some inanimate instrument to convey His message, that would not take away for a moment the importance of the message . . . What is the answer to be? Perhaps some of you say, 'I do not choose to return an answer'. But it is not

410

optional with you whether you will or not ... All truth coming from God demands, nay receives an answer from every soul who listens to it; that very refusal to return an answer *is* an answer of defiance. It is saying back to God, 'Mind your own business, I don't want your will. I have chosen my path. I am busy about other matters. I shall not return an answer to *your* messages.' That very attitude is an answer of defiance! You cannot help yourself; your soul *must* respond to the truth one way or the other. You have heard that inward voice; you have seen that inward light. Now you must say 'yes' or 'no'. You can never go back to where you stood before—*never!* Now what does the Lord want with you? He wants first to do something *in* you. Then He wants you to present yourselves that He may do something *by* you ... The Voice in you is saying, 'Come to Me; bring that poor, stained, wretched, up-and-down, in-and-out, unbelieving doubting soul of yours to Me ... I will empower you henceforth to live in obedience to My commands ... to walk before Me as my beloved child, in holiness and righteousness all your days ...'"

This and much more was solemnly and lovingly spoken. Catherine reasoned, reproved, beseeched. The time melted away, the meeting's end was at hand. In the stillness that settled over the whole assembly the people sat as if under a spell. It was at this point of a meeting that she always felt the burden of her message most. Tenderly she said, "I may not have spoken of your particular difficulty. Never mind. Apply the truth to yourself ... Will you rise up and say in your heart, 'Yes, Lord, I accept, I submit ...' 'Oh,' you say, 'I don't know what He will want next.' No, we none of us know that, but we know that we shall be safe in His hands ..."[126]

Her voice, vibrant to the last with love to God and man, suddenly ceased. The people before her did not know that most of them would never hear it again. Catherine herself did not know that she would preach only once or twice more. Reading the record of her words, and knowing what was to follow, one cannot avoid feeling that she was speaking for herself as much as for anyone in the Colston Hall that night when she said, "*Yes, Lord, I accept. I submit.*" William Booth's little wife was fifty-nine. It was twenty-eight years since she opened her lips in public, prepared by God to become Mother in Israel, Mother of The Salvation Army, Mother of Nations.

BOOK SEVEN

The Last Enemy

"The last enemy that shall be destroyed is death."

—St. Paul.

"Thy will be done; only let me be Thine, whether suffering or in health, whether living or dying."

—In Catherine's Journal at seventeen.

"All our enemies have to be conquered by *faith*, not by realization, and is it not so with the last enemy, death?"

—To Commissioner Booth-Clibborn from her death-bed.

"It is faith that brings power . . . daring to believe the written Word with or without feeling."

—In a letter to her parents.

"I cast the responsibility on God . . . He Who is so faithful in time will not fail us in eternity! Nor in the dark valley that lies between."

—In a letter to Mr. Denny.

"Don't be concerned about your dying: only go on living well, and the dying will be all right."

—From her last message to Salvationists.

". . . there is nothing like the light of eternity to show us what is real and what is not."

—In a love-letter to William Booth.

"I consider the first and fundamental and all comprehensive principle of Christ's salvation . . . that every act of our lives, every relationship into which we enter, should be centred and bounded by God and His glory."

—In her address at her daughter Emma's wedding.

"Give me grace to cry in all life's conflicts and changes and temptations, and in death's final struggle as my Saviour did 'Father, Glorify Thyself'."

—From love-letter to William Booth.

"No matter how advanced in holiness, every dying saint rests his soul on the Blood of Christ."

—From a public address.

"My soul acquiesces in God's providence. I can, I do, submit and all within me says, 'Thy will be done'."

—Love-letter to William Booth.

"A denouncer of iniquity . . . Thank God I have been that! That is what is wanted in the world today, denouncers; denouncers of iniquity."

—Message when on death-bed to a young officer.

1

Looking back it seems to me that Catherine Booth's life was to an extraordinary degree marked by the unpredictable. She was a delicate child, prostrated at fourteen by spinal trouble, at seventeen her lungs were affected, yet she became the mother of eight healthy children and in addition to her responsibilities for her home sustained, after the birth of her fourth child, the burden of continual preaching. Were the records not indisputable it would be easier to doubt than to believe the story of her endurance on the physical plane alone, but if the emotional strain entailed be included the demands made upon her were surely beyond mere human strength? Further this delicate child, without formal education or informed guidance, yet made her way through such a maze of church history and dogmatical disputations as, together with a profound and intimate knowledge of the Bible, equipped her intellectually for mastery in argument of her hearers, many of them highly educated.

We need to consider the times in which Catherine lived to estimate the revolutionary nature of her action when she defied the most rigid of conventions—religious custom—by breaking into the hush of a Sunday morning service asking permission to speak! We need to remember, too, that she was temperamentally timid, shrinking from publicity. Not even William who knew her best could have predicted her action.

Catherine was rapturously in love with her William and continued to be. In youth she felt that any hardship was to be preferred to separation. Yet she denied herself the company of the beloved with a persistence that might well suggest indifference were there not proof to the contrary. About this she met regret as she looked back from her death-bed. In one of the long nights of waking and suffering she turned with pleading eyes to Bramwell's wife; they were alone together, Florence acting as nurse to relieve Emma. The younger woman heard the still beautiful voice, gentle but charged with longing, the sound of it dying away into silence between the short phrases as if her thoughts were dwelling in the past. "I regret—I have not got more happiness out of my life—I see I should have done—I advise you not to be such a slave to any work—as to have no time to love one another—to make one another as happy as possible."[1] No time! The inexorable words were written by her own hand across the door leading to many of life's innocent joys.

The love-letters reveal a very practical minded young woman who envisaged the responsibilities of the future, the importance of being able to provide for children and their education and for old age.

Yet it was Catherine who encouraged William to ignore her needs and their children's when the decision to step out of security to become itinerant preachers was taken. And again, when William felt he must stay to work in Whitechapel, it was she who responded with that steadfast, "We have trusted the Lord once for our support and we can trust Him again."

Even her spiritual life ran an unpredicted course. Cradled in the Methodist teaching of the experience of conversion, it did not become alive in her until she was seventeen, nor had she joined the Methodist Church at that time. She sought with passionate desire a token in confirmation of her faith. But faith so hardly come by for her was rarely rewarded by exaltation; faced with a sea of contrary circumstances no instant miracle divided the waters for her, rather it seemed at times that they rose about her as she passed. And here also I found the unexpected. God did not reveal Himself to her as I should have thought that He would. As I look at her unfolded life dare I suggest a reason? Is it that a more sentient response to her faith might have upset the balance of her free spirit? To those capable of intense emotion danger lies in incontrovertible proof. Independence of spirit, vital to love, whether the object be human or divine, may be imperilled by too clear an apprehension and the precious faculty of reason be overwhelmed by fanaticism; then love itself may become more oppressive than hate. Catherine was continually driven by God out from the familiar to the unknown, and every new departure in her life demanded a new act of faith in God. She was not allowed to hear a voice, nor to see a "safe" way ahead. To every fresh call and in the presence of every threatened loss or sorrow her response had to be "I will trust and not be afraid." And now, at life's close, after all this walking by faith, will she be granted a "sign"? Will she like Stephen be allowed to *see* the heavens opened and Christ there? Or will she be required to go to the last step of her earthly journey walking by faith alone?

2

Those who loved her were not aware that Catherine was to a noticeable degree more ill than often before. Everyone had grown accustomed to her mastery of bodily weakness and to her recuperative power. It was not until the Bristol two days' meetings that Bramwell heard from his mother of a swelling in her breast. He was the first to whom she spoke of it. Significant this of her love's home. The chill of fear must not whisper in that sanctuary. William must be spared; he must not feel the shadow while the substance was uncertain. Remembering Mrs. Mumford's suffering and death, Bramwell at once urged that "the best advice possible should be obtained. Although," he says, "my mother did not seem at all to share in my anxiety." He ought surely to have known her better by now! The fact that when the time came she insisted upon going alone to see the specialist shows how deep was her dread. Immediately upon her return to London an appointment was made through Dr. Heywood Smith* with Sir James Paget.† It was on Tuesday February 21, 1888, that she set forth in the familiar "four-wheeler" to trundle the long slow journey across London. After thorough examination Sir James Paget—he was very kind but also very frank—"unhesitatingly pronounced the tumour to be of a cancerous type". He advised an immediate operation. Calmly Catherine told him her objections. She explained that in a long experience she had never met one case in which the use of the knife had resulted in a cure. She asked, "How long, then, am I likely to live?" Sir James, not knowing her, attempted to hedge, but quietly persisting, Catherine repeated her question. Finally he told her that in his opinion about eighteen months or "at the utmost two years."

"Two years . . . at the utmost two years. . . ." The cab is in motion again on its return journey. Solitary within she looks out of the window, on one side, on the other. She said, "It seemed that the sentence of death had been passed upon everything." Anguish sprang into life with the thought, "I shall not be there to nurse William in his last hour." Is not love's fiercest torment ever in its impotence? Nothing is too hard to bear while love can *help*. It is when love is helpless that the heart is ready to break. The cab crawls on. No! It flies now, towards home, towards William! "Two years . . . I shall not be there." She tells us that her heart was swept with "unutterable yearning" . . . for William, for the children, for the Army. And now she is on her knees. Did she remember the cab where she and William first saw each into the heart of each? When "it seemed . . . that henceforth the current of our lives must flow together?" I think she remembered. William was at her side then, and she had seen love's future, its togetherness. *Now,* she is alone and sees the parting that will end their earthly companionship.

> *The thousand sweet, still joys of such*
> *As, hand in hand, face earthly life.*‡

She does not want to die. Her mind and heart are so vividly alive,

* Dr. Heywood Smith, physician; suffered for the part he took in helping the Booths in the Purity Crusade.
    † Sir James Paget (1814-1899), surgeon and lecturer, St. Bartholomew's Hospital, London.
    ‡ Matthew Arnold, *Farewell*.

O

so aware of her love's capacity for loving. And, there is so much that she could do, wants to do, wants to see done. She weeps. She prays. We do not know how long she knelt alone praying, but we do know, for William tells us, that when the cab drew up outside their home and he ran down the steps to meet her, she was able to smile up at him. "Drawing me into the room," he tells, "she unfolded gradually to me the result of the interview. I sat down speechless. She rose from her chair and came and knelt beside me, saying, 'Do you know what was my first thought? That I should not be there to nurse you at your last hour'. . . ."[2] Poor William! He sits as one stunned, while she kneels there close to him, caressing, talking. "She talked," William says, "like a heroine, like an angel to me; she talked as she had never talked before. I could say little or nothing. It seemed as though a hand were laid upon my very heart-strings."[3] And now they kneel together hand in hand as at their betrothal. They pray.

William was due to leave on the very night of that black day for meetings in Holland. He tells, "She would not hear of my remaining at home for her sake." Loving-wise Catherine! She well knew how the activity entailed by the meetings would shield him from the full blast of the tempest now rising for all who loved her. On the way to the station the General called in at Headquarters (there were no telephones in those days) to speak to Bramwell, who, according to bad custom, was working there until it should be time for him to leave to conduct a half-night of prayer at Notting Hill. So it was at "101" that Bramwell heard the doctor's verdict from his father. The great building is empty about them; the street outside deserted, as the two men talk and weep. Before they part father and son kneel to pray. I picture them there; these two, so near in love to her and to each other, now united afresh by these new bonds of their grief. Catherine understood them both and, by the illuminating prescience of her love for them, saw their importance to one another in their great task of making and leading The Salvation Army. It is just as she would wish that when they feel the first chill of her approaching absence they should draw closer to each other. To the end of their lives on earth they spoke of her as if she were but lately gone from them. She seemed still to enter into their plans and hopes. Questions were debated as if what she would think were still important. Their love for her kept alive for them a sense of her presence.

Because his conflict was, at its core, the same for a vast number of Catherine's spiritual children, I include here some account of her son's experience that night, recorded by him at the time. It is not unique, rather is it typical. The links between the early day Salvationists and William Booth and his wife were so strongly allied to family relationships that it seemed natural and proper at the time, that the world-wide family should be brought, as it were, to the bedside of their "Mother", and the experiences of her sons and daughters shared with Catherine's and William's spiritual children. In the little book he wrote Bramwell tells, "I left at once for Notting Hill to lead a half-night of prayer ... The long ride across the city was filled with the darkest and most sorrowful thoughts, and in the meeting I found it impossible to throw off my burden ... after inviting seekers for holiness to come to the penitent-form and several had responded, I spoke to one—I received one of the great lessons of my lifetime from her lips. She was a woman of middle life, apparently a Christian of many years' experience, but now deeply moved, and all she could say amidst her sobs ... was, 'Oh, Lord, I want to be willing —make me willing—let me be willing.' I knelt down beside her, all the gathering storm seemed already to be bursting over me; all that my beloved mother had been and was and could be ... crowded itself on the dark horizon of my soul. I can never forget those moments. Could I for myself say, 'Not my will, but Thine be done'? The seeker at my side went on praying and crying 'Lord make me willing—let me say it'. And at last I cried it also! I joined my prayers to hers. ... Her spoken distress and agony of soul were made a guide and beacon amid the storm and darkness of a terrible trial of my faith."[4]

"We look at one another through our tears and cannot speak," Emma wrote to her mother a day or two after that visit to Sir James Paget. Her phrase well described the condition of the family, of all the household. Catherine was loved by them all, and they all felt that *she* understood their grief. There was a kind of rest of heart for them in that knowledge. One senses it in Emma's words, when continuing her letter she says, "But, loved one, *you* will know how we feel."[5] William said of that time, "It was the realization of *our* grief that filled her heart." From the very first she perceived that her suffering and death would be, as it were, Satan's instrument to challenge the faith and submission of those who loved her. It was not only her dying, it was the unanswered "why" that tormented each heart and it became her care to help them in this testing.

Catherine sent William to Holland on that bleak February night for his own sake, but also because she had already resolved that they all must be helped by her to go on with "the war". Within a few days she had laid her commands upon her two best beloveds. With William and Bramwell, General and Chief-of-Staff of The Salvation Army, she made "a sort of compact", Bramwell recorded, that business of an anxious kind, which we might, from a desire to save her from pain, keep from her, was still to be brought forward; so that while she could she was to hold her loved place in the councils of the Army, "and many decisions which later proved to be of the utmost importance ... were arrived at beside her sick-bed."[6] Further consultations with doctors, and especially with her husband and family, only confirmed Catherine's decision not to submit to operation. Bramwell spoke of his mother as being "strongly and firmly opposed

419

to it . . . We around her were also influenced by the risk of operation arising from the weak condition of her heart. . . ."⁷

After the first shock of the disclosure Catherine's strength diminished. Her public work almost ceased. Some things were decided upon in direct consequence of her condition. Katie and her husband were called from France to see her. Ballington and his wife in the U.S.A were asked to arrange a visit. The day of Emma's marriage was fixed. She had just become engaged to Commissioner Tucker, a widower, pioneer of the Army's work in India. Announcing her decision in *The War Cry* Catherine said, "The recent serious change in my prospect of health (unless the Lord intervenes) has led me to desire that the marriage should take place at an earlier date than had been intended, so that I might have the surer prospect of taking part. . . ."⁸ The wedding day was made the occasion of a great demonstration in the interest of missionary work. The series of meetings described as *Two Days with God* had continued at various centres fortnightly throughout the spring. William led these, aided by one or more of his family and others. The *claims of God and the heathen world upon every follower of Christ,* was the advertised topic for the two days' meetings arranged in London, one in St. James's Hall, and the following day in the Congress Hall. The morning of the second day was decided upon as Emma's marriage service. It was the tenth of April, William's birthday (he was fifty-nine) and the anniversary of the day when he and Catherine had first lifted love's eyes to one another. In what deeps of love and sorrow they must have greeted that morning in 1888. But the day was to be faced with courage for Emma's sake, and for the people, their Army children, who, by nine a.m., were flocking towards the hall. A missionary meeting, announced as an *Indain Durbar,* was to take place at night, and the pillars of the vast hall were decked, we are told, to resemble palm trees. The bridegroom had brought a dark-skinned contingent from India to greet the bride, and to plead India's cause. Bandsmen and others on the slope behind the platform wore yellow, red, or blue turbans. A huge strip of calico across one side of the hall bore the words "The heathen for His inheritance", and on the other "They shall come from the East and the West". Reserved seat ticket holders (at 5s to help India) were admitted first, and among these were some of the Booths' oldest and staunchest friends. *The War Cry* named many; I name some, without whose aid the Army could not have advanced so rapidly. Samuel Morley was dead, but up the steps and through the great pillars of the portico came Mr. R. C. Morgan of *The Christian,* William's first "backer" in Whitechapel, Mr. Billups of pre-Whitechapel days, Dr. and Mrs. Heywood Smith, Mr. Denny's sons, Mr. Crossley of Manchester, Mr. Willett of Brighton, Mr. George Studd lately home from China. The crowd followed until every corner was packed with people and the

420

windows of the hall opening into the Training College were raised and the class-rooms beyond filled, and still there were people in Linscott Road. These would wait to see "the family" arrive. A pavement artist had drawn a picture of the bride, and reaped a good reward in pence.

The General, by way of apology for the over-crammed hall, said: "Heaven is the only place where there can be a crowd without a crush!" He conducted the wedding ceremony. Everybody looked happy, or tried to. When Catherine, whose right arm was in a sling, rose to speak all hearts moved in sympathy towards her. She was perhaps the least perceptibly distressed among them. That fine command of self, perfected now, subordinated all to the opportunity "to reach hearts". Her opening words said so, "I feel sure, dear friends, that you are not expecting me to say much this morning. The few words I do say I should like to be as the first words I think I said twenty-eight years ago, when I opened my public commission . . . that they should *reach your hearts* and inspire every father and mother here to present their children to God . . . As I listened to these articles of marriage of The Salvation Army,* and remembered, as I did, that some persons thought them rather too strict, too severe, I looked back upon my own wedding day. I am very sorry that there was not an organization that would have voiced the desires, and purposes, and aspirations of my soul on that occasion, as those desires and aspirations have been voiced this morning; for God is my witness that these have not one whit exceeded those which swelled my own heart that day." She went on to say that from her youth she had held that "whatever we do . . . we should do all to the glory of God. I had embraced that idea of Christianity early and I can say before God and in my own conscience, that I sought to carry out that principle, and by His grace— His wonderful grace—though I have not always come up to my own ideal, yet . . . I have . . . kept His interests first, as I do now this morning in this marriage. I believe my precious child will do the same."

Then, with a power and vigour that surprised all, she spoke of God's fulfilment of His promise and purpose in her own life; and used her own experience to make a plea that "You should thus present yourselves, your children, your all; for you know we all have a world to give up. It does not signify how we are trained or what were the particular circumstances of our antecedent life, there comes a crisis, a moment when every human soul which enters the Kingdom of God has to make its choice of that Kingdom in preference to *everything* that it holds and owns as its world; to give up all that,

* See *The Salvation Army Ceremonies,* Salvationist Publishing and Supplies, Ltd.

and to embrace and choose God." The Army Mother was almost at the end of what she would say on that April morning, and what she said is of utmost significance to Salvationists today, and for so long as there are sinners left in the world. "Pray for us all, and pray for this Salvation Army, because we believe it is the highest embodiment of Jesus Christ's ideas, the nearest approximation to His work now in the world ... I believe that we are about the very business which He set His people to do—the very identical work. There are plenty of people about all other kinds of work ... helpful to humanity ... I say 'Amen, God bless you', but *that* is not the particular work Jesus Christ set His people to do. The great characteristic of His people in the world was that they were to be *saviours of men*—Salvationists."[9]

There seemed, at this time, to be a rallying of Catherine's strength. Possible, was it, to hope? To those at a distance, watching for news of her, it seemed so; seemed so, even to those close at hand. In May she went with William to the *Two Days with God* held in Glasgow City Hall and was able to take part. At Exeter Hall, London, another two days' meetings were held on June 4 and 5. Catherine spoke on the morning of both days. William called for a day of "fasting and prayer." The whole Army was praying for her. Multitudes felt as William did when he wrote in his diary, "It seems incredible that she should die ... and there are a good many people at the present moment who are strongly believing that this sickness after all is not unto death."[10] Hope for her recovery was springing in many hearts in those May-June days.

Dr. Joseph Parker* invited Catherine to preach in the City Temple.† On the morning of Thursday, June 21, 1888, that pleasant spacious meeting-house was filled in all its parts, including fringes and aisles. Mr. Denny read the Scripture chosen for the basis for her theme. Catherine Booth stood at the reading-desk of the roomy pulpit, a frail looking little woman, one time "most timid and bashful of all Christ's disciples", *now*, in a living sense of the words, and to an extent unprecedented in the history of mankind, "Mother of Nations", the first woman since New Testament days whose message reached millions of her fellow creatures.

The mere records of her words cannot account for their effect. Judged as orator, teacher, advocate, she was among those who excel, but still there was something *more*, something between her and her hearers, known to them alone. Gunning, distinguished Hollander, religious teacher and author, had listened to the foremost speakers of his day and he declared, "Above them all, to my mind, stands

* Dr. Joseph Parker (1830-1892), English Congregational Minister. Famed preacher, author of *People's Bible*.
† Destroyed by German bombs and since rebuilt.

Catherine Booth. I cannot exactly describe the secret of the extraordinary, captivating power of her words, but her address remains unforgettable. Right from the beginning to the end she brought me into the personal presence of Jesus Christ. From the moment she opened her mouth she took possession of her listeners' hearts, and seemed to speak to them, not from without but from within."[11] In her congregation that June morning sat a young American, Dr. Parkes Cadman. Forty years afterwards when he was himself a preacher of world fame he still held her words in mind. He said of them, "I have not heard since, anything which moved me more deeply than that remarkable address, lasting at least one hour and a quarter, delivered in the purest English, with faultless diction, in a voice like the pealing of a silver bell across a still lake." The people assembled to hear her knew that death had her by the hand but, in this her last address, Catherine Booth had almost nothing to say about herself and little to say about the Army; she was swept on in a torrent of desire for *the salvation of the world*. At the end she sank down utterly spent. It was nearly an hour before she could be moved. The crowd went decorously away and Catherine Booth lived in silence that last spell she would spend in a pulpit.

Here are some of her words, as apt today as on the morning she spoke them, pertinent to this book because they are an epitome of her faith and teaching. Here in her simple logical fashion, she opened her thoughts and we may see what she believed and what was her life's purpose. Here, too, spoke the Mother who would, with her last breath, raise up children of the Spirit, like-minded, for the honour of Christ and the salvation of the world. She spoke of *the duty of spreading Christianity throughout the world* ... "I think there would be no division of opinion with respect to two or three facts ... the first is, we have made very *poor progress so far, even in making known Christ* as a Saviour from sin and hell. I have been appalled and amazed at the comparatively few I have met, who have understood that the realization of the forgiveness of sins is possible! ... They do not appear to know that Jesus Christ is a positive, *present* Saviour. ... Perhaps on no point has The Salvation Army suffered persecution more than on this one point of its teaching: that it proclaims a Saviour not only willing to pardon but who does pardon absolutely, and who communicates a sense of that pardon by His Holy Spirit to the hearts of those who truly repent and sincerely believe. And that He not only washes their past sins away, but has the power to keep them from their sins, and will, if they trust in Him, enable them to live in righteousness and holiness all their lives, walking in obedience to His commands, keeping that inner law— the law of Christ—which is the most perfect law and fulfils all others ... As I have looked round our towns and cities, and observed the marks of misery depicted on thousands of faces I meet with, I feel, oh, for a trumpet voice! Oh, for some mighty herald that would get up on every kerb-stone, or every other available space, and proclaim to this poor world, full of hungry souls, that there *is* peace, pardon, purity for them, and power in a living Saviour to keep them from sin ...

"There can be no dispute, I suppose, as to the fact that we have made very poor progress in the conversion of the world. Not only has our progress been slow in making a Saviour known, but in bringing people to Him where He has been made known ... Sin, and the outcome of sin, which is misery, are everywhere prevalent, just as much amongst the rich as amongst the poor, amongst the educated as amongst the illiterate. Sin and misery everywhere—changed in its outward forms since apostolic days ... but, however genteel and civilized evil may be, it is evil still, and whether an evil heart beats under a broadcloth coat or a fustian jacket, it brings forth the same bitter fruits of sorrow ... From the manner in which many speakers and writers arrogate all civilization in the world to Christianity one would imagine that they had forgotten there was a civilization in existence long before Christ appeared on the scene. I grant that civilization follows in the wake of Christianity; but Christ did not come to *civilize* the world, but to *save* it, and to bring it back to God. ... If I understand the Bible rightly, it appeals alike to civilized and uncivilized. It makes no distinction between the sinfulness of civilized and uncivilized men ... Let us, therefore, be careful to distinguish between civilization and Christianity, and do not let us arrogate to ourselves all the civilization of the world, for it does not belong to us. We have nothing to boast of short of salvation. We have not a single disciple, baptized person, or professing Christian to be thankful for who has not experienced a change of heart; who has not been made out of falsehood into truth, out of dishonesty into honesty, out of uncleanness into purity; who is not transformed in the spirit of his mind, and renewed again after the likeness of God. Oh, that God may use me to be the means of imprinting this on your minds and of helping you, in future, not to be satisfied with, or glory over, anything short of this in connection with all your religious work! Jesus Christ came, I say, to rectify men's hearts ... when you have got man right with God you will soon get him right with humanity, with himself, and in all his relationships ... Then it follows that, if this be true, all missionary, ministerial, evangelistic, or Salvation Army effort that fails in accomplishing this is a farce and a failure ...

"All who know anything of the salvation of God must feel with me here; that if we cannot cover the earth with the knowledge of it, then we should cover as much as we can ... I think we are bound to do this for the peace, purity, goodwill, beneficence, truth and justice which always follow in the wake of true Christianity.

'Ah,' you say, 'these things do not follow in the wake of all Christianity.' But I am talking about the genuine thing, Christ's Christianity, and I say, if these results do *not* follow, it is a bastard Christianity ....Real Christianity inculcates and implants the love that worketh no ill of any kind to its neighbour; the love that seeks the good even of its enemies...*That is real Christianity*, and wherever that goes peace and goodwill are found...

"Are not we who love the Lord Jesus Christ bound to do something for *His* sake?...Will He be satisfied with a paltry percentage of the human race, as the result of the travail of His soul Who tasted death for every man, and Who wills that all men should be saved ...He wants His prodigal children brought home. He won't ask you where you worshipped, or what creed you professed; but He *will* ask for His prodigals—those whom you have won for Him. Will you not set to work to do something for His sake?...God has arranged to save men by *human* instrumentality and if we have not succeeded in the past we are not to throw the blame on Him...If Christians were only half as diligent as husbandmen the world would have been saved long ago...What is wanted, I say, is a force of spiritually equipped and determined men and women to *take the world for God*...

"Look at the world again for a minute. Here are the millions of men entrenched in their wickedness; entrenched behind all manner of refuges of lies, enamoured of their sins...There they are, satisfied with their sin so far, because, poor things, they won't allow themselves to think...How are you going to get them down from their tower of self-satisfaction, sin and pleasure? Do you think they are coming down by your saying, 'Here, come along; hear me; let me preach to you. Come and be converted'? Oh, no, the Christian church has been trying that game too long. The people are *far too busy*. They turn round and tell you so...Listen to what Jesus Christ commissioned His disciples to do. Not to ensconce themselves in comfortable buildings and invite the people to come, and then, if they would not come, leave them alone to be damned. No! No! He said, 'Go ye,' which means 'go after them'. 'Where, Lord?' 'Into all the world.' 'What to do?' 'Preach the Gospel to every creature.' 'Where, Lord?' '*Where the creatures are*. Follow them.' If ever you are to get this work done it will be by *pressing* God's truth upon the attention of men and making them hear, and think, and feel; and it must be done by men and women who have themselves experienced and are living in the practice of what they preach...A great deal of the truth preached nowadays would not cut the wings off a fly, much less pierce asunder the soul and spirit. You must preach God's justice and vengeance against sin, as well as His love for the sinner. You must preach hell as well as heaven. You must let your Gospel match the intuitions of humanity, or you may as well throw it in the sea...The great want in this day is *truth*...Tell a man the truth about himself, then the truth about God, then the truth about his obligation to others. That is, if you believe the things I have been saying are true ... If it is not true, be done with it. If it is true, act upon it!"

In closing came the only words in her address which may be linked with her condition. She said, "When we come to face eternity, and look back on the past, what will be our regret? That we have done so much? Oh no! That we have done so little ... Friends, take these few words home to your closet, and ask the Spirit of God if they are so ... and go and bring forth fruit accordingly! May God bless and help you; and may we meet at the right hand of the Throne, for Jesus' sake, Amen!"[12]

4

Salvationists and friends gathered at the Alexandra Palace on July 9, 1888, for the Annual Day of Thanksgiving. The Army Mother looked on for a few minutes from a distance. She felt "unutterable things". Whatever hopes her dear ones and friends harboured for her, *she* looked steadily forward to the limit set for her life on earth. She knew that she would never again see her Army children gathered for prayer and praise on a "Palace Day". The next year she sent a message. She said, "My heart is filled with wonder and thanksgiving in remembrance of the mighty things God has done ... I picture to myself your happy faces, and listen to your joyous songs, my heart goes out in a fervent prayer that this day may prove the renewing of your inward strength ... "[13]

The months following the discovery of Catherine's illness brought a series of uncertainties; helpful, mainly, to cloud with hope the blinding glare of inevitability from those who loved her. Treatments were tried; the dear patient was "seen" by one expert after another, but on the whole Sir James Paget's verdict stood unchallenged. The seeming increase of strength that had made the last preachings possible now flagged. The active right hand became incapacitated. She could no longer make her pen fly over the pages. She must dictate, and though her letters were as usual taken up with the one to whom she wrote, or with the "blessed war", we may legitimately read into a sentence here and there an echo of what she was saying to herself about herself; for instance in this letter to Captain Charlotte Stirling, "I pray continually that His grace may prove sufficient for you, not only till the end of this iniquitous imprisonment, but for a valiant and victorious fight with the powers of darkness to the end of your life ... I would specially warn you against allowing your present distressing circumstances to cast you down, or lead you to fear that this event has happened outside the divine programme. I know how cunningly Satan can misrepresent our very highest blessings and honours, making them appear as misfortunes ... Try to leave the interests of the war and the fate of your comrades in the hands of your Great Commander ... Don't let Satan make you afraid that the great and most comprehensive promises are not for you."[14]

Catherine's knowledge of the devil's tactics prepared her to meet the "last enemy". For her faith included the recognition of the existence of a spirit at enmity with God and working for the destruction of man. From a child she had been, as it were, on speaking terms with the devil. Strange as it may seem to some, I am convinced that her belief in the devil, and familiarity with his ways, strengthened the loving, believing submission of her spirit to God as she went down to death. Stead observed, "Her belief in the devil was a constant tonic which supplemented the stimulus and the energy of her abounding faith in the ever-present reality of the active love of God."[15]

The sea was one of Catherine's loves: "The great and beautiful sea." She had herself already chosen a Home of Rest for Officers. It was the last house on the east cliff of a quiet little town on the Essex coast, Clacton *then* being in sharp contrast to Clacton *now*, There she went for a long stay. Before her return from the coast to London, it had become clear that a quieter and more secluded dwelling than the home-cum-headquarters on Clapton Common would be necessary. A house was taken on a newly developed estate near Hadley Wood. Here, from Clacton, the dear sufferer came amd gained some refreshment in the restful surroundings. Mr. Billups, oldest among her friends, supplied a horse and brougham. She was able to receive visitors, and among them Stead, who wrote, "Dear Bramwell, I was with your mother last night and had a very good time ... I would like to go back. One thing I am quite sure of and that is that it is a sin ... not to have an intelligent and sympathetic stenographer or a person with a long memory constantly within call of your mother. If I had no other work I would volunteer for the post in order to secure for the benefit of the Army her reflections upon all things ... Pray pardon my vehemence[16] ..." This suggestion was followed. (Later, at Clacton, screens were arranged near the door so that Catherine did not know when a shorthand writer was present.) Conferences on Salvation Army affairs were held in her room. A small house nearby had been acquired for Bramwell so that he could be at hand daily. To Hadley Wood came Ballington and his wife and baby son, on a brief visit from his Salvation Army charge in the U.S.A. Lucy, Catherine's youngest daughter, was in close and loving waiting on her mother. For duties needing more trained care, Captain Carr (a nurse) took charge and was at Mrs. Booth's side to the last. She was a gentle, firm woman, one of those "born" nurses. "Carr ... you have been good to me—more than a nurse—you have been a daughter,"[17] Catherine said to her when the end was near. In the spring of 1889 a new method of treatment by electric needles was under consideration. It was declared to be a "successful remedy for cancer" and had been favourably reported on in the *British Medical Journal*. Investigations showed that some patients seemed to have been cured. In May Catherine underwent a series of these electric treatments, given under an anaesthetic. Much intense suffering was involved and signs of improvement were soon seen to be but temporary.

Meantime Emma, with her first-born, returned from India. Lucy had fallen ill. Florence (Bramwell's wife) records of her presence, "Emma is ... such a strength of love and kindness."[18] The shock and strain of the electric treatment had a bad effect on the heart, and Catherine was much more manifestly ill. The doctors said, "Back to the sea." For how long? "Four or five weeks." But the sick woman knew better. On her way to Liverpool Street Station she talked of her experiences among the people; talked of that first "campaign" in Rotherhithe; of her meetings in the East End and in the West End. Driving leisurely along the streets, she looked her last upon the great city. Catherine was withdrawing from the multitude to whom her life had been devoted, to lie where she could see out over the far spaces of the waters and look farther still, forward to the eternal shore. After her arrival she wrote, slowly now, with her left hand, a brief note to William: "My dearest Love, just a few lines to say I am some better today. The journey aggravated the thing very much and I have suffered a good deal, but am better today. I like the place very much. I see what you mean more than ever I did, by being retired and shut off from the public gaze—if only it were nearer London so that you could get easier, I should propose that we took it and lived here while I need a home. The south room is too hot for me to go in now, and I feel sure will be as warm a winter room as I should find anywhere, having the south and west sun. However, we shall talk it over when you come. I am so sorry to hear you were feeling so down, tho' not surprised. Bless you. I wish I could cheer you. I could cry all the time if I allowed myself ... but I battle against it, and try to be as cheerful as I can for your sake. I know I have loved you and do still, as much as any wife living ... The Lord Himself bless and comfort you and bring you to me once more in peace ..."

They talked over her proposal and it gave William a brief happiness to arrange for the Clacton house to be their home, as she wished. A gift from Mr. Frank Crossley made it possible. The Booths rented the house from The Salvation Army. A suitable staff was installed, and offices arranged so that the General and others could be at work without disturbing Mrs. Booth. Staff-Captain Beard, an honorary Salvation Army officer of comfortable means, provided a carriage for her use. She had always enjoyed driving. The sea, the country, the skies, all were beautiful to her. But less than six weeks after her arrival in Clacton came the morning when, having started out, she asked to be driven back. "This will be my last drive, Emma," she said as they went into the house together. After this there were little strolls along the cliff, sometimes leaning on William's arm, but by October there was no longer strength to rise, and she was confined to her bed, placed at her wish so that from it she had a view of the sea. I have found one more scrap to William, characteristically undated, "My darling One, I never thought of you wanting a line or you should have had [a] better one, but you will accept this, just to assure you of my fullest and most satisfying assurance of your unalterable and eternal love to me. I have never doubted the possession of all your heart from the day you first declared it mine. We were wed for ever and though I go first you will soon follow and we shall find our all again in that eternal day, Amen, Amen. Good-bye darling till then. I shall be the first to greet you on the eternal shore with all our children and thousands of spiritual children from all lands. Yours as ever. Catherine."

The only alleviation of the now increasing bouts of pain came from the excitement of hearing news of the Army. This was especially so in the long, often sleepless, nights. "And so it came about," Bramwell's narrative tells, "that . . . news of the Lord's battle in some struggling little outpost or dismal slum, the tidings of a new conquest for the Cross from Ceylon or New York, succeeded in . . . bringing back to the dear worn features the radiance of her own days of victorious contact with the enemy." From time to time all her family and many of her visitors brought this kind of news. But even so, the very love of the fight that quickened her life's pulse intensified her grief. Bramwell says, "She mourned her coming withdrawal from the battlefield, with many tears and in deep dark anguish of spirit . . . It was in these inner conflicts that she seemed sometimes to suffer more than when the cancer rendered her whole body a house of torture."[19] To Mrs. Irvine* one of her spiritual children, Catherine had written years before, "My dear friend, this is the lesson that life is designed to teach us, that *God is enough for us.*,"[20] The lesson is not yet fully learned by her own heart. This slow dying; this conscious laying down of arms in the midst of battle: this bitter draught of love's impotence is the cup she must drink. And because her love's spring is in *God,* this last conflict must centre on Him. This is the anguish: God *could* help, "Lord, if Thou wilt, Thou canst . . ." and the answer is *He will not.*

How simple now faith's walk in the past appears as in her helplessness she looks out from her "prison" over the restless waters. How joyful now seem battles with the "world . . . and the devil"—the *flesh* had long since been made subservient. But now? Now the

* *née* Billups.

"poor body" was to become, as it were, the wood of her love's cross. She was always a little scornful and greatly impatient of the limitations of the flesh and its demands. "If only I had a better body," she used to say. Now, on the common cross of pain, she is to prove for herself and to demonstrate to others that death, no less than life, "is designed to teach us that God is enough for us". She knows the pattern of death ordained for her. As Stead put it, she received "two years' notice to quit". Not for her the sudden call, the swift parting, nor the gentle fading of faculties that creeps on life in old age; but when her powers of heart and mind are in full vigour, her influence at its highest, she is ordered off the field, to lie helpless, racked by pain and dying by inches. She had heard the word spoken "signifying by what death ... [she] should glorify God." It was not a premonition but a fact to be faced in the cold, clear light of reality. She wrote for the 1889 Self-Denial Appeal, "If the Lord were to ask me to deny myself of almost all I possess how easy it would be in comparison with what He requires from me just now, for I am realizing more fully than ever how much harder it is to suffer than to serve; nevertheless my soul bows in submission to my Heavenly Father."[21] This was no figure of speech. Strong-willed, independent, mothering Catherine Booth exemplified in her life to the last, her own definition of her faith, "I don't believe in any religion apart from doing the will of God." In death, and especially on the way to death, her life testifies that to do God's will is still her supreme desire.

Someone said to me, "The doctrine of 'doing' was the Booths' bane." A grain of truth this: two grains perhaps, applied to Catherine. It is because her love is so prolific of ideas, her capacity to see what *ought* to be done for people, so clear so confident (at least to herself) that to be deprived of power to act is, for her, a kind of second death. Impossible to think of her lying on her death-bed, mind and heart so alert, and not remember that half whimsical, half indignant, "How can I see the poor things going wrong and not put them right?" Here is pain for her: she is now no longer able to *do* anything. Is not love's service love's joy? And may not love's last sacrifice to God be to offer up that joy? To cease from serving? To be loving only? To testify in these new conditions that "God is enough"? To bow to Divine Love's ordinance, though the reasonableness of it be hidden? To believe though she could not see! She wrote once, "How precious it is when we see as well as believe but yet more blessed to *believe* and *not* see. Lord! work this determined, obstinate, blind, unquestioning, unanswering faith in me."[22] I think that that prayer was answered as she took her slow, painful way out of mortality. God gave her for her dying a secret spring of strength that made her independent of outward signs. *"I feel the power to leave all in the hands of God."* She had felt that power at seventeen when she thought death was near and now at sixty when death is ordained she still felt it and nothing can rob her of the possession.

She divined that her dear ones coveted for her a sign from heaven at the last. Her logical turn of thought, so baffling in life's beginnings, helped her now. She wants to lead all who loved her to the same conclusions. "One of the hardest lessons that I have had to learn," she said to her son-in-law Arthur Clibborn, "one that I think I have been learning more effectively the last few years, is to discern between faith and realization. They are entirely distinct the one from the other, and if I have had to conquer all through life by naked faith ... I can only expect that it shall be the same now. All our enemies have to be conquered by *faith*, not by realization, and is it not so with the last enemy, death? Therefore, ought I not to be willing, if it be God's will, even to go down into the dark valley without any realization, simply knowing that I am His and that He is mine? And thus repeat in the last struggle my life-lesson? Yes, if it please the Lord to deal with me thus, I am quite willing. I can accept it. And however blessed it would be to see His face, if He deprives me of that sight, I am willing it should be so. How can I conquer by faith fully, unless I go on to the end without realization, simply trusting in His eternal covenant?"[23]

Catherine positively refused all opiates. Not until August 1890 did she consent to occasional injections of morphia. She was determined that if possible her mind should be at her command to the end. Pain was the price she would pay that she might still tell her love, and as her son put it "occupy herself with matters concerning 'the war'." She had her heart's desire. Begbie could not bring himself to quote William's diary describing her sufferings. As our thoughts dwell with her through the last lap of her life, we should keep in mind that pain had become a permanent ingredient of it. It is in the midst of suffering that talking to a small group of visiting officers she says, "I don't want you to regard this affliction as having come upon me in consequence of my work. I don't think it has. We don't understand God's dealings in this world ... We shall never understand till we get beyond death's flood. I am afraid that a good deal of the religion of this day has put suffering quite out of its account. It does not seem to recognize that God has anything to do in the way of pruning and disciplining His saints through the furnace of affliction ... and through them of influencing others. Look at the martyrs! Think what they endured."[24] On another occasion when a visitor, sympathizing, said, "I wish I could bear it for you." Catherine replied, "Ah, but perhaps, then, God's purpose toward *me* would not be answered."

431

5

Who shall say that it was not of God's mercy to William Booth, as well as to those he succoured, that on his way home at midnight on a cold winter's day early in 1888, he saw men lying in the recesses of a London bridge? What he saw led to the vast and various undertakings known now throughout the world as the Men's Social Work of The Salvation Army.

From the first, to him, horrific discovery that men were "sleeping out all night on the stones" to the decision to *act* was but a matter of hours. Bramwell, who had looked in for "business" with his father before breakfast, found him in his dressing-room and was given a dramatic account of the night's discovery. Before the General had finished dressing he had given Bramwell orders, "Go and do something ... get hold of a warehouse and warm it, and find something to cover them."[25] Thus "shelters" for men, and their quickly following benevolent derivatives, came into being. The Booths tackled the venture with their native vehemence. They gathered masses of information; and the more they discovered, the greater the need was seen to be. Opening the first night-shelter was like diverting an underground stream, bringing the dark and sluggish waters to the surface. At first there seemed danger that the new "doings" might be flooded before channels for the oncoming stream could be prepared. Begbie, telling the story of William Booth, recounts, "The Shelter and Food Depots which he had set up in 1888 were besieged by crowds of the homeless whom he could not house, and of the hungry whom he could not feed."[26] Perhaps the first beneficiary of what came to be known as the Darkest England Scheme was its heart-broken founder! Begbie called the book *In Darkest England and the Way Out*,* written to launch the scheme, "at once the burden and the blessing of William Booth",[27] while he must wait for his wife's death. It helped to sustain them both. Writing it was reserved for William's hours at Clacton; much of it was actually written in the sick-room, where he and Catherine discussed their notions and read together what he had written.

Late in November 1889 there were two days' meetings at Exeter Hall, followed by two days' Staff Officers Councils. A deputation of eighteen officers went to Clacton to see the Army Mother. The party travelled down under a leaden sky through snow-covered country. The gloom without, one of them said, seemed to accord with the

* Sir Henry Stanley's book *In Darkest Africa* had just been published, 1890.

sorrowful looks of the little company. Mrs. Booth had passed a very suffering night, but one of the visitors reported that there was "less trace on her beloved features than we had feared." Because there was not room for chairs the officers knelt round the bed. The Army flag was draped at its head. Emma led the singing of "Oh, Thou God of every nation, we now for Thy blessing call . . . Bless our Army." The words, written (in 1882) by Colonel William Pearson, well expressed the desires of those early-day leaders, especially the second verse which runs

> *Fill us with Thy Holy Spirit;*
> *Make our soldiers white as snow;*
> *Save the world through Jesus' merit,*
> *Satan's kingdom overthrow.*
> *Bless our Army!*
> *Send us where we ought to go.*[28]

Cadman, by then Colonel, was to lead in prayer, but he and all were weeping. It was a moment before he could recover himself, and then he poured out his heart to God and "his prayer seemed to nerve and compose all present". Colonel Dowdle, formerly a railway guard, said a few words, "We rejoice to be able in the name of the Council, to express our loyalty to the General, to the whole of his family, and to yourself." Commissioner Howard—who became the Army's second Chief-of-Staff—told about the meetings and "our determination to stand by the first principles of the Army . . . upon which you and the General founded your work . . . our form of constitution and government. We have determined . . . that there must be no distinction between the spirit in which we transact business and that in which we conduct a holiness meeting . . . we must and will do all in the name of the Lord Jesus; in the power of the Holy Ghost."[29]

At first the Army Mother was too overcome to speak; but after a moment she said, ". . . I should have to be a great deal more stoical than I am, not to be deeply touched by this manifestation of your affection." After forceful words about the Army's principles, she went on, "I am surer than ever that they are right principles, indeed that they are the only principles by which to push successfully the *salvation of the world* . . . the persecution, opposition and misrepresentation that we do receive, rather than being any discouragement to us, should on the contrary be regarded as the glorious proof . . . that we are on the right lines, doing the work to which Jesus Christ has called us . . ." Of herself she said, "Realizing that I must soon leave the battlefield, it has been a special joy to me to know that there are so many *young* in the ranks . . . who, when we have left the field, will leap into our places and go on with the war." Looking

433

affectionately round upon the men and women, whose faces turned to her were wet with tears, she said, "I value your expression of affection . . . I thank God that, notwithstanding all the defects and imperfections I see in my life and work as I look back . . . I can say that by His grace I have always kept the interests of His Kingdom first." As they left, each touched her hand. Colonel Barker alluded to his conversion under the old railway arch in Bethnal Green, and spoke of his work in Australia. She replied, "Give the Australian soldiers my love. Tell them that I look on them and care for them just as for my English children, and expect them to gather in many, many a prodigal child who has wandered away from his Father's house."[30]

In December strength seemed to be failing. Heart attacks became more frequent and left her exhausted. There were serious haemorrhages, and on the doctor's advice the family was summoned. On December 15, 1889, William wrote in his diary: "My darling had a night of agony. When I went into her room at 2 a.m. . . . they were endeavouring to staunch a fresh haemorrhage . . . After a slight improvement another difficulty set in . . . After several painful struggles there was a great calm, and we felt the end had come. The whole household gathered in her room. My darling thought herself to be dying . . . The beautiful, heavenly expression on the countenance of the beloved sufferer, her marvellous calmness and self-possession, the words of semi-inspiration . . . made an impression on the hearts of all present such as could never be erased."[31]

More than once the household was gathered in Catherine's room, when she spoke a word of farewell to each, sometimes light-heartedly as to Mrs. Dutton, cook in the Booth household for years, saying with a smile, "Stand where I can see you, Dutton. I am going to eat the angels' food. I shall never be faint any more." Mrs. Dutton was weeping as Catherine said that Emma and the General would advise her about her wayward son. "They will help you to be a little tender with Tommy. I wish I could have seen the boy. Tell him it pays to be good, and he ought not to risk losing his soul. Don't be afraid of boring him . . . people who won't serve God ought to be bored. Bore him until he gives in. Give my love to your mother and your poor old father, too. Is he ready?" Pausing for Mrs. Dutton's "Yes, ma'am."[32] Later, of heaven, she said to William, "I feel like flying. I don't believe I shall be fastened up in a corner . . . I shall come progging about if I can." Railton came in and turning to him she said, "I shall see your mother. What shall I say to her?" Soon they were singing together

My God, I am Thine;
What a comfort divine,
What a blessing to know that my Jesus is mine![33]

434

It was in the words of this verse that assurance of her own salvation had come to Catherine as a girl; the song was for her a psalm of triumph and often sung at her bedside. Once she turned to William and said, "Don't you remember in Cornwall how they used to sing it?" adding, "I have not been able to sing, but I shall soon be able now." Her inability to sing had been a little grief to her ever since she and William met. Mrs. Oliphant* entered the room during the singing and in response to a call from Catherine came and knelt at the bedside. "Célestine, you must do credit to your Dutch history, and be as brave as a brick for the Lord. They were a brave lot, those old Dutch. Strengthen your husband's hands. When he is weak, you must be strong ... God has seen the sincerity of your father's heart, and He has brought you as a family into The Salvation Army ... Hold on ... God could save the world in a few years if all His people were faithful."[34]

On December 19 she sent a brief message to her Army children in all lands, "The waters are rising, but so am I. I am not going under, but over. Don't be concerned about your dying: only go on living well, and the dying will be all right."[35] Another time she said to William, "Pray with me a moment. It always does me good. Put your hand on my head." The strain of all this was fearful; William would pace up and down after coming from his wife's room, weeping, saying, "I don't understand it!" 'and then fall upon his knees in an excess of grief.[36] Bramwell wrote, "Her state of exhaustion seemed to leave no possible hope of her spending Christmas Day on earth. Throughout its hours her family waited for her last word ..." But to the amazement of all including the doctors, towards the evening of Boxing Day she began to revive. From now on there was a rhythmic recurrence of periods of intense pain and exhaustion, in any of which her physicians considered that she might die.

Once when her husband and children stood around her bed listening to one of those "farewells", she said, "I am so disgusted with myself in many respects. I don't want you to publish [abroad] what I have done ... if only I had had more faith I might have achieved so much."[37] Every time she spoke to visiting groups of Salvationists, words slipped in that show her thoughts dwelling on the little she was, and the wonder of God's work in her. Eagerly now that life was finished, as when her activity was at the peak, she attributed all its good to God; and wanted those watching dear ones, wanted all the world, to see as clearly as she herself saw, in the revealing light of life's evening, that it was not God's fault she did not do more —do better. She spoke lovingly of the absent. Kissing a letter from Katie she murmured, "My darling first-born girl, she is a brave

---

* Célestine Schoch, daughter of Staff-Captain and Mrs. Schoch, Honorary Dutch officers. Her sister married Herbert Booth. See page 443.

beautiful soul." Of her brother she said to Eva, "Write to Uncle John . . . I have tried hard for his soul, but he would not yield . . . Eva, you will write him? Tell him I kept his photograph on the mantelpiece until the last."

Contemplating the wonders of the world to come, Catherine talked, without a hint of embarrassment, of speaking "in the celestial language to Abraham, Job, David and Paul", and with the same naturalness up to her last hour on earth, she gave everyday doings their due place. She did not discard life because death was at hand. To her there was nothing in time antagonistic to eternity. God, who bid us pray for daily bread, would not, she was sure, be affronted by a practical "I shall ask Jesus to give you a fine day for my funeral, Emma, so that you mayn't take cold."

At one moment she seemed to her watching loved ones to be almost within sight of the heavenly city, and to be done with earth's affairs. "You are drawing near the end with me, Emma! Don't you realize, as we approach it together, the immortality of the soul? The soul can never die. As soon as this poor decaying body falls off, I feel, I know, that my soul will spring forth into life still more abundant."[38] But quite as definitely, at another moment, her thoughts were of things down here. "Herbert, let the coffin be plain —such as will be in keeping with the life I have lived." Or again, when her daughter was helping Carr to dress the breast, "You need not hurry, Emma! there is plenty of time. I have no train to catch . . . now, but the chariot." "When will the boys come?" Told "At eight", she said, "Then I shall wait till they come and afterwards I shall sleep . . . . it is only going to sleep you know . . . and Eva don't forget that man with the handcuffs on. Find him. Go to Lancaster jail . . . tell him your mother prayed, when she was dying, for him, and that she had a feeling in her heart that God would save him. And tell him, hard as ten years are, it will be easier with Christ than . . . without [Him] . . . I did want to have done something for the prisons and for the asylums."[39]

Bramwell brought Catherine quietness of spirit when no other could. Her very love for William made her want to spare him and when her distress seemed for the moment beyond endurance, she called for Bramwell. His sensitive, imaginative nature made his mother's pain, the mystery of it, a continuing torment in him. The repeated journeys down to Clacton for a few hours at her bedside were an exhausting addition to the work in which they were all engaged, most of all for Bramwell, because on him lay the heavy burden of administration in addition to his public work. He would often rush down to spend the night, or most of it, with his mother, leaving for Headquarters by the early morning train, only to repeat the journey next evening. "Kiss Mama for me once every hour till I come again," he wrote to Emma; and it was to Emma, years later, that he wrote, "Tomorrow will be the fourth. I shall join with you on this day of great mystery in renewing every covenant we have taken in the past, of faithfulness to God and to that One we loved and love."[40]

Of course it was their love that multiplied their grief. It may seem strange today to find both love and grief so freely expressed. This came largely from Catherine's example. She loved and never hid her love. The spontaneous expression of love for her husband and children was "her way" and they all grew up like that. To *The War Cry* William wrote, "The mystery . . . of God's dealings with us . . . is past finding out. The permitting this terrible disease to come upon my dear wife . . . and to allow her to come down to Jordan again and again, during the last seven days, has been more perplexing still . . . Only on Friday last she fell into one of those death-faints with which we are growing quite familiar . . . she murmured, 'I am in His arms, He will not let me drop'. And yet on that very night there came a strange rallying to life."[41] Even in the midst of this, there were seasons of joy. William wanted to hold these hours for memory, and tried to record them in his diary. Once he wrote, "I sent them all out, resolving to have the remainder of the night alone with her. What passed that night can never be revealed. It will never be half remembered by myself . . . It was a renewal, in all its tenderness and sweetness and a part of its very ecstasy, of our first love. It seemed, I believe to us both, in spite of all . . . a repetition of some of those blissful hours we spent together in the days of our betrothal. Oh, the wonderful things! We were in Jordan together . . . I saw how exhausted she was . . . when I made as though I would leave her she upbraided me in the gentlest . . . manner, by saying . . . 'It will soon be over and what matters a few hours shorter or longer now? I have done with the body . . .' "[42] Of another such occasion when they were alone William records, "She took hold of my hand almost at the very beginning, and took the ring off her finger, and slipping it on to mine, said: 'By this token we were united for time, and by it now we are united for eternity.' "[43]

Many times she thought death was at hand. Bracing herself for the parting seemed to revive life in her. More than once she bade them, "Take hands with me, I cannot get hold of all your hands, so Emma will be on one side, and," turning to William, "you, Pa, the other . . . I shall feel I have got hold of you all till the Light meets me . . . Love one another . . . Stand fast together . . . What does it matter what the world says about me? Not a bit, not an atom." Bramwell wrote of the love that beamed in her beautiful face, and she spoke, looking from one to another, "Oh, be not faithless; I have been so wanting in faith . . . If I had had more faith and been more courageous. . ." Tears flowed from her eyes. "Have faith in God. Don't be afraid of the devil . . . I am going into the dark

437

valley believing..."[44] Then, after a pause she said to William, "Let us have a song my precious One—my dearest," and again the sound of singing drifted through the house and her favourites were repeated over and over again, "My Jesus, I love Thee, I know Thou art mine...I will love Thee in life, I will love Thee in death and praise Thee as long as Thou lendest me breath". Between the verses she spoke some particular word to this one or that one as thoughts arose in her mind. "Bramwell, I have had your boy here [his children had each been brought for a last kiss and blessing]. Mind how you train your children. What is it that Jesus said? They are in the world. I pray not that Thou shouldest take them out of the world but keep them from the evil..."

At one of these "partings" Catherine said, "You who have joined hands with me, as we stand in the midst of this Jordan, there are not stones that we can set up as an altar, but...promise me that you will be faithful to The Salvation Army...You promise?...All of you?" All respond. "Say it one at a time...that I may know your voices." Bramwell first answering, she said, "I gave you up to God when you were younger than your baby downstairs, and consecrated you to be a preacher of holiness..." Herbert promises and his mother responds, "I believe you will." And so from each, to each, a word. Bramwell says, "No sudden glimpse through the gates of heaven, had they opened for her quickly, could have borne such transcendent testimony of our [Christian] faith as the way in which it sustained her...through constantly repeated death-partings."[45]

To everyone's amazement she gained a little strength. By January 30, 1890, she had rallied enough to hear an Army band play and afterwards to receive the bandsmen. They come marching along the grassy cliff top, playing Salvation Army tunes. Standing in the chill sunshine, under the window of the room in which the Army Mother lies, they play one of her son Herbert's compositions: its words familiar now in half a dozen languages to Salvationists all over the world:

> *Grace there is my every debt to pay,*
> *Blood to wash my every sin away,*
> *Power to keep me spotless day by day,*
> *For me, for me!*[46]

(Eleven years before this visit there was only one brass band in The Salvation Army, composed of a father and his three sons. In 1890, 8,550 bandsmen had been added to their number.) Herbert Booth, who has been campaigning with the band, is present and recounts for *The War Cry*, "Mrs. Booth had summoned strength and consented to see the band lads (twenty-eight)...They piled their instruments in the garden, left their coats and shoes in the hall, and mounted the

438

staircase jacketed in red and holding their white helmets in their hand ... They formed in a semi-circle round the bed ... The bandmaster [a converted drunkard] wept, but could not speak." He had brought a letter, signed by himself, which he handed to Herbert to read. I quote a few lines of it: "We wish to assure you, as you near the land of song and of all kinds of music, that the Army bands exist ... with the sole purpose of luring Satan's slaves to the service and happiness of their true Master, Jesus Christ ... We have sorrowed over the terrible suffering ... of your mysterious illness, yet our faith has been strengthened ... Reckon on us on earth and in heaven as your loving and faithful children ... Signed, on behalf of The Salvation Army bandsmen of the world, Harry Appleby, Bandmaster."[47]

All Catherine said in reply is worth consideration. Here is part: "It is very kind of you to come and play to me ... I have enjoyed it ... I wish I were stronger that I might say more of what is in my heart ... especially the importance of keeping your music spiritual, and using it for the one end ... I had always regarded music as *all* belonging to God. Perhaps some of you have heard me say in public that there will not be a note of music in hell, it will all be in heaven, and God ought to have it all here ... The church has strangely lost sight of the value of music as a religious agency. I think God has used the Army to resuscitate and awaken—to create it in fact, and while the bandsmen of The Salvation Army realise it to be as much their service to blow an instrument as it is to sing or pray ... and while they do it in the same spirit, I am persuaded it will become an ever-increasing power amongst us. But the moment you, or any other bandsmen, begin to glory in the excellence of the *music alone*, apart from spiritual results, you will begin at that moment, to lose your power ... You see, when you separate the divine from the human, it ceases to have any power over souls. Don't forget that. I never expected to hear any more earthly music. A fortnight ago I thought I was almost within hearing of the heavenly ... but here I am, shunted, for what purpose I don't know, but one purpose has been to see your faces. [I think she smiled on them at this moment?] I think you have formed far too high an estimate of me and of my work; but any blessing I can be to you ... I give it to you with all my heart. I feel you are my lads. May God bless you all and keep you—keep you all faithful and make you all valiant soul-winners."[48] The General then came in. He shook each man by the hand, and said a few words, and all knelt. The bandmaster, who had not been able to command himself sufficiently to read his letter, was now able to pray, spontaneously telling out his feelings, "Dear Lord, we have very little human strength and ability, but such as we have shall be Thine. Our precious Mother shall not be disappointed in us, and her trust shall not be deceived; but we, by Thy grace, shall be a credit to our dear General and Mother ... We pray that Thou wouldst bless our Mother. Thou knowest that out of our hearts we cannot find words to express our desire, but we leave it all with Thee . . ."[49] The bandmaster stops—they wait in silence, as if expecting. "Oh, Lord, we can only ask Thee to bless everyone in this room." Catherine was praying now, "Deal with every heart in Thine own way for the perfecting of that heart and for the full devotion of all its powers to Thee and to Thy Kingdom for ever. Oh, do not let one in this room ever wander away from the narrow path . . . give us the joy of meeting, every one of us, on the other side of that River, the *one* River that we must all cross, and we will praise Thee with louder voices on the other side . . . Through Jesus Christ our Lord. Amen."[50]

Quietly the men filed out. Food was provided. It was growing dusk in the winter afternoon, as, standing under her window, they played their farewell. The music swelled in triumphant crescendo for the refrain, "Christ is all, yes, all-in-all, My Christ is all-in-all." It melted away, and into the silence rose a tenor voice, full and clear. A bandsman was singing:

> *I stood beside a dying bed,*
> *There lay a saint with aching head,*
> *Waiting the Master's call.*
> *I asked her whence her strength was given;*
> *She looked triumphantly to heaven,*
> *And whispered, "Christ is all".*

Like the sound of an organ, all the men's voices took up the refrain:

> *Christ is all, yes, all-in-all,*
> *My Christ is all-in-all.*[51]

And so once more Catherine had spoken to the hearts of her hearers.

It is the same for the group of officers from ten countries, who were in the last company, apart from her family, to gather in her presence. In a moment she had *their* thoughts drawn out to the world's need. "From my very childhood I have felt a peculiar interest in the spread of the Gospel abroad . . . litttle thinking that God would ever use me to put a measure of this missionary spirit into a people who would go to the very darkest corners of the earth! I always looked upon the work of Jesus Christ as being world-wide. I believed in my inmost soul that 'He tasted death for every man', and, therefore, it seemed to me, that He intended, at least, every man and woman to *hear* about it." And now there was a sense of suppressed power in her voice. "How often I have felt while lying

440

here, thinking of our officers toiling and conquering all over the world, if I could but have them all together ... and speak to every heart just as I feel! Oh, how I would strive to make them realize the value of souls and the verities of eternity."[52]

6

Catherine was still alive when the Army's twenty-fifth anniversary was celebrated. Twenty-five years, that is, from the time William Booth first preached in Whitechapel. It was only *twelve* years since The Salvation Army got its Deed of Constitution and its name! More than fifty thousand people poured through the turnstiles into the Crystal Palace; the Alexandra Palace was not large enough. It was a tremendous day of marches and music. Few distinct impressions of it remain in the memory of a child then six years old, but those that do are clear, and here is one. She is seated towards the front of the huge central transept. It is gorged with people for "The Great Assembly", and a crowd, standing close packed, stretches away on either side of the enclosure which is filled with seats. The child remembers this crowd outside the partition, for she walked through a narrow lane in its midst on her way to the meeting, and she could hear the sound of its singing joining in the mighty volume that rose through the echoing glass dome when the meeting began. She sees the mountain-side of faces towering up behind the platform. The steep orchestra, including the space round the organ loft, is packed to its utmost limits with uniformed singers and bandsmen. The glitter of instruments and the kind of dull roar, as the movement of rising for singing spread about her, are a clear-cut memory. She remembers, too, that "hugeous" band, and what little sound it made. The sound of the brass was swallowed up by a different sound. A sound that seemed to fill the whole world, the sound of a vast sea of song. The child shivers and feels like crying. At the end of the verses the singing is still going on in the distant parts of the building, not quite in tune, and lagging behind in time. There are movements ... kneeling, rising, but what form the service takes is quite lost to her. Until, in deep blue letters on a white background, words begin to creep across from one side of the orchestra front to the other: fixed high, and unrolling, a calico strip is drawn along, to be rolled up on the opposite side, so that a phrase is visible at one time. The silence is like cotton wool. Sharp sounds echo from far away in other parts of the Palace only to make the near stillness more still. "My dear children and friends," the unrolling is stayed a moment, the little girl knows who the words are from, *she* is one of the "children" (only she remembers 'My dear

441

child', the phrase belongs to that *one*, her grandmother) and now the words are moving on; and there is another kind of movement; a dim rustling, an uncertain sorrowful sound; suddenly the great building is full of it, as it had been of the mighty sound of singing, only there are no verse ends. It goes on and on, it is not loud yet it fills every second with sound, it wavers, falls, rises. Someone *might* scream and be heard; the child feels anyone might scream . . . but no one does. Handkerchiefs fustle and flutter all over the mountain side of faces on the orchestra, *everyone* is weeping: all the people round her and the child too . . . and the words go on rolling; passing, pausing . . . "My dear children and friends, my place is empty, but my heart is with you. You are my joy and my crown . . . Go forward. Live holy lives. Be true to the Army. God is your strength. Love and seek the lost . . . I am dying under the Army flag. It is yours to live and fight under . . . I send you my love and blessing. Catherine Booth."[53]

While she lingered Catherine's thoughts went out to her Army children. She sent messages, through her visitors and to *The War Cry* as: "Tell them that in helping to pioneer this new movement I have come through many clouds and storms, but now, as I stand with my feet in Jordan, I am more than ever satisfied that the Lord has led me . . . Tell my comrades that I feel lost in wonder . . . that He should have condescended to use so feeble an instrument in accomplishing His loving purposes. That I give Him *all*, all the glory, and that my last exhortation is that they should know nothing among men but Christ and Him crucified: that they should set no store on any other treasure . . . have no higher purpose in life than the bringing of lost sinners to His feet."

Or as: "Tell them that the only consolation for a Salvationist on his dying-bed is to feel he has been a *soul-winner* . . . beseech them to redeem their time, for we can do but little at our best."[54] Once, to the family, placing her hand on William's head, she said, "I used to ask the Lord that we might both be taken at the same time until afterwards I felt it to be so selfish, and then I did not ask Him for it any more." To me, that last phrase in its simplicity is like a snapshot taken unawares, revealing her spirit's habit of submission.

All this time the General and the family went back and forth to Clacton from their Salvation Army duties—all save Emma and the frail Marie, who remained with their mother. And so it came about that though death was expected and watched for, when it was *really* at hand, Catherine's aliveness misled them all including the doctors. Stead gave his impression of her vitality when he last saw her, less than three weeks before her death. He spoke of her "cheery, confident defiant conversation". It was Sunday evening, September 14. "The air was filled with stillness, the lapping of the rippling waves on the beach below being hardly audible. In pain that ever and anon increased to anguish . . . she spoke to me for the last time . . . Her

442

spirit was still as high, her interest still intense, even her sense of humour as quick and keen as in the days when she had held listening thousands by the power of her eloquence and the consuming passion of her love."⁵⁵ I like to think of them talking on that soft evening, and of their being merry together, and of their praying together. Stead knelt by her bedside "pouring out his soul" and the last words he heard her speak were to ask God's blessing on him— almost the last, but not quite, for as he was leaving her room she exclaimed, "Try to raise up mothers. *Mothers are the want of the world.*"

To one of her visitors, a young officer, she said, "When you have done your very best, and done all you can, *then* you must roll the responsibility back on to God. I wish I had done it more. I have taken things too much to heart. I was made of an anxious nature." The practical side of Catherine's mind had not always been able to counteract her too vivid imagination. This was perhaps a weakness in her? A flaw not fully compensated for by grace? To William a little time before she died, she said, "You have not a very vivid realization, dear darling ... I have too much, more than has been of use. You have often said, 'What is the use of torturing yourself when you cannot prevent it?' ... There is the *trouble,* when you are made so I am."

On September 18, the Booth's youngest son, Herbert, was married to Captain Cornelie Schoch.* She had served two years as a Salvation Army Officer and had several times visited Mrs. Booth. William Booth, who conducted the wedding ceremony in the Congress Hall, read Catherine's message, prefacing it by a reference to her suffering state, "... yet her spirit is just as strong as ever". After a word of congratulation and blessing to "my dear son and daughter", Catherine said, "... as I cannot stand in my old place and say these words, I send them by my dear husband ... so far as my poor blessing is of value, I send it to you all. I again thank you for your prayers and sympathy, and again express my oft-repeated hope to meet you in heaven. I am no less interested in this world because I am waiting here on the threshold of the other [for my Lord's bidding]Oh, believe me, its sorrows and its sin, its opportunities and its responsibilities, are *realities*, which claim all your powers and all your influence for the service of Him who has redeemed it. God be with you! Yours, till the Morning, Catherine Booth."⁵⁶

William was in Lancashire for a series of meetings, the family scattered on their various "battlefields" when Bramwell received a premonition that his mother's death was imminent. He recorded it at the time. "So far as human judgment could discern," he said, "our

* Cornelie Schoch, daughter of a distinguished officer in the Dutch Army. He and his wife became Salvationists with several of their children.

mother might have been left with us for weeks." On the night of Tuesday, September 30, he was on his way home from leading a meeting and having missed the last train to Hadley Wood he had to walk from New Barnet. "I was alone. My road passed for about a mile through a dense wood, always deserted on a dark night such as this, and as I was tired I did not hasten. An intense consciousness of the ... nearness of God came over me; and, leaving my mind free, so to speak, to receive any impression, my thoughts turned, as they had turned so many times before, to that chamber by the sea in which my beloved mother lay dying. I saw all the scene as I had so often seen it, the open windows, the bed, the pillows, the small table with the Bible and flowers ... the dear worn face, and it all seemed to say to me, 'The time is at hand.' ... and looking up in the darkness I cried out: 'Lord, it is well. Thy will be done.' "[57]Bramwell was at Headquarters at eight-thirty, the next morning, October 1, where he found his father, who had travelled from the North by night, already at work. There being no word of any unusual development at Clacton, he did not accompany his father when he left to catch the three o'clock train down. But on Thursday William wired, "Much worse come by next train." Another serious haemorrhage had occurred. Absent members of the family were sent for. Florence arrived on the last train. By evening the doctor said the immediate danger was past. The September sunshine had given place to storm. All night the deeps roared in a hurricane of wind and rain. At six in the morning Bramwell was called to his mother's room. Pain had come on with terrifying force. "Could I be lifted out of this bed, Bramwell?" Catherine asked. "It would not be much trouble to you all, would it?" Bramwell's heart failed him, he could not speak: it was Emma who gently persuaded her mother that to move would be but to increase her suffering. After a moment, turning to Emma she asked, "Have I anything more I ought to do, Emma?" No, all is done. Almost her last audible prayer was, "Lord, let the end be easy for Emma's sake." Her last order was to the watchers at her side and repeated with emphasis, "Take it in turns—in turns". She then said a few tender words to Bramwell and sank into a deep sleep. During the afternoon she roused. Bramwell records, "We gathered to sing one or two favourite verses," among these a chorus which Katie had written and which Catherine loved to hear:

> *We shall walk through the valley of the shadow of death,*
> *We shall walk through the valley in peace,*
> *For Jesus Himself shall be our Leader*
> *As we walk through the valley in peace.*

Bramwell's narrative continues, "Each time we came to the word *peace*, Catherine raised her hand. Toward evening she slept again and

444

we waited." At ten o'clock at night came a revival of strength. Without the storm still raged. Within, the family gathered, though they did not know it, for the last vigil. Singing pleased her—what would they not have done to please? With trembling lips, for sorrow and singing do not go well together, they sang some of the old songs, Rock of Ages,

> While I draw this fleeting breath,
> When my eyes shall close in death,
> When I soar to worlds unknown,
> See Thee on Thy judgment throne;
> Rock of ages, cleft for me,
> Let me hide myself in Thee.

For a time she seemed unconscious of their presence, then, with clear utterance she said, "Emma, let me go darling". Emma replied, "Yes, we will, we will." And her mother spoke in prayer "Now? Yes, now Lord, come now." "The singing seemed to be a joy to her, and so again we joined in,

> Calvary's stream is flowing so free,
> Flowing for you and me.

'Go on,' she said, when we reached the end of the verse, and so over and over again we sang,

> Jesus, my Saviour, has died on the tree
> Died on the tree for me, Hallelujah."[58]

About midnight William embraced her and she was able to speak a few words of endearment to him. It was a moment of deepest sorrow. Again there was singing. The great hymn "Now I have found the ground wherein sure my soul's anchor may remain" helped them all.

> O Love, Thou bottomless abyss,
> My sins are swallowed up in Thee!
> Covered is my unrighteousness,
> Nor spot of guilt remains on me,
> While Jesus' Blood, through earth and skies,
> Mercy, free, boundless mercy, cries.[59]

After this verse she spoke once more, "Do you believe?" she asked Bramwell. "Yes!" came his answer. She called for prayer. "Lord Jesus, we thank Thee for Thy Presence," prayed Bramwell. "We beseech Thee to help us in this experience so new to us, in this separation ... Lord help us. Thou hast conquered death ..." As his son ceased, William Booth continued, asking for his Beloved's

445

release without further suffering, "Oh Lord, we have trusted Thee for this. Add this to Thy thousand other mercies." Catherine raised her hand once or twice. For a moment none understood, and then it was seen she was pointing to a text on the wall. "My grace is sufficient for thee." This was her last testimony to God's faithfulness.

At about two o'clock in the morning Eva arrived, having had to drive from Colchester. Her mother recognized her at once and tenderly greeted her, then fell asleep. She roused about three, after a moment Emma said, "Jesus is calling you." Catherine replied with sweet emphxasis, "Amen. Amen."[60]

On crept the night. It was Saturday, October 4. At nine a.m. the doctor found her stronger than on the night before, but soon after noon life ebbed gently lower. Her hand lay in William's. Lovers now must part. Each of the family kissed her brow, her lips moved as her eyes searched out Bramwell's. The beloved William had been committed to his care. Again they sang: they were kneeling around her bed now.

> *My mistakes His free grace doth cover,*
> *My sins He doth wash away:*
> *These feet which shrink and falter*
> *Shall enter the Gates of Day.*[61]

And still holding her hand, William once more gave her up to God. Bramwell says, "A gleam of joyful recognition passed over the brightening countenance," as she spoke William's name. Their eyes met, held, the last kiss of earthly love was given and, without further movement, breathing gradually ceased. Catherine Booth, William's little wife—Mother of his eight "beauties", Mother of The Salvation Army, Mother of Nations—had gone Home. She had faced the last enemy and proved that in life and in death "God is enough for us."

7

Catherine Booth had done with the body. But for a day or two longer that poor remnant of her drew people. In the centre of the Congress Hall, under a red canopy, was placed the coffin, slightly raised at the head, so that through the glass window let into it, the people passing in two streams, one on either side, might look upon her for the last time. Catherine's Bible, her Army bonnet and the flag from the head of her bed were on the foot of the coffin to which was affixed a brass plate inscribed:

Catherine Booth
The Mother of The Salvation Army
Born 17th January 1829
Died 4th October 1890
"More than conqueror"

Above, a large card bore in bold letters a phrase from one of her messages, "Love one another and meet me in the Morning".

At eleven o'clcock on Tuesday morning, October 7, Commissioner Howard led a brief meeting with officers and friends present by invitation. Doors were then opened to the public. From time to time her favourite songs were sung by companies of officers inside the adjoining Training College building, whence windows, opened for the occasion gave upon the hall. All day, until ten at night, the people passed. By Sunday night more than fifty thousand had been counted. Some had come long journeys; many had been saved through the Army Mother's preaching. Crowds came who, though still in sin, knew and loved her. Men and women were won to God as they knelt near the coffin, one of these was a disreputable woman, who had once struck Catherine as she left a meeting, and with whom Catherine had pleaded in vain for a decision to come to the Saviour. Mary, Bramwell's five-year-old daughter, knelt there too. She remembers vividly "how beautiful Grandmama looked". While her mother was speaking to her and her sister Catherine about heaven, the child felt that she was not good enough to go there and began to cry. The three knelt down and with her mother's arm around her Mary prayed and gave her heart to Jesus. She has always looked back to that moment as the beginning of her life of faith.

A reporter commented, "All classes of society were represented ... but oh, the poor! Never before have I experienced so melting and harrowing a time as, one after another, numbers of them passed along, their quivering lips and tearful eyes betraying the fact that they recognized in the death of Mrs. Booth the loss of a personal friend."[62]

On Monday, October 13, a pall of fog hung over London. On that day the Army Mother's funeral service was held in Olympia. Through the gloom the people poured in one continuous stream from three to six. There were special trains and buses. Every seat in the enormous building was occupied, and a crowd of people stood. More than thirty-six thousand persons passed through the turnstiles. The fog without had drifted in so that even the then newfangled electric lighting was dimmed. The vast silent company was directed by means of huge signs displayed from a raised square platform near one end. The printed Order of Service, distributed to all, gave

447

clear instructions when the congregation was to rise, sing, pray, respond and read in silence extracts from Catherine Booth's addresses appealing to the saved and unsaved. There were no electric aids to amplify sounds in those days. The Salvation Army Household Troops Band played the funeral march written for the occasion by Herbert Booth, Catherine's youngest son. He wrote the words too; they were appropriate to the Mother of The Salvation Army:

> *Summoned home! the call has sounded*
> *Bidding a soldier his warfare cease.*

Thus the verse begins, and after each is the repeated refrain:

> *Strife and sorrow over,*
> *The Lord's true faithful soldier*
> *Has been called to go*
> *From the ranks below*
> *To the conquering host above.*[63]

From the back of the great structure came the procession, headed by flags of the nations where the Army was "at war". All standards were hung with pennants of white ribbon. A white arm-band with a red "S" surmounted by a red crown was the only sign of mourning for Salvationists. Army flags followed carried by twelve men and twelve women soldiers of the first and second Army corps, following them, twelve men and twelve women local officers bearing flags, then men and women officers with corps flags, including the first Army flag to fly, which had been presented by Catherine to the Coventry Corps. A representative group of officers of all ranks preceded Captain Carr, Catherine's devoted nurse, who carried the flag beneath which the Army Mother had died. The coffin, borne by staff officers, came next followed by William Booth and his family. As the procession reached the platform, the coffin was rested on a dais below, the flags moved on around the platform where William Booth and his family took their places. Massed brass bands played the melody Rockingham chosen for the first song. After the gentle opening bars the music mounted higher and higher like a lament, to drop again as tens of thousands of voices joined to sing Isaac Watts' hymn, "When I survey the wondrous Cross, on which the Prince of Glory died." The meeting closed with an invitation to all who were willing to make a whole-hearted surrender of themselves to God, to signify it by rising to their feet. In all parts of the building, one by one, hundreds stood, while the immense concourse sang:

448

The funeral service at Olympia

Bramwell, his wife Florence, and their children about the time of
Catherine's death. Standing at the back, holding her grandmother's
photograph, is the author, Catherine Bramwell-Booth

Memorial bust to Catherine Booth
at her birthplace, Ashbourne in Derbyshire

Just as I am, Thou wilt receive,
Wilt welcome, pardon, cleanse, relieve,
Because Thy promise I believe,
O lamb of God, I come![64]

At the end of the meeting the flags that framed the platform moved off. Back through the throng passed the procession in a silence that was itself an expression of affection and sympathy. And almost as silently the crowd melted out into the foggy autumn night.

There was fog again the next day when early in the morning officers and bands mustered on the Embankment to form the procession to the grave. It was led by flags of the first hundred corps. These were followed by field officers, slum officers, social wing officers, battalion on battalion, bearing high over their heads banners inscribed with phrases from Catherine Booth's last words. The Army march, on that October day, was four thousand strong, and it passed through a throng such as, it was said, had not been seen in London since the funeral of the Duke of Wellington. At the International Headquarters the procession parted to take in the high flat, flag-draped dray on which the coffin rested. William Booth followed standing alone in an open carriage. His sons Bramwell and Herbert, mounted, rode on either side. (Ballington was in the U.S.A.) In following carriages came William's daughters and after them Bramwell's little girls. They were in white and wore a white shoulder sash marked with a crimson cross and crown, as their aunts did. Last came Captain Carr and the household. On to the sound of singing and music the funeral procession moved through the city streets crowded as far as eye could reach; past the Royal Exchange, through Shoreditch, Dalston, to Abney Park Cemetery. The gates of the Bank of England were closed as were the shops. Stands had been erected in shop windows, upper windows were filled with onlookers and hundreds of spectators lined roof tops. Police had set barriers at side streets on the route to contain the crowds. The slow march paced the four miles of the journey, flanked by a dense crowd that stretched without interruption from the city to the gates of the cemetery in Stoke Newington. And all the way the people wept! Tears ran unchecked down the face of a mounted policeman riding at the side of the procession. As the tall, grey-bearded figure of William Booth came into view, many cried out "God bless you".

Admission to the cemetery was by ticket and was restricted to ten thousand persons. Stands seating fifteen hundred people had been erected behind the raised platform where the family and others had their places. Bands played subdued but not melancholy music while the crowd assembled. Singing of hymns, prayers, and admonitions, which had already become familiar at Salvation Army funerals, each

449

P

had a place. The ceremony was conducted by Commissioner Railton, who in his clear strong voice spoke the words of the first hymn, "Rock of ages, cleft for me . . ." Led by the band the great company broke into song. Commissioner Howard read from the Bible. Major Musa Bhai from India prayed. Staff-Captain Annie Bell Divisional Commander for Canterbury, sang a solo—"When the roll is called in heaven, and the host shall muster there, I will take my place among them and their joys and triumphs share." Katie, Emma and others spoke, but it was natural that the attention of the crowd centred upon William Booth. All who had loved Catherine were kin to him in that hour. "It was a most touching sight," the *Daily Telegraph* reported, "when the tall, upright General came forward in the gathering darkness . . . He spoke manfully, resolutely and without the slightest trace of affectation. Not a suspicion of clap-trap marred the dignity of the address. He spoke as a soldier should who had disciplined his emotion, without effort and straight from the heart."

Some of what William said at Catherine's graveside follows. "My beloved Comrades and Friends, You will readily understand that I find it a difficulty to talk to you this afternoon, To begin with, I could not be willing to talk without an attempt to make you hear, and sorrow does not feel like shouting." William then spoke of the throng of people through which he had passed, who had bared their heads and blessed him. "My mind has been full of two feelings . . . the feeling of sorrow and the feeling of gratitude. Those who know me—and I don't think I am very difficult to understand—and those who knew my darling, my beloved, will, I am sure, understand how it is that my heart should be rent with sorrow.

"If you had had a tree that had grown up in your garden, under your window, which for forty years had been your shadow from the burning sun, whose flowers had been the adornment and beauty of your life, whose fruit had been almost the very stay of your existence, and the gardener had come along and swung his glittering axe and cut it down before your eyes, I think you would feel as though you had a blank—it might be a big one—but a little blank in your life!

"If you had had a servant who, for all this long time, had served you without fee or reward, who had administered, for very love, to your health and comfort, and who had suddenly passed away, you would miss that servant!

"If you had had a counsellor who in hours—continually occurring—of perplexity and amazement, had ever advised you, and seldom advised wrong; whose advice you had followed and seldom had reason to regret it; and the counsellor, while you are in the same intricate mazes of your existence, had passed away, you would miss that counsellor!

"If you had had a friend who had understood your very nature, the rise and fall of your feelings, the bent of your thoughts, and the purpose of your existence; a friend whose communion had ever been pleasant—the most pleasant of all other friends, to whom you had ever turned with satisfaction—and your friend had been taken away, you would feel some sorrow at the loss!

"If you had had a mother for your children who had cradled and nursed and trained them for the service of the living God, in which you most delighted; a mother indeed . . . and that darling mother had been taken from your side, you would feel it a sorrow!

"If you had had a wife, a sweet love of a wife, who for forty years had never given you real cause for grief; a wife who had stood with you side by side in the battle's front, who had been a comrade to you, ever willing to interpose herself between you and the enemy and ever the strongest when the battle was fiercest, and your beloved one had fallen before your eyes, I am sure there would be some excuse for your sorrow!

"Well, my comrades, you can roll all these qualities into one personality and what would be lost in each I have lost, all in one. There has been taken away from me the delight of my eyes, the inspiration of my soul . . . yet, my comrades, my heart is full of gratitude . . . that the long valley of the shadow of death has been trodden . . . gratitude because God lent me for so long a season such a treasure. I have been thinking, if I had to point out her three qualities to you here, they would be: First, she was *good*. She was washed in the Blood of the Lamb. To the last moment her cry was, 'A sinner saved by grace'. She was a thorough hater of shams, hypocrisies, and make-believes. Second, she was *love*. Her whole soul was full of tender, deep compassion. I was thinking this morning that she suffered more in her lifetime through her compassion for poor dumb animals than some doctors of divinity suffer for the wide, wide world of sinning, sorrowing mortals! Oh, how she loved, how she compassioned, how she pitied the suffering poor! How she longed to put her arms round the sorrowful and help them! Lastly, she was a *warrior*. She liked the fight. She was not one who said to others, 'Go!' but 'Here, let *me* go!' . . .

"My comrades, I am going to meet her again. I have never turned from her these forty years for any journeyings on my mission of mercy but I have longed to get back, and have counted the weeks, days, and hours which should take me again to her side. When she has gone away from me it has been just the same. And now she has gone away for the last time. What, then, is there left for me to do? . . . My work plainly is to fill up the weeks, the days, and the hours, and cheer my poor heart as I go along with the thought that, when I have served my Christ and my generation according to the will of God— which I vow this afternoon I will, to the last drop of my blood— then I trust that she will bid me welcome to the skies, as He bade her. God bless you all. Amen."[65]

As the coffin was lowered the crowd sang a favourite verse of Catherine's from a hymn written by her son Herbert,

Blessèd Lord, in Thee is refuge,
Safety for my trembling soul,
Power to lift my head when drooping
'Midst the angry billows' roll.
I will trust Thee,
All my life Thou shalt control.

Commissioner Railton spoke the words of committal: "As it has pleased Almighty God to promote our dear Mother from her place in The Salvation Army to the mansion prepared for her above, we now commit her body to this grave—earth to earth, ashes to ashes, dust to dust—in the sure and certain hope of seeing her again on the Resurrection Morning."[66]

Following The Salvation Army Order of Service Railton then called out, "God bless and comfort all the bereaved ones", at which the crowd around the grave answered with a shout "Amen". Again Railton's voice is raised, "God help us who are left to be faithful unto death." And again the shout startled the silence, "Amen." Once more Railton called out, "God bless The Salvation Army" and this time the people answered with a mighty rush of sound, "Amen". As it died away the concourse stirred as with a sigh. The graveside meeting closed with a dedication in which all present were invited to join.

Bramwell Booth led the prepared words, repeated after him phrase by phrase in solemn earnestness by the crowd: "Blessed Lord, we do solemnly promise, here by the side of this open grave, and before each other, that we will be true to our cause, and valiant in Thy service, that we will devote ourselves to the great end of saving souls, that we will be faithful to Thee, faithful to one another, and faithful to a dying world, till we meet, our beloved Mother, in the Morning. Amen."[66]

There was a moment of silence. All stood motionless; then at a signal the flags were raised, the white ribbons floated out a little, the bandsmen lifted their instruments in preparation for the closing song. The chorus was often sung at the Army Mother's bedside. She liked its note of personal triumph, "Victory for *me*". It was as she would have wished that her Army children should turn from her grave with a battle song. William Booth and his family stepped down from the platform and away into the dusk, as the Salvationists sang Herbert Booth's song of victory:

To the front! the cry is ringing;
To the front! your place is there;
In the conflict men are wanted,

452

Men of hope and faith and prayer.
Selfish ends shall claim no right
From the battles post to take us;
Fear shall vanish in the fight,
For triumphant God will make us.

CHORUS:

No retreating, hell defeating,
Shoulder to shoulder we stand;
God, look down, with glory crown
Our conquering band.
Victory for me
Through the Blood of Christ, my Saviour;
Victory for me
Through the precious Blood.

To the front! the fight is raging;
Christ's own banner leads the way;
Every power and thought engaging,
Might divine shall be our stay.
We have heard the cry for help
From the dying millions round us,
We've received the royal command
From our dying Lord who found us.

To the front! no more delaying,
Wounded spirits need thy care;
To the front! thy Lord obeying,
Stoop to help the dying there.
Broken hearts and blighted hopes,
Slaves of sin and degradation,
Wait for thee, in love to bring
Holy peace and liberation.[67]

BIBLIOGRAPHY

BEGBIE, HAROLD, *Life of William Booth*, 2 vols., Macmillan, London, 1920.

BOOTH, CATHERINE, *Aggressive Christianity*, The Salvation Army, London, 1891 (Published 1880).

—— *Church and State*, London, 1890 (First published 1883).

—— *Godliness*, London, 1890 (First published 1881).

—— *Life and Death*, London, 1890 (First published 1883).

—— *Popular Christianity*, London, 1887.

—— *Practical Religion*, London, 4th edn., 1891.

—— *Reminiscences* (unpublished).

BOOTH, BRAMWELL, *Echoes and Memories*, 1926 edn., Salvationist Publishing and Supplies, London (First published Hodder and Stoughton, London, 1925).

—— *On the Banks of the River; or, Mrs. Booth's Last Days*, The Salvation Army, London, 1894, 1900, 1911.

—— *These Fifty Years*, Cassell, London, 1929.

BOOTH, WILLIAM, *Training of Children*, The Salvation Army, London.

BOOTH-TUCKER, F. de L., *The Life of Catherine Booth*, 3 vols., The Salvation Army, London, 1893.

—— *The Consul*, The Salvation Army, New York, 1903.

BRAMWELL-BOOTH, CATHERINE, *Bramwell Booth*, Rich and Cowan, London, 1933.

BUTLER, JOSEPHINE, *The Salvation Army in Switzerland*, Dyer, London, 1883.

The Christian Mission Magazine. Ed. William Booth (1868-1869 *East London Evangelist*, 1870-1879 *Christian Mission Magazine*).

CHURCHILL, WINSTON, *My Early Life*, Butterworth, London, 1930.

COOK, ALICE I., *Life of Mrs. Booth* (pamphlet).

ERVINE, ST. JOHN, *God's Soldier: General William Booth*, 2 vols., Heinemann, London, 1934.

JOY, EDWARD, H., *The Old Corps*, Salvationist Publishing and Supplies, London, 1944.

LYTTELTON, OLIVER, *The Memoirs of Lord Chandos*, The Bodley Head, London, 1962.

The Musical Salvationist, vols. 1-3, The Salvation Army, London.

Orders and Regulations for Soldiers of The Salvation Army, Salvationist Publishing and Supplies, London, 1943.

PETRI, LAURA, *Catherine Booth och Salvationismen*, Sweden, 1925.

RAILTON, GEORGE SCOTT, *Twenty-one Years*, The Salvation Army, London, *c*. 1886.

The Salvation Army Ceremonies, Salvationist Publishing and Supplies, London, 1925 edn.

The Salvation Army Song Book, Salvationist Publishing and Supplies, London, 1930, 1953 edns.

STAFFORD, ANN, *The Age of Consent*, Hodder and Stoughton, London, 1964.

STEAD, W. T., *Mrs. Booth of The Salvation Army*, Nisbet, London, 1900.

STRAHAN, JAMES, *The Maréchale*, New York, 1921 (First edition 1914).

WALLIS, HUMPHREY, *The Happy Warrior: The Life-Story of Commissioner Cadman*, Salvationist Publishing and Supplies, London, 1928.

The War Cry of The Salvation Army 1880-1890.

REFERENCES

CM   Catherine Mumford
CB   Catherine Booth
WB   William Booth

Book 1

1 Reminiscences
2 *Ibid.*
3 *Ibid.*
4 *Last Days,* p. 126
5 CM to WB 13.6.1853
6 Stead, p. 24
7 CM to WB May 1853
8 Reminiscences
9 *Orders and Regulations for Soldiers* (1943) chap. 4, sect. 8
10 Reminiscences
11 *Last Days,* p. 70
12 CM to WB 22.5.1852
13 *Ibid.* May 1853
14 *Ibid.* 13.2.1855
15 Reminiscences
16 *Ibid.*
17 CM to WB 16.1.1853
18 Petri, p. 129
19 Stead, p. 31
20 Reminiscences
21 Begbie, vol. 1, p. 125
22 CM to WB December 1853
23 *Practical Religion,* p. 135
24 CM to WB 16.1.1853
25 Jacques Lusseyran, *And There Was Light* (1964), p. 2
26 *Aggressive Christianity,* How Christ Transcends the Law, p. 9
27 CM to WB 16.1.1853
28 Petri, p. 113
29 *Life and Death,* p. 30
30 *Ibid.,* p. 30
31 Reminiscences
32 *Aggressive Christianity,* p. 10
33 Reminiscences
34 *War Cry* 21.4.1888
35 *Life and Death,* pp. 64-70
36 CM to WB 1.12.1853
37 *Ibid.* 20.3.1853
38 *Thomas Aquinas,* Everyman's Library (Dent), p. 215
39 CM to WB 1858
40 CM to her mother May 1847
41 Reminiscences
42 *Methodist Times* 1890
43 Reminiscences
44 Booth-Tucker, vol. 1, pp. 117-23
45 Begbie, vol. 1, p. 126
46 Reminiscences
47 CM to WB January 1854
48 CM's Journal 14.5.1847

Book 2

1 Reminiscences
2 Begbie, vol. 1, p. 89
3 *Ibid.,* p. 104
4 Reminiscences
5 Begbie, vol. 1, p. 129
6 *Ibid.,* p. 118
7 *Ibid.,* p. 115
8 Reminiscences
9 *Ibid.*
10 *Ibid.*
11 *Ibid.*
12 CM to WB 3.4.1853
13 WB to CM undated
14 Reminiscences
15 WB to CM undated
16 *Ibid.*
17 *Ibid.*
18 CM to WB 11.5.1852
19 WB to CM undated
20 *Ibid.*

457

21	CM to WB 13.5.1852	70	CM to WB 27.2.1853
22	*Ibid.*	71	WB to CM undated
23	*Ibid.*	72	CM to WB 6.3.1853
24	Begbie, vol. 1, pp. 130-1	73	*Ibid.* January 1854
25	CM to WB May 1852	74	*Ibid.* 20.3.1853
26	Reminiscences	75	*Ibid.* 30.3.1853
27	WB to CM 1852 undated	76	*Ibid.* 3.4.1853
28	CM to WB 22.5.1852	77	*Ibid.* 1853 undated
29	Reminiscences	78	*Ibid.* undated
30	*Ibid.*	79	*Ibid.* 12.4.1853
31	CM to WB 17.3.1853	80	WB to CM undated
32	Reminiscences	81	CM to WB May 1853
33	*Ibid.*	82	*Ibid.* May 1853
34	*Ibid.*	83	*Ibid.* June 1853
35	*Ibid.*	84	*Ibid.*
36	CM to WB 17.3.1853	85	*Ibid.*
37	*Ibid.* 5.12.1852	86	WB to CM undated
38	*Ibid.* 18.10.1853	87	CM to WB June 1853
39	*Ibid.* 12.2.1855	88	*Ibid.* 30.3.1853
40	Rt. Rev. Phillips Brooks, D.D.	89	*Ibid.* 30.6.1853
	Sermons, vol. 5, p. 45	90	*Ibid.* 3.7.1853
41	Begbie, vol. 1, pp. 161, 157,	91	*Ibid.* 2.8.1853
	145	92	*Ibid.* September 1853
42	Ervine, vol. 1, p. 58	93	*Ibid.* 15.9.1853
43	CM to WB June 1853	94	*Ibid.* 21.9.1853
44	*Ibid.* 4.1.1854	95	*Ibid.* 24.9.1853
45	Reminiscences	96	*Ibid.* 28.9.1853
46	WB to CM undated	97	*Ibid.* 13.10.1853
47	Petrie, p. 124	98	*Ibid.* October 1853
48	WB to CM 17.11.1852	99	WB to CM undated
49	CM to WB 5.12.1852	100	*Ibid.* undated 1853
50	*Ibid.* 12.12.1852	101	CM to WB 18.7.1853
51	*Ibid.* 16.12.1852	102	WB to CM September 1853
52	*Ibid.* 17.12.1852	103	Begbie, vol. 1, p. 199
53	*Ibid.* 19.12.1852	104	CM to WB 8.11.53
54	*Ibid.* 27.12.1852	105	CM to WB 23.11.1853
55	*Ibid.* 1.1.1853	106	*Ibid.* undated 1853
56	*Ibid.* 7.1.1853	107	*Ibid.* November 1853
57	*Ibid.* 10.1.1853	108	*Ibid.* 1.12.1853
58	*Ibid.* 16.1.1853	109	*Ibid.* December 1853
59	*Ibid.* undated	110	*Ibid.* 1.1.1854
60	*Ibid.* 7.2.1853	111	WB to CM 24.5.1855
61	WB to CM undated	112	*Ibid.* undated
62	CM to WB 8.2.1853	113	CM to WB 1854
63	*Ibid.* 24.10.1854	114	*Ibid.* 4.1.1854
64	*Ibid.* 1.12.1853	115	*Ibid.* 6.1.1854
65	*Ibid.* 12.2.1855	116	WB to CM undated
66	*Ibid.* June 1853	117	CM to WB 18.1.1854
67	WB to CM undated	118	Begbie, vol. 1, p. 72
68	*Ibid.* 1886 undated	119	WB to CM January 1854
69	CM to WB 20.2.1853	120	CM to WB 5.1.1854

121 *Ibid.* 4.2.1854
122 Begbie, vol. 1, p. 225
123 *Ibid.* vol. 1, p. 226
124 Reminiscences
125 CM to WB 12.6.1854
126 WB to CM undated
127 Mr. Josiah Bates, *New Connexion Magazine,* 1854
128 CM to WB 12.6.1854
129 *Ibid.* September 1854
130 *Ibid.* 2.9.1854
131 *Ibid.* 4.9.1854
132 *Ibid.* 6.9.1854
133 *Ibid.* 13.9.1854
134 WB to CM undated
135 Begbie, vol. 1, p. 231
136 WB to CM 5.1.1855
137 *Ibid.* 13.1.1855
138 *The Staffordshire Sentinel*
139 WB to CM 29.1.1855
140 WB to CM 30.1.1855
141 CM to WB 5.2.1855
142 *Ibid.* 6.2.1855
143 WB to CM 9.2.1855
144 CM to WB 12.2.1855
145 WB to CM 12.2.1855
146 CM to WB 13.2.1855
147 WB to CM 21.2.1855
148 CM to WB 22.2.1855
149 *Ibid.* 1.3.1855
150 WB to CM 6.4.1855
151 CM to WB 5.4.1855
152 *Ibid.* 9.4.1855
153 WB to CM 12.4.1855
154 *Ibid.* 28.4.1855
155 *Ibid.* 4.5.1855
156 *Ibid.* 11.5.1855
157 *Ibid.* 15.5.1855
158 *Ibid.* 22.5.1855
159 CM to WB undated
160 WB to CM 24.5.1855
161 *Ibid.* 1.6.1855
162 *Ibid.* 8.6.1855
163 CB to her mother 7.7.1855
164 CB to WB 8.8.1855
165 WB to CB 4.8.1855
166 CB to WB 6.8.1855
167 *Ibid.* 8.8.1855
168 *Ibid.* 8.8.1855
169 *Ibid.* August 1855
170 *Ibid.* 22.8.1855
171 Chorus 427 Song Book 1930 edn.
172 Chorus of Song 802, *Ibid.* 1953 edn.
173 German Song Book no. 301
174 Reminiscences
175 CB to WB 11.9.1855
176 CB to her mother 9.10.1855
177 *Ibid.* undated
178 *Ibid.* 9.10.1855
179 *Ibid.* October 1855
180 *Ibid.* 5.11.1855
181 Begbie, vol. 1, p. 296
182 *These Fifty Years,* p. 25
183 CB to her mother October 1855
184 CB to her parents 22.10.1855
185 CB to her mother 24.10.1855
186 *Ibid.* October 1855
187 *Ibid.* October 1855
188 CB to her parents 2.11.1855
189 *Ibid.* November 1855
190 *Ibid.* 22.11.1855
191 *Ibid.* 12.11.1855
192 *Ibid.* 5.11.1855
193 *Ibid.* 7.12.1855
194 *Ibid.* December 1855
195 *Ibid.* December 1855
196 CB to her mother 18.12.1855
197 CB to her parents 13.12.1855
198 *Ibid.* 31.12.1855
199 CB to her mother 3.1.1856
200 *Ibid.* 16.1.1856
201 *Ibid.* January 1856
202 CB to her parents 5.2.1856
203 *Ibid.* February 1856
204 *Ibid.* 11.2.1856
205 *Ibid.* undated
206 *Ibid.* 7.3.1856
207 CB to her mother undated
208 Reminiscences
209 CB to her mother undated
210 *Ibid.*
211 CB to her mother 27.10.1856
212 Rev. B. Turnock. Booth-Tucker, vol. 1, p. 262
213 CB to her mother
214 WB's Diary 11.1.1857
215 WB to CB undated
216 *Ibid.*
217 *Ibid.*

218 *Ibid.*
219 CB to her mother undated
220 CB and WB to her parents
     11.4.1857
221 CB to her mother 31.5.1857
222 Begbie, vol. 1, p. 307
223 CB to her mother undated
224 Reminiscences. Booth-Tucker,
     vol. 1, p. 294
225 CB to her mother 21.6.1857
226 Stead, p. 112
227 WB to CB undated
228 Reminiscences
229 WB to CB undated
230 Begbie, vol. 1, p. 346
231 *Echoes and Memories,* p. 7
232 WB to CB undated
233 CB to WB 2.11.1886
234 WB to CB undated
235 CB to WB 29.10.1886
236 WB to CB undated 1886
237 CB to WB 12.10.1886
238 WB to CB undated
239 *These Fifty Years,* p. 18

BOOK 3

1   CB to her mother 26.8.1855
2   *These Fifty Years,* p. 35
3   CB to her mother undated
4   *Ibid.* undated
5   *Ibid.* undated
6   WB to Mrs. Mumford undated
7   CB to her parents 7.12.1857
8   *Ibid.* 23.12.1857
9   *Ibid.* 6.1.1858
10 *Ibid.* February 1858
11 CB to her mother undated
    1858
12 *Ibid.* undated 1858
13 *Ibid.* undated
14 Reminiscences
15 *Practical Religion,* pp. 125-7
16 Ervine, vol. 1, p. 219
17 CB to her mother 18.9.1859
18 *Ibid.* undated
19 CB to her parents 25.12.1859
20 *Ibid.*
21 Ervine, vol. 1, p. 224
22 CB to her parents undated

23 CB to her mother undated
24 *Aggressive Christianity
     Witnessing for Christ,*
     pp. 14-5
25 CB to WB 13.9.1854
26 *Aggressive Christianity,
     Witnessing for Christ,*
     pp. 16-17
27 The Salvation Army *Staff
     Review* 29.1.1929
28 Stead, p. 168
29 WB to CB 12.4.1855
30 *The Star* October 1890
31 *The Methodist Recorder* 1890
32 *Daily Graphic* 1890
33 *These Fifty Years,* pp. 10 34
34 Booth-Tucker, vol. 1, p. 363
35 *Aggressive Christianity
     Witnessing for Christ,* p. 18
36 CB to her mother 23.7.1860
37 *Ibid.* 16.8.1860
38 *Ibid.* 23.8.1860
39 CB to WB undated
40 CB to her mother 31.8.1860
41 *Ibid.* 20.9.1860
42 CB to her parents September
     1860
43 CB to WB 13.9.1860
44 *Ibid.* 17.9.1860
45 *Ibid.* 17.9.1860 second letter
46 *Ibid.* 19.9.1860
47 CB to her parents 24.9.1860
48 CB to WB 27.9.1860
49 *Ibid.* 1.10.1860
50 *Ibid.* 4.10.1860
51 CB to her parents 12.11.1860
52 CB to her mother November
     1860
53 *Ibid.* 30.11.1860
54 CB to her daughter Catherine
     9.3.1890
55 CB to her parents 31.12.60
56 Song Book 1953 edn. Doctrine
     No. 10
57 From the *Book of Common
     Prayer*
58 CM's Journal 8.7.1847
59 *Ibid.* 28.11.1847
60 Dean Inge, *Evening Standard*
     9.3.1943
61 CB to WB 16.1.1853

62 *Ibid.* 7.2.1853
63 *Ibid.* 28.8.1860
64 CB to her parents undated
        Monday 1860
65 *Ibid.* 21.1.1861
66 *Ibid.* undated
67 *Ibid.* 4.2.1861
68 *Ibid.* 11.2.1861
69 *Ibid.* 22.2.1861
70 *Ibid.* 29.3.1861
71 *Ibid.* April 1861
72 *Ibid.* undated
73 *Ibid.* undated
74 Reminiscences
75 *Ibid.*
76 CB to her parents June 1861
77 Ervine, vol. 1, p. 248
78 CB to her mother 24.6.1861
79 CB to her parents undated
80 WB to CB undated
81 *Ibid.* undated
82 Booth-Tucker, vol. 1, p. 426
83 CB to her mother 18.7.1861
84 *Church and State,* p. 67
85 Reminiscences
86 CB to her parents undated
87 *Ibid.* 2.9.1861
88 *Ibid.* undated
89 CB to her mother undated
90 Booth-Tucker, vol. 2, pp. 39-40
        Wesleyan Times
91 *Ibid.,* pp. 43-4
92 *Ibid.,* p. 57
93 CB to her mother undated
        1862
94 Booth-Tucker, vol. 2, p. 68
95 *Ibid.,* vol. 1, p. 284
96 CB to her parents undated
97 *Ibid.* 23.2.1863
98 CB to her mother February
        1863
99 *Ibid.* 1.4.1863
100 WB's Diary 21.6.1863
101 *Ibid.* 17.6.1863
102 CB to her parents undated
103 *Ibid.* 8.12.1863
104 Booth-Tucker, vol. 2, p. 101
105 CB to her parents 16.12.1863
106 *Ibid.* 29.2.1864
107 CB to her mother March 1864
108 Begbie, vol. 1, p. 321

109 WB to CB undated
110 *Ibid.*
111 *Ibid.*
112 *Ibid.*
113 *Ibid.*
114 *Ibid.*
115 *Ibid.*
116 *Ibid.*
117 *Ibid.*
118 CB to her parents 27.9.1864
119 R. C. Morgan to WB 8.3.1875
120 CB to R. C. Morgan 11.5.1875
121 Booth-Tucker, vol. 2, p. 113
        The Gospel Guide
122 Reminiscences
123 *Ibid.*
124 *Ibid.*
125 Ervine, vol. 1, p. 284
126 Begbie, vol. 1, p. 366
127 *Ibid.,* p. 362
128 Booth-Tucker, vol. 2, p. 138
129 Begbie, vol. 1, pp. 371-2
130 Article by WB in the *Christian*
131 Editor of the *Christian* 1865
132 Booth-Tucker, vol. 2, p. 145
133 Reminiscences
134 *The Methodist Recorder*
        October 1890
135 Booth-Tucker, vol. 2, p. 153
136 Begbie, vol. 1, p. 357
137 Booth-Tucker, vol. 2, p. 192
138 *The East London Evangelist,*
        vol. 1, p. 102, 1868
139 *Ibid.,* vol. 1, p. 1
140 CB to Mrs. Billups undated
141 *Bramwell Booth,* p. 41
142 Booth-Tucker, vol. 2, pp. 215-7
143 CB to Father Ignatius 1868
144 Booth-Tucker, vol. 2, p. 219
145 Begbie, vol. 1, p. 354
146 Booth-Tucker, vol. 2, p. 222
147 Samuel Rutherford: *Loveli-
        ness of Christ,* p. 30
148 CB to Mrs. Billups 27.8.1873

BOOK 4

1 *Commissioner Cadman,* p. 56
2 Stead, p. 199
3 *Ibid.,* pp. 6-7

4 *Christian Mission Magazine* May 1870
5 Begbie, vol. 1, p. 101
6 *Church and State,* pp. 59-60
7 Stead, pp. 83-8
8 *Christian Mission Magazine* 1.5.1870
9 Stead, p. 166
10 CB to the Editor of *Methodist New Connexion Magazine;* Booth-Tucker, vol. 1, p. 172
11 *Aggressive Christianity,* World's Need, pp. 5, 6
12 *Christian Mission Magazine* May 1876, p. 238
13 *Ibid.* May 1870, p. 74
14 *Ibid.* May 1871, p. 74
15 *Ibid.*
16 *Ibid.* May 1872, p. 74
17 WB to Bramwell July 1872
18 CB to Mrs. Billups undated
19 *Ibid.* March 1873
20 *Christian Mission Magazine* 1873, p. 169, *Chatham News*
21 *These Fifty Years,* p. 95
22 Commissioner George Railton to CB 21.7.1873
23 Booth-Tucker, vol. 2, pp. 316-7
24 *Christian Mission Magazine* May 1875, p. 176
25 *Ibid.,* p. 183
26 Stead, p. 216
27 *Christian Mission Magazine* May 1875, pp. 183-4
28 CB to Bramwell 1875 undated
29 *Bramwell Booth,* p. 95
30 *Church and State,* p. 76
31 *Ibid.,* p. 41; *Practical Religion,* pp. 37-9
32 *Church and State,* p. 15
33 *Lord Chandos,* p. 165
34 *These Fifty Years,* p. 22
35 CB to Mrs. Billups 1876
36 CB to Bramwell 17.4.1876
37 CB to Mrs. Billups 4.5.1876
38 *Ibid.* undated
39 Bramwell to his mother 19.10.1876
40 *Christian Mission Magazine* 1877 July, p. 177
41 *Ibid.* 1877, p. 181
42 CB to Mrs. Billups undated
43 Booth-Tucker, vol. 3, 1882, p. 167
44 *Christian Mission Magazine* 1877, p. 265
45 CB to Mrs. Billups undated
46 *Ibid.*
47 *Christian Mission Magazine* 1878, p. 14
48 Begbie, vol. 1, p. 439
49 *Christian Mission Magazine* 1878, pp. 236, 240
50 CB to Mrs. Billups 25.10.1878
51 Stead, pp. 76-83
52 *Ibid.,* p. 214
53 *Church and State,* pp. 32-4, 67
54 *Ibid.,* pp. 82-5
55 CB to Katie 1878
56 Reminiscences
57 CB to Emma undated
58 *Church and State,* pp. 54-6
59 WB to Bramwell 5.8.1874
60 *Christian Mission Magazine* June 1879, p. 143
61 *Coventry Times* 1878; *Christian Miss. Mag.,* p. 283
62 *Christian Mission Magazine* 1878, p. 286
63 WB to Bramwell 1.10.1878
64 *Christian Mission Magazine* December 1878, p. 316
65 CB to Mrs. Billups undated
66 Bramwell to Mrs. Billups 27.7.1879
67 CB to Mrs. Billups undated
68 *Christian Mission Magazine* June 1879, p. 145
69 *Northern Echo* 1879
70 *Church and State,* pp. 20-3
71 CB to Bramwell undated 1879
72 *Ibid.* 24.3.1879
73 *Ibid.* 12.4.1876
74 *Christian Mission Magazine* 1879, p. 288
75 CB to Stead, p. 207
76 *Northern Echo* 1879
77 WB to Bramwell 16.3.1877
78 *Church and State,* pp. 25, 52

79 CB to Mrs. Billups 17.6.1879
80 *The War Cry* 12.2.1880
81 CB to Mrs. Billups undated
82 *The Old Corps,* pp. 12, 13
83 John Bright to CB 3.5.1882
84 *Church and State,* p. 19
85 CB to Mrs. Billups undated
86 *Ibid.* undated
87 Booth-Tucker, vol. 3, p. 167
88 CB to Mrs. Billups undated
89 *Saturday Review, Christian Mission Mag.* May 1879, pp. 199, 201
90 CB to Frank Crossley
91 *Church and State,* p. 53
92 *The War Cry* 9.10.1880
93 *Ibid.* 9/16/23.10.1880
94 Begbie, vol. 2, p. 82
95 Josephine Butler to CB 1882
96 Bramwell to his mother 10.5.1879
97 *Church and State,* p. 38
98 CB to Mrs. Billups undated
99 CB to Mr. Reed 27.5.1879
100 Booth-Tucker, vol. 3, p. 88-90
101 *Ibid.,* p. 51
102 CB to Mrs. Billups 15.5.1880
103 Stead, p. 230
104 *Life and Death,* p. 44
105 Stead, p. 168
106 *Ibid.,* p. 231
107 *Popular Christianity,* pp. 96-9
108 *Ibid.,* p. 134
109 J. C. Carlile, *My life's little day*
110 *These Fifty Years,* pp. 35, 37
111 Begbie, vol. 2, p. 28
112 CB to Mrs. Billups 20.5.1880
113 *These Fifty Years,* p. 37
114 Stead, pp. 167-8
115 CB to Mrs. Billups 3.5.1876
116 *Ibid.* undated
117 *Ibid.* 2.7.1880
118 *Ibid.* 31.8.1880
119 *Church and State,* pp. 3, 4, 8, 6
120 CB to Bramwell 7.3.1875
121 Stead, p. 215
122 *Ibid.,* p. 180

BOOK 5

1 *These Fifty Years,* p. 21

2 Booth-Tucker, vol. 3, pp. 413-4
3 CB to WB 13.6.1853
4 Stead, p. 122
5 CB to her mother undated
6 *Practical Religion,* pp. 4, 5, 8
7 CB to her mother 15.5.1857
8 *Practical Religion,* p. 15
9 *Ibid.,* p. 7
10 CB to Mrs. Billups undated
11 *Practical Religion,* p. 24
12 CB to her mother May 1859
13 *Practical Religion,* p. 24
14 Mrs. Booth to Mrs. Mumford undated
15 CB to Bramwell 15.8.1861
16 *Ibid.* 18.9.1861
17 CB to her mother undated
18 *Ibid.* undated
19 *Bramwell Booth,* p. 24
20 Reminiscences
21 *These Fifty Years,* p. 26
22 CB to her mother undated
23 CB to WB 4.9.1854
24 CB to her mother undated
25 *Ibid.*
26 *These Fifty Years,* p. 10
27 *My Early Life,* p. 18
28 WB to Mrs. Mumford undated
29 Reminiscences
30 *These Fifty Years,* pp. 28-9
31 *Ibid.,* p. 28
32 *Practical Religion,* p. 26
33 *Last Days,* p. 59
34 *These Fifty Years,* p. 60
35 Reminiscences
36 *Life and Death,* p. 88
37 *These Fifty Years,* p. 61
38 Reminiscences
39 *These Fifty Years,* p. 63
40 CB to her mother undated
41 *Practical Religion,* pp. 21-4
42 *The Consul,* p. 25
43 *Last Days,* p. 84
44 *Practical Religion,* p. 26
45 WB to CB undated
46 *Ibid.*
47 Begbie, vol. 1, p. 348
48 *Practical Religion,* pp. 25-6
49 Stead, p. 142
50 *Ibid.,* p. 211
51 Begbie, vol. 1, p. 347

52   *Echoes and Memories,* p. 15
53   Begbie, vol. 1, p. 345
54   *Ibid.*
55   CB to her parents 22.11.1855
56   *Training of Children*
57   *Practical Religion,* p. 7
58   *These Fifty Years,* p. 29
59   *Ibid.,* p. 29
60   WB to CB undated
61   *These Fifty Years,* p. 29
62   CB to her mother undated
63   CB to Bramwell 18.9.1877
64   Begbie, vol. 1, p. 349
65   Mrs. Bramwell Booth Article
     in *The Officer,* Magazine
     of The Salvation Army
66   Begbie, vol. 1, p. 351
67   Booth-Tucker, vol. 2, p. 44
68   *Bramwell Booth,* p. 24
69   *Practical Religion,* p. 19
70   Begbie, vol. 1, p. 347
71   CB to her mother 24.11.1863
72   *Ibid.* undated
73   *Ibid.*
74   *Ibid.*
75   *Practical Religion,* p. 31
76   Booth-Tucker, vol. 3, p. 334
77   *Life and Death,* p. 11
78   CB to Bramwell 15.8.1861
79   *Bramwell Booth,* p. 37
80   *Ibid.,* p. 131
81   CB to Bramwell 9.2.1871
82   CB to Mrs. Billups undated
83   *The Consul,* p. 27
84   CB to Emma undated
85   CB to Herbert 24.9.1877
86   *Practical Religion,* pp. 6-7
87   CB to Ballington 7.4.1876
88   *These Fifty Years,* pp. 29-30
89   Booth-Tucker, vol. 1, p. 254
90   *Practical Religion,* pp. 27-8
91   Booth-Tucker, vol. 1, p. 127
92   *Bramwell Booth,* p. 1
93   WB to Mr. Cory 1869 undated
94   CB to Katie undated
95   Ballington to his mother
     undated
96   CB to Ballington undated
97   *Ibid.* 3.3.1879
98   *Ibid.* 1875 undated
99   *Ibid.* 1877 undated
100 *Ibid.* 2.3.1876
101 *Ibid.* 1877 undated
102 *Ibid.* 15.5.1876
103 *Ibid.* 7.4. 1876
104 *Ibid.* undated 1877
105 *Ibid.*
106 *Ibid.* 13.9.1876
107 Emma to Bramwell undated
108 CB to Bramwell 4.4.1876
109 CB to Ballington 12.5.1878
110 *Ibid.* undated scrap
111 *Ibid.* undated
112 Petri, p. 132
113 CB to a Lady Friend undated
114 CB to Emma undated
115 *Ibid.*
116 CB to Ballington 1.6.1878
117 *The War Cry* 19.2.1887
118 Booth-Tucker, vol. 2,
     pp.359-61
119 CB to Katie 17.9.1874
120 *Ibid.* 12.4.1876
121 *Ibid.* 13.4.1876
122 CB to Bramwell 31.7.1876
123 CB to Katie and Emma
     23.12.1876
124 *Ibid.* 1.1.1877
125 CB to Katie 30.1.1877
126 *Ibid.* undated
127 *Ibid.* 1.8.1877
128 *Ibid.* 6.11.1877
129 Rev. James Strahan, D.D.,
     The Maréchal, p. 33
130 CB to Mrs. Billups 11.5.1877
131 CB to Emma undated
132 Emma to her mother undated
133 CB to Emma undated
134 *Ibid.*
135 *Ibid.*
136 CB to Mrs. Billups 9.2.1877
137 WB to Bramwell undated
138 CB to Bramwell 2.7.1876
139 WB to CB undated
140 CB to Bramwell 17.4.1873
141 CB to Mrs. Billups 1874
142 *These Fifty Years,* pp. 12, 37
143 CB to Bramwell 7.3.1875
144 Bramwell to his mother
     9.3.1875
145 CB to Bramwell 23.11.1877
146 *Ibid.* undated

147 *Ibid.* undated
148 *Ibid.* 1877
149 *Ibid.* 21.2.1877
150 CB to Ballington 1877
151 CB to Bramwell 2.3.1877
152 *Ibid.* 8.3. 1877
153 Bramwell to his mother
    March 1877
154 CB to Bramwell 8.9.1877
155 Bramwell to his mother
    18.9.1877
156 CB to Bramwell 11.9.1877
157 *Ibid.* October 1877
158 *Ibid.* 3.10.1877
159 *Ibid.* November 1877
160 CB to Mrs. Billups 15.5.1880
161 Booth-Tucker, vol. 3, p. 95
162 Stead, p. 122
163 *Church and State,* p. 69

Book 6

1 *The War Cry* 17.2.1881
2 *Ibid.*
3 *Ibid.*
4 CB to Mrs. Billups February
    1881
5 *Church and State,* p. 70
6 CB to Herbert undated
7 CB to Mrs. Reed 9.9.1880
8 *Ibid.* 25.9.1880
9 Petri, p. 129
10 CB to WB 20.3.1853
11 *The War Cry* 5.12.1885
12 *Twenty-one Years,* p. 202
13 *Aggressive Christianity,*
    The Holy Ghost, p. 5
14 *Ibid.* Adaptation, p. 4
15 Booth-Tucker, vol. 2, p. 424
16 *Popular Christianity,* p. 150
17 *Ibid.,* pp. 18-21
18 *Aggressive Christianity,*
    ch. 1, p. 6
19 *Church and State,* pp. 71-2
20 *Ibid.,* pp. 10, 11
21 *Practical Religion,* pp. 104-8
22 *Godliness,* pp. 93, 94
23 *Popular Christianity,* pp. 76-80
24 *Aggressive Christianity,* Filled
    with the Spirit, pp. 3, 8

25 *Practical Religion,* p. 95
26 *Aggressive Christianity,*
    Adaptation of Measures,
    p. 13
27 *Ibid.,* How Christ Transcends
    the Law, pp. 10-11
28 *Ibid.,* Adaption of Measures,
    pp. 11, 12
29 *Church and State,* pp. 30-2
30 *The Salvation Army*
    Ceremonies 1925 ed., p. 20
31 *Popular Christianity,* 112-3,
    116-7
32 *The War Cry* 21.4.1883
33 Booth-Tucker, vol. 3, p. 426
34 *Church and State,* pp. 12, 13
35 Booth-Tucker, vol. 3, p. 325
36 *The Christian World* 1890
37 *Twenty-one Years,* p. 248
38 *Ibid.,* pp. 52, 53
39 Begbie, vol. 2, pp. 111-2
40 CB to Mrs. Billups 14.4.1881
41 *Ibid.* September 1881
42 *The War Cry* 29.9.1881
43 CB to Bramwell 29.5.1878
44 Bramwell to his mother
    6.12.1881
45 CB to Dr. Soper 1.2.1882
46 *The Salvation Army Soldiers*
    Regulations, p. 79
47 *The Daily Chronicle* October
    1882
48 Booth-Tucker, vol. 3, p. 192
49 CB to Mrs. Billups April 1882
50 Booth-Tucker, vol. 3, p. 190
51 CB to Mrs. Billups undated
52 Booth-Tucker, vol. 3, p. 190
53 *The War Cry* 9.12.1882
54 *Ibid.*
55 CB to Katie undated
56 CB to Emma undated
57 CB to Bramwell undated
58 *The Salvation Army in*
    Switzerland, p. 190
59 *Ibid.,* p. 26
60 *Ibid.,* p. 208
61 *Ibid.,* p. 213
62 *Ibid.,* p. 217
63 Katie to Mrs. Josephine Butler
    19.9.1883

64 *The War Cry* 29.9.1883; 3.10.1883
65 CB to the Rt. Hon. W. E. Gladstone
66 CB to Katie 19.9.1883
67 *Ibid.* undated
68 *The Salvation Army in Switzerland*, p. 262
69 *The Times* 23.10.1883
70 *Ibid.* 27.10.1883
71 *The War Cry* 3.10.1883
72 CB to WB undated
73 Katie to her mother 19.9.1883
74 *Wesleyan Times* 1865
75 *Echoes and Memories*, p. 117
76 Bramwell to his wife Florence 11.6.1885
77 Josephine Butler to CB undated
78 Booth-Tucker, vol. 3, p. 264
79 *The War Cry* 22.7.1885
80 *Echoes and Memories*, p. 121
81 Begbie, vol. 2, p. 44
82 *The War Cry* 22.7.1885
83 *Ibid.*
84 *Ibid.*
85 *Ibid.* 1.8.1885
86 CB to Her Majesty Queen Victoria
87 Booth-Tucker, vol. 3, p. 265
88 CB to the Rt. Hon. W. E. Gladstone
89 CB to Emma undated
90 *Ibid.* 5.7.1885
91 *Ibid.* 1885
92 *Ibid.* undated
93 *The War Cry* 18.7.1885
94 *Ibid.* 29.7.1885
95 *Ibid.*
96 *The Daily News* 18.8.1885
97 *The Christian* article by Mrs. Josephine Butler
98 CB to Lady Cairns 22.12.1885
99 *The War Cry* 24.10.1885
100 Stead, pp. 200-3
101 *Age of Consent*, p. 24
102 Begbie, vol. 1, p. 357
103 *Popular Christianity*, p. 53
104 Stead, p. 197
105 *Ibid.*, p. 206
106 *Church and State*, p. 12

107 *Ibid.*, p. 50
108 Petri, p. 151
109 Stead, p. 192
110 CB to Mrs. Billups 12.5.1877
111 *Aggressive Christianity*, Filled with the Spirit, p. 9
112 Stead, p. 164
113 *The War Cry* 28.8.1886
114 Narrative by Brigadier M. Asdell
115 CB to Ballington 19.10.1879
116 *Life of Mrs. Booth*, p. 40
117 *The War Cry* 18.9.1886
118 CB to Mr. Denny undated
119 Booth-Tucker, vol. 3, pp. 335-6
120 CB to Bramwell 18.10.1877
121 *The War Cry* 19.2.1887
122 *The Freeman* 6.8.1887
123 Song Book No. 382, 1953 edn.
124 *The War Cry* 11.2.1888
125 CB to Emma 30.1.1888
126 *The War Cry* 10.3.1888

Book 7

1 Mrs. Bramwell Booth's Diary 9.12.1889
2 Booth-Tucker, vol. 3, p. 352
3 *Ibid.*, p. 353
4 *Last Days*, p. 20
5 Booth-Tucker, vol. 3, p. 353
6 *These Fifty Years*, p. 22
7 Booth-Tucker, vol. 3, p. 355
8 *The War Cry* 24.3.1888
9 *Ibid.* 21.4.1888
10 Begbie, vol. 2, p. 106
11 Article by Lieut.-Commissioner Gauntlett in *The Staff Review* of The Salvation Army
12 Booth-Tucker, vol. 3, pp. 362-74
13 *The War Cry* 20.7.1889
14 CB to Captain C. Stirling 25.10.1888
15 Stead, p. 232
16 Stead to Bramwell 29.12.1888
17 Booth-Tucker, vol. 3, p. 406
18 Mrs. Bramwell Booth's Diary 14.5.1889

19 *Last Days,* pp. 49-50
20 CB to Mrs. Irvine, Petri, p. 173
21 *The War Cry* 28.9.1889
22 CB to Mrs. Billups 27.8.1873
23 *The War Cry* 4.1.1890
24 *Last Days,* pp. 71, 72
25 *Bramwell Booth,* p. 284
26 Begbie, vol. 2, p. 92
27 *Ibid.*
28 Song Book No. 556 1953 edn.
29 *The War Cry* 7.12.1889
30 *Ibid.*
31 Booth-Tucker, vol. 3, p. 400
32 *Last Days,* p. 81
33 Song Book No. 284 1953 edn.
34 *Last Days,* p. 82
35 *The War Cry* 25.12.1889
36 Begbie, vol. 2, p. 105
37 *Last Days,* pp. 78-9
38 Booth-Tucker, vol. 3, p. 417
39 *Last Days,* pp. 79-80
40 Bramwell to Emma 3.10.1895
41 *The War Cry* 4.1.1890
42 Begbie, vol. 2, pp. 106-7
43 *Ibid.*
44 *Last Days,* p. 78
45 *Ibid.,* p. 75
46 Song Book No. 228, 1953 edn.
47 *Last Days,* p. 64
48 *Ibid.,* pp. 65-6
49 *Ibid.,* p. 67
50 *Ibid.,* p. 67
51 *The Musical Salvationist,*
      vol. 2, p. 33
52 *Last Days,* pp. 70-2
53 Booth-Tucker, vol. 3, p. 385
54 *Ibid.,* vol. 3, p. 416
55 *Last Days,* p. 128
56 Booth-Tucker, vol. 3, p. 413
57 *Last Days,* pp. 92-3
58 *Ibid.,* pp. 96-8
59 Song Book No. 776
60 Booth-Tucker, vol. 3, p. 430
61 *Last Days,* p. 100
62 Booth-Tucker, vol. 3, p. 442
63 Song Book No. 821, 1953 edn.
64 *Ibid.,* No. 217
65 Booth-Tucker, vol. 3,
      pp. 458-61
66 *Last Days,* p. 121
67 Song Book No. 692, 1953 edn.

INDEX

Abney Park Cemetery, Stoke Newington, 449–52

Age of Consent by C. B., 399[100]

Aggressive Christianity by C. B., 455; refs. to extracts 457, 460, 462, 465–6

Aldersgate Street, 330

Alexandra Palace, 408, 426, 441

Analogy of Religion by Dr. Butler, 28

Animal friends, 21–2, 25–6, 28, 32–3, 97, 293, 311–12

Annual Self-Denial Appeals, 366, 430

Appleby, Harry (bandmaster), 439–40

Aquinas, St. Thomas, 40[38]

Armstrong, Eliza, 397

Arnold, Matthew, 417 (*and footnote*)

Asdell, Brigadier Marianne, 404–5

Ashbourne, Derbyshire, 17–22

Australia, 252, 329, 353, 370, 434

Bachus, 87, 96

Bailey, Mr. (Longton, Staffs.), 135, 145

Balls, Mr. (cab-driver), 404

Band of Hope, 176

Baptists, 163, 218, 226, 235, 243

Barker, Colonel James, 329, 434

Barry, Glam., 221

Bates, Josiah, 128–9, 137

Bath, Mayor of, 281

Beard, Staff Captain, 428

Becquet, Captain, 381

Begbie, Harold, *Life of William Booth*, 163, 455; refs. to extracts 457–67

Belgium, 390

Bell, Staff-Captain Annie, 450

Bermondsey, 226

Bethnal Green, 243, 256, 434

Billups, Mr., 220, 244, 387, 420, 427

Billups, Mrs., 220–21, 386–7, 409; refs. to correspondence, 461–6

Billups, Miss, *see* Mrs. Irvine

Birmingham, 162–3, 204, 221–3

Blackwood, Sir Arthur, 277–8, 353

Booth, Mrs. (W. B.'s mother), 59, 66, 129, 153–4, 163, 191

Booth, Misses (W.B.'s sisters), 97, 145, 163

Booth, Ballington, childhood 165, 175–6, 181, 194–5, 212; home Mission work 259, 270, 273, 275, 281, 288, 290; student 325–31, 333–4, 336; U.S.A. and marriage 406, 420, 427, 449 (*passim*)

Booth, Mrs. Catherine (*née* Mumford), background and youth 17–55; betrothal and marriage 60–145; children 161, 165, 177, 184, 216, 223, 231, 235; faith and beliefs 360–8, 423–6; first writing 23; first sermon 187; journal 16, 40–47, 55, 198; preacher 187–94, 202–6, 213–29 *et seq.*; propagandist 234–6, 239–43; silver wedding 346–7; valedictions 433–48

Booth, Catherine (Katie), *see* Mrs. Clibborn

Booth, Mrs. Coraline Herbert (née Schoch), 435 (*footnote*), 443

Booth, Emma Moss, *see* Mrs. Tucker

Booth, Evelyn Cory (Eva), 231, 320, 338, 347, 395, 436, 446

Booth, Mrs. Florence Bramwell (*née* Soper), 9, 317, 354 (*footnote*), 355, 371–4, 389, 391, 415, 428, 444

Booth, Herbert Howard (Bertie), childhood and home, 216, 306, 322, 340, 348; school 327, 334, 336; France 355; marriage 443; preacher and hymn-writer 409, 438–9, 448, 452–3 (*passim*)

471

1878- flag